Microsoft

W9-BZP-813

Building Microsoft® Access Applications

John L. Viescas

PUBLISHED BY
Microsoft Press
A Division of Micro Corporation
One Microsoft Way 98052-6399
Redmond, Washin

Copyright © 20 y John L. Viescas

All rights rese d. No part of the contents of this book may be reproduced or transmitted in any form or by any mean ithout the written permission of the publisher.

Library of ngress Control Number 2004118058

Printed a bound in the United States of America.

1 2 3 5 6 7 8 9   QWT   9 8 7 6 5

Dist uted in Canada by H.B. Fenn and Company Ltd.

A P catalogue record for this book is available from the British Library.

icrosoft Press books are available through booksellers and distributors worldwide. For further information about international editions, contact your local Microsoft Corporation office or contact Microsoft Press International directly at fax (425) 936-7329. Visit our Web site at www.microsoft.com/ learning/. Send comments to *mspinput@microsoft.com*.

Microsoft, ActiveX, FrontPage, Georgia, Microsoft Press, Outlook, PivotChart, PivotTable, PowerPoint, Tahoma, Verdana, Visual Basic, and Windows are either registered trademarks or trademarks of Microsoft Corporation in the United States and/or other countries.

The example companies, organizations, products, domain names, e-mail addresses, logos, people, places, and events depicted herein are fictitious. No association with any real company, organization, product, domain name, e-mail address, logo, person, place, or event is intended or should be inferred.

Acquisitions Editor: Alex Blanton and Hilary Long
Project Editor: Kristine Haugseth
Production Manager: Curtis Philips, Publishing.com
Technical Editor: Steve Saunders
Copy Editor: Andrea Fox
Indexer: Rebecca Plunkett

Body Part No. X10-87117

For Suzanne. You know I wouldn't be able to do this without you.

Contents at a Glance

Table of Contents

What do you think of this book?
We want to hear from you!

Microsoft is interested in hearing your feedback about this publication so we can continually improve our books and learning resources for you. To participate in a brief online survey, please visit: *www.microsoft.com/learning/booksurvey/*

What do you think of this book?
We want to hear from you!

Microsoft is interested in hearing your feedback about this publication so we can continually improve our books and learning resources for you. To participate in a brief online survey, please visit: *www.microsoft.com/learning/booksurvey/*

Acknowledgments

Although I'm ultimately responsible for the content of any book I write, the finished product doesn't make it out the door without the help of many people at Microsoft Learning (Microsoft Press) and Publishing.com. First, many thanks to the editorial and technical team at Microsoft Press—Sandra Haynes, Kristine Haugseth, Carl Diltz, and Elizabeth Hansford. Special thanks go to Alex Blanton who helped me refine the idea for the book and get it accepted for publication. And the folks at Publishing.com did another superb job of editing and producing the book. Curt Philips deserves special mention as the project manager— I don't know when he found time to eat and sleep during the final push. Thanks also to Andrea Fox, who kept all my commas in order, and Rebecca Plunkett, who built the index.

Thanks to Teresa Hennig, the President of the Pacific Northwest Access Developers Group, who gave me permission to use the group name in the Membership Tracking sample application (the member names are fictitious) and reviewed the sample as I built it. Thanks also to my son, Mike Viescas, who helped me develop the concept for the Customer Support sample application.

Very early in the project, I asked for feedback from my fellow Microsoft Access Most Valuable Professionals (MVPs) on my ideas for the design and user interface chapters. Several also volunteered to allow me to use their names as instructors in the Registration Management sample application. I apologize to any of you who don't like the courses you ended up teaching in the database—the courses were assigned using a random append query! The MVPs who contributed are:

Marshall Barton	Duane Hookom[*]	Kenneth Snell[*]
Jeff Boyce	Larry Linson	John Spencer
Allen Browne[*]	Graham Mandeno[*]	Douglas Steele[*]
Sandra Daigle[*]	Arvin Meyer[*]	Bruce M. Thompson
Victor Delgadillo[*]	John Nurick	Tony Toews
Van T. Dinh[*]	Brendan Reynolds	Lynn Trapp[*]
Alex Dybenko	Luiz Rocha[*]	John Vinson[*]
Tom Ellison	Steve Schapel[*]	Joan Wild
Joe Fallon[*]	Ben M. Schorr	
Dirk Goldgar[*]	M.L. "Sco" Scofield[*]	

[*] Instructors in the Registration Management sample database.

Many thanks to you all!

John Viescas
Austin, Texas
November, 2004

About the CD

The companion CD that ships with this book contains tools and resources to help you get the most out of *Building Microsoft Access Applications*.

What's on the CD

Your *Building Microsoft Access Applications* CD includes the following:

- **Sample Databases**   This section contains the four databases described in the book: the Membership Tracking database, Inventory Management database, Customer Support database, and Registration Management database.

- **eBook**   In this section you'll find the electronic version of *Building Microsoft Access Applications*.

- **Readme.txt**   This file on the companion CD provides detailed information about the files on the CD. The files on the CD are designed to be accessed through Microsoft Internet Explorer (version 5.01 or later).

> **Note**   Please note that the links to third-party sites are not under the control of Microsoft Corporation, and Microsoft is therefore not responsible for their content, nor should their inclusion on this CD be construed as an endorsement of the product or the site.
>
> Also, software provided on this CD is only in the English language and may be incompatible with non-English-language operating systems and software.

Sample Applications

Parts 2 through 5 of this book show you how to design and build four of the most common types of business applications. You can find the sample databases in the Sample Databases area of the CD.

- **Membership Tracking** (Membership.mdb and MembershipData.mdb). This application demonstrates how to maintain a member list for an organization, log membership renewal and dues payments, and track activities. This application also shows you how to contact members using automation with Microsoft Outlook.

- **Inventory Management** (Inventory.mdb, and InventoryData.mdb). Although some of the sample data in this application is based on the venerable Northwind example that has shipped with every version of Microsoft Access, the Inventory Management sample application goes far beyond the basic features of a typical "order entry" database. It not only tracks customer orders but also allocates inventory from stock, generates vendor purchase orders for items not in stock, posts received purchase order items to inventory (and to any related customer order), and tracks customer payments. The application includes an example that dynamically creates a sales analysis chart in Microsoft Excel.

- **Customer Support** (Support.mdb and SupportData.mdb). This application is similar in some ways to Membership Tracking, but it tracks support issues and the resolution of issues rather than activities. This application demonstrates a technique for "pushing the envelope" to support 50 or more concurrent users, as discussed in Chapter 3, "Designing a Client/Server Application." This application also shows you how to perform data analysis by linking to Microsoft Excel.

- **Registration Management** (Registration.mdb and RegistrationData.mdb). This application illustrates how to manage registrations for a school or a seminar. It limits the number of registrants for each session, verifies that a registrant has signed up to attend prerequisite sessions or courses, and manages wait lists. You can use this application as a template for any application that must manage limited resources that are available only for specific time periods (such as hotel rooms or airline flights and seats). This application includes sending registration notices using Microsoft Outlook.

Caution   The sample applications were compiled and saved using Microsoft Access 2002 (XP). If you open any of the samples using Access 2000 or Access 2003, the startup code warns you that the Visual Basic project is no longer compiled. Before working in the sample, you should open any module in the Visual Basic Editor, choose Compile from the Debug menu, and save the result to obtain the best results.

The examples in this book assume you have installed Microsoft Office 2000, Microsoft Office XP (2002), or Microsoft Office 2003, not just Microsoft Access. Several examples also assume that you have installed all optional features of Access through the Microsoft Office Setup program. If you have not installed these additional features, you might not be able to run the samples from the companion CD. The dialog boxes illustrated in this book were captured with the Office Assistant turned off. If you have the Office Assistant turned on, some of your dialog boxes will appear differently.

All the sample databases are in Access 2000 file format, so you can open and run them using Access 2000, Access 2002 (XP), or Access 2003. You will not be able to open the samples using Access 97 or earlier. Although the code was developed and compiled using Access 2002, all the screen illustrations were created using Access 2003 with the **Use Windows Themed Controls on Forms** option enabled. If you run the sample application using Access 2000 or 2002, the forms will look slightly different on your system.

Note   Please note that the person names, company names, e-mail addresses, and Web site addresses in these databases are fictitious. (The one exception is the instructor names in the Registration Management sample database—these are names of actual Microsoft Access MVPs, and their names are used with permission.) Although I preloaded all databases with sample data, some of the sample databases also include a special form (zfrmLoadData) that has code to load random data into the tables based on parameters that you supply.

Using the CD

To use the companion CD, insert it into your CD-ROM or DVD drive. Accept the license agreement that is presented to access the Start menu. If AutoRun is not enabled on your system, run StartCD.exe located in the root of the CD or refer to the Readme.txt file. The menu provides you with links to the resources available on the CD and also to the Microsoft Learning Support Web site.

Caution   The electronic version of the book included on this CD is provided in Portable Document Format (PDF). To view this file, you will need Adobe Acrobat or Adobe Reader. For more information about these products or to download the free Adobe Reader, visit the Adobe Web site at *http://www.adobe.com*.

System Requirements

The following minimum system requirements are necessary to run the CD:

- Microsoft Windows XP or later or Windows 2000 Professional with Service Pack 3 or later

- Pentium 233-MHz personal computer; Pentium III or faster processor recommended

- At least 128 megabytes (MB) of RAM for Microsoft Access 2003; other Access versions might vary

- At least 75 MB of hard disk space for copying the sample applications from the CD to your computer's hard drive

- CD-ROM or DVD drive

- Super VGA (800 × 600) or higher-resolution monitor; XGA (1024 × 768) recommended for the sample applications

- Microsoft Internet Explorer 5.01 or later

- Microsoft Mouse or compatible pointing device

Note An Internet connection is necessary to access the Web sites cited in this book. The Internet functionality of Access also requires that you have dial-up or broadband Internet access; dial-up and other charges might apply to your Internet access.

Support Information

Every effort has been made to ensure the accuracy of the book and the contents of the companion CD. For feedback on the book content or the companion CD, fill out the Online Survey referenced on the CD.

Microsoft Press provides corrections for books through the World Wide Web at *http://www.microsoft.com/learning/support/*. To connect directly to the Microsoft Press Knowledge Base and enter a query regarding a question or issue that you might have, go to *http://www.microsoft.com/learning/support/search.asp.*

For support information regarding Microsoft Access, you can connect to Microsoft Technical Support on the Web at *http://support.microsoft.com/.*

Introduction

With all five versions of my *Running Microsoft Access* books and my latest *Microsoft Office Access 2003 Inside Out* title, I included one or more complete sample applications to help illustrate the concepts that I describe in the books. However, there has never been enough space in the 1,000 or more pages of these book to fully explore how the applications work while also documenting the many features of Access itself. Adventuresome readers can explore the samples in detail to learn more, but the reader must try to discern how it all fits together by studying the table designs and relationships and by reading the comments that I always include in the code.

I can't tell you how many times I've seen developers struggling to implement some of the more complex features in various common applications. These struggles often end in frustration after long threads in Internet newsgroups or in one of the many available Web-based forums (such as Yahoo Groups). So, I decided to create complete samples of four of the most common applications and explore the toughest issues in depth in a separate book. You are holding the result in your hand.

You might be asking, "How did you decide which applications to build?" First, I drew on my more than 10 years' experience as a Microsoft Most Valuable Professional (MVP) answering questions in the public newsgroups and forums. (Disclaimer: I am not now and never have been an employee of Microsoft.) I also consulted my fellow MVPs and members of the Access development and support staffs. Finally, I decided to provide solutions for the most common business problems, so you won't find a sample database in this book to help you keep track of your personal book or record collection.

For those of you who think Microsoft Access is just a development tool for casual users, I think the complexity of the four sample applications will convince you otherwise. I built all four applications in less than eight months. Although my long experience with Access certainly contributed to my productivity, I can't imagine building a set of four complex applications in less time with any other development tool.

Who Can Use This Book

This book is not for the rank beginner. I assume the reader of this book has been working with Access for a while and has worked through at least one of the "big" books on Microsoft Access—such as my *Running Microsoft Access 2000* or *Microsoft Office Access 2003 Inside Out*. So, this book will not teach you the fundamentals of query, form, or report design or coding in Visual Basic. Although this book covers common table design problems and recommended design techniques in Chapter 1, "Designing Your Tables," you should have also studied accepted relational database design techniques in depth elsewhere. (You can find a list of suggested reading in Appendix A, "Recommended Reading.")

You will find this book useful if you are tasked with creating an Access application that is similar to any of the four discussed in this book. You might even find that you can use one of the sample applications as a starting template for your application. Even if the application you need to build isn't similar to one of the four in this book, you most likely will find in one of the samples the solution for some complex tasks you need to perform. For example, if you need to allocate a resource, you can see ways to solve variations of this problem in both the Registration Management and Inventory Management applications. If you need examples of automating tasks with Microsoft Excel or Microsoft Outlook, you can find examples in all four sample applications.

Although I created the samples using Access 2002 (version 10), all the sample databases are in Access 2000 format. You should be able to open and run the samples and view the design of objects using Access 2000 (version 9) or later.

> **Note** I compiled and saved the sample code using Access 2002. The sample databases avoid using version-dependent elements such as ActiveX controls or the Visual Basic libraries for Microsoft Office or other Microsoft Office products. If you want to run the samples using a different version of Access, you should first open any module in the Visual Basic Editor, verify that the library references are correct by choosing References from the Tools menu, and then compile and save the project.

What's in This Book

Building Microsoft Access Applications is divided into five major parts:

- Part 1 discusses overall table design, user interface design, and client/server issues.

  - Chapter 1 focuses on common table design problems and recommended design techniques for designing tables for an Access application. You should already be familiar with the basic concepts of relational table design before reading this chapter.

  - Chapter 2 describes recommended techniques for building the user interface for your application.

  - Chapter 3 explains the considerations for building an efficient client/server application that can support multiple users. This chapter also describes advanced techniques you can use to support 50 or more simultaneous users.

- Part 2 shows you how to build a membership application.

  - Chapter 4 describes the Membership Tracking application and explains the table design.

  - Chapter 5 shows you how to detect, and warn users about, potentially duplicate names and how to ensure that names are stored in proper case.

❑ Chapter 6 discusses how to track membership activities, including meeting and committee meeting attendance.

❑ Chapter 7 explains how to track membership expiration, collect dues, and report dues status.

❑ Chapter 8 shows you how to print meeting and dues expiration notices and send the notices using Microsoft Outlook.

■ Part 3 discusses how to design and build a sales and inventory management application (think Northwind on steroids).

❑ Chapter 9 describes the Inventory Management application, including business rule assumptions and the supporting table design.

❑ Chapter 10 shows you how to allocate an ordered item to an order from available inventory.

❑ Chapter 11 describes how to generate purchase orders to bring product stock up to minimum levels. It also shows you how to generate purchase orders linked to open customer orders when there is insufficient stock to fill an order.

❑ Chapter 12 explains how to log the vendor invoice for a purchase order, mark the items received, and post them to inventory. When a purchase order has a related customer order, you'll learn a technique for simultaneously marking the customer order as allocated.

❑ Chapter 13 shows you how to create customer invoices and mark the allocated products sold in inventory.

❑ Chapter 14 describes how to produce packing lists, invoices, and inventory reports and explores ways to analyze and chart sales using automation features of Microsoft Excel.

■ Part 4 explains the intricacies of a customer support application, including techniques for supporting 50 or more simultaneous users.

❑ Chapter 15 describes the Customer Support application and shows you how to build both shared and local tables.

❑ Chapters 16 explores how to organize customer information, including tracking the products owned and warranty expiration.

❑ Chapter 17 describes how to capture support cases, assign them for resolution, and log support events.

❑ Chapter 18 shows you how to create reminders for a support case, track outstanding reminders, and mark reminders complete.

❑ Chapter 19 describes ways to report and analyze support cases, including using automation features of Microsoft Excel.

- Part 5 explores how to manage a technical school or seminar with a registration management application.

  - Chapter 20 describes a technology school registration management business model and shows you how to design the supporting tables.

  - Chapter 21 explores how to leverage the power of Visual Basic to automatically schedule courses and course sections.

  - Chapter 22 shows how to validate and confirm a registration request while managing section attendance limits and verifying prerequisites.

  - Chapter 23 describes how to print or e-mail registration confirmations and the class schedule for instructors.

  - Chapter 24 discusses how to generate and send out student invoices.

This book also includes five appendixes that contain important reference information:

- Appendix A lists additional books that are recommended as part of any Access application developer's complete library.

- Appendix B describes the schemas (table layouts) of the four sample applications.

- Appendix C lists the Visual Basic functions most commonly used in Access applications.

- Appendix D is a complete reference to SQL as implemented in desktop databases. It also contains notes about differences between SQL supported natively by Access and SQL implemented in SQL Server.

- Appendix E describes generic features that you might want to use in any Access application.

Conventions Used in This Book and the Sample Databases

As you work through the book, you'll encounter various conventions to describe the syntax you should use. In the sample databases, you'll find that I have used standard naming conventions for object and variable names. This section describes those conventions.

SQL Syntax Conventions

The following conventions are used in the descriptions of SQL statement syntax in Appendix D, "Understanding SQL." These conventions do not apply to code examples listed within the text; all code examples appear exactly as you'll find them in the sample databases. Except as noted below, you must enter all symbols, such as parentheses and colons, exactly as they appear in the syntax line.

Convention	Meaning
Bold	Bold type indicates keywords and reserved words that you must enter exactly as shown. Microsoft Visual Basic understands keywords entered in uppercase, lowercase, and mixed case type. Access stores SQL keywords in queries in all uppercase, but you can enter the keywords in any case.
Italic	Italicized words represent variables that you supply.
Angle brackets < >	Angle brackets enclose syntactic elements that you must supply. The words inside the angle brackets describe the element but do not show the actual syntax of the element. Do not enter the angle brackets.
Brackets [ ]	Brackets enclose optional items. If more than one item is listed, the items are separated by a pipe character (|). Choose one or none of the elements. Do not enter the brackets or the pipe; they're not part of the element. Note that Visual Basic and SQL in many cases require that you enclose names in brackets. When brackets are required as part of the syntax of variables that you must supply in these examples, the brackets are italicized, as in *[MyTable].[MyField]*.
Braces { }	Braces enclose one or more options. If more than one option is listed, the items are separated by a pipe character (|). Choose one item from the list. Do not enter the braces or the pipe.
Ellipsis ...	Ellipses indicate that you can repeat an item one or more times. When a comma is shown with an ellipsis (,...), enter a comma between items.
Underscore _	You can use a blank space followed by an underscore to continue a line of Visual Basic code to the next line for readability. You cannot place an underscore in the middle of a string literal. You do not need an underscore for continued lines in SQL, but you cannot break a literal across lines.

Object and Variable Naming Conventions

In any application, it's a good idea to prefix the names of objects and variables so that when the names appear in queries or code, the intended use of the object is clear. For example, when constructing queries, a FROM clause that includes Customers or Products doesn't tell you whether those names refer to a table or a query. Names like tblCustomers or qryProducts are more meaningful. Likewise, a variable named Q isn't very informative, but a variable named intQ tells you the data type of the variable is Integer. Following are the naming prefixes used in the sample applications and their meanings.

Naming Conventions Used for Access Objects

Object Type	Object Prefix	Meaning
Table	tbl	A table object.
	tlkp	A table containing lookup values for the foreign key in another table.
	tvw	A table containing a local view of data from the shared data file.
	ztbl, zttbl, or zztbl	A working or system table for the application.
Query	qry	A standard select query, usually a record source for a form.
	qlkp	A query on a lookup table, usually the row source for a combo box or list box.
	qupd	An update query.
	qapp	An append (insert) query.
	qdel	A delete query.
	qmak	A make table query.
	qtot	A totals query.
	qxtb	A crosstab query.
	zqry, zqupd, zqapp, zqdel	Queries used by application code.
	qxmpl or qryXmpl	Sample queries referenced in the book but not used by the application.
Form	frm	A form to edit data.
	fpop	A form that opens in pop-up mode.
	fdlg	A form that opens in Dialog mode.
	fsub	A form used as a subform.
	frmXmpl, fsubXmpl	Sample forms referenced in the book but not used by the application.
	zfrm, zfdlg	Sample or system forms not normally displayed to the user.

Object Type	Object Prefix	Meaning
Report	rpt	A report to display data.
	rsub	A report used as a subreport.
	rptXmpl, rsubXmpl	Sample reports referenced in the book but not used by the application.
Module	mod	A standard module. (Class modules have no prefix.)
	zmod	A module containing sample code not used by the application.

> **Note**   Within the sample databases, you'll find that I always use prefixes but don't always strictly follow the suggested linkage between prefix and meaning. For example, you'll probably find some totals queries that have a *qry* prefix instead of a *qtot* prefix.

Naming Conventions for Access Form and Control Names

Prefix	Meaning
btn or opt	An option button.
bx	A rectangle.
chk	A check box.
cmb	A combo box.
cmd	A command button.
fsub	A subform and subform control.
img	An image control.
lbl	A label.
ln	A line.
lst	A list box.
og	An option group.
ole	A bound or unbound object frame.
pag	A page on a tab control.
pbk	A page break.
tab	A tab control.
tgl	A toggle button.
txt	A text box.

Naming Conventions for Variables

Variable Type	Prefix	Meaning
Data	byt	Byte data type.
	bln	Boolean data type.
	int	Integer data type.
	lng	Long data type.
	sng	Single data type.
	dbl	Double data type.
	cur	Currency data type.
	dec	Decimal data type.
	dat	Date data type.
	str	String data type.
	var	Variant data type.
Objects	obj	A generic object.
	db	A Database object.
	rst	A Recordset object.
	tdf	A TableDef object.
	qdf	A QueryDef object.
	frm	A Form object.
	rpt	A Report object.

Part I
Designing Your Application

Chapter 1

Designing Your Tables

As discussed in the Introduction, this book assumes that you understand how to design tables for a relational database like Microsoft Access. In truth, a single chapter cannot teach you all you need to know about table design. See Appendix A for some recommendations of books you should consider reading to improve your design skills.

However, no book on building database applications would be complete without some discussion of the most common errors, why these errors are bad, and what you can do to fix them. This chapter also discusses design techniques unique to Access that you can employ to make your application run more smoothly.

You can find many of the recommendations in this chapter scattered throughout several chapters in either my *Running Microsoft Access 2000* (Microsoft Press, 1999) or *Microsoft Office Access 2003 Inside Out* (Microsoft Press, 2003) book. However, those books focus on the mechanics of creating tables and relationships, and offer design recommendations primarily in sidebars or notes. This chapter assumes that you already understand the mechanics of table and relationship design in Microsoft Access, and instead provides a discussion of specific design techniques you can use to improve your table structures. In fact, you can apply many of the lessons learned in this chapter to designing any relational database structure.

Note Before writing this chapter, I polled my fellow Microsoft Access MVPs for suggestions about topics that I should include. (You can find a list of all who participated in the Acknowledgments section at the beginning of this book.) Although we could all agree on certain fundamental principles, we had some rather interesting (and sometimes heated) discussions about some of the design recommendations that I proposed. You can find the topics upon which we all reached consensus in the next section, "Avoiding Common Problems." "Using Good Design Techniques," page 23, includes recommendations that you should consider when designing your tables, but you should apply only those that make sense for your specific application.

Avoiding Common Problems

Even experienced Access developers occasionally commit design errors. If you have been developing Access applications for a while, you have probably already learned how expensive a small design error can be after you have designed dozens of forms and reports and need to implement a new feature. If your tables were well designed, adding a new feature is easy. If you took any shortcuts, making changes is costly and time consuming. This first section describes the 10 most common problems and how to avoid them.

Problem #1: Creating Compound Fields

Especially if you have imported data from another source, you might find that some fields contain data that should be broken into multiple fields. A very common problem is using a compound field for an address that contains house or building number, street name, apartment or suite number, city, region or state, postal code, and country—perhaps formatted with carriage returns to print as a single value on mailing labels or envelopes. Another common error is storing a person's full name in a single field.

This is great for a word processing application, but it's a bad idea for a database. If the postal code is embedded within a long string, how will you sort the records by postal code? How can you find records for a specific city? How can you sort on a person's last name or search on last name if it's embedded within a long string? Sure, you can use a LIKE search, but that is very inefficient. And you certainly cannot build an index on any of the parts to improve performance.

Figure 1-1 shows you a typical record layout with compound fields and suggests a more appropriate layout for the same data in a database table. If you study the relational model for database design, this process of separating compound fields into simple ones is called decomposing data into *atomic* values.

The better design allows you to search and index on discrete values, and you can always re-create the more complex values using string concatenation. Of course, your final design depends on how your application needs to use the data. Some applications might require even further granularity—such as splitting out the house or building number into a separate field or adding a person's title.

Bad:

CustName	CustAddress
John Allen Smith, Jr.	1234 Main Street, Suite 5A, Oakland, CA, 94622, USA

Better:

CustLName	CustFName	CustName	CustSuffix	CustAddress1
Smith	John	Allen	Jr.	1234 Main Street

CustAddress2	CustCity	CustRegion	CustPostal	CustCountry
Suite 5A	Oakland	CA	94622	USA

Figure 1-1   Decomposing complex fields into atomic values.

Problem #2: Including Repeating Groups

A *repeating group* is a set of one or more columns that appears multiple times in a table definition. That is, the table design includes multiple columns that all have the same kind of data. Figure 1-2 shows a simple repeating group of classes in which each particular student is enrolled.

StudentID	Period1	Period2	Period3	Period4	Period5	Period6
55	Algebra	History	French	Physics	Phys Ed	Comp Sci
68	Geometry	French	Chemistry	Soccer	Orchestra	Debate
87	Geography	Math I	German	Biology	Speech	Band

Figure 1-2   A simple repeating group of classes for which a student is registered.

Repeating groups *can* be useful for displaying or analyzing data. In fact, you'll often see repeating groups in a spreadsheet or in a PivotTable. However, they're terrible for storing data in a relational database. For example, how would you find out how many students are registered for each subject? If you know the subject names in advance, you can certainly search for rows that have a particular subject in any of the class periods and then count the rows. But you would have to run a separate query for each known subject and then UNION the results to get the complete answer. Also, if the school decides to add a seventh class period, the table design must be changed. And if some students attend only part time, the table will contain rows with empty and unused columns, thereby wasting space in the table.

To correctly store data like this in a relational table, you need to "un-pivot" the grid and use the repeating group column names as data values. Figure 1-3, on the next page, shows the data in Figure 1-2 restructured for a relational table.

StudentID	Period	Subject
55	1	Algebra
55	2	History
55	3	French
55	4	Physics
55	5	Phys Ed
55	6	Comp Sci
68	1	Geometry
68	2	French
68	3	Chemistry
68	4	Soccer
68	5	Orchestra
68	6	Debate
87	1	Geography

Figure 1-3   The correct design for a class registration table that avoids repeating groups.

When you restructure the table in this way, finding out how many students are registered for each subject is easy.

```
SELECT Subject, Count(StudentID) As SubjectCount
FROM StudentRegistrations
GROUP BY Subject;
```

If the school decides to add an early "zero" class period or a late seventh class period, the table structure does not need to be changed because the new period numbers are simply new values in the Period column.

Tip   You can often identify repeating groups by examining the field names. You probably have a repeating group if any of the following is true:

■ Field names are similar and differ only by the presence of a numeric or alphabetic suffix or prefix.

■ Field names are lists of the names of months in a year, days in a week, or hours in a day.

■ Field names are descriptions of the same type of object. For example, apples, pears, bananas, and peaches are all fruits. Mathematics, history, biology, and rhetoric are all course names.

Note that a repeating group isn't always just one field repeated several times. Repeating groups can also be sets of two or more fields repeated in a table design. Extending the example shown in Figure 1-2, a table containing StudentID, Period1Class, Period1Instructor, Period1Classroom, Period2Class, Period2Instructor, Period2Classroom, and so on contains sets of three fields repeated several times in the table design. This table structure not only contains compound repeating groups but also includes the problem of including fields for multiple subjects in a single table, as discussed in the next section.

Problem #3: Putting Multiple Subjects in One Table

Each table should describe one and only one subject or action. An example of a common error is including the full name and address information for the customer of each order in the Orders table rather than placing the customer information (a separate subject) in its own table. When you fail to create a separate table, you repeat data unnecessarily, potentially introduce errors, and must potentially update many rows in the Orders table if you want to correct the spelling of a customer name or update a billing address.

To consider another example, assume that the table shown previously in Figure 1-2 not only has the repeating group for classes (Period1Class, Period2Class, and so forth) but also has additional fields within each group: Period1Instructor, Period1Classroom, Period2Instructor, Period2Classroom, and so on. If Period1Instructor contains a person's name and Period1Classroom contains a classroom name and location, these are quite probably separate subjects that belong in their own tables. You should have a separate table for Instructors and include only the primary key value from a specific row in that table as the foreign key in this table to link the class registration to the details about the instructor. Likewise, Classrooms (and perhaps Buildings) should also be separate subject tables, and the specific class location in the class registration row should be a foreign key link to those tables.

You can perform a simple test to find multiple subjects in one table: Can I change the value of any field (other than the primary key) in this table and not have to change a similar value anywhere else in my database? Note, however, that it is acceptable to copy certain values to dependent tables depending on your business rules. For example, an Order Detail record might include a *copy* of the Price from the Products table because that copy represents the price at the time the order was placed. Or, an Order might need a Shipping Address that could be different from the customer's address at the time the order is placed.

I call this type of data *Point in Time* data—data that was current at a specific time. The copy of the Price in the Order Detail record is the price that was *current at the time the order was placed*, but the Price in the Products table is always the current price. The price in the Order Detail table is not a duplicate field because its meaning is different from the price in the Products table. Likewise, the Shipping Address is the location to which the order was shipped, but the Address in the Customers table is always the customer's current mailing address.

If you look at the table shown previously in Figure 1-3, you might conclude that the Subject column is actually a separate subject that should be in its own table. If the subject has additional related information, such as the grade level or full course description, you should probably have a separate table containing this information. In this case, the contents of the Subject column in the sample could well be the foreign key that links to the Subjects table containing the details about each subject—provided it is also the primary key in the Subjects table.

See the discussions about artificial primary keys in "Using Good Design Techniques," page 23, for tips about defining primary keys and foreign keys.

Problem #4: Oversimplifying Your Tables

It's also possible to oversimplify or "over-normalize" your table design. Did you create a separate table for customer addresses, but each customer has only one address? Did you create a separate table for "categories" or "types," but that table contains only the one field? Perhaps you have oversimplified your table design. Consider the table designs in Figures 1-4 and 1-5.

You should always be suspicious of tables that contain a single field or an AutoNumber primary key and a single field. Why is a subject in its own table if it contains only one descriptive field? In both cases shown in Figures 1-4 and 1-5 the table for contact types has only one field. However, note the referential integrity relationship shown between contact types and contacts. The referential integrity relationship ensures that a customer type cannot be entered in the Contacts table that does not exist in the ContactTypes table, so the ContactTypes table might be a valid use of a table with a single field. Keep in mind that you could achieve the same result by defining a validation rule on the ContactType field in the Contacts table, but using a separate table like this provides the flexibility to add a new valid contact type in the future by adding a row to ContactTypes without having to modify the Contacts table design.

In Figure 1-4, you can see two sets of addresses and phone numbers. Is this an invalid repeating group? If the application never needs to track more than two addresses (work and home), and most contacts have both a work address and a home address, this design is more efficient than creating a separate table of addresses because the application can fetch names and addresses without having to join two tables. Figure 1-5 shows an alternative design that can accommodate an unlimited number of addresses and phone numbers for any one contact. Should the phone numbers remain in the Contacts table in case you have no address for a contact? Should phone numbers be in a separate table altogether? It probably makes sense to leave the mobile phone number field in the Contacts table in any case—very few people have more than one mobile phone number.

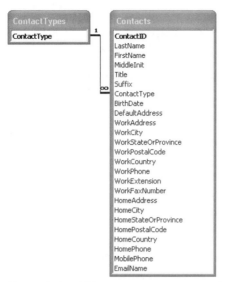

Figure 1-4   Tables to store contacts and contact types.

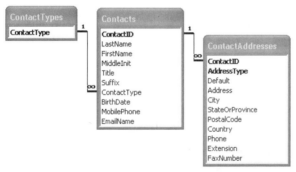

Figure 1-5   Tables to store contacts, contact types, and multiple contact addresses.

What's the correct answer? As the French would say, "ça depend" ("it depends"). The bottom line is you must fully understand the data you need to store in your tables and how that data will be used.

- Do not create a separate table where doing so forces you to always join two or more tables to solve most problems.

- Do create a separate table when you might need to store an unknown and unrestricted number of related items (addresses and phone numbers in this example) for another subject table.

- Do create a separate table to hold repeating groups as rows when you must perform an analysis on the members of the groups—such as counting the phone numbers in a particular area code.

Problem #5: Segmenting Tables

When you're working with large amounts of data in a spreadsheet, you are often forced to segment your data in some way because the number of rows that you can store in a worksheet is limited. You might segment your active data by a date range (perhaps sales details by month) or by some other natural value such as sales region or department.

Segmenting data in a database application is a bad idea. First, you must either design separate queries, forms, and reports to edit and view the segmented data, or you must write code to dynamically load the desired recordset from the correct segment. Second, if you want to analyze data across more than one segment (for example, analyze the sales data for a full year from several monthly files), you must use a union query to gather the data from multiple segments, and union queries can be very slow.

Although you are limited to a total of 2 gigabytes in a single JET .mdb file, you can easily store several hundred thousand rows within this limitation. You can also place a single very large table in its own .mdb file, define other supporting tables in another .mdb file, and use linked tables to your application to bring all the data together. If you are using SQL Server to store your data—other than the Microsoft SQL Server Desktop Engine (MSDE), which is also limited to a total of 2 gigabytes—you are limited only by the amount of available hard drive space on the server.

You might argue that segmented tables make it easier to secure data so that users can have access only to those segments to which they have authority. However, you can solve this problem when all data is in a single large table by creating With OWNERACCESS queries that filter the rows in Access, or by defining secured views in SQL Server.

So, other than for historical summary tables, it does not make sense to segment your active data into separate tables for an Access application. Of course, you should define indexes on fields that might be used by your application to filter the data for a specific task or user. For example, if some users should be able to work with data only from their own department, you should define an index on the department field.

Problem #6: Storing Calculated Values

Do not store calculated values in your tables. It is preferable to perform the appropriate calculation in a query because Access provides no mechanism in the database engine to automatically maintain a calculated value for you. The simple test for compound subjects applies here as well. If changing a field value means you must also change a dependent field, that second field is probably a calculated value.

Note, however, that including a calculated value might be necessary for performance reasons—such as maintaining the current sum of items in inventory over thousands of inventory transaction rows. You should plan such a calculated value carefully. In the forms you provide to update the other fields in the calculation, you must write code to recalculate the value and save it. You might also need to write verification code that the user can run periodically to ensure that the stored calculated values match what's in the fields that participate in the calculation. Keep in mind that if you allow access to your application tables outside your application code, users might change values that would result in your calculated value being incorrect.

Problem #7: Defining Field Lookup Properties

Microsoft Access for Windows 95 introduced the ability to define lookup properties for fields in tables to allow you to predefine how you want the field displayed in a datasheet, form, or report. For example, if you have a DepartmentID field in an Employees table that stores the foreign key value of the department for which the employee works, you can display the department name rather than the number value when you look at the data. If you're displaying a Yes/No field, you can provide a drop-down list that shows options for "invoiced" and "not invoiced" instead of yes and no or true and false. Using a lookup—a combo box or list box on a form to select primary key values from a related table to set a foreign key—is not a bad idea in some instances. For example, you can open the frmOrders form in the Inventory Management application (Inventory.mdb), and you'll see combo boxes for both Customer and Tax Status. However, I avoid defining lookup properties for fields in my tables unless the "looked up" value is also the foreign key.

In Chapter 3, "Designing a Client/Server Application," you'll learn that using a combo box or list box to display a row source of several thousand rows is detrimental to obtaining good client/server performance. Chapter 3 also shows you techniques to either minimize the number of rows or use an alternate method to choose a value from a lookup.

First and foremost, a lookup masks the actual underlying value for sorts and searches. If you open tblOrders in the Inventory application, as shown on the next page in Figure 1-6, you can see that it has no lookup properties defined for any of the fields. You see the numeric value of the CustomerID foreign key field (the Caption property for the field is set to Customer), not customer names, and you see the numeric tax status code, not a text description.

To see how a lookup on customer name appears, open qxmplLookup in the Inventory application, as shown in Figure 1-7, on the next page.

You can now see the customer name instead of the CustomerID field value, and opening the combo box list shows you additional useful information about each customer. However, if you look at this query in Design view, you'll find that the query is sorted in ascending order on the CustomerID field. Do you think "Ottilies Käseladen" should appear before "Great Lakes Food Market" if the query is sorted correctly? The query output is correctly sorted on the underlying numeric customer ID value, not the name.

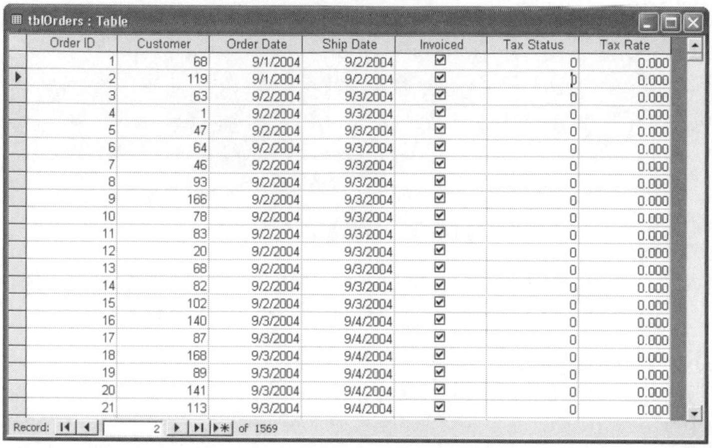

tblOrders : Table

Order ID	Customer	Order Date	Ship Date	Invoiced	Tax Status	Tax Rate
1	68	9/1/2004	9/2/2004	☑	0	0.000
2	119	9/1/2004	9/2/2004	☑	0	0.000
3	63	9/2/2004	9/3/2004	☑	0	0.000
4	1	9/2/2004	9/3/2004	☑	0	0.000
5	47	9/2/2004	9/3/2004	☑	0	0.000
6	64	9/2/2004	9/3/2004	☑	0	0.000
7	46	9/2/2004	9/3/2004	☑	0	0.000
8	93	9/2/2004	9/3/2004	☑	0	0.000
9	166	9/2/2004	9/3/2004	☑	0	0.000
10	78	9/2/2004	9/3/2004	☑	0	0.000
11	83	9/2/2004	9/3/2004	☑	0	0.000
12	20	9/2/2004	9/3/2004	☑	0	0.000
13	68	9/2/2004	9/3/2004	☑	0	0.000
14	82	9/2/2004	9/3/2004	☑	0	0.000
15	102	9/2/2004	9/3/2004	☑	0	0.000
16	140	9/3/2004	9/4/2004	☑	0	0.000
17	87	9/3/2004	9/4/2004	☑	0	0.000
18	168	9/3/2004	9/4/2004	☑	0	0.000
19	89	9/3/2004	9/4/2004	☑	0	0.000
20	141	9/3/2004	9/4/2004	☑	0	0.000
21	113	9/3/2004	9/4/2004	☑	0	0.000

Record: 2 of 1569

Figure 1-6 The tblOrders table in the Inventory application has no lookup properties defined for fields.

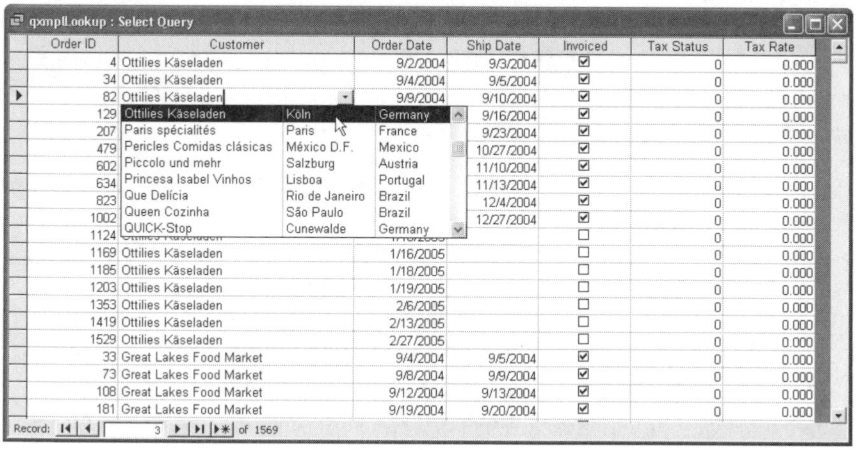

qxmplLookup : Select Query

Order ID	Customer	Order Date	Ship Date	Invoiced	Tax Status	Tax Rate
4	Ottilies Käseladen	9/2/2004	9/3/2004	☑	0	0.000
34	Ottilies Käseladen	9/4/2004	9/5/2004	☑	0	0.000
82	Ottilies Käseladen	9/9/2004	9/10/2004	☑	0	0.000
129			9/16/2004	☑	0	0.000
207			9/23/2004	☑	0	0.000
479			10/27/2004	☑	0	0.000
602			11/10/2004	☑	0	0.000
634			11/13/2004	☑	0	0.000
823			12/4/2004	☑	0	0.000
1002			12/27/2004	☑	0	0.000
1124				☐	0	0.000
1169	Ottilies Käseladen	1/16/2005		☐	0	0.000
1185	Ottilies Käseladen	1/18/2005		☐	0	0.000
1203	Ottilies Käseladen	1/19/2005		☐	0	0.000
1353	Ottilies Käseladen	2/6/2005		☐	0	0.000
1419	Ottilies Käseladen	2/13/2005		☐	0	0.000
1529	Ottilies Käseladen	2/27/2005		☐	0	0.000
33	Great Lakes Food Market	9/4/2004	9/5/2004	☑	0	0.000
73	Great Lakes Food Market	9/8/2004	9/9/2004	☑	0	0.000
108	Great Lakes Food Market	9/12/2004	9/13/2004	☑	0	0.000
181	Great Lakes Food Market	9/19/2004	9/20/2004	☑	0	0.000

Ottilies Käseladen	Köln	Germany
Paris spécialités	Paris	France
Pericles Comidas clásicas	México D.F.	Mexico
Piccolo und mehr	Salzburg	Austria
Princesa Isabel Vinhos	Lisboa	Portugal
Que Delícia	Rio de Janeiro	Brazil
Queen Cozinha	São Paulo	Brazil
QUICK-Stop	Cunewalde	Germany

Record: 3 of 1569

Figure 1-7 The qxmplLookup query has lookup properties defined for the CustomerID field. The query is sorted on the CustomerID field, but the result appears to not be in the correct sequence because the lookup masks the underlying value.

You can actually click in the Customer column and then click the Sort Ascending button on the toolbar to see the rows in sequence by customer name, not customer ID. When you do this, Access sets the OrderBy property of the query to something strange:

```
Lookup_CustomerID.CustomerName
```

The field CustomerName does not exist in the query at all! Clearly, a field name prefixed with "Lookup_" has special meaning to Access. To correctly honor the sort request, Access is forcing the JET engine to perform a hidden join with the tblCustomers table so that it can sort on what you see rather than the actual underlying value.

To see one of the other bad side effects of lookup properties, open the frmOrders form in the Inventory application, click in the Customer field, and click the Find button (binoculars) on the toolbar. The first order should be for customer Around the Horn (unless you've reloaded the sample data), so you should be able to find all customers whose names begin with the letter *A*. Type that letter in the Find What box, choose **Start of Field** in the Match box, clear the **Search Fields As Formatted** option, and click Find Next. Your result should look like Figure 1-8.

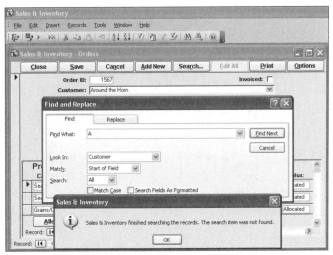

Figure 1-8   Displaying an apparently incorrect Find result in a combo box lookup.

The problem, of course, is Access is searching on the underlying numeric customer ID value (to which the combo box is bound), not what you see displayed in the control. So, there is no match for a numeric value starting with the letter *A*. Of course, you can execute the Find command again, but first select the **Search Fields As Formatted** option. You'll find the records you want, but Access is performing the Find on the looked-up values, not the actual field value. If you have ever performed a Find on a very large table using the **Search Fields As Formatted** option, you know that using this option is very slow and inefficient.

As with a query, you can click in the Customer field on the form, click the Sort Ascending button, and see a correct result sorted on the looked-up value. If you ask Access to do this in the frmOrders form, you can find out what really happened by opening the Immediate window (press Ctrl+G) and entering

```
?Forms!frmOrders.OrderBy
```

Visual Basic will respond

```
Lookup_cmbCustomerID.CustomerName
```

The name of the combo box control is "cmbCustomerID." Again, the "Lookup_" prefix has a special meaning. Access is performing a hidden join with the row source of the combo box (a query on tblCustomers) to be able to sort the rows by what you see. Interestingly, the record source of the frmOrders form uses a query that does include tblCustomers along with tblOrders, so the extra join is redundant and wasteful of resources.

You can also highlight the customer name in the combo box and click the Filter By Selection button on the toolbar to see only the orders for that customer. Again, you can find out what happened by going to the Immediate window and entering

```
?Forms!frmOrders.Filter
```

Visual Basic will respond with something like

```
((Lookup_cmbCustomerID.CustomerName="Alfreds Futterkiste"))
```

As it did with the sort on the combo box, Access is forcing the JET engine to do an extra hidden join on the row source of the combo box to get the correct result. Even worse, unless you've secured your database to disallow Modify Design permission on your forms, Access silently saves the modified Filter and OrderBy properties when the user closes the form! If your code depends on the contents of the Filter property to correctly filter related objects (such as a report to display the currently filtered orders or customers), your code will likely break if you try to borrow the form filter. Another form might not have a cmbCustomerID control, and reports don't understand the strange "Lookup_" filter syntax.

What about the Lookup Wizard entry under Data Type in table Design view? I recommend that you *never* use this wizard. It often builds strange SQL for the Row Source property, it always defines a relationship between the table you're editing and the lookup table, and it defines additional indexes on both fields. If the lookup table contains only a few rows, the index is a waste of time and resources. As you probably know, there's a limit of 32 indexes on a table. I have seen some cases where I haven't been able to build all the indexes I need because the wizard built these unnecessary indexes.

Finally, if you have secured your data, using a lookup forces you to grant permissions not only on the record source of the form but also the row source of all combo boxes. If you use a With OWNERACCESS query as the row source, filters and sorts will fail because the hidden join required to do a filter or sort on a lookup control does not directly use the query.

For more details about the evils of lookup properties, go to http://www.mvps.org/access/ lookupfields.htm.

Problem #8: Defining Validation Rules Without Validation Text

The ability to define validation rules for both fields and tables in an Access database is a great feature. However, if you specify a validation rule but no validation text, Access generates an ugly and cryptic message that your users might not understand. The tblPOProducts table has a complex validation rule that prohibits setting the Invoiced field to True without also supplying an InvoiceNumber, and vice versa. Without any validation text defined, violating this rule results in the interesting error message shown in Figure 1-9.

Figure 1-9   What the user sees when a complex validation rule has no companion validation text.

A user seeing this message is likely to be completely bewildered and have no idea what is wrong. Unless you like getting lots of support calls, I recommend that you always enter a custom validation text message whenever you specify a validation rule. Figure 1-10 shows the actual validation text defined for this rule.

Figure 1-10   Validation text can describe what's wrong in terms a user can understand.

Of course, you must be careful to write validation text that you're confident your users will understand. A simple message such as "You entered an invalid value" probably won't solve the problem, either!

Problem #9: Incorrectly Using Data Types

Designing tables for your application is a big challenge. You must not only identify the subject for each table, the attributes (fields) required to define each subject, and the relationships between subjects, but also select the best data type for storing each attribute. Table 1-1 summarizes the data types available in an Access desktop (.mdb) database.

Table 1-1   Access Data Types

Data Type	Usage	Size
Text	Alphanumeric data	Up to 255 characters
Memo	Alphanumeric data—sentences and paragraphs	Up to about 1 gigabyte (but controls to display a memo are limited to the first 65,535 characters)
Hyperlink	A link address to a document or file on the World Wide Web, on an intranet, on a local area network (LAN), or on your local computer	Up to about 1 gigabyte
Number	Numeric data	1, 2, 4, 8, or 16 bytes
AutoNumber	Unique value generated by Access for each new record	4 bytes (16 bytes for Replication ID)
Currency	Monetary data, stored with 4 decimal places of precision	8 bytes

Table 1-1   **Access Data Types**

Data Type	Usage	Size
Yes/No	Boolean (true/false) data; Access stores the numeric value zero (0) for false, and minus one (–1) for true.	1 bit
Date/Time	Dates and times	8 bytes
OLE Object	Pictures, graphs, or other ActiveX objects from another Windows-based application	Up to about 2 gigabytes

Storing Character Data

For character data, you should normally select the Text data type. You can control the maximum length of a Text field by setting the Field Size property. Use the Memo data type only for long strings of text that might exceed 255 characters.

The Memo data type has some serious limitations, as listed here:

- Although later versions of Access allow you to define an index on a field of the Memo data type, Access indexes only the first 255 characters of each field.

- You cannot use a Memo field in a union query.

- If you include a Memo field in a totals (aggregate) query and use the field in the Group By clause, Access displays only the first 255 characters of the field in the query output.

- Form and report controls in an Access application can display only the first 65,535 characters stored in a Memo field.

- Unless you have installed the latest version of the JET database engine (SP 8 or later), Access in many cases truncates Memo fields to 256 characters when importing from or exporting to Excel. You can obtain the latest JET database engine update via Windows Update.

The Hyperlink data type lets you store a simple or complex link to an external file or document. Internally, Hyperlink is a Memo data type with a special flag set to indicate that it is a link—so the limitations that apply to the Memo data type also apply to Hyperlink. The link can contain a Uniform Resource Locator (URL) that points to a location on the World Wide Web or on a local intranet. It can also contain the Universal Naming Convention (UNC) name of a file on a server on your local area network (LAN) or on your local computer drives. The link can point to a file that is in Hypertext Markup Language (HTML) or in a format that is supported by an ActiveX application on your computer.

The link itself can have up to four parts:

- An optional descriptor that Access displays in the field when you're not editing the link. The descriptor can start with any character other than a pound sign (#) and must have a pound sign as its ending delimiter. If you do not include the descriptor, you must start the link address with a pound sign.

- The link address expressed as either a URL (beginning with a recognized Internet protocol name such as http: or ftp:) or in UNC format (a file location expressed as \\server\share\path\filename). If you do not specify the optional descriptor field, Access displays the link address in the field. Terminate the link address with a pound sign (#).

- An optional subaddress that specifies a named location (such as a cell range in a Microsoft Excel spreadsheet or a bookmark in a Microsoft Word document) within the file. Separate the subaddress from the ScreenTip with a pound sign (#). If you entered no subaddress, you still must enter the pound sign delimiter if you want to define a ScreenTip.

- An optional ScreenTip that appears when you move your mouse pointer over the hyperlink.

For example, a hyperlink containing all four items might look like the following:

```
Viescas Download Page#http://www.viescas.com/Info/links.htm#Downloads#Click to see the files
you can download from Viescas.com
```

A hyperlink that contains a ScreenTip but no optional subaddress might look like this:

```
Viescas.com Books#http://www.viescas.com/Info/books.htm##Click to see recommended books on
Viescas.com
```

Storing Numbers

When you select the Number data type, you should think carefully about what you enter as the Field Size property because this property choice will affect precision as well as length. (For example, integer numbers do not have decimals.)

Note   The table design grid in Access allows you to define fields that can store numbers, including AutoNumber, Byte, Currency, Decimal, Double, Integer, Long Integer, and Single. You can find AutoNumber and Currency listed as separate data types in the Data Type list in the top part of the design grid, but all the other data types are subtypes of the Number data type, and you indicate the data type you want by setting the Field Size property. Internally, each of these numeric types is unique—the JET database engine does not have a Number data type with subtypes. So, when you see the text in this book reference the Single data type, it means the Number data type in the table design grid with the Field Size property set to Single.

The AutoNumber data type is specifically designed for automatic generation of primary key values. (See "Avoid Artificial Primary Keys in Tables," page 26, to learn why I think this is a bad idea.) Depending on the settings for the Field Size and New Values properties you choose for an AutoNumber field, you can have Access create a sequential or random long integer. You can include only one field using the AutoNumber data type in any table. If you define more than one AutoNumber field, Access displays an error message when you try to save the table.

Table 1-2 lists the available Field Size settings for the Number and AutoNumber data types.

Table 1-2   Field Size Properties for Numeric Fields

Data Type	Options, Description
Number	**Byte.** A single-byte integer containing values from 0 through 255.
	Integer. A 2-byte integer containing values from –32,768 through +32,767.
	Long Integer. A 4-byte integer containing values from –2,147,483,648 through +2,147,483,647.
	Single. A 4-byte floating-point number containing values from -3.4×10^{38} through $+3.4 \times 10^{38}$ and up to seven significant digits.
	Double. An 8-byte floating-point number containing values from -1.797×10^{308} through $+1.797 \times 10^{308}$ and up to 15 significant digits.
	Replication ID.[*] A 16-byte globally unique identifier (GUID).
	Decimal. A 12-byte integer with a defined decimal precision that can contain values from -10^{28} through $+10^{28}$. The default precision (number of decimal places) is 0 and the default scale (total number of digits) is 18. You can store up to 28 significant digits in the Decimal field size.
AutoNumber	**Long Integer.** A 4-byte integer containing values from –2,147,483,648 through +2,147,483,647 when New Values is Random or from 1 to +2,147,483,647 when New Values is Increment.
	Replication ID. A 16-byte globally unique identifier (GUID).

[*]   In general, the Replication ID field size should be used only in a database that is managed by the Replication Manager.

Single and Double data types use an internal storage format called floating point that can handle very large or very small numbers but is somewhat imprecise. If the number you need to store contains more than 7 significant digits for Single or more than 15 significant digits for Double, the stored number will be rounded. For example, if you try to save 10,234,567 in a Single, the actual value stored will be 10,234,570. Likewise, Access stores 10.234567 as 10.23457 in a Single. If you want absolute fractional precision, use the Decimal or Currency data type instead.

In addition, floating-point numbers store the fractional part of any number as the sum of negative powers of two. That is, the first bit to the right of the decimal point is 0.5, the second bit is 0.25, the third bit is 0.125, and so on. You're more likely to get an imprecise fractional number using a Single data type because that data type has a maximum of only 24 bits (1 bit is used for the sign and 7 bits are used for the exponent) in which to resolve an accurate fractional value. You're also more likely to see a precision error when you multiply two fractional values. For example, you can go to the Immediate window (Ctrl+G) and enter

Visual Basic responds with the correct answer:

```
3.7329996
```

However, if you force one of the numbers to a Single data type, you can see the effect of imprecise representation of the fractional value. Try entering

```
?CSng(1.131212) * 3.3
```

Visual Basic responds with an imprecise answer:

```
3.73299958705902
```

Floating-point numbers are particularly nasty when you're attempting to calculate precisely rounded numbers—such as a percentage of a currency amount rounded to pennies. In general, you should use Single and Double only in scientific applications or applications that must deal with extremely large or extremely small numbers.

Use the Currency or Decimal data type to obtain a precise value—up to 4 decimal places for Currency and up to 28 decimal places for Decimal. You should generally use the Currency data type for storing money values, but you can also use it to store any number for which you need precisely 4 decimal places.

What makes Currency and Decimal precise is the fact that Access stores the entire number as an integer, but with an assumed number of decimal, not binary, digits to the right of the decimal point. For example, Access stores the number 1.131212 in a Decimal field with scale 12 and precision 8 as the integer value 000113121200. Access keeps track of the fact that the decimal place occurs 8 digits in from the right, and the math processor (actually a component of Windows) makes the appropriate adjustment when you multiply or divide decimal values.

For more information about problems with calculations using numeric data types in Access, go to http://www.fmsinc.com/tpapers/math/index.html.

The Yes/No data type in Access is actually a Byte numeric field. Use the Yes/No data type to hold Boolean (true or false) values. This data type is particularly useful for flagging accounts paid or not paid or orders filled or not filled. When a Yes/No field contains a zero, Access interprets the value as False or No. When a Yes/No field is nonzero, Access interprets the value in most cases as True or Yes. In fact, you can test any numeric field for True in a query, and the query will return all rows that have a nonzero value in the field.

If you assign True or Yes to a Yes/No field, Access turns on all the bits in the byte. (All bits on in a Byte field is the numeric value −1.) If you assign a False or No to a Yes/No field, Access sets all the bits to 0.

> **Caution**   If you upsize your application tables to SQL Server in the future, be aware that SQL Server stores a Yes/No data type as a single bit. A False is still 0, but a True value is 1, not −1. If you explicitly test for −1 as a True value, your test will fail on data that has been upsized.

Storing Dates and Times

The Date/Time data type is useful for calendar or clock data and has the added benefit of allowing calculations in seconds, minutes, hours, days, months, or years. Internally, the Date/Time data type is a Double floating-point number. The integer portion is the number of days since December 30, 1899 (negative values represent days prior to that date), and the fractional portion is a fraction of a day, accurate to seconds. When you store only a time value in a Date/Time field, the integer portion is 0, and the fractional portion contains the time. For example, Access stores the value for 12:00 noon as 0.5.

Of course, Access never displays the underlying numeric value for a Date/Time field in the user interface. You can control what portion of the value Access displays by setting the Format property for the field. If you don't specify a format, Access displays the Date/Time value using the Short Date format defined in the regional settings section of Windows Control Panel. Many novice users think that what they see in the user interface is what is actually stored in the field. Access always stores a full Date/Time value even though the application might be displaying only month and year.

Unless you restrict what users can enter with an input mask, a user can enter both a date and time component into a field that displays only the date portion. If you do not restrict what a user can enter, you might obtain incorrect results when you create a query (or a search string in code) that includes criteria to search only for date values. For example, to search for rows in the month of January 2005, you might enter the following criteria for a Date/Time field:

```
tblSales.DateSold BETWEEN #01 JAN 2005# And #31 JAN 2005#
```

This criteria is equivalent to entering

```
tblSales.DateSold >= #01 JAN 2005# And tblSales.DateSold <= #31 JAN 2005#
```

If users have been entering a time as well as a date, you will potentially not see all the records for the last day of the month because the simple date value for January 31, 2005, is a simple integer value that is less than a Date/Time value of January 31, 2005, 9:15 A.M.—an integer plus a fraction that represents 9:15 A.M. To correctly perform the search, you should use the following:

```
tblSales.DateSold >= #01 JAN 2005# And tblSales.DateSold < #01 FEB 2005#
```

When you understand the internal format of the Date/Time data type, you can subtract one Date/Time value from another to obtain the interval between the two values. (You can also use the *DateDiff* function, but subtracting is more efficient.)

You can also add Date/Time values that contain a time component to calculate a total time—but be aware that when the total exceeds 24 hours, the total time overflows into the date portion of the Date/Time value. For example, adding 9 hours (9:00 A.M.) and 4 hours (4:00 A.M.) yields 13 hours (1:00 P.M.), but adding 14.5 hours (2:30 P.M.) and 16 hours (4:00 P.M.) yields 1 day and 6.5 hours (which equates to December 31, 1899, 6:30 A.M.). However, because you know the internal representation of Date/Time is days and fractions of days, you can add a series of elapsed times and then multiply by 24 (the number of hours in a day) to obtain the total elapsed hours and fractions of hours.

Arithmetic operations with Date/Time values follow these rules:

- Adding or subtracting two Date/Time values yields a Date/Time value.

- Adding or subtracting a number to or from a Date/Time value yields a Date/Time value. For example, you can add 1 to "today" to calculate "tomorrow," or you can subtract the integer portion of a Date/Time value (using the *Int* function) from itself to obtain the time component.

- Multiplying a Date/Time value by a number or dividing a Date/Time value by a number yields a Double data type.

> **Tip**   When you create a sum of elapsed times in a query or report, and the total time might exceed 24 hours, you can display the correct result by using this expression (substitute the name of your summary field for *TotElapsed*):
>
> ```
> Format((Int([TotElapsed]) * 24) + Hour([TotElapsed]), "#,##0") & ":" &
> Format([TotElapsed], "nn:ss")
> ```
>
> The *Int* function extracts the integer number of days, the *Hour* function extracts the hours that are less than a day, and the second *Format* function extracts the minutes and seconds.

Storing Objects

The OLE Object data type allows you to store complex data, such as pictures, graphs, or sounds, which can be edited or displayed through a dynamic link to another Windows-based application. For example, Access can store and allow you to edit a Microsoft Word document, a Microsoft Excel spreadsheet, a Microsoft PowerPoint presentation slide, a sound file (.wav), a video file (.avi), or pictures created using the Paint or Draw application.

Be aware, however, that Access stores not only the object but also a "thumbnail" of the object in bitmap format to enable it to display a representation of the object in a bound object frame in a form or report. As a result, storing compacted images in formats such as JPEG or GIF can require much more space in your .mdb file than the size of the original file because of the space occupied by the bitmap thumbnail.

Also, if you attempt to display an OLE Object field on a Web page, your browser cannot handle the internal format of the OLE Object data type. To solve both problems, consider using a Text or Hyperlink field to store a link to the OLE Object. To display a picture object stored as a text link on a form or report, you can write code to load the object path into an image control.

In summary, consider the following five points when deciding on a data type:

1. Understand the limitations of the Memo data type when sorting on a Memo field, using a Memo field in union or totals queries, and exporting a Memo field before choosing the Memo data type to store text that might be longer than 255 characters.

2. Do not use Single or Double when your application requires precise calculations; use Currency or Decimal instead.

3. Understand how SQL Server handles the Yes/No data type differently if you need to upsize your data.

4. Know the storage format of the Date/Time data type so that you create correct search criteria and use it in calculations.

5. Use a link to external objects rather than storing object data in your tables.

Problem #10: Naming Fields Incorrectly

Microsoft Access gives you lots of flexibility when it comes to naming your fields. A field name can be up to 64 characters long and can include any combination of letters, numbers, spaces, and special characters except a period (.), an exclamation point (!), an accent grave (`` ` ``), and brackets ([ ]); however, the name cannot begin with a space and cannot include control characters (ANSI values 0 through 31).

In general, you should give your fields meaningful names and should use the same name throughout for a field that occurs in more than one table. You should avoid using field names that might also match any name internal to Microsoft Access or Visual Basic. For example, all objects have a Name property, so it's a good idea to qualify a field containing a name by calling it something like CustomerName or CompanyName. You should also avoid names that are the same as built-in functions, such as *Date*, *Time*, *Now*, or *Space*. See Microsoft Access Help for a list of all the built-in function names.

Although you can use spaces anywhere within names in Access, you should try to create field names and table names *without* embedded spaces. Most SQL databases to which Access can attach do not support spaces within names. If you ever want to move your application to a client/server environment and store your data in an SQL database such as Microsoft SQL Server or Oracle, you'll have to change any names in your database tables that have an embedded space character.

Using Good Design Techniques

As you can see from the previous section, avoiding design mistakes saves you time and effort later as you develop or change your application. However, you can also greatly improve the way your application works and enhance your users' experience by employing additional design techniques as you build your tables in Access.

Avoid Allowing Both Null and Zero Length Values in Text

Relational databases support a special value in fields, called a *Null*, that indicates an unknown value. In contrast, you can set Text, Memo, or Hyperlink fields to a zero-length string to indicate that the value of a field is known but the field is empty.

Why is it important to differentiate Nulls (unknown values) from zero-length strings? Here's an example: Suppose you have a database that stores the results of a survey about automobile preferences. For questionnaires on which there is no response to a color-preference question, it is appropriate to store a Null. You don't want to match responses based on an unknown response, and you don't want to include the row in calculating totals or averages.

On the other hand, some people might have responded "I don't care" for a color preference. In this case, you have a known "no preference" answer, and a zero-length string might be appropriate. You can match all "I don't care" responses and include the responses in totals and averages.

But you should not allow a Text, Memo, or Hyperlink field to be both Zero Length (Allow Zero Length property set to Yes) and Null (Required property set to No and no setting in the Validation Rule property) unless you truly want to be able to store either an empty string or a Null. The user interface in Access displays both a Null and a zero-length string ("") the same way (both appear blank), so allowing both can be confusing to the user. In truth, you should probably store "No Preference" rather than allow both a Null or Zero Length String value because the user won't be able tell the difference when looking at the data displayed in a datasheet, form, or report.

You can join tables on zero-length strings, and two zero-length strings will compare to be equal. However, for Text, Memo, and Hyperlink fields, you must be sure that the Allow Zero Length property is set to Yes to allow users to enter zero-length strings. Otherwise, Access converts a zero-length or all-blank string to a Null before storing the value. In fact, Access removes all trailing blanks from any text string before storing the string. So, if you type nothing but blanks in a field and save the record, Access reduces the string to zero length—and stores a Null if Allow Zero Length is No. If you also set the Required property of a character field to Yes, Access stores a zero-length string if the user enters either "" (two double quotes with no space) or nothing but blanks in the field.

Nulls have special properties. A Null value cannot be equal to any other value, not even to another Null. This means you cannot join (link) two tables on Null values. Also, the question

"Is A equal to B?" when A, B, or both A and B contain a Null can never be answered "yes." The answer, literally, is "I don't know." Likewise, the answer to the question "Is A not equal to B?" is also "I don't know." Finally, Null values do not participate in aggregate calculations involving such functions as *Sum* or *Avg*. You can test a value to determine whether it is a Null by comparing it to the special keyword NULL or by using the *IsNull* built-in function.

> **Caution**   As of Access version 10 (also known as Access XP or Access 2002), Microsoft changed the default setting for the Allow Zero Length property of Text, Memo, and Hyperlink fields to Yes. If you do not require an entry in a character field (either by setting the Required property to Yes or by defining a validation rule), you should be sure to reset the Allow Zero Length property to No.

Use a Validation Rule Instead of Required = Yes

You certainly should take advantage of the validation features in Access to ensure that users supply a valid value for fields in your tables. When you want to require that a user enter a value, but you don't need to perform any other validation, you might be tempted to set the Required property of the field to Yes. However, when a user fails to supply a value or attempts to clear a required value, Access displays a cryptic message as shown in Figure 1-11.

Figure 1-11   Access displays a confusing error message when you set Required to Yes and the user fails to provide a value.

Instead of setting the Required property to Yes, set the Validation Rule property to **Is Not Null** and include an appropriate message in the Validation Text property. When you leave the Required property set to No and define an Is Not Null validation rule, Access displays your more meaningful message, as shown in Figure 1-12.

Figure 1-12   When you set the Validation Rule property to **Is Not Null**, you can define a more meaningful error message that Access displays when the user fails to enter a value.

Note that you must leave the Required property set to No because Access checks Required before testing the validation rule.

Never Define Subdatasheets for Tables (or Queries)

You should set the Subdatasheet Name property to [None] in the Table Properties window for all tables and leave the property blank in the Query Properties window for all queries. If you define a subdatasheet, Access also fetches the rows in the subdatasheet when you open the table or query. This can have a huge negative performance impact if the table is linked over a network.

If you're using linked tables and the database containing the data has no relationships defined, in some cases Access will scan all other tables looking for a related table based on key names. This scanning process can take from several seconds to up to a minute before Access gives up and finally displays the data.

Also, if you have secured your tables, all users must have permissions to both the table(s) displayed in the main datasheet as well as all of the tables in any subdatasheet.

> **Caution**   Consider also that any production application should not allow the user to see table or query datasheets because you cannot enforce complex business rules. Any data validation in a table or query datasheet depends entirely on the validation and referential integrity rules you defined for your tables because you cannot define any Visual Basic code behind tables or queries.

Know That Referential Integrity Creates Extra Indexes

When you design your tables, you should always take advantage of the referential integrity feature in Access to ensure that the relationships between your tables are enforced. However, you should understand that Access always builds a hidden system index on the foreign key(s) in the dependent table—it needs to do this to be able to enforce the integrity rule. Also, this additional index counts toward the maximum number of 32 indexes that you can define for each table.

Access does not display these extra indexes in the Indexes window in a table's Design view. The only way to discover the indexes is to examine the Indexes collection of the table by using Visual Basic. For example, if you open the tblPOProducts table in the InventoryData.mdb database in Design view and open the Indexes window, you can see three defined indexes—the primary key, an index on the LineNo field, and an index on the Posted field. To find out the actual count of indexes, open the Immediate window (press Ctrl+G) and enter

```
?CurrentDb.TableDefs("tblPOProducts").Indexes.Count
```

Visual Basic will tell you that there are actually six indexes defined! The additional indexes support the referential integrity relationships to the tblProducts table, the tblPurchaseOrder table, and the tblVendorProducts table. In the InventoryData.mdb database, I created a little function that you can copy to any other database and run to list all tables and their indexes. You can find this function in the modExamples module in the Inventory and Membership sample databases. The code follows:

```
Public Function ListIndexes()
Dim db As DAO.Database, tdf As DAO.TableDef
Dim idx As DAO.Index, fld As DAO.Field
  ' Point to this database
  Set db = DBEngine(0)(0)
  ' Loop through all tables
  For Each tdf In db.TableDefs
    ' Skip system and hidden tables
    If (tdf.Attributes And (dbSystemObject + dbHiddenObject)) = 0 Then
      ' Display the table name and index count
      Debug.Print "Table: " & tdf.Name, _
        " No. Indexes: " & tdf.Indexes.Count
      ' Loop through all indexes for this table
      For Each idx In tdf.Indexes
        ' Display the index name
        Debug.Print "  Index: " & idx.Name
        ' Loop through all fields in this index
        For Each fld In idx.Fields
          ' Display the field name
          Debug.Print "    Field: " & fld.Name
        Next fld
      Next idx
    End If
  Next tdf
  Set fld = Nothing
  Set idx = Nothing
  Set tdf = Nothing
  Set db = Nothing
End Function
```

You might well ask: "Because I can't see the hidden index, I might define the index again in the table's Design view. Does this create an unnecessary index in my database and waste space and resources?" Yes, that will create another index definition (which counts toward the total of 32 for the table), but Access recognizes when another index already exists with the same attributes, so the "duplicate" index is only an alias to the actual physical index. Access does use up a little space for the index definition, but it doesn't waste any space or resources creating another physical index. To actually delete the index, you would need to delete both the index that you can see in the table's Design view and the referential integrity rule.

Avoid Artificial Primary Keys in Tables

One of the critical rules of database design is each table must have a primary key to uniquely identify each row. If you adhere strictly to relational theory, you'll collect all the attributes (fields) for a subject (table) and then identify one or more sets of attributes that are potentially unique for each row—these are called *candidate keys*. From the set of candidate keys, you should choose the simplest key (one field if possible) to use as the actual primary key.

But in the real world, identifying a simple candidate key is often difficult if not impossible. For example, the typical customer table might have first name, middle initial, last name, address, city, region, postal code, country, phone number, fax number, and e-mail fields. Certainly the combination of first name and last name might be a candidate key, but the instant you encounter a second person with the same name at a different address, that candidate key fails. You could try adding another field, such as e-mail address, but this, too, fails when you encounter a customer who has no e-mail address.

Many Access developers simply give up, throw an AutoNumber field in the table, and define it as the primary key. I used to use AutoNumber in this manner all the time, but I have found that falling back on AutoNumber as a primary key creates a meaningless value (every field in a table should have meaning and be directly related to the subject of the table) and is just plain lazy. Because this artificial key is meaningless, there's a great temptation to never display it to the user at all.

I sometimes use a generated number as a primary key, but I display it to the user, and I write code to generate the "next" number for a new row. Also, whenever possible, I define one or more other fields in the table to be unique, or I write code to check for potential duplicates. For example, in the Inventory application, the tblProducts table has a numeric product ID field, but it also has a unique index defined on the combination of product category and description. So, a user cannot define two products with the exact same name in the same category. In the Membership Tracking application, each member has an application-generated numeric member ID field, but code in the form to edit members uses a Soundex comparison to check for a potentially duplicate name when adding a new record.

A purist might ask, "In the Inventory application, why not use the natural combination of the Category and Description fields as the primary key of the tblProducts table?" I chose to use a simple application-generated number to avoid carrying a compound key down to many related tables. If I were to use the combination of the Category and Description fields as the primary key, I would have to put copies of these two longer fields in all the dependent tables—tblOrderProducts, tblVendorProducts, tblPOProducts, and tblInventory.

I do expose the Product ID field to the user everywhere in the application. Over time, users will come to know that Jack's New England Clam Chowder is also product number 41. And if the application is ever extended in the future to use bar codes to track inventory, I'll need an associated numeric value to generate the codes stamped on incoming and outgoing shipments.

In truth, in a real inventory application, you'll probably have an actual product identifier (perhaps one provided by your suppliers) that you can use without reservation. Even large vendors like Amazon.com generate artificial keys for many products (they call it an ASIN), but they do use a "real" value wherever possible—such as the ISBN for books they sell. And many retailers use an in-house generated product number—called an SKU or Stock Keeping Unit—to uniquely identify the products they sell. But the point is even these "artificial" numbers have meaning. The best way to find out if a neighborhood branch of a department store has a particular dress in a specific size and color is to know that product's SKU when you call. If I want to create a link to a product on Amazon.com on my Web site, I must know that product's ASIN.

The following sections discuss some of the additional pitfalls of using artificial primary keys.

Avoid Artificial Primary Keys in Lookup Tables

As noted in "Oversimplifying Your Tables," page 8, it is quite common to create a lookup table that contains nothing more than a list of valid values for one field in a dependent table. Rather than hard-code a value list in a validation rule for the field in the dependent table, you can control the list of values by defining a referential integrity rule between the lookup table and the dependent table. Adding a new valid value later is easy—you add a row to the lookup table rather than change the dependent table design.

Consider the two pairs of tables shown in Figure 1-13.

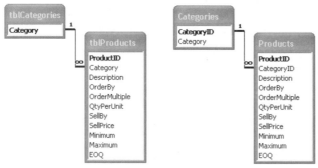

Figure 1-13   Two ways to use a lookup table to control the contents of a single field in a dependent table.

It's a common mistake to create table definitions that look like the second pair, and the CategoryID field is usually a meaningless AutoNumber field. First and foremost, the design on the right encounters all the problems previously discussed in "Defining Field Lookup Properties," page 11. Remember, you're probably going to display the Category field in any combo box but bind the control to the CategoryID field, so any sort or filter the user applies generates an inefficient hidden join to the lookup table. Second, you're not likely to ever expose the numeric value to the user—it's the category description that has meaning, not the number.

You might try to argue that an AutoNumber or long integer key stores and indexes more efficiently than a varying length description field. Although that is true, the benefits of using the real text value far outweigh the small additional overhead of the text field. Unless you have hundreds of thousands of categories (not likely), you're not going to notice the difference either in the space required to store the data or the time it takes to index and search text instead of a number.

I must confess that I used to build many such single-value lookup tables with an AutoNumber primary key and a description. I finally broke the habit when a client asked me to build an application that provided a custom synchronization between a master database in the home office and several remote users. An administrator in the home office inadvertently deleted a lookup value that was being used by remote users, and there was no way to put it back—short of a brute-force insert query—with the original numeric ID.

The administrator tried to define the "category" again, but the system assigned it a new number under the covers. The data wouldn't synchronize correctly anymore because the data coming in from remote users contained an invalid category identifier number that was forever gone from the main system. If I had used the description value as the primary key (resulting in a table with a single field), it would have been simple for the administrator to re-insert the missing value. I didn't discover this problem until long after the application had gone into production. I ended up writing a lot of unnecessary code and some special data entry forms to solve the problem.

Do Not Use AutoNumber for Identifiers That Should Be Consecutive or That Have a Special Meaning

If you have worked with the AutoNumber data type at all, you know that it's easy to end up with missing numbers—and not just because a user has deleted some rows. When a user starts to create a new row in a table that has a sequential AutoNumber field, Access generates the next number. If the user decides to use the Esc key to clear edits and abort the new row, that number is lost forever.

Sometimes, missing numbers in a sequence are no problem. However, particularly if you're working with accounting data (such as checks, debits, credits, invoices, or purchase orders), maintaining a strict number sequence with no gaps can be very important.

Your business rules might dictate that your application generates numbers that have meaning and are in sequence. For example, in the Inventory application, a purchase order number for a related customer order is the order number followed by a three-digit sequence number. If the purchase order is generated to restock products to minimum inventory levels, the number is the digit 9 followed by the four-digit year number and a three-digit sequence number. You can look at a purchase order number and immediately identify the purpose of the order. The number has meaning—something you can't achieve with an AutoNumber.

Avoid Artificial Primary Keys in Child Tables

When you have a set of related tables that have a cascading relationship down three or more levels, it's often tempting to create an artificial simple primary key (often with an

AutoNumber) at lower levels to avoid having to cascade a compound primary key. Don't do it. Consider the two sets of tables in Figure 1-14.

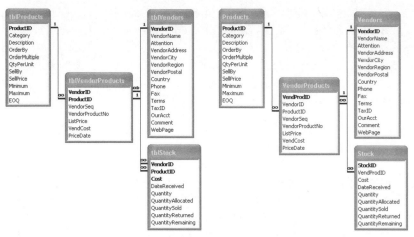

Figure 1-14   The correct and incorrect way to cascade relationships down three or more levels.

Again, the second design on the right is incorrect. Sure, VendorProducts and Stock have simple one-field primary keys, but at what cost? If I'm looking at a Stock record, what is the product in stock? Which vendor supplied the product? I'm forced to perform a join with the next table up the chain to answer these questions. Also, if I want the product description or the vendor name, I must join all three tables. I need the VendorID and ProductID in the VendorProducts table anyway, so why not use both fields as a compound primary key instead of using an artificial key? As you can see, using an artificial key masks the true identity of the parent rows when you navigate down to the third level.

In the correct design on the left, I have almost all the information about a stock entry that I need in the single tblStock table. If I need the product description, I can join tblProducts with tblStock and avoid the intermediate table. The same is true if I need the vendor name—I can join just two tables, not three. Yes, there's an ugly three-field compound key in tblStock, but the identity of the parent rows is unmistakable. (The Cost field is part of the primary key so that the application can track inventory valuation by each item's original cost and vendor.)

Turn Off Track Name AutoCorrect

Access version 9 (Access 2000) introduced a new feature called AutoCorrect for desktop databases (.mdb file extenstion) that attempts to automatically propagate changes you make to field names, table names, and query names to other dependent objects. You can enable this feature for individual databases, and the feature is turned on by default for new databases. AutoCorrect does a relatively good job of correcting field and table or query name changes. However, it won't fix references to these objects in Visual Basic code, and it misses name changes in certain types of expressions. It also won't fix changes to field names in linked tables.

To enable or disable this feature, open your database and choose Options from the Tools menu. Click the General tab to see the options as shown in Figure 1-15.

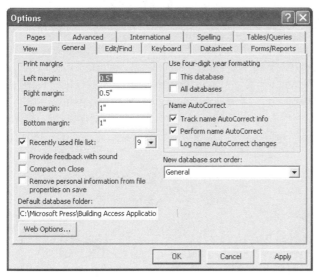

Figure 1-15   Setting the AutoCorrect options for an Access desktop database.

As you are developing your application, you might find it useful to turn on these options. Select **Track name AutoCorrect info** to instruct Access to generate the internal identifiers it uses to propagate name changes. Select **Perform name AutoCorrect** to instruct Access to check queries, forms, and reports each time you open them and automatically correct any names that have changed. Note that AutoCorrect works whether you open the object in Design view or in standard view—Datasheet view for queries; Form, PivotTable, or PivotChart view for forms; and Print Preview for reports. Select **Log name AutoCorrect changes** to ask Access to create a table called Name AutoCorrect Log containing rows that tell you the object type, object name, control name, property name, and old and new values for every change.

However, because this feature runs whenever you open any dependent object, it's a bad idea to leave this feature activated in a database that you distribute to users. If you change, for example, a field name in a table without opening and closing all objects that use that field, users must have Modify Design permission for all objects to be able to successfully run your application. In addition, the internal tracking codes take up additional (though nominal) space in your desktop database file.

And finally, if you enable **Perform name AutoCorrect**, you will not have any idea what changes Access makes on your behalf unless you also enable **Log name AutoCorrect changes** because Access makes the changes without notifying you. It doesn't even prompt you to save a changed object after you open it, make no changes yourself (other than the ones performed by AutoCorrect), and close it. It's this last "silent change" feature that causes me to recommend that you turn it off even when you're developing your application. To turn off this feature for the current database, clear the **Track name AutoCorrect info** option in the Options dialog box.

Use the Description Property Wisely

Entering a Description property for every field in your table helps document your application. Because Access also displays the description on the status bar, paying careful attention to what you type in the Description field can later pay big dividends as a kind of mini-help for the users of your database. Also, since this data propagates automatically, you probably don't want to type something nonsensical or silly. Typing **My boss told me to add this field, but I don't have a clue why** is probably not a good idea—it will show up later on the status bar!

Create Meaningful Captions

As noted in "Naming Fields Incorrectly," page 22, you should avoid using blanks in field names. This rule applies both to field names in tables and to alias field names in queries. (Remember, you create an alias field name in a query using an AS clause after an expression in the Select clause or by typing a name, a colon, and an expression on the Field line in the query design grid.) In the absence of a Caption property definition, Access uses the field name as the caption in attached labels on forms and reports or as column headings in Datasheet view.

When a field name is a single meaningful word, you probably don't need to define a Caption property. However, if the field name is a compound name (such as QtyOnHand) or follows a company naming standard for fields (naming standards often result in names meaningful to the developer but not the user), you should define a caption so that you don't accidentally display the nonfriendly field name anywhere in your application.

Understand the Interaction Between Format and Input Mask

Perhaps second only to the misunderstanding about the difference between how a Date/Time data type is stored and displayed (discussed earlier in this chapter) is the confusion about the difference between the Format property and the Input Mask property. The salient points are as follows:

- When a control or field has only a Format property, that property controls how Access displays the data when the control or field does not have the focus and the field has a value or has a default value on a new row. The format might not display all the data stored in the field or control—for example, a format might display only the year portion of a Date/Time field. When you move the focus to the field or control, Access removes the format and displays the actual data.

- When a control or field has only an Input Mask property, that property controls both how Access displays the data when the control or field does not have the focus and what you can enter when you begin typing data in the control or field. If the field contained data before you defined the input mask or you insert data into the field without using the mask (perhaps with an insert query), the input mask might not display all the data.

- When you define an input mask for a text field, you can optionally instruct the mask to store any formatting characters in addition to the data you type. Access includes the formatting characters only when you update the field by typing in it with the mask active.

- When you define both a format and an input mask for a control or field and the format matches the input mask, Access displays the data using the format when the control or field does not have the focus, and it activates the input mask when you enter a control or field that already has data or a default value. If you tab into a control or field that does not have any data, the input mask appears as soon as you begin to type.

Notice that this all works nicely when the format and input mask are compatible—they display the same number of characters in the same pattern. But you should *never* define an input mask that doesn't match the Format property. The bad news is you can accidentally define an input mask that's not compatible in a Date/Time field even though you have defined no format. Here's what happens when Format and Input Mask properties are not compatible:

- The Format property takes precedence over the Input Mask property when the control or field contains data or a default value—whether the control or field has the focus or not.

- If you begin typing in a control or field that has data or a default value, the format disappears, but you will not see the input mask. However, you must enter characters that are compatible with the input mask that you cannot see. If you attempt to save a value that does not match the input mask, Access displays an error.

- If you begin typing in an empty control or field, the input mask appears and controls what you can enter. The Format property displays the result when you move the focus away from the control or field.

- The Date/Time data type is a special case. Even though you might not have defined a format, Access displays the data formatted with the General Date format. If your input mask does not match this format, the control or field acts as though the format and input mask are not compatible. The problem is the General Date format might display a date, a time, or both, depending on what is stored in the control or field. You might define an input mask to enter the date only, but if the field contains a time component, the field acts as though it has an incompatible format and input mask.

To help you understand this interaction more clearly, I created a small table in the data file for the Inventory sample application (InventoryData.mdb). The table, which is named ztblFormatInputMask, has five long integer fields and one row containing the value 1234567 in all five fields. Here's how the fields are defined and what happened when I tried to enter data in a new row:

Field One

The Format property is set to 0-00000-0, the Input Mask property is set to 000\-0\-000;1;n (not compatible), and the Default Value property is 0.

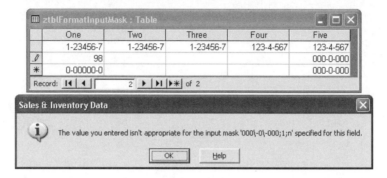

This is the worst-case scenario. The input mask never appears because the field has a default value that the Format property displays. When I tried to tab away from this field without entering the number of digits required by the input mask, Access displayed the ugly message you see.

Field Two

The Format property is set to 0-00000-0, the Input Mask property is set to 000\-0\-000;1;n (not compatible), and there is no Default Value.

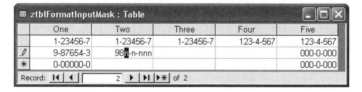

The input mask worked correctly when I first began to enter data because the field has no default value, but it won't work for fields that already have data. Notice that field One now displays the data using the format, not the input mask. Also, as you can see in the first row, Access formats any data that I enter in field Two using the format, not the input mask, when the field does not have the focus.

Field Three

The Format property is set to 0-00000-0, and there is no Default Value.

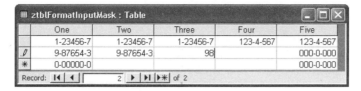

This demonstrates a simple Format property. Notice that the format disappeared when I began typing, but the row above shows the field is formatted correctly.

Field Four

The Input Mask is set to 000\-0\-000;1;n, and there is no Default Value.

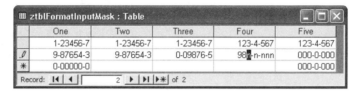

This demonstrates a simple Input Mask property. Notice that the input mask was activated as soon as I began typing, and the field in the row above displays the data formatted with the input mask.

Field Five

The Format property is set to 000-0-000, the Input Mask property is set to 000\-0\-000;1;n (compatible), and the Default Value is 0.

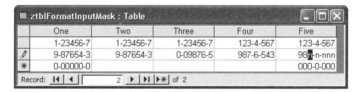

This demonstrates correct behavior because the format is compatible with the input mask. The field in the row above is actually being formatted by the Format property, and the field where I'm entering data shows the input mask activated.

The Bottom Line: Know Thy Data and Its Usage

As you have read through this chapter, you've encountered many "ifs, ands, and buts." This is intentional. If a "rule" truly doesn't apply to the way you need to use the data in your application, don't use it. But that assumes that you really know the application requirements inside and out.

In any database design exercise, it's absolutely critical that you thoroughly understand what your application needs to do and the business rules it needs to enforce. Look at the "classic" order entry application problem for a minute as an example. Will the price of a product never change over time? If that's true (it probably isn't), then you don't need to save a copy of the price in the order detail rows. Does the company need to track product price changes over time? If so, you probably need a separate product price table that includes the price effective date, and you need to write code to look up the current price at the time an order is placed.

Is a product provided by only one vendor, or can you find the same or equivalent product from an alternate vendor? If an equivalent product is acceptable, do you need another table to track which products are equivalent to each other? If your business rules dictate that the second and subsequent purchase of the same product in one order receives a discount (buy one, get the second at half off), do you reflect the discount in a single order detail row, or must the salesperson enter the second purchase in another row at a discount?

As you create a database design, don't be afraid to ask a lot of questions or "think outside of the box." And don't be afraid to question *everything* your user tells you. Do you really need only one address for a customer? Can a registrar override the requirement for prerequisite courses to register a student for an advanced course? Will your business requirements ever change? I can answer the last question for you—the answer is YES!

Chapter 2
Creating the User Interface

In my more than 12 years of working with Microsoft Access, I've seen many examples of a workable user interface for an Access application. I've also seen some unmitigated disasters. As Alexander White so eloquently stated, "I can make an ugly document very easily. I own a computer and layout software."[1]

When I think of the user interface of an Access application, my primary focus is on the design of the forms and toolbars and the ways I provide users to navigate through my application. Reports are certainly important, but application designers often must either try to emulate an existing paper form or create a report that clearly prints the result the user wants. So, in a certain sense, the user is going to dictate the layout of reports.

Most comprehensive books about Access show you *how* to build forms and toolbars, but they don't really address how to create a user interface that is attractive, intuitive, and easy to use. This book assumes that you already know how to build forms and toolbars. This chapter focuses on principles you should follow not only to make your users productive but also to make them happy they're using your application.

Designing Look and Feel

You can certainly make your user interface look very sophisticated in Access. For example, I've seen a sample contact management application in which all the forms look like pages from a spiral-bound planner notebook. But you don't have to create exotic-looking forms to have a

---

1. Alexander White, *Type in Use* (New York: W. W. Norton & Company, 1999). p. 8.

cohesive look and feel. This section describes some fundamental principles for designing forms using colors, fonts, graphics, and visual clues.

Using Colors

When I first started designing forms in Access version 1, most monitors that worked with Windows 3.1 could display a maximum of only 256 colors at a time on a 640 × 480 pixel screen. In fact, the built-in color palette in Access offered only 16 different colors, many of which were quite ugly. So, early Access applications tended to stick with shades of gray for the form background, black or white for text, and a judicious use of primary colors such as blue, red, or yellow to highlight some items. If you included a picture on a form, you had to be sure that it used colors only from the standard Windows 256-color palette. If you didn't, the colors would appear dithered on the screen.

How times have changed! Even the most basic computer system that can run Windows XP can display more than 16 million colors. Your color choice is now virtually limitless, but in some ways that simply gives you more options to design forms that look really ugly. How about mauve letters on a chartreuse background? I don't think so, at least not for a professional application.

Figure 2-1 shows you the built-in Color dialog box with the Define Custom Colors panel open on the right. You can open this dialog box by selecting any color property in the form's Design view and clicking the Build button next to the property. Click the Define Custom Colors button to see the color palette. Access gives you a choice of 48 basic colors, including a couple of shades of gray. You can also define up to 16 additional custom colors to use in a form's palette, choosing from any one of more than 16 million colors by moving the cursor in the large window on the right with your mouse. You also select a custom color by setting the Hue, Sat (saturation), and Lum (luminance) values, or the Red, Green, and Blue values.

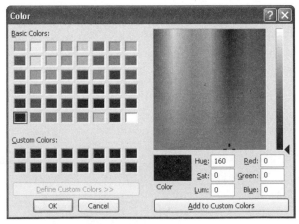

Figure 2-1   The Color dialog box.

Understanding Basic Color Guidelines

Despite the fact that you now have a huge color palette, I recommend that you keep your color choices simple. Although there are no hard and fast rules, here are some guidelines you should consider:

- Choose a simple color scheme consisting of two or three colors plus black and white (and shades of those colors) and use it consistently throughout your application.

- Use highlight colors sparingly and only when it's important to call attention to a message or object.

- Be sure to provide sufficient contrast for text—dark letters on a light background or vice versa.

- Because a significant portion of the population is red-green color-blind, avoid using red on green or vice versa, particularly for text.

For "industrial strength" applications such as the Inventory Management sample application (Inventory.mdb), I like to use a basic "shades of gray" look, with an occasional bright blue or red as a highlight color for important messages. Figure 2-2 shows you the frmCustomers form in the Inventory application that uses a very simple and straightforward color scheme and layout throughout.

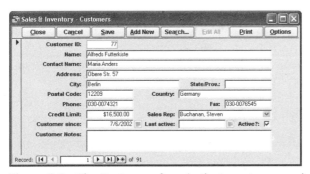

Figure 2-2   The Customers form in the Inventory sample application is designed with a simple color scheme.

For many applications, I like to use a simple but more modern-looking design. I like the blue-on-blue look of the built-in Sumi Painting AutoFormat (choose AutoFormat from the Format menu when you're in form design), but I adjust some of the defaults to suit my particular style. For example, I like associated labels on forms to be right aligned to the left of the related control, and I prefer the caption to end with a colon. Figure 2-3 on the next page shows you a sample form designed using this technique from the Membership Tracking sample application.

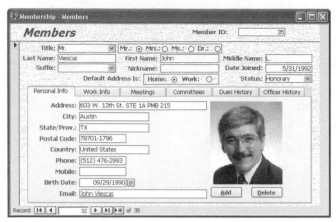

Figure 2-3   The forms in the Membership sample application use a color scheme based on the Sumi Painting built-in AutoFormat.

You can find additional color schemes in the other sample databases. The one design technique common to all of them is all the forms within a particular application use the same colors and graphic design elements. In short, the forms all look like they belong in the same application.

I have seen (and have built myself) some applications that use a different color scheme for different major tasks. For example, I have as a client a small business that sells engine parts in one side of the business and engine maintenance (including parts) in another part of the business. I designed one application that handles both major functions, but the background of the forms in the parts area is a different color from the forms that handle the maintenance tasks. The user can see at a glance which sub-business he's working in.

Working with System Colors

In addition to using the broad palette of colors offered by the Color dialog box, you can specify special color codes that instruct Access to use one of the colors the user has set in the Windows Display dialog box. In fact, if you open many of the forms in the Inventory application in Design view, open the Properties window, and find the Back Color property, you'll find a negative number: −2147483633. This happens to be a special code number that means to use the color set in Windows for button faces and other 3-D objects. Table 2-1 shows a list of color code numbers that you can use to set colors in your forms and controls to match those set in Windows objects.

If you want your application to exactly match your user's Windows color scheme, you can set the Fore Color and Back Color properties of your form controls to match these special settings. The easiest way to accomplish this is to create a template form, set the defaults for the form sections and each of the controls, and then enter that form name in the **Form template** box on the Forms/Reports tab of the Options dialog box.

Table 2-1   Color Codes to Match Windows Objects

Visual Basic Constant Name	Code	Meaning
vbScrollBars	–2147483648	Scroll bar color
vbDesktop	–2147483647	Desktop color
vbActiveTitleBar	–2147483646	Color of the title bar for the active window
vbInactiveTitleBar	–2147483645	Color of the title bar for the inactive window
vbMenuBar	–2147483644	Menu background color
vbWindowBackground	–2147483643	Window background color
vbWindowFrame	–2147483642	Window frame color
vbMenuText	–2147483641	Color of text on menus
vbWindowText	–2147483640	Color of text in windows
vbTitleBarText	–2147483639	Color of text in caption, size box, and scroll arrow
vbActiveBorder	–2147483638	Border color of active window
vbInactiveBorder	–2147483637	Border color of inactive window
vbApplicationWorkspace	–2147483636	Background color of multiple-document interface (MDI) applications (the color of the area under the toolbars in Access)
vbHighlight	–2147483635	Background color of items selected in a control
vbHighlightText	–2147483634	Text color of items selected in a control
vbButtonFace or vb3DFace	–2147483633	Color of shading on the face of command buttons and other 3-D objects
vbButtonShadow or vb3DShadow	–2147483632	Color of shading on the edge of command buttons and other 3-D objects.
vbGrayText	–2147483631	Dimmed (disabled) text
vbButtonText	–2147483630	Text color on push buttons
vbInactiveCaptionText	–2147483629	Color of text in an inactive caption (a caption in a window that does not have the focus)
vb3DHighlight	–2147483628	Highlight color for 3-D display elements
vb3DDKShadow	–2147483627	Darkest shadow color for 3-D display elements
vb3DLight	–2147483626	Next lightest 3-D color after the highlight color
vbInfoText	–2147483625	Color of text in ToolTips
vbInfoBackground	–2147483624	Background color of ToolTips

You must be careful, however, if you combine a Windows color with a color from the Color dialog box palette—for example, choosing a Windows color for the Back Color property and a normal color value for the Fore Color (font color) property. The user controls the selection of the Windows colors. If the user sets the Windows color you're using in the Back Color property to a dark color, and you use a dark color (such as black) for the font, your caption might not be readable.

You especially need to be aware of this problem because Access does not allow you to set a background color for command button controls and toggle button controls. These controls do not have a Back Color property and are always displayed using the Windows Button Face color (–2147483633). When you set the Fore Color property to a normal color value, the user can select a Windows Button Face color that makes your caption on the button unreadable.

You also need to pay attention to the colors you select in your label controls. The default Back Style property for labels is Transparent in both the Normal and Standard templates in all recent versions of Access. Also, the default Fore Color (font color) property is 0 or black in these templates in some versions of Access. The transparent background of the label lets the color of the area on which you place the label to show through.

This is a problem for labels that you place on tab control pages because tab controls have no Back Color property—Access displays the surface of the tab pages using the Windows Button Face color. It's also a problem for labels placed directly on any section of a form because the Normal template (defined in the Options dialog box) and the Standard template (which you can choose in AutoFormat on the Format menu when you're in the form's Design view) set the background color of form sections to the Windows Button Face color. (A new form inherits the Normal template when you select **Create form in Design view** in the Database window or choose Design View in the New Form dialog box.)

> **Note**   You could change the Back Style property of your labels from Transparent to Normal, but then the background color you have chosen will be displayed as a solid rectangle behind the text in the label. Unless this background color matches the color of the area on which you have placed the label, the label control design area will be visible to the user.

Table 2-2 shows you the default Fore Color property settings for toggle button controls, command button controls, and label controls in both the Normal and the Standard templates in the three most recent versions of Access. The settings that present a problem are italicized in the table.

Table 2-2   Fore Color Settings by Version and Template

Access Version	Template	Toggle Button Control	Command Button Control	Label Control
2000	Normal	Windows Button Text	Windows Button Text	*Black*
	Standard	Windows Button Text	*Black*	Black
2002	Normal	Windows Button Text	Windows Button Text	*Black*
	Standard	*Black*	*Black*	Windows Button Text
2003	Normal	Windows Button Text	Windows Button Text	*Black*
	Standard	*Black*	*Black*	*Windows Button Text*

When the default Fore Color property is Windows Button Text, you're still somewhat at the mercy of your user. But when you set the Back Color property to Windows Button Face (or that's the default because of the control type or the setting in the template you select), the user isn't likely to pick a color combination that makes captions difficult to read everywhere in Windows.

> **Note** The captions on the tabs of a tab control are not a problem because Access displays the background of the tabs using the Windows Button Face color and the text in the captions on the tabs using the Windows Button Text color.

So, how do you fix this problem? You could define a custom form template with the Fore Color property for label controls, toggle button controls, and command button controls set to the Windows Button Text color. You could also modify the built-in Standard template. If you don't want to be bothered with doing either of these, or you need to fix existing forms after the fact, you can run a small Visual Basic function to fix all your forms in one pass. You can find the following code in the modExamples module in the Inventory sample database:

```
Public Function FixCaptionColors()
Dim aob As AccessObject
Dim frm As Form
Dim ctl As Control
  ' Ignore any errors
  On Error Resume Next
  ' Loop through all the forms
  For Each aob In CurrentProject.AllForms
    ' Open the form in Design view, but hidden
    DoCmd.OpenForm aob.Name, acDesign, , , , acHidden
    ' Point to the form
    Set frm = Forms(aob.Name)
    ' Loop through all controls
    For Each ctl In frm.Controls
      ' If it's a label, command button, or toggle button
      If (ctl.ControlType = acLabel) Or _
          (ctl.ControlType = acCommandButton) Or _
          (ctl.ControlType = acToggleButton) Then
        ' .. and the Fore Color is black
        If ctl.ForeColor = 0 Then
          ' Change it to Windows Button Text color
          ctl.ForeColor = vbButtonText
        End If
      End If
    Next ctl
    ' Clear the control object
    Set ctl = Nothing
    ' Close and save any changes
    DoCmd.Close acForm, aob.Name, acSaveYes
  Next aob
  ' Clear the Access object
  Set aob = Nothing
  ' .. and the Form object
  Set frm = Nothing
End Function
```

Of course, this procedure won't help you if you've chosen some other dark color (such as the dark blue used in the Sumi Painting template) as the font color for labels, toggle buttons, and command buttons. The procedure fixes only controls that have a black Fore Color setting. You will be at your users' mercy if they decide to set a dark color for button faces—but at least you'll know how to solve the problem (tell them to fix their Windows colors) when you get the support call.

> **Tip**   You can change the color of the pages on a tab control (but not the tabs themselves) by setting the Back Style property to Transparent. When you do this, the background color of the section or the graphic defined in the Picture property of the form "bleeds through" the transparent pages. (This doesn't work in Access 2003 if you have chosen the **Use Windows Themed Controls on Forms** option on the Forms/Reports tab in the Options dialog box.) Be careful when you do this and are working in form Design view. If you click the surface of the page, you will select the section that contains the tab control, not the page. To select the page (for example, to add a control to the page), you must click the tab for the page.

Selecting Fonts

You can have almost as much fun with fonts as you can with colors. Windows XP comes with at least 25 different fonts, and a full installation of Microsoft Office gives you more than 100 additional fonts to work with. You can also find thousands of fonts on the Internet, either to purchase or for free. So, it's easy to go "font crazy."

Don't. Most applications will look the best with only one or two fonts used throughout. You should also be consistent in your use of fonts. You might choose one stylized or italicized font for title labels, a serif font for control labels, and a sans serif font for data display. A serif font has tiny horizontal short strokes added at the top and bottom of vertical strokes in letters—this paragraph's text uses a serif font. A sans serif font does not have these embellishments—the chapter titles, headings, and the text of the tip on this page use a sans serif font.

If you know that all your users have a full installation of Office, you can feel confident using any of the fonts you find on your machine—unless you have also installed some custom fonts. If you're not sure, you should stick with the standard fonts installed with Windows. Table 2-3 lists the most common fonts you'll find in Windows.

Be extremely careful if you choose to use a custom font not provided by either Windows or Office. If you decide to do this, you must be sure to install the custom font on your users' machines. I have a large selection of extra fonts installed on one of my machines—including fonts called Andy, Bickley Script, and Parade. I created a sample form with three label controls, each one using one of these custom fonts. Below each label control, I placed an image control that displays a bitmap showing what the font really looks like.

Table 2-3   **Common Fonts Installed with Windows**

Serif	Sans Serif
Courier*	Arial
Courier New*	Arial Black
Georgia	Comic Sans
MS Serif	Franklin Gothic Demi
Palatino Linotype	Impact
Roman	Lucida Console*
Sylfaen	Microsoft Sans Serif
Times New Roman	Modern
	MS Sans Serif
	Tahoma
	Trebuchet MS
	Verdana

*   These are monospaced fonts that are suitable for code listings or simulating the look produced by a typewriter.

If you open frmXmplFonts in the Membership database on your machine, it will probably look like Figure 2-4. This gives you an idea of what can happen if you use a custom font that isn't on your user's machine. The second instance of each pair is an actual graphic of the correct font, which always displays correctly, while the first instances are text formatted for the font in question and thus depend on the fonts being installed on each user's computer.

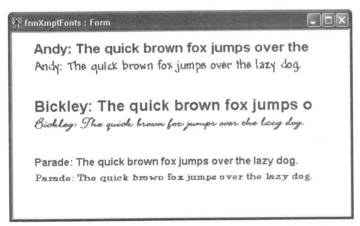

Figure 2-4   A demonstration of how Access displays fonts that aren't installed on the machine.

When a font doesn't exist on a machine, Windows tries to substitute an equivalent font that is available. As you can see in Figure 2-4, it doesn't often do a very good job. Not only do the fonts chosen in the label controls look nothing like the originals in the image controls immediately below each label, but also two of the alternate selections don't even fit in the designed label control.

Including Visual Clues

Your user interface design can include visual clues that help the user understand what they can or should do in the various parts of your application. Some ways to do this include the following:

- Surround groups of related controls with rectangles, or separate them on separate pages of a tab control. For example, in the Inventory application when you ask to print a product or inventory item, the Print Options dialog box appears. Related items in the dialog box are surrounded with rectangles as shown here. So, the user knows to choose one of the top two and one of the bottom three options.

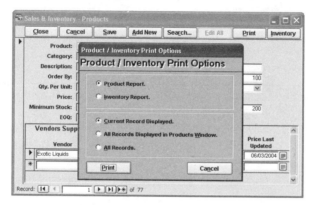

- Give the user a visual clue when the form is a pop-up or modal (dialog box) form, such as using a darker background or by adding a dark border around the form. For example, all the modal forms in the Membership application that open from a combo box NotInList event have a dark blue border around the detail area as shown here.

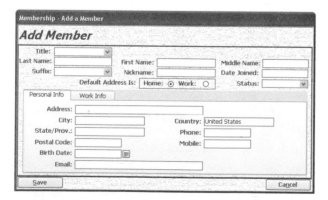

- Distinguish between controls that are updatable (Locked property set to No) and those that are not. For example, make unlocked controls sunken and locked ones flat, or place locked controls in the header or footer of the form. The frmInventory form in the Inventory sample application (shown next) does not allow the user to enter data in

Product ID, Category, Highest Cost, Qty. In Stock, or Qty. On Hand on the outer form. It also does not let the user change Qty Alloc., Qty. Sold, Qty. Returned, or Qty. Available on the subform. The user can see which controls are available because the locked controls appear flat and the enabled controls appear sunken.

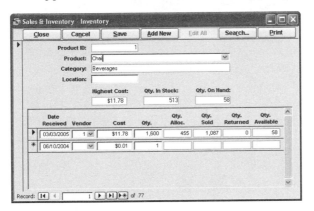

Dealing with Windows XP Themes in Access 2003

One of the new features in Access 2003 is the ability to set an option called **Use Windows Themed Controls on Forms**. You can set this option by choosing Options from the Tools menu and then selecting the Forms/Reports tab. Note that this option is set by default for any new database that you create with Access 2003. If the user sets Display Properties in Windows XP SP1 or later to use the Windows XP theme on the Themes tab and Windows XP Style for windows and buttons on the Appearance tab, Access applies the theme settings to all controls except labels, images, object frames, subforms, lines, and rectangles.

As you read in the previous section, one of my visual clue recommendations is to use the Sunken setting of the Special Effect property to highlight controls where the user can change the data. Access 2003 defeats this special effect when it applies the Windows XP theme. The result is all your controls that you have carefully designed with a sunken or etched special effect will appear flat.

To avoid this problem, you need to know the rules that Access uses to determine when to apply the Windows XP theme. You can then slightly alter your settings so that a control that you want to remain sunken or etched displays that way regardless of whether the **Use Windows Themed Controls on Forms** option is active or not. Table 2-4 on the next page explains the rules Access follows to apply the Windows XP theme.

So, you can defeat the application of the Windows XP theme by violating any one of the following rules—such as setting the Border Color to 1 (an unnoticeably lighter shade of black). Similar to the problem of setting Fore Color properties discussed earlier, you could define a custom form template with the Border Color for text box controls, combo box controls, and list box controls set to 1. You could also modify the built-in Standard template. If you don't

Table 2-4   Property Settings to Inherit the Windows XP Theme

Property	Setting
Special Effect	Sunken, Flat, or Etched.
	If the value is set to Flat, the Border Style property must not be set to Transparent in order to inherit the theme.
Border Style	Solid or Transparent.
	If the value is set to Transparent, the Special Effect property must not be set to Flat in order to inherit the theme.
Border Color	0 or –2147483640 (system color that corresponds to the default font color for dialog boxes)
Border Width	Hairline, 1, or 2
	The Border Width setting is ignored for check boxes and option buttons.

want to be bothered with doing either of these, or you need to fix existing forms after the fact, you can run a small Visual Basic function to fix all your forms in one pass. You can find the following code in the modExamples module in the Inventory sample database:

```
Public Function FixXPSpecialEffects()
Dim aob As AccessObject
Dim frm As Form
Dim ctl As Control
  ' Ignore any errors
  On Error Resume Next
  ' Loop through all the forms
  For Each aob In CurrentProject.AllForms
    ' Open the form in Design view, but hidden
    DoCmd.OpenForm aob.Name, acDesign, , , , acHidden
    ' Point to the form
    Set frm = Forms(aob.Name)
    ' Loop through all controls
    For Each ctl In frm.Controls
      ' If the control is designed with a special effect,
      If (ctl.Properties("SpecialEffect") = 2) Or _
        (ctl.Properties("SpecialEffect") = 3) Then
        ' Funky trick to turn off XP Theme
        ctl.Properties("BorderColor") = vbBlack + 1
      End If
    Next ctl
    ' Clear the control object
    Set ctl = Nothing
    ' Close and save any changes
    DoCmd.Close acForm, aob.Name, acSaveYes
  Next aob
  ' Clear the Access object
  Set aob = Nothing
  ' .. and the Form object
  Set frm = Nothing
End Function
```

Using Graphics

You can certainly use graphics to enhance the appearance of your forms. As noted earlier, the one exception to using a custom font is to include the font in a bitmap logo that you include on one or more of your forms. Here are some additional guidelines:

- When you want to display a graphic image on your forms, use the image control, not the unbound object frame control. The image control uses far fewer resources because it does not call the registered application for the image type to display the picture. Instead, it embeds the binary bitmap definition directly into your form.

- If you choose to define a background picture for forms, use a simple bitmap image that can be defined in a small file. Large and complex images take up space in each form definition when you choose the default Embedded setting for the Picture Type property. If you choose Linked for the Picture Type property, you must be sure to install the picture in the exact location referenced by the Picture property on the user's machine.

- Consider using icons or bitmaps for command buttons, toggle buttons, and tab control tabs. If you do this, make sure that your use of icons is consistent—for example, use the same icon for a Close button everywhere. Simple 16 × 16 pixel icons work best for the application icon or tab control tabs. For images on command buttons or toggle buttons, use a bitmap sized so that Access does not have to shrink or expand it.

- If your application will run using Access 2002 or later, you can define an application icon that appears in place of the standard Access object icon on all your forms and reports. To define this icon, choose Startup from the Tools menu, put the name of the icon file in the Application Icon box, and select the **Use as Form and Report Icon** option.

Architectural Issues

You can design some of the nicest-looking forms in the world, but if you don't pay attention to how your application is structured—how your forms are sized and how you provide navigation to various parts of the application—your users will find your application difficult to understand and use. The following sections describe architectural techniques you can employ to make your application more user friendly.

Sizing Forms

Although most modern video cards support a standard resolution of 1024 × 768 or greater, you cannot always trust that your user has chosen this resolution or higher or hasn't restored the Access application window so that it doesn't take up the entire screen. Your code can certainly execute a call to the Windows *GetSystemMetrics* function to find out the current screen resolution, but then what? Although samples abound that demonstrate how to dynamically change the size of forms as they are loaded or resized based on the screen resolution, I've found that they all have several shortcomings. At a minimum, these routines execute a lot of code, including several calls to Windows functions, so they can significantly slow down your application.

For this reason, I try to design all my forms so that they fit on an 800 × 600 pixel screen resolution. Using this smaller size forces me to carefully consider how much I include on each form. In a way, it keeps me from making my forms too cluttered. Also, many of my applications allow the user to have several form windows open at the same time. If the user has set a higher screen resolution, the smaller form sizes allow for positioning forms so that they don't stack on top of one another.

The one negative aspect of using smaller forms is the temptation to use the smallest font sizes (8 point or smaller) to try to cram more information in a smaller space. If the user has chosen a very high resolution (such as 1280 × 1024) on a small display (17 inches or less), the smaller fonts will be hard to read.

Tip   To help design forms that conform to the available space on a computer running at either 800 × 600 or 1024 × 768 resolution, I designed two template forms that are sized to fill the application workspace without triggering any scroll bars. I sized these forms assuming that the application has a standard menu bar and toolbar, the user has only the standard Windows Start button at the bottom of the screen, and the application is maximized. You can find these forms saved in the various sample databases as zsfrm800x600 and zsfrm1024x768. To use these forms, import them into the application you are building and open either one in Form view. Open a form you have built that you want to check in Form view and make sure it doesn't extend beyond the edges of the template form.

Planning Navigation

Since the dawn of computing, many studies have been undertaken to attempt to determine which user interfaces work best to minimize confusion and make an application easy to use. In general, when you're designing a way for your users to navigate through your application, it's best to never present them with more than six to ten options at one time. If you think about it, the standard Form view menu bar has only nine menu options (File, Edit, View, Insert, Format, Records, Tools, Window, and Help). When the focus is on the Database window, Access shows you seven menus. And the Visual Basic Editor gives you ten menus.

So, how do you provide navigation in an application that has dozens of potential tasks or navigation paths? The answer is to subcategorize the tasks and make it easy for the user to navigate through logical paths to a specific task. This is exactly why the menus in a Microsoft application drop down and often provide a tree of submenus.

You might ask, "But the standard File menu for the Database window has 14 options plus links to the recently opened files. How does that fit into the idea that 10 or fewer is good?" If you've been using Office applications for a long time, you might remember that Microsoft introduced adaptive menus in Office 2000. Microsoft introduced this feature to minimize the number of choices users have to view in the ever more complex Office applications. This option is turned on by default, and it limits the number of options a user sees in a menu by displaying only the most commonly or recently used items. When this option is active, the built-in menus typically display no more than six options unless the user clicks the arrow at the bottom of the list to show all options.

Designing Navigation Forms

So, how should you apply this guideline to your application? I like to have my applications start by displaying a classic switchboard form, but I never put more than seven or eight command buttons on this form. When the application is very complex, I provide buttons that take the user to major task categories. Figure 2-5 shows you the main switchboard in the Inventory sample application.

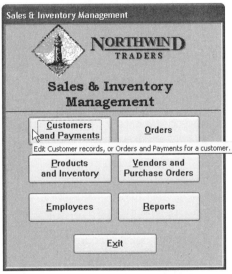

Figure 2-5   The main switchboard form in the Inventory sample application offers seven options.

As you can see, this main switchboard form provides options to go to Customers and Payments, Orders, Products and Inventory, Vendors and Purchase Orders, Employees, and Reports, and to exit the application. If you click any of the first three buttons, the application shows you a pop-up selection form, like the one shown in Figure 2-6 on the next page, that lets you specify a filter and select the specific option you need.

When you first run this application, you might not realize that clicking Customers and Payments on the first switchboard will also offer the option to edit orders for a specific customer. But notice that the command button on the main switchboard shown in Figure 2-5 also offers ToolTip text that displays more information when you move the pointer over the button.

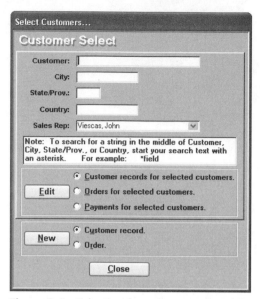

Figure 2-6   Selecting from Customers and Payments suboptions in the Inventory sample application.

> **Tip**   When I'm first planning the navigation layout of an application, I draw a navigation tree on paper, with the six to eight main categories that I plan to implement as the first nodes of the tree right under the main switchboard. I then work down the tree and plan where to include options to get to all of the features in the application. I will also sometimes note cross-paths—ways to jump from one major branch to another. For example, in the Inventory sample application when you are editing orders, you can click an Options button in the Orders window that displays a dialog box giving you options to jump to related invoices, payments, purchase orders, or vendor invoices.

Providing Keyboard Shortcuts

Not everyone is proficient with a mouse, and some people (particularly employees doing lots of data entry) prefer to do as many tasks as possible using the keyboard. So, you should design your forms so that, if they wish, your users can perform all tasks from the keyboard and not have to touch their mouse.

You can start with your switchboard forms. So that users doesn't have to click command buttons using their mouse, provide a keyboard shortcut for every command button by including an ampersand in the caption just before the letter that you want to be the shortcut key. This allows the user to press Alt and the letter to "click" the command button. If you look back at Figure 2-5, you can see that I defined keyboard shortcuts for all the command buttons. The user can get to Customers and Payments by pressing Alt+C.

Option groups also present a challenge. Although Access lets the user tab from control to control, pressing Tab when the focus is on one option in an option group moves the focus to the next control rather than to the next option in the group. Some users might figure out that you can use the arrow keys to move from option to option once the focus is in an option group, but that's not necessarily intuitive. You can help the user out by defining a shortcut key in the label attached to the option button. You do this the same way that you do for command button captions—place an ampersand just before the letter you want to be the shortcut key. As you can see in Figure 2-6, I defined shortcut keys (the underlined letter is the shortcut key) for all the option buttons. The user can choose **Orders for selected customers** by pressing Alt+O and then press Alt+E to "click" the Edit button.

Of course, you should try to make sure that all the shortcut keys on a form are unique from one another. If you don't do that, Access selects the first available option when you press the shortcut key the first time, and subsequent duplicate options when you press the shortcut key again. In the example form shown in Figure 2-6, I purposefully used the letter C twice so that you can see what happens. If you press Alt+C once, the form will highlight the **Customer records for selected customers** option. If you press Alt+C again, you'll close the form because that's the shortcut key for the **Close** button.

Creating Custom Menus and Toolbars

You don't want your users fiddling around in the design of your forms and reports, so you should always build custom menus and toolbars for your applications. For example, Figure 2-7 shows the built-in Form view menu bar that includes an option to switch to Design view on the View menu. That figure also shows you the custom form menu bar that I built for several of the sample applications. It has no View menu at all, and the File menu includes only the options applicable to editing data on a form.

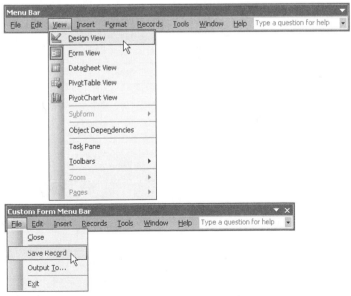

Figure 2-7   Comparing the built-in form menu bar with a custom one.

To build a custom menu bar, toolbar, or shortcut menu, you can choose Customize from the Tools menu. This opens the Customize dialog box shown in Figure 2-8 and makes all the visible menus and toolbars editable.

Figure 2-8   The Customize dialog box lets you define new menu bars, toolbars, and shortcut menus.

Click the New button to start defining a new toolbar. You can set the toolbar properties to make it a menu bar or toolbar, or add it to the list of shortcut menus. You can drag and drop any of the commands that you find on the Commands tab, or you can create custom menu entries or toolbar buttons. You can also copy existing commands or menus from any open menus or toolbars.

When you want to borrow an item from an existing toolbar, be sure to hold down the Ctrl key when you drag and drop the item from an existing toolbar or menu bar to your new one. When you hold down the Ctrl key, Access makes a copy of the item instead of moving it. If you don't do that, you'll be modifying the existing toolbar. Also, when you copy a built-in top-level menu (either from an available menu bar or from the Built-In Menus category), Access does *not* make an independent copy of the original. So, if you copy a menu and then change some of its properties (for example, you delete one of the commands from the menu), you're also affecting the built-in menu. So, you must use the New Menu command to start building custom root menu entries rather than copy existing File, View, Tools, or other menus.

To read about the full details of how to build custom menus, toolbars, and shortcut menus, see Chapter 24 in Microsoft Office Access 2003 Inside Out *(Microsoft Press, 2003).*

The Bottom Line: Know Your Users and Their Needs

This chapter certainly doesn't cover all you need to know about creating user interfaces. You could be a really artful designer, know all the tricks you can use to your advantage in Access, create a user interface that looks great, and still end up with an application that your users hate!

As with designing your tables, if you don't understand how the business runs and what the users need to do, you'll just be spinning your wheels. Are your users experienced computer users? Do many of the tasks require intensive keyboard entry? Do any of your users have disabilities? Do all of your users have the same operating system and screen resolution? Do you need to build a different user interface for managers? (You might need to build a separate reports-only front end database for managers that lets them search and print the data but not edit it.) As you apply what you have learned in this chapter, you probably need to ask all those questions and many more.

Chapter 3
Designing a Client/Server Application

Unless you're building an application for your own use or creating a specialized application for a single user, you need to understand the best ways to allow multiple users to share your application. One of the key reasons developers move an application from Excel to Access is the need to allow multiple users to share and update the same data at the same time. With Excel, unless you have marked the workbook for sharing, only one user can have the workbook file open for editing at a time. Even when you share a workbook, Excel either saves the last change to a cell without warning or asks the user to resolve the conflict. But database systems are designed to share the data, and multiple users can be editing data in the same table at the same time.

In this chapter, you'll explore the various client/server architectures you can employ. You'll also learn how to design your application to minimize network resources and conflicts. Finally, you'll learn about advanced techniques that you can use to allow your application to be shared by 50 or more users at the same time—even when you're still using the JET desktop engine to manage the data.

Understanding Access Client/Server Architectures

To allow multiple users to run your application at the same time and share the data, you must make the data available on a server accessible to all the users. The biggest mistake you can make when you want multiple users to run your application is to place a single desktop database file (.mdb) on a server file share. When you do that, a copy of Access must still run on each desktop, and each user's copy must fetch not only the data but also the query, form, report, and module definitions over the network. This additional traffic over the network slows down not only your application but also any other applications or tasks needing to send data over the network (such as sending a report to a network printer).

Also, because some user actions (such as applying a filter to a form) actually change a form definition, Access must be able to periodically save a form back to the shared database. When that happens, Access on the user's machine must be able to temporarily acquire exclusive access to the object. If your application needs to create temporary objects such as a working table or query, a user will see a locking error if another user is in the same part of the application at the same time. If any error occurs on the network while Access is trying to save an object, your shared database can become corrupt.

You can, however, design the architecture of your Access application to provide efficient sharing of data. Figure 3-1 shows you the most common client/server architectures for an Access application.

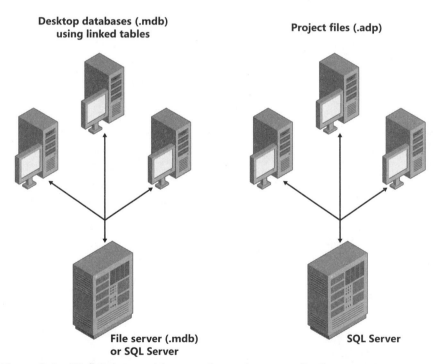

Desktop databases (.mdb) using linked tables

Project files (.adp)

File server (.mdb) or SQL Server

SQL Server

Figure 3-1 Client/server architectures for an Access application.

The most commonly used and simplest to develop architecture, shown on the left of Figure 3-1, involves giving each user a copy of a desktop database file (.mdb or .mde) that contains only local tables and the definitions for the queries, forms, reports, and modules that define your application. This desktop database file uses linked tables to connect to the shared data residing in either another desktop database file (.mdb) or in Microsoft SQL Server.

Keep in mind that Access running with the JET database engine is fundamentally a desktop database. Although JET provides many data management capabilities similar to what you'll find in a full-fledged database system such as SQL Server, it's really only a very smart file manager that understands SQL. So, all requests for data execute on the client machine, and the JET engine makes low-level file requests to the file system. When the data is in a shared file on a file server, those requests must be sent over the network, and the necessary physical file pages must be sent by the server to the desktop machine for further processing by the JET engine. This is in sharp contrast to a true database system like SQL Server where the client sends an SQL command, the server finds the data, and the client receives only the requested rows from the server.

Access 2000 introduced a new type of application file—an Access project (.adp) shown on the right side of Figure 3-1—that allows your application to connect directly to a Microsoft SQL Server database. Access 2002 greatly improved the stability and features available in project files. You can design SQL Server tables directly from Access, and you can design and work with SQL Server views, stored procedures, and functions defined in the SQL Server database. You should certainly consider using this architecture if your application needs to manage very large amounts of data or needs to support more than 20 concurrent users.

Because you're working directly with SQL Server with a project file, communication with the server is potentially more efficient because all the work to fetch and update data is done by the server. However, designing an application to work with SQL Server is more complex. For example, you must be careful to assign a unique name to any temporary table that you create because all data is shared—you cannot access or create tables on the user's local machine. And you can still create a very inefficient application if you do not employ techniques to minimize the amount of information transferred over the network.

Programming for Client/Server Architecture

Regardless of whether you're using a desktop database file (.mdb) on a file server or SQL Server to manage your data, you should design your application to request only the data needed for each specific task. If, for example, you design forms that always open to display all available records in the table you want to edit, you are transmitting far more data over the network than might be needed for a specific task. It's the network that is the slowest component in a client/server application, so the less information that your application transmits over the network, the better your application will run. The following sections describe techniques that you can implement in any client/server architecture to accomplish the goal of transmitting only the data absolutely needed for each task.

> **Note**   All the sample applications included with this book use the simpler client/server archi-
> tecture that stores the data in a desktop database file (.mdb) on a file server and uses linked
> tables in the application code running on the client. When an application using this architec-
> ture is well designed, it can easily be upsized to an Access project file (.adp) and SQL Server. For
> details about upsizing a desktop application to a project, see Chapter 24 in *Microsoft Office
> Access 2003 Inside Out* (Microsoft Press, 2003).

Filtering Forms and Reports

When you first start building applications using Access, it's very simple to select a table you
want to edit and run the Form Wizard to create a form that edits all the data. As you become
a bit more experienced, you might create a query first that includes data from related tables
(such as Customer information for an Order) and then build your form. These techniques
work fine for a single-user application, but they are potentially disastrous when you're editing
data stored on a server and your application is shared by multiple users.

Remember that the key to designing an efficient client/server application is minimizing the
amount of data sent to or fetched from the server. When your forms always open displaying all
the available data and the user needs to work with only one or two records, you're asking
Access and the database system to do far more work than is necessary. The same is true when
you open a report that needs to display or print only a few records. If your tables contain tens
of thousands of rows, your application performance will be terrible.

The best way to focus the user on the task at hand and fetch only the rows the user needs is
to force the user to enter some criteria that specifies or narrows down what records are
needed. In all the sample applications, you'll find that you cannot click a button on the main
application switchboard to open a form editing all records. For example, when you click the
Orders button on the main switchboard in the Inventory Management sample application,
the application displays a pop-up filter window that forces you to narrow your choices, as
shown in Figure 3-2.

Notice that the form automatically fills in the name of the currently signed-on sales representative. If you open the Customer list, you'll find that the form has also filtered the list of customers to only those assigned to the current sales representative. When I designed the form,
I set the Default Value property of the From Date text box control to =Date()–90, and the
Default Value property of the To text box control to =Date(), but the user can set a wider or
narrower range if necessary. If the user tries to clear all the criteria and then click Edit
Unbilled or Edit All, the application code refuses to proceed. The application also requires
the user to select a customer before clicking the New button, and it opens frmOrders in Data
Entry mode, thus avoiding fetching any records from the database at all.

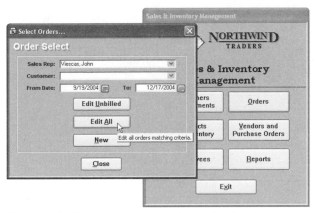

Figure 3-2   The Inventory sample application forces you to specify filtering criteria for Orders.

Here's the code behind the Edit All button that builds and tests the filter:

```
Private Sub cmdAll_Click()
Dim strWhere As String
  ' Open all orders for the selected customer
  ' Set an error trap
  On Error GoTo cmdAll_Err
  ' Call the predicate builder
  strWhere = BuildPredicate()
  ' If returned nothing, then done
  If strWhere = "" Then Exit Sub
  ' Close the form if it is open
  If IsFormLoaded("frmOrders") Then
    If vbYes = MsgBox("The Orders window is already open.  " & _
      "This search will cancel any pending edits in that " & _
      "window, close it, and " & _
      "attempt to reopen with the criteria you specified." & _
      vbCrLf & vbCrLf & "Are you sure you want to proceed?", _
      vbQuestion + vbYesNo + vbDefaultButton2, gstrAppTitle) Then
      ' Close using the form's Cancel routine
      Forms!frmOrders.cmdCancel_Click
    Else
      Exit Sub
    End If
  End If
  ' Open frmOrders hidden to check if any records found
  DoCmd.OpenForm FormName:="frmOrders", WhereCondition:=strWhere, _
    WindowMode:=acHidden
  If Forms!frmOrders.RecordsetClone.RecordCount = 0 Then
    ' No orders for selected customers
    MsgBox "There are no orders for the " & _
      "customer criteria you specified.", _
      vbInformation, gstrAppTitle
    DoCmd.Close acForm, "frmOrders"
    Exit Sub
  Else
    Forms!frmOrders.Visible = True
```

```
   End If
   ' Close myself
   DoCmd.Close acForm, Me.Name

cmdAll_Exit:
  Exit Sub

cmdAll_Err:
  ErrorLog Me.Name & "_cmdAll", Err, Error
  MsgBox "Unexpected error: " & Err & ", " & Error, _
    vbCritical, gstrAppTitle
  Resume cmdAll_Exit
End Sub
```

And here's the *BuildPredicate* function (that you can find in the form's module) called by the Edit All command button code:

```
Private Function BuildPredicate() As String
Dim varWhere As Variant
  ' Initialize to Null
  varWhere = Null
  ' If specified a company value
  If Not IsNothing(Me.cmbCustomerID) Then
    ' .. build the predicate
    varWhere = "CustomerID = " & Me.cmbCustomerID
  End If
  ' Do dates next
  If Not IsNothing(Me.txtFromDate) Then
    If Not IsDate(Me.txtFromDate) Then
      MsgBox "You must enter a valid 'From' date.", _
        vbExclamation, gstrAppTitle
      Me.txtFromDate.SetFocus
      Exit Function
    End If
    ' .. build the predicate
    ' Note: taking advantage of Null propogation
    '  so we don't have to test for any previous predicate
    varWhere = (varWhere + " AND ") & "[OrderDate] >= #" & _
      Format(Me.txtFromDate, "dd mmm yyyy") & "#"
  End If
  If Not IsNothing(Me.txtToDate) Then
    If Not IsDate(Me.txtToDate) Then
      MsgBox "You must enter a valid 'To' date.", _
        vbExclamation, gstrAppTitle
      Me.txtToDate.SetFocus
      Exit Function
    End If
    ' Make sure To is later or equal to From
    If Not IsNothing(Me.txtFromDate) Then
      If Me.txtToDate < Me.txtFromDate Then
        MsgBox "'To' Date must not be earlier than 'From' Date.", _
          vbExclamation, gstrAppTitle
        Me.txtToDate.SetFocus
        Exit Function
      End If
    End If
```

```
      End If
    ' .. build the predicate
    ' Note: taking advantage of Null propogation
    '   so we don't have to test for any previous predicate
    varWhere = (varWhere + " AND ") & "[OrderDate] <= #" & _
      Format(Me.txtToDate, "dd mmm yyyy") & "#"
  End If
  ' Finally, do Sales Rep
  If Not IsNothing(Me.cmbSalesRep) Then
    ' .. build the predicate
    varWhere = (varWhere + " AND ") & "[SalesRepID] = " & Me.cmbSalesRep
  End If
  ' Check to see that we built a filter
  If IsNothing(varWhere) Then
    MsgBox "You must enter at least one search criteria.", _
      vbInformation, gstrAppTitle
    Exit Function
  End If
  ' Return the filter string
  BuildPredicate = varWhere
End Function
```

> **Note**   Notice that this sample code uses the WhereCondition parameter of the OpenForm command. This technique works equally as well in an Access project (.adp) as long as the form you are opening uses a table or a view as its record source. Access sets the form's ServerFilter property using the filter you specify, which causes the form to send the filter to the server. If the form uses a stored procedure or function as its record source, Access must send a command to the server to execute the procedure, and the procedure returns all the rows unfiltered. Access must then apply your filter to the rows the server sends back, so you increase rather than reduce network traffic when you use a filter in this way. To filter a form or report based on a stored procedure or function, you should include parameters in the procedure and set the form or report Input Parameters property. For more details about input parameters, see Chapter 19 in *Microsoft Office Access 2003 Inside Out*.

Filtering Lookup Values

Combo box controls and list box controls are a good way to look up related values to set a foreign key or to provide a list of potential values for a filter. But keep in mind that for every combo box or list box that uses a table or a query as its row source, Access must fetch data from the shared data file to fill in the row values. If the table or query returns thousands of rows from a table on the server and the user needs to select only one value, you're asking Access to do more work than necessary. You can deal with this problem in one of two ways: filter the row source or provide an alternative lookup method.

> **Note**   Another alternative is to use a local copy of a lookup table as the row source of a combo box or list box control. See "Pushing the Envelope," page 85, for details.

Restricting Rows in a Combo Box or List Box

The good news is Access optimizes the fetching of the row source for a combo box or list box. Combo boxes are especially efficient because Access doesn't fetch the entire row source until the user begins to type in the box or opens the list. (Access does look up any bound value as you move from row to row.) However, if the row source contains thousands of rows, Access might need to fetch a lot of data over the network as the user searches for the desired value in the list.

Filtering an unbound combo box or list box is relatively easy using a parameter query. For example, the Customer combo box shown in Figure 3-2 has the following query set for its row source:

```
PARAMETERS Forms!fpopOrderSelect!cmbSalesRep Long;
SELECT NullID As CustomerID, "< All Customers >" As CustomerName,
"" As City
FROM tblDummy
UNION ALL SELECT tblCustomers.CustomerID, tblCustomers.CustomerName,
tblCustomers.City
FROM tblCustomers
WHERE (tblCustomers.Active=True) AND
((tblCustomers.SalesRepID = [Forms]![fpopOrderSelect]![cmbSalesRep]) OR
([Forms]![fpopOrderSelect]![cmbSalesRep] Is Null))
ORDER BY CustomerName;
```

Of course, the name of the form is fpopOrderSelect, and the name of the combo box containing the SalesRepID is cmbSalesRep. Code in the form's Load event initially sets the Sales Rep to the ID of the currently signed-on employee and requeries the Customer combo box—which effectively filters the customer list to only those assigned to the current employee. When the user selects a different sales rep (the signed-on employee can look at orders entered by other employees), code in the AfterUpdate event of the cmbSalesRep combo box control requeries the Customer combo box control, causing the query shown above to run again and fetch the customers for the newly selected sales rep.

> **Tip**   You might be wondering why the row source of the Customer combo box is a union query. The tblDummy table has exactly one row with a long integer field set to Null. I union this Null value with the real list to generate an entry that allows the user to clear the combo box by setting it to Null. You might find this technique particularly useful on any search parameter form.

But what about filtering a lookup list for data entry? In a sales and inventory database, you might have thousands of products. If you provide a combo box on the order entry form that allows the user to pick the product to be ordered, the combo box might delay a second or two when the user tries to open the list to select a product to sell. If your products are categorized, it would make sense to require the user to pick a category first, and then pick a product from a shorter list.

Only 77 products are in the Inventory sample database, but the Orders form does require you to select a category before adding a product to an order. You can see how this works by starting the application (open the frmSplash form), signing on as me, clicking Orders, and searching for all unbilled orders in the month of February 2005. The first order that appears (if you haven't changed the sample data) has 10 products ordered. You can go to the new record row in the Products subform, select Dairy Products for Category, and then open the Product list. You should see only the 10 products that are in that category, as shown in Figure 3-3.

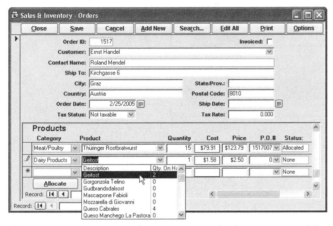

Figure 3-3 You must select a category before you can pick a product on the Orders form in the Inventory sample database.

As you might guess, some of the code running behind the subform sets up the combo box to display the restricted list of products. But the subform is a form in Continuous Form view, which presents a special problem when working with filtered combo boxes. Although you can see more than one row in a continuous form, there's actually only one copy of the combo box control. If you filter the combo box to show products from a certain category, the combo box for any other row for a product in a different category will go blank because the product on the other row is no longer in the row source.

To solve this problem, you must include the lookup table in the record source for the form and use a text box that overlays the display portion of the combo box to show the real value from every row. The record source for the fsubOrderProducts form is as follows:

```
SELECT tblOrderProducts.OrderID, tblOrderProducts.LineNo,
tblProducts.Category, tblOrderProducts.ProductID,
tblProducts.Description, tblProducts.SellPrice,
tblOrderProducts.VendorID, tblVendors.VendorName,
tblOrderProducts.Quantity, tblOrderProducts.OrderPONo,
tblOrderProducts.OrderPOLineNo, tblOrderProducts.InvoiceNo,
tblOrderProducts.Cost, tblOrderProducts.Price, tblOrderProducts.Status,
tblOrderProducts.DateAlloc, tblProducts.OrderMultiple AS PROM
FROM tblProducts INNER JOIN
    (tblOrderProducts LEFT JOIN tblVendors
```

```
            ON tblOrderProducts.VendorID = tblVendors.VendorID)
ON tblProducts.ProductID = tblOrderProducts.ProductID;
```

If you open the fsubOrderProducts form in Design view, click on Category and drag down, and then click on Description and drag down, you'll reveal the two overlay text boxes, as shown in Figure 3-4.

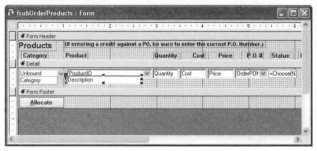

Figure 3-4   The problem with filtered combo boxes on a continuous form can be solved by using overlaid text boxes.

You can see that the text box sitting on top of the unbound cmbCategory combo box always displays the category from the current row. Likewise, the Description text box sitting atop the cmbProductID combo box displays the product description of the current row (the displayed text in the underlying combo box). The rest of the work happens in code behind the form, which is as follows:

```
Private Sub CategoryName_Enter()
  ' Move focus to category combo box behind this text box
  ' when user enters this field
  Me.cmbCategory.SetFocus
End Sub

Private Sub cmbCategory_AfterUpdate()
  ' Filter the product list based on the new category
  Me.cmbProductID.RowSource = "SELECT * FROM qlkpProducts " & _
    "WHERE Category = '" & Me.cmbCategory & "'"
End Sub

Private Sub Description_Enter()
  ' Push focus to combo box behind this control
  Me.cmbProductID.SetFocus
End Sub

Private Sub Form_Current()
Dim strSQL As String
  ' Sync up the category combo
  Me.cmbCategory = Me.Category
  ' Reset the Row source for the products combo box
  If Not IsNothing(Me.Category) Then
    ' If got a good category, then use it as filter
    Me.cmbProductID.RowSource = "SELECT * FROM qlkpProducts " & _
      "WHERE Category = '" & Me.cmbCategory & "'"
```

```
    Else
      ' No category - return an empty set
      ' (will be reset by Category AfterUpdate)
      Me.cmbProductID.RowSource = "SELECT * FROM qlkpProducts " & _
        "WHERE ProductID IS NULL"
      End If
' Other code not related to this issue here …
End Sub
```

The Enter event code for the two overlay text box controls makes sure that should the user click into the control, the focus immediately goes to the combo box control behind it. (The two text box controls are not in the tab order.) The AfterUpdate event code for the cmbCategory combo box resets the row source of the cmbProductID combo box to match the newly selected category. And finally, as the user moves from row to row, the form Current event code keeps the cmbProductID row source in sync with the category on that row.

Resetting the Row Source property does requery the combo box and forces Access to look up the bound value for the row, but the result is a series of tiny probes to the database instead of a large fetch when the user needs to add a product to an order.

Providing an Alternate Lookup Method

In some cases, you might not be able to logically filter a very large list that you need for a combo box control or list box control. One alternative is to pop open a separate search criteria form for the list every time the user needs to select a new value, but that could become tedious for the user. Another alternative is to provide an unbound text box where the user can begin to type the name they want. You can write code to monitor the keystrokes and do individual quick probes to the database to find the closest matching value and display it. If the user presses Enter or tabs out of the control, your code can set the foreign key value for the name the code looked up as the user was typing.

Although the Membership Tracking sample database has only 35 members defined (using a combo box to look up all member names would be reasonable), the application does contain one form that demonstrates this technique. Open the Membership Tracking application (Membership.mdb), and open the frmMeetings form. In the sample data, I am not registered yet in the first meeting in September 2004. Click the Attendees button on the frmMeetings form, and in the Attendee Options dialog box, select the **Open the meeting sign-in form** option and click Go to open the frmMemberAttendance form. The general purpose of this form is to allow someone sitting at the meeting registration desk to sign in members as they arrive by simply typing in each member's name. When the correct name appears, the user can press Enter or Tab to add the member to the registration list for the meeting and then verify other information on file while the member is still standing there.

In the **Sign In, Please** box, begin typing the first three characters of my last name—**vie**. As soon as you type the third character, the text box fills in my name, as shown in Figure 3-5 on the next page. (The figure shows the data for the previously signed-in member in the main area of the form.) Press Enter or Tab, and the code behind the form adds my attendance record and displays the information from my record in the tblMembers table so that you can edit it.

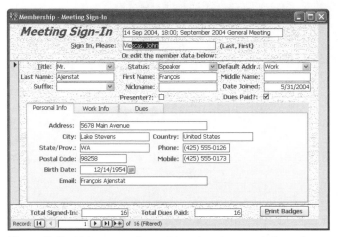

Figure 3-5   Using an unbound text box to search for values.

Access signals several events as a user types in a text box. These events include KeyDown, KeyPress, Change, and KeyUp. The KeyDown event occurs when the users presses any key. In this event, you can also detect whether the user is holding down the Shift, Ctrl, or Alt key. When you don't want the key to be delivered to the control—for example, to prevent the user from tabbing out of the control or using Page Up or Page Down in the control—you can set the Keycode to 0 to instruct Access to act as though the user didn't press the key.

The KeyPress event occurs when a character is about to be delivered to the control. This event does not occur, for example, when the user presses one of the arrow keys or the Backspace key. The Change event occurs when a key the user pressed changes the value of the text displayed in the control—for example, the user typed a letter or number or pressed the Backspace key to delete a character. Note that the Value property of the control doesn't change until the user moves out of the control and thereby commits the change to the control. However, you can examine the Text property of the control to find out what's currently displayed. Finally, the KeyUp event occurs when the user releases the key.

All the work to make the lookup happen occurs in the Change and KeyDown events for the text box. The KeyDown event occurs first, so that event procedure gets to look at the Keycode and determine if the user pressed the Backspace or Delete key. If the user is correcting data in the text box using these keys, it doesn't make sense for the Change event procedure to do anything with these keystrokes—what's in the Text property of the control might not be what the user needs to look up. Below is the start of the KeyDown event procedure for the sign in text box. The code sets a module variable—intChangeOff—to let the Change event procedure know that it shouldn't process the next keystroke.

```
Option Compare Database
Option Explicit
```

```
Dim lngMemberID As Long, intChangeOff As Integer, strName As String

Private Sub txtSignIn_KeyDown(KeyCode As Integer, Shift As Integer)
Dim strName As String, strWhere As String, intI As Integer
Dim strLast As String, strFirst As String, varID As Variant
Dim rst As DAO.Recordset, lngNewMember As Long
  ' Trap some keys and tell Change to ignore
  If (KeyCode = vbKeyDelete) Or (KeyCode = vbKeyBack) Then
    ' Delete or backspace - ignore
    intChangeOff = True
    ' Reset the saved memberID
    lngMemberID = 0
    Exit Sub
  End If
```

When the user types a character that needs to be examined, the KeyDown event leaves the intChangeOff variable set to False. The Change event procedure looks at the current value of the Text up to the position of the cursor (indicated by the SelStart property). As long as the text box contains at least three characters and what the user types changes the leading part of the text, the code attempts to find the matching name. For example, the procedure won't begin to look up the name until the user types at least the third character of the last name—the letter *e* in my last name. The code finds me when the user types the letter *e*—it fills in the rest of my name but leaves the cursor sitting between the *e* and the first letter *s*. If the user next types an *s* to replace the letter already there, the code doesn't do another lookup because typing an *s* in the fourth position isn't actually changing what the procedure already found, but the procedure does refill the text box with the found name and positions the cursor again. Below is the beginning of the code in the Change event procedure that performs these tasks.

```
Private Sub txtSignIn_Change()
Dim strText As String, intI As Integer, strLast As String, strFirst As String
Dim strWhere As String, intStart As Integer
Dim db As DAO.Database, rst As DAO.Recordset
  ' If change is firing because of this code
  If intChangeOff = True Then
    ' Bail
    Exit Sub
  End If
  ' Do nothing until the text is at least 3 characters
  If Len(Me.txtSignIn.Text) < 3 Then
    Exit Sub
  End If
  ' Attempt to do a lookup on the name up to SelStart
  If Me.txtSignIn.SelStart > 0 Then
    ' Save the start
    intStart = Me.txtSignIn.SelStart
    ' Get the characters up to the cursor
    strText = Left(Me.txtSignIn.Text, Me.txtSignIn.SelStart)
    ' If the leading characters didn't change
    '  (User typed a character that matches what was already displayed)
    If strText = Left(strName, intStart) Then
      ' Don't bother to do another lookup
      ' Put the name back
```

```
      Me.txtSignIn = strName
      ' Make sure intStart not > new length
      If intStart > Len(Me.txtSignIn.Text) Then
        intStart = Len(Me.txtSignIn.Text)
      End If
      ' Put the cursor back by setting SelStart
      Me.txtSignIn.SelStart = intStart
      ' Select to end of text
      Me.txtSignIn.SelLength = Len(Me.txtSignIn.Text) - intStart
      ' Done
      Exit Sub
    End If
```

If the code has not yet found a matching name or the user types a different character in the text box, the Change event parses out the last name and first name by looking for the separating comma. If the user entered a last name, a comma, and a first name, the procedure searches for an exact match on the last name (the text up to the comma) and a wildcard match on the first part of the first name. If the text contains no comma, the procedure performs a wildcard search on the last name only. It then attempts to look up that name in the tblMembers table.

> **Tip**   If you want to change this code to search for something like a company name where the name the user types might appear in the middle of the string (the actual name is "The Blue Yonder Company," but the user typed "Blue"), you can add the wildcard character (*) to both ends of the search string.

If the procedure can't find the name, it doesn't change what the user typed, but it does clear the lngMemberID and strName module variables to indicate that the name typed cannot be found. Here's the code in the Change event procedure that parses the name and performs the lookup:

```
    ' Find any comma
    intI = InStr(strText, ",")
    If intI > 0 Then
      strLast = Trim(Left(strText, intI - 1))
      strFirst = Trim(Mid(strText, intI + 1))
      strWhere = "[LastName] = '" & strLast & _
      "' And [FirstName] Like '" & strFirst & "*'"
    Else
      strLast = Trim(strText)
      strWhere = "[LastName] Like '" & strLast & "*'"
    End If
    ' Point to this database
    Set db = DBEngine(0)(0)
    ' Try to get the member ID and name
    Set rst = db.OpenRecordset("Select MemberID, LastName, FirstName " & _
      "FROM tblMembers WHERE " & strWhere & _
      " ORDER BY LastName, FirstName")
    ' If got one,
    If Not rst.EOF Then
      ' Update this textbox
```

```
        ' Can't change the Text property because that
        '  fires the stupid Change event again!
        ' Save the new name
        strName = rst!LastName & ", " & rst!FirstName
        Me.txtSignIn = strName
        ' Make sure intStart not > new length
        If intStart > Len(Me.txtSignIn.Text) Then
          intStart = Len(Me.txtSignIn.Text)
        End If
        ' Put SelStart back
        Me.txtSignIn.SelStart = intStart
        ' Select to end of text
        Me.txtSignIn.SelLength = Len(Me.txtSignIn.Text) - intStart
        ' Update the saved member ID
        lngMemberID = rst!MemberID
      Else
        ' Not found - clear saved member ID
        lngMemberID = 0
        ' .. and name
        strName = ""
      End If
      ' Close the recordset
      rst.Close
      Set rst = Nothing
      Set db = Nothing
    Else
      ' Nothing to search on - clear the saved member ID
      lngMemberID = 0
    End If
End Sub
```

When the user presses the Tab key or the Enter key to indicate a desire to accept the displayed value, the KeyDown event gets to look at those keystrokes first. Neither of these keys changes the value of the text, so the code doesn't need to tell the Change event to not process the keystroke. If the user pressed either of these keys, the remaining code in the KeyDown event first checks to see if the Change event code found a matching member ID. If the code in the Change event previously found a match, the code in the KeyDown event attempts to look up that member ID in the form's recordset, which is editing rows in the tblMemberAttend table. If the member ID isn't in the recordset, the member isn't yet signed in to the current meeting. The code adds the member (explained in Chapter 6, "Tracking Member Activities"), checks for dues paid (explained in Chapter 7, "Tracking Member Status"), and positions to the new record so the user can verify current address and contact information. If the attendance record already exists, the code positions the form display to that record.

Finally, if the Change event did not previously find a match on the name, the code in the Key-Down event asks the user if this is a new member. If the user replies Yes, the code sets up a search string to verify that the record has been added and opens the fdlgMemberAdd form and passes that form the text the user entered. If the user successfully adds a new member record with the name originally entered, the code then branches back up to add the member attendance record for that new user. The remaining code in the KeyDown event procedure that performs all these tasks is as follows:

```
  ' If Tab or Enter,
  If (KeyCode = vbKeyTab) Or (KeyCode = vbKeyReturn) Then
    ' Assume they meant to update the control
    ' Set an error trap
    On Error GoTo txtSignIn_Error
UserAdded:
    ' If got a member ID
    If Not IsNothing(lngMemberID) Then
      ' Get a copy of the recordset
      Set rst = Me.RecordsetClone
      ' See if the row exists
      rst.FindFirst "MemberID = " & lngMemberID
      ' If not found
      If rst.NoMatch Then
        ' Save the memberID locally
        lngNewMember = lngMemberID
  ' ** Several lines of code to insert a member
  ' ** attendance record - explained in Chapter 6.

  ' ** Several lines of code to check dues ...
  ' ** Explained in Chapter 7.
      Else
        ' Position to the found row
        Me.Bookmark = rst.Bookmark
      End If
      ' Clear the recordset
      Set rst = Nothing
    Else
      ' Member wasn't previously found by the Change event
      ' See if there is some text
      If Len(Trim(Me.txtSignIn.Text)) > 5 Then
        ' OK, got at least 5 characters - see if they want to add
        strName = Trim(Me.txtSignIn.Text)
        ' Build the verification search string
        ' See if there's a comma
        intI = InStr(strName, ",")
        ' If yes,
        If intI > 0 Then
          ' Parse out the last name
          strLast = Trim(Left(strName, intI - 1))
          ' Parse out the first name
          strFirst = Trim(Mid(strName, intI + 1))
          ' Build the test predicate
          strWhere = "[LastName] = '" & strLast & _
            "' And [FirstName] = '" & strFirst & "'"
        Else
          ' Build a simple last name predicate
          strWhere = "[LastName] = '" & Trim(strName) & "'"
        End If
        ' Verify that they want to add the new Member
        If vbYes = MsgBox("Member " & strName & " is not defined. " & _
          "Do you want to add this Member?", _
```

```
      vbYesNo + vbQuestion + vbDefaultButton2, gstrAppTitle) Then
      ' Open the add a Member form and pass it the new value
      DoCmd.OpenForm "fdlgMemberAdd", DataMode:=acFormAdd, _
        WindowMode:=acDialog, OpenArgs:=strName
      ' Code will wait until "add" form closes
      '  - now verify that it got added!
      varID = DLookup("MemberID", "tblMembers", strWhere)
      ' If not
      If IsNull(varID) Then
        ' Ooops
        MsgBox "You failed to add a Member that matched " & _
          "what you entered.  Please try again.", _
          vbInformation, gstrAppTitle
      Else
        ' Save the new ID
        lngMemberID = varID
        ' Loop back up to try again with the newly added row
        GoTo UserAdded
      End If
    End If
  End If
  ' Tell the user there's a problem.
  MsgBox "The name you entered does not exist!", _
    vbExclamation, gstrAppTitle
  End If
  ' Tell Change to ignore this keystroke
  intChangeOff = True
  Exit Sub
End If
' Not ignoring key, so turn off ignore flag
intChangeOff = False
txtSignIn_Exit:
  Exit Sub

txtSignIn_Error:
  ' Make sure Echo is on
  Application.Echo True
  ' Not supposed to error - tell user
  MsgBox "Unexpected Error: " & Err & ", " & Error
  ' Log it
  ErrorLog Me.Name & "_txtSignin_KeyDown", Err, Error
  ' Bail
  Resume txtSignIn_Exit
End Sub
```

Understanding Additional Optimizations

As you have read so far, most of the optimizations you can implement for client/server applications are centered around minimizing the amount of data you transmit between the client machine and the server when editing data on forms. This section discusses additional points to consider.

Never Open the Same Record for Editing in Multiple Forms

In some applications, one or more subject tables legitimately have dozens of fields. It's very tempting to provide one form to edit some of the most frequently used fields and another to edit other fields. Unless you're careful to make sure that the user can edit in only one form at a time, the user can end up with edits pending for the same record in two different places. Access treats this as though two different users are editing the same record at the same time. If the user has multiple edits pending for the same record, saves one, and then attempts to save the other, Access displays the confusing error message shown in Figure 3-6.

Figure 3-6   The warning message Access displays when a user has edited the same record in two different forms at the same time.

> **Note**   Access will also display this message if a user starts to edit a record, another user edits and saves the exact same record, and then the first user attempts to save the record. This is likely to happen only when a table contains a few records, a user starts an edit on a record that some other user also needs to change, waits a long time, and then tries to save. You can trap that error in the form Error event and look for error code 7787. When you encounter that error, you can display your own error message and clear the edits on the form so the user can start over.

The real solution is to use the tab control to allow all fields to be edited on one form. Place the most commonly used fields on the first page of the tab and hide other fields behind other tabs. The user can change the data in fields on one tab and click to another tab to continue editing without problems.

Use a Local Table for Complex Report Data

When a report contains dozens or hundreds of pages and includes calculations that reference group totals (such as a percentage of the total), Access might need to fetch the data for the report from the server multiple times as the user scrolls through the pages and then scrolls back in Print Preview. If the record source of the report is complex and involves three or more tables, the user might also experience noticeable delays when moving between the pages of the report.

You should consider loading the data for this type of report into a local table before opening the report bound to that local table. This working table does not need to follow the design rules for active tables—that is, it can contain repeating groups and data from multiple subjects. You should also consider using this technique when the user needs to print a series of complex reports and all the reports need the same data. Fetch the data from the server once into your local tables, and then open the series of reports.

In Chapter 19, "Reporting and Analyzing Support Cases," you'll discover that all the reports in the Customer Support application use data loaded into local tables.

Avoid More Than Three Subforms on a Form

When your application opens a form that contains multiple subforms, Access must fetch not only the data for the outer form but also the data for each of the subforms, even if the user cannot see all the subforms (perhaps because they're on tab control pages). Even if you are careful to filter the outer form, Access must open multiple threads to the server to be able to fetch all the data. So, for most applications, three subforms is a reasonable limit to avoid performance problems. Although you can nest subforms up to 10 levels deep, you should also avoid nesting more than three levels (a subform on a form that's also the subform on another form). The critical point is that any one form should open no more than four form objects—the outer form and three subforms on that form, or the outer form with one simple subform and a second subform with another form as a subform on that form.

If you have rummaged around in the sample databases, you might have discovered the frmMembers form in the Membership Tracking application (Membership.mdb) that has *four* subforms on a tab control (Meetings, Committees, Dues History, and Officer History), as shown in Figure 3-7. (The other two tabs edit fields in the tblMembers row.) OK, I'm guilty as charged! My justification (or my excuse) is the subforms on the Committees and Officer History tabs are unlikely to have many rows (if any at all) for most members. In truth, if this is a large group with hundreds of rows in each subform for each member, I should find another way to solve the problem.

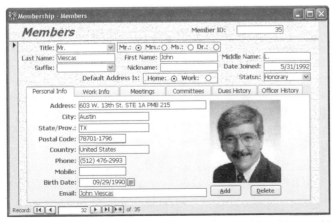

Figure 3-7   The frmMembers form in the Membership Tracking application uses four subforms on a tab control.

If you find that a form like this one performs poorly in a client/server application, you can redesign the form to use only one subform control and provide an option group with toggle button controls to simulate the tab control. When the user clicks a button asking for data in a different subform, code that responds to the option group AfterUpdate event can show/hide the appropriate controls and dynamically load the correct subform into the single subform control. You can find a sample form that demonstrates this technique in the Membership Tracking sample database (Membership.mdb). Open the database and then open the frmMembersOneSubform form, as shown in Figure 3-8.

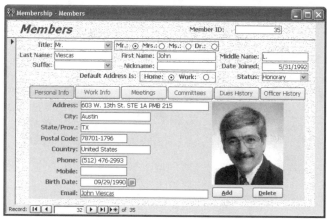

Figure 3-8   The frmMembersOneSubform form in the Membership Tracking database displays data from multiple related tables using only one subform.

This form uses an option group control with toggle button controls to simulate a tab control. You can click each of the buttons to see the other information about each member. When you click the Meetings, Committees, Dues History, or Officer History buttons, the AfterUpdate event of the option group control hides and reveals controls using the Visible property of each and, if necessary, loads the proper form into the Source Object property of the single subform control. The trick is to layer the controls properly so you don't have to fiddle with too many Visible properties. Figure 3-9 shows you the form in Design view with the layers pulled away from each other.

The bottom layer is an image control that has its background set to light gray and all the controls for the Personal Info button placed on top. The next layer is another image control (imgPersonalCover) with the controls for the Work Info button on top of that. The final layer is the subform that initially displays the fsubMemberAttend form–the data corresponding to the Meetings button. The subform control is the top layer because you cannot send a subform control behind other controls–it always displays on top. The form also has a tiny text box control–txtSafe–that's not in the tab sequence and is tucked in the corner of the form header. This control provides a place to park the focus while the code that responds to changes in the option group control works. You can't change any property of a control that has the focus.

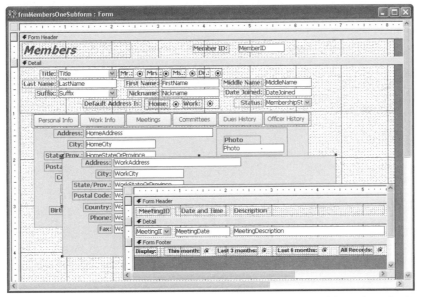

Figure 3-9   The underlying layers of the frmMembersOneSubform form in the Membership Tracking sample database.

Hiding the Personal Info is easy—as long as the imgPersonalCover control is visible, it will hide those controls. The code, however, must hide and reveal each of the controls for the Work Info button individually. You can find the code that performs this magic in the AfterUpdate event procedure for the option group control. The code is as follows:

```
Private Sub optTabs_AfterUpdate()
  ' User "clicked" a "tab"
  ' Hide and reveal stuff
  ' Put the focus in a safe place
  Me.txtSafe.SetFocus
  Select Case Me.optTabs
    Case 1
      ' Personal Info
      ' Hide the subform
      Me.fsubForm.Visible = False
      ' Hide all the "work" controls
      Me.WorkAddress.Visible = False
      Me.WorkCity.Visible = False
      Me.WorkCountry.Visible = False
      Me.WorkExtension.Visible = False
      Me.WorkFaxNumber.Visible = False
      Me.WorkPhone.Visible = False
      Me.WorkPostalCode.Visible = False
      Me.WorkStateOrProvince.Visible = False
      ' Unhide the personal info by hiding the
      ' covering image
      Me.imgPersonalCover.Visible = False
      ' Put the focus on the first Personal control
      Me.HomeAddress.SetFocus
```

```
Case 2
  ' Work Info
  ' Hide the subform
  Me.fsubForm.Visible = False
  ' Hide the Personal info by unhiding the
  ' covering image
  Me.imgPersonalCover.Visible = True
  ' Unhide all the "work" controls
  Me.WorkAddress.Visible = True
  Me.WorkCity.Visible = True
  Me.WorkCountry.Visible = True
  Me.WorkExtension.Visible = True
  Me.WorkFaxNumber.Visible = True
  Me.WorkPhone.Visible = True
  Me.WorkPostalCode.Visible = True
  Me.WorkStateOrProvince.Visible = True
  ' Put the focus on the first work control
  Me.WorkAddress.SetFocus
Case 3
  ' Meeting Info
  ' Load the meeting subform, if necessary
  If Me.fsubForm.SourceObject <> "fsubMemberAttend" Then
    Me.fsubForm.SourceObject = "fsubMemberAttend"
  End If
  ' Reveal the subform to hide everything else
  Me.fsubForm.Visible = True
  ' Put the focus there
  Me.fsubForm.SetFocus
Case 4
  ' Committee Info
  ' Load the committee subform, if necessary
  If Me.fsubForm.SourceObject <> "fsubMemberCommittee" Then
    Me.fsubForm.SourceObject = "fsubMemberCommittee"
  End If
  ' Reveal the subform to hide everything else
  Me.fsubForm.Visible = True
  ' Put the focus there
  Me.fsubForm.SetFocus
Case 5
  ' Dues
  ' Load the dues subform, if necessary
  If Me.fsubForm.SourceObject <> "fsubMemberDues" Then
    Me.fsubForm.SourceObject = "fsubMemberDues"
  End If
  ' Reveal the subform to hide everything else
  Me.fsubForm.Visible = True
  ' Put the focus there
  Me.fsubForm.SetFocus
Case 6
  ' Officer history
  ' Load the officer subform, if necessary
  If Me.fsubForm.SourceObject <> "fsubMemberOfficer" Then
    Me.fsubForm.SourceObject = "fsubMemberOfficer"
  End If
  ' Reveal the subform to hide everything else
```

```
        Me.fsubForm.Visible = True
        ' Put the focus there
        Me.fsubForm.SetFocus
    End Select
End Sub
```

Dealing with Complex Subforms: A Case History

For one client, I designed a very complex form that allowed the client to edit all the information for a work order to remanufacture large diesel engines. Each work order could have a log of the work performed, a list of the parts used, the labor charged to the work order, trip charges to go to the client site to perform the repair, services charged at a package price, and charges for work subcontracted out to other vendors—six subforms in total. I knew before I started that attempting to load data into all seven forms (the outer form and six subforms) might take minutes, not seconds.

My solution was to use only two subform controls. In the first subform, I loaded the parts subform—data required for virtually every work order. When the form opened, the second subform was bound to the labor data—the second most likely to be used set of related data. I placed the two subforms on top of each other and sized them exactly the same. Instead of a tab control, I used an option group control (similar to the frmMembersOneSubform that you can find in the Membership Tracking database) with a set of toggle button controls lined up to look like tabs. When the user clicked Parts or Labor, the code in the option group control AfterUpdate event set the Visible property of the two subforms appropriately. If the user needed to edit any of the other four categories, the code made the second subform visible and loaded the requested subform into it by setting its Source Object property.

Just for fun, I also created a test form with six embedded subforms. Loading a work order that had dozens of rows in each of the related categories took nearly 2 minutes over a 100BT network. My two-subform solution loaded in 5 seconds or less.

Be Careful Where You Place the Linked Data File

If you have many files on the server that manages your desktop database (.mdb) data file, the server probably has a complex folder structure. Unfortunately, Access can take several orders of magnitude longer when it attempts to establish a connection to a file that's buried several folders deep rather than connect to a file saved in the root folder or in a folder only one level deep. Performance slows significantly when the file is in a folder more than two levels deep and/or the total length of the path name is very long. This is true even when the share that you're using points directly at the folder containing the file. The file server must still maintain locks on the real folder tree, not just the single folder.

One folder that can be particularly misleading is the My Documents folder that exists on every Windows machine. That folder really exists at C:\Documents and Settings*user name*\My Documents on most machines—three levels deep in the folder structure. If you're having performance problems using linked tables to a desktop database file (.mdb) on a server, try moving the file to the root folder or a folder only one level down.

Validating Links on Startup

When you're using linked tables in a desktop database (.mdb or .mde), you should always include startup code that verifies the links and restores them if necessary. You might need to do this if the user chose a different logical drive name for the share that contains the data file. If the link to the server is down, the application should inform the user and exit gracefully.

All the sample databases include code that runs in the startup form (the frmSplash form in all samples) that performs this task. The core of the procedure is the *CheckConnect* function that you can find in modStartup in all the sample databases. The procedure begins by finding all the attached tables and testing them by opening a recordset on the table. Note that the code leaves one recordset open during this process to avoid the overhead of rebuilding the connection for each table. This is a technique you can use whenever you are going to open and close several recordsets over a short period of time and no bound form is open. When you leave one recordset open, the subsequent open commands reuse the already established connection. The code is as follows:

```
Public Function CheckConnect() As Integer
' This function called directly by frmCopyright to verify
' connections.
' It is also called by function CheckStartup (called from frmSplash)
' It calls functions AttachAgain and GetFileName as needed
Dim db As DAO.Database, rst As DAO.Recordset, tdf As DAO.TableDef
Dim rstV As DAO.Recordset, intFirst As Integer, intI As Integer
Dim strFilePath As String, strPath As String, varRet As Variant

  ' Set an Error trap
  On Error GoTo CheckConnect_Err
  ' Point to this database
  Set db = DBEngine(0)(0)
  ' Turn on the progress meter on the status bar
  varRet = SysCmd(acSysCmdInitMeter, "Verifying data tables...", _
    db.TableDefs.Count)
  ' Loop through all TableDefs
  For Each tdf In db.TableDefs
    ' Looking for attached tables
    If (tdf.Attributes And dbAttachedTable) Then
      ' Try to open the table
      ' Use alternate recordset if already processed the first
      If intFirst = True Then
        Set rst = tdf.OpenRecordset()
        ' This one OK - close it
        rst.Close
        ' And clear the object
```

```
          Set rst = Nothing
        Else
          ' Doing the first one - use alternate
          ' recordset and leave it open to speed up the process
          Set rstV = tdf.OpenRecordset()
          ' OK - set "first processed" flag
          intFirst = True
        End If
      End If
      ' Update the progress counter
      intI = intI + 1
      varRet = SysCmd(acSysCmdUpdateMeter, intI)
  Next tdf
  ' Got through them all - clear the progress meter
  varRet = SysCmd(acSysCmdClearStatus)
  ' Close the "first" recordset
  rstV.Close
  ' and clear it
  Set rstV = Nothing
  ' Set a good return
  CheckConnect = True

CheckConnect_Exit:
  Exit Function
```

If any of the open commands fail, the error trap causes execution to resume at the CheckConnect_Err label (shown below). The code resets any error and sets a new error trap to take a different action if the attempt to refresh the links fails. Because I expect that you'll run all the sample databases from your local drive, the code next checks to see if it can find the data file in the same path as the current database. The public constant gstrDataFile contains the expected name of the data file for the application. The code is as follows:

```
CheckConnect_Err:
  ' Clear the error
  Err.Clear
  ' Set new error trap
  On Error GoTo CheckConnect_Err2
  ' If we successfully got the "first" one open
  If intFirst = True Then
    ' Close and clear it
    rstV.Close
    Set rstV = Nothing
  End If
  ' Clear the status bar
  varRet = SysCmd(acSysCmdClearStatus)
  ' First, try to use the current path of this database
  strPath = CurrentProject.Path
  strFilePath = strPath & "\" & gstrDataFile
  ' Use DIR to see if the data file is here
  If Not IsNothing(Dir(strFilePath)) Then
    ' Call the generic re-attach code
    If AttachAgain(strFilePath) = -1 Then
      ' Got a good re-attach
      ' Set OK return
```

```
    CheckConnect = True
    ' Done
    Exit Function
  End If
End If
```

If the code cannot find the file locally, it displays a message telling you to locate the file using the Open File dialog box that is about to appear. When you click OK in the MsgBox dialog box, the code continues and calls the *GetFileName* function that uses the ComDlg class module (not shown) to tell Windows to open the standard Open File dialog box. Unless you click Cancel in that dialog box, the *GetFileName* function returns a new path and file name. If you do not locate a file, the code issues a warning that you probably won't be able to open any of the linked tables or run the application. The code is as follows:

```
' No success to this point
' Tell the user about the problem
' - about to show an open file dialog box
MsgBox "There's a temporary problem connecting to the " & _
  gstrShortTitle & " data.  " & _
  "Please locate the " & gstrShortTitle & _
  " data file in the following dialog box.", _
  vbInformation, gstrAppTitle
' Set up the default file name
strFilePath = gstrDataFile
' Call the file dialog function
If Not (GetFileName(strFilePath)) Then
  ' Tell user of error
  MsgBox "You failed to select the correct file.  WARNING: " & _
    "You may not be able to open any of the linked tables " & _
    "or run the application.  You can open frmCopyright or " & _
    "the startup form (frmStartup) to try again.", _
    vbCritical, gstrAppTitle
  ' Set Failed return
  CheckConnect = False
  ' Done
  Exit Function
End If
```

When you locate a file, the code opens the frmReconnect form that displays a simple message telling you that the attempt to relink the tables is in progress. It calls the *AttachAgain* function one last time with the new file name. If that fails, the code issues a final warning message and exits. The code at the end of the procedure is the second error trap that executes if any of this code generates an error. The code is as follows:

```
' Open the "info" form telling what we're doing
DoCmd.OpenForm "frmReconnect"
' .. and be sure it has the focus
Forms!frmReconnect.SetFocus
' Try calling the attach code again
If AttachAgain(strFilePath) = 0 Then
  MsgBox "Relinking of attached tables failed.  The file " & _
    gstrDataFile & " must " & _
```

```
        " be in the folder you located and cannot be renamed." & _
        vbCrLf & vbCrLf & "You can open frmCopyright to try again.", _
        vbCritical, "Building Microsoft Access Applications"
      ' Close and bail
      CheckConnect = False
      Exit Function
    End If
    ' Close the reconnect "splash" form
    DoCmd.Close acForm, "frmReconnect"
    ' All OK
    CheckConnect = True
    Exit Function

CheckConnect_Err2:
    ' Got an unexpected error
    ' Tell user-
    MsgBox "Unexpected error checking attached tables. " & Err & _
      ", " & Error, vbCritical
    ' Log it
    ErrorLog "CheckConnect", Err, Error
    ' Bail
    CheckConnect = False
    ' Close the info form if it is open
    If IsFormLoaded("frmReconnect") Then DoCmd.Close acForm, "frmReconnect"
    ' ... bail
    Resume CheckConnect_Exit
End Function
```

In either the case where the code finds the file in the local folder or when you specify a path and file via the Windows Open File dialog box, the code calls the *AttachAgain* function to reattach the linked tables. Similar to the code in the *CheckConnect* function, this procedure loops through all the tables in the TableDefs collection looking for attached tables. When it finds one, it updates the Connect property of the TableDef object to point to the new location and uses the RefreshLink method to try to validate the new location. If Access cannot successfully perform the RefreshLink, it generates an error that is handled by the code at the Err_Attach label. The procedure might have successfully relinked some of the tables at the point of the failure, but when any RefreshLink fails, the procedure doesn't try any other tables and exits to the calling procedure with a False (failure) return. If the code manages to loop through all the tables successfully, it returns True to the calling procedure to indicate that the entire relink was successful. The code is as follows:

```
Public Function AttachAgain(strFilePath As String) As Integer
' This is a generic function that accepts a new path name
'  and attempts to refresh the links of all attached tables
' Input: File Path name as C:\SomeFolder\SomeSubFolder\SomeDB.mdb
' Output: True if successful
Dim db As DAO.Database, tdf As DAO.TableDef, rst As DAO.Recordset
Dim varRet As Variant, intFirst As Integer
Dim intI As Integer, intK As Integer, intL As Integer
    ' Get a pointer to the database
    Set db = DBEngine(0)(0)
    ' Set the "first table" indicator
```

```
      intFirst = True
      ' Turn on the progress meter
      varRet = SysCmd(acSysCmdInitMeter, "Reconnecting Data...", _
         db.TableDefs.Count)
      ' Set an error trap
     On Error GoTo Err_Attach
      ' Attempt to reattach the tables
     intI = 0 ' Reset the status meter counter
     For Each tdf In db.TableDefs
         ' Looking for attached tables
         If (tdf.Attributes And dbAttachedTable) Then
            ' Change the Connect property to point to the new file
            tdf.Connect = ";DATABASE=" & strFilePath
            ' Attempt to refresh the link definition
            tdf.RefreshLink
            ' If the first table, then open a recordset
            '  to make this go faster
            If (intFirst = True) Then
               Set rst = db.OpenRecordset(tdf.Name)
               intFirst = False
            End If
         End If
         ' Update the status counter
         intI = intI + 1
         ' .. and update the progress meter
         varRet = SysCmd(acSysCmdUpdateMeter, intI)
         ' And pause for a sec so the status bar updates
         DoEvents
      Next tdf
      ' Done - clear the progress meter
      varRet = SysCmd(acSysCmdClearStatus)
      ' Clear the object variables
      Set tdf = Nothing
      rst.Close
      Set rst = Nothing
      Set db = Nothing
      ' Return attach successful
      AttachAgain = True
   Attach_Exit:
      Exit Function
   Err_Attach:
      ' Uh, oh - failed.  Write a log record
      ErrorLog "AttachAgain " & strFilePath, Err, Error
      ' Clear the progress meter
      varRet = SysCmd(acSysCmdClearStatus)
      ' Clear the object variables
      Set tdf = Nothing
      Set db = Nothing
      ' Return attach failed
      AttachAgain = False
      ' Exit
      Resume Attach_Exit
   End Function
```

Pushing the Envelope

You can use the techniques that you've learned to this point in this chapter to successfully build a client/server application with desktop database files (.mdb) that can support up to 20 simultaneous users. These techniques also work best when you need to share less than 200 megabytes of data. If you need to support more users or need to store more data, you can take one of two paths: upsize your application to SQL Server, or radically restructure how your desktop application works.

Most developers choose to upsize. But if your company (or your client) doesn't want to move up to the cost of SQL Server (both the cost of the software and the extra expertise needed to manage SQL Server on an ongoing basis), you can "push the envelope" with a desktop database architecture.

The sample Customer Support application demonstrates one way to design a client/server application that can support more simultaneous users with an Access application that uses a desktop database file (.mdb) to store the data. If you open the application database file (Support.mdb) and look at the list of tables, as shown in Figure 3-10, you'll see what looks like local copies of some of the linked tables stored within the database.

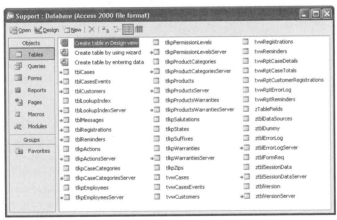

Figure 3-10   The list of tables in the Customer Support application.

For example, you can find customer support case data in both the tblCases table and the tvwCases table. The data in the tlkpEmployees table appears to be the same as the data in the tlkpEmployeesServer table. Here's what's happening:

- For tables that the application updates frequently (such as those for customers, support cases, support case events, product registrations, and reminders), the application fetches from the server only the data that the user needs to edit. The application uses a combination of bound and unbound forms to present the data and to allow the user to edit it. When a form is bound to data, it uses a copy of the data that the application has fetched into a local table. (The local tables containing a subset of data from the server have a name beginning with "tvw" (short for table view). To save the data, the application collects the changes from the unbound form and writes those changes back to the copy on the server.

■ For tables that won't change very often (such as those for employees, case action codes, products, product categories, and so on), the application keeps an exact copy of the data stored on the server. The application periodically checks the status of records on the server that might have been updated by other users and refreshes the local copies only when necessary. In the Customer Support sample application, these tables have names beginning with "tlkp" (lookup tables).

Taking this approach isn't for the faint of heart. If you look behind the forms and into the code modules in the Customer Support database, you'll find lots of code that is necessary to manage the movement of data from and to the shared data file on the server. As you'll learn later in Part 4, "Implementing a Customer Support Application," the actual tasks implemented in the application are quite simple.

Editing Data Locally

What allows the Customer Support application to handle 50 or more users is the fact that the application severely limits the need to work with data in the data file on the server. Unlike a classic client/server application using linked tables, the application is designed to never edit data directly from the server. Only a few of the forms, combo boxes, and list boxes are directly bound to data, and the bound data all resides in a local table containing a copy of the data.

Examining an Unbound Form

You can actually open several of the forms directly from the Database window. For example, you can open the frmCustomers form that the application uses to display and edit customer data, and it will look like Figure 3-11.

Notice that the form is completely blank. However, the form does display customer information when you open it from the application. The application forces the user to choose from a local list of customer records that the application fetches from the server in response to search criteria. The user can pick the one record that's needed, and code in the application opens the frmCustomers form and tells the form which record to fetch.

In Chapter 16, "Organizing Customer Information," you'll learn how the application manages customer information. To see the frmCustomers form with a specific customer displayed for editing, be sure the frmCustomers form is not open, press Ctrl+G to open the Immediate window, and enter the following command:

```
DoCmd.OpenForm "frmCustomers", OpenArgs:="65"
```

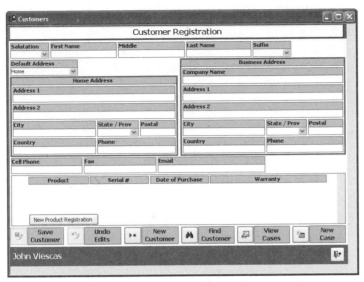

Figure 3-11 The frmCustomers form shows no data when you open it from the Database window.

The argument passed to the form tells it to locate and load the information about the customer whose customer ID is 65. When you go back to the Access window, you should see the form with the data displayed for the requested customer, as shown in Figure 3-12.

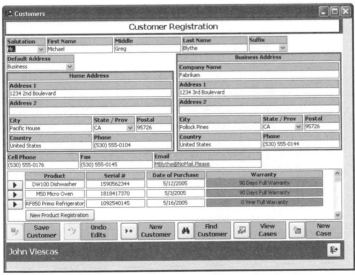

Figure 3-12 The frmCustomers form displaying data for customer number 65.

Note The application doesn't ever reveal the customer ID value to the user because the actual number assigned to each customer is irrelevant. The user always searches for customers by name, phone number, or e-mail address. However, the application internally uses the customer ID to efficiently identify the correct record.

The only bound data in the form is the product list in the subform window. If you change any of the data, code behind the form reveals an informational message in the blank area next to the Default Address label telling you that you need to click the Save Customer button (the button with the disk and pencil icon) to save your changes. You can click any of the arrows in the list of products in the subform window, and the application opens the frmRegistrations form to display the details about the customer's registered product.

Loading Data to Edit

Each form that allows the user to edit unbound data must fetch the requested record and set the controls on the form to display the data. This is in stark contrast to a normal bound form where the form fetches the records and displays the data in bound controls. Each form contains a *fctReLoadRecord* function that is specific to the data the user can edit in the form, but the operation of this function is very similar across all forms.

The *fctReLoadRecord* function depends on the value of a hidden control to either indicate that the user is editing a new record (the control contains 0 or Null), or specify the unique identifier of the record that should be loaded. In the frmCustomers form, the txtCustomerID text box control serves this purpose. You can open the frmCustomers form in Design view and find the txtCustomerID text box with its Visible property set to No just to the left of the new record command button. When the form opens, the form's Open event procedure saves the customer ID value that was passed in the OpenArgs argument in the txtCustomerID control and calls the *fctReLoadRecord* function to fetch the data to display.

The beginning of the function checks to see if the txtCustomerID control contains nothing (is 0 or Null). When the ID is nothing, the code clears all the editable controls by setting them to Null. In some forms, the code in this section sets the equivalent of a default value (for example, the current date and time) in some controls. Basically, the code is simulating what Access does when the users chooses to move to a new record in a bound form. The code is as follows:

```
Function fctReLoadRecord() As Boolean
' Called when the form opens, the user asks to start a new
'   record, or the user cancels an edit after a save failed.
' Function either clears all editable controls or reloads
'   the customer specified by the current CustomerID.
  On Error GoTo errfctReLoadRecord
  ' If CustomerID is empty,
  If IsNothing(Me.txtCustomerID) Then
    ' .. clear the form to create an empty record
    Me.cmbSalutation = Null
    Me.txtCFirst = Null
    Me.txtCMiddle = Null
    Me.txtCLast = Null
    Me.cmbCSuffix = Null
    Me.txtHomeAddress1 = Null
    Me.txtHomeAddress2 = Null
    Me.txtHomeCity = Null
    Me.cmbHomeStateOrProvince = Null
```

```
Me.txtHomePostal = Null
Me.txtHomeCountry = Null
Me.txtHomePhone = Null
Me.txtBusinessName = Null
Me.txtBusinessAddress1 = Null
Me.txtBusinessAddress2 = Null
Me.txtBusinessCity = Null
Me.cmbBusinessStateOrProvince = Null
Me.txtBusinessPostal = Null
Me.txtBusinessCountry = Null
Me.txtBusinessPhone = Null
Me.txtCellPhone = Null
Me.txtFax = Null
Me.txtEmail = Null
```

When the txtCustomerID text box control contains a value, the code calls another public function—*LoadRecord*—that is used by all forms to load data from a requested table into the form. (You can find the *LoadRecord* function in the modRecordEditor module.) In this case, the code calls that function, passing parameters that identify the name of the calling form, the name of the table containing the data to load, the identifier of the record requested, and a title to use in error messages. If the record load fails, the code exits.

Next, the code calls the *fctRefreshReg* function (that you can find in the module for the frmCustomers form) that clears the tvwRegistrations table and uses an insert query to load the product registration data for the current customer into that table. If you look at the design for the fsubCustomersRegistrations form that is the subform on the frmCustomers form, you'll find that it is bound to a query on the local tvwRegistrations table. (The code for the *fctRefreshReg* function is described later in this chapter.) Finally, the code marks the record saved, hides the label that informs the user when the record has been changed, requeries the subform to display the new data in the tvwRegistrations table, and exits. The code is as follows:

```
Else
    ' Otherwise, load the record using the CustomerID
    ' Call the function that loads the record
    If LoadRecord("frmCustomers", "tblCustomers", _
      Me.txtCustomerID, "Customer") = False Then
        ' Got an error - bail
        Exit Function
    End If
    ' Load the related registrations into the view table
    If fctRefreshReg(Me.txtCustomerID) = False Then
        ' Got an error - bail
        Exit Function
    End If
End If
'After loading the new record,
'  set the Boolean 'saved' markers to true (or saved).
blnSaved = True
' .. and hide the save instruction label
Me.lblSaveCustomer.Visible = False
```

```
'Refresh the sub form display
Me.fsubCustomersRegistrations.Requery
' Return success
fctReLoadRecord = True
okfctReLoadRecord:
 Exit Function
errfctReLoadRecord:
 ' Got an error - set failure
 fctReLoadRecord = False
 ' Display and log the error
 ErrTryingTo "load the customer data"
 Resume okfctReLoadRecord
End Function
```

The *LoadRecord* function is one of several functions you'll find in the modRecordEditor module that help manage unbound data. Most of these functions use a local table that defines how to map fields in each table to controls on the forms that edit them. The table also identifies which fields must have a value (Required), which fields must always be saved (isSaved), and which field is the primary key (isID). Table 3.1 shows you a sample of some of the rows that control how the code works with customer data.

Table 3-1   Sample Data from the ztblFormReq Table

FilterName	FieldName	ControlName	Description	Required	isID	isSaved
frmCustomers	CFirst	txtCFirst	First Name	Yes	No	Yes
frmCustomers	CLast	txtCLast	Last Name	Yes	No	Yes
frmCustomers	CMiddle	txtCMiddle	Middle Initial	No	No	Yes
frmCustomers	CustomerID	txtCustomerID	Customer ID	No	Yes	No

> **Note**   All the tables have a primary key defined using the AutoNumber data type to simplify acquiring a unique key when adding new records. This avoids an additional probe to the server to determine the previous high value when inserting a row. As a consequence, the ID fields in the tables are not marked required or saved in the ztblFormReq table.

As you saw earlier, the *fctReLoadRecord* function in the frmCustomers form calls the *LoadRecord* function in the modRecordEditor module to fetch the data for a specific customer ID. The *LoadRecord* function uses information from the ztblFormReq table to know which fields to fetch from the tblCustomers table and which controls should be assigned each field value. The code begins by verifying that the target form named in the strFormName parameter is open. The code next fetches the rows from the ztblFormReq table for the specified form. The code then searches within the rows for the one that indicates the primary key of the table—the isID field is True—and saves the name of the key field. Note that if any of these operations fail, the code raises an error, which causes the error code at the end of the function to display and log the error and exit. The code is as follows:

```
Public Function LoadRecord(strFormName As String, strTableName As String, _
  lngRecordID As Long, Optional strRecordDesc As String = "form") _
  As Boolean
'*********************
'LoadRecord - loads a record as requested by any open form
'Inputs:
'    strFormName - The name of the form making the request
'    strTableName - The name of the table to load the record from
'    lngRecordID - The identifier for the record to be loaded
'    strRecordDesc (optional) - A description of the record to load
'Output:
'    Returns a Boolean value to indicate if the record was loaded or not
'********************
Dim db As DAO.DataBase
Dim rstF As DAO.Recordset
Dim rst As DAO.Recordset
Dim frm As Form
Dim strSQL As String
Dim strIDName As String
  ' Set an error trap
  On Error GoTo errLoadRecord
  ' Make sure the form specified is open
  If IsFormLoaded(strFormName) = False Then
    ' Form should be there - raise an error
    Err.Raise vbObjectError + 1024, , _
      "Invalid call to Load Record function."
  Else
    ' Get a pointer to the form
    Set frm = Forms(strFormName)
  End If
  ' Point to this database
  Set db = DBEngine(0)(0)
  ' Get the rows that tell us what to load
  strSQL = "SELECT FR.* FROM ztblFormReq AS FR " & _
    "WHERE FR.FilterName = '" & strFormName & "'"
  Set rstF = db.OpenRecordset(strSQL)
  ' Make sure there are some
  If rstF.EOF Then
    ' Close the recordset
    rstF.Close
    ' Raise an error
    Err.Raise vbObjectError + 1025, , _
      "No field rows found for requested form."
  End If
  ' Find out the primary key of the table to update
  rstF.FindFirst "isID = True"
  ' If not found
  If rstF.NoMatch Then
    ' Close the recordset
    rstF.Close
    ' Raise an error
    Err.Raise vbObjectError + 1026, , _
      "Key field not found for record load."
  End If
  ' Save the name of the key field
```

```
strIDName = rstF!FieldName
' Go back to start of the recordset
rstF.MoveFirst
```

Now that the code knows the name of the primary key field, it opens the one record needed from the data file on the server to fill the controls in the form. The code then loops through all the rows for the form in the ztblFormReq table, using the control name and field name information to assign the values from the record to the controls in the form. After processing all fields, the code closes all recordsets and returns the value of the primary key to the calling procedure. The code is as follows:

```
' Get the record to load
strSQL = "SELECT TBL.* FROM " & strTableName & " AS TBL " & _
    "WHERE TBL." & strIDName & " = " & lngRecordID
Set rst = db.OpenRecordset(strSQL, dbOpenDynaset, dbSeeChanges)
' If not found,
If rst.EOF Then
    ' Close the recordsets
    rstF.Close
    rst.Close
    ' Raise an error
    Err.Raise vbObjectError + 1027, , _
        "Record requested to load not found."
End If
' Loop through all the fields
Do While Not rstF.EOF
    ' Set the form control value from the field
    frm(rstF.Fields("ControlName")) = _
        rst.Fields(rstF.Fields("FieldName"))
    ' Move to next row
    rstF.MoveNext
' Loop until done
Loop
' Close out
rst.Close
rstF.Close
LoadRecord = True
okLoadRecord:
' Clean up
Set rstF = Nothing
Set rst = Nothing
Set db = Nothing
Set frm = Nothing
Exit Function
errLoadRecord:
' Trapped an error - set failed return
LoadRecord = False
' Display and log the error
ErrTryingTo "load the " & strRecordDesc & " record"
Resume okLoadRecord
End Function
```

This code is specifically designed to make a single connection to the data in the file on the server, quickly fetch the single record needed, grab the field values, and then disconnect. As a result, the application code running on each workstation is using the network and the shared data file for only a few milliseconds. The user might work on the fetched record for several minutes before needing to connect to the shared data file again to save any changes.

In this design, the workstation code maintains no permanent connection to the server. A classic client/server application that uses linked tables has a connection as long as any form is open. Keep in mind that Access refreshes any open recordset based on the Refresh Interval setting on the Advanced tab in the Options dialog box (choose Options from the Tools menu). You can certainly change this setting, but most developers leave the Refresh Interval set to the default 60 seconds.

In some cases, 60 seconds is too long. But choosing a lower number in a standard client/server application can severely impact performance. If the user opens a form and then goes off to lunch, that form's recordset is being refreshed by Access once a minute. Constant polling contributes to limiting the typical client/server application to no more than 20 users.

Validating and Saving Unbound Data

One of the challenges of using unbound data is that your forms won't automatically trap data type, data length, and validation rule violations as the user enters data into the form. You must write code to validate the data as the user enters it. You can certainly trap errors when you try to write the data to the shared data file, but that might be too late for the user to fix the problem easily.

The Customer Service application implements rudimentary data validation on each form. Wherever possible, the form controls have either a Format property or Input Mask property or both defined. Even when a control is unbound, Access won't let the user type data that doesn't match the Format or Input Mask property. For example, you can enter only a value recognizable as a date in a control that has its Format property set to Short Date. If you try to type something that Access doesn't recognize as a date/time value, Access displays an error message.

In addition to taking advantage of the Format and Input Mask properties, code in the After-Update event of all the controls that can contain text calls a validation function to test that the user hasn't entered text longer than the field in the table accepts. You can find several examples in the frmCustomers form. For example, code in the AfterUpdate event procedure for the txtCellPhone text box control makes sure that the user doesn't enter more than 20 characters. The code also calls the fctDirty function in the form module to mark the record changed. The code is as follows:

```
Private Sub txtCellPhone_AfterUpdate()
  ' Call the length validator
  Call CheckFieldSize(Me.txtCellPhone, "Cell Phone", 20)
  ' Mark the record changed
  fctDirty
End Sub
```

The applicaton uses the *CheckFieldSize* function that you can find in the modRecordEditor module to verify the field length for controls on many of the forms. The calling procedure passes the control to be verified, a descriptor to use in an error message, and the maximum length allowed. The function tests the length of the data in the current value of the control, shortens it to the maximum length if it is too large, and warns the user that the data has been truncated. The code is as follows:

```
Public Function CheckFieldSize(ctl As Control, strFieldName As String, _
  intMaxSize As Integer)
' This function checks the length of a value entered in a control.
' Inputs: Control object to validate
'         Name of the field for warning message
'         Maximum length
' Output: Data truncated to max length, if necessary
Dim strValue As String
Dim strMsg As String
  ' Set an error trap
  On Error GoTo errCheckFieldSize
  ' Get the value of the control
  strValue = Nz(ctl.Value, "")
  ' See if user typed too much
  If Len(strValue) > intMaxSize Then
    ' Warn the user -
    strMsg = "The " & strFieldName & _
      " field can only accept a maximum of " & _
      intMaxSize & " characters. " & _
      "The field value has been truncated to the maximum size."
    Call CustomError(strMsg)
    ' .. and truncate the value
    ctl.Value = Left(ctl.Value, intMaxSize)
  End If
okCheckFieldSize:
  Exit Function
errCheckFieldSize:
  ErrTryingTo "validate field " & strFieldName
  Resume okCheckFieldSize
End Function
```

Each form that allows the user to edit unbound data also has a function, *fctCheckSaved*, that verifies and saves any changes. This function runs whenever the user clicks the Save Record button, asks to begin a new record after changing an existing one, or clicks the Close button to close the form.

The function first checks to see if the ID field on the form (the txtCustomerID text box in the case of the frmCustomers form) has a value. If it has no value, the code assumes that the user is saving a new record. If it has a value, the code in some forms next creates any calculated values that should be saved in the record. In the case of the frmCustomers form, the code creates the calculated CustomerName value by concatenating the first and last names with an intervening blank. Next, the code checks the blnSaved module variable to determine if any value has been changed by the user. If no changes need to be saved, the code returns a confirmation that the data is saved and exits. The code is as follows:

```
Public Function fctCheckSaved() As String
'This code checks that the required information is complete and then
'saves the record and flags the linked table for an update
Dim strErrMsg As String
Dim blnNewRec As Boolean
Dim lngID As Long
  ' Set an error trap
  On Error GoTo errfctCheckSaved
  ' If no customer ID yet,
  If IsNothing(Me.txtCustomerID) Then
    ' Set the new record flag
    blnNewRec = True
  Else
    ' Have a customer ID - save it
    lngID = Me.txtCustomerID
    blnNewRec = False
  End If
  'Make sure the composite Customer Name field is properly filled
  Me.txtCustomerName = Me.txtCFirst & " " & Me.txtCLast
  'If the current record already saved,
  If blnSaved = True Then
    ' Confirm saved and exit
    fctCheckSaved = "Saved"
```

When the user has changed any data on the form, the code calls the *ValidateRecord* function that you can find in the modRecordEditor module, passing to the function the name of the form and the value of the filter to be used to verify the data. Remember from Table 3-1 that the ztblFormReq table has a Required field that indicates which fields must have values in the record to be saved. As you'll see later in this section, the *ValidateRecord* function returns an empty string if it finds no errors and a string containing the fields that failed the validation if any required fields do not have data. When the *ValidateRecord* function returns an error string, the *fctCheckSaved* function displays the error and exits. The code is as follows:

```
  Else
    ' Validate the customer data - returns ZLS if successful
    strErrMsg = ValidateRecord("frmCustomers", "frmCustomers")
    ' If the error string not empty,
    If strErrMsg <> "" Then
      ' Set up the message to display
      strErrMsg = "The record could not be saved " & _
        "because the following fields are not complete: " & _
        vbCrLf & strErrMsg & vbCrLf & "What would you like to do?"
      ' Display the message - if user clicked cancel,
      If CustomError(strErrMsg, OkCancel, "Could not save record", _
        Question) = "Cancel Changes" Then
        ' Return that edit was canceled
        fctCheckSaved = "Cancel"
        ' Clear all data to a new screen
        Call fctReLoadRecord
```

```
        Else
          ' User clicked - OK, wants to work on it some more
          ' Return that edit failed, but still dirty
          fctCheckSaved = "Ok"    'The user chose to keep working.
          ' Make sure record not marked saved
          fctDirty
        End If
```

When all required fields have a value, the code calls the *SaveRecord* function that you can find in the modRecordEditor module, passing it the name of the form, the filter value for the ztblFormReq table, the name of the table in the shared data file on the server to update, the ID of the record to update (0 if adding a new record), and a descriptive string for error messages. (The missing parameter you see in the code below is an optional local table name where the function saves a copy of the updated record.) The *SaveRecord* function returns the nonzero value of the ID of the record if the save is successful. When the function returns a successful save value, the code sets the blnSaved module variable and hides the informative message on the form telling the user to click the Save button. The code is as follows:

```
        Else
          ' No error messages, so save the record
          ' *** Additional code here explained in Chapter 16 ***
          'This might take a while...
          DoCmd.Hourglass True
          'If there was no error message,
          '  and the record hasn't been saved then:
          ' Save the Customer - returns the CustomerID if successful
          lngID = SaveRecord("frmCustomers", "frmCustomers", _
            "tblCustomers", lngID, , "Customer")
          ' If customer save successful.
          If lngID <> 0 Then
            ' Save the Customer ID in the form control
            Me.txtCustomerID = lngID
            ' Set up return success
            fctCheckSaved = "Saved"
            ' Turn on the saved flag
            blnSaved = True      'The current record is saved
            ' Hide the "click to save" message
            Me.lblSaveCustomer.Visible = False
          End If
        End If
      End If
      'Done!
okfctCheckSaved:
    ' Make sure hourglass is off
    DoCmd.Hourglass False
    Exit Function
errfctCheckSaved:
    ' Display and log error
    ErrTryingTo "save customer data"
    ' Clear the record so we don't get an unending loop
    fctReLoadRecord
    Me.txtCustomerID = 0
    Resume okfctCheckSaved
End Function
```

The *ValidateRecord* function is quite simple. After verifying that the calling form is open, the code fetches the rows from the ztblFormReq table that have the Required field set to True for the specified table filter. The code processes each row, testing that the related form control has a value. When it finds any missing values, it creates an error string message that lists the fields that must have values, using the descriptive field from the ztblFormReq table. When the code has finished processing all rows, it returns the contents of the error string—but the string is empty if there were no missing required fields. The code is as follows:

```
Public Function ValidateRecord(formname As String, _
  FilterName As String) As String
'********************
'ValidateRecord - Validates a record using the required fields list in
'  the ztblFormReq table.
'Inputs:
'  FormName - The name of the form making the request
'Output:
'  Returns a string containing the failed validation information
'  -- empty if no validation failed.
'********************
Dim db As DAO.DataBase
Dim rst As DAO.Recordset
Dim frm As Form
Dim strSQL As String
Dim strErrMsg As String
  ' Set an error trap
  On Error GoTo errValidateRecord
  ' Make sure the form specified is open
  If IsFormLoaded(formname) = False Then
    ' Form should be there - raise an error
    Err.Raise vbObjectError + 99, , _
      "Invalid call to Validate Record function."
  Else
    ' Get a pointer to the form
    Set frm = Forms(formname)
  End If
  ' Point to this database
  Set db = DBEngine(0)(0)
  ' Set up to find the required fields for the current form
  strSQL = "SELECT FR.* FROM ztblFormReq AS FR " & _
    "WHERE FR.Required = True AND FR.FilterName = '" & _
    FilterName & "'"
  ' Get the list of required fields
  Set rst = db.OpenRecordset(strSQL)
  ' Process all the rows
  Do While Not rst.EOF
    ' Use the name of the control from the recordset
    '  to test that the form control contains a value
    If IsNothing(frm(rst!ControlName)) Then
      ' Value is missing - add it to the error message
      strErrMsg = strErrMsg & " -" & _
        rst.Fields("Description") & vbCrlf
    End If
    ' Process the next one
```

```
    rst.MoveNext
  Loop
  ' Close the recordset
  rst.Close
  ' Return the error string
  ValidateRecord = strErrMsg
okValidateRecord:
  Set rst = Nothing
  Set db = Nothing
  Set frm = Nothing
  Exit Function
errValidateRecord:
  ' Return an error string
  ValidateRecord = "Error"
  ' Display and log the error
  strErrMsg = "The following error occured while " & _
    "trying to verify the form information: " & _
    vbCrLf & "Error Number: " & Err.Number & vbCrLf & _
    "Error Description: " & Err.Description
  Call CustomError(strErrMsg, , "Error verifying form information", Severe)
  ' Bail
  Resume okValidateRecord
End Function
```

Finally, let's take a look at the *SaveRecord* function in the modRecordEditor module. As you might expect, the code is the reverse of the *LoadRecord* function—this function writes data to the tables instead of fetching data from the tables. The code also handles inserting new records, and it can optionally write the same data to both the master copy in the shared data file on the server as well as to any local mirror copy in the application database.

The code begins by verifying that the specified calling form is loaded. It then fetches the rows from the ztblFormReq table for the specified table filter. These rows indicate either fields that must be saved or the ID field of the table. The code searches the recordset for the ID field and saves the field name. If any of these operations fail, the code raises an error to call the error handling code at the end of the function. Finally, the code either saves any nonzero record ID or sets a new record flag. The code is as follows:

```
Public Function SaveRecord(strFormName As String, _
  strFilterName As String, strTableName As String, _
  Optional lngRecordID As Long, _
  Optional strLocalTableName As String, _
  Optional strRecordDesc As String = "form") As Long
'*********************
'SaveRecord - saves a record as requested by any open form
'Inputs:
'    strFormName - The name of the form making the request
'    strTableName - The name of the table to save the record to
'    lngRecordID (optional) - The identifier for the record to be saved.
'        If a lngRecordID is provided, then the save is an edit;
'        otherwise a new record is created.
'    strLocalTableName (optional) - The name of the local table
'        that also must be updated.
```

```
'     strRecordDesc (optional) - A description of the record to save
'Output:
'    Returns a long integer value containing the
'       saved record ID (0 if the save failed or was cancelled)
'********************
Dim db As DAO.DataBase
Dim rstF As DAO.Recordset
Dim rst As DAO.Recordset
Dim frm As Form
Dim strSQL As String
Dim strIDName As String
Dim intI As Integer
Dim blnNew As Boolean
Dim blnTrans As Boolean
    ' Set an error trap
    On Error GoTo errSaveRecord
    ' Make sure the form specified is open
    If IsFormLoaded(strFormName) = False Then
      ' Form should be there - raise an error
      Err.Raise vbObjectError + 4096, , _
        "Invalid call to Save Record function."
    Else
      ' Get a pointer to the form
      Set frm = Forms(strFormName)
    End If
    ' Point to this database
    Set db = DBEngine(0)(0)
    ' Get the list of fields to update
    strSQL = "SELECT FR.* FROM ztblFormReq AS FR " & _
      "WHERE (FR.isSaved = True " & _
      "Or FR.isID = True) " & _
      "AND FR.FilterName = '" & strFilterName & "'"
    ' .. and open a recordset on it
    Set rstF = db.OpenRecordset(strSQL)
    ' Make sure there are some
    If rstF.EOF Then
      ' Close the recordset
      rstF.Close
      ' Raise an error
      Err.Raise vbObjectError + 4097, , _
        "No field records found for requested table."
    End If
    ' Get the name of the ID field
    rstF.FindFirst "isID = True"
    ' If not found
    If rstF.NoMatch Then
      ' Close the recordset
      rstF.Close
      ' Raise an error
      Err.Raise vbObjectError + 4098, , _
        "ID field not found for record save."
    End If
    ' Save the name of the ID field
    strIDName = rst!FieldName
    ' If passed a record ID
```

```
If Not lngRecordID = 0 Then
  ' Set the new record flag to false
  blnNew = False
Else
  ' No ID - set the new record flag
  blnNew = True
End If
```

Next, the code starts a transaction to ensure that both the linked data file and the local copy are updated or neither is updated if any error is encountered. The code starts a loop to first process the linked table and then the local table on the second pass. On the first pass, the code determines if a new record is needed and opens a recordset to either insert a new row or fetch the existing row filtered by the ID value specified. When the code is in the second pass through the loop, it checks to see if the optional local table name was supplied and, if so, prepares a new record to insert or fetches the local table record. When updating an existing record, the code raises an error if the record cannot be found in either the linked table or the local table. The code is as follows:

```
' Start a transaction to ensure both updates work
BeginTrans
blnTrans = True
' Loop twice to process server on the first pass
'   and optional local copy on the second pass
For intI = 1 To 2
  ' If we're on the first pass,
  If intI = 1 Then
    ' And adding a record,
    If blnNew = True Then
      ' Open the server table for insert only
      Set rst = db.OpenRecordset(strTableName, dbOpenDynaset, _
        dbAppendOnly)
      ' .. and start a new record
      rst.AddNew
    Else
      ' Fetch the record to update from the server
      strSQL = "SELECT " & strTableName & ".* FROM " & strTableName & _
        " WHERE " & strTableName & "." & strIDName & " = " & lngRecordID
      Set rst = db.OpenRecordset(strSQL, dbOpenDynaset, dbSeeChanges)
      ' Make sure we got it
      If rst.EOF Then
        ' Close the recordset
        rst.Close
        ' Raise an error
        Err.Raise vbObjectError + 4099, , _
          "Record requested to update on server not found."
      End If
      ' Put it in Edit mode
      rst.Edit
    End If
  Else
    ' Second pass - see if there's a local table to update
    If strLocalTableName <> "" Then
      ' Yes - and if new record,
```

```
     If blnNew = True Then
       ' Open the local table for insert only
       Set rst = db.OpenRecordset(strLocalTableName, dbOpenDynaset, _
         dbAppendOnly)
       ' .. and start a new record
       rst.AddNew
       ' Copy the lngRecordID set on the server
       rst(strIDName) = lngRecordID
     Else
       ' Not a new record - fetch the record to update
       strSQL = "SELECT " & strLocalTableName & ".* FROM " & _
         strLocalTableName & _
         " WHERE " & strLocalTableName & "." & _
         strIDName & " = " & lngRecordID
       Set rst = db.OpenRecordset(strSQL)
       ' Make sure we got it
       If rst.EOF Then
         ' Close the recordset
         rst.Close
         ' Raise an error
         Err.Raise vbObjectError + 4100, , _
           "Local record requested to update not found."
       End If
       ' Put it in Edit mode
       rst.Edit
     End If
   Else
     ' No local table - Done
     Exit For
   End If
 End If
```

The remainder of the code within the two-pass loop processes the rows from the ztblFormReq table and uses the information in the rows to fetch the value in a control on the form and assign it to the correct field in the recordset being updated. Just before saving the changed record, the code saves the ID of the record. Because all the tables use an AutoNumber data type as the ID field, the JET database engine sets the ID of any new record as soon as any field value is assigned. After executing the two loops to process the linked and local tables, the code commits the transaction to make all changes permanent and returns the ID of the record saved. The code is as follows:

```
' Go to the first field record
rstF.MoveFirst
' Loop and process all the fields
Do While Not rstF.EOF
  ' Update only the ones where isSaved = True
  If rstF!isSaved Then
    ' Copy the form control value to the field
    rst(rstF!FieldName) = _
      frm(rstF!ControlName)
  End If
  ' Process the next field
  rstF.MoveNext
```

```
        ' Loop until done
        Loop
        ' Save the record ID
        lngRecordID = rst(strIDName)
        ' Save the record
        rst.Update
        ' Close the recordset
        rst.Close
    ' Go process the possible second one
    Next intI
    ' Good to here - commit the transaction
    CommitTrans
    blnTrans = False
    ' Close the fields recordset
    rstF.Close
    ' Return the ID of the record saved
    SaveRecord = lngRecordID
okSaveRecord:
    ' Clean up
    Set rstF = Nothing
    Set rst = Nothing
    Set db = Nothing
    Set frm = Nothing
    Exit Function
errSaveRecord:
    ' Set an error return
    SaveRecord = 0
    ' If a transaction started
    If blnTrans = True Then
        ' Roll it back
        blnTrans = False
        Rollback
    End If
    ' Display and log the error
    ErrTryingTo "save the " & strRecordDesc & " record"
    Resume okSaveRecord
End Function
```

Again, the application is connecting to the shared data on the server only for the few milliseconds required to fetch, update, and save the record. No permanent connection to the shared data file exists after the update completes.

Loading Related Data into a Local Table for Viewing

For many tasks in a database application, you as the developer need to present the user with a list of items to view or edit. Obvious examples include list boxes and combo boxes that provide lookup values. Another common example is a subform that displays a list of rows from a table related to the single row displayed in the outer form—for example, the order details for an order, the contact events for a support case, or the products owned by a customer.

In Figure 3-12 on page 87, you can see a list of products owned by the customer being edited in the outer form. Because the design of this application seeks to avoid binding any forms or controls to the shared data on the server, the application must load the data into a local table. If you look at the design of the fsubCustomersRegistrations form in the Customer Support sample database (Support.mdb), you'll find that the form is bound to the local tvwRegistrations table, not the linked tblRegistrations table. In fact, if you open the tvwRegistrations table in Datasheet view, you'll find records for only one customer ID, not the entire set of records in the tblRegistrations table.

Code in the frmCustomers form loads selected data into the local tvwRegistrations table when the application opens the form to edit a specific customer. In "Loading Data to Edit" on page 88, you learned that the *fctReLoadData* function in the module for the frmCustomers form calls the *fctRefreshReg* function to load the data used by the subform. The code deletes all previous rows in the tvwRegistrations table and then executes an insert query to fetch the rows from the tblRegistrations table on the server for the current customer. The code is as follows:

```
Function fctRefreshReg(lngID As Long) As Boolean
' Called from the fctReLoadRecord function
'  to reload the local view of the registrations for
'  the current customer.  Input: CustomerID
Dim db As DAO.DataBase
  ' Set an error trap
  On Error GoTo ErrRefresh    'Enable error trapping
  ' Point to this database
  Set db = DBEngine(0)(0)
  ' Empty the local Call Events table (delete everything).
  db.Execute "DELETE * FROM tvwRegistrations", dbFailOnError
  ' Update the table with the registrations
  '  from the source table on the server
  db.Execute "INSERT INTO tvwRegistrations " & _
    "SELECT tblRegistrations.* FROM tblRegistrations " & _
    "WHERE tblRegistrations.CustomerID = " & lngID
  'Refresh the view of the registrations on the form
  Me.fsubCustomersRegistrations.Requery
  ' Clear the database object
  Set db = Nothing
  ' Return successful
  fctRefreshReg = True
RefreshOk:
  Exit Function
ErrRefresh:
  ' Error - set failure
  fctRefreshReg = False
  ' Display and log the error
  ErrTryingTo "reload customer product registrations"
  ' Bail
  Resume RefreshOk
End Function
```

Again, the application connects to the server for a few milliseconds to retrieve the rows needed to display on the form. Once the form is open, the application has no permanent connection to the server, so it avoids tying up valuable network resources.

Using and Refreshing Local Lookup Tables

In addition to local tables that the application loads with data to edit as needed, the application also maintains several tables that are mirror images of the data in the shared file on the server. These tables have the following characteristics:

- The data is not changed frequently.

- The data is needed often to fill lookup lists—combo boxes, list boxes, and some subforms.

- The tables are much smaller than the active tables that are updated frequently.

The tables with these characteristics in the Customer Support application include:

- The list of lookup tables (tblLookupIndex)

- The list of final actions for customer support cases (tlkpActions)

- The list of employees who can sign on to the application (tlkpEmployees)

- The list of issue categories for support case events (tlkpCaseCategories)

- The list of permissions granted to each employee (tlkpPermissionLevels)

- The list of product categories (tlkpProductCategories)

- The list of products (tlkpProducts)

- The list of warranties available for each product (tlkpProductsWarranties)

- The list of warranties offered (tlkpWarranties)

Because the application frequently needs to fetch and display the entire list of available rows from these tables, it doesn't make sense to go to the server to refresh the list every time the application opens a form containing a list box or combo box that needs the data. However, other users might update the data, so the application needs a mechanism to periodically check for updates and reload the local copies.

When the Customer Support application starts up, it runs the *fctLookupUpdate* function that you can find in the modStartup module in the sample Support.mdb database. This function uses information in the tblLookupIndex and tblLookupIndexServer tables to determine which tables need to be refreshed. These tables contain one row per lookup table, and each row lists the name of the local table, the name of the server linked table, and an update index counter for each update made to the table, as shown in Table 3-2.

Each time the application writes a change to any of the tables, it increments the update index in both the local copy and the copy on the server. When another copy of the application starts on another machine, the *fctLookupUpdate* function compares its local tblLookupIndex table with the copy on the server to quickly determine which tables need updating. The code in the function does this by opening a recordset on a query that joins the two lookup update tables

Table 3-2   Sample Data from the tblLookupIndex Table

TableName	ServerTableName	UpdateIndex
tblLookupIndex	tblLookupIndexServer	1
tlkpActions	tlkpActionsServer	1
tlkpEmployees	tlkpEmployeesServer	1
tlkpCaseCategories	tlkpCaseCategoriesServer	1
tlkpPermissionLevels	tlkpPermissionLevelsServer	1
tlkpProductCategories	tlkpProductCatetoriesServer	1
tlkpProducts	tlkpProductsServer	1
tlkpProductsWarranties	tlkpProductsWarrantiesServer	1
tlkpWarranties	tlkpWarrantiesServer	1

and compares the UpdateIndex fields. For each record returned where the update index doesn't match, the code deletes the old data in the local copy and executes an insert query to refresh the data from the copy on the table. The code also updates its local UpdateIndex field to match the value on the server. The code is as follows:

```
Public Function fctLookupUpdate()
Dim dbs As DAO.DataBase, rst As DAO.Recordset, strSQL As String
  ' Reload the "lookup" tables - all the tables
  '  whose names begin with "tlkp" as well as the
  '  tblLookupIndex table.
  ' Function called periodically to refresh the local
  ' copies of these tables with any updates others
  ' have made to the data on the server.
  ' Set an error trap
  On Error GoTo errfctLookupUpdate
  ' Point to this database
  Set dbs = DBEngine(0)(0)
  ' Build query to find updated tables -
  '  The table tblLookupIndexServer on the server
  '  contains the latest "lookup index" for each
  '  lookup table.  Query finds tables with a higher
  '  index than the local copy.
  strSQL = "SELECT LI.TableName, LI.ServerTableName, LI.UpdateIndex " & _
    "FROM tblLookupIndexServer AS LI " & _
    "INNER JOIN tblLookupIndex " & _
    "ON LI.LookUpID = tblLookupIndex.LookUpID " & _
    "WHERE LI.UpdateIndex > [tblLookupIndex].[UpdateIndex] "
  ' Open a recordset on the query
  Set rst = dbs.OpenRecordset(strSQL)
  ' If we have some records
  Do While Not rst.EOF
    ' Clear the local copy
    strSQL = "DELETE " & rst!TableName & ".* FROM " & rst!TableName
    dbs.Execute strSQL, dbFailOnError
    ' Fetch the latest rows from the server
    strSQL = "INSERT INTO " & rst!TableName & _
      " SELECT " & rst!ServerTableName & _
      ".* FROM " & rst!ServerTableName
```

```
          dbs.Execute strSQL, dbFailOnError
          ' Update the local update index counter
          strSQL = "UPDATE tblLookupIndex " & _
            "SET tblLookupIndex.UpdateIndex = " & rst!UpdateIndex & _
            " WHERE tblLookupIndex.TableName = '" & rst!TableName & "'"
          dbs.Execute strSQL, dbFailOnError
          ' Process the next
          rst.MoveNext
        Loop
        ' Close out
        rst.Close
        Set rst = Nothing
        Set dbs = Nothing
okfctLookupUpdate:
        Exit Function
errfctLookupUpdate:
        ' Log the error and tell the user
        ErrTryingTo "update lookups"
        ' Bail
        Resume okfctLookupUpdate
End Function
```

Of course, checking for updates when the application starts makes perfect sense. But what if a user leaves the application running for days at a time? If you look at the design of the frmCSMain form that is the main switchboard for the application, you'll find a Timer event procedure. This procedure runs every 4 minutes, and every third time (once every 12 minutes), the code calls the *fctLookupUpdate* function to refresh the local tables.

To see how the application manages the updates to these lookup tables, you can open the frmDBAdminProducts form, as shown in Figure 3-13. This form is designed in Continous Form view to display all the available products. The user can filter the list by setting filter values in the form's footer section. The user must click one of the selector buttons (the right arrow next to each row) to copy the data into the unbound area in the form's header section to be able to make changes.

Although this form could allow the user to edit the data directly from the local lookup table, it's more reliable to use unbound data because any updates must be written to both the local copy and the linked copy on the server. Like all the other unbound editing forms, this form has an *fctCheckSaved* function to validate and save the data. After calling the *ValidateRecord* function to check for data in required fields, the code calls the *SaveRecord* function to save the record. However, note that the code provides both the local table name and the linked table name to update. Finally, the code calls the *FlagLookup* function that you can find in the modRecordEditor module to update the lookup index values for the table it just changed. Note that the code protects the calls to the two data update functions with a transaction to ensure that either all changes are saved successfully or none are.

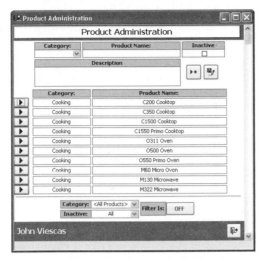

Figure 3-13   Using a form to edit data in a system lookup table.

The code is as follows:

```
Private Function fctCheckSaved()
' This code checks that the required information
' is complete and then saves the record and
' flags the linked table for an update
Dim strMsg As String, blnTrans As Boolean
  ' If already saved,
  If blnSaved = True Then
    ' Return success
    fctCheckSaved = "Saved"
    ' and exit
    Exit Function
  End If
  ' Set an error trap
  On Error GoTo errfctCheckSaved
  ' Call record validation to check for required data
  strMsg = ValidateRecord("frmDBAdminProducts", "frmDBAdminProducts")
  ' Return message is zero length string (ZLS) if OK
  If strMsg <> "" Then
    ' Build the error message
    strMsg = "The record could not be saved because " & _
      "the following fields must be completed: " & _
      vbCrLf & vbCrLf & strMsg & vbCrLf & _
      "What would you like to do?"
    ' Ask the user what to do
    If CustomError(strMsg, OkCancel, "Save Product Record", _
      Question) = "Cancel Changes" Then
      ' User gives up - return cancel
      fctCheckSaved = "Cancel"
```

```
         Else
           ' User wants to continue edit - return OK
           fctCheckSaved = "Ok"
         End If
         ' Make sure still marked not saved
         blnSaved = False
      Else
         ' No error - Start a transaction to protect all updates
         BeginTrans
         blnTrans = True
         '  Call the record saver to
         '  update both the remote table
         '  and the local copy.
         If SaveRecord("frmDBAdminProducts", "frmDBAdminProducts", _
            "tlkpProductsServer", Me.txtProductID, _
            "tlkpProducts", "Product") <> 0 Then
            ' Got a nonzero answer - OK
            ' Return success
            fctCheckSaved = "Saved"
            ' Mark the record saved
            blnSaved = True
            ' Flag the lookup table that we have changed it!
            If FlagLookup("tlkpProductsServer", True) = True Then
               ' Both changes done - commit all changes
               CommitTrans
               blnTrans = False
               ' Rebuild my recordset to show any added record
               Me.Requery
            Else
               ' Failed to flag - rollback!
               Rollback
               blnTrans = False
               ' Return failure
               fctCheckSaved = "OK"
               ' Leave record marked not saved
               blnSaved = False
            End If
         Else
            ' Something failed -
            Rollback
            blnTrans = False
            fctCheckSaved = "Ok"
            ' Leave record marked not saved
            blnSaved = False
         End If
      End If
   End If
   'Done!
okfctCheckSaved:
   ' Make sure hourglass is off
   DoCmd.Hourglass False
   Exit Function
errfctCheckSaved:
   ' If a transaction in process,
```

```
    If blnTrans = True Then
      ' Clear it
      blnTrans = False
      ' and roll it back
      Rollback
    End If
    ' Display and log error
    ErrTryingTo "save customer data"
    ' Clear the record so we don't get an unending loop
    Me.txtProductID = 0
    fctReLoadRecord
    Resume okfctCheckSaved
End Function
```

The *FlagLookup* function that you can find in the modRecordEditor module is very simple.
The code first fetches the record from the tblLookupIndexServer table for the lookup table
that was just updated. It adds 1 to the value of the UpdateIndex field and writes the record
back. If the caller asked to update the local lookup index table as well, the code uses an
update query to change the UpdateIndex field to match the value it just saved in the linked
table to the server data. The code is as follows:

```
Public Function FlagLookup(strSvrTblName As String, _
  Optional blnSetLocal As Boolean) As Boolean
'********************
' FlagLookup - Updates the value for a specific
' table record in the lookup table. This tells all
' other user copies to update their local table
' versions the next time the value is checked.
'Inputs:
'    strSvrTblName - The name of the server
'                    table to increment by 1
'    blnSetLocal - Indicates whether the local table
'                  should also be incremented
'    (False if the local version is already up to date)
'********************
Dim db As DAO.DataBase
Dim rst As DAO.Recordset
Dim strSQL As String
Dim intIndex As Integer
Dim blnTrans As Boolean
  ' Set an error trap
  On Error GoTo errFlagLookup
  ' Point to this database
  Set db = DBEngine(0)(0)
  ' Start a transaction to protect both updates
  BeginTrans
  blnTrans = True
  ' Fetch the index row for the specified table on the server
  strSQL = "SELECT tblLookupIndexServer.UpdateIndex " & _
    "FROM tblLookupIndexServer " & _
    "WHERE tblLookupIndexServer.ServerTableName = '" & strSvrTblName & "'"
  Set rst = db.OpenRecordset(strSQL, dbOpenDynaset, dbSeeChanges)
```

```
' Edit the record to lock it
rst.Edit
' Get the current index value
intIndex = rst!UpdateIndex
' Add 1
intIndex = intIndex + 1
' Change the value in the record
rst!UpdateIndex = intIndex
' Save it
rst.Update
' Close the recordset
rst.Close
' If we need to update the local copy, too...
If blnSetLocal = True Then
  ' Use an UPDATE query
  strSQL = "UPDATE tblLookupIndex " & _
    "SET UpdateIndex = " & intIndex & _
    " WHERE tblLookupIndex.ServerTableName = '" & strSvrTblName & "'"
  db.Execute strSQL, dbFailOnError
End If
' Done - commit the updates
CommitTrans
blnTrans = False
' Return success
FlagLookup = True
okFlagLookup:
  Set rst = Nothing
  Set db = Nothing
  Exit Sub
errFlagLookup:
  ' Got an error - display and log it
  ErrTryingTo "flag the " & strSvrTblName & " lookup"
  Resume okFlagLookup
End Sub
```

In Part 4, "Implementing a Customer Support Application," you'll learn all the details about how the application is designed to track customers, capture support issues and events, track follow-up contacts, and report statistics on issue trends. However, it should be clear at this point that the Customer Support application also teaches you how to minimize contact with the shared data stored on a server in order to maximize the number of users your application can support.

The Bottom Line: Keep the Wire "Cool"

If you walk away with nothing else in this chapter, you should understand that minimizing the amount of data transmitted over the network—keeping the wire "cool," not "hot"—is the key to a successful client/server application. You cannot create a classic single-user application and then just put it on the server for multiple users to share. You can probably split a simple single-user application into a "code" database file (containing queries, forms, reports, and modules) with linked tables to tables in a "data" database file on a file server and successfully deploy the application for three to five users. When you need to support more users, you might need to completely rewrite or revamp your application design.

So, if you know in advance that your application must eventually support multiple users, design how the application code works with client/server architecture in mind from the beginning. When you remember that the main purpose of a database is to share data, nearly every application you write will someday "grow up" to be shared by more than one user. So, even if you think you're building a simple single-user application, you'll be better off using good client/server coding techniques from the start.

Part II
Building a Membership Tracking Application

Chapter 4

The Membership Tracking Application

Any organization that has members, holds meetings, sends out notices, and collects dues can use the Membership Tracking application. Examples include a book club, a homeowners' association, or a software user group. Within a company, a similar application might also be usable by any ongoing task force (perhaps without the dues component) to track members assigned to the task force and the meetings held by the task force. Additional types of organizations that might use this application include:

- Neighborhood association
- School club
- Parent-teacher association
- Political action group
- Cub Scouts, Brownies, Girl Scouts, or Boy Scouts
- City council task force
- Genealogy club
- Social club
- Language club—such as L'Alliance Française
- Officers' wives clubs

And the list goes on and on.

Understanding the Membership Tracking Application

The Membership Tracking application in this book is specifically modeled after the activities and subjects that might be tracked by a software user group. In fact, Teresa Hennig, the president of the Pacific Northwest Access Developers Group (PNWADG) based in the Seattle area, graciously allowed me to use the group name, discussed with me some of the tasks that they track in their own membership database, and provided me with sample meeting agendas. Although the sample you'll find on the companion CD isn't actually used by PNWADG, it's based on a real-world example.

Identifying Tasks and Data

Whenever you begin to design an application, you should start by making lists of the tasks that the application must support and the data needed by those tasks. You should interview the potential users and determine how they're performing the tasks without a database or find out what they expect the database to do for them. Here are the tasks implemented in the Membership Tracking application:

- Enter member information, including home address, work address, e-mail address, and membership status.

- Collect information about the committees that perform work outside the general meetings.

- Track which members belong to which committees.

- Log both general and committee meetings.

- Track which members attended which meetings.

- Print a badge for each member when they sign in to a meeting.

- Identify which members are or were officers of the group and when they served in each position.

- Create the agendas for both general and committee meetings.

- Send out notices to the appropriate members for upcoming meetings.

- Specify special announcements to be included in meeting notices.

- Track dues paid by members.

- Inform members when their membership is about to expire.

- Print a membership roster.

- List the current officers.

- Display or print current committees.

- Print a membership expiration list.

> **Note**   Although not specifically included in this sample application, you could easily add tables to store meeting minutes and track the group's budget and expenditures.

From the preceding list, you can begin to identify the subjects and actions that should be represented by tables in the application. These include the following:

- Members
- Committees
- Committee Members
- Meetings
- Meeting Agendas
- Meeting Announcements
- Meeting Attendees
- Officers
- Dues

When you see a subject name that lists the simple name of two other subjects, such as Committee Members, that subject is probably going to be the many-to-many link between Members and Committees. Likewise, Meeting Attendees (Attendee is another name for Member) is also a many-to-many link.

You might think that you don't need a separate subject for Officers, but note one of the tasks listed previously that stated: "Identify which members are or were officers of the group and *when they served in each position*." If you need to know only which members are currently officers, you could do that with an attribute (column) in the Members subject (table). But the requirement to also keep the history of past officers suggests that Officers should be a separate subject. So, you can see that understanding both the tasks required and the data for those tasks is critical to designing the application correctly. You cannot do one without the other.

Understanding Business Rules

As you identify the tasks that need to be supported by your application, you'll also learn something about the business rules that restrict those tasks. For example, the first task in the previous section states that the Member information should include both home and work address. Do you have a business rule that states that information is always to be mailed to the business address if it is available? Or, should you also store some indication from the member about which is the preferred address? In the sample application, I included a DefaultAddress field (an integer code indicating whether home or work is the default) in the tblMembers table and made it required, thus enforcing the rule that the members should indicate a preference.

The best way to discover business rules is to ask questions. Some of the questions that I considered as I designed the application (and the answer I chose for each) are as follows:

- Can a member belong to more than one committee? Yes.

- Can a committee have more than one chair? Yes.

- Can a member hold more than one office at at time? No.

- Can more than one member hold the same office at the same time? No.

- Should a member name be saved in all capitals, all lowercase, or proper case? Proper case.

- Can a member have more than one member identifier? No.

- Are general meetings always held on the same day of every month? No. (Actually, PNWADG meets on the third Tuesday of every month.)

- Should all announcements be listed either before or after the agenda for a meeting? The user can choose the position of the announcement, before or after the agenda.

- Must all agenda topics have a speaker? No.

- Are any membership types complimentary? Yes, honorary members and invited speakers do not have to pay dues.

- Are the dues rates the same for all members? Yes. (This might not be true for a homeowners' association.)

- Will the dues rates change over time? Yes.

- Can a member renew for a period of more or less than a year? Yes.

- Do you need to keep a history of dues rates? Yes.

- Do members with complimentary memberships have the same rights and privileges as active members? No, but not enforced within the application. The application does print separate Speaker and Guest name badges when a member signs in.

- Can members who owe dues attend a meeting? Yes, but they are issued a Guest badge unless they bring their dues up to date.

- Can a member sign in as both a Speaker and a Guest at a meeting? No.

- Are dues payable at the same time every year? No, dues payments extend membership for 6 or 12 months from the date paid or the last expiration date. (PNWADG actually runs on an annual basis with all dues owing in January.)

Keep in mind that no question is too trivial, and sometimes you have to think "outside the box" to conjure up questions that your user or client needs to answer. Think like a good investigative reporter and find out not only what the user needs to do, but also when they need to do the task, where they need to be when they do the task, how they need to perform the task, and, most importantly, *why* they need to do it.

Designing the Tables

If you have identified all the tasks, the data required for all the tasks, and all the business rules, designing the tables you need to store and manage the data should be easy. You should never sit down and start creating tables without all the necessary background information. If some of the data exists in other files (such as a spreadsheet), create your properly normalized tables first, and then figure out what you need to do to import the existing data into your correct table structure.

From the list of subjects you determined earlier, you can see that the Membership Tracking application needs the following tables:

- tblMembers
- tblCommittees
- tblMemberCommittees
- tblMeetings
- tblMeetingAgenda
- tblMeetingAnnouncements
- tblMemberAttend
- tblOfficers
- tblDues

When you study the answers to the business rule questions, you can see that you probably need some additional supporting tables. These tables include:

tblDuesRates   to track the history of rates and different rates for different renewal periods.

tlkpMembershipStatus   to list the valid member status settings.

tlkpOfficerType   to store the officer titles for the organization.

tlkpTitles   to provide a list of common name titles, such as Mr., Mrs., Dr., and so forth.

tlkpSuffixes   to provide a list of common name suffixes, such as Jr., Sr., III, and so on.

> **Tip**   As you explore the sample databases, you'll notice that I have prefixed object names to indicate their usage. For example, tables names beginning with "tbl" indicate main data tables, "tlkp" tables are tables containing lookup data, and tables with names beginning with the letter "z" are working tables that the user cannot edit. Likewise, queries beginning with "qry" are primary record sources, and queries beginning with "qlkp" are ones used as row sources for list box controls and combo box controls. Forms beginning with "fdlg" are ones that open in Dialog mode, "fpop" indicates pop-up forms, "frm" indicates main editing forms, and "fsub" indicates forms that are used as subforms. You might find that a naming convention like this helps you organize the objects in a large application.

Now, you're ready to begin defining the tables you need and the relationships between them. As you create the tables, you should also define as many of the business rules as possible using the validation rule features of Access. Figure 4-1 shows you the final design for the tables in the Membership Tracking application. You can find a detailed listing of the fields and indexes in Appendix B, "Sample Database Schemas."

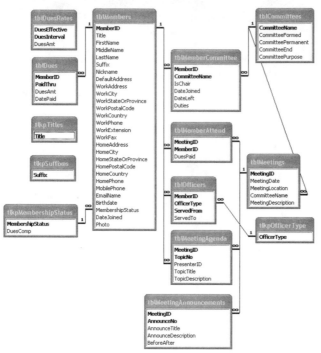

Figure 4-1   The tables in the Membership Tracking application.

The table design for the Membership Tracking application is actually quite simple. In some of the other sample applications, you'll see that nine main tables won't even begin to describe the data for the application. In the remainder of this part of the book, you can explore specific tasks implemented in the Membership Tracking sample database (Membership.mdb) that you can use in any similar application that you build.

Chapter 5

Verifying Names

Whenever you need to store person names in a database, you should make an effort to help the user avoid duplicate entries and enter names in the correct combination of uppercase and lowercase letters. The Membership Tracking application is a classic example of an application that stores person names. This chapter discusses two techniques you can implement to make data entry easier and more accurate.

Detecting Duplicate Names

The rules of normalization tell you that you should, whenever possible, choose a simple set of natural values as the primary key of your tables. When you're dealing with person names and addresses, finding a simple combination of fields that will always be unique is usually difficult if not impossible. So, you end up generating an artificial primary key—usually an integer number—to uniquely identify each row.

But how do you help the user ensure that a new person about to be added isn't already in the database? You can certainly perform a lookup on first name and last name to discover if someone else is already in the database with the name about to be saved. That certainly is a good start, but what about the case where the user enters a name that is similar? Is Jack McDonald the same person as John MacDonald?

Genealogists have to deal with "near matching" names when searching old record archives. Many old records were hand-written, and the person recording the data was very likely getting the information from someone barely literate who had no clue how to correctly spell the name. So, the person creating the record just guessed. To deal with this problem, the U.S. National Archives and Records Administration (NARA) created a formula, called Soundex, that generates a matching code based on the sounds of letters, not the exact spelling. This formula produces a four-character code, and when the codes for two names match, it's likely that the names are very similar and sound alike.

You can perform exact name matching, or you can use Soundex codes to try to identify potentially duplicate last names and warn the user before saving a new row. To see how this works, open the frmMembers form in the Membership sample database (Membership.mdb). Go to a new record, choose any Title, and type **Eriksen** in the Last Name field. Type any first name you like and click the Save Record button on the toolbar (or choose Save Record from the File menu). Figure 5-1 shows you how the application responds. Note that the application found a Gail Erickson in the database who is clearly not the same person. However, the code checks last name only because checking both last name and first name is not likely to find potential duplicates—such as the Jack McDonald and John MacDonald example noted earlier. (The Soundex code for Jack is J200, and the Soundex code for John is J500.)

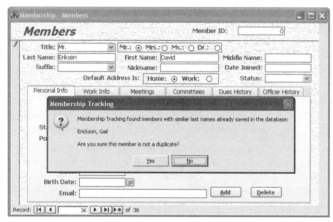

Figure 5-1 Code that checks for similar names using Soundex warns you when another person in the database has a potentially matching name.

Microsoft SQL Server has a native *Soundex* function, but Access does not. However, you can create a Public *Soundex* function in any standard module and then call it from anywhere in your application, including queries. You can find the code you need in the modUtility module in all the sample databases. The code is as follows:

```
Function Soundex(strName As String) As String
'-----------------------------------------------------------
' Input: A string
' Outputs: U.S. National archive "Soundex" number
'    This number is useful to find similar last names
' Created By: JLV 03/01/2003
' Last Revised: JLV 06/27/2005
'-----------------------------------------------------------
' A Soundex code is the first letter, followed by
' three numbers derived from evaluating the remaining
' letters.  Vowels (including Y) and the letters H and W
' are ignored.  When consecutive letters return the
' same numeric code, the number appears only once.
' When two letters with the same code are separated only
' by H or W, the second letter is ignored.
' Letters are translated to numbers as follows:
```

```
'    B, P, F, V = 1
'    C, S, G, J, K, Q, X, Z = 2
'    D, T = 3
'    L = 4
'    M, N = 5
'    R = 6
' If the final code after examining all letters is less
' than three digits, the code is padded with zeros.
' Working variables:
' String to build the code, string to hold code number
Dim strCode As String, strCodeN As String
' Length of original string, last code returned, looping integer
Dim intLength As Integer, strLastCode As String, intI As Integer
   ' Save the first letter
   strCode = UCase(Left(strName, 1))
   ' Save its code number to check for duplicates
   strLastCode = GetSoundexCode(strCode)
   ' Calculate length to examine
   intLength = Len(strName)
   ' Create the code starting at the second letter.
   For intI = 2 To intLength
      strCodeN = GetSoundexCode(Mid(strName, intI, 1))
      ' If two letters that are the same are next to each other
      ' only count one of them
      If strCodeN > "0" And strLastCode <> strCodeN Then
         ' Different code number, add to the result
         strCode = strCode & strCodeN
      End If
      ' If this is not the special "skip" code (H or W)
      If strCodeN <> "0" Then
         ' Save the last code number
         strLastCode = strCodeN
      End If
   ' Loop
   Next intI
   ' Check the length
   If Len(strCode) < 4 Then
      ' Pad zeros
      strCode = strCode & String(4 - Len(strCode), "0")
   Else
      ' Make sure not more than 4
      strCode = Left(strCode, 4)
   End If
   ' Return the result
   Soundex = strCode
End Function
```

The *Soundex* function calls the *GetSoundexCode* function to calculate the numeric value of each letter examined. The code is as follows:

```
Private Function GetSoundexCode(strChar As String) As String
'-------------------------------------------------------------
' Input: One character
' Output: U.S. National archive "Soundex" number
'    for the specified letter
```

```
' Created By: JLV 03/01/2003
' Last Revised: JLV 06/27/2005
'------------------------------------------------------------
  Select Case strChar
    Case "B", "F", "P", "V"
     GetSoundexCode = "1"
    Case "C", "G", "J", "K", "Q", "S", "X", "Z"
      GetSoundexCode = "2"
    Case "D", "T"
      GetSoundexCode = "3"
    Case "L"
      GetSoundexCode = "4"
    Case "M", "N"
      GetSoundexCode = "5"
    Case "R"
      GetSoundexCode = "6"
    Case "H", "W"
      ' Special "skip" code
      GetSoundexCode = "0"
  End Select
End Function
```

To perform the last name similarity check, I added code to the BeforeUpdate event procedure of the frmMembers form. For a new record, the code opens a recordset that looks for any other member records that have the same Soundex code for the last name as the last name in the record about to be saved. When the recordset finds any matches, the procedure displays all the potential duplicates and gives the user a chance to cancel the save. The code is as follows:

```
Private Sub Form_BeforeUpdate(Cancel As Integer)
Dim varID As Variant
Dim rst As DAO.Recordset, strNames As String
  ' If on a new row,
  If (Me.NewRecord = True) Then
    ' Check for similar name
    If Not IsNothing(Me.LastName) Then
      ' Open a recordset to look for similar names
      Set rst = DBEngine(0)(0).OpenRecordset( _
        "SELECT LastName, FirstName FROM " & _
        "tblMembers WHERE Soundex([LastName]) = '" & _
        Soundex(Me.LastName) & "'")
      ' If got some similar names, issue warning message
      Do Until rst.EOF
        strNames = strNames & rst!LastName & ", " & rst!FirstName & vbCrLf
        rst.MoveNext
      Loop
      ' Done with the recordset
      rst.Close
      Set rst = Nothing
      ' See if we got some similar names
      If Len(strNames) > 0 Then
        ' Yup, issue warning
        If vbNo = MsgBox(gstrAppTitle & " found members with similar " & _
          "last names already saved in the database: " & _
          vbCrLf & vbCrLf & strNames & _
```

```
            vbCrLf & "Are you sure this member is not a duplicate?", _
            vbQuestion + vbYesNo + vbDefaultButton2, gstrAppTitle) Then
            ' Cancel the save
            Cancel = True
          End If
        End If
      End If
    End If
    ' Additional code not related to this example ...
End Sub
```

> **Note**   Throughout the sample code, you'll see me use DBEngine(0)(0) (equivalent to
> DBEngine.Workspaces(0).Databases(0)—the first database in the first workspace) to set a
> pointer to the current database. In the help files, Microsoft recommends using CurrentDb
> instead because it makes an independent copy of the current database object, and you're less
> likely to run into conflicts if multiple users have the same database open at the same time.
> However, it's a bad idea to let multiple users run the same copy of your code because doing so
> is more likely to result in locking conflicts and corruption of your database. Also, CurrentDb is
> much slower because it reloads and revalidates all the objects in the database. If you imple-
> ment the client/server architecture recommended in Chapter 3, each user has his or her own
> copy of the database where this code executes, so conflicts are not an issue.

As you might recall, setting the Cancel parameter to True tells Access to not save the record.
The user can then either clear the duplicate record or make any corrections before saving the
record.

Ensuring Names Are in Proper Case

When users type in names, some might use the Shift key to properly capitalize names as they
enter them. But if you want to ensure that names are entered in proper case (perhaps to
ensure that names appear correctly on name badges or in correspondence), you can add some
code to your forms to assist the user. If you start to enter a new member in the frmMembers
form in the Membership database (Membership.mdb) and enter the name in all lowercase,
the application prompts you with an appropriate correction, as shown on the next page in
Figure 5-2.

If you're familiar with the *StrConv* function, you might think that using it with the
vbProperCase argument would be useful to verify uppercase and lowercase letters in a name,
but you'd be wrong. Open the Immediate window by pressing Ctrl+G, and type the following:

```
?StrConv("macdonald", vbProperCase)
```

The function responds with:

```
Macdonald
```

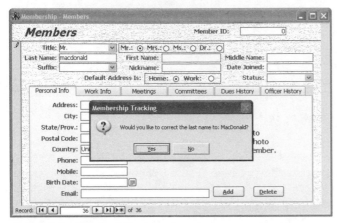

Figure 5-2   The frmMembers form prompts you with a suggested correction when you do not enter a name in proper case.

The *StrConv* function also doesn't handle embedded apostrophes (O'Brien) or periods (J.R.) either. Several years ago, I decided to write a custom function that does a better job with names like this. You can find my *SetUpper* function in the modUtility module in any of the sample databases. The code is as follows:

```
Function SetUpper(ByVal varFixCase As Variant) As Variant
'----------------------------------------------------------
' Inputs: A string containing a person name
' Outputs: Updates the string to "proper" case
' Created By: JLV 07/31/1998
' Last Revised: JLV 08/10/2005
'----------------------------------------------------------
  Dim i As Integer
  Dim intSkip As Integer
  Dim intASC As Integer
  Dim strUpper As String
  Dim strLast As String
  ' Make sure the argument is a string
  If VarType(varFixCase) <> vbString Then
    SetUpper = Null
    Exit Function
  End If
  strUpper = varFixCase
  strLast = " "     ' set starting "last" character to blank
  ' First, set everything to lowercase
  strUpper = LCase$(strUpper)
  ' Loop through each character, 1 at a time
  For i = 1 To Len(strUpper)
    ' First, see if we're skipping some letters (special cases)
    If intSkip > 0 Then
      intSkip = intSkip - 1   ' Yes.  Decrement skip count
    Else
      ' If "last" character was a blank (or start of string),
      ' do some special tests for "O'", "Mc", and "Mac"
      If strLast = " " Then
```

```
            If Len(strUpper) - i > 2 Then   ' If at least 3 characters left
              ' Then if the next two are O' (as in O'Brien)
              ' or Mc (as in McDonald)
              If Mid$(strUpper, i, 2) = "o'" Or _
                Mid$(strUpper, i, 2) = "mc" Then
                 ' Make the "O" or "M" uppercase
                 Mid$(strUpper, i, 1) = UCase$(Mid$(strUpper, i, 1))
                 intSkip = 1      ' and set up to skip the next character
              End If
              ' Or if the next three are Mac  (as in MacDougal)
              If Mid$(strUpper, i, 3) = "mac" Then
                 ' Make the "M" upper case
                 Mid$(strUpper, i, 1) = UCase$(Mid$(strUpper, i, 1))
                 intSkip = 2       ' and set up to skip the next 2 characters
              End If
            End If
          End If
        ' If not skipping characters
        If intSkip = 0 Then
          ' Not a special case, so see if "last"
          ' was a letter or an apostrophe
          ' Use the ASCII value to avoid having to do binary compares
          intASC = Asc(strLast)
          ' 39 = ', 97 = a, 122 = z, 65 = A, 90 = Z,
          ' 224 and higher are foreign language letters (like à or ö)
          ' except 247, which is a division sign (÷)
          If intASC = 39 Or (intASC >= 97 And intASC <= 122) Or _
            (intASC >= 65 And intASC <= 90) Or _
            (intASC >= 224 And intASC <= 246) Or (intASC >= 248) Then
            ' If previous character was a letter or
            ' apostrophe, then leave this one alone
          Else
            ' If previous WASN'T a letter or apostrophe, Upper this one
            Mid$(strUpper, i, 1) = UCase$(Mid$(strUpper, i, 1))
          End If
          ' Save this character for next go-around
          strLast = Mid$(strUpper, i, 1)
        End If
      End If
    Next i
  End Function
```

As you might suspect, the code that checks the last name uses the *SetUpper* function to create a comparison value. Because the comparison must be case-sensitive (all comparisons in an Access database are case-insensitive by default), you must use the *StrComp* function to ask for a true binary compare. Here's the code in the AfterUpdate event of the LastName control on frmMembers:

```
Private Sub LastName_AfterUpdate()
Dim strUpper As String
  ' Get the corrected uppercase
  strUpper = SetUpper(Me.LastName)
  ' See if it matches what the user entered
  If StrComp(strUpper, Me.LastName, vbBinaryCompare) <> 0 Then
```

```
      ' Ask the user if this code should fix it
      If vbYes = MsgBox("Would you like to correct the last name to: " & _
        strUpper & "?", vbQuestion + vbYesNo, gstrAppTitle) Then
        Me.LastName = strUpper
      End If
  End If
End Sub
```

Of course, you could just update the name with the corrected value without asking the user, but the *SetUpper* function might get it wrong. For example, the *SetUpper* function will correct Mackey to MacKey. You must weigh that possibility against the potential annoyance of asking the user to verify the correction for each name. The user can avoid the prompt by entering the name in the correct case to begin with.

As you might imagine, you can apply the techniques described in this chapter to any application that must store people's names. In the next chapter, you'll learn how the Membership Tracking sample application tracks member activities.

Chapter 6
Tracking Member Activities

As you learned in Chapter 4, the Membership Tracking application is designed to not only save information about members, officers, meetings, and committees but also keep track of which members are active in the group—which ones regularly attend meetings. To make this information useful, you need to create forms that make it easy to capture the data and reports that help you analyze activity over selected periods of time.

Logging Activities

In Chapter 3, you explored the frmMemberAttendance form that demonstrates an alternative way to look up values in a list by capturing characters as the user types in an unbound text box. It's this form that provides a simple way to capture member attendance as each member walks into a meeting. The form not only registers the member in the current meeting but also gives the person entering the data the opportunity to correct information about each member. As you'll learn in the next chapter, it also alerts the user when a member's dues are not current and provides a way to immediately accept a payment and extend the membership.

You can see how the form works by opening the Membership database (Membership.mdb). After the initial splash form closes (frmCopyright), open the frmMeetings form and move to the meeting record you want to work with. Click the Attendees button at the bottom of that form, select the **Open the meeting sign-in form** option in the Attendee Options window, and click Go. Figure 6-1, on the next page, shows you the frmMemberAttendance form opened for the October 2004 general meeting and displaying the first attendee who has already signed in.

This form looks like it is primarily used to edit the member data. Except for the text box in the form header that lists the related meeting, it doesn't look like it has anything to do with members attending meetings at all. The secret is this form is actually based on a query that joins the tblMembers table with the tblMemberAttend table.

The SQL for the query is as follows:

```
SELECT tblMemberAttend.MeetingID, tblMemberAttend.MemberID, tblMemberAttend.DuesPaid,
tblMembers.Title, tblMembers.LastName, tblMembers.FirstName, tblMembers.MiddleName,
tblMembers.Suffix, tblMembers.Nickname, tblMembers.DefaultAddress, tblMembers.WorkAddress,
tblMembers.WorkCity, tblMembers.WorkStateOrProvince, tblMembers.WorkPostalCode,
tblMembers.WorkCountry, tblMembers.WorkPhone, tblMembers.WorkExtension, tblMembers.WorkFax,
tblMembers.HomeAddress, tblMembers.HomeCity, tblMembers.HomeStateOrProvince,
tblMembers.HomePostalCode, tblMembers.HomeCountry, tblMembers.HomePhone,
tblMembers.MobilePhone, tblMembers.EmailName, tblMembers.Birthdate,
tblMembers.MembershipStatus, tblMembers.DateJoined
FROM tblMembers
INNER JOIN tblMemberAttend
ON tblMembers.MemberID = tblMemberAttend.MemberID
ORDER BY tblMembers.LastName, tblMembers.FirstName;
```

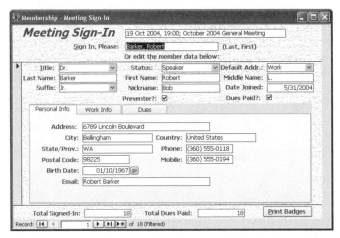

Figure 6-1   The frmMemberAttendance form tracks members who attend a specific meeting.

For each row in tblMembers, many rows can exist in tblMemberAttend. The target table in any query for additions and deletions is the one on the many side of the relationship. But you don't see a control for either tblMemberAttend.MeetingID or tblMemberAttend.MemberID— so how does this work? If you remember from Chapter 3, you can type a person's last name and first name in the **Sign In, Please** box, and code behind the form either finds the existing attendance record for the member name you entered or adds a new record.

The code to do this runs when you press Enter or Tab in the **Sign In, Please** box, indicating you accept the name that the form has found for you. It first attempts to find an existing member attendance record for the member ID for the current meeting that matches the name you entered. If it doesn't find that the member is already registered, it makes a copy of the form's recordset from the form's RecordsetClone property and inserts in a new row the member ID that it found and the meeting ID acquired from the companion frmMeetings form that is open. It then requeries the form so that the form's recordset now contains the new row and positions you to that row by finding the row in the form's recordset and using the Bookmark property to move to the new row. Below is the bit of code in the KeyDown event procedure for the txtSignIn text box control that inserts the new attendance row for you:

```
If (KeyCode = vbKeyTab) Or (KeyCode = vbKeyReturn) Then
    ' Assume they meant to update the control
    ' Set an error trap
    On Error GoTo txtSignIn_Error
UserAdded:
    ' If got a member ID
    If Not IsNothing(lngMemberID) Then
      ' Get a copy of the recordset
      Set rst = Me.RecordsetClone
      ' See if the row exists
      rst.FindFirst "MemberID = " & lngMemberID
      ' If not found
      If rst.NoMatch Then
        ' Save the memberID locally
        lngNewMember = lngMemberID
        ' Insert a new row into the attendance table
        rst.AddNew
        ' Set the Meeting ID
        rst!MeetingID = varMeetingID
        ' Set the Member ID
        rst!MemberID = lngNewMember
        ' Save it!
        rst.Update
        ' Turn off painting
        Application.Echo False
        ' Requery me
        Me.Requery
        ' Get the recordset again
        Set rst = Me.RecordsetClone
        ' Find the row we just added
        rst.FindFirst "MemberID = " & lngNewMember
        ' Should not be nomatch
        If rst.NoMatch Then
          ' Signal our own error
          Err.Raise 3999, "Membership.Form_frmMemberAttendance", _
            "Record just added was not found."
        Else
          ' Move me to the added row
          Me.Bookmark = rst.Bookmark
        End If
        ' Turn on painting again
        Application.Echo True
```

So, the user doesn't have to worry at all about selecting a member ID or making sure that the new record contains the meeting ID currently displayed in the frmMeetings form. Because Access lets you edit fields on the one side of a many-to-one relationship query, you can verify and correct all the member information displayed on the form.

Reporting Activities

After you make it easy to enter member attendance, you need to give the user the ability to analyze that activity. The chairman of the membership committee might be particularly interested in how many meetings each member has attended in the last six months or year and the date of the last meeting attended. If the data is sorted properly, it should be easy to identify which members should be contacted or marked inactive.

When you first look at the problem, you might consider building a totals query that joins the tblMembers, tblMemberAttend, and tblMeetings tables, finds out the last meeting date (using the Max aggregate function on MeetingDate) and the count of meetings attended. But if you do that, you'll get data only for members who have been to a meeting within the date range of interest. You really want to list all members and then find the statistics for any meetings attended. You might be tempted to define an outer join from tblMembers to tblMemberAttend so that you will see all members and any related rows from tblMemberAttend, as shown in Figure 6-2.

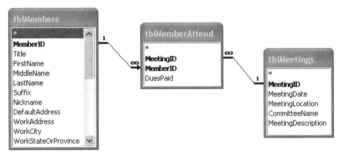

Figure 6-2   Attempting to fetch data for all members and any related member attendance records.

There are two problems with this technique. First, you need to filter the meeting attendance data to look at meetings only for a specific time period. You cannot add a filter to rows on the "right" side of a "left" join and get the right answer because Access honors the join criteria first and then applies the filter. The join might fetch all members, but adding a filter on the MeetingDate field will exclude any members that did not attend any meeting in the selected time period.

Second, because you need a one-to-many and many-to-one join, the query engine will tell you that "The SQL statement could not be executed because it contains ambiguous outer joins." The error message also suggests that you create a query on the two tables that do not participate in the outer join, and then use that query in another query to perform the final outer join. Using separate queries is the correct way to solve both problems.

> **Tip**   Whenever you need an aggregate calculation (Min, Max, Avg, Sum, or Count) on only a few fields in a totals query that returns many grouped fields, you can obtain a more efficient result by breaking out the aggregate calculations into a separate query that is grouped on a primary key value. The query engine must build a temporary index to solve a Group By operation on many fields, so you're asking the engine to do far more work than necessary if you group on 10 or more fields, particularly if some of those fields are not indexed. When you perform the aggregate calculations in a separate query and then use that query in another query that fetches the remaining fields you need, your query will execute much faster, particularly in a client/server application.

In the sample application you can find the qryMemberActivity query that finds the last date any meeting was attended and counts the number of meetings. The query also includes parameters that point to controls on the fdlgDateReportParm form to filter the result to the time period of interest. Figure 6-3 shows you the query.

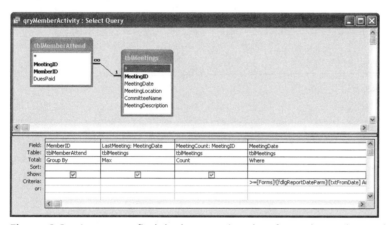

Figure 6-3   A query to find the last meeting date for each member and count meetings.

Keep in mind that the MeetingDate field contains both a date and a time. To find all records within a date span using date parameter values, you must construct the criteria to include any meeting on the last date. The full criteria on the MeetingDate field is as follows:

```
>=[Forms]![fdlgReportDateParm]![txtFromDate] And
<([Forms]![fdlgReportDateParm]![txtToDate]+1)
```

Note that I added 1 to the "to" date parameter and used a less than comparison. This ensures that the result includes any record up to midnight of the end of the date range. If I were to compare less than or equal to the date, the query would not return any rows on the last date that also have a time component because that date/time value will be larger than just the date value.

The final query needed for the report is qryRptMemberActivity. This query fetches (and formats) the data needed from the tblMembers table and uses an outer join to the qryMemberActivity query to include any available statistics for each member. The SQL of the qryRptMemberActivity query is as follows:

```
PARAMETERS [Forms]![fdlgReportDateParm]![txtFromDate] DateTime,
[Forms]![fdlgReportDateParm]![txtToDate] DateTime;
SELECT ([Title]+" ") & [FirstName] & " " & ([MiddleName]+" ") & [LastName] & (", "+[Suffix])
AS MemberName, tblMembers.MembershipStatus, tblMembers.LastName, tblMembers.FirstName,
Replace(Mid([EmailName],InStr([EmailName],"MailTo:")+7),"#","") AS Email,
tblMembers.DateJoined, qryMemberActivity.LastMeeting, qryMemberActivity.MeetingCount,
[Forms]![fdlgReportDateParm]![txtFromDate] AS [From],
[Forms]![fdlgReportDateParm]![txtToDate] AS [To]
FROM tblMembers
LEFT JOIN qryMemberActivity
ON tblMembers.MemberID = qryMemberActivity.MemberID;
```

> **Tip**   Notice that I explicitly declared the parameters needed by the qryMemberActivity query. Although most parameter queries can run successfully without an explicit parameter declaration, including the declaration helps ensure that the supplied parameter value can be used successfully by the query. When you design a parameter query to prompt the user for values, the query won't continue until the user enters a value that matches the declared data type. Some types of parameter queries, such as a crosstab query, won't run at all without an explicit parameter declaration.

I assembled the parts of the MemberName field in the query, but I could have also done so using an expression in a report control. I included the separate LastName and FirstName fields so that the report could sort the names correctly for members that have the same last meeting date. I also stripped out the superfluous delimiters and the MailTo: prefix so that the e-mail address could be displayed in the report as plain text. Finally, I included the two parameter values as fields so that the report could display them.

To see the final result, you can start the application by opening the frmSplash form, clicking the Reports button on the main switchboard, and clicking the Member Activity button on the reports switchboard. (You can also open the frmReports form—the reports switchboard form—directly from the Database window.) You'll see a dialog box asking you for a date range for the Member Activity report. The sample database contains meeting records for September 2004 through January 2005, so you should select dates that include these dates. Click Print in the dialog box to see the report, as shown in Figure 6-4.

Membership - Member Activity

Member Activity

From: 9/1/2004
To: 1/31/2005

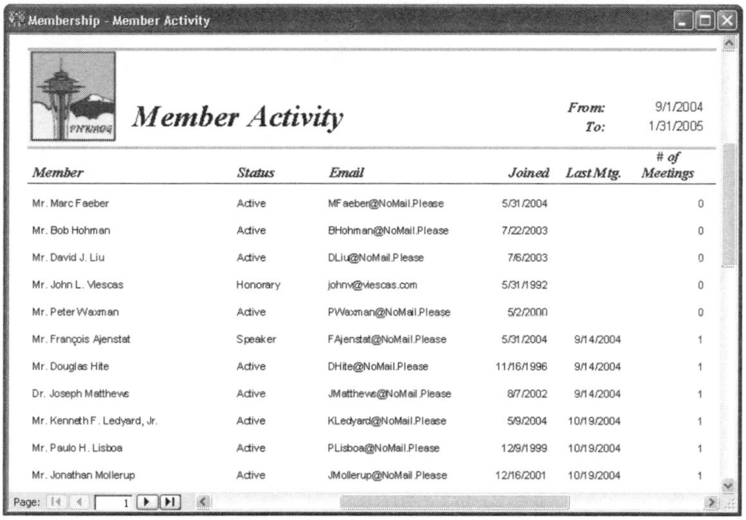

Member	Status	Email	Joined	Last Mtg.	# of Meetings
Mr. Marc Faeber	Active	MFaeber@NoMail.Please	5/31/2004		0
Mr. Bob Hohman	Active	BHohman@NoMail.Please	7/22/2003		0
Mr. David J. Liu	Active	DLiu@NoMail.Please	7/6/2003		0
Mr. John L. Viescas	Honorary	johnv@viescas.com	5/31/1992		0
Mr. Peter Waxman	Active	PWaxman@NoMail.Please	5/2/2000		0
Mr. François Ajenstat	Speaker	FAjenstat@NoMail.Please	5/31/2004	9/14/2004	1
Mr. Douglas Hite	Active	DHite@NoMail.Please	11/16/1996	9/14/2004	1
Dr. Joseph Matthews	Active	JMatthews@NoMail.Please	8/7/2002	9/14/2004	1
Mr. Kenneth F. Ledyard, Jr.	Active	KLedyard@NoMail.Please	5/9/2004	10/19/2004	1
Mr. Paulo H. Lisboa	Active	PLisboa@NoMail.Please	12/9/1999	10/19/2004	1
Mr. Jonathan Mollerup	Active	JMollerup@NoMail.Please	12/16/2001	10/19/2004	1

Page: 1

Figure 6-4 The Member Activity report showing members who have missed the last several meetings.

The chairman of the membership committee might want to contact Marc Faeber, Bob Hohman, David Liu, and Peter Waxman to see if they still want to be active members. You can also see that some members have attended only one of the last several meetings. (Yes, I'm an honorary member of the Pacific Northwest Access Developers Group, but I live in Austin now, so don't often have a chance to attend a meeting!)

Chapter 7

Tracking Member Status

Every organization needs some level of funds to run, whether it be something as mundane as paying for postage stamps and stationery, or something as expensive as paying for meeting space. Many organizations acquire the funds they need by charging a membership fee or annual dues. Nonprofit organizations accept pledges and donations. So, it's important to not only accurately record dues or donations paid but also track payment status and report dues or pledges owed in a timely manner.

The Membership Tracking sample application assumes dues can be paid at any time, and dues can be paid to renew for various numbers of months, which you can define in the tblDuesRates table. The actual Pacific Northwest Access Developers Group, on which the sample is modeled, charges annual dues only and collects those dues each January. Perhaps after they see how easy it is to implement a rolling dues payment plan, they'll change how they collect their dues.

Entering Dues Rates and Payments

Whenever a user enters a dues payment, you could require that the user manually specify the current dues rate. You could also set a default value for the dues rate, but the user would have to correct that each time if the rate has changed, or you would need to modify your application. A simpler method is to provide a dues rates table that contains at least one row with the current rate. When you do that, the user can change the current rate at any time, and you can look up that value to supply the current value as the default in any new payment record.

But if you're going to provide a dues rates table, you might as well allow the user to keep a history of rate changes over time. Your table could also allow the user to specify different renewal intervals. It's a bit more complex to find and load the latest rates, but doing so provides an additional level of integrity for the dues amounts charged.

The Membership application includes a tblDuesRates table. You can examine the contents of this table by opening the frmDuesRates form, as shown in Figure 7-1. Note that when running the application, the user can access this form by clicking the Code Tables button on the main switchboard, and then clicking the Dues Rates button on the Code Tables switchboard.

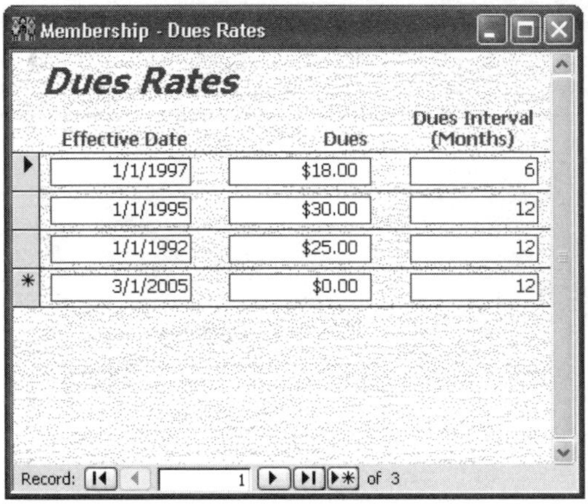

Figure 7-1   The frmDuesRates form allows you to view and edit the contents of the tblDuesRates table in the Membership application.

As you can see, the annual dues were $25.00 starting in January 1992, increased to $30.00 in January 1995, and an option for a six month membership was added in 1997. Now all you need to know is how to pick up the most recent dues rates from this list and make them available to the user.

In the Member Activity report that is shown in Figure 6-4 on page 135, you can see several members at the top of the list who haven't been active for a while. Let's assume you edited those member records and set their status to Inactive. A few days later, you receive a dues payment from Peter Waxman, so you need to enter the payment in the database and renew his membership. To see how this works, perform the following steps:

1. Open the Membership application (Membership.mdb) and open the frmMembers form.

2. Find the record for Peter Waxman and set his status to Inactive.

3. Click on the Dues History tab and select the All Records option.

4. Go to the last record—the new record row—enter a date a few days earlier than the current date (perhaps the date you received the payment) in the Date Paid column, and then open the Paid Thru list.

You should see a result similar to that shown in Figure 7-2.

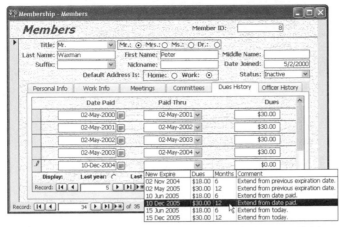

Figure 7-2   The Membership application calculates available renewal dates using the information from the tblDuesRates table.

Because it's clear from the activity report that this user hasn't attended any meetings since his dues last expired, you'll probably want to renew his membership from the payment date rather than extend his old membership. Go ahead and save his dues payment (press Shift+Enter or move to another record)—we'll see how that affects signing in to a meeting later in this chapter.

The list that you see is generated by code running in the fsubMemberDues subform. The code depends on a query that returns the current rate in each different renewal interval, and then it generates the combo box row source as a value list for each rate. The qryCurrentDuesRates query fetches the current rates, and the SQL for that query is as follows:

```
SELECT tblDuesRates.DuesEffective, tblDuesRates.DuesAmt, tblDuesRates.DuesInterval
FROM tblDuesRates
WHERE tblDuesRates.DuesEffective =
(Select Max([DuesEffective])
FROM tblDuesRates As DR2
WHERE DR2.[DuesEffective] <= Date()
And DR2.[DuesInterval] = tblDuesRates.DuesInterval)
ORDER BY tblDuesRates.DuesInterval;
```

The list is created by the *SetupPaidThru* function in the form's module that is called each time you move to a new row (from the Current event) and each time you change the value in the DatePaid field (from that control's AfterUpdate event). The code begins by setting the heading information in the combo box Row Source property (which also clears any previous entries) and then verifying that a valid MemberID exists in the outer form, as follows:

```
Private Function SetupPaidThru() As Integer
Dim db As DAO.Database, rst As DAO.Recordset, rstDues As DAO.Recordset
Dim datMemberPaidThru As Date, strRowSource As String
    ' Called by other procedures to set up the Row Source for cmbPaidThru
    ' Procedure fetches the current dues intervals and rates from
```

```
' qryCurrentDuesRates and sets up the following valid "Paid Thru"
' choices:
'  1) Renewal extension from this members last paid thru date
'  2) Renewal extension from the date paid
'  3) Renewal extension from today
'
' The combo box has four columns:
'  1) New Expire date
'  2) Dues amount
'  3) Length of renewal in months
'  4) Comment indicating reason for choice

' Set an error trap
On Error GoTo SetupPaidThru_Error
' Clear the current Row Source - headings only
Me.cmbPaidThru.RowSource = "'New Expire';'Dues';'Months';'Comment'"
' If there's not a valid member ID
If IsNothing(Me.Parent.MemberID) Then
  ' Bail
  Exit Function
End If
```

Next, the function opens the qryCurrentDuesRates query and verifies that it returns at least one row.

```
' Point to this database
Set db = DBEngine(0)(0)
' Open a recordset on the current dues rates
Set rstDues = db.OpenRecordset("qryCurrentDuesRates")
' If no records, close and bail
If rstDues.RecordCount = 0 Then
  ' Close
  rstDues.Close
  Set rstDues = Nothing
  Set db = Nothing
  Exit Function
End If
```

The function fetches the most recent dues payment record for the current member, and if any payment exists, generates one row in the combo box for each current renewal rate. These are the first two data rows you see in Figure 7-2.

```
' Get the last dues renewal
Set rst = db.OpenRecordset("SELECT Top 1 * FROM tblDues " & _
  "WHERE MemberID = " & Me.Parent.MemberID & _
  " ORDER BY PaidThru DESC")
' If there's a record
If Not rst.EOF Then
  ' Save the member's last paid thru date
  datMemberPaidThru = rst!PaidThru
  ' Loop through dues rates to generate combo box rows
  Do Until rstDues.EOF
    ' Set up the next row of data
    strRowSource = strRowSource & ";'" & _
```

```
        Format(DateAdd("m", rstDues![DuesInterval], datMemberPaidThru), _
        "dd mmm yyyy") & _
        "';'" & Format(rstDues!DuesAmt, "Currency") & "';'" & _
        rstDues!DuesInterval & "';" & _
        "'Extend from previous expiration date.'"
      rstDues.MoveNext
    Loop
  End If
' Close the member recordset
rst.Close
Set rst = Nothing
```

The next piece of code repositions back to the beginning of the current dues rates recordset
and creates the renewal options for the date paid that you entered (the third and fourth rows
in Figure 7-2).

```
' Move back to start of current dues rates recordset
rstDues.MoveFirst
' If there's a date paid
If Not IsNothing(Me.DatePaid) Then
  ' Create rows for "Extend from date paid"
  Do Until rstDues.EOF
    ' Set up the next row of data
    strRowSource = strRowSource & ";'" & _
      Format(DateAdd("m", rstDues![DuesInterval], Me.DatePaid), _
      "dd mmm yyyy") & _
      "';'" & Format(rstDues!DuesAmt, "Currency") & "';'" & _
      rstDues!DuesInterval & "';" & _
      "'Extend from date paid.'"
    rstDues.MoveNext
  Loop
End If
```

Finally, if the date paid is different from today's date, the code creates rows for renewal options
from today (the last two rows in Figure 7-2).

```
' Move back to start of current dues rates recordset
rstDues.MoveFirst
' Create today rows only if DatePaid <> Today
If Me.DatePaid <> Date Then
  ' Create "today" rows
  Do Until rstDues.EOF
    ' Set up the next row of data
    strRowSource = strRowSource & ";'" & _
    Format(DateAdd("m", rstDues![DuesInterval], Date), "dd mmm yyyy") & _
      "';'" & Format(rstDues!DuesAmt, "Currency") & "';'" & _
      rstDues!DuesInterval & "';" & _
      "'Extend from today.'"
    rstDues.MoveNext
  Loop
End If
' Close out
rstDues.Close
Set rstDues = Nothing
```

```
  Set db = Nothing
  ' Set the rest of the row source
  Me.cmbPaidThru.RowSource = Me.cmbPaidThru.RowSource & strRowSource
  ' Indicate success
  SetupPaidThru = True
SetupPaidThru_Exit:
  ' Done
  Exit Function
SetupPaidThru_Error:
  ' Tell user there was an error
  MsgBox "Unexpected error setting up Paid Thru list: " & _
    Err & "," & Error, _
    vbCritical, gstrAppTitle
  ' Log it
  ErrorLog Me.Name & "_SetupPaidThru", Err, Error
  ' Bail
  Resume SetupPaidThru_Exit
End Function
```

An experienced programmer might ask why I didn't load the renewal options from the qryCurrentDuesRates query into an array in memory rather than loop through the recordset three times. To use an array, the code would have to dynamically allocate the memory using the ReDim statement and then read through the recordset at least once to load the array. Notice that the code doesn't close and reopen the recordset—it merely repositions to the beginning of the recordset each time. Unless you have dozens of renewal options, Access will load the entire recordset into memory, so moving through the recordset in this way is more efficient than allocating and loading additional memory.

Detecting Dues Not Paid

In the previous section, you entered a dues payment for Peter Waxman, but there are other members in the database whose dues are not current. To see what happens when one of these members signs in to a meeting, open the frmMeetings form. Go to the last meeting—a general meeting in January 2005—and click the Attendees button. In the Attendee Options dialog box, select the **Open the meeting sign-in form** option and click Go.

If you haven't changed the sample data, you should see 19 members already signed in to this meeting. In the **Sign In, Please** box, type the letters **wax** (the first three letters of Peter Waxman's last name), and press Enter. If you entered a dues payment as instructed in the previous section, the application should create an attendance record and issue no warnings, as shown in Figure 7-3.

Next, try to sign in Douglas Hite. Press Alt+S to return to the **Sign In, Please** box, type the letters **hit**, and press Enter. The application creates an attendance record, but warns you that dues are not paid, as shown in Figure 7-4.

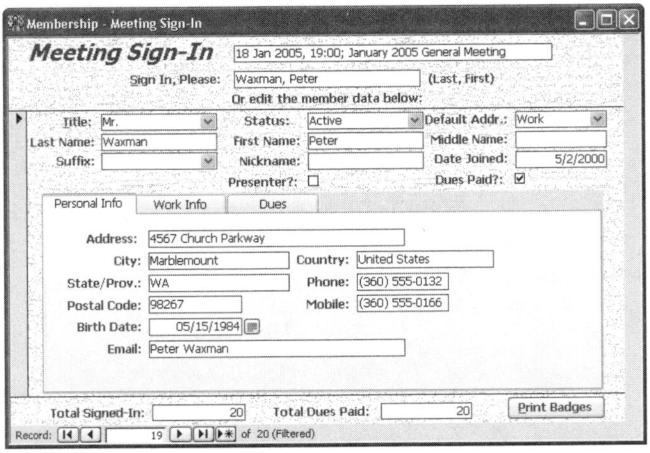

Figure 7-3   Recording the attendance of a member whose dues are paid.

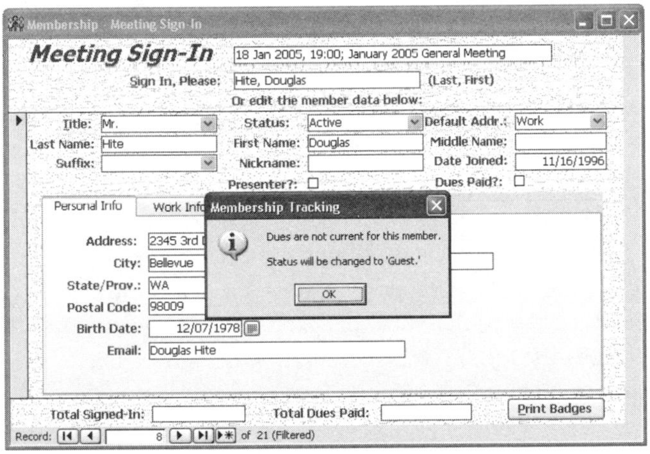

Figure 7-4   The Membership application warns you when a member whose dues are unpaid signs in to a meeting.

After you click OK, the application code changes the Status field to Guest as promised, and puts the focus on the Dues tab. You can ask the member if he'd like to renew his dues and immediately enter the renewal if he chooses to do so.

The code that makes this happen is in the KeyDown event of the **Sign In, Please** text box. After the procedure detects that you have pressed Tab or Enter, it adds the new member attendance record. It then performs a check to see if dues are paid through the current meeting date. The code is as follows:

```
' See if dues are paid - or Complimentary
If (IsNull(DLookup("MemberID", "tblDues", _
  "MemberID = " & lngNewMember & _
  " And PaidThru >= #" & frmMtg.MeetingDate & "#"))) And _
  (Me.MembershipStatus.Column(1) = "0") Then
```

```
' Issue message
MsgBox "Dues are not current for this member." & _
  vbCrLf & vbCrLf & "Status will be changed to 'Guest.'", _
  vbInformation, gstrAppTitle
' Make sure Dues are clear
Me.DuesPaid = False
' Save the change
Me.Dirty = False
' Change the status
DBEngine(0)(0).Execute "UPDATE tblMembers " & _
  "SET MembershipStatus = 'Guest' " & _
  "WHERE MemberID = " & lngNewMember, dbFailOnError
' Put focus on the Dues tab
Me.TabCtl0.Value = 2
Else
  ' Set dues paid
  Me.DuesPaid = True
  ' Save the change
  Me.Dirty = False
  ' Put focus on Title
  Me.Title.SetFocus
End If
```

The MembershipStatus combo box control has a Row Source property that displays the status (the displayed text), and also fetches the DuesComp field (not displayed) in the second column. The DuesComp field will be True (–1) for a status that is complimentary (Honorary and Speaker members), but False (0) for a member status that should pay dues. The *DLookup* function attempts to find a dues payment row for the current member that has a PaidThru date greater than or equal to the meeting date. If no record is found and the member's current status is one that should pay dues, the code issues the warning message, updates the record in tblMembers to Guest, and puts the focus on the Dues tab. If dues have been paid, the code sets the DuesPaid field in the attendance record to True and saves the change.

> **Tip**   The Access help topic on the Dirty property notes that the property is read/write—which means you can update the property from code. However, the help topic doesn't tell you what happens when you change the property. If the Dirty property is True (meaning the current record has been changed but not saved), you can set the property to False, and Access saves the changed record. Using this technique is not only more efficient but also safer than using RunCommand acCmdSaveRecord. When you use the RunCommand method, the command applies to whatever has the focus, which in a complex form with several subforms might not save what you intended. Setting the Dirty property of a specific form to False always saves the record being edited by that form.

If Doug decides to pay his dues, code in the AfterUpdate event of the Dues subform runs to verify that the dues are current. If the dues are paid, the code sets the record in tblMemberAttend to paid and updates the members status to Active.

The code is as follows:

```
Private Sub Form_AfterUpdate()
Dim db As DAO.Database, strSQL As String
  ' Set an error trap
  On Error GoTo AfterUpdate_Err
  ' See if member is paid now
  If Not IsNull(DLookup("MemberID", "tblDues", _
    "MemberID = " & Me.MemberID & _
    " And PaidThru >= #" & Form_frmMeetings.MeetingDate & "#")) Then
    ' Dues table says they've paid, set it - using a query
    Set db = DBEngine(0)(0)
    ' Set up the query
    strSQL = "UPDATE tblMemberAttend Set DuesPaid = -1 " & _
      "WHERE MemberID = " & Me.MemberID & _
      " AND MeetingID = " & Me.Parent.MeetingID
    ' Execute it
    db.Execute strSQL, dbFailOnError
    ' If current status is not Active
    If (Me.Parent.MembershipStatus <> "Active") Then
      ' Change the status to Active
      strSQL = "UPDATE tblMembers SET MembershipStatus = 'Active' " & _
        "WHERE MemberID = " & Me.MemberID
      ' Execute it
      db.Execute strSQL, dbFailOnError
    End If
    ' Refresh the parent
    Me.Parent.Refresh
    ' Clear the object
    Set db = Nothing
  End If
AfterUpdate_Exit:
  Exit Sub
AfterUpdate_Err:
  ' Tell user about error
  MsgBox "Unexpected error: " & Err & ", " & Error, _
    vbCritical, gstrAppTitle
  ' Log it
  ErrorLog Me.Name & "_Form_AfterUpdate", Err, Error
  ' Bail
  Resume AfterUpdate_Exit
End Sub
```

Reporting Dues Status

You can also find out which members will owe dues as of a certain date by creating a report that uses a parameter query. First, you need a query that finds the last expiration date for each member. You can find qryDuesExpire in the sample database, as shown in Figure 7-5 on the next page, that returns the Max PaidThru date for each MemberID.

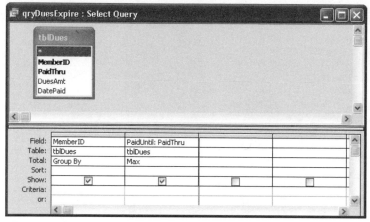

Figure 7-5   A query that finds the latest dues expiration date for each member.

You can use this query in a parameter query that fetches member data to determine whose dues will expire as of a specific date. You can find the qryRptDuesExpire query in the sample database, and the SQL for the query is as follows:

```
PARAMETERS [Forms]![fdlgDuesExpireParm]![txtExpireDate] DateTime;
SELECT ([Title]+" ") & [FirstName] & " " & ([MiddleName]+" ") & [LastName] & (", "+[Suffix])
AS MemberName, tblMembers.LastName, tblMembers.FirstName, tblMembers.MembershipStatus,
tlkpMembershipStatus.DuesComp, Choose([DefaultAddress],[WorkAddress],[HomeAddress]) AS
StreetAddr, Choose([DefaultAddress],[WorkCity] & ", " & [WorkStateOrProvince] & " " &
[WorkPostalCode],[HomeCity] & ", " & [HomeStateOrProvince] & " " & [HomePostalCode]) AS CSZ,
tblMembers.WorkPhone, tblMembers.WorkExtension, tblMembers.WorkFax, tblMembers.HomePhone,
tblMembers.MobilePhone, Replace(Mid([EmailName],InStr([EmailName],"MailTo:")+7),"#","") AS
Email, qryDuesExpire.PaidUntil, [Forms]![fdlgDuesExpireParm]![txtExpireDate] AS ExpireBy
FROM tlkpMembershipStatus INNER JOIN (tblMembers LEFT JOIN qryDuesExpire ON
tblMembers.MemberID = qryDuesExpire.MemberID) ON tlkpMembershipStatus.MemberShipStatus =
tblMembers.MembershipStatus
WHERE (((tlkpMembershipStatus.DuesComp)=False) AND ((qryDuesExpire.PaidUntil) Is Null Or
(qryDuesExpire.PaidUntil)<[Forms]![fdlgDuesExpireParm]![txtExpireDate]));
```

In addition to assembling the parts of the member name into one field, the query uses the *Choose* function to display the correct default address and city, state, and postal code for each member. The query uses an outer join from tblMembers to qryDuesExpire because some members might not have any dues payment records. You want to look at all member records regardless of whether the member has ever paid dues. Finally, the WHERE clause eliminates any members that have a complimentary dues status and includes members with no dues record or whose latest dues record has a PaidUntil date that is earlier than the date you entered in the parameter.

The fdlgDuesExpireParm form is a simple dialog box form that lets you enter the date you want to test, as shown in Figure 7-6.

Figure 7-6   The parameter form referenced by the query that returns members whose dues have expired by the date entered.

To run the report that displays the members whose dues will expire by the date you select, open the frmReports form (or click Reports on the main switchboard form), and click the Upcoming Dues button. The report opens the fdlgDuesExpireParm form, and the report runs when you click the Print button on that form. If you run the report with a date in February 2005, you should see the result shown in Figure 7-7.

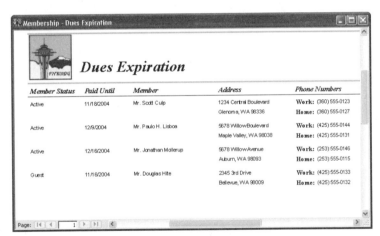

Figure 7-7   The Dues Expiration report.

The real key to the report is the query that is its record source, the qryRptDuesExpire query shown earlier. However, the report also shows you an interesting way to resolve parameters for the report with a user-friendly form. This technique depends on the fact that a report doesn't start to open its record source until after the report Open event completes. So, you can open a dialog box form in that event and hide the form after the user enters the parameter. Hiding the form allows the Open event to complete, but you must leave the form open so that the parameter in the record source can be resolved without further prompting the user. Here is the code in this report's Open event:

```
Private Sub Report_Open(Cancel As Integer)
    ' Open the parameter dialog box
    DoCmd.OpenForm "fdlgDuesExpireParm", WindowMode:=acDialog
    ' If the user closed the form (canceled)
```

```
    If Not IsFormLoaded("fdlgDuesExpireParm") Then
        ' Cancel this report
        Cancel = True
    End If
End Sub
```

Notice that the code checks to be sure the form is still open. If you click the Cancel button on the form, it closes. When the form is no longer open, the Open event code discovers this by calling the *IsFormLoaded* function that you can find in the modUtility module. When the form is no longer open, the code cancels the Open event, and the report never appears. If you execute a DoCmd.OpenReport for this report in code elsewhere (this command is executed in the Click event procedure for the cmdDues command button on the frmReports form), you'll also need an error trap in that code to trap the 2501 cancel error or ignore errors. If you don't do that, the code that issued the DoCmd.OpenReport will cause Access to display an error to the user if the user cancels the Dues Expiration dialog box.

Chapter 8
Sending Out Notices

In the previous chapter, you learned techniques for tracking member status and dues payments and reporting members whose dues have expired. But you probably don't want to wait until a member shows up at the next meeting to try to collect dues. As you've worked with the Membership Tracking database, you've probably noticed that it's easy to enter meeting agendas and announcement information for each meeting. But you also want to be to be able to send notices to members in advance of each meeting—either via regular mail or by e-mail. This chapter shows you how to solve both of these problems.

Printing Notices

Today many people have computers and e-mail addresses. But for some types of organizations, a large percentage of the membership might not have a computer or an e-mail address. So, any membership application needs a way to print out notices that can be mailed to members.

Printing Dues Expiration Letters

To construct a letter to send to members whose dues have expired or are about to expire, you need much of the same information that you gathered for the Dues Expiration report in Chapter 7, "Checking Member Status," in the qryRptDuesExpire query. Because you're mailing a letter, you don't need the phone numbers included in that report. Also, you should include a parameter that obtains a date value from a form specifically designed for sending out notices. You can find a query designed for this purpose, qryRptDuesExpireLetter, in the Membership sample database (Membership.mdb). The SQL for the query is as follows:

```
PARAMETERS [Forms]![fdlgNoticeChoices]![txtDate] DateTime;
SELECT tblMembers.MemberID, ([Title]+" ") & [FirstName] & " " & ([MiddleName]+" ") & [LastName]
& (", "+[Suffix]) AS MemberName, tblMembers.LastName, tblMembers.FirstName,
tblMembers.Nickname, NZ([NickName],[FirstName]) AS Salutation, tblMembers.MembershipStatus,
tlkpMembershipStatus.DuesComp, Choose([DefaultAddress],[WorkAddress],[HomeAddress]) AS
```

```
StreetAddr, Choose([DefaultAddress],[WorkCity] & ", " & [WorkStateOrProvince] & " " &
[WorkPostalCode],[HomeCity] & ", " & [HomeStateOrProvince] & " " & [HomePostalCode]) AS CSZ,
Replace(Mid([EmailName],InStr([EmailName],"MailTo:")+7),"#","") AS Email,
qryDuesExpire.PaidUntil, [Forms]![fdlgNoticeChoices]![txtDate] AS ExpireBy
FROM tlkpMembershipStatus
INNER JOIN (tblMembers
LEFT JOIN qryDuesExpire
ON tblMembers.MemberID = qryDuesExpire.MemberID)
ON tlkpMembershipStatus.MembershipStatus = tblMembers.MembershipStatus
WHERE (((tlkpMembershipStatus.DuesComp)=False) AND ((qryDuesExpire.PaidUntil) Is Null Or
(qryDuesExpire.PaidUntil)<[Forms]![fdlgNoticeChoices]![txtDate]));
```

> **Note**   You don't need the e-mail address to mail a dues expiration letter, but you'll see later that I use this same query to send the notices by e-mail.

> **Tip**   As you can see in the qryRptDuesExpireLetter query, the MemberName field concatenates the Title, FirstName, MiddleName, LastName, and Suffix fields and includes appropriate spacing and punctuation. However, many member records might not have a Title, Middle-Name, or Suffix. In a string expression in Access, you can use either the & operator or the + operator to concatenate strings. The difference is the & operator ignores Null values and returns all the non-Null values concatenated together. The + operator, however, returns nothing if any part of the expression is Null—also known as Null propagation. The expression for the MemberName field takes advantage of Null propagation provided by the + operator to eliminate the space after Title and MiddleName if either is Null and to eliminate the comma and space before Suffix if that is Null.

Remember that the qryDuesExpire query returns the latest dues expiration date for each member, but some members (such those who have attended meetings only as a guest) might have never paid dues at all. This is why you must include not only records with an expiration date earlier than the parameter date but also records that have no expiration date (Is Null).

In each letter, it would also be nice to include a list of the current renewal options so that the member can choose a dues amount and related renewal extension length. You might remember from Chapter 7 that the qryCurrentDuesRates query returns the current rate for each different renewal interval. You can combine that query with the records from the qryDuesExpire query to calculate a new expiration date for each interval for each member. If the member has never paid dues, you can display an informative message about the expiration of any first-time payment of dues. You can find the qryRsubDuesExpireLetter query that fetches these rows in the Membership sample database. The SQL for the query is as follows:

```
SELECT qryDuesExpire.MemberID, [DuesInterval] & " months" AS [Renew For],
qryCurrentDuesRates.DuesAmt, NZ(DateAdd("m",[DuesInterval],[PaidUntil]),[DuesInterval] & "
months from date paid.") AS [Renew Until]
FROM qryDuesExpire, qryCurrentDuesRates
WHERE NZ(DateAdd("m",[DuesInterval],[PaidUntil]),Date())>=Date()
ORDER BY qryDuesExpire.MemberID, qryCurrentDuesRates.DuesInterval;
```

The query uses the *DateAdd* function to add the number of months specified in the DuesInterval field from the qryCurrentDuesRates query to the member's last expiration date. When the member has never paid dues, the *DateAdd* function returns a Null value. The *NZ* function examines that value, and if it is Null, substitutes a message that dues will expire [DuesInterval] months from the date the member first pays dues. The query also eliminates any rows where adding the renewal interval to the last paid until date would result in a date in the past.

Notice that there is no join specification in the From clause of this query. This query matches each row from the qryDuesExpire query with each row in the qryCurrentDuesRates query. You know that the qryDuesExpire query returns exactly one row per member, and the qryCurrentDuesRates query returns one row per available renewal interval. When you use this query as the record source for a subreport in a letter for each member, you can link the subreport on the MemberID field to display the renewal options pertinent for each member.

As with most reports, designing the query that the report needs is the hard part. The design of the rsubDuesExpireLetter report is quite simple. It displays the Renew For, DuesAmt, and Renew Until fields calculated by the qryRsubDuesExpireLetter query. Figure 8-1 shows you the design of this report that is embedded in the final report that produces the letter.

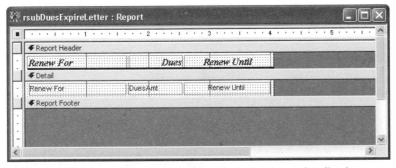

Figure 8-1 The rsubDuesExpireLetter report that is used to list dues renewal options for each member.

The report to print the letter (rptDuesExpireLetter) is fairly straightforward. Figure 8-2, on the next page, shows you the design of this report.

The salutation line uses an expression that includes the Salutation field calculated in the query (use the Nickname field unless it is null; otherwise use the FirstName field). The expression is as follows:

```
="Dear " & [Salutation] & ":"
```

Code that executes when the report opens uses the qryCurrentTreasurer query to fetch the name of the member who is the treasurer as of the date you print the report. It also loads the two template messages stored in the ztblDuesMessages table (one for new members, and one for current members) into module variables. The SQL for the qryCurrentTreasurer query is as follows:

```
SELECT tblOfficers.OfficerType, tblOfficers.ServedTo, [FirstName] & " " & ([MiddleName]+" ")
& [LastName] & (", "+[Suffix]) AS MemberName
FROM tblMembers
INNER JOIN tblOfficers
ON tblMembers.MemberID = tblOfficers.MemberID
WHERE (((tblOfficers.OfficerType)="Treasurer") AND ((tblOfficers.ServedTo) Is Null Or
(tblOfficers.ServedTo)>=Date()));
```

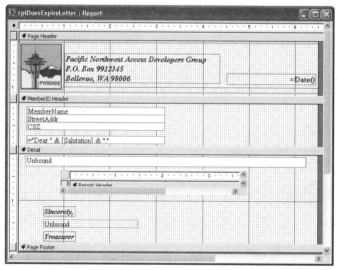

Figure 8-2   The rptDuesExpireLetter report in Design view.

The Format event procedure for the Detail section creates the text of the letter and assigns that text to the unbound text box control at the top of the Detail section. This text box control has its Can Grow property set to Yes, so the text box expands to display all the text when you view or print the report. Code in that event procedure also inserts the treasurer name in the unbound text box that you see below the subreport control. The code in the Format event of the Detail section that inserts both the text of the letter and the treasurer name is as follows:

```
Option Compare Database
Option Explicit
' Place to save treasurer name in Open
Dim strTreasurer As String
' Place to save the new member message
Dim strNewMemberMsg As String
' Place to save the expired dues message
Dim strDuesExpireMsg As String
Private Sub Detail_Format(Cancel As Integer, FormatCount As Integer)
Dim strExpire As String
  ' Set the treasurer name
  Me.txtTreasurer = strTreasurer
  ' If a Guest or never paid dues
```

```
    If (Me.MembershipStatus = "Guest") Or _
      IsNull(Me.PaidUntil) Then
      ' Make letter an offer to join
      Me.txtMsg = strNewMemberMsg
    Else
      ' If already expired
      If Me.PaidUntil < Date Then
        ' Set expired on
        strExpire = "Your membership expired on " & _
          Format(Me.PaidUntil, "mmmm d, yyyy")
      Else
        ' Set will expire
        strExpire = "Your membership expires on " & _
          Format(Me.PaidUntil, "mmmm d, yyyy")
      End If
      ' Set the message
      Me.txtMsg = strExpire & ".  " & strDuesExpireMsg
    End If
End Sub
```

The module variables strTreasurer, strNewMemberMsg, and strDuesExpireMsg are set by
code in the report Open event procedure. The code first opens a query that returns the current treasurer name based on today's date. The code then opens the ztblDuesMessages table
that contains the text to be displayed for current and new members. Using a table in this way
allows the user to modify the messages printed in the dues expiration report without having
to change the report design. The code is as follows:

```
Private Sub Report_Open(Cancel As Integer)
Dim rst As DAO.Recordset
  ' Get the current Treasurer name
  Set rst = DBEngine(0)(0).OpenRecordset("qryCurrentTreasurer")
  If Not rst.EOF Then
    strTreasurer = rst!MemberName
  End If
  ' Close out
  rst.Close
  ' Now open the template table
  Set rst = DBEngine(0)(0).OpenRecordset("ztblDuesMessages")
  ' Process the rows
  Do Until rst.EOF
    ' Decide which template we're loading
    Select Case rst!Template
      ' New member
      Case "New Member"
        ' Save the template
        strNewMemberMsg = rst!TemplateText
      ' Existing member
      Case "Current Member"
        ' Save the template
        strDuesExpireMsg = rst!TemplateText
    End Select
    ' Get the next row
    rst.MoveNext
  Loop
```

```
    ' Close out
    rst.Close
    Set rst = Nothing
End Sub
```

You can run this report by starting the application (open the frmSplash form) and clicking the Notices button on the main switchboard. The application opens the fdlgNoticeChoices form—remember, this form is referenced in the record source of the report. Select Dues Expiration Notice, choose a date, select Print Notices, and click Go, as shown in Figure 8-3, to see the report.

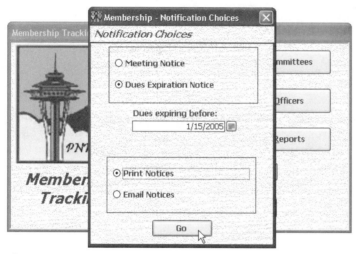

Figure 8-3 Running the Dues Expiration Notice report.

The code that responds to clicking the command button is simple. It examines the options you picked and either opens the appropriate report or calls a procedure to generate e-mails.

Printing Meeting Announcements

The Pacific Northwest Access Developers Group sends out regular notices about upcoming meetings. The group secretary will often include various special announcements as well as the actual agenda of the meeting. Some of these announcements should display or print before the agenda items (such as a notice about a meeting location change or special topic that should receive special attention), and some of the announcements should print after the agenda items at the end of the notice (such as a thank you to a sponsor who has provided door prizes).

You can see how the secretary enters agenda items and announcements for a meeting by opening the frmMeetings form in the Membership application. Figure 8-4 shows you the agenda items for one of the meetings, and Figure 8-5 shows you the announcements.

Note that the announcements subform lets the secretary specify whether the announcement is to appear before or after the agenda items. The Before / After combo box actually stores the number 0 for Before and the number 2 for After.

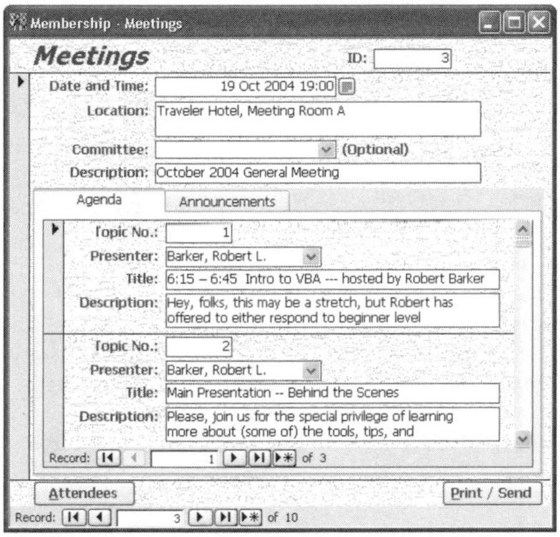

Figure 8-4   Entering agenda items for a meeting.

Figure 8-5   Entering announcements for a meeting.

To produce all the rows you need for a meeting announcement in the correct order, you can use a union query to select the before rows for announcements, the agenda items, and the after rows for announcements. To put the rows in the correct sequence, you can generate a number literal with a value of 1 to put the agenda rows in the middle. (Now you know why before announcements are 0 and after announcements are 2!) The query that performs this task is qryRptMeetingAnnouncement, and the SQL for the query is as shown on the next page.

```
SELECT tblMeetings.MeetingID, tblMeetings.MeetingDate, tblMeetings.MeetingLocation,
tblMeetings.CommitteeName, tblMeetings.MeetingDescription,
tblMeetingAnnouncements.AnnounceNo, tblMeetingAnnouncements.AnnounceTitle,
tblMeetingAnnouncements.AnnounceDescription, tblMeetingAnnouncements.BeforeAfter
FROM tblMeetings
INNER JOIN tblMeetingAnnouncements
ON tblMeetings.MeetingID = tblMeetingAnnouncements.MeetingID
WHERE tblMeetingAnnouncements.BeforeAfter=0
UNION ALL
SELECT tblMeetings.MeetingID, tblMeetings.MeetingDate, tblMeetings.MeetingLocation,
tblMeetings.CommitteeName, tblMeetings.MeetingDescription, tblMeetingAgenda.TopicNo,
tblMeetingAgenda.TopicTitle, tblMeetingAgenda.TopicDescription, 1 AS BeforeAfter
FROM tblMeetings
INNER JOIN tblMeetingAgenda
ON tblMeetings.MeetingID = tblMeetingAgenda.MeetingID
UNION ALL
SELECT tblMeetings.MeetingID, tblMeetings.MeetingDate, tblMeetings.MeetingLocation,
tblMeetings.CommitteeName, tblMeetings.MeetingDescription,
tblMeetingAnnouncements.AnnounceNo, tblMeetingAnnouncements.AnnounceTitle,
tblMeetingAnnouncements.AnnounceDescription, tblMeetingAnnouncements.BeforeAfter
FROM tblMeetings
INNER JOIN tblMeetingAnnouncements
ON tblMeetings.MeetingID = tblMeetingAnnouncements.MeetingID
WHERE tblMeetingAnnouncements.BeforeAfter=2
ORDER BY MeetingID, BeforeAfter, AnnounceNo;
```

> **Note**   You might be tempted to create a report that uses a query on the tblMeetings table and uses subreports for the records from the tblMeetingAgenda table and the tblMeeting-Announcements table. However, when a subreport generates more data rows than will fit on a page, producing headers at the top of subsequent pages will be difficult. It's much easier to create a single recordset that joins the tblMeetings table with either the tblMeetingAgenda table or the tblMeetingAnnouncements table and not use subreports.

Because all the work is done by the query, the report layout is simple. Figure 8-6 shows you the design of the rptMeetingAnnouncement report.

The MeetingID Header section has the Force New Page property set to Before Section, and the Repeat Section property set to Yes. The AnnounceNo Header section also has its Repeat Section property set to Yes so that all the details of the meeting and the title of each topic will print again at the top of a new page when the announcement or agenda item description overflows a page.

You can print a meeting announcement either by clicking the Notices button on the main switchboard or by opening the meeting you want and clicking the Print/Send button (as shown in Figure 8-4) on the Meetings form. In either case, you'll see the fdlgNoticeChoices form shown earlier in Figure 8-3, but you'll also see a combo box to select the meeting to print when you select the Meeting Notice option. Figure 8-7 shows you the first part of the announcement for the October 2004 general meeting.

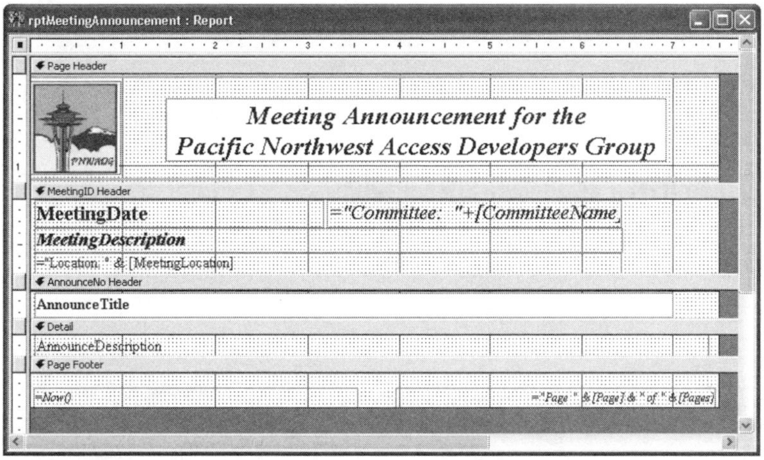

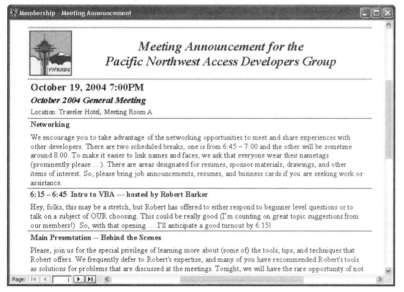

Figure 8-6   The design of the rptMeetingAnnouncement report.

Figure 8-7   The Meeting Announcement report.

Sending Notices by E-Mail

You might think that mailing notices is old technology in this modern era of the Internet and e-mail, and you might be right. The good news is that designing the two reports to send out dues expiration notices and meeting announcements has laid the groundwork for creating e-mails that serve the same function.

To make your e-mails look their best, you should format them as HTML so that you can use various fonts and include graphics. You could painstakingly write the HTML code you need in the procedure that formats and sends your e-mails. Or, you could use an HTML editor such as Microsoft FrontPage to design a template and then store the pieces of the template you need in a table. I chose the latter method, and you can find the parts of the templates used in the next two sections saved in the ztblHTMLTemplates table.

Sending Dues Expiration Notices by E-Mail

Because I decided to use templates to build the HTML, I first built a sample Web page for the dues expiration messages. You can find this template file in the sample files saved as DuesExpireTemplate.html. Figure 8-8 shows you the template displayed in Microsoft Internet Explorer.

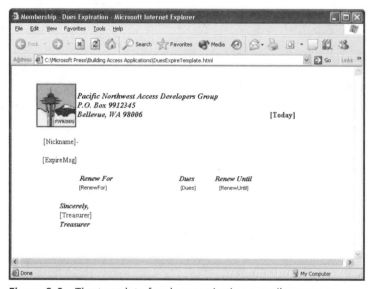

Figure 8-8   The template for dues expiration e-mail messages.

You can see that I embedded keywords in the HTML ([Today], [Nickname], [ExpireMsg], and so on) to make it easy to customize each message. You can find the template broken into three pieces as records in the ztblHTMLTemplates table—the top part of the message including the Nickname and ExpireMsg keywords, the renewal option line that might appear several times, and the signature lines.

You can try this out by starting the application (open the frmSplash form), clicking Notices on the main switchboard, selecting Dues Expiration Notice in the Notification Choices dialog box, selecting an expiration date, selecting the option to Email Notices (the default), and click-ing the Go button. You might see several e-mails generated, but unless you've entered dues payments to bring all members up to date, you should see at least one. Because all the e-mail addresses in the database are fictitious, the code in the application merely displays the e-mail messages rather than sending them. Figure 8-9 shows you a formatted message.

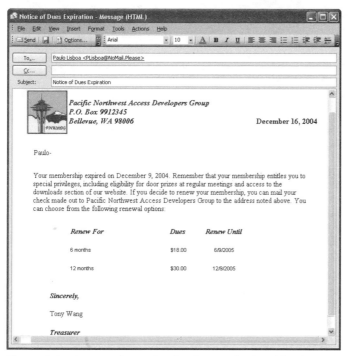

Figure 8-9   An e-mail sent by the dues expired notification procedure.

Although I set up template records in advance to make assembling the e-mail message easier, the code that performs this task in the fdlgNoticeChoices form isn't simple at all. The code is in the *DuesEmail* function in the form's module, and that function is called from the procedure that responds to clicking the Go button when you select the Dues Expiration Notice and Email Notices options. The first part of the function gets the current treasurer's name and the two different dues messages—similar to the code in the rptDuesExpireLetter report you saw earlier. It borrows the query for that report to find out all the members whose dues expire by the date specified on the form. Note that to open a parameter query in code, you must first open the QueryDef object, set the parameter, and then open a recordset on the QueryDef. When the code finds no members with dues expiring by the specified date, it displays a message and exits. The code is as follows:

```
Private Function DuesEmail() As Integer
Dim db As DAO.Database, qd As DAO.QueryDef, rstRenew As DAO.Recordset
Dim rstTemplate As DAO.Recordset, rstData As DAO.Recordset
Dim strTo As String, strTitle As String, strHTML As String
Dim strWork As String, strTreasurerName As String
    ' Set an error trap
    On Error GoTo DuesEmail_Err
    ' Point to this database
    Set db = DBEngine(0)(0)
    ' Get the current Treasurer name
    Set rstData = db.OpenRecordset("qryCurrentTreasurer")
    If Not rstData.EOF Then
```

```
        strTreasurerName = rstData!MemberName
    End If
    ' Close out
    rstData.Close
    ' Now open the dues messages table
    Set rstData = db.OpenRecordset("ztblDuesMessages")
    ' Process the rows
    Do Until rstData.EOF
      ' Decide which template we're loading
      Select Case rstData!Template
        ' New member
        Case "New Member"
          ' Save the template
          strNewMemberMsg = rstData!TemplateText
        ' Existing member
        Case "Current Member"
          ' Save the template
          strDuesExpireMsg = rstData!TemplateText
      End Select
      ' Get the next row
      rstData.MoveNext
    Loop
    ' Close out
    rstData.Close
    ' Get the query that the report uses
    Set qd = db.QueryDefs("qryRptDuesExpireLetter")
    ' Set its parameter
    qd.Parameters(0) = Me.txtDate
    ' Open the recordset
    Set rstData = qd.OpenRecordset
    ' See if any records
    If rstData.RecordCount = 0 Then
      ' Tell the user
      MsgBox "No member dues expire before the date you specified.", _
        vbInformation, gstrAppTitle
      ' Close out
      rstData.Close
      Set rstData = Nothing
      Set qd = Nothing
      Set db = Nothing
      ' Bail
      Exit Function
    End If
```

Next, the code opens the HTML template records for the dues expiration notice. This code expects the template to be broken into three parts:

1. A header with the logo, address, date, person name, message body, and the heading of the dues renewal table.

2. The dues renewal line, which the code might use multiple times.

3. The footer that contains the treasurer name.

The code processes each member's dues expiration record (for members whose dues expire by the date you specified) by fetching the first part of the template and filling in the date, person name, and expiration message. Notice that the *Replace* function works well to find the template keywords and replace them with the actual text. The code is as follows:

```
' Open the HTML template for email
Set rstTemplate = db.OpenRecordset( _
  "SELECT * FROM ztblHTMLTemplates " & _
  "WHERE Template = 'Dues' " & _
  "ORDER By TemplateSeq")
' Process the members one at a time
Do Until rstData.EOF
  ' Make sure we're at the start of the template records
  rstTemplate.MoveFirst
  ' Grab the first part
  strWork = rstTemplate!TemplateHTML
  ' Put in today's date
  strWork = Replace(strWork, "[Today]", Format(Date, "mmmm d, yyyy"))
  ' Put in the person's first name or nickname
  strWork = Replace(strWork, "[Nickname]", rstData!Salutation)
  ' If a Guest or never paid dues
  If (rstData!MembershipStatus = "Guest") Or _
    IsNull(rstData!PaidUntil) Then
    ' Make letter an offer to join
    strMsg = strNewMemberMsg
  Else
    ' If already expired
    If rstData!PaidUntil < Date Then
      ' Set expired on
      strExpire = "Your membership expired on " & _
        Format(rstData!PaidUntil, "mmmm d, yyyy")
    Else
      ' Set will expire
      strExpire = "Your membership expires on " & _
        Format(rstData!PaidUntil, "mmmm d, yyyy")
    End If
    ' Set the message
    strMsg = strExpire & ".  " & strDuesExpireMsg
  End If
  ' Replace the message in the HTML
  strWork = Replace(strWork, "[ExpireMsg]", strMsg)
  ' Stuff what we have so far in the HTML variable
  strHTML = strWork
```

Next, the code gets the second part of the template to fill in the renewal option lines. The code opens the renewal options recordset for this member, using the same query that is also the record source for the rsubDuesExpireLetter subreport. Using the template, it fills in the Renew For, Dues, and Renew Until values and adds each row one at a time to the HTML built to this point. The code is as follows:

```
' Move to the next template row
rstTemplate.MoveNext
' Open a recordset on the renew options for this person
```

```
Set rstRenew = db.OpenRecordset("SELECT * FROM " & _
    "qryRsubDuesExpireLetter " & _
    "WHERE MemberID = " & rstData!MemberID)
' Loop and insert the options
Do Until rstRenew.EOF
    ' Get the template for the expire option rows
    strWork = rstTemplate!TemplateHTML
    ' Put in Renew For months
    strWork = Replace(strWork, "[RenewFor]", rstRenew![Renew For])
    ' Put in Dues
    strWork = Replace(strWork, "[Dues]", _
        Format(rstRenew!DuesAmt, "Currency"))
    ' Put in new expire date
    strWork = Replace(strWork, "[RenewUntil]", rstRenew![Renew Until])
    ' Add to the HTML
    strHTML = strHTML & strWork
    ' Get the next renewal option
    rstRenew.MoveNext
Loop
' Close the renewal recordset
rstRenew.Close
Set rstRenew = Nothing
```

Finally, the code gets the last part of the template for this member's message, fills in the treasurer name, and calls the *SendOutlookMsg* function to send the message on its way. The code is as follows:

```
' Get the last piece of the template
rstTemplate.MoveNext
' Get the HTML
strWork = rstTemplate!TemplateHTML
' "sign" the letter
strWork = Replace(strWork, "[Treasurer]", strTreasurerName)
' Finish the HTML
strHTML = strHTML & strWork
' Send the email
If Not (SendOutlookMsg("Notice of Dues Expiration", _
    rstData!FirstName & " " & rstData!LastName & _
    "<" & rstData!Email & ">", strHTML)) Then
    ' Got failure - tell the user
    MsgBox "Notice to " & rstData!FirstName & " " & _
        rstData!LastName & " failed.", vbCritical, gstrAppTitle
End If
' Move to the next member record
rstData.MoveNext
Loop
' Close the member data and template
rstData.Close
Set rstData = Nothing
rstTemplate.Close
Set rstTemplate = Nothing
Set qd = Nothing
Set db = Nothing
' All worked - return success
DuesEmail = True
```

```
DuesEmail_Exit:
  Exit Function
DuesEmail_Err:
  ' Tell user about an error
  MsgBox "Unexpected error: " & Err & ", " & Error, _
    vbCritical, gstrAppTitle
  ' Bail
  Resume DuesEmail_Exit
End Function
```

You can find the code for the *SendOutlookMsg* function in the modOutlook module. If you look at the references for the Membership project (open the Visual Basic Editor and choose References from the Tools menu), you'll find that I did not include a reference to the Outlook library. I did this so you can run this application on any machine that has Microsoft Outlook 2000, 2002, or 2003 installed. If I referenced a specific library, none of the code would run on a machine that had another version installed because the project would have a library reference error.

To make this code work, I used a coding technique called *late binding*. Rather than declare objects from the Outlook library, I declared the objects I need simply As Object. The code uses the *CreateObject* function to start a copy of Outlook and get a reference to its Application object. The code then uses the CreateItem method of the Application object to create a new e-mail message, set its Subject property, the To or BCC property, and the HTMLBody property using the parameters passed to the function. Finally, the code executes the Display method to show you the result. The code is as follows:

```
Option Compare Database
Option Explicit
Const olMailItem = 0
Public Function SendOutlookMsg(strSubject As String, strTo As String, _
    strHTML As String, Optional intUseBCC As Integer = 0) As Integer
' Function to send an email message using Outlook
' Inputs: Subject of the message
'         List of valid "To" email addresses
'         HTML for the body of the message
'         Send using BCC flag (optional)
' Output: True if successful
' Note: This demo version only formats and displays a new
'       message.  Use ObjMail.Send instead of .Display
'       to actually send the message
Dim objOL As Object, objMail As Object
  ' Set an error trap
  On Error GoTo SendOutlookMsg_Err
  ' Get a pointer to Outlook - late binding
  Set objOL = CreateObject("Outlook.Application")
  ' Create a new email
  Set objMail = objOL.CreateItem(olMailItem)
  ' Set the subject
  objMail.Subject = strSubject
  ' Set To or BCC
  If intUseBCC = True Then
```

```
      objMail.BCC = strTo
  Else
      objMail.To = strTo
  End If
  ' Insert the HTML of the message
  objMail.HTMLBody = strHTML
  ' Display it
  objMail.Display
  ' Done - clear objects
  Set objMail = Nothing
  Set objOL = Nothing
  ' Return true
  SendOutlookMsg = True
SendOutlookMsg_Exit:
  Exit Function
SendOutlookMsg_Err:
  ' Log the error
  ErrorLog "SendOutlookMsg", Err, Error
  ' Bail
  Resume SendOutlookMsg_Exit
End Function
```

Tip   If you look carefully at the templates I created for the HTML the code builds, you'll notice that the code embeds the logo by making a reference to a graphics file on my Web site. The HTML code is as follows:

```
<img src="http://www.viescas.com/PNWADGLogoSmall.gif" width="89" height="94">
```

Although you can include an image directly in an HTML format e-mail message from the user interface and send the graphic embedded in the message, doing so from code is extremely tricky. You must first add the graphic as an attachment and then establish a Messaging Application Programming Interface (MAPI) session for the mail item so that you can change the attributes of the attachment to mark it embedded and create the Content ID (CID) you need to be able to reference the image within your HTML. Unfortunately, some of the methods you must use in the MAPI session are undocumented, and I'm always loath to recommend such techniques. You can read more about this technique at fellow Outlook MVP Sue Mosher's Web site: *http://www.outlookcode.com/d/code/htmlimg.htm*.

Sending a Meeting Announcement by E-Mail

As you might suspect, I also used an HTML template to construct a meeting announcement. You can find this template file saved as MeetingAnnouncementTemplate.html in the sample files. Figure 8-10 shows you the template displayed in Microsoft Internet Explorer.

You can see that I embedded keywords in the HTML ([MeetingDate], [Committee], [MeetingDescription], and so on) to make it easy to customize the message. You can try this out by opening the frmMeetings form, selecting one of the general meetings (they are more interesting), clicking the Print/Send button, and clicking the Go button in the Notification Choices dialog box. As noted earlier, because all the e-mail addresses in the database are fictitious, the code in the application merely displays the e-mail message rather than sending it. For meetings, the code also places the e-mail addresses on the Bcc line of the message. Figure 8-11 shows you a formatted meeting announcement. You can click on any of the topic lines to jump to that topic or announcement because the code generates internal hyperlinks to bookmarks.

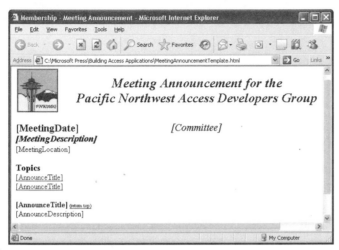

Figure 8-10   The template for meeting announcement messages.

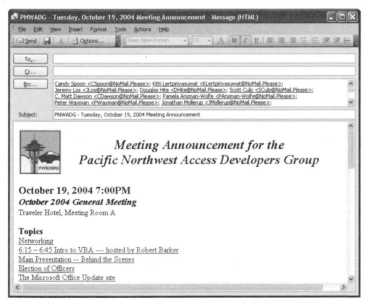

Figure 8-11   A meeting notice ready to send via e-mail.

In some ways, the code to assemble this message is somewhat less complex because it has to generate only one message to multiple recipients. However, the code to assemble the topic index and the topics is trickier. You can find the code in the *AnnouncementEmail* function in the code module for the fdlgNoticeChoices form. The code begins by opening a recordset on the same union query used by the rptMeetingAnnouncement report, but filtered for the MeetingID that you selected on the form. If the recordset contains no records, the code tells the user and exits. The code is as follows:

```
Private Function AnnouncementEmail() As Integer
Dim db As DAO.Database, rstAnnounce As DAO.Recordset
Dim rstTemplate As DAO.Recordset, rstData As DAO.Recordset
Dim strTo As String, strTitle As String, strHTML As String
Dim strWork As String, strBody As String, strTopics As String
Dim strTopicIndexTemp As String, strTopicTemp As String, strFootTemp As String
Dim intTopicNo As Integer, datMtgDate As Date
  ' Set an error trap
  On Error GoTo AnnounceEmail_Err
  ' Point to this database
  Set db = DBEngine(0)(0)
  ' Open the query that the report uses
  ' -- filtered on the meeting selected
  Set rstAnnounce = db.OpenRecordset("SELECT * " & _
    "FROM qryRptMeetingAnnouncement WHERE MeetingID = " & Me.cmbMeeting)
  ' See if any records
  If rstAnnounce.RecordCount = 0 Then
    ' Tell the user
    MsgBox "The meeting you selected has no announcement " & _
      "or agenda records.", vbInformation, gstrAppTitle
    ' Close out
    rstAnnounce.Close
    Set rstAnnounce = Nothing
    Set db = Nothing
    ' Bail
    Exit Function
  End If
```

Next, the code assembles a list of recipients. If the meeting is for a committee, the code uses the qryAnnounceEmailCommittee query to fetch the current members of the committee. If the meeting is a general meeting, the code uses the qryAnnounceEmail query to get a list of all members except those with Inactive status. The code is as follows:

```
  ' Get the list of members
  ' If a committee meeting,
  If Not IsNothing(rstAnnounce!CommitteeName) Then
    ' Get the list of members on this committee
    Set rstData = db.OpenRecordset( _
      "SELECT * FROM qryAnnounceEmailCommittee " & _
      "WHERE CommitteeName = '" & rstAnnounce!CommitteeName & _
      "' AND ((DateLeft Is Null) Or (DateLeft > #" & _
      rstAnnounce!MeetingDate & "#))")
    ' Make sure we have some
    If rstData.RecordCount = 0 Then
      ' Ask if they want to send to entire list or bail
      If vbYes = MsgBox("There are no members currently assigned " & _
        "to the " & rstAnnounce!CommitteeName & " Committee.  Do you " & _
        "want to send an announcement to all members?", _
```

```
            vbQuestion + vbYesNo + vbDefaultButton2, gstrAppTitle) Then
              ' Close this one
              rstData.Close
              ' Open for all members
              Set rstData = db.OpenRecordset("qryAnnounceEmail")
          Else
              ' Close out
              rstData.Close
              Set rstData = Nothing
              rstAnnounce.Close
              Set rstAnnounce = Nothing
              Set db = Nothing
              ' Bail
              Exit Function
          End If
      End If
  Else
      ' Open a recordset on all active members
      Set rstData = db.OpenRecordset("qryAnnounceEmail")
  End If
  ' Build the "To" list
  Do Until rstData.EOF
      ' Add an email name
      strTo = strTo & rstData!FirstName & " " & _
          rstData!LastName & _
          "<" & rstData!Email & ">" & ";"
      ' Get the next record
      rstData.MoveNext
  Loop
  ' Close the recordset
  rstData.Close
  Set rstData = Nothing
```

Next, the code opens the HTML template records for the meeting announcement. This code expects the template to be broken into four parts:

1. A header with the logo, meeting date and time, committee name, meeting description, meeting location, and the header of the topics list.

2. The topics index line.

3. The topic title and full description, which the code uses once per topic.

4. The footer to close out the HTML.

The code gets the header and replaces all the relevant template marker fields with the data from the first row in the announcement recordset. The code is as follows:

```
  ' Open the HTML template for email
  Set rstTemplate = db.OpenRecordset( _
      "SELECT * FROM ztblHTMLTemplates " & _
      "WHERE Template = 'Announcement' " & _
      "ORDER By TemplateSeq")
  ' The first record has the header - copy it
  strHTML = rstTemplate!TemplateHTML
```

```
' Insert the date
strHTML = Replace(strHTML, "[MeetingDate]", _
  Format(rstAnnounce!MeetingDate, "mmmm dd, yyyy h:nnampm"))
' Insert the Committee, if any
strHTML = Replace(strHTML, "[Committee]", _
  Nz(("Committee: " + rstAnnounce!CommitteeName), ""))
' Add the meeting description
strHTML = Replace(strHTML, "[MeetingDescription]", _
  rstAnnounce!MeetingDescription)
' Finally, do the location
strHTML = Replace(strHTML, "[MeetingLocation]", _
  rstAnnounce!MeetingLocation)
' Save the meeting date
datMtgDate = rstAnnounce!MeetingDate
```

Next, the code gets the topic index and topic detail templates. It then loops through all the topics in the announcement recordset, adding a line to the topic index (which will appear in a block at the beginning of the message), and a block to the topic body for each row (which all appear after the topic index block). As it adds each topic, it increments a topic number counter so that it can set up unique bookmarks and hyperlinks within the HTML. The code is as follows:

```
' Load the rest of the template text
rstTemplate.MoveNext
' Record 2 is the Topic Index Template
strTopicIndexTemp = rstTemplate!TemplateHTML
rstTemplate.MoveNext
' Record 3 is the Topic Detail Template
strTopicTemp = rstTemplate!TemplateHTML
rstTemplate.MoveNext
' Record 4 is the footer
strFootTemp = rstTemplate!TemplateHTML
' Close the template recordset
rstTemplate.Close
Set rstTemplate = Nothing
' Now process all the topics, building indexes as we go
Do Until rstAnnounce.EOF
  ' Build the index first - add 1 to counter
  intTopicNo = intTopicNo + 1
  ' Get the index template - insert the link key
  strWork = Replace(strTopicIndexTemp, "[TopicKey]", _
    "Topic" & intTopicNo)
  ' Insert the Topic Title
  strWork = Replace(strWork, "[AnnounceTitle]", _
    rstAnnounce!AnnounceTitle)
  ' Add it to the existing topics
  strTopics = strTopics & strWork
  ' Now, do the topic body - insert link key
  strWork = Replace(strTopicTemp, "[TopicKey]", _
    "Topic" & intTopicNo)
  ' Insert the Topic Title
  strWork = Replace(strWork, "[AnnounceTitle]", _
    rstAnnounce!AnnounceTitle)
  ' Insert the topic detailed description
```

```
      strWork = Replace(strWork, "[AnnounceDescription]", _
        rstAnnounce!AnnounceDescription)
      ' Add it to the existing topic body
      strBody = strBody & strWork
      ' Get the next record
      rstAnnounce.MoveNext
    Loop
    ' Close the recordset
    rstAnnounce.Close
    Set rstAnnounce = Nothing
    Set db = Nothing
```

Finally, the code assembles the pieces of the message and calls the *SendOutlookMsg* function to send the message. The code is as follows:

```
    ' Got the pieces built, now assemble them
    strHTML = strHTML & strTopics & strBody & strFootTemp
    ' Send the email
    If Not (SendOutlookMsg("PNWADG - " & Format(datMtgDate, "Long Date") & _
      " Meeting Announcement", _
      strTo, strHTML, True)) Then
      ' Got failure - tell the user
      MsgBox "Sending meeting notice failed.", vbCritical, gstrAppTitle
    End If
    ' All worked - return success
    AnnouncementEmail = True
AnnounceEmail_Exit:
    Exit Function
AnnounceEmail_Err:
    ' Tell user about an error
    MsgBox "Unexpected error: " & Err & ", " & Error, _
      vbCritical, gstrAppTitle
    ' Bail
    Resume AnnounceEmail_Exit
End Function
```

This concludes the review of features specific to the Membership Tracking application. As you explore the forms and reports in the application, you're likely to discover additional interesting features that you can use in any application. You can find some of these features described in Appendix E, "Implementing Generic Features." The next part of this book discusses the complex Inventory Management sample application.

Part III
Creating an Inventory Management Application

Chapter 9

The Inventory Management Application

At least once a month in the newsgroups or one of the e-groups, I see a post from someone wanting help building an inventory management application. Some even assume they can take the venerable Northwind sample database and adapt it to their needs. Although the Products table in Northwind does have columns for Units In Stock, Units on Order, and Reorder Level, there's no code to verify that an order request can be filled or to automatically reduce stock levels when a product is added to an order. There are also no tables to handle purchase orders to vendors.

Although you can generate most of the missing tables by using the Inventory Control sample database template included with Access, you would have to do a lot of work to merge the two designs. You would also need to write a lot of complex code to automate the posting of received items into inventory and to the orders that requested those items. So, I usually politely reply that what the user wants to do is very complicated, and it's not possible to provide the answers via posts in a newsgroup or replies to e-group messages.

When you think of an inventory management application, you probably have the perception that such an application is useful only if you're selling stocked items and tracking purchase orders sent to vendors. But, as a general concept, inventory management applies to any situation where you buy items from one or more vendors and ultimately sell, dispose of, or loan out the items. Here are just a few of the applications:

- Dispensing pharmaceuticals in a hospital
- Tracking products in a grocery store
- Managing a car dealer parts department
- Loaning books in a library

- Tracking your household goods for insurance and tax purposes

- Managing pet inventory and supplies in a pet store

- Renting and selling movies or CDs in a media store

- Tracking merchandise you buy and sell on an online auction Web site

- Managing a clothing boutique

And I'm sure you can think of a few more!

Understanding the Inventory Management Application

The Inventory Management application that you can find on the companion CD included with this book (Inventory.mdb) is loosely based on the concept of the Northwind sample database that has shipped with every version of Access. So, the customers and products and vendors will seem familiar, and the structure of many of the tables is similar to the ones you'll find in Northwind.

But this sample goes far beyond what you can do with Northwind or the Inventory Control template. When you add a product to a customer order, you can run a procedure to allocate available stock from inventory. If not enough of the product exists in inventory, you can generate a purchase order to send to the relevant vendor. When you receive a product on a purchase order, you can not only post it into inventory but also allocate it to the customer order that is waiting for the product to arrive. So, you could call this sample application "Northwind on Steroids."

Identifying Tasks and Data

You might think that an order entry and inventory management application is so common that you could build the tables, design the queries, forms, and reports, and write all the code without thinking about going through a formal application design process—but you would be wrong. Just like creating any other database application, you should start by making lists of the tasks that the application must support and the data needed by those tasks. You should interview the potential users and determine how they're performing the tasks without a database or find out what they expect the database to do for them. You'd be surprised how many different ways there are to look at sales and inventory management.

Here are the tasks implemented in the Inventory Management application:

- Define product categories.

- Enter product information, including description, list price, quantity to order by (pallet, case), and quantity to sell by (case, each) for all products available.

- Specify the minimum stocking level for each product.

- Generate purchase orders for products that are below minimum stocking level.

- Track which products have ever been ordered or stocked in inventory.

- Enter vendor information.

- Identify which vendors supply which products, and which vendor is the preferred vendor for each product.

- Print purchase orders.

- Enter the vendor invoice received with a shipment.

- Print vendor invoices.

- Define basic employee (sales representative) information and specify a password that allows that employee to sign on to the application.

- Enter customer information, including the assigned sales representative.

- Create new orders for customers and specify the taxable status for each order.

- Enter products for each order, including the quantity ordered and the current list price.

- Verify current stock for each product ordered and post the quantity from inventory to the order.

- When insufficient stock exists in inventory for a product ordered, create a purchase order to the appropriate vendor.

- Post received products for which the price has been confirmed by a vendor invoice both to inventory and, if necessary, to the related customer order.

- Enter returned products on each order, verify the original order quantity, and post the returned product back into inventory or to a purchase order to return to the vendor.

- Print a packing list for each customer order.

- Create invoices for each customer order, including invoices that indicate which products are on back order.

- Print customer invoices.

- Post customer payments to invoices.

- Print lists of customers, vendors, and products.

- Produce a sales report that shows total sales and gross profit by product and category.

- Chart sales percentages by category.

From this list, you can begin to identify the subjects and actions that should be represented by tables in the application. These include the following:

- Categories

- Products

- Vendors
- Vendor Products
- Purchase Orders
- Purchase Order Products
- Vendor Invoices
- Inventory
- Product Stock
- Employees
- Customers
- Orders
- Order Products
- Customer Invoices
- Customer Payments

When you see a subject name that lists the simple name of two other subjects, such as Vendor Products or Purchase Order Products, that subject is probably going to be the many-to-many link between the two other subjects. So, Vendor Products is the many-to-many link between Vendors and Products, and Purchase Order Products is the many-to-many link between Purchase Orders and Products. As you'll see later in the final design, the Product Stock table is actually a many-to-many link between Vendor Products and Inventory.

You might wonder why the application needs separate Products and Inventory tables. But notice the requirement to "Track which products have ever been ordered or stocked in inventory." The Products table is a catalog of all products that can be ordered from a vendor. The Inventory table contains only those products that have ever been ordered or carried in stock. For example, a vendor might announce the availability of a new line of cheeses. You add those products to the Products table so that customers and sales representatives can see that these new products can be ordered. However, you don't create an Inventory record until you receive a customer order for the product, order it from the vendor, place it in stock, and then sell it to the customer. You can see that understanding both the tasks required and the data for those tasks is critical to designing the application correctly. You cannot do one without the other.

Understanding Business Rules

As you identify the tasks required to be supported by your application, you'll also learn something about the business rules that restrict those tasks. From the discussion in "Identifying Tasks and Data," you can already surmise one business rule: The Products table contains all products that are possible to order, and the Inventory table contains products that have ever been ordered or are now in inventory.

A sales and inventory application is, by its very nature, complex. Some business rules are self-evident—for example, you can't ship a product that isn't in inventory. But a particular business might have dozens of ancillary rules that will ultimately affect the way you design the application. The best way to discover business rules is to ask questions. Some of the questions that I considered as I designed the application (and the answer I chose for each) are as follows:

- Can a product be ordered more than once in an order? Yes.

- Can a customer return a product? Yes.

- Can a customer return a product that hasn't been ordered in the current order? No.

- Can a customer return more of a product than has been ordered? No.

- Can a product quantity requested in an order be changed after that quantity has been allocated from inventory? No, the user must enter a new request for the same product.

- How is a product tracked in inventory? By product, vendor, and original cost.

- If a customer orders more of a product than is available in inventory at a single original cost, can the order be filled? If the total available in inventory (at different original costs) is sufficient to fill the order, the order must contain multiple product rows to track the original costs and, therefore, the profit in each order. (As you'll learn in Chapter 10, "Ordering Items from Inventory," the allocation process automatically splits the original product request into multiple rows when the requested product is available in inventory at multiple costs.)

- If the quantity requested for a product is greater than the amount in inventory, must the entire amount be ordered from a vendor? No, the product request must be split into multiple rows, the amount available allocated to some rows, and the remainder placed on order.

- Is the customer charged a restocking fee for returning a product? No.

- Should the application be able to track products ordered in one quantity from a vendor, but sold in a smaller quantity to customers? Yes, the application must be able, for example, to order from a vendor by the case but sell individual items from the case to the customer.

- Given the answer to the previous question, are quantities tracked in inventory by the vendor order amount or by the customer sale amount? Inventory is kept in customer sales units—for example, a vendor order of two cases containing 24 individual items each is entered into inventory as 48 items received from the vendor.

- Must a customer order be complete before you can bill it? No, the application must be able to create one bill for items shipped (showing items on back order) and additional bills for the remaining items when the items become available.

- Can items received on a vendor purchase order be posted to inventory before an invoice is received from the vendor? No, the vendor invoice must be posted first to ensure the correct cost per item is reflected in inventory.

- Are all purchase orders related to a customer order? No, the application must also be able to create an order for stock to bring stock levels to the minimum specified for each product.

- When posting received items in a purchase order related to a customer order, must the order entry clerk manually post the items received in the customer order as well? No, the application must detect when a purchase order is for a customer order, post the received item into inventory, and then mark the item allocated on the customer order automatically.

- Is it possible to post a partial shipment received on a purchase order? Yes, as long as a vendor invoice has been created for the received items.

- Can the price be changed for an allocated item in a customer order? Yes, but not if the item has been billed.

- Can a product be billed at two different prices in the same order? Yes, but the application should warn the user and provide an opportunity to correct the different prices.

- Can the user change an order that has been final billed? No, but the application should provide a way to remove the final status from an order.

- Can the user change the quantity of an item already allocated or billed? No.

- Can a customer order be billed to one address but shipped to another? Yes.

- Does the application automatically pass along shipping charges from vendors for purchase orders related to the customer order? No, but the user can enter an adjustment amount in a customer invoice to cover such fees.

- Can the user add products to a purchase order related to a customer order? Yes, and the application should automatically create the related product row in the customer order.

- Can the order entry clerk enter a price for a product that is less than the inventory cost? No.

- Can the user specify a price that represents an exorbitant markup? Yes, but the application should warn the user when the price entered is more than three times the cost.

- Can the user delete products from a customer order? Yes, as long as the product is not on order or allocated and no credit (return) row exists for the same product in the order. If the product is already on order or allocated, the user must enter a credit record. If a credit row exists, the credit must be deleted first.

- Can the user delete products from a purchase order? Yes, as long as the product hasn't been received or invoiced from the vendor.

Keep in mind that no question is too trivial, and sometimes you have to think "outside the box" to conjure up questions that your user or client needs to answer. Think like a good investigative reporter and find out not only what the user needs to do, but also when they need to do the task, where they need to be when they do the task, how they need to perform the task, and, most importantly, *why* they need to do it.

Designing the Tables

If you have identified all the tasks, the data required for all the tasks, and all the business rules, designing the tables you need to store and manage the data should be straightforward. You should never sit down and start creating tables without all the necessary background information. If some of the data exists in other files (such as a spreadsheet), create your properly normalized tables first, and then figure out what you need to do to import the existing data into your correct table structure.

The difficult part about designing tables for a sales and inventory application is providing a way to track the status of products in customer orders, inventory, and vendor purchase orders. For example, you need to be able to determine if a product in a customer order is requested, on order, allocated from inventory, or billed, and the user should be restricted from making certain changes when the status is something other than requested. In inventory, you must be able to determine the quantity placed in inventory, the quantity allocated to customer orders, the quantity billed, and the quantity returned. In a vendor purchase order, a product is on order, received, invoiced by the vendor, and then finally posted to inventory.

The typical way to design a sales and inventory database is to create one or more tables to track transactions that log the amounts moving into and out of inventory. These transactions can log the product, date and time of the transaction, the related purchase order or customer order, and the amount ordered, received, or sold. In fact, if you create a database using the Inventory Control template that you can install with Access, you'll find that it includes an Inventory Transactions table for this purpose. The bad news is the template provides only a Purchase Orders form to enter "on order" transactions. There's no example of how to create a transaction to note that the product has been received or sold.

When you create a design that includes only transaction tables, you must sum the activity from all previous transactions for a product to find out what's currently in inventory. As you can imagine, after tens of thousands of transactions are accumulated, this process can be very slow. Some designs deal with this problem by providing a procedure that periodically creates total transactions for each product—perhaps once a month or once a quarter. A total transaction summarizes the quantities ordered, received, returned, and billed to the customer as of a specific date. The application must still find the last total transaction for a product and sum all detail transactions since that total was created to find the current inventory amount.

The sample Inventory Management application provided with this book does use transaction tables—the tblOrderProducts table and the tblPurchaseOrderProducts table—but it also maintains a calculated current total in the tblStock table. Although this would seem to violate the rule that you should avoid calculated values stored in tables, the tblStock table exists to eliminate the performance problems you might encounter summing thousands of transaction rows each time the application needs to know the current stock levels.

To ensure that the totals in the tblStock table are accurate, the application must not allow the user to change one of the transaction rows after it has been posted to inventory. The application must also provide some complex procedures to post items from the two transaction tables. These procedures use the transaction management features of the Access database engine (BeginTrans, CommitTrans, and Rollback) to ensure that the transaction tables stay synchronized with the tblStock table. You'll learn more about how these procedures work in the remaining chapters in this part of the book.

From the list of subjects you determined earlier, you can see that the Inventory Management application needs the following tables:

- tblCategories
- tblProducts
- tblVendors
- tblVendorProducts
- tblPurchaseOrders
- tblPOProducts
- tblVendInvoices
- tblInventory
- tblStock
- tblEmployees
- tblCustomers
- tblOrders
- tblOrderProducts
- tblCustInvoices
- tblCustomerPayments

Now, you're ready to begin defining the tables you need and the relationships between them. As you create the tables, you should also define as many of the business rules as possible using the validation rule features of Access. Figure 9-1 shows you the final design for the tables for the sales tracking part of the Inventory Management application.

Figure 9-2 shows you the tables for the inventory tracking portion of the Inventory Management application. You can see that tblProducts is the key link between the two major functions. You can find a detailed listing of the fields and indexes for all the tables in Appendix B, "Sample Database Schemas."

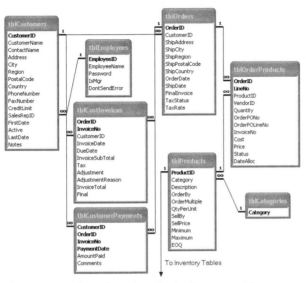

Figure 9-1   The sales tables in the Inventory Management application.

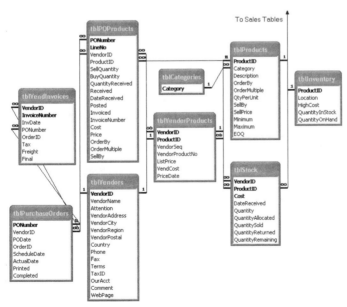

Figure 9-2   The inventory tables in the Inventory Management application.

As you can see, the table and relationship design is significantly more complex than the design for the Membership Tracking application that you studied in the previous part of this book. In the remainder of this part of the book, you can explore specific tasks implemented in the Inventory Management sample database (Inventory.mdb). Each chapter explores the tables needed for a particular set of tasks and the code that performs those tasks.

Chapter 10

Ordering Items from Inventory

Most sample order entry databases (such as Northwind) focus on how to track customer orders, but they do nothing to manage inventory. Of course, for order entry to work correctly products must be in stock before an order entry clerk can successfully order a product for and ship it to a customer. So, you might be wondering why this book covers ordering items from inventory before discussing how inventory gets stocked. In some sense, this is a bit of a "which came first—the chicken or the egg" situation. Let's assume that you built this application to automate an existing paper process and manually loaded into the relevant tables the stock that was already on hand. This chapter explains the design and code needed to add a product request to an order, validate the request, and allocate available products in inventory to the request.

Understanding the Tables Involved

As noted in the previous chapter, the critical aspect of an inventory management application is being able to track the status of requests in the transaction tables. For example, you need to be able to determine if a product in a customer order is requested, on order, allocated from inventory, or invoiced. In inventory, you must be able to determine the quantity received in inventory, the quantity allocated to customer orders, the quantity sold, and the quantity returned.

So, the tables involved in moving products from inventory to an order (or returning products from an order to inventory) must be able to reflect the current status of both a product request in an order (the tblOrderProducts table) and the products available in inventory (the tblInventory and tblStock tables). Table 10-1, on the next page, explains the purpose of each field in the tblOrderProducts table.

Table 10-1   The Fields in the tblOrderProducts Table

Field Name	Data Type	Description
OrderID	Long Integer	Related customer order identifier.
LineNo	Integer	Unique transaction line number.
ProductID	Long Integer	Related product requested in this transaction.
VendorID	Long Integer	Related ID of the vendor who provided this product. This value is set by the allocation process.
Quantity	Integer	Quantity requested in this transaction. Can be negative when returning a product, but cannot be zero.
OrderPONo	Long Integer	Related ID of the purchase order generated to fill this request when the product is not in stock. This value is set by the allocation process.
OrderPOLineNo	Integer	Related transaction line number in the purchase order. This value is set by the allocation process.
InvoiceNo	Text, Field Size 2	The suffix of the related customer invoice when the product has been invoiced. This value is set by the invoicing process. (See Chapter 13.)
Cost	Currency	Original vendor cost of the product. This value is set by the allocation process.
Price	Currency	Initially, the list price of the product, but the user can change this value.
Status	Integer	0 = None (on request)
		1 = On Order
		2 = Allocated
		3 = Invoiced
		This value is set by the allocation and invoicing processes.
DateAlloc	Date/Time	Date the product request was filled from inventory. This value is set by the allocation process.

Note   The application tracks items in inventory by product, vendor, and cost. The application copies these values in the tblOrderProducts table to maintain an exact link to the related inventory record and to make it easy to calculate the profit on each product sold.

The tblInventory table provides a calculated summary of all products that have ever been in stock. Table 10-2 explains each field in that table.

Table 10-2   The Fields in the tblInventory Table

Field Name	Data Type	Description
ProductID	Long Integer	Related product ID.
Location	Text, Field Size 20	The warehouse storage location of the product. This is the only field in this table that can be changed by the user.
HighCost	Currency	The highest vendor cost ever paid for this product. This value is set by the purchase order posting process. (See Chapter 12.)
QuantityInStock	Long Integer	The quantity of the product that should be in the warehouse, which includes amounts allocated to product requests that have not yet been shipped and invoiced. This value is set by the allocation, purchase order posting, and invoicing processes.
QuantityOnHand	Long Integer	The quantity available to sell, which does not include amounts allocated to product requests. This value is set by the allocation, purchase order posting, and invoicing processes.

And finally, the tblStock table reflects the details of products in inventory by product, vendor, and cost. This table can be used to calculate the current value of the product inventory. Table 10-3 explains the fields in that table.

Table 10-3   The Fields in the tblStock Table

Field Name	Data Type	Description
VendorID	Long Integer	Related ID of the vendor who provided this product. This value is set by the purchase order posting process.
ProductID	Long Integer	Related product ID. This value is set by the purchase order posting process. (See Chapter 12.)
Cost	Currency	Original vendor cost of the product. This value is set by the purchase order posting process.
DateReceived	Date/Time	Date the item was posted to stock. This value is set by the purchase order posting process.
Quantity	Long Integer	Total quantity received. This value is set by the purchase order posting process.
QuantityAllocated	Long Integer	Quantity currently allocated to a product request but not yet shipped and invoiced. This value is set by the allocation and invoicing processes.
QuantitySold	Long Integer	Quantity shipped and invoiced to an order. This value is set by the invoicing process.
QuantityReturned	Long Integer	Quantity returned to the vendor on a purchase order. This value is set by the purchase order posting process.
QuantityRemaining	Long Integer	Quantity remaining available to sell. This value is set by the allocation, purchase order posting, and invoicing processes.

Notice that the user cannot modify many of the fields in these tables. To keep the values correct and synchronized, code in the application must handle the required simultaneous updates within a transaction. The code must also validate data as the user enters it, particularly for new product requests for an order. The code that does this is explained in the remaining sections in this chapter.

Validating a Product Order Transaction

Because so many of the fields in these tables must be managed by code, you must take steps to ensure that users cannot edit fields or records that should be locked down. You can accomplish part of the work by setting the Locked property of some controls to Yes. However, you must also dynamically change the locked status of fields depending on the status of individual product order records. And you must validate the data that the user enters to ensure that the posting procedures can handle what the user requests.

Preventing Users from Editing Processed Records

As you'll learn later in Chapter 13, "Creating Customer Invoices," the user can create a partial invoice when only some products are available in inventory. After all products become available to ship, the user can create a final invoice, which marks the order completed. The simplest dynamic change that you can control in code is to ensure that orders that have been final invoiced cannot be changed. If you open the Inventory Management application (Inventory.mdb), open the frmOrders form, move to the last record (which should be an invoiced order for Richter Supermarkt, as shown in Figure 10-1), and try to change anything in that order or the products shipped with the order, you'll find all the controls locked. In fact, you can't even go to the new row in the Products subform window and add any product requests to the order.

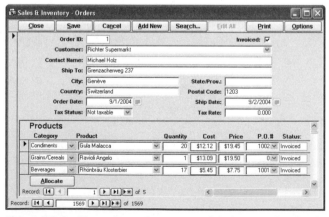

Figure 10-1   You cannot change any data in an order that has a final invoice.

You can go back to the first record—an order for Around the Horn that hasn't been invoiced—and find that you can edit most fields. The code that makes this happen is in the Current event procedure of the frmOrders form. The beginning part of the code sets the Enabled property of the command buttons in the form header based on whether the form is on a new record, has a filter applied, or is in Data Entry mode. If the form is on a new record, the procedure calls the *LockAll* procedure to unlock all editable controls; otherwise, the code asks the *LockAll* procedure to lock the controls based on whether the order is marked invoiced. (If FinalInvoice is True, the *LockAll* procedure locks all controls.) The code is as follows:

```
Public Sub Form_Current()
  ' Set up availability of the command buttons
  Me.cmdSearch.Enabled = Not (Me.NewRecord)
  Me.cmdAddNew.Enabled = Not (Me.NewRecord)
  Me.cmdEditAll.Enabled = (Me.FilterOn Or Me.NewRecord Or Me.DataEntry)
  Me.cmdPrint.Enabled = Not (Me.NewRecord)
  Me.cmdOptions.Enabled = Not (Me.NewRecord)
  ' Unlock controls if new record
  If Me.NewRecord Then
    LockAll False
  Else
    ' Otherwise, lock based on final invoice
    LockAll Me.FinalInvoice
  End If
End Sub
```

The *LockAll* procedure that you can find in the form's module first moves the focus to a tiny text box control in the upper left corner of the form header. It does this because code cannot change the properties of a control that has the focus. It then loops through all the controls in the Detail section of the form, Section(0), and sets the Locked property of all text box controls, combo box controls, and subform controls unless the control has a Tag property set to Lock. (If you examine the Tag property of the OrderID, FinalInvoice, and ContactName controls, you'll find the Tag property set to Lock so that the *LockAll* procedure doesn't change the original locked status of these controls.) It also sets the Enabled status for any command buttons it finds. If the parameter passed to the procedure is True, the procedure locks and disables controls. If the parameter is False, it unlocks and enables controls. The code is as follows:

```
Private Sub LockAll(intLocked As Integer)
Dim ctl As Control
  On Error Resume Next
  ' Move the focus to a control that won't be affected
  Me.txtSafe.SetFocus
  ' Set Locked for all text boxes, combo boxes, and subforms
  ' in Detail section based on parameter
  For Each ctl In Me.Section(0).Controls
    Select Case ctl.ControlType
      Case acTextBox, acComboBox, acSubform
        ' Don't change if Tag says "Lock"
        If Not (ctl.Tag = "Lock") Then
          ctl.Locked = intLocked
```

```
        End If
      Case acCommandButton
        ctl.Enabled = Not (intLocked)
    End Select
  Next ctl
  Set ctl = Nothing
  ' Put the focus back
  Me.cmbCustomerID.SetFocus
End Sub
```

In the first order for Around the Horn, the code in the Current event of the outer form should
unlock the subform control. However, you'll find that you cannot change any of the existing
product records because they have all been allocated from inventory—they have all been processed by the allocation procedure. But you can go to the new record in the subform and enter
a new product.

The code that handles this is in the Current event of the fsubOrderProducts form that is the
subform for the frmOrders form. The code unlocks all controls on a new record, but locks all
controls if the status is on order, allocated, or invoiced (the Status field is greater than zero).
Note that the code does allow you to change the price in a record as long as it has not been
invoiced. The code is as follows:

```
  ' If on a new row,
  If Me.NewRecord Then
    ' Unlock everything
    Me.cmbCategory.Locked = False
    Me.cmbProductID.Locked = False
    Me.Quantity.Locked = False
    Me.Price.Locked = False
  Else
    ' Not a new record ...
    ' If on order, allocated, or invoiced,
    If (Me.Status > 0) Then
      ' Lock down Category, Product, PO Number, and Quantity
      Me.cmbCategory.Locked = True
      Me.cmbProductID.Locked = True
      Me.cmbOrderPONo.Locked = True
      Me.Quantity.Locked = True
      ' Also lock Price if already invoiced
      If (Me.Status = 3) Then
        Me.Price.Locked = True
      Else
        Me.Price.Locked = False
      End If
    Else
      ' Status is nothing, so leave unlocked
      Me.cmbCategory.Locked = False
      Me.cmbProductID.Locked = False
      Me.Quantity.Locked = False
      Me.Price.Locked = False
    End If
  End If
```

Validating the Price

Although users can change the price of any product until it has been invoiced, you certainly want to validate any price that the user enters. You can find out how this works in the frmOrders form. Open that form and go to any order that hasn't been invoiced yet. Go to the new record in the subform, choose a category, choose a product, enter any quantity greater than zero, and then enter a price that's less than the cost the application found for you. Try to tab away from the control to save the new value, and the application responds as shown in Figure 10-2.

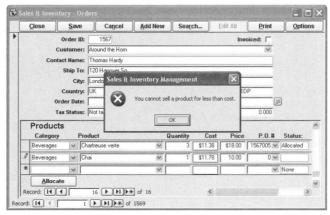

Figure 10-2 The Inventory Management application won't let you sell a product for less than cost.

You also don't want the user to enter a ridiculously high price. Click OK in the previous error dialog box and see what happens when you enter a very high price (more than three times the cost). The application responds as shown in Figure 10-3.

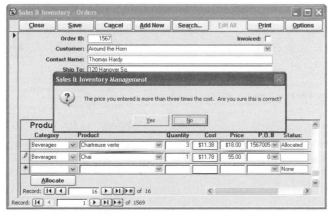

Figure 10-3 The Inventory Management application warns you when you attempt to enter a very high price.

Notice that the default button for the warning message is the No button just in case the user hastily presses Enter without reading the message. The user can still choose to accept the high price by clicking the Yes button. The code that performs these validations is in the BeforeUpdate event procedure for the Price text box control.

The code is as follows:

```
Private Sub Price_BeforeUpdate(Cancel As Integer)
  On Error GoTo PBU_Bail
  ' Disallow a price less than cost
  If Me.Price < Me.Cost Then
    MsgBox "You cannot sell a product for less than cost.", _
      vbCritical, gstrAppTitle
    Cancel = True
    Me.Price.SetFocus
    Exit Sub
  End If
  ' Warn if price is more than three times the cost
  If Me.Price > (Me.Cost * 3) Then
    If vbYes = MsgBox("The price you entered is more than " & _
      "three times the cost.  " & _
      "Are you sure this is correct?", _
      vbQuestion + vbYesNo + vbDefaultButton2, gstrAppTitle) Then
      Exit Sub
    End If
    Cancel = True
  End If
PBU_Bail:
  Exit Sub
End Sub
```

Validating the Product Quantity

The application doesn't need to validate any positive product quantities in a customer order—although it might make sense to check and warn when the user enters a very large number. Of course, a product request transaction should never have a quantity of zero. However, when the user wants to return products by entering a negative quantity, the application must perform some special validations.

Validating a Return to Inventory

As noted in the business rules in Chapter 9, "The Inventory Management Application," the application does allow a negative quantity to indicate a product being returned. When the user enters a negative quantity, the application must verify the following:

- The quantity being returned is not greater than the sum of the quantity on order, allocated, or invoiced for the product being returned.

- Because the application tracks the original cost charged by the vendor for each product, when the product has been allocated at multiple inventory costs, the user must select the cost, and the quantity returned cannot be greater than the amount allocated at that cost.

To see how this works, you can open the frmOrders form in the Inventory Management application. Unless you have modified the sample data, the first order you see should be an order for customer Around the Horn with 15 product request rows that hasn't been invoiced. If you scan down the product rows, you'll find two rows for the Chartreuse verte beverage product. The customer requested a quantity of seven, and the allocation procedure found four in inventory and generated a purchase order for the remaining three, so the original request was split into two rows. The amount requested on a purchase order was received and posted both to inventory and the customer order. You'll learn more about the posting process in Chapter 12, "Posting Received Items into Inventory."

Go to the new record in the Products subform window, select that beverage product, and try to return 8 or more in the Quantity field. The application responds as shown in Figure 10-4.

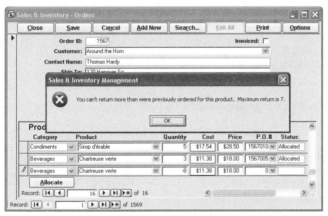

Figure 10-4   The Inventory Management application won't let you return more than was ordered.

The code to perform these checks runs in the BeforeUpdate event of the Quantity text box control. The code depends on a working table and an append query to find the previously ordered, allocated, or invoiced records for the product being returned. The query that loads the table is zqappOrderProductReturn, which sums the quantity for all product rows other than the current row by vendor and cost. The SQL of the query is as follows:

```
PARAMETERS OrderParm Long, ProductParm Long, LineParm Short;
INSERT INTO zttblOrderProductReturn
(OrderID, ProductID, QuantityRequired, Cost, Price, ListPrice, VendorID)
SELECT tblOrderProducts.OrderID, tblOrderProducts.ProductID, Sum(tblOrderProducts.Quantity)
AS SumOfQuantityRequired, tblOrderProducts.Cost, Max(tblOrderProducts.Price) AS MaxOfPrice1,
Max(tblOrderProducts.Price) AS MaxOfPrice, tblOrderProducts.VendorID
FROM tblOrderProducts
WHERE (((tblOrderProducts.Status)>0) AND ((tblOrderProducts.LineNo)<>[LineParm]) AND
((tblOrderProducts.OrderID)=[OrderParm]) AND ((tblOrderProducts.ProductID)=[ProductParm]))
GROUP BY tblOrderProducts.OrderID, tblOrderProducts.ProductID, tblOrderProducts.Cost,
tblOrderProducts.VendorID;
```

Notice that the query contains three parameters to select the current order, the current product, and all product request lines other than the line the user is currently editing. The query also includes only rows that have been placed on order, allocated, or invoiced (Status > 0).

The BeforeUpdate procedure of the Quantity text box control performs these validations. First the procedure verifies that the quantity entered is not zero. (The Default Value property of the Quantity field is set to 1.) If the quantity is greater than zero, no further checks are required. When the quantity is less than zero, the code clears a working table, opens the zqappOrderProductReturn query, sets the three parameters, and executes the query to load the current data into the working table. The code is as follows:

```
Private Sub Quantity_BeforeUpdate(Cancel As Integer)
Dim db As DAO.Database, qd As DAO.QueryDef, rst As DAO.Recordset
  ' Don't allow a quantity of zero
  If Me.Quantity = 0 Then
    MsgBox "You can't enter a zero quantity.", vbCritical, gstrAppTitle
    Cancel = True
    Exit Sub
  End If
  ' No check needed when ordering an item (positive quantity)
  If Me.Quantity > 0 Then Exit Sub
  ' Price and quantity matching on a return!
  Set db = DBEngine(0)(0)
  ' Clear the working table
  db.Execute "Delete * From zttblOrderProductReturn"
  ' Get the template query
  Set qd = db.QueryDefs("zqappOrderProductReturn")
  ' Set the parameters
  qd!OrderParm = Me.OrderID
  qd!ProductParm = Me.ProductID
  qd!LineParm = Me.LineNo
  ' Insert the net sum of orders for this product
  qd.Execute
  ' Make sure the tabledefs collection is refreshed
  db.TableDefs.Refresh
```

The code then checks the number of rows in the table. When more than one row exists (indicating this product has been requested at different costs or from different vendors), the code opens the fdlgPickOrderReturnCost form that is bound to the table just loaded by the zqappOrderProductReturn query. The working table has a True/False field called ThisOne that indicates the row the user chose. Code in the fdlgPickOrderReturnCost form ensures that the user selects one and only one row.

When the user closes that form, the code following the DoCmd.OpenForm statement runs. (When code opens a form in Dialog mode, the code halts until the form closes or hides.) The code in the BeforeUpdate event then finds the row the user selected, sets the selected cost, price, and vendor in the current product record, and then verifies that the amount being returned is not greater than the amount already requested. If the amount is too large, the code informs the user and cancels saving the new quantity. The code is as follows:

```
' See if more than one
Select Case db.TableDefs("zttblOrderProductReturn").RecordCount
  Case Is > 1
    ' Yes, open the "pick the cost" form
    DoCmd.OpenForm "fdlgPickOrderReturnCost", acNormal, , , , acDialog
    ' Code continues when form closes -
    ' open a recordset on the working table
    Set rst = db.OpenRecordset("Select [Cost], [Price], " & _
      "[ListPrice], [VendorID], " & _
      "[QuantityRequired] From zttblOrderProductReturn " & _
      "Where [ThisOne] = True")
    If rst.EOF Then
      MsgBox "Unexpected error choosing return price.", _
        vbCritical, gstrAppTitle
      Cancel = True
      Exit Sub
    End If
    ' Set the cost, price, and vendor ID
    Me.Cost = rst!Cost
    Me.Price = rst!Price
    Me.VendorID = rst!VendorID
    ' .. but check to see that quantity wanted to return
    ' is not more than ordered
    If Abs(Me.Quantity) > rst!QuantityRequired Then
      MsgBox "You can't return more than were ordered for " & _
        "this product at the cost you selected.  " & _
        "Maximum return at this cost is " & _
        rst![QuantityRequired] & ".", vbCritical, gstrAppTitle
      Cancel = True
    End If
    rst.Close
    Set rst = Nothing
```

When only one row exists (all previous order rows were at the same cost), the code fetches that row, sets the cost, price, and vendor, and performs the same quantity check. The code is as follows:

```
  Case 1
    ' Only one - fetch that row
    Set rst = db.OpenRecordset("Select [Cost], [Price], " & _
      " [ListPrice], [QuantityRequired], [VendorID] " & _
      "From zttblOrderProductReturn")
    ' Set the cost, price, and vendor ID
    Me.Cost = rst!Cost
    Me.Price = rst!Price
    Me.VendorID = rst!VendorID
    ' .. but check that enough previously ordered
    If Abs(Me.Quantity) > rst!QuantityRequired Then
      MsgBox "You can't return more than were " & _
        "previously ordered for this product.  " & _
        "Maximum return is " & rst![QuantityRequired] & ".", _
        vbCritical, gstrAppTitle
      Cancel = True
    End If
```

```
        rst.Close
        Set rst = Nothing
```

And finally, when no previous rows exist, the code displays an appropriate error message and cancels the save. You can see this message by trying to return any product that is not already in the order. The code is as follows:

```
    Case 0
        ' None - not on order, allocated, or returned
        MsgBox "You cannot return any of this product because " & _
          "it has not been previously " & _
          "ordered, allocated, or invoiced in this order.", _
          vbCritical, gstrAppTitle
        Cancel = True
  End Select
End Sub
```

Validating a Return to a Purchase Order

When the user wants to return a product previously ordered, and the product came partly from inventory and partly from a purchase order issued on behalf of the customer, the user can choose to send the product directly back to the purchase order by selecting a purchase order number in the P.O.# combo box control. For the return to be valid, the request record must meet the following criteria:

- The quantity must be negative. Entering positive values is controlled by the allocation procedure when you mark a product received on a purchase order.

- The quantity must be an even multiple of the value in the QtyPerUnit field in the tblProducts table. For example, the application might have had to order an entire case of the product (perhaps 12 units) to satisfy a request for a quantity of five. The vendor won't accept individual product returns, so the application must return full cases on the purchase order—even multiples of 12.

- The product must exist in the selected purchase order. Code in the AfterUpdate event of the Product combo box control (not shown) helps ensure this by setting the RowSource property of the P.O.# combo box control to purchase orders for the current order that contains the requested product.

- The quantity must be less than or equal to the amount provided by the purchase order.

To see how this works, you can modify the return row you were testing earlier to return 11 or fewer in the Quantity field. Tab to the P.O.# field and select the purchase order number—1567005. Figure 10-5 shows you the result.

The code that performs this check is in the BeforeUpdate event procedure of the cmbOrder-PONo combo box control. The code first checks to see that you have entered a negative quantity because you cannot specify a purchase order number when you're ordering products. (The P.O.# values you see on rows with positive quantities were generated by the purchase order creation process. See Chapter 11, "Generating Purchase Orders," for details.) The record source for the fsubOrderProducts form includes the OrderMultiple field from the tblProducts table, renamed to PROM. The code next verifies that the negative quantity you specified is an even multiple of this order multiple. Note that the order multiple is the count of individual sale items that exist in each item that can be ordered from a vendor—for example, a case might contain 12 or 24 individual products to sell.

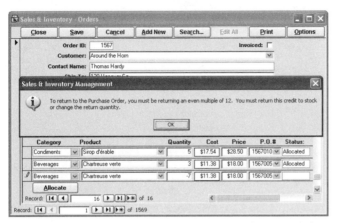

Figure 10-5   The Inventory Management application makes sure that you return full cases to a purchase order.

Finally, even though the row source for the combo box control should contain only purchase order numbers for the current order and product, the code verifies that the product actually exists in the purchase order and checks that the amount being returned is not greater than the total in the purchase order. The code is as follows:

```
Private Sub cmbOrderPONo_BeforeUpdate(Cancel As Integer)
Dim varQty As Variant
Dim strProductA As String, curMinPrice As Currency
  On Error GoTo cmbOrderPONo_BeforeUpdate_ERR
  If Me.Quantity >= 0 Then
    MsgBox "You can't set a P.O. Number unless you are " & _
      "returning products.  " & _
      "(Quantity Required must be negative.)", vbCritical, gstrAppTitle
    Cancel = True
    Exit Sub
  End If
  ' Verify that return to the PO is an even multiple of the Order Multiple
  If Me.Quantity Mod Me.PROM <> 0 Then
    MsgBox "To return to the Purchase Order, " & _
      "you must be returning an even " & _
      "multiple of " & Me.PROM & _
      ".  You must return this credit to stock " & _
      "or change the return quantity.", vbInformation, gstrAppTitle
    Cancel = True
    Exit Sub
  End If
```

```
' Check if Product exists on selected PO
varQty = DSum("SellQuantity", "tblPOProducts", _
  "[PONumber] = " & Me.cmbOrderPONo & _
  " AND [ProductID] = " & Me.ProductID)
' If got a quantity,
If Not IsNull(varQty) Then
  ' Verify that quantity to return isn't more than ordered
  If varQty < Abs(Me.Quantity) Then
    MsgBox "You cannot return more than was ordered " & _
      "in the Purchase Order specified.  Amount ordered was " & _
      varQty & ".  Press Esc, correct the returned amount, " & _
      "then choose this purchase order again.", _
      vbCritical, gstrAppTitle
    Cancel = True
  End If
Else
  ' Quantity was null, so didn't find the Product at all!
  MsgBox "The product you want to return was not ordered from the " & _
    "P.O. Number you selected.", vbCritical, gstrAppTitle
  Cancel = True
End If
cmbOrderPONo_BeforeUpdate_Exit:
  Exit Sub
cmbOrderPONo_BeforeUpdate_ERR:
Dim lngErr As Long, strError As String
  lngErr = Err
  strError = Error
  ErrorLog Me.Name & "_cmbOrderPONo_BeforeUpdate", lngErr, strError
  MsgBox "Unexpected error: " & lngErr & ", " & _
    strError & " has been logged.", vbCritical, gstrAppTitle
  Resume cmbOrderPONo_BeforeUpdate_Exit
End Sub
```

Validating a Product Request Before Saving It

As you can see from the preceding section, the application includes several code procedures to validate the quantity as the user enters data in the Products subform in the Orders form. Even when the data passes all these validations, the application still needs to perform some final checks before allowing the user to save the row.

The code that performs these final checks is in the BeforeUpdate event procedure of the fsubOrderProducts form. First, the code generates the next line number for the product request when the user is creating a new row. Next, if the user has specified a purchase order number, the code double-checks that the user is returning the product. The user could have entered a negative amount, set a purchase order number, and then changed the quantity to a positive value before saving the row. Although the code in the BeforeUpdate event of the Quantity text box could also check for a nonblank purchase order number when the quantity is positive, I chose to do this final check in the form's BeforeUpdate event.

After verifying the purchase order number and quantity, the code checks for a cost set to zero and warns the user. Finally, when the user is returning a product, the code checks for the existence of a companion purchase order if the user has not specified a purchase order number. If a purchase order exists, the code confirms that the user wants to return the product to inventory rather than to the vendor. The code is as follows:

```
Private Sub Form_BeforeUpdate(Cancel As Integer)
Dim varAmt As Variant, strProductA As String, varAmt2 As Variant
Dim strMsg As String, lngQty As Long
Dim varLine As Variant
  ' If on a new row
  If Me.NewRecord Then
    ' Calculate the next order line number
    varLine = DMax("LineNo", "tblOrderProducts", "[OrderID] = " & _
      Me.Parent!OrderID) + 1
    If IsNull(varLine) Then varLine = 1
    ' Set the line number for the new row
    Me.LineNo = CInt(varLine)
  End If
  ' Double-check if PO, then quantity must be negative
  If Not IsNothing(Me.OrderPONo) Then
    If Me.Quantity > 0 Then
      MsgBox "You can't set a P.O. Number unless you are " & _
        "returning Products.  " & _
        "(Quantity Required must be negative.)", vbCritical, gstrAppTitle
      Cancel = True
      Exit Sub
    End If
  End If
  ' Special check for cost at 0
  If Me.Cost = 0 Then
    If vbYes <> MsgBox("Are you SURE you want to set " & _
      "Cost to ZERO for this Product?", _
      vbQuestion + vbYesNo, gstrAppTitle) Then
      Cancel = True
      Exit Sub
    End If
  End If
  ' If returning an item
  If Me.Quantity < 0 Then
    ' Attempting a return -- do some special checks
    ' If no PO Number specified
    If IsNothing(Me.OrderPONo) Then
      ' Check to see if there are POs for this Order
      If 0 = DCount("*", "tblPurchaseOrders", "[OrderID] = " & _
        Me.Parent!OrderID) Then Exit Sub
      ' Otherwise, confirm they want to credit to inventory
      If vbYes = MsgBox("You entered a credit amount, " & _
        "but no PO number.  " & _
        "The Products you are returning will be " & _
        "placed in inventory when you " & _
        "'post' Products for this Order.  " & _
        "Do you want to credit to a Purchase " & _
        "Order instead?", vbQuestion + vbYesNo, gstrAppTitle) Then
        Cancel = True
        Exit Sub
```

```
      End If
    End If
  End If
End Sub
```

Verifying Rows to Be Deleted

The fsubOrderProducts form also needs to control which records the user can delete. Deletions should be allowed (or disallowed) according to the following rules:

- A product request that has not been placed on order, allocated, or invoiced can be deleted.

- A product request that has been allocated or invoiced cannot be deleted. The user must enter a return transaction.

- When the item is on order and a positive amount, no return records (negative quantity) can exist. The user must delete the return records first. Remember that code in the BeforeUpdate event procedures for the Quantity text box control and the cmbOrder-PONo combo box control verifies that sufficient quantity exists in the order to allow the return quantity. If the user were allowed to delete positive amount rows, the check for the return amount would be invalid.

- If the user deletes a row that is on order, the application must be sure that the related row in the purchase order is also deleted.

Most of this work is done in the form's Delete event procedure. You might recall that when a user selects multiple rows and presses the Delete key, the Delete event runs once for each row selected, and that event can cancel the deletion of one or more of the individual rows. The code in the Delete event cannot delete related purchase order rows because the user might cancel the entire deletion when Access asks that the deletion be confirmed. When the deletion process is complete, the form's AfterDelConfirm event runs, and if the deletion was successful, code in that procedure can synchronize the related purchase order.

The code in the Delete event first checks to see if the row has not been placed on order, allocated, or invoiced (Status = 0). If so, the delete is allowed to proceed. Next, the procedure checks the Status field to see if the request has been allocated or invoiced. If so, the code displays an error message and cancels the delete. If the status is on order and the quantity is positive, the code checks to see if any return records exist in the order for the same product. If so, the code displays an error message that informs the user that the return rows must be deleted first. Finally, when the row is on order and all other verifications are satisfied, the code places information about the related purchase order row into an array in memory. The code is as follows:

```
Option Compare Database
Option Explicit
Option Base 1
Dim mintNukePO As Integer, mintNukeCount As Integer, mlngPONum(100) As Long
```

```
Dim mintPOLine(100) As Integer, mlngProductID(100) As Long
Dim mintFound(100) As Integer

Private Sub Form_Delete(Cancel As Integer)
  ' If it's not on order, then OK to delete
  If (Me.Status = 0) Then Exit Sub
  ' If it's been allocated or invoiced, then no can do
  If (Me.Status > 1) Then
    MsgBox "You can't delete a Product that has been " & _
      "allocated from inventory or invoiced.  " & _
      "Enter a credit instead.", vbCritical, gstrAppTitle
    Cancel = True
    Exit Sub
  End If
  If Me.Quantity > 0 Then ' if deleting a positive amount,
  ' .. then check to be sure there's no credits outstanding
    If 0 <> DCount("*", "tblOrderProducts", "[OrderID] = " & _
      Me.Parent!OrderID & _
      " And [ProductID] = " & Me.ProductID & " And [Quantity] < 0" & _
      " And [Status] = 0") Then
      MsgBox "You can't delete an ordered Product " & _
        "that has credits outstanding.  " & _
        "Delete the credits first.", vbCritical, gstrAppTitle
      Cancel = True
      Exit Sub
    End If
  End If
  ' Set up to adjust the PO after the delete is complete
  If (mintNukePO = False) Then
    mintNukePO = True
    mintNukeCount = 0
  End If
  ' Get the next index into the delete PO arrays
  mintNukeCount = mintNukeCount + 1
  ' Redim all the arrays - can delete until Access
  '  runs out of memory!
  ReDim Preserve mlngPONum(mintNukeCount)
  ReDim Preserve mintPOLine(mintNukeCount)
  ReDim Preserve mlngProductID(mintNukeCount)
  ReDim Preserve mintFound(mintNukeCount)
  ' Save the PO data - see AfterDelConfirm for the PO sync code
  mlngPONum(mintNukeCount) = Me.OrderPONo
  mintPOLine(mintNukeCount) = Me.OrderPOLineNo
  mlngProductID(mintNukeCount) = Me.ProductID
  mintFound(mintNukeCount) = False
End Sub
```

If the Delete event procedure adds purchase order row information to the array, the
AfterDelConfirm event procedure processes the information to delete the related purchase
order rows. That code runs only when Access informs the procedure that the delete completed without any errors. That code finds each purchase order product row entered into the
array by the form's Delete event procedure and deletes them all. You can find that code in the
module for the fsubOrderProducts form.

Allocating Available Inventory

As you look at the products listed in the Orders form, you can see that the user cannot touch the Status field. The only way to allocate products to a customer order or return products from an order is to ask the application to run the allocation procedure.

Returning and Ordering from the User's Perspective

You can see how this works by entering a few new order request lines. Open the frmOrders form and leave the form positioned on the first order that isn't invoiced. (This is the same order for Around the Horn used for examples earlier in this chapter.) Remember that earlier you tried to enter more of the Chartreuse verte beverage product than was previously ordered. Go ahead and create a return row with a quantity of −6 and select No when the application asks you if you want to return the quantity to a purchase order. On the next row, create a new request for a quantity of 12 for the Perth Pasties product in the Meat/Poultry category. Unless you have modified the original sample data, there should be only 8 of that product in inventory, so you will be able to see what happens when you order more than is available. The order should now look like Figure 10-6.

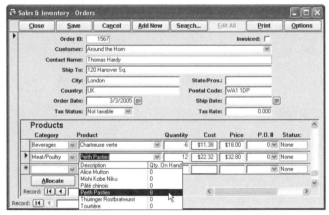

Figure 10-6   Entering a product return and a request for another product that is more than is currently in inventory.

When an order has one or more rows that have a status of None, the user can click the Allocate button to ask the application to process the product requests for the order. You can click the Allocate button after adding the two rows shown in Figure 10-6, and the application runs the allocation process.

Because you asked for more of the Perth Pasties product than is in inventory, the application shows you a dialog box that asks you if you want to generate purchase orders. If you click Yes, the application displays a dialog box that lists all the unfulfilled product requests and asks you to verify the vendor you want to use for each product. In the sample database each product has only one vendor, so you can click the Done button in that dialog box to confirm the default selection. The application creates the necessary purchase orders, opens the purchase order report to display those orders, and displays a final confirmation dialog box. You can click OK to close the dialog box and close the report to return to the order, which should now look like Figure 10-7.

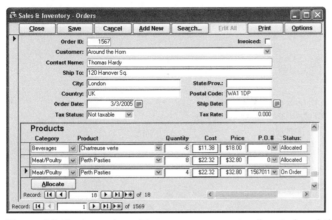

Figure 10-7   An order with two new requests allocated and the remaining quantity that was not available placed on order.

The allocation process marked the returned product Allocated—which for a return means the product is now back in inventory ready to sell to another customer. Notice that the allocation process split your original request for 12 Perth Pasties into a row that allocates the 8 that were available in inventory and another row that shows the 4 that had to be ordered from the vendor. In Chapter 11, you'll learn how the purchase order was generated, and in Chapter 12, you'll find out how to post items received on a purchase order, both to inventory and to any related order.

Running the Allocation Process

The code that starts the allocation process is in the Click event procedure for the Allocate command button. The code first attempts to move the focus off the command button by moving the focus back to the control indicated by Screen.PreviousControl. In some cases, the SetFocus command fails if the previous control was a check box control or a control on a tab control, so the local error trap avoids the error. Next, the code calls the *SaveIt* procedure within the form's module to ensure that any changes have been saved. The code then checks to find out if any records need to be processed in the current order (Status = 0) by using a parameter query. The procedure then calls the *AllocateProducts* function (located in the modInventory module) to perform the work. That function returns True (−1) if all requests were satisfied, False (0) if the allocation failed (perhaps because of an error in the database), and a +1 if the allocation succeeded but some purchase orders were generated. The code is shown on the next page.

```
Private Sub cmdAllocate_Click()
Dim intReturn As Integer, db As DAO.Database
Dim qdA As DAO.QueryDef, rsA As DAO.Recordset
  ' User has requested to allocate / order products
  ' Set local error trap while trying to put focus back
  On Error Resume Next
  Screen.PreviousControl.SetFocus
  ' Set error trap
  On Error GoTo cmdAllocate_ERR
  ' Make sure the last edit is saved
  If Not SaveIt() Then Exit Sub
  ' Point to this database
  Set db = DBEngine(0)(0)
  ' Get the query that find products Status = None
  Set qdA = db.QueryDefs("zqryOrderProductSelect")
  ' Set the parameter for this order
  qdA![OrderParm] = CLng(Me.Parent!OrderID)
  ' See if records found
  Set rsA = qdA.OpenRecordset()
  ' If none, tell them and exit
  If rsA.RecordCount = 0 Then
    MsgBox "Nothing to allocate.", vbInformation, gstrAppTitle
    rsA.Close
    Set rsA = Nothing
    Exit Sub
  End If
  rsA.Close
  Set rsA = Nothing
  ' Call the allocate function and pass it this order ID
  intReturn = AllocateProducts(CLng(Me.Parent!OrderID))
  ' Check the return value
  Select Case intReturn
    ' True = All OK
    Case -1
      ' Requery myself to show updated status
      Me.Requery
      MsgBox "Products allocation completed successfully!", _
        vbInformation, gstrAppTitle
    ' False return - some error occurred
    Case 0
      MsgBox "An error occurred while attempting to allocate " & _
        "Products for this order.", vbExclamation, gstrAppTitle
    ' 1 = allocated, but built some Purchase Orders
    Case 1
      MsgBox "Not all Products were in inventory.  " & _
        "One or more purchase orders " & _
        "were generated.", vbInformation, gstrAppTitle
  End Select
cmdAllocate_Exit:
  Exit Sub
cmdAllocate_ERR:
Dim lngErr As Long, strError As String
  lngErr = Err
  strError = Error
  ErrorLog Me.Name & "_cmdAllocate", lngErr, strError
```

```
    MsgBox "Unexpected error: " & lngErr & ", " & strError & _
      " has been logged.", vbCritical, gstrAppTitle
    Resume cmdAllocate_Exit
End Sub
```

Understanding the AllocateProducts Procedure

As you might imagine, the *AllocateProducts* function is very complex. You can find this function in the modInventory module in the Inventory Management sample database.

Procedure Initialization

The beginning part of the function declares all the variables and evaluates the optional date parameter. Next, it opens a recordset on the order row and locks it by editing the row. (When you edit a row in code, the JET engine places a lock on the row.) It does this so that in a multi-user environment two users don't try to allocate products to the same order at the same time. If another user tries to allocate to the same order at the same time, the request to edit the order row fails and raises an error.

Next, the code cleans out the zttblProductsToOrder working table by deleting all its rows. (Code later in the procedure writes rows to this table for products for which there was an insufficient quantity available in inventory. If the user decides to create purchase orders, this table is used by the *GenProductsPO* function, described in Chapter 11, to create the purchase orders.) Finally, the code starts a transaction, opens a recordset on the unallocated rows in the order using the zqryOrderProductSelect parameter query, and opens a recordset on the tblInventory table. The code is as follows:

```
Function AllocateProducts(lngOrder As Long, _
   Optional intSilent As Integer = 0, _
   Optional varDate As Variant) As Integer
' Inputs: Order ID
'         Optional "run silent" indicator (used by zfrmLoadData)
'         Optional process date (used by zfrmLoadData)
' Output: Returns "True" (-1) if all Products allocated successfully
'         Returns +1 if Products allocated and purchase order(s) generated
'         Returns "False" (0) if an error occurs
' Technique:
' This routine attempts to allocate the required Products.
' Uses "zqryOrderProductSelect" to find Products where Status not
' On Order, Allocated, or Invoiced. If Product is being returned (negative
' quantity), posts to Inventory or the original PO as appropriate.
' If Product is being ordered (positive quantity), allocates from stock
' in inventory.  At end of allocation if some still not allocated from
' inventory, then stuffs the unordered Products in ztTblProductsToOrder
' and calls the common PO build routine.
' Note: When called from zfrmLoadData, intSilent is True - procedure will
'         open no forms and will not display any errors. zfrmLoadData also
'         passes the date it wants to use as the allocation / PODate date.
Dim db As DAO.Database, qd As DAO.QueryDef, qdA As DAO.QueryDef
Dim rsA As DAO.Recordset, rsI As DAO.Recordset, rsS As DAO.Recordset
```

```
Dim rst As DAO.Recordset, rsP As DAO.Recordset, rsC As DAO.Recordset
Dim varQuantity As Variant, intQuantityReq As Integer
Dim varRet As Variant, intEditA As Integer, intRecCount As Integer
Dim intI As Integer, intSomeError As Integer, intSomeLeft As Integer
Dim intCount As Integer, intQty As Integer, intMult As Integer
Dim intL As Integer, curMinPrice As Currency, curCost As Currency
Dim curPrice As Currency, varCost As Variant, varPrice As Variant
Dim lngPO As Long, lngVendor As Long, intTrans As Integer
Dim lngProductID As Long, lngThisLine As Long, intAddedSome As Integer
Dim intDoPO As Integer, datAllocDate As Date, lngVend As Long
Dim rstW As DAO.Recordset, strSQL As String, strMsg As String
  On Error Resume Next
  ' Set up for default false return
  AllocateProducts = 0
  ' Set up the allocation date
  datAllocDate = Date
  ' If passed a date variable
  If Not IsMissing(varDate) Then
    ' .. and it's a valid date
    If IsDate(varDate) Then
      ' Use the parameter value
      datAllocDate = varDate
    End If
  End If
  ' Point to this database
  Set db = DBEngine(0)(0)
  ' Open the Order and lock it!
  Set rstW = db.OpenRecordset("Select OrderID From tblOrders " & _
    "Where OrderID = " & lngOrder)
  If rstW.EOF Then
    If Not intSilent Then
      MsgBox "Unexpected error: Can't find Order #" & _
        lngOrder, vbCritical, gstrAppTitle
    End If
    Exit Function
  End If
  ' Lock the order by editing it
  rstW.Edit
  If Err <> 0 Then
    strMsg = "Error trying to edit Order #" & lngOrder
    strMsg = strMsg & ".  Someone else may be editing this Order."
    If Not intSilent Then MsgBox strMsg, vbExclamation, gstrAppTitle
    Exit Function
  End If
  ' Set an error trap
  On Error GoTo AllocOrderProducts_ERR
  ' Clean out working table to store Products not in stock
  db.Execute "Delete * FROM zttblProductsToOrder;", dbFailOnError
  ' Turn on the hourglass and start a transaction
  DoCmd.Hourglass True
  BeginTrans
  intTrans = True
  ' Open a recordset on Products to allocate
  Set qdA = db.QueryDefs("zqryOrderProductSelect")
  qdA![OrderParm] = lngOrder
```

```
Set rsA = qdA.OpenRecordset()
' Open the Inventory table
Set rsI = db.OpenRecordset("tblInventory")
' Get count of Products to allocate rows for SysCmd
rsA.MoveLast
intRecCount = rsA.RecordCount
rsA.MoveFirst
' Show a progress meter
varRet = SysCmd(acSysCmdInitMeter, "Updating Inventory...", intRecCount)
```

Returning Products

The next section of code begins a large loop to process each order product row one at a time. The first part of the code deals with rows that have a negative quantity—the user wants to return the product to inventory or to the related purchase order.

Returning Products to Inventory   If the row has no purchase order number, the code finds the inventory record and locks it. Next, the code fetches the stock row for the specified product, cost, and vendor. If the product was allocated at a specific cost, then it should be returned to the same cost record. If the record is not found, the code displays an error message and deletes the row from the order because it is invalid.

When the correct stock record is found, the code adds the negative quantity to the quantity previously allocated and recalculates the quantity remaining in the stock record. Finally, the code updates the inventory record for the product to reflect the new quantity in stock and quantity on hand, and sets the status of the order product row to Allocated. The code is as follows:

```
' Loop through all Products to allocate, deduct from stock,
'  and adjust master Inventory row
Do Until rsA.EOF
  ' If returning products, ...
  If rsA![AmtNeeded] < 0 Then
    ' See if return is to a Purchase Order
    If IsNothing(rsA!OrderPONo) Then
      ' If no PO to credit, then return to inventory
      intQty = rsA![AmtNeeded]
      ' Find the inventory record
      rsI.FindFirst "ProductID = " & rsA!ProductID
      If rsI.NoMatch Then
        ' Ooops -- can't find the inventory record to return
        ' the Product!
        intSomeError = True
        strMsg = "Error attempting to return Product # "
        strMsg = strMsg & rsA!ProductID & " to inventory."
        strMsg = strMsg & "  Inventory record not found."
        strMsg = strMsg & "  The Order record has been deleted."
        If Not intSilent Then MsgBox strMsg, _
          vbCritical, gstrAppTitle
        ' Delete the Order row
        rsA.Delete
      Else
```

```
' Found the Inventory row - edit it to lock it
rsI.Edit
' Find the matching Stock row for an inventory return
strSQL = "Select * From tblStock Where ([ProductID] = "
strSQL = strSQL & rsA!ProductID
strSQL = strSQL & ") And ([Cost] = " & rsA!Cost & ")"
' If there's a VendorID, then also filter for vendor
If Not IsNothing(rsA!VendorID) Then
  strSQL = strSQL & " AND ([VendorID] = " & _
    rsA!VendorID & ")"
  lngVendor = rsA!VendorID
End If
' Open the Stock recordset
Set rsS = db.OpenRecordset(strSQL)
If rsS.EOF Then
  ' Ooops -- can't find the stock row to return
  ' the Product!
  intSomeError = True
  strMsg = "Error attempting to return Product # "
  strMsg = strMsg & rsA!ProductID & " to stock."
  strMsg = strMsg & "  Stock record that matches the "
  strMsg = strMsg & "vendor and cost not found."
  strMsg = strMsg & "  The Order record has been deleted."
  If Not intSilent Then MsgBox strMsg, _
    vbCritical, gstrAppTitle
  ' Delete the Order row
  rsA.Delete
Else
  ' Return the Products to the Stock record
  rsS.Edit
  ' Subtract from Allocated amount -
  ' product now available back in stock
  ' NOTE: QuantityAllocated can be negative if
  '       previously allocated product was already
  '       invoiced.  Will correct when invoiced item credited.
  rsS!QuantityAllocated = rsS!QuantityAllocated + _
    rsA!AmtNeeded
  rsS!QuantityRemaining = rsS!Quantity - _
    (rsS!QuantityAllocated + rsS!QuantitySold + _
    rsS!QuantityReturned)
  lngVendor = rsS!VendorID
  rsS.Update
  intQuantityReq = 0
End If
rsS.Close
' Refresh the master inventory totals...
rsI.Edit
' Using a query here so that this routine will
' see the updated quantities within the transaction.
Set qd = db.QueryDefs("zqrySumStockParm")
qd!ItemToFind = rsA!ProductID
Set rst = qd.OpenRecordset()
' Update the calc values in the Inventory row.
If Not rst.EOF Then
  rsI!HighCost = rst!MaxCost
```

```
        rsI!QuantityInStock = rst!Available
        rsI!QuantityOnHand = rst!Remain
    Else
        rsI!QuantityInStock = 0
        rsI!QuantityOnHand = 0
    End If
    rst.Close
    Set rst = Nothing
    qd.Close
    Set qd = Nothing
    rsI.Update
    ' Update the Order status
    rsA.Edit
    rsA!Status = OrderStatus.Allocated
    rsA!DateAlloc = datAllocDate
    rsA!VendorID = lngVendor
    rsA.Update
End If
```

Returning Products to a Purchase Order   When the code encounters a row that is returning a quantity to a purchase order, it does not update stock at all. Instead, it inserts a new return row in the related purchase order. The change to inventory levels and posting the order allocated occur later when the user marks the credit received, enters the vendor invoice credit information, and requests that the purchase order be posted. You can find out how the purchase order posting process works in Chapter 12. The code to create the new purchase order row is as follows:

```
Else
    ' There's a PO Number, so credit back to the PO!
    ' Open a recordset on PO Products to insert the row
    Set rsP = db.OpenRecordset("zqryPOProductsForAlloc", _
        dbOpenDynaset, dbAppendOnly)
    ' Insert a new PO Product row to queue up the credit
    ' Get "next" line no --
    '   must use recordset inside a transaction!
    Set rsC = db.OpenRecordset("Select Max([LineNo]) " & _
        "As [LastLineNo] " & _
        "From tblPOProducts " & _
        "Where [PONumber] = " & rsA!OrderPONo)
    If IsNull(rsC!LastLineNo) Then
        intL = 1
    Else
        intL = rsC!LastLineNo + 1
    End If
    rsC.Close
    rsP.AddNew
    rsP!PONumber = rsA!OrderPONo
    ' Setting the PO Number should "autolookup"
    ' the Vendor ID from the PO
    If IsNothing(rsP!POVend) Then
        ' Ooops - means the PO does not exist!
        If Not intSilent Then
            MsgBox "Error attempting to credit product # " & _
```

```
                        rsA!ProductID & " to purchase order # " & rsA!OrderPONo & _
                        ".  The Purchase Order cannot be found.  " & _
                        "The PO Number in the Order has been zeroed.", _
                        vbCritical, gstrAppTitle
                    End If
                    intSomeError = True
                    rsA.Edit
                    ' Zero out the PO Number
                    rsA!OrderPONumber = 0
                    rsA.Update
                    ' Discard the PO Product row
                    rsP.Close
                    Set rsP = Nothing
                Else
                    ' OK - have a good PO, so set the rest of the fields
                    rsP!LineNo = intL
                    ' copy Vendor ID from the Purchase Order
                    rsP!VendorID = rsP!POVend
                    lngVendor = rsP!POVend
                    ' Copy the Product ID
                    rsP!ProductID = rsA!ProductID
                    ' Save the quantity required
                    intQty = rsA![AmtNeeded]
                    ' .. and the order multiple
                    ' (number of sell units in one purchase unit)
                    intMult = rsA![OrderMultiple]
                    ' Set the return quantity
                    rsP!SellQuantity = intQty
                    ' If the quantity is an even multiple
                    If intQty Mod intMult = 0 Then
                        ' Do an integer divide to get the amount to order
                        rsP!BuyQuantity = intQty \ intMult
                    Else
                        ' else round up to the next buy amount
                        rsP!BuyQuantity = (intQty \ intMult) + 1
                    End If
                    ' Set the order by ("case", "pallet")
                    rsP!OrderBy = rsA![OrderBy]
                    ' Set the sell by ("each", "case")
                    rsP!SellBy = rsA![SellBy]
                    ' Set the order multiple
                    rsP!OrderMultiple = intMult
                    ' Use the vendor cost
                    rsP!Cost = rsP!VendCost
                    ' Use price from the order
                    rsP!Price = rsA!Price
                    ' Save the new PO Product row
                    rsP.Update
                    rsP.Close
                    Set rsP = Nothing
                    ' Update the Order status
                    rsA.Edit
                    ' Put the vendor we found in the order
                    rsA!VendorID = lngVendor
                    ' Set the related PO line number
```

```
    rsA!OrderPOLineNo = intL
    ' Mark the status "on order"
    rsA!Status = OrderStatus.OnOrder
    rsA.Update
    ' Finally, get the PO and unset its Completed flag
    db.Execute ("Update tblPurchaseOrders " & _
      "Set [Completed] = False " & _
      "Where [PONumber] = " & rsA!OrderPONo)
  End If
End If
' End of code to process returns
```

Allocating Products from Inventory

The remainder of the code deals with requests to sell products to an order—the quantity requested is positive. First, the code attempts to find the inventory record for the product and verify that the quantity on hand is greater than zero. If the record doesn't exist or the quantity on hand is zero, there is no inventory to allocate.

When the code does find that inventory exists, it opens a recordset on the stock records that have a quantity remaining greater than zero in ascending sequence by the date any inventory last arrived for the product for each vendor and cost. Sorting this way implements a FIFO (first in, first out) strategy for inventory management. If your organization uses LIFO (last in, first out), sort the recordset by date in descending sequence.

When the code finds a stock record with quantity available, it processes only one record because each order record can have only one cost. If the quantity available in that record is sufficient to fill the order, the code updates the stock, order, and inventory records and sets the intQuantityReq variable to 0 to indicate the code is done with the current order row. If the quantity isn't sufficient, the code takes what is available and changes the Quantity value in the order row. It also updates the stock and inventory records. The code is as follows:

```
Else
' Start of code to process positive allocations
  ' Quantity is positive -- go try to allocate from inventory
  intQuantityReq = rsA!AmtNeeded
  ' Find the Product in the master inventory table
  rsI.FindFirst "ProductID = " & rsA!ProductID
  If Not rsI.NoMatch Then
    ' We found the inventory row -- check for quantity available
    If rsI!QuantityOnHand > 0 Then
      ' Looks like some in stock,
      ' so open a recordset on the stock rows
      strSQL = "Select * From tblStock"
      strSQL = strSQL & " Where [ProductID] = " & rsA!ProductID
      strSQL = strSQL & " AND QuantityRemaining > 0"
      strSQL = strSQL & " ORDER BY [DateReceived]"
      ' Recordset plucks off the oldest rows first
      Set rsS = db.OpenRecordset(strSQL)
      If Not rsS.EOF Then
        rsS.Edit
```

```
    ' If this stock record has enough, then ...
    If intQuantityReq <= rsS!QuantityRemaining Then
        ' .. pluck the Products from this stock row and we're done
        ' Add the quantity needed to Stock Allocated
        rsS!QuantityAllocated = rsS!QuantityAllocated + _
            intQuantityReq
        ' Reduce quantity remaining by quantity needed
        rsS!QuantityRemaining = rsS!QuantityRemaining - _
            intQuantityReq
        ' Save the record
        rsS.Update
        ' Got it all - set required to zero
        intQuantityReq = 0
    Else
        ' .. otherwise, grab what's available
        ' Take whatever is remaining and add it to allocated
        rsS!QuantityAllocated = rsS!QuantityAllocated + _
            rsS!QuantityRemaining
        ' Reduce required by amount that was remaining
        intQuantityReq = intQuantityReq - _
            rsS!QuantityRemaining
        ' Set remaining to zero
        rsS!QuantityRemaining = 0
        ' Save the record
        rsS.Update
    End If
    ' Save the cost for updating the Order row
    curCost = rsS!Cost
    ' Save the vendor ID for updating the Order row
    lngVendor = rsS!VendorID
    rsS.Close
    ' We're going to update the Order, so edit the row
    rsA.Edit
    ' Update the Order with what we found in stock...
    ' If quantity remaining, then this will
    '   reduce the original quantity
    rsA!AmtNeeded = (rsA!AmtNeeded - intQuantityReq)
    ' Set in the allocated found cost
    rsA!Cost = curCost
    ' Set this amount allocated
    rsA!Status = OrderStatus.Allocated
    ' Set the allocation date
    rsA!DateAlloc = datAllocDate
    ' Update the Vendor ID
    rsA!VendorID = lngVendor
    ' Save the Order record
    rsA.Update
    ' Refresh the master inventory totals...
    rsI.Edit
    ' Using a query here so that this routine '
    '   will see the updated quantities
    '   within the transaction.
    Set qd = db.QueryDefs("zqrySumStockParm")
    qd!ItemToFind = rsA!ProductID
    Set rst = qd.OpenRecordset()
```

```
            ' Update the "unnormalized" calc values
            '  in the Inventory row.
            If Not rst.EOF Then
              rsI!HighCost = rst!MaxCost
              rsI!QuantityInStock = rst!Available
              rsI!QuantityOnHand = rst!Remain
            Else
              rsI!QuantityInStock = 0
              rsI!QuantityOnHand = 0
            End If
            rst.Close
            qd.Close
            ' Update the inventory master
            rsI.Update
          End If
        End If
      End If
```

If the first stock record found does not have enough to satisfy the original request, the intQuantityReq variable contains the amount remaining to allocate. If some of the requested amount was allocated, then the code creates a new row in the order recordset that reflects the amount remaining to allocate. Because the code doesn't close the order recordset, the new row appears at the end of the original recordset. The code repositions to the row just processed and then moves to the next row. The new row just added will eventually get processed for the remaining amount as the code loops through each order record. The code is as follows:

```
      ' See if any remaining to allocate
      If intQuantityReq > 0 Then
        ' Did we allocate any on the current row?
        If rsA!Status = OrderStatus.Allocated Then
          ' Yes - need to create a new row
          '  with remaining quantity!
          ' Save the line number to get back
          lngThisLine = rsA!LineNo
          ' Save values for new row
          lngProductID = rsA!ProductID
          curCost = rsA!Cost
          curPrice = rsA!Price
          ' Now, add a new Order row!
          ' This is a cool trick in DAO - the new row will come up for
          '  processing at the end of the current recordset, so we'll
          '  keep looking for available Stock records at other costs until
          '  we either allocate all requested or end up with a leftover
          '  amount to stuff in a Purchase Order.
          rsA.AddNew
          intAddedSome = True
          ' Set the order ID
          rsA!OrderID = lngOrder
          ' Use a query to find the current largest line number
          Set rst = db.OpenRecordset("Select Max([LineNo]) As MaxLine " & _
            "From tblOrderProducts Where [OrderID] = " & lngOrder)
          rsA!LineNo = rst![MaxLine] + 1
          rst.Close
```

```
             ' Set up Product ID, quantity, and prices
             rsA!ProductID = lngProductID
             rsA!Cost = curCost
             rsA!Price = curPrice
             rsA!AmtNeeded = intQuantityReq
             rsA!Status = OrderStatus.None
             ' Save the new Order Products row with
             '   remaining unallocated amount
             rsA.Update
             ' Reposition on the original line number to '
             '  continue processing!
             rsA.FindFirst "[LineNo] = " & lngThisLine
             If rsA.NoMatch Then    ' Should not occur!
               Error 3999
             End If
           End If
         End If
       End If
       ' Finished processing the current Order record - get the next
       rsA.MoveNext
       intI = intI + 1
       ' Update the status meter
       varRet = SysCmd(acSysCmdUpdateMeter, intI)
    Loop
```

Finalizing Allocation

After processing all the order rows, including any that were inserted because it took more than one stock record to find sufficient quantity, the code commits all updates performed to this point. This ensures that all updates to the tblOrderProducts, tblInventory, tblStock, and tblPOProducts tables are completed together. If there were no non-fatal errors, the code sets a True return value. If any rows were inserted to the order, the code verifies that the frmOrders form is open and then requeries the subform so that it displays the new rows. The code is as follows:

```
    ' Done with all Order rows - clear the status bar
    varRet = SysCmd(acSysCmdClearStatus)
    ' Commit what we've done
    CommitTrans
    intTrans = False
    ' Close off recordsets
    rsA.Close
    Set rsA = Nothing
    rsI.Close
    Set rsI = Nothing
    rstW.Close
    Set rstW = Nothing
    ' Turn off the hourglass
    DoCmd.Hourglass False
    ' If got no warnings, then set up to return success
    If Not (intSomeError) Then AllocateProducts = True
    ' If we added some Order rows
    If (intAddedSome = True) Then
```

```
' If Order form loaded (it should be, but just checking)
If IsFormLoaded("frmOrders") Then
  ' Requery the subform
  Forms!frmOrders!fsubOrderProducts.Requery
End If
End If
```

Finally, the code uses a parameter append query to copy the data for any unallocated rows to the working table cleared at the beginning. If the query found some rows, the code tells the user that some product requests didn't have sufficient stock in inventory and asks if the user wants to create purchase orders. If the user replies Yes, the code calls the *GenProductsPO* function to create purchase orders and put the remaining product requests on order; otherwise, the code leaves the unprocessed order rows in the customer order. You will learn how the *GenProductsPO* function works in the next chapter.

Notice that the code at the end of the function after the AllocOrderProducts_ERR label is the general error trap to catch any fatal errors. It tells the user about the error, logs it, and if a transaction has been started, rolls back all updates made up to the point of the error. This ensures that either all updates are successful or no updates are saved. No tables will be partially updated. The code is as follows:

```
' See if any left unallocated - run the "append leftovers" query
Set qd = db.QueryDefs("zqappOrderProductsToOrder")
qd![OrderParm] = lngOrder
qd.Execute
' See if there are any rows
If DCount("*", "ztTblProductsToOrder") <> 0 Then
  ' Yes - set a flag
  intSomeLeft = True
  ' Ask if user wants to create Purchase Orders
  ' But auto-create PO if called from zfrmLoadData
  If intSilent Then
    intDoPO = vbYes
  Else
    intDoPO = MsgBox("Insufficient stock in inventory for one " & _
      "or more Products required for this order.  " & _
      "Do you want to generate purchase orders for this order?", _
      vbQuestion + vbYesNo, gstrAppTitle)
  End If
  If intDoPO = vbYes Then
    ' Turn off local error trapping
    On Error GoTo 0
    ' Call the Product PO generator - pass the silent flag
    If GenProductsPO(lngOrder, intSilent, datAllocDate) Then
      ' Indicate Purchase Orders created
      AllocateProducts = 1
      intSomeLeft = False
    End If
  End If
End If
If (intSomeLeft = True) Then
  If Not intSilent Then MsgBox "Some Products were not allocated, " & _
```

```
        "but you cancelled PO creation.", vbInformation, gstrAppTitle
    End If

    ' Let the DBEngine catch up with all this work
    DBEngine.Idle dbFreeLocks

    ' Done
    Exit Function

AllocOrderProducts_ERR:
    ' Display and log any errors
    If Not intSilent Then MsgBox "Unexpected Error: " & Err & _
        ", " & Error, vbCritical, gstrAppTitle
    ErrorLog "AllocateProducts", Err, Error
    On Error Resume Next
    ' If a transaction was started, roll it back
    If (intTrans = True) Then Rollback
    ' Clear the status bar
    varRet = SysCmd(acSysCmdClearStatus)
    ' Turn off the hourglass
    DoCmd.Hourglass False
    ' Bail!
    Exit Function

End Function
```

After studying this chapter, perhaps you're beginning to understand why the original Northwind sample database contains no examples to manage inventory and purchase orders. In the next chapter, you'll learn how the Inventory Management application manages purchase order creation and editing.

Chapter 11

Generating Purchase Orders

In the previous chapter, you learned about the processes in the Inventory Management application that handle allocating products from inventory to a customer order or returning products from a customer order to a purchase order or to inventory. Three critical processes remain: ordering products from a vendor by issuing a purchase order, receiving ordered products from a vendor and posting them into inventory and potentially to a customer order, and billing and shipping products to customers. This chapter discusses the design components in the sample application that handle the creation of purchase orders.

Understanding the Tables Involved

As you learned in the last chapter, when the business represented by the Inventory Management sample application receives an order from a customer, the application allows the user to enter the customer order transactions into the tblOrderProducts table. When the business needs to order more products from a vendor, it needs to create an order—in business terms, a purchase order—to send to the vendor. This business, in effect, becomes a customer of the vendor.

To be able to track orders sent to vendors, the application must track information about each purchase order and each product requested in the purchase order. The application must also allow the user to edit and create new purchase orders. The tables required are very similar in concept to the tblOrders and tblOrderProducts tables that the application uses to track orders received from customers, but these new transaction tables are tracking orders going out to vendors. Table 11-1, on the next page, explains the purpose of each field in the tblPurchaseOrders table.

Table 11-1 The Fields in the tblPurchaseOrders Table

Field Name	Data Type	Description
PONumber	Long Integer	Unique purchase order number. Orders for stock are in the format 9yyyynnn. (The leading 9 helps ensure that all orders for stock appear after all customer orders.) Orders for a customer order are in the format oooonnn, where ooooo is the related customer order number. This value is generated by the application.
VendorID	Long Integer	Related vendor for this purchase order.
PODate	Date/Time	Date the purchase order was issued.
OrderID	Long Integer	Related customer order number (if any).
ScheduleDate	Date/Time	Date products are expected to be received.
ActualDate	Date/Time	Date the products were received.
Printed	Yes/No	This purchase order has been printed and sent. This field is set by the application when the order is printed, and it is reset when the user adds a new product request to the order.
Completed	Yes/No	All items on the purchase order have been received. This field is set by the application when all products have been posted to inventory.

For this business, a purchase order must contain a request for one or more products in each order, and those products must be ones supplied by the vendor to whom the purchase order is directed. Table 11-2 explains the purpose of each field in the tblPOProducts table that stores the information for each product.

Table 11-2 The Fields in the tblPOProducts Table

Field Name	Data Type	Description
PONumber	Long Integer	Related purchase order number.
LineNo	Integer	Unique line number for this product.
VendorID	Long Integer	Related vendor for this purchase order. This value is copied by the application from the vendor ID specified in the tblPurchaseOrders table.
ProductID	Long Integer	Product ordered in this transaction row.
SellQuantity	Integer	Quantity to sell to customer or place into inventory, in inventory stocking units.
BuyQuantity	Integer	Quantity ordered from the vendor, in vendor purchase units. This field is calculated by the application using the OrderMultiple information for the product in the tblProducts table.
QuantityReceived	Integer	Quantity actually received, in inventory stocking units.
Received	Yes/No	The item has been received.
DateReceived	Date/Time	Date the item was received.

Table 11-2   The Fields in the tblPOProducts Table

Field Name	Data Type	Description
Posted	Yes/No	Item has been posted into inventory. Item has also been posted to the related customer order, if any. This field is set by the purchase order posting process. (See Chapter 12, "Posting Received Items into Inventory," for details.)
Invoiced	Yes/No	Item has been invoiced by the vendor. This field cannot be edited when editing a purchase order, but it can be set when editing a vendor invoice. See Chapter 12 for details.
InvoiceNumber	Text, length 20	Vendor's invoice number. This field is set by the application when the user enters a vendor invoice for this purchase order and marks this transaction Invoiced. See Chapter 12 for details.
Cost	Currency	Price the vendor charged per inventory stocking unit.
Price	Currency	Current list price charged to the customer per inventory stocking unit.
OrderBy	Text, length 15	Vendor purchase unit description (Case, Pallet, etc.) copied by the application from the related row in the tblProducts table.
OrderMultiple	Integer	Number of inventory stocking units per vendor purchase unit copied by the application from the related row in the tblProducts table.
SellBy	Text, length 15	Inventory stocking unit description (Each, Case, etc.) copied by the application from the related row in the tblProducts table.

Notice that the Posted field cannot be set by the user. Also, the application sets the vendor InvoiceNumber field when the user adds this transaction to a vendor invoice by marking it Invoiced. You'll learn more about creating a vendor invoice and posting received products to inventory in the next chapter.

Validating a Purchase Order Transaction Row

As you learned in the previous chapter, the application must strictly control what the user can edit in a customer order. The same is true for purchase orders. As you'll learn later in this chapter, most purchase orders are created either when insufficient stock items are found in inventory during the allocation process or when the user requests that orders be generated to bring stock up to minimum levels.

A user can edit existing purchase orders, create new ones, and, in some cases, delete existing purchase orders. Because much of the data in both the tblPurchaseOrders and tblPOProducts tables must be controlled by application processes in order to maintain synchronization between purchase order, customer order, stock, and vendor invoice data, the forms provided to edit the data in these tables must enforce some restrictions. The restrictions are as follows:

- The user cannot edit the PODate, ScheduleDate, or VendorID fields for a purchase order that has a matching vendor invoice, is marked completed, or is for a customer order.

- The user cannot edit any product request records in a purchase order for a customer order that has a final invoice.

- The VendorID field cannot be changed when the user has opened the purchase order form from the Vendor Options form (fdlgVendorOptions) requesting to edit purchase orders for the currently displayed vendor or to create a new purchase order for the currently displayed vendor.

- The ProductID, BuyQuantity, Cost, Received, DateReceived, and QuantityReceived fields cannot be changed in a product request record when the product has already been invoiced or posted to inventory.

- The user cannot change the ProductID field or the BuyQuantity field in a product request for a customer order.

- When the user attempts to create a product credit record to return a product to the vendor, the product must have been ordered on the purchase order, the quantity returned must be less than or equal to the quantity ordered, and the credit cost must match the purchase cost.

- The quantity received in a product request record cannot be more than the quantity ordered and cannot be zero.

- The user cannot delete a product request that has been posted to inventory.

- The user cannot delete a product request in a purchase order for a customer order. The user must delete the request in the customer order instead.

The following sections explain how these rules are enforced by Visual Basic code in the frmPurchaseOrder and fsubPurchaseProducts forms.

Preventing Users from Editing Processed Rows

To explore how the application restricts what the user can do, you can open the Inventory Management application (Inventory.mdb) and then open the frmPurchaseOrder form. Unless you have modified the sample data, the first purchase order displayed should be PO Number 1001, as shown in Figure 11-1.

Because this order has a matching vendor invoice, is marked completed, and is for a customer order, you'll find that the only field you can change in the order is the Actual Date field. Actually, any one of the three conditions locks the fields in the purchase order. In addition, because the purchase order is for a customer order that is final, you cannot change any of the data or insert a new product request in the subform window that edits the related product request records.

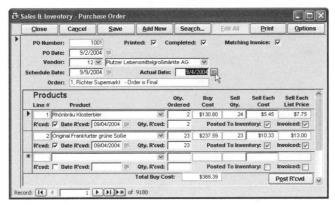

Figure 11-1 The frmPurchaseOrder form restricts what the user can do based on the status of the order displayed.

The code that locks and unlocks controls is in the Current event of the frmPurchaseOrder form. Remember that the Current event occurs each time the user moves to a new record, so the locking changes with each new record displayed. The first part of the code in the Current event requeries the Product combo box control so that it is filtered to display only products supplied by the current vendor.

The code then executes a call to DLookup to find out if any vendor invoices exist for the current purchase order. If invoices exist, the code sets the Matching Invoice check box and hides a label control containing a message reminding the user to create invoices before attempting to post received products. Next, the code enables or disables command buttons in the form header depending on whether the form is on a new record or a filter has been applied. The code sets the locked status of the controls using the matching invoice and completed indicators and the existence of an OrderID for the purchase order. If the order is for a customer order and that order has a final invoice, the code locks the Products subform. Finally, the code locks the vendor ID controls if a default value exists for the VendorID combo box control. The default value is set by the form's Open event procedure when the form was opened from the Vendor Options dialog form (fdlgVendorOptions). The code is as follows:

```
Private Sub Form_Current()
Dim intMatchInv As Integer
  ' Set an error trap
  On Error GoTo Error_Form_Current
  ' Requery the product row source for current vendor
  Me.fsubPurchaseProducts.Form!cmbProductID.Requery
  ' Get matching invoices - can't use DLookup directly in
  '   the Control Source of chkMatchInv because of
  '   timing problems - must execute it here.       .
  If IsNothing(Me.PONumber) Then
    intMatchInv = 0
    Me.lblNote.Visible = False
  Else
    intMatchInv = Not IsNothing(DLookup("[PONumber]", _
      "tblVendInvoices", "[PONumber] = " & Me.PONumber))
```

```
      If intMatchInv = True Then
        Me.lblNote.Visible = False
      Else
        Me.lblNote.Visible = True
      End If
    End If
    Me.chkMatchInv = intMatchInv
    ' Set up availability of the command buttons and controls
    ' Disable some command buttons if on new record
    Me.cmdSearch.Enabled = Not (Me.NewRecord)
    Me.cmdAddNew.Enabled = Not (Me.NewRecord)
    Me.cmdPrint.Enabled = Not (Me.NewRecord)
    Me.cmdOptions.Enabled = Not (Me.NewRecord)
    ' Enable "edit all" if filtered, on a new record, or in data entry mode
    Me.cmdEditAll.Enabled = (Me.FilterOn Or Me.NewRecord Or Me.DataEntry)
    ' Disable PODate, schedule date, and vendor combo boxes
    '  if Completed, a matching Vendor invoice exists, or for an Order
    Me.PODate.Locked = (intMatchInv Or Nz(Me.Completed, 0) Or _
      (Not IsNothing(Me.OrderID)))
    Me.cmdPODateCal.Enabled = Not (intMatchInv Or Nz(Me.Completed, 0) Or _
      (Not IsNothing(Me.OrderID)))
    Me.ScheduleDate.Locked = (intMatchInv Or Nz(Me.Completed, 0) Or _
      (Not IsNothing(Me.OrderID)))
    Me.cmdSchedDateCal.Enabled = Not (intMatchInv Or Nz(Me.Completed, 0) Or _
      (Not IsNothing(Me.OrderID)))
    Me.VendorID.Locked = (intMatchInv Or Nz(Me.Completed, 0) Or _
      (Not IsNothing(Me.OrderID)))
    Me.cboVendor.Locked = (intMatchInv Or Nz(Me.Completed, 0) Or _
      (Not IsNothing(Me.OrderID)))
    ' Disable the subform if the order is final
    If (Me.FinalInvoice = True) Then
      Me.fsubPurchaseProducts.Locked = True
    Else
      Me.fsubPurchaseProducts.Locked = False
    End If
    ' Also lock the vendor controls if a default value set
    '    by OpenArgs in the Load procedure
    If Not IsNothing(Me.VendorID.DefaultValue) Then
      Me.VendorID.Locked = True
      Me.cboVendor.Locked = True
    End If
Exit_Form_Current:
  Exit Sub
Error_Form_Current:
  mlngErr = Err
  mstrError = Error
  ErrorLog "frmPurchaseOrder.Form_Current", mlngErr, mstrError
  MsgBox "Unexpected error " & mlngErr & ", " & mstrError & _
    " has been logged.", vbCritical, gstrAppTitle
  Resume Exit_Form_Current
End Sub
```

The fsubPurchaseProducts form (the form you see in the subform window on the Purchase Order form) also controls what you can edit in the form based on the status of the purchase order and the individual product requests. If you followed the steps to add a product request for customer order number 1567 in the previous chapter, you can find that purchase order to see how you are restricted. Open the frmOrders form, scroll down in the list of products until you find the request for Perth Pasties that has an On Order status, and double-click the P.O.# combo box control. The frmPurchaseOrder form should open and display purchase order 1567011 for vendor G'day, Mate, as shown in Figure 11-2.

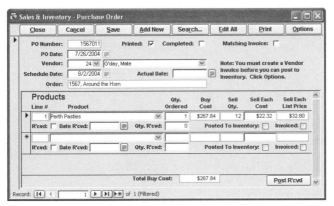

Figure 11-2   A purchase order for a customer order that hasn't been completed yet.

If you didn't create this purchase order in Chapter 10, you can do so now by following these steps:

1. Open the frmOrders form and navigate to any order that has not yet been invoiced.

2. Go to the new record in the Products subform, select any category and product in that category, and request a quantity that is more than was indicated in stock in the Product combo box list.

3. Click the Allocate button and click Yes when the application asks you if you want to create a purchase order.

4. Click Done in the Verify Vendor dialog box.

5. Return to the order after closing the purchase order report that was opened by the purchase order creation process and double-click the P.O.# combo box on the new product purchase order record that the application created for you.

The application then displays the Purchase Order form, where you should find that you can change received, date received, and quantity received, but you cannot change the product or the quantity ordered. The code that controls what you can do is in the Current event procedure of the fsubPurchaseProducts form. The code begins by unlocking all controls and exiting if you have clicked in the new row. If the current product request has been invoiced by the vendor or posted to inventory, the code locks all controls. If the purchase order is for a customer order, the code locks only the cmbProductID combo box control and the BuyQuantity text box control. The code is as shown on the next page.

```
Private Sub Form_Current()
  On Error GoTo Error_Form_Current
  ' Unlock everything by default
  Me.cmbProductID.Locked = False
  Me.BuyQuantity.Locked = False
  Me.Cost.Locked = False
  Me.Received.Locked = False
  Me.DateReceived.Locked = False
  Me.cmdDateReceivedCal.Enabled = True
  Me.QuantityReceived.Locked = False
  ' If on a new row, then we're done
  If Me.NewRecord Then Exit Sub
  ' If posted or invoiced,
  If Me.Posted Or Me.Invoiced Then  ' .. lock all controls
    Me.cmbProductID.Locked = True
    Me.BuyQuantity.Locked = True
    Me.Cost.Locked = True
    Me.Received.Locked = True
    Me.DateReceived.Locked = True
    Me.cmdDateReceivedCal.Enabled = False
    Me.QuantityReceived.Locked = True
  ' Otherwise, if no order ID
  ElseIf Not IsNull(Me.Parent.OrderID) Then  ' .. then allow all edits
    'Not posted, but do have Order ID
    ' Lock ProductID and Quantity, but edit all else
    Me.cmbProductID.Locked = True
    Me.BuyQuantity.Locked = True
  End If
Exit_Form_Current:
  Exit Sub
Error_Form_Current:
  mlngErr = Err
  mstrError = Error
  ErrorLog Me.Name & ".Form_Current", mlngErr, mstrError
  MsgBox "Unexpected error " & mlngErr & ", " & mstrError & _
    " has been logged.", vbCritical, gstrAppTitle
  Resume Exit_Form_Current
End Sub
```

Validating the Quantity Requested

As you learned in Chapter 10, the Inventory application must validate the quantity on a customer order when it is negative (indicating a product being returned) to ensure that the product being returned has been ordered in the customer order and that the quantity being returned isn't larger than the quantity previously ordered. The application must perform an identical validation for purchase orders.

To see how this works, open the Inventory application (Inventory.mdb) and then open the frmPurchaseOrder form. Click the Search button and ask for all purchase orders for customer order number 1569. This customer order does not have a final bill, so you should be able to edit all the purchase orders. In the first purchase order for this customer order, you should see an order for 11 of Grandma's Boysenberry Spread. On the second line in the Products window, try selecting one of the other products from this vendor and entering a negative quantity. When you tab out of the Qty. Ordered text box control, the application displays the error message shown in Figure 11-3, and it won't let you leave the Qty. Ordered text box control until you correct the quantity or press Esc to clear your edits.

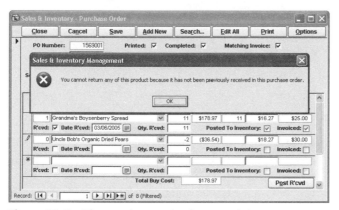

Figure 11-3   The purchase order form won't let you return a product that hasn't been ordered.

You can press Esc until the new row clears and then try to return more than 11 of the Grandma's Boysenberry Spread product. When you try to leave the Qty. Ordered text box control, the application tells you that you cannot return more than 11. The code to perform these checks runs in the BeforeUpdate event of the BuyQuantity text box control in the fsubPurchaseProducts form. The code depends on a working table and an append query to find the previously received records for the product being returned. The query that loads the table is zqappPOProductReturn, which sums the quantity for all product rows other than the current row by vendor and cost. The SQL of the query is as follows:

```
PARAMETERS POParm Long, ProductParm Long, LineParm Short;
INSERT INTO zttblOrderProductReturn ( OrderID, ProductID, QuantityRequired, Cost, Price,
VendorID )
SELECT tblPOProducts.PONumber, tblPOProducts.ProductID, Sum(tblPOProducts.BuyQuantity) AS
SumOfBuyQuantity, tblPOProducts.Cost, tblProducts.SellPrice, tblPOProducts.VendorID
FROM tblProducts INNER JOIN tblPOProducts ON tblProducts.ProductID = tblPOProducts.ProductID
WHERE (((tblPOProducts.Received)=-1) AND ((tblPOProducts.LineNo)<>[LineParm]) AND
((tblPOProducts.PONumber)=[POParm]) AND ((tblPOProducts.ProductID)=[ProductParm]))
GROUP BY tblPOProducts.PONumber, tblPOProducts.ProductID, tblPOProducts.Cost,
tblProducts.SellPrice, tblPOProducts.VendorID;
```

Notice that the query contains three parameters to select the current purchase order, the current product, and all product request lines other than the line the user is currently editing. The query also includes only rows that have been received (Received=-1).

The BeforeUpdate procedure of the BuyQuantity text box control (its label is Qty. Ordered on the form) performs the validations. First the procedure verifies that the quantity entered is not zero. (The Default Value property of the BuyQuantity field is set to 1.) If the quantity is greater than zero, no further checks are required. When the quantity is less than zero, the code clears a working table, opens the zqappPOProductReturn query, sets the three parameters, and executes the query to load the current data into the working table. The code is as follows:

```
Private Sub BuyQuantity_BeforeUpdate(Cancel As Integer)
Dim qd As DAO.QueryDef, rst As DAO.Recordset
  If Me.BuyQuantity > 0 Then Exit Sub
  ' Price and quantity matching on a return!
  ' We're borrowing the same temp table used for OrderProducts
  db.Execute "Delete * From zttblOrderProductReturn"
  ' Get the template query
  Set qd = db.QueryDefs("zqappPOProductReturn")
  ' Set the parameters
  qd!POParm = Me.PONumber
  qd!ProductParm = Me.ProductID
  qd!LineParm = Me.LineNo
  ' Insert the net sum of purchase order lines for this product
  qd.Execute
  ' Refresh the Tabledefs collection to see the added rows
  db.TableDefs.Refresh
```

The code then checks the number of rows in the table. When more than one row exists (indicating this product has been received at different costs—not likely but possible), the code opens the fdlgPickPOReturnCost form that is bound to the table just loaded by the zqappPOProductReturn query. The working table has a True/False field called ThisOne that indicates the row the user chose. Code in the fdlgPickPOReturnCost form ensures that the user selects one and only one row.

When the user closes that form, the code following the OpenForm command runs. (When code opens a form in Dialog mode, the code halts until the form closes or hides.) The code in the BeforeUpdate event then finds the row the user selected, sets the selected cost in the current product record, and then verifies that the amount being returned is not greater than the amount received. If the amount is too large, the code informs the user and cancels saving the new quantity. The code is as follows:

```
  ' See if more than one
  Select Case db.TableDefs("zttblOrderProductReturn").RecordCount
    Case Is > 1
      ' Yes, open the "pick the cost" form
      DoCmd.OpenForm "fdlgPickPOReturnCost", acNormal, , , , acDialog
      ' Code continues when form closes
      ' - open a recordset on the working table
      Set rst = db.OpenRecordset("Select [Cost], [Price], " & _
        [ListPrice], [VendorID], " & _
        "[QuantityRequired] From zttblOrderProductReturn " & _
        "Where [ThisOne] = True")
      If rst.EOF Then
        MsgBox "Unexpected error choosing return price.", _
          vbCritical, gstrAppTitle
        Cancel = True
        Exit Sub
      End If
```

```
      ' Set the selected cost
      Me.Cost = rst!Cost
      ' .. but check to see that quantity wanted to return
      ' is not more than received
      If Abs(Me.BuyQuantity) > rst!QuantityRequired Then
        MsgBox "You can't return more than were " & _
          "previously received at the cost you selected.  " & _
          "Maximum return at this cost is " & rst![QuantityRequired] & _
          ".", vbCritical, gstrAppTitle
        Cancel = True
      End If
      rst.Close
      Set rst = Nothing
```

When only one row exists (all previous purchase order rows were at the same cost), the code fetches that row, sets the cost, and performs the same quantity check. The code is as follows:

```
    Case 1
      ' Only one cost record - get it
      Set rst = db.OpenRecordset("Select * From zttblOrderProductReturn")
      ' Set the cost
      Me.Cost = rst!Cost
      ' .. but check that enough previously received
      If Abs(Me.BuyQuantity) > rst!QuantityRequired Then
        MsgBox "You can't return more than were " & _
          "previously received for this product.  " & _
          "Maximum return is " & rst![QuantityRequired] & ".", _
          vbCritical, gstrAppTitle
        Cancel = True
      End If
      rst.Close
      Set rst = Nothing
```

And finally, when no previous rows exist, the code displays an appropriate error message and cancels the save. This is the message you can see in Figure 11-3. The code is as follows:

```
    Case 0
      ' No records - cannot return it!
      MsgBox "You cannot return any of this product because " & _
        "it has not been previously " & _
        "received in this purchase order.", vbCritical, gstrAppTitle
      Cancel = True
  End Select
End Sub
```

The one other immediate quantity check performed in the fsubPurchaseProducts form occurs in the BeforeUpdate event of the QuantityReceived text box control. If Received is selected, then the code verifies that the quantity is not zero. The code is as shown on the next page.

```
Private Sub QuantityReceived_BeforeUpdate(Cancel As Integer)
  On Error GoTo Error_QuantityReceived_BeforeUpdate
  ' If Received checked
  If (Me.Received = True) Then
    ' Quantity cannot be zero
```

```
      If Me.QuantityReceived = 0 Then
        MsgBox "Quantity received cannot be zero.", vbCritical, gstrAppTitle
        Cancel = True
        Exit Sub
      End If
    End If
Exit_QuantityReceived_BeforeUpdate:
  Exit Sub
Error_QuantityReceived_BeforeUpdate:
  mlngErr = Err
  mstrError = Error
  ErrorLog Me.Name & ".QuantityReceived_BeforeUpdate", mlngErr, mstrError
  MsgBox "Unexpected error " & mlngErr & ", " & mstrError & _
    " has been logged.", vbCritical, gstrAppTitle
  Resume Exit_QuantityReceived_BeforeUpdate
End Sub
```

Validating a Product Request Before Saving It

Although the BeforeUpdate event procedures for the BuyQuantity and QuantityReceived text boxes in the fsubPurchaseProducts form perform some preliminary checks, some final validation must be performed just before any new row or any changed row is saved. These checks are performed in the BeforeUpdate event procedure for the fsubPurchaseProducts form.

First, the procedure verifies that the quantity ordered (the BuyQuantity field) is not zero. Although the tblPOProducts table also has a field validation rule to enforce this, it's more efficient to catch the problem in the form. If the quantity is less than zero, the code checks that the quantity received is not larger than the quantity ordered and that the quantity received is not positive. If the quantity received passes the checks, the code performs one final check using the *DSum* function to ensure that the amount being returned is not more than was ordered. The code to perform these checks is as follows:

```
Private Sub Form_BeforeUpdate(Cancel As Integer)
Dim varQty As Variant, strSearch As String
Dim varNum As Variant
  On Error GoTo Error_Form_BeforeUpdate
  ' First, verify BuyQuantity against Quantity Received
  Select Case Me.BuyQuantity
    ' Can't specify zero
    Case 0
      MsgBox "Quantity Ordered cannot be zero.", vbCritical, gstrAppTitle
      Cancel = True
      Exit Sub
    ' If less than zero (returning products)
    Case Is < 0
      ' .. and Qty received is less than buy quantity
      If Me.QuantityReceived < Me.BuyQuantity Then
        MsgBox "Quantity Credited can't be " & _
          "larger than Quantity Returned.", _
          vbCritical, gstrAppTitle
        Cancel = True
        Exit Sub
```

```
          End If
          ' .. or Qty received is positive
          If Me.QuantityReceived > 0 Then
            MsgBox "Quantity Received can't be positive " & _
              "when Quantity Ordered is negative.", _
              vbCritical, gstrAppTitle
            Cancel = True
            Exit Sub
          End If
          ' Quantities look OK
          ' Do a final check to make sure more was ordered
          ' than is being returned
          strSearch = "[PONumber] = " & Me.PONumber & " AND [LineNo] <> " & _
            Me.LineNo & " AND [ProductID] = " & Me.ProductID
          varQty = DSum("BuyQuantity", "tblPOProducts", strSearch)
          If Not IsNull(varQty) Then
            If varQty >= (-Me.BuyQuantity) Then Exit Sub
          End If
          MsgBox "You can't return more of an item " & _
            "than you have ordered in this PO.", _
            vbCritical, gstrAppTitle
          Cancel = True
          Exit Sub
```

When the quantity ordered is positive, the quantity received cannot be more than the quantity ordered, and the quantity received cannot be negative. The code to verify this is as follows:

```
        ' If quantity is positive
        Case Is > 0
          ' Make sure that Qty received isn't greater
          If Me.QuantityReceived > Me.BuyQuantity Then
            MsgBox "Quantity Received can't be " & _
              "larger than Quantity Ordered.", _
              vbCritical, gstrAppTitle
            Cancel = True
            Exit Sub
          End If
          ' .. and Qty received is not negative
          If Me.QuantityReceived < 0 Then
            MsgBox "Quantity Received can't be negative " & _
              "when Quantity Ordered is positive.", _
              vbCritical, gstrAppTitle
            Cancel = True
            Exit Sub
          End If
      End Select
```

Finally, the code checks to see if this is a new record. If it is, the code generates the next line number for the purchase order and sets it in the record. Also, if the purchase order is for a customer order, the code verifies that the user wants to add the product request via the purchase order and warns that the record can later be deleted only via the customer order. The code is as shown on the next page.

```
        ' If on a new record
        If Me.NewRecord Then
          ' Get and set the next line number
          varNum = DMax("LineNo", "tblPOProducts", _
            "[PONumber] = " & Me.Parent.PONumber)
          If IsNull(varNum) Then
            Me.LineNo = 1
          Else
            Me.LineNo = varNum + 1
          End If
          ' .. and if on a new record for a customer order
          If (Not IsNothing(Me.Parent.OrderID)) Then
            ' Verify the user really wants to do this
            If vbNo = MsgBox("Are you sure you want to add product " & _
              Me.cmbProductID.Column(1) & " to this purchase order " & _
              "for customer order " & Me.Parent.txtOrder & "?" & _
              vbCrLf & vbCrLf & "(You must open the customer order " & _
              "to delete the request if you change your mind later.)", _
              vbQuestion + vbYesNo + vbDefaultButton2, gstrAppTitle) Then
              ' Cancel the save
              Cancel = True
              ' Tell the user what to do next
              MsgBox "Press Esc to clear your edits.", _
                vbInformation, gstrAppTitle
            End If
          End If
        End If
Exit_Form_BeforeUpdate:
    Exit Sub
Error_Form_BeforeUpdate:
    mlngErr = Err
    mstrError = Error
    ErrorLog Me.Name & ".Form_BeforeUpdate", mlngErr, mstrError
    MsgBox "Unexpected error " & mlngErr & ", " & mstrError & _
      " has been logged.", _
      vbCritical, gstrAppTitle
    Cancel = True
    Resume Exit_Form_BeforeUpdate
End Sub
```

Verifying Rows to Be Deleted

When a product has been posted to inventory, the user should not be allowed to delete the product request because a complex process is required to synchronize the stock and inventory records. Instead, the user must enter a credit record and then post that credit to inventory.

Also, as you learned in Chapter 10 in "Verifying Rows to Be Deleted" on page 198, there's a complex process involved to make sure the customer order and purchase order are synchronized when deleting a row. I could have duplicated that process in the fsubPurchaseProducts form, but I decided to disallow deleting a row when the purchase order is for a customer order. The application instructs the user to delete the request via the customer order in that case. You can find the code that performs these checks in the Delete event of the fsubPurchaseProducts form. The code is as follows:

```
Private Sub Form_Delete(Cancel As Integer)
  On Error GoTo Error_Form_Delete
  If (Me.Posted = True) Then
    MsgBox "Can't delete a posted item.", vbCritical, gstrAppTitle
    Cancel = True
    Exit Sub
  End If
  If Not IsNull(Me.Parent.OrderID) Then
    MsgBox "Can't delete a Product from a Purchase Order " & _
      "associated with an Order.  " & _
      "Revise the Order instead.", vbCritical, gstrAppTitle
    Cancel = True
    Exit Sub
  End If
Exit_Form_Delete:
  Exit Sub
Error_Form_Delete:
  mlngErr = Err
  mstrError = Error
  ErrorLog Me.Name & ".Form_Delete", mlngErr, mstrError
  MsgBox "Unexpected error " & mlngErr & ", " & mstrError & _
    " has been logged.", vbCritical, gstrAppTitle
  Resume Exit_Form_Delete
End Sub
```

Synchronizing Inserted Requests

The application does allow the user to add new product request rows in a purchase order for a customer order. However, to ensure that the customer order reflects the same information, code in the fsubPurchaseProducts form inserts the new row in the customer order on behalf of the user. You can try this out by adding a request for another product in purchase order number 1569001 shown earlier. When you try to save the row, the application warns you that you'll be able to delete the request only via the customer order if you change your mind later, as shown in Figure 11-4 on the next page.

You saw the code that produces this warning earlier in "Validating a Product Request Before Saving It" on page 226. After you click Yes, the application allows the row to be saved. You can double-click the Order text box on the purchase order to open the related customer order. If you scroll to the bottom of the list of products requested, you'll find a new request for the product you requested—the customer order and the purchase order are synchronized correctly.

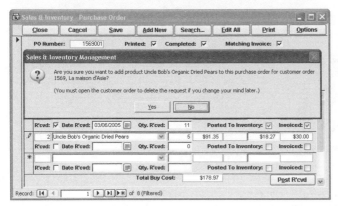

Figure 11-4   The application warns you when you add a product request in a purchase order for a customer order.

You can find the code that synchronizes the data in the AfterUpdate event procedure for the fsubPurchaseProducts form. The code uses the Execute method of a database object to run an Insert SQL command. The code is as follows:

```
Private Sub Form_AfterInsert()
Dim varLinNo As Variant
  On Error GoTo Error_Form_AfterInsert
  DoCmd.Hourglass True
  ' If there's an order, then stuff the new row there, too!
  If Not IsNothing(Me.Parent.OrderID) Then
    varLinNo = DMax("[LineNo]", "tblOrderProducts", _
      "[OrderID] = " & Me.Parent.OrderID) + 1
    If IsNull(varLinNo) Then varLinNo = 1
    db.Execute "INSERT INTO tblOrder Products " & _
      "(OrderID, LineNo, ProductID, VendorID, Quantity, OrderPONo, " & _
      "OrderPOLineNo, Cost, Price, Status) " & _
      "VALUES(" & Me.Parent.OrderID & ", " & varLinNo & ", " & _
      Me.ProductID & ", " & Me.Parent.VendorID & _
      ", " & Me.SellQuantity & ", " & _
      Me.PONumber & ", " & Me.LineNo & ", " & Me.Cost & ", " & _
      DLookup("SellPrice", "tblProducts", _
      "ProductID = " & Me.ProductID) & ", " & _
      OrderStatus.OnOrder & ")", dbFailOnError
  End If
  ' If Orders is open
  If IsFormLoaded("frmOrders") Then
    ' Requery the subform
    Forms!frmOrders!fsubOrderProducts.Requery
  End If
Exit_Form_AfterInsert:
  DoCmd.Hourglass False
  Exit Sub
Error_Form_AfterInsert:
  mlngErr = Err
  mstrError = Error
  ErrorLog Me.Name & "_AfterInsert", mlngErr, mstrError
```

```
      MsgBox "Unexpected error attempting to sync Order with this PO: " & _
        mlngErr & ", " & mstrError & " has been logged.", _
        vbCritical, gstrAppTitle
      Resume Exit_Form_AfterInsert
End Sub
```

Creating Purchase Orders for Customer Orders

In Chapter 10 in "Allocating Available Inventory" on page 200, you saw how the allocation process splits a request for more of a product than is currently in inventory into a request for the available amount and a second row for the amount that will have to be ordered from a vendor. Also in Chapter 10 in "Understanding the AllocateProducts Procedure" on page 203, you learned that the *AllocateProducts* function tests for unallocated products at the end of the process and offers to call a procedure (GenProductsPO) to create purchase orders. For review, the code at the end of the *AllocateProducts* function is as follows:

```
' See if any left unallocated - run the "append leftovers" query
Set qd = db.QueryDefs("zqappOrderProductsToOrder")
qd![OrderParm] = lngOrder
qd.Execute
' See if there are any rows
If DCount("*", "ztTblProductsToOrder") <> 0 Then
  ' Yes - set a flag
  intSomeLeft = True
  ' Ask if user wants to create Purchase Orders
  ' But auto-create PO if called from zfrmLoadData
  If intSilent Then
    intDoPO = vbYes
  Else
    intDoPO = MsgBox("Insufficient stock in inventory for one " & _
      "or more Products required for this order.  " & _
      "Do you want to generate purchase orders for this order?", _
      vbQuestion + vbYesNo, gstrAppTitle)
  End If
  If intDoPO = vbYes Then
    ' Turn off local error trapping
    On Error GoTo 0
    ' Call the Product PO generator - pass the silent flag
    If GenProductsPO(lngOrder, intSilent, datAllocDate) Then
      ' Indicate Purchase Orders created
      AllocateProducts = 1
      intSomeLeft = False
    End If
  End If
End If
```

The query that the code executes loads the zttblProductsToOrder working table that drives the purchase order generation process. The table contains the product ID required, the related line number in the tblOrderProducts table, the default or preferred vendor for the product, the product description, the quantity needed for the customer order, and the order by, order multiple, and sell by values for the product. The SQL for the query is as follows:

```
PARAMETERS OrderParm Long;
INSERT INTO zttblProductsToOrder ( ProductID, LineNo, VendorID, ProductDescription, Quantity,
OrderBy, OrderMultiple, SellBy )
SELECT tblOrderProducts.ProductID, tblOrderProducts.LineNo, tblVendorProducts.VendorID,
tblProducts.Description, tblOrderProducts.Quantity, tblProducts.OrderBy,
tblProducts.OrderMultiple, tblProducts.SellBy
FROM tblProducts
INNER JOIN (tblOrderProducts
  LEFT JOIN tblVendorProducts
  ON tblOrderProducts.ProductID = tblVendorProducts.ProductID)
ON tblProducts.ProductID = tblOrderProducts.ProductID
WHERE (((tblOrderProducts.Quantity)<>0) AND ((tblOrderProducts.Status)=0) AND
((tblOrderProducts.OrderID)=[OrderParm]) AND ((tblVendorProducts.VendorSeq)=
(Select Min(VendorSeq)
From tblVendorProducts As P
Where P.[ProductID] = tblOrderProducts.[ProductID]) Or (tblVendorProducts.VendorSeq) Is
Null));
```

Note that the query finds the preferred or default vendor using a subquery that finds the vendor with the lowest sequence number.

The *GenProductsPO* function can generate purchase orders for a customer order or purchase orders to bring stock up to minimum stocking levels. The function uses the zttblProducts-ToOrder table for both processes to know which products to order. If the first parameter, lngOrder, is not zero, the function creates purchase orders for the customer order specified in the parameter. Later in this chapter, in "Ordering for Stock" on page 237, you'll see how the application works to create orders for stock and pass a zero lngOrder parameter.

The first part of the *GenProductsPO* function (after all the variable declarations) checks to see if an optional date has been passed as a parameter. This function can be called from the code in the zfrmLoadData form that lets you reload sample data, and you can specify a range of dates to process. If no date is provided, the function uses the current date for the purchase orders it generates. Next, the code opens the fdlgPOProducts form to allow the user to verify the products to be ordered. When the function has been called to generate purchase orders for a customer order, it passes a parameter to the form to disallow deleting records. If the user decides to cancel the purchase order generation process at this point, the function exits.

Next, the function opens the recordsets it needs on the tblPurchaseOrders and tblPOProducts tables and generates the starting number for the new purchase orders. Purchase orders for customer orders use the customer order number with a three-digit suffix to provide up to 999 purchase orders per customer order. To process the products to order, the function opens a query that uses the zttblProductsToOrder table. For customer orders, the zqryProductsTo-OrderWOrder query includes information from the related records in tblOrderProducts, and the query is constructed so that the code can update the companion customer order row. The code is as follows:

```
Function GenProductsPO(lngOrder As Long, Optional intSilent As Integer, _
  Optional varDate As Variant) As Long
'
'   This function gives the user the opportunity to validate the vendors
'   for products to order and to confirm generation of Purchase Orders
'
'   Input:  Order ID if from Order build
'           Zero in lngOrder if ordering for stock
'
'   Output: Returns True to the caller if user cancels the edit form.
'           If user confirms, then builds one purchase order per vendor
'           found in zttblProductsToOrder.  If generating for an order,
'           Inserts OrderID and updates the matching tblOrderProducts row.
'           Returns the number of the first PO generated.
'           Returns False if an error occurred
'
' Note: When called from zfrmLoadData, intSilent is True
'       - procedure will open
'       no forms or reports and will not display any errors.
'       zfrmLoadData also passes the date it wants to use as the PO date.
'
Dim db As DAO.Database
Dim rstPO As DAO.Recordset, rstPOProducts As DAO.Recordset
Dim rstPToOrder As DAO.Recordset, qd As DAO.QueryDef
Dim varRet As Variant, lngPOCount As Long
Dim lngPONum As Long, lngI As Long, intLine As Integer
Dim lngFirstPONum As Long, lngThisVend As Long
Dim intQty As Integer, intMult As Integer
Dim curPrice As Currency, intTrans As Integer
Dim lngBaseNum As Long, varPONo As Variant
Dim strWhere As String, varPOList As Variant
Dim intNoMessages As Integer, datToday As Date
  On Error GoTo GenProductsPO_ERR
  GenProductsPO = False
  ' Set up the PO date
  datToday = Date
  ' If passed a date variable
  If Not IsMissing(varDate) Then
    ' .. and it's a valid date
    If IsDate(varDate) Then
      ' Use the parameter value
      datToday = varDate
      ' And set the default schedule date
      gdatPOSchedDate = varDate + 7
    End If
  End If
  ' If called in "silent" mode from zfrmLoadData
  If intSilent Then
    ' Clear the global cancel PO flag
    gintPOProductCancel = 0
  Else
    ' Open the Products to order edit form
    If IsNothing(lngOrder) Then
      ' If no Order ID (ordering for stock),
      ' then open normally (allow deletes)
```

```
      DoCmd.OpenForm "fdlgPOProducts", acNormal, , , acEdit, acDialog
    Else
      DoCmd.OpenForm "fdlgPOProducts", acNormal, , , _
        acEdit, acDialog, "NoDelete"
    End If
  End If
  ' If user clicked cancel, then done
  If gintPOProductCancel Then
    GenProductsPO = True
    Exit Function
  End If
  DoEvents
  Set db = DBEngine(0)(0)
  ' Open Purchase order for Insert Only
  Set rstPO = db.OpenRecordset("tblPurchaseOrders", _
    dbOpenDynaset, dbAppendOnly)
  ' Open Purchase order Products for Insert Only
  Set rstPOProducts = db.OpenRecordset("tblPOProducts", _
    dbOpenDynaset, dbAppendOnly)
  ' Set up the "next" PO Number
  If IsNothing(lngOrder) Then
    ' Order for stock - use year as the base with a "9" prefix
    lngBaseNum = ((Year(datToday)) * 1000) + 90000000
  Else
    ' Use Order ID as Product of the number if for a specific order
    lngBaseNum = lngOrder * 1000
  End If
  strWhere = "[PONumber] > " & lngBaseNum & _
    " AND [PONumber] < " & lngBaseNum + 1000
  varPONo = DMax("[PONumber]", "tblPurchaseOrders", strWhere) + 1
  If IsNull(varPONo) Then varPONo = lngBaseNum + 1
  lngPONum = varPONo
  ' Clear the PO list to print
  varPOList = Null
  lngFirstPONum = lngPONum
  ' Get the list of Products to order
  If Not IsNothing(lngOrder) Then
    Set qd = db.QueryDefs("zqryProductsToOrderWOrder")
    qd![OrderNo] = lngOrder
    Set rstPToOrder = qd.OpenRecordset()
  Else
    Set rstPToOrder = db.OpenRecordset("zqryProductsToOrder")
  End If
  rstPToOrder.MoveLast   ' Get record count
  lngPOCount = rstPToOrder.RecordCount
  varRet = SysCmd(acSysCmdInitMeter, _
    "Creating Purchase Orders...", lngPOCount)
  rstPToOrder.MoveFirst
```

Both queries on the zttblProductsToOrder table deliver the rows in vendor ID and product ID sequence. The code loops through all the rows to create one purchase order per vendor. When the code encounters a new vendor ID, and it isn't the first one, the code commits the transaction created for the previous purchase order and adds the purchase order number to the list to print later. The code then starts a new transaction for the next purchase order and creates the row in the tblPurchaseOrders table. The code is as follows:

```
Do Until rstPToOrder.EOF
  ' If record for different vendor
  If lngThisVend <> rstPToOrder![ThisVend] Then
    ' .. and this isn't the first one
    If lngThisVend <> 0 Then
      ' Commit the PO insert
      CommitTrans
      intTrans = False
      ' Save the PO Number to print later
      varPOList = (varPOList + ", ") & lngPONum
      ' Increment the PO number
      lngPONum = lngPONum + 1
    End If
    ' Start a new PO - First, create a purchase order row
    ' Protect everything with a transaction
    BeginTrans
    intTrans = True
    rstPO.AddNew
    rstPO!PONumber = lngPONum
    rstPO!PODate = datToday
    rstPO!ScheduleDate = gdatPOSchedDate
    rstPO!VendorID = rstPToOrder![ThisVend]
    rstPO!Printed = True
    If lngOrder <> 0 Then rstPO!OrderID = lngOrder
    rstPO.Update
    intLine = 0
  End If
  lngThisVend = rstPToOrder![ThisVend]
```

Next, the code creates one row per product in the tblPOProducts table. To calculate the amount to be ordered from the vendor, the code rounds up the buy quantity to the next even multiple of the order multiple. It does this because the customer order might need a quantity less than the amount that the user must order from the vendor. For example, a customer might need a quantity of 5, but the vendor supplies the product only in a full case containing 24 products. When generating purchase orders for a customer order, the code edits the row in the zqryProductsToOrderWOrder query, updates the actual quantity ordered, adds the purchase order number, line number, and vendor ID, and sets the status to On Order. The code is as follows:

```
  ' Next, add the Products for this PO
  rstPOProducts.AddNew
  rstPOProducts!PONumber = lngPONum
  intLine = intLine + 1
  rstPOProducts!LineNo = intLine
  rstPOProducts!VendorID = lngThisVend
  rstPOProducts!ProductID = rstPToOrder![ProductID]
  intQty = rstPToOrder![Quantity]
  intMult = rstPToOrder![OrderMultiple]
  rstPOProducts!SellQuantity = intQty
```

```
' Calculate the purchase amount -
' We often sell in quantities smaller than we can order
If intQty Mod intMult = 0 Then
    rstPOProducts!BuyQuantity = intQty \ intMult
Else
    rstPOProducts!BuyQuantity = (intQty \ intMult) + 1
End If
rstPOProducts!OrderBy = rstPToOrder![OrderBy]
rstPOProducts!SellBy = rstPToOrder![SellBy]
rstPOProducts!OrderMultiple = intMult
rstPOProducts!Cost = rstPToOrder![VendCost]
rstPOProducts!Price = rstPToOrder![ListPrice]
rstPOProducts.Update
' If creating for an order
If Not IsNothing(lngOrder) Then
    ' edit the tblOrderProducts portion
    rstPToOrder.Edit
    rstPToOrder!OrderQty = intQty
    rstPToOrder!OrderPONo = lngPONum
    rstPToOrder!OrderPOLineNo = intLine
    rstPToOrder!VendorID = lngThisVend
    ' Set status to "on order"
    rstPToOrder!Status = OrderStatus.OnOrder
    rstPToOrder.Update
End If
' Update the status meter
lngI = lngI + 1
varRet = SysCmd(acSysCmdUpdateMeter, lngI)
rstPToOrder.MoveNext
Loop
```

After processing all the product request rows, the code commits the last purchase order and adds the purchase order number to the list to print. If not called from the code in the zfrmLoadData form, the intSilent variable will be False, so the code opens the rptPurchase-Order report and filters it for the list of new purchase orders produced. The code returns the number of the first purchase order produced, closes all recordsets, and exits. The code at the end of the procedure handles any errors encountered. The code is as follows:

```
' Commit the final PO
CommitTrans
DBEngine.Idle dbFreeLocks
' Add the last PO number to the filter string
varPOList = (varPOList + ", ") & lngPONum
' If not in "silent" mode,
If Not intSilent Then
    ' Open the purchase orders we created in Print Preview
    DoCmd.OpenReport "rptPurchaseOrder", acViewPreview, _
        WhereCondition:="[PONumber] IN (" & varPOList & ")"
End If
GenProductsPO_Exit_Print:
    ' Return the number of the first PO generated
    GenProductsPO = lngFirstPONum
    rstPToOrder.Close
    Set rstPToOrder = Nothing
```

```
        rstPO.Close
        Set rstPO = Nothing
        rstPOProducts.Close
        Set rstPOProducts = Nothing
GenProductsPO_Exit:
    varRet = SysCmd(acSysCmdClearStatus)
    Exit Function
GenProductsPO_ERR:
Dim strError As String, lngErr As Long
    ' Save the error codes
    strError = Error
    lngErr = Err
    ' Turn off error trapping
    On Error Resume Next
    ' intTrans indicates a transaction needs to be rolled back
    If (intTrans = True) Then Rollback
    ' Clear the status bar
    varRet = SysCmd(acSysCmdClearStatus)
    ' Make sure the hourglass is off
    DoCmd.Hourglass False
    ' Log the error
    ErrorLog "GenProductsPO", lngErr, strError
    ' Tell the user if not in silent mode
    If Not intSilent Then MsgBox "Unexpected error: " & _
        lngErr & ", " & strError & _
        "  Error has been logged.", _
        vbCritical, gstrAppTitle
    Resume GenProductsPO_Exit
End Function
```

Ordering for Stock

Many of the available products have a minimum stocking level defined. The idea is to keep the most popular products in stock so that customer orders aren't delayed waiting for a shipment from the vendor. Depending on the order activity, the business might want to execute an "order for stock" to bring stock to minimum levels once a month, once a week, or even once a day.

To see how this works, you need to sign on to the application. Open the frmSplash form and then sign on as any of the employees (the password is the employee last name unless you have changed it). On the main switchboard, click Vendors and Purchase Orders. On the Vendors, Purchase Orders, and Invoices pop-up form (fpopOptionsVendorPO), click Purchase Orders. On the Select Purchase Orders pop-up form (fpopPurchaseOrderSelect), click the Stock button. This takes you to the Order for Inventory dialog box form (fdlgPOStockOptions), as shown in Figure 11-5 on the next page, where you can choose to bring the stock to minimum levels for all vendors or a specific vendor.

Click the Create PO button, and code behind the form calculates the inventory shortages and calls the *GenProductsPO* function. You'll see the function open the Products to Order – Verify Vendor form (fdlgPOProducts) so that you can make sure you're ordering the products from the correct vendor. You can click the Print List button to print a list of the products about to be ordered (rptProductsToOrder). Click the Done button to generate the purchase orders, and the *GenProductsPO* function creates the purchase orders and opens a filtered report (rptPurchaseOrder) to print all the new purchase orders.

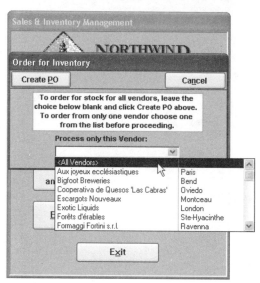

Figure 11-5   Ordering for stock for all vendors or a specific vendor.

The code that executes when you click the Done button on the fdlgPOStockOptions form uses a query template to calculate the products that are below minimum stock levels. The zqappOrderForInvTemplate query uses another query, zqtotOnOrderForInventory, to take into account products already on order but not yet posted to inventory. The query calculates the quantity to order as an even multiple of the economic order quantity (the EOQ field). The economic order quantity for most products is probably a single case or pallet, but some vendors might offer a large discount when ordering in multiples of 3 or 5—the economic order quantity. The SQL for the query template is as follows:

```
INSERT INTO zttblProductsToOrder ( ProductID, VendorID, ProductDescription, Quantity, OrderBy,
OrderMultiple, SellBy )
SELECT tblProducts.ProductID, tblVendorProducts.VendorID, tblProducts.Description,
IIf([EOQ]=0,[Minimum]-NZ([QuantityOnHand],0),
  IIf(([Minimum]-NZ([QuantityOnHand],0)) Mod [EOQ]=0,
  (([Minimum] NZ([QuantityOnHand],0))\[EOQ])*[EOQ],
  ((([Minimum]-NZ([QuantityOnHand],0))\[EOQ])+1)*[EOQ])) AS QtyToOrder, tblProducts.OrderBy,
tblProducts.OrderMultiple, tblProducts.SellBy
FROM ((tblProducts
LEFT JOIN zqtotOnOrderForInventory
ON tblProducts.ProductID = zqtotOnOrderForInventory.ProductID)
LEFT JOIN tblInventory
ON tblProducts.ProductID = tblInventory.ProductID)
LEFT JOIN tblVendorProducts
ON tblProducts.ProductID = tblVendorProducts.ProductID;
```

When you click the Create PO button (the name of the control is cmdGo) on the fdlgPOStock-Options form, Access runs the Click event procedure for the button. The procedure clears the zttblProductsToOrder table, opens the template query, and appends an appropriate WHERE clause to the SQL depending on whether you have chosen all vendors or a specific vendor. The WHERE clause includes a test to include only those products that are below minimum stocking level. The code then executes that query to load records into the zttblProductsToOrder table. If the query added one or more records to the table, the code calls the *GenProductsPO* function with a zero order ID parameter to indicate purchase orders should be created for stock orders. The code is as follows:

```
Private Sub cmdGo_Click()
Dim db As DAO.Database, qd As DAO.QueryDef
Dim lngReturn As Long, varRet As Variant
Dim strSQL As String
On Error GoTo cmdStock_ERR
  ' Point to this database
  Set db = DBEngine(0)(0)
  ' Inform user on status bar
  varRet = SysCmd(acSysCmdSetStatus, _
    "Calculating Inventory product shortages...")
  ' .. and turn on hourglass to indicate this might take a sec.
  DoCmd.Hourglass True
  ' Clear out the working table
  db.Execute "DELETE * FROM zttblProductsToOrder", dbFailOnError
  ' Open the append query template
  Set qd = db.QueryDefs("zqappOrderForInvTemplate")
  ' Get the SQL string
  strSQL = qd.SQL
  ' Strip off the ending semi-colon
  strSQL = Left(strSQL, InStr(strSQL, ";") - 1)
  ' Check for vendor ID and add the correct WHERE clause
  If IsNothing(Me!cmbVendorID) Then
    strSQL = strSQL & _
      " WHERE (((tblVendorProducts.VendorSeq)=(Select Min(VendorSeq) " & _
      "From tblVendorProducts As P " & _
      "Where P.[ProductID] = tblProducts.[ProductID]) " & _
      "Or (tblVendorProducts.VendorSeq) Is Null) AND " & _
      "((NZ([QuantityOnHand],0)+IIf(IsNull([SumOfQuantity]),0," & _
      "IIf([SumOfQuantity]<0,0,[SumOfQuantity])))<[Minimum]));"
  Else
    strSQL = strSQL & _
      " WHERE ((tblVendorProducts.VendorID= " & Me!cmbVendorID & _
      " Or tblVendorProducts.VendorID Is Null) AND " & _
      "(tblVendorProducts.VendorSeq=" & _
      "(Select Min(VendorSeq) From tblVendorProducts As P " & _
      "Where P.[ProductID] = tblProducts.[ProductID]) Or " & _
      "tblVendorProducts.VendorSeq Is Null) AND " & _
      "((NZ([QuantityOnHand],0)+IIf(IsNull([SumOfQuantity]),0," & _
      "IIf([SumOfQuantity]<0,0,[SumOfQuantity])))<[Minimum]));"
  End If
  ' Execute the resulting SQL
  db.Execute strSQL, dbFailOnError
  ' Clear the status message and hourglass
```

```
        varRet = SysCmd(acSysCmdClearStatus)
        DoCmd.Hourglass False
        ' Refresh the Tabledefs collection to see the added rows
        db.TableDefs.Refresh
        ' See if we got any products to order for stock
        If db.TableDefs!zttblProductsToOrder.RecordCount = 0 Then
            ' Nope - let user know
            MsgBox "No products in inventory are below minimum stock level.", _
                vbInformation, gstrAppTitle
        Else
            ' Yes - hide me and call the PO generation function
            Me.Visible = False
            DoEvents
            ' Zero argument indicates "order for stock"
            lngReturn = GenProductsPO(0)
            ' True (-1) indicates user clicked cancel;
            ' False (0) indicates error occurred
            ' Otherwise returns PONumber from first PO generated
            If lngReturn < 1 Then MsgBox "No products were ordered.", _
                vbInformation, gstrAppTitle
        End If
        DoCmd.Close acForm, Me.Name
        Exit Sub
    cmdStock_ERR:
    Dim lngErr As Long, strError As String
        lngErr = Err
        strError = Error
        ErrorLog Me.Name & "_cmdGo_Click", lngErr, strError
        MsgBox "Unexpected error: " & lngErr & ", " & strError & _
            " has been logged.", vbCritical, gstrAppTitle
        Exit Sub
    End Sub
```

Now that you understand how the application edits and generates purchase orders, the next step is to see how received products get posted to inventory and to customer orders. The next chapter will show you how to do just that.

Chapter 12

Posting Received Items into Inventory

In the previous chapter, you learned how a user can create a new purchase order or edit an existing one, and how the application generates purchase orders either for customer requests or to restock inventory to minimum levels. Upon receipt of the purchase order, the vendor should ship the requested products and send an invoice. This chapter explains how the application allows the user to enter the vendor invoice (to ensure that the correct cost is recorded in inventory), mark a product received and invoiced, and post the received products to inventory and any related customer order.

Entering Vendor Invoices

Because inventory is tracked by product, vendor, and cost, the user must verify and enter the cost charged by the vendor before posting received products into inventory. To understand the mechanism for entering a vendor invoice, open the Inventory Management application (Inventory.mdb) and after the opening form closes, open the frmPurchaseOrder form. If you followed the steps in the previous chapter to create purchase orders for stock, you can find several open purchase orders at the end of the recordset. Click the Last Record button on the form and then move back through the recordset until you find a purchase order that has two or three products on order. Click the Options button to open the Purchase Order Options dialog box, choose the **New Invoice for current Purchase Order** option, and click the Invoices button as shown in Figure 12-1 on the next page.

The code that responds to the button click opens the frmVendorInvoices form and passes the vendor ID and purchase order number to that form so that it can set default values. The frmVendorInvoices form starts a new invoice, sets the vendor ID and purchase order number using the data passed by the Purchase Order Options dialog box, and displays all the product records from the purchase order that haven't been invoiced. The user can enter a unique vendor invoice number and click Save, as shown in Figure 12-2, to save the new invoice.

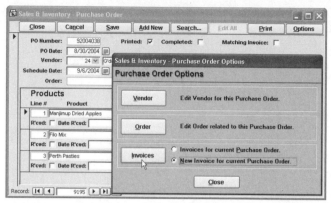

Figure 12-1 Asking the application to create a new vendor invoice for the current purchase order.

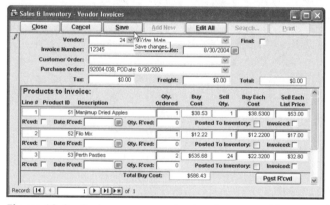

Figure 12-2 Saving a new vendor invoice created for a purchase order.

> **Note** You can see in Figure 12-2 that a quantity of 2 is on order for the Perth Pasties product, but the sell quantity is 24. If you were to look up the product record for Perth Pasties, you would find that the vendor sells this product in cases containing 12 items but this company resells the product individually to customers. So 2 ordered from the vendor results in 24 items to sell to customers in inventory.

The user can now enter any tax or freight charges from the vendor. The user can also mark which products have been received, update the date received, indicate a smaller quantity received than ordered if receiving a partial shipment, correct the cost and list price indicated by the vendor, and select which products appear on this vendor invoice by choosing the Invoiced box. When the user changes the quantity received, the subform updates the Buy Cost field and the total in the subform. As you'll learn later, the product posting process sets the Posted To Inventory box after the products have been posted.

Note that the application lets the user create more than one vendor invoice for a purchase order. A vendor might send an invoice for a partial shipment and later send another invoice for the items on back order. After the user marks the invoice final, the form shows only those products that were marked invoiced on the current vendor invoice. The user can later create another vendor invoice for any products remaining.

The form and the subform enforce a number of business rules. These rules are as follows:

- The user cannot change a vendor invoice marked final but can clear the final indicator to edit the invoice again.

- If the user selects a customer order, the user can choose a purchase order only for the selected vendor and customer order.

- If the invoice is not marked final, the subform displays all product request rows from the related purchase order that are either for the current vendor invoice or have not been invoiced. When the invoice is marked final, the subform displays only the product request rows for the current invoice.

- When the subform has related product request rows, the user cannot change the vendor, customer order, or purchase order number.

- The user can neither insert nor delete product request rows.

- If a product has been posted to inventory, the user cannot change the quantity ordered, cost, price, received, received date, quantity received, or invoiced fields.

- If the related purchase order is for a customer order, the user cannot change the quantity ordered field.

- The user cannot change the vendor unless neither a customer order nor a related purchase order has been specified.

- The user cannot save a vendor invoice that has no vendor or purchase order specified.

- The user cannot delete a vendor invoice marked final or that has related products posted to inventory.

- The quantity ordered cannot be changed to a value larger than originally specified in the original purchase order. The user must make such changes via the purchase order.

- The quantity received cannot be zero in a row marked received and it cannot be more than was ordered.

- When a quantity received is negative (credit for a returned product), the amount returned cannot be more than the total ordered.

- The cost and price must be greater than zero, and the price must be greater than the cost.

- The user cannot mark invoiced a product request that has a zero cost or price.

The following sections describe how theses rules are enforced by the application.

Controlling What the User Can Edit

Enforcing the business rule that disallows the user from inserting or deleting product request rows requires no code at all. You can open in Design view the fsubVendInvoiceProducts form that is the subform in the frmVendorInvoices form. Look at the Allow Additions and Allow Deletions properties, and you'll find both set to No. Enforcing the remaining rules requires Visual Basic code that you can find in the modules for the two forms.

Locking and Unlocking Controls in the Outer Form

As the user moves from one invoice to another in the frmVendorInvoices form, Access runs the code in the form's Current event procedure. The code in this procedure checks the status of the invoice about to be displayed and changes various properties to control what the user can see or do.

The beginning part of the procedure changes the availability of the command buttons in the form header. These buttons simplify executing certain actions, but not all buttons are appropriate at all times—for example, performing a search doesn't make sense when on a new record. When the user moves to a new record, the code disables the Search, Add New, and Print buttons. If the form has a filter applied, the user has moved to a new record, or the form is in Data Entry mode, the code makes the Edit All button available to make it simple for the user to remove the filter or exit Data Entry mode.

Next, the code calls the *AddCharges* procedure, explained later in "Updating the Displayed Total," page 252, to calculate the total for the current record and display it in an unbound control on the form. The code calls the *LockAll* procedure with a False argument to unlock all the editable controls. This procedure is nearly identical to the one you saw in Chapter 10, "Ordering Items from Inventory," for the frmOrders form. The code is as follows:

```
Private Sub Form_Current()
  On Error GoTo Error_Form_Current
  ' Set up availability of the command buttons
  Me.cmdSearch.Enabled = Not (Me.NewRecord)
  Me.cmdAddNew.Enabled = Not (Me.NewRecord)
  Me.cmdEditAll.Enabled = (Me.FilterOn Or Me.NewRecord Or Me.DataEntry)
  Me.cmdPrint.Enabled = Not (Me.NewRecord)
  ' Update the total
  AddCharges
  ' Start by unlocking all controls
  LockAll False
```

Next, if the form is on a new record, the code examines the record source of the subform and sets it to the qryVendInvoiceProducts query if necessary. This query includes all product request rows from the related purchase order that match the current vendor invoice or that have not been invoiced yet. If the vendor ID has a default value (because the form was opened from the Purchase Order Options dialog box), the code sets the RowSource property of the

PONumber combo box control to filter it for the default vendor specified; otherwise, it sets the RowSource property to include all purchase orders. The code is as follows:

```
' If in Add mode, then set subform record sources
'    and combo box row sources
If (Me.NewRecord = True) Then
    ' Make sure subforms include rows with Null invoice number
    If Me.fsubVendInvoiceProducts.Form.RecordSource <> _
       "qryVendInvoiceProducts" Then
        Me.fsubVendInvoiceProducts.Form.RecordSource = _
          "qryVendInvoiceProducts"
    End If
    ' If there's a default value for Vendor
    If Not IsNothing(Me.cmbVendorID.DefaultValue) Then
        ' Make sure the PO Combo is filtered on it
        Me.PONumber.RowSource = "qlkpPOForVendInvoiceParm"
    Else
        ' Set to display all purchase orders
        Me.PONumber.RowSource = "qlkpPOForVendInvoice"
    End If
    Exit Sub
End If
```

When the form is not on a new record, the code makes sure the default values for the customer order and purchase order number are cleared. These might have been set when the form loaded if the form was opened to create a vendor invoice for a specific purchase order and that purchase order has a related customer order. Next, the code sets the RowSource property of the PONumber combo box control to filter it for the current vendor. If the vendor invoice has been marked final, the code calls the *LockAll* procedure with a True argument to lock all editable controls, sets the RecordSource property of the subform to filter the rows on both purchase order number and vendor invoice number, and exits. Otherwise, the code sets the RecordSource property of the subform to display all product request rows from the matching purchase order that either match the current vendor invoice or that have no invoice number. Finally, if the subform contains rows, the code locks the vendor, customer order, and purchase order controls. The code is as follows:

```
' Not a new row - clear Defaults for Order, PO Number
Me.OrderID.DefaultValue = ""
Me.PONumber.DefaultValue = ""
' Make sure the PONumber Row Source is current
Me.PONumber.RowSource = "qlkpPOForVendInvoiceParm"
' If this has been marked final,
If Me.Final Then
    '    then lock all controls
    LockAll True
    ' Make sure subforms show only matching rows
    If Me.fsubVendInvoiceProducts.Form.RecordSource <> _
       "qryVendInvoiceProductsNoNull" Then
        Me.fsubVendInvoiceProducts.Form.RecordSource = _
          "qryVendInvoiceProductsNoNull"
    End If
```

```
        ' .. and exit
        Exit Sub
      Else
        ' Make sure subforms include rows with Null invoice number
        If Me.fsubVendInvoiceProducts.Form.RecordSource <> _
          "qryVendInvoiceProducts" Then
            Me.fsubVendInvoiceProducts.Form.RecordSource = _
              "qryVendInvoiceProducts"
        End If
      End If
      '  If there are products in the subform,
      '  Then don't let 'em change VendorID, OrderID, or PO
      If (Me.fsubVendInvoiceProducts.Form.RecordsetClone.RecordCount <> 0) Then
        Me.cmbVendorID.Locked = True
        Me.cmbVendor.Locked = True
        Me.OrderID.Locked = True
        Me.PONumber.Locked = True
      End If
Exit_Form_Current:
      Exit Sub
Error_Form_Current:
      mlngErr = Err
      mstrError = Error
      ErrorLog Me.Name & ".Form_Current", mlngErr, mstrError
      MsgBox "Unexpected error " & mlngErr & ", " & _
        mstrError & " has been logged.", _
        vbCritical, gstrAppTitle
      Resume Exit_Form_Current
End Sub
```

You can find similar code in the form's AfterUpdate event procedure that resets the command buttons in the form header and locks or unlocks controls and changes the subform record source depending on the value of the Final field.

Locking and Unlocking Controls in the Subform

Although the outer form locks the entire subform when the vendor invoice is final, code in the subform controls what the user can do when the subform is editable. You can find the code that controls what the user can do in the Current event procedure of the fsubVendInvoice-Products form. When a new row receives the focus, the code checks to see if the product request has been posted or invoiced. If so, the code locks all the editable controls—the BuyQuantity (Qty. Ordered), Cost (Buy Each Cost), Price (Sell Each List Price), Received, DateReceived, and QuantityReceived fields. It also locks Invoiced if the row is Posted. If the product is not posted to inventory and the vendor invoice has no related customer order, the code unlocks all these controls. Finally, if the product is not posted but the vendor invoice does have a related customer order, the code locks the BuyQuantity control (this amount should be set from the customer order) and unlocks all the others. The code is as follows:

```
Private Sub Form_Current()
  On Error GoTo Error_Form_Current
  ' If posted or invoiced,
```

```
    If (Me.Posted = True) Or (Me.Invoiced = True) Then
      ' .. lock all controls
      Me.BuyQuantity.Locked = True
      Me.Cost.Locked = True
      Me.Price.Locked = True
      Me.Received.Locked = True
      Me.DateReceived.Locked = True
      Me.QuantityReceived.Locked = True
      ' Lock Invoiced only if also posted
      Me.Invoiced.Locked = Me.Posted
    ' Not posted or invoiced -- if no Order ID
    ElseIf IsNull(Me.Parent.OrderID) Then
      ' .. then allow all edits
      Me.BuyQuantity.Locked = False
      Me.Cost.Locked = False
      Me.Price.Locked = False
      Me.Received.Locked = False
      Me.DateReceived.Locked = False
      Me.QuantityReceived.Locked = False
      Me.Invoiced.Locked = False
    'Not posted or invoiced, but do have Order ID
    Else
      ' Lock Quantity, but edit all else
      Me.BuyQuantity.Locked = True
      Me.Cost.Locked = False
      Me.Price.Locked = False
      Me.Received.Locked = False
      Me.DateReceived.Locked = False
      Me.QuantityReceived.Locked = False
      Me.Invoiced.Locked = False
    End If
Exit_Form_Current:
  Exit Sub
Error_Form_Current:
  mlngErr = Err
  mstrError = Error
  ErrorLog Me.Name & ".Form_Current", mlngErr, mstrError
  MsgBox "Unexpected error " & mlngErr & ", " & mstrError & _
    " has been logged.", _
    vbCritical, gstrAppTitle
  Resume Exit_Form_Current
End Sub
```

To ensure that the locking status changes immediately whenever the user changes the Invoiced field or saves the record, this code is also called from the *Invoiced_AfterUpdate* and *Form_AfterUpdate* procedures.

Verifying Vendor ID Changes

The user can also open the frmVendorInvoices form and click the Add New button to create a new invoice. However, if the user has also set either the customer order (OrderID) or purchase order (PONumber) fields, the vendor cannot be changed because these other fields are dependent on the value of the vendor ID. The code that enforces this is in the BeforeUpdate event procedure for the cmbVendorID combo box control. Because the form includes the cmbVendor combo box control that is also bound to the vendor ID but displays the vendor name, this code is called from that control's BeforeUpdate event as well. The code is as follows:

```
Private Sub cmbVendorID_BeforeUpdate(Cancel As Integer)
  On Error GoTo Error_cmbVendorID_BeforeUpdate
  ' OK to change vendor on new row
  If (Me.NewRecord = True) Then Exit Sub
  ' OK to reset Vendor if both OrderID and PONumber are empty
  If IsNothing(Me.OrderID) And IsNothing(Me.PONumber) Then Exit Sub
  ' Tell the user what to do
  MsgBox "You can't change the Vendor ID unless " & _
    "the PO Number is blank.  " & _
    "Press Esc or choose Undo on the toolbar, delete this Invoice, ' " & _
    "and create it again.", vbCritical, gstrAppTitle
  Cancel = True
Exit_cmbVendorID_BeforeUpdate:
  Exit Sub
Error_cmbVendorID_BeforeUpdate:
  mlngErr = Err
  mstrError = Error
  ErrorLog Me.Name & ".cmbVendorID_BeforeUpdate", mlngErr, mstrError
  MsgBox "Unexpected error " & mlngErr & ", " & mstrError & _
    " has been logged.", vbCritical, gstrAppTitle
  Cancel = True
  Resume Exit_cmbVendorID_BeforeUpdate
End Sub
```

Validating Final Status

When the user decides to mark a vendor invoice final, code in the frmVendorInvoices form verifies that the user has also specified a vendor ID, an invoice number, and a related purchase order number. If any of these fields is empty, the code disallows marking the invoice final. You can find the code in the BeforeUpdate event procedure for the chkFinal check box control. The code is as follows:

```
Private Sub chkFinal_BeforeUpdate(Cancel As Integer)
  ' See if trying to set Final
  If (Me.chkFinal = True) Then
    ' .. Check that there's a Vendor
    If IsNothing(Me.VendorID) Then
      MsgBox "You cannot mark an invoice final until " & _
        "you specify a vendor.  Press Esc to clear your edit.", _
        vbCritical, gstrAppTitle
      Cancel = True
      Exit Sub
    End If
    ' .. Check that there's an Invoice Number
    If IsNothing(Me.InvoiceNumber) Then
      MsgBox "You cannot mark an invoice final until " & _
        "you specify an invoice number.  Press Esc to clear your edit.", _
        vbCritical, gstrAppTitle
```

```
        Cancel = True
        Exit Sub
    End If
    ' .. and a Purchase Order Number
    If IsNothing(Me.PONumber) Then
        MsgBox "You cannot mark an invoice final until " & _
            "you specify a related Purchase Order.  " & _
            "Press Esc to clear your edit.", _
            vbCritical, gstrAppTitle
        Cancel = True
        Exit Sub
    End If
```

If the user has supplied the required fields, the code also checks to see if any related product request rows from the purchase order have been associated with the vendor invoice. It does this by using the *DLookup* function to search for a row in the tblPOProducts table that has a matching vendor ID, purchase order number, and vendor invoice number. If the code finds no rows, it warns the user and asks whether the invoice should be marked final with no related product rows. If the user responds No (the default button in the message box), the code cancels the edit. The code is as follows:

```
    ' Now see if there are any related Invoiced rows
    If IsNothing(DLookup("PONumber", "tblPOProducts", _
        "VendorID = " & Me.VendorID & _
        " And PONumber = " & Me.PONumber & _
        " And InvoiceNumber = '" & Me.InvoiceNumber & "'")) Then
        ' None - see if they really want to mark Final
        If vbNo = MsgBox("You have marked no products Invoiced in " & _
            "the related Purchase Order.  Are you sure you want to " & _
            "mark this Invoice Final?", _
            vbYesNo + vbQuestion + vbDefaultButton2, gstrAppTitle) Then
            Cancel = True
            MsgBox "Press Esc to clear your edit.", vbOKOnly, gstrAppTitle
        End If
    End If
End If
End Sub
```

Fixing a Changed Invoice Number

After creating a vendor invoice and marking several related product rows for the invoice, the user might discover that the invoice number has been misentered. The frmVendorInvoices form allows the user to make this change, but verifies that the user really means to do this. If so, the code saves the old invoice number and sets a module variable to let the form's AfterUpdate event procedure know that the related product request rows must also be changed.

You can find the code that detects the change in the BeforeUpdate event procedure for the InvoiceNumber text box control. The code does nothing if the form is on a new record that hasn't been saved yet. It detects a change by comparing the current value of the InvoiceNumber text box control to its OldValue property. The OldValue property contains the original value of the control before the user made any changes. The code asks the user to verify the change. The code saves the old value and sets the mintChangeInvoice variable if the user confirms the change; otherwise, it cancels the edit. The code is as follows:

```
Private Sub InvoiceNumber_BeforeUpdate(Cancel As Integer)
  On Error GoTo Error_InvoiceNumber_BeforeUpdate
  ' Do nothing on a new record
  If (Me.NewRecord = True) Then Exit Sub
  ' If they're changing the invoice number
  If Me.InvoiceNumber <> Me.InvoiceNumber.OldValue Then
    ' Verify that they really want do do this
    If vbYes = MsgBox("Are you SURE you want to change " & _
      "this invoice number?", _
      vbYesNo + vbQuestion + vbDefaultButton2, gstrAppTitle) Then
      ' Let After Update know invoice number changed
      mintChangeInvoice = True
      ' Save the old value to re-sync any invoiced products
      mstrOldInvoice = Me.InvoiceNumber.OldValue
    Else
      ' User changed mind - cancel the update
      Cancel = True
      ' And make sure the "changed" flag is off
      mintChangeInvoice = False
    End If
  End If
Exit_InvoiceNumber_BeforeUpdate:
  Exit Sub
Error_InvoiceNumber_BeforeUpdate:
  mlngErr = Err
  mstrError = Error
  ErrorLog Me.Name & ".InvoiceNumber_BeforeUpdate", mlngErr, mstrError
  MsgBox "Unexpected error " & mlngErr & ", " & mstrError & _
    " has been logged.", _
    vbCritical, gstrAppTitle
  Cancel = True
  Resume Exit_InvoiceNumber_BeforeUpdate
End Sub
```

After the user finally saves the record, Access executes the form's AfterUpdate event procedure. As mentioned earlier, some of the code in this procedure resets the command buttons and controls and sets the subform record source. Within this procedure, you can also find the code that detects a change to the invoice number and executes an update query to fix the invoice number in the related product request rows in the tblPOProducts table. (It can't test the OldValue property of the InvoiceNumber text box at this point because OldValue equals the current value after the row has been saved.) The code is as follows:

```
  ' Did the user change the invoice number?
  If mintChangeInvoice Then
    ' Yes - update POProducts with the new value
    Set db = DBEngine(0)(0)
    strSQL = "UPDATE tblPOProducts SET [InvoiceNumber] = '" & _
      Me.InvoiceNumber & _
```

```
        "' WHERE [PONumber] = " & Me.PONumber & _
        " AND [InvoiceNumber] = '" & mstrOldInvoice & "';"
      db.Execute strSQL, dbFailOnError
      ' Reset the changed flag
      mintChangeInvoice = False
      ' Requery the subform to reflect the new linked number
      Me.fsubVendInvoiceProducts.Requery
   End If
```

You might wonder why I didn't create a relationship between the tblVendInvoices table and the tblPOProducts table and depend on the cascade update feature to make the invoice number change automatically. I could have defined a unique index on the VendorID, Invoice-Number, and PONumber fields in the tblVendInvoices table and then related those fields to the matching ones in the tblPOProducts table. However, the application must be able to create rows in tblPOProducts independently. If I were to create this relationship, the application would not be able to add rows in tblPOProducts without a related row in tblVendInvoices existing first. Because the vendor invoices aren't created until long after the purchase order is created, this relationship and use of the cascade update feature are not possible.

Validating an Invoice Before Saving It

Before a vendor invoice can be saved, it must have a vendor ID, an invoice number, and a related purchase order number. The application performs these checks in the form's BeforeUpdate event procedure. If any of these items are missing, the procedure diplays an error message and cancels the save. The code is as follows:

```
Private Sub Form_BeforeUpdate(Cancel As Integer)
  On Error GoTo Error_Form_BeforeUpdate
  ' Before saving a row
  ' .. Check that a vendor is specified
  If IsNothing(Me.VendorID) Then
    MsgBox "You must specify a vendor!", vbCritical, gstrAppTitle
    Me.cmbVendor.SetFocus
    Cancel = True
  End If
  ' .. Check that there's an Invoice Number
  If IsNothing(Me.InvoiceNumber) Then
    MsgBox "You must specify an invoice number!", vbCritical, gstrAppTitle
    Me.InvoiceNumber.SetFocus
    Cancel = True
  End If
  ' .. and a Purchase Order Number
  If IsNothing(Me.PONumber) Then
    MsgBox "You can't enter an invoice without a related PO.  " & _
      "Go create the Purchase Order first!", vbCritical, gstrAppTitle
    Me.PONumber.SetFocus
    Cancel = True
  End If
  ' Make sure total is updated
  AddCharges
Exit_Form_BeforeUpdate:
```

```
  Exit Sub
Error_Form_BeforeUpdate:
  mlngErr = Err
  mstrError = Error
  ErrorLog Me.Name & ".Form_BeforeUpdate", mlngErr, mstrError
  MsgBox "Unexpected error " & mlngErr & ", " & mstrError & _
    " has been logged.", _
    vbCritical, gstrAppTitle
  Cancel = True
  Resume Exit_Form_BeforeUpdate
End Sub
```

Note that the code also calls a procedure named *AddCharges* to ensure that the invoice total displayed in an unbound text box is up to date. The next topic explains how that procedure works.

Updating the Displayed Total

In general, you should not store a calculated value in your tables unless the performance of your application would otherwise suffer significantly. In many cases, you can include an expression in a query to calculate and display a value. However, the invoice total for a vendor invoice includes not only taxes and shipping charges but also the total cost of all product requests that have been marked related to the invoice. The code module for the frmVendor-Invoices form includes a procedure named *AddCharges* that calculates this total.

The procedure first checks to see if any related rows exist in the tblPOProducts table by using the *DCount* function to count the rows in a query filtered with parameters for the current vendor invoice. If rows exist, the code uses the *DSum* function to calculate the total cost of products marked invoiced. It then adds the tax and freight amounts to that total and updates the unbound text box on the form. The code is as follows:

```
Public Sub AddCharges()
Dim curCostP As Currency, varCost As Variant
  ' Sub used by other procedures to calculate and display the invoice total
  On Error GoTo Error_AddCharges
  ' See if any products assigned to this invoice yet.
  If DCount("*", "qryVendInvoiceProductsNoNull") <> 0 Then
    ' Yes - attempt to sum the cost
    varCost = DSum("[BuyCost]", "qryVendInvoiceProductsNoNull")
    ' If not a null return, save it
    If Not IsNothing(varCost) Then curCostP = varCost
  End If
  ' Update the displayed total
  Me.txtTotal = curCostP + Me.Tax + Me.Freight
Exit_AddCharges:
  Exit Sub
Error_AddCharges:
  mlngErr = Err
  mstrError = Error
  ErrorLog Me.Name & ".AddCharges", mlngErr, mstrError
  MsgBox "Unexpected error " & mlngErr & ", " & mstrError & _
```

```
      " has been logged.", _
        vbCritical, gstrAppTitle
    Resume Exit_AddCharges
End Sub
```

Note that the procedure is declared public. Any public procedure in a form module can be called by code in other modules as a method of the form's class. As you'll see later, code in the AfterUpdate event of the fsubVendInvoiceProducts form calls this procedure as a method of the frmVendorInvoices form to update the total each time the user changes a row in the subform. You can see how this works by entering a freight amount or choosing Invoiced for any of the product request rows and then clicking the Save button on the form shown earlier in Figure 12-2. Your result should look something like Figure 12-3.

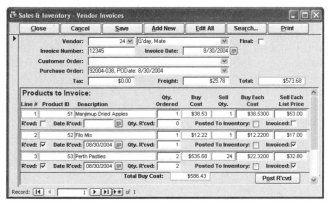

Figure 12-3   The vendor invoices form updates the calculated total whenever you save a change in the outer form or the subform.

Note that the total displayed on the outer form isn't the sum of the Total Buy Cost on the subform plus the Freight. The Total Buy Cost on the subform is the total potential cost of all items in the related purchase order, not just the ones marked Invoiced for this vendor invoice. The totals will match when the user marks the invoice Final.

> **Tip**   You might be wondering why the code doesn't open a recordset on the qryVend-InvoiceProductNoNull query. This query includes parameters that reference controls on the frmVendorInvoices form. To open a recordset in code on a parameter query, you must first open the query's QueryDef object, set its parameters, and then open the query. However, the Domain functions (such as *DLookup*, *DCount*, and *DSum*) when called from Visual Basic code are able to resolve the parameters for you, so it's simpler to let the Domain function do the work.

Controlling Invoice Deletion

Unless the user has marked the vendor invoice final or one or more products have been posted to inventory for the invoice, the application lets the user delete an invoice. Similar to cascading a changed invoice number shown earlier in "Fixing a Changed Invoice Number" on page 249, the application must reset to Null the InvoiceNumber field in the related tblPOProducts rows when the user deletes the invoice.

Code in the form's Delete event procedure first checks to see if the invoice is marked final. If it is, the code warns the user and cancels the delete. Next, the code uses the *DSum* function to find out if any related products have been posted to inventory for the current vendor invoice. (The Posted field is 0 for items not posted and −1 for posted items, so the sum will be nonzero if any are posted.) If products have been posted to inventory, the code tells the user and cancels the delete. If no products have been posted, the code asks the user to verify the delete and then saves the invoice number and purchase order number to be used by the form's AfterDelConfirm event procedure. The code is as follows:

```
Private Sub Form_Delete(Cancel As Integer)
  On Error GoTo Error_Form_Delete
  ' Disallow the delete if marked final
  If (Me.Final = True) Then
    MsgBox "You can't delete a vendor invoice " & _
      that you have marked 'final.'", _
      vbInformation, gstrAppTitle
    Cancel = True
  End If
  ' If any related products are posted
  If DSum("Posted", "qryVendInvoiceProductsNoNull") <> 0 Then
    ' Tell the user and cancel
    MsgBox "You cannot delete a vendor invoice " & _
      "that has invoiced products that have been " & _
      "posted to inventory.", vbCritical, gstrAppTitle
    Cancel = True
    Exit Sub
  End If
  ' Save the invoice # for AfterDelConfirm
  mstrThisInvNo = Me.InvoiceNumber
  ' Save the PONumber for AfterDelConfirm
  mlngOldPONumber = Me.PONumber
  ' Ask if they want to delete!
  If vbNo = MsgBox("Are you sure you want to delete this invoice?", _
    vbQuestion + vbYesNo + vbDefaultButton2, gstrAppTitle) Then
    Cancel = True
  End If
Exit_Form_Delete:
  Exit Sub
Error_Form_Delete:
  mlngErr = Err
  mstrError = Error
  ErrorLog Me.Name & ".Form_Delete", mlngErr, mstrError
  MsgBox "Unexpected error " & mlngErr & ", " & mstrError & _
```

```
          " has been logged.", _
            vbCritical, gstrAppTitle
        Cancel = True
        Resume Exit_Form_Delete
End Sub
```

When the delete process has completed, Access runs the form's AfterDelConfirm event procedure and passes it a Status parameter that indicates whether the delete was successful. If the
procedure detects that the delete completed successfully (Status = acDeleteOK), it executes an
update query to clear the invoice number in all related rows in the tblPOProducts table. The
code is as follows:

```
Private Sub Form_AfterDelConfirm(Status As Integer)
Dim db As DAO.Database
    On Error GoTo Error_Form_AfterDelConfirm
    ' If delete is OK
    If (Status = acDeleteOK) Then
        ' Make sure we set to Null all "invoiced" PO Products!
        Set db = DBEngine(0)(0)
        db.Execute "UPDATE tblPOProducts SET InvoiceNumber = Null " & _
            "WHERE PONumber = " & mlngOldPONumber & _
            " And InvoiceNumber = '" & mstrThisInvNo & "'", dbFailOnError
    End If
Exit_Form_AfterDelConfirm:
    Exit Sub
Error_Form_AfterDelConfirm:
    mlngErr = Err
    mstrError = Error
    ErrorLog Me.Name & ".Form_AfterDelConfirm", mlngErr, mstrError
    MsgBox "Unexpected error " & mlngErr & ", " & mstrError & _
        " has been logged.", _
        vbCritical, gstrAppTitle
    Resume Exit_Form_AfterDelConfirm
End Sub
```

As noted earlier, this works similarly to the correction of a changed invoice number. The code
can't perform the fix until the delete is confirmed as completed with no errors. Again, using a
referential integrity rule would not work because a rule would delete the dependent rows
rather than set the key value to Null. This code allows the user to delete an invoice entered in
error without deleting the product request rows.

Validating Changes in Related Purchase Order Products Rows

In addition to locking and unlocking controls, code in the fsubVendInvoiceProducts form
validates quantities, cost, and the invoiced status and copies cost and price changes to related
records in other tables.

Verifying Quantities

Remember that in Chapter 11, "Generating Purchase Orders," extensive code exists in the fsubPurchaseProducts form to validate quantities requested. The primary purpose of the vendor invoices form is to verify the cost charged by the vendor and mark items invoiced, not to enter or adjust quantities ordered. The BuyQuantity control could be locked to prevent all changes. However, on an order for stock, the user might need to increase the quantity requested to be able to accept an overshipment from the vendor or to decrease the credit requested if the vendor credit received was less.

The code that verifies the quantity the user enters is in the BeforeUpdate event procedure for the BuyQuantity text box control. If the new value is negative, the code disallows the change if the previous value was positive or the previous value was for a smaller credit. This allows the user to decrease the amount of a credit requested but not increase it. If the new value is positive, the code disallows the change if the previous value was negative or the previous value was for a larger requested amount. This allows the user to increase the amount requested but not decrease it. The code is as follows:

```
Private Sub BuyQuantity_BeforeUpdate(Cancel As Integer)
  On Error GoTo Error_BuyQuantity_BeforeUpdate
  ' NOTE:  Buy Quantity is locked if the item is
  '        posted or there's a related Order
  ' Allow only an increase of a purchased (not returned) item
  '  or decrease of a returned item.
  ' Force user to make all other changes via the Purchase Order
  ' If the new value is negative
  If Me.BuyQuantity < 0 Then
    ' Disallow change from positive to negative
    If Me.BuyQuantity.OldValue > 0 Then
      MsgBox "You can't change Buy Quantity from positive to negative.", _
        vbCritical, gstrAppTitle
      Cancel = True
      Exit Sub
    End If
    ' Disallow net increase of returned item
    If Me.BuyQuantity < Me.BuyQuantity.OldValue Then
      MsgBox "You can't increase the amount of returned " & _
        "items in Vendor Invoice edit. " & _
        "Change the amount in the related Purchase Order.", _
        vbCritical, gstrAppTitle
      Cancel = True
      Exit Sub
    End If
  Else
    ' New value is positive - if old was negative, disallow
    If Me.BuyQuantity.OldValue < 0 Then
      MsgBox "You can't change Buy Quantity from negative to positive.", _
        vbCritical, gstrAppTitle
      Cancel = True
      Exit Sub
    End If
```

```
    ' If decreasing the amount ordered, disallow
    If Me.BuyQuantity < Me.BuyQuantity.OldValue Then
      MsgBox "You can't decrease the amount of ordered items " & _
        "in Vendor Invoice edit. " & _
        "Change the amount in the related Purchase Order.", _
        vbCritical, gstrAppTitle
      Cancel = True
      Exit Sub
    End If
  End If
Exit_BuyQuantity_BeforeUpdate:
  Exit Sub
Error_BuyQuantity_BeforeUpdate:
  mlngErr = Err
  mstrError = Error
  ErrorLog Me.Name & ".BuyQuantity_BeforeUpdate", mlngErr, mstrError
  MsgBox "Unexpected error " & mlngErr & ", " & mstrError & _
    " has been logged.", _
    vbCritical, gstrAppTitle
  Cancel = True
  Resume Exit_BuyQuantity_BeforeUpdate
End Sub
```

Code in the fsubVendInvoiceProducts form also verifies the quantity received. If the user has indicated that the product has been received, the code disallows a quantity of zero. You can find the code in the BeforeUpdate event procedure for the QuantityReceived text box control, as follows:

```
Private Sub QuantityReceived_BeforeUpdate(Cancel As Integer)
  ' If setting received,
  If (Me.Received = True) Then
    ' .. quantity can't be zero.
    If Me.QuantityReceived = 0 Then
      MsgBox "Quantity received cannot be zero.", vbCritical, gstrAppTitle
      Cancel = True
    End If
  End If
End Sub
```

Validating Cost

When marking a requested product invoiced, the user can correct the cost to match what the vendor actually charged. The user can enter any cost (Buy Each Cost) as long as it is greater than zero and less than the price (Sell Each List Price). The code that validates this is in the BeforeUpdate event procedure for the Cost text box control, as follows:

```
Private Sub Cost_BeforeUpdate(Cancel As Integer)
  ' Negative or zero cost not allowed
  If Me.Cost <= 0 Then
    MsgBox "Cost cannot be negative or zero.", vbCritical, gstrAppTitle
    Cancel = True
  End If
  ' Cost can't be more than Price
```

```
    If Me.Cost >= Me.Price Then
      MsgBox "Cost must be less than Price.", vbCritical, gstrAppTitle
      Cancel = True
    End If
End Sub
```

Validating the Invoiced Flag and
Relating the Product Request to the Invoice

When the user marks a requested product invoiced, code in the fsubVendInvoiceProducts form validates the request to make sure that an invoice number is available and that cost (Buy Each Cost) and price (Sell Each List Price) are not zero. The code that performs these validations is in the BeforeUpdate event procedure of the Invoiced check box control, as follows:

```
Private Sub Invoiced_BeforeUpdate(Cancel As Integer)
  On Error GoTo Error_Invoiced_BeforeUpdate
  ' If invoiced, then make sure there's an Invoice Number
  '   and cost and price are not zero.
  If (Me.Invoiced = True) Then
    If IsNothing(Me.Parent.InvoiceNumber) Then
      MsgBox "You must specify an Invoice Number " & _
        "before marking any Products invoiced!", _
        vbExclamation, gstrAppTitle
      Cancel = True
      Exit Sub
    End If
    If (Me.Cost = 0) Or (Me.Price = 0) Then
      MsgBox "You can't mark an item invoiced that doesn't " & _
        "have a cost and a price.", _
        vbExclamation, gstrAppTitle
      Cancel = True
      Exit Sub
    End If
  End If
Exit_Invoiced_BeforeUpdate:
  Exit Sub
Error_Invoiced_BeforeUpdate:
  mlngErr = Err
  mstrError = Error
  ErrorLog Me.Name & ".Invoiced_BeforeUpdate", mlngErr, mstrError
  MsgBox "Unexpected error " & mlngErr & ", " & mstrError & _
    " has been logged.", _
    vbCritical, gstrAppTitle
  Cancel = True
  Resume Exit_Invoiced_BeforeUpdate
End Sub
```

After the user selects the Invoiced check box control, code in the form must change the InvoiceNumber field to reflect the new invoiced status and potentially set the Received, DateReceived, and QuantityReceived fields. You can find the code that performs these tasks in the AfterUpdate event procedure of the Invoiced check box control. If the user set Invoiced to True (selected the check box), the code must copy the InvoiceNumber field from the parent form to correctly relate the current row to the vendor invoice. If the product request isn't also marked Received, the code sets the Received, QuantityReceived, and DateReceived fields. If the user clears the Invoiced check box, the code clears the related InvoiceNumber field to disassociate the product request row from the vendor invoice. Finally, the code calls the form's Current event procedure (explained earlier) to reset the locking status of controls based on the new value of Invoiced. The code is as follows:

```
Private Sub Invoiced_AfterUpdate()
  ' If marking Invoiced,
  If (Me.Invoiced = True) Then
    ' Auto-copy Invoice Number from Parent
    Me.InvoiceNumber = Me.Parent.InvoiceNumber
    ' If not also received
    If Not (Me.Received = True) Then
      ' Set Received
      Me.Received = True
      ' Update the received date
      Me.DateReceived = Date
      ' .. and set Qty Received = amount ordered
      Me.QuantityReceived = Me.BuyQuantity
    End If
  Else
    ' .. otherwise, clear the invoice number
    Me.InvoiceNumber = Null
  End If
  ' Call Current to reset locking
  Form_Current
End Sub
```

Verifying a Changed Product Row Before Saving It

Although the BeforeUpdate event procedures for the BuyQuantity (Qty. Ordered) and QuantityReceived text boxes in the fsubVendInvoiceProducts form perform some preliminary checks, some final validation must be performed just before any new row or any changed row is saved. These checks are performed in the BeforeUpdate event procedure for the fsubVendInvoiceProducts form.

First, the procedure verifies that the quantity ordered (the BuyQuantity field) is not zero. Although the tblPOProducts table also has a field validation rule to enforce this, it's more efficient to catch the problem in the form. If the BuyQuantity value is less than zero (the product is being returned), the code checks that the quantity received is not less than the quantity ordered and that the quantity received is not positive. Note that when dealing with negative numbers, when the first number is less than the second one, the first number represents a "larger" negative value. If the quantity received passes the checks, the code performs one final check using the *DSum* function to ensure that the amount being returned is not more than was ordered. The code to perform these checks is as follows:

```
Private Sub Form_BeforeUpdate(Cancel As Integer)
Dim strSearch As String, varQty As Variant
```

```
On Error GoTo Error_Form_BeforeUpdate
' Verify BuyQuantity against Quantity Received
Select Case Me.BuyQuantity
  ' Can't specify zero
  Case 0
    MsgBox "Quantity Ordered cannot be zero.", vbCritical, gstrAppTitle
    Cancel = True
    Exit Sub
  ' If less than zero (returning products)
  Case Is < 0
    ' .. and Qty received is less than buy quantity
    If Me.QuantityReceived < Me.BuyQuantity Then
      MsgBox "For a vendor invoice credit, the Quantity Received " & _
        "can't be less than Quantity Ordered.", _
        vbCritical, gstrAppTitle
      Cancel = True
      Exit Sub
    End If
    ' .. or Qty received is positive
    If Me.QuantityReceived > 0 Then
      MsgBox "Quantity Received can't be positive " & _
        "when Quantity Ordered is negative.", _
        vbCritical, gstrAppTitle
      Cancel = True
      Exit Sub
    End If
    ' Quantities look OK
    ' Do a final check to make sure more was ordered
    ' than is being returned
    strSearch = "[PONumber] = " & Me.PONumber & " AND [LineNo] <> " & _
      Me.LineNo & " AND [ProductID] = " & Me.ProductID
    varQty = DSum("BuyQuantity", "tblPOProducts", strSearch)
    If Not IsNull(varQty) Then
      If varQty >= (-Me.BuyQuantity) Then Exit Sub
    End If
    MsgBox "You can't return more of an item than you " & _
      "have ordered in the Purchase Order.", _
      vbCritical, gstrAppTitle
    Cancel = True
    Exit Sub
```

When the quantity ordered is positive, the quantity received cannot be more than the quantity ordered, and the quantity received cannot be negative. The code to verify this is as follows:

```
  ' If quantity is positive
  Case Is > 0
    ' Make sure that Qty received isn't greater
    If Me.QuantityReceived > Me.BuyQuantity Then
      MsgBox "Quantity Received can't be " & _
        "larger than Quantity Ordered.", _
        vbCritical, gstrAppTitle
      Cancel = True
      Exit Sub
    End If
    ' .. and Qty received is not negative
```

```
      If Me.QuantityReceived < 0 Then
        MsgBox "Quantity Received can't be negative " & _
          "when Quantity Ordered is positive.", _
          vbCritical, gstrAppTitle
        Cancel = True
        Exit Sub
      End If
  End Select
Exit_Form_BeforeUpdate:
  Exit Sub
Error_Form_BeforeUpdate:
  mlngErr = Err
  mstrError = Error
  ErrorLog Me.Name & ".Form_BeforeUpdate", mlngErr, mstrError
  MsgBox "Unexpected error " & mlngErr & ", " & mstrError & _
    " has been logged.", _
    vbCritical, gstrAppTitle
  Cancel = True
  Resume Exit_Form_BeforeUpdate
End Sub
```

Copying Cost and Price Changes to Related Rows

One of the primary purposes of entering the vendor invoice for products received is to verify the cost charged by the vendor and, if available, any new suggested list price. If the user changes the cost or price—both derived from the last known values for the product in the tblVendorProducts table, the application should update those values so that any future customer orders or purchase orders reflect the most current values.

First, the application must detect changes to the Cost and Price text box controls. It does this via code in the AfterUpdate event procedures for these controls. When the user changes the cost, the application sets a module variable to notify the form's AfterUpdate event procedure that the change must be propagated to the related tables. It also estimates a new list price by adding a standard 20% markup to the new price. It asks the user if the list price should also be changed to the new value. The user might know a new list price that is different, so he or she can choose to ignore the list price change and enter a new price manually. The code for the AfterUpdate event procedure of the Cost text box control is as follows:

```
Private Sub Cost_AfterUpdate()
Dim curPrice As Currency
  On Error GoTo Error_Cost_AfterUpdate
  ' Notify Form AfterUpdate that cost has changed
  intCostPriceChange = True
  ' Calculate "standard" markup= 20%
  curPrice = CCur(CLng(Me.Cost * (1 + 0.2) * 100) / 100)
  ' If Price less than standard markup
  If curPrice > Me.Price Then
    If vbYes = MsgBox("Do you also want to automatically " & _
      "change the Price from " & _
      Me.Price & " to " & curPrice & "?", _
      vbYes + vbQuestion + vbDefaultButton2, gstrAppTitle) Then
```

```
      Me.Price = curPrice
    End If
  End If
Exit_Cost_AfterUpdate:
  Exit Sub
Error_Cost_AfterUpdate:
  mlngErr = Err
  mstrError = Error
  ErrorLog Me.Name & ".Cost_AfterUpdate", mlngErr, mstrError
  MsgBox "Unexpected error " & mlngErr & ", " & mstrError & _
    " has been logged.", _
    vbCritical, gstrAppTitle
  Resume Exit_Cost_AfterUpdate
End Sub
```

Handling a list price change is much simpler. The AfterUpdate event procedure for the Price text box control merely sets the module variable to notify the form's AfterUpdate event procedure and exits. The code is as follows:

```
Private Sub Price_AfterUpdate()
  ' Let Form AfterUpdate know price has changed
  intCostPriceChange = True
End Sub
```

After Access saves the changes, it runs the AfterUpdate event procedure of the form. First, the event procedure calls the form's Current event procedure (described earlier) to reset the locking status of controls based on the newly saved values. If the AfterUpdate event procedure for either the Cost or Price text box control has set the intCostPriceChange module variable to True, the code starts a transaction and executes an update query to change the vendor default values for the current product. It also executes an update query to change the cost and price for any other rows in the tblPOProducts table for the current purchase orders that have not yet been posted to inventory. The code is as follows:

```
Private Sub Form_AfterUpdate()
Dim curSumCostP As Currency, curSumTotal As Currency
Dim qd As DAO.QueryDef, rst As DAO.Recordset, rstStock As DAO.Recordset
Dim frm As Form
Dim strSQL As String, intLineNo As Integer, intTrans As Integer
  On Error GoTo Error_Form_AfterUpdate
  ' Call Current code to set locking
  Form_Current
  ' We think we detected a cost change, so...
  If (intCostPriceChange = True) Then
    ' Turn on the hourglass
    DoCmd.Hourglass True
    ' Protect in a transaction
    BeginTrans
    intTrans = True
    ' Make sure vendor cost is in sync
    strSQL = "UPDATE tblVendorProducts SET [ListPrice] = " & Me.Price & _
      ", [VendCost] = " & Me.Cost & ", [PriceDate] = " & Date & _
      " WHERE [VendorID] = " & Me.Parent.VendorID & _
```

```
                  " AND [ProductID] = " & Me.ProductID
           db.Execute strSQL, dbFailOnError
           ' Update the cost and price for ALL OTHER
           ' unposted PO line items for this same Product
           strSQL = "UPDATE tblPOProducts SET tblPOProducts.Cost = " & Me.Cost & _
              ", tblPOProducts.Cost = " & Me.Cost & _
              ", tblPOProducts.Price = " & Me.Price & _
              " WHERE tblPOProducts.PONumber = " & Me.PONumber & _
              " AND tblPOProducts.ProductID = " & Me.ProductID & _
              " AND tblPOProducts.Posted = 0 AND tblPOProducts.LineNo <> " & _
              Me.LineNo
           db.Execute strSQL, dbFailOnError
           ' Commit all changes
           CommitTrans
           intTrans = False
           ' .. and reset the cost/price change flag
           intCostPriceChange = False
       End If
   Exit_Form_AfterUpdate:
     DoCmd.Hourglass False
     Exit Sub
   Error_Form_AfterUpdate:
     mlngErr = Err
     mstrError = Error
     ErrorLog Me.Name & ".Form_AfterUpdate", mlngErr, mstrError
     MsgBox "Unexpected error " & mlngErr & ", " & mstrError & _
       " has been logged.", _
       vbCritical, gstrAppTitle
     ' If we started a transaction, then roll it back
     If (intTrans = True) Then Rollback
     intTrans = False
     ' If we were in the middle of a cost/price update
     If (intCostPriceChange = True) Then
       ' Tell the user
       MsgBox "Unable to change related Products cost for this Vendor.  " & _
         "Try changing the Cost for Product " & _
         Me.ProductID & " again!", vbCritical, gstrAppTitle
       intCostPriceChange = False
     End If
     Resume Exit_Form_AfterUpdate
   End Sub
```

The importance of this code is the user does not need to find the product and the vendor in
the frmProducts form and make the change to the cost and price manually. The application
assumes that the new cost and price are the latest values and performs the update
automatically.

Posting to Inventory and Customer Orders

In Chapter 10, you learned how requesting in a customer order more of a product than is in
inventory and then attempting to allocate the product gives the user the option to create a purchase order for the missing products. Open the Inventory sample database (Inventory.mdb)

and after the opening form closes, open the frmOrders form. If you followed the steps in Chapter 10, you should see at the bottom of the products list for the first order a request for a quantity of 4 Perth Pasties with a status of On Order and a purchase order number indicated in the P.O.# column, as shown in Figure 12-4.

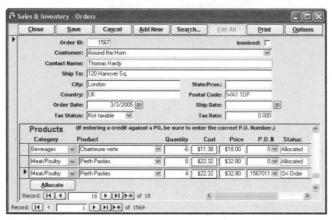

Figure 12-4   A customer order that has a requested product on order.

If you did not follow the steps in Chapter 10, you can navigate to any open order, go to the new record row in the Products window, add a request for a product, and ask for a quantity that is greater that what is indicated in inventory when you choose the product in the Product combo box. (You can see the current quantity in inventory when you open the Product combo box.) Click the Allocate button and then click the Yes button when the allocation process asks you if you would like to generate purchase orders. Click the Done button in the Verify Vendor dialog box and then close the purchase order report when the application displays it.

You can open the purchase order by double-clicking the purchase order number in the P.O.# column. Remember, to post items to inventory, you must first create a vendor invoice and verify the cost and price. Click the Options button on the Purchase Order form, choose the **New Invoice for current Purchase Order** option, and click the Invoices button. Type any non-blank value you like in the Invoice Number field on the Vendor Invoices form, mark the product on order as Invoiced in the Products to Invoice area of the form, and click the Save button. Your forms should now look something like Figure 12-5.

You're now ready to post the product into inventory—and to the customer order. You can click the Post R'cvd button on the Vendor Invoices or the Purchase Order form to add the received items to inventory and satisfy the customer request. When you return to the Orders form, you should find the request now marked Allocated in the customer order.

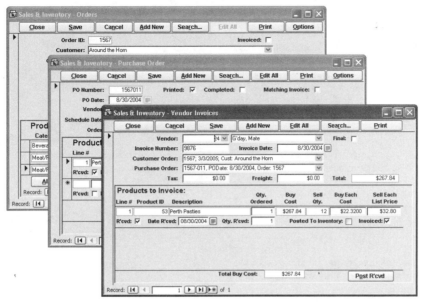

Figure 12-5   Marking a product request Invoiced and ready to post to inventory.

Triggering the Posting Process

The code to call the product posting process is very similar in both the Purchase Order and the Vendor Invoices windows. In the previous section, you learned that the AfterUpdate event procedure for the fsubVendInvoiceProducts form might run two update queries to change the price. Because many events run asynchronously in Access, the Click event procedure for the cmdPost command button must wait until the updates complete before calling the product posting function.

The code first makes sure that the subform contains some product request records by checking the RecordCount property of the form's RecordsetClone object. If records exist, the code next executes a Do loop that runs until the intCostPriceChange module variable is reset to False by the form's AfterUpdate event procedure. Before entering the loop, the code calls the *Timer* function to obtain the current time in seconds. The Do loop continues until either the module variable is reset or the *Timer* function returns a value that is more than 5 seconds after the loop started. Within the loop, the code executes the DoEvents statement to release the processor to handle other pending events—such as the AfterUpdate event procedure for the form. When the loop completes, the code calls the *PostPOProducts* function to do the actual posting work, passing it the VendorID, PONumber, and OrderID fields from the parent form. The code is as follows:

```
Private Sub cmdPost_Click()
Dim sglTime As Single
  On Error Resume Next
  ' Attempt to put focus back on previous control
```

```
Screen.PreviousControl.SetFocus
On Error GoTo Error_cmdPost_Click
' Make sure the current row is saved - this might
'  trigger cost and price update queries.
If Not SaveIt() Then Exit Sub
' If no rows, then bail out
If Me.RecordsetClone.RecordCount = 0 Then Exit Sub
' This may take a sec - show the hourglass
DoCmd.Hourglass True
' Wait up to 5 seconds for form after_update to complete!
sglTime = Timer
' intCostPriceChange will be true while updates still in process
Do While (intCostPriceChange = True)
  ' Wait up to 5 seconds
  If ((Timer - sglTime) > 5) Then Exit Do
  ' Release the CPU so other tasks can run
  DoEvents
Loop
' Call the post code - Exit if failure return
If Not PostPOProducts(Me.Parent.VendorID, _
  Me.Parent.PONumber, Me.Parent.OrderID) Then
  DoCmd.Hourglass False
  Exit Sub
End If
' Rebuild my recordset to show the new status
Me.Requery
Exit_cmdPost_Click:
  DoCmd.Hourglass False
  Exit Sub
Error_cmdPost_Click:
  mlngErr = Err
  mstrError = Error
  ErrorLog Me.Name & ".cmdPost_Click", mlngErr, mstrError
  MsgBox "Unexpected error " & mlngErr & ", " & mstrError & _
    " has been logged.", _
      vbCritical, gstrAppTitle
  Resume Exit_cmdPost_Click
End Sub
```

As you'll see in the next section, the *PostPOProducts* function issues appropriate messages for any errors, so the code in this procedure merely exits if the function returns a False return code indicating a failure. If the function completed successfully, this code requeries the current form to make sure the form displays the updated posted status.

Posting Received Products

To post a received product to inventory, the application must update the tblPOProducts, tblInventory, and tblStock tables. If the purchase order was generated to satisfy a customer order request, the code must also update the tblOrderProducts table. You can find the *PostPOProducts* function that performs these actions in the modInventory module.

Initializing and Validating the Data to Be Posted

The *PostPOProducts* function begins by opening a recordset on the tblPOProducts table for the specified purchase order to fetch rows that have been marked received and invoiced but not posted. If the recordset is empty, the code displays an informational message and exits. Next, the code scans the records about to be posted for any items that have an indicated cost of 10 cents or less or items that have a price that is less than a 20% markup over cost. If the code finds either problem, it warns the user and gives the user an opportunity to cancel the post and correct the prices. The code is as follows:

```
Function PostPOProducts(ByVal lngVendorID As Long, _
  ByVal lngPONumber As Long, ByVal varOrderID As Variant, _
  Optional intSilent As Integer = 0) As Integer
' This code "posts" to inventory all products marked
'    received on a Purchase Order
' When the PO is also for an Order, updates the
'    companion tblOrderProducts rows.
' Inputs: VendorID, PONumber, and OrderID
' Output: True if successful.  All products must "post" to be successful
'
' Note: When called from zfrmLoadData, intSilent is True
'       - procedure will not display any errors.
'       zfrmLoadData also passes the date it wants to use as the post date.
'
Dim db As DAO.Database, rstPOProducts As DAO.Recordset, _
  rstStock As DAO.Recordset
Dim rstOrder As DAO.Recordset, rstOrderProducts As DAO.Recordset, _
  qd As DAO.QueryDef
Dim rstPORedo As DAO.Recordset, lngNextLine As Long, intRedo As Integer
Dim intRedoThis As Integer, lngDiffB As Long, lngDiffS As Long
Dim rstInventory As DAO.Recordset, curAvgCost As Currency, _
  curPrice As Currency
Dim lngNextOrderLine As Long, intKeepQty As Integer
Dim varRet As Variant, lngRealQty As Long, intOrderYes As Integer, _
  intNotEnough As Integer
Dim intSell As Integer, intTrans As Integer, curMinPrice As Currency, _
  curCost As Currency
Dim curListPrice As Currency
  On Error GoTo POPost_ERR
  Set db = DBEngine(0)(0)
  ' See if there are any unposted Products in this Purchase Order
  ' Will post only those marked Received and Invoiced
  ' - cost not verified until invoiced.
  ' Sort by product and then by received descending to post returns last
  Set rstPOProducts = db.OpenRecordset("SELECT tblPOProducts.*, _
    tblProducts.SellPrice " & _
    "FROM tblProducts INNER JOIN tblPOProducts " & _
    "ON tblProducts.ProductID = tblPOProducts.ProductID " & _
    "WHERE PONumber = " & lngPONumber & " AND (Received = True) " & _
    "AND (Posted = False) AND (Invoiced = True)" & _
    "ORDER BY tblPOProducts.ProductID, QuantityReceived DESC;")
  If rstPOProducts.RecordCount = 0 Then
    rstPOProducts.Close
```

```
    Set rstPOProducts = Nothing
    If Not intSilent Then
      MsgBox "Nothing to post for this Purchase Order." & _
        vbCrLf & vbCrLf & _
        "(Note: You must create a Vendor Invoice " & _
        "to verify inventory costs " & _
        "before you can post received items to inventory.)", _
        vbInformation, gstrAppTitle
    End If
    PostPOProducts = True
    Exit Function
  End If
' Skip error checks if running in "silent" mode
If Not intSilent Then
  ' Check for any ridiculously cheap Products!
  rstPOProducts.FindFirst "[Cost] < .11"
  If Not (rstPOProducts.NoMatch) Then
    If vbNo = MsgBox("WARNING!  You are attempting to post " & _
      "Products to inventory " & _
      "that have an indicated cost of 10 cents or less." & _
      vbCrLf & vbCrLf & "Are you SURE you want to proceed?", _
      vbCritical + vbYesNo + vbDefaultButton2, gstrAppTitle) Then
      PostPOProducts = False
      rstPOProducts.Close
      Set rstPOProducts = Nothing
      Exit Function
    End If
  End If
' Check for any Products priced at more than four times cost!
rstPOProducts.FindFirst "([Cost] * 4) < [Price]"
If Not (rstPOProducts.NoMatch) Then
  If vbNo = MsgBox("WARNING!  You are attempting to post " & _
    "Products to inventory that " & _
    "have an indicated price of more than four times the cost." & _
    vbCrLf & vbCrLf & "Are you SURE you want to proceed?", _
    vbCritical + vbYesNo + vbDefaultButton2, gstrAppTitle) Then
    PostPOProducts = False
    rstPOProducts.Close
    Set rstPOProducts = Nothing
    Exit Function
  End If
End If
' Finally check for any Products where
'   Cost * 1.2 > Price (less than 20% markup)
rstPOProducts.FindFirst "([Cost] * 1.2) > [Price]"
If Not (rstPOProducts.NoMatch) Then
  If vbNo = MsgBox("WARNING!  You are attempting to post " & _
    "Products to inventory that have " & _
    "an indicated price less than cost times 1.2 (20% markup)." & _
    vbCrLf & vbCrLf & "Are you SURE you want to proceed?", _
    vbCritical + vbYesNo + vbDefaultButton2, gstrAppTitle) Then
    PostPOProducts = False
    rstPOProducts.Close
    Set rstPOProducts = Nothing
    Exit Function
```

```
        End If
      End If
    End If
rstPOProducts.MoveFirst
```

> **Note**   In Chapter 10, you learned that the *AllocateProducts* function can be called from the zfrmLoadData form that you can use to load random sample data into the database. Code in the the zfrmLoadData form also calls the *PostPOProducts* function. When that form loads the data, it sets the optional intSilent variable to True so that these functions skip some error testing and do not display any messages. When operating normally, the functions do not run in this "silent" mode.

Next, the code empties the zttblPOAddProducts working table that it uses to save the data for rows where less was received than was ordered, opens a recordset for append only on that table, and calculates the next line number in the purchase order to be able to insert these rows. The code opens a recordset on the tblStock table filtered on products for the specified vendor. If the purchase order is for a customer order, the code opens a recordset on the row in the tblOrders table and locks it to prevent other users from changing the order while this code executes. The code also opens a recordset on the tblOrderProducts table for the specified customer order. Finally, the code starts a transaction to ensure that either all updates are saved or none are saved if an error is encountered. The code is as follows:

```
' Clear out the "redo" PO Products table
db.Execute "Delete * From zttblPOAddProducts", dbFailOnError
' Open it ready to save "extra" order lines when received < ordered
Set rstPORedo = db.OpenRecordset("zttblPOAddProducts", _
  dbOpenDynaset, dbAppendOnly)
' Calculate the "next" line for this PO for possible insertions
lngNextLine = DMax("[LineNO]", "tblPOProducts", _
  "[PONumber] = " & lngPONumber) + 1
' Open a recordset on tblStock for this Vendor
Set rstStock = db.OpenRecordset("SELECT * FROM tblStock " & _
  "WHERE VendorID = " & lngVendorID)
' Set up to update customer order
If Not IsNothing(varOrderID) Then
  ' Set up to trap immediate error
  On Error Resume Next
  ' Open the Order and LOCK IT!
  Set rstOrder = db.OpenRecordset("Select [OrderID], " & _
    "tblOrders.[CustomerID] " & _
    "From tblOrders INNER JOIN tblCustomers " & _
    "ON (tblOrders.CustomerID = tblCustomers.CustomerID) " & _
    "WHERE [OrderID] = " & varOrderID)
  If rstOrder.EOF Then
    If Not intSilent Then MsgBox "Unexpected error: " & _
      Can't find Order #" & _
      varOrderID, vbCritical, gstrAppTitle
    ' Close out
    rstPOProducts.Close
    Set rstPOProducts = Nothing
```

```
      rstPORedo.Close
      Set rstPORedo = Nothing
      rstOrder.Close
      Set rstOrder = Nothing
      PostPOProducts = False
      Exit Function
  End If
  ' Lock the Order so no one can dink with it
  rstOrder.Edit
  If Err <> 0 Then
      If Not intSilent Then MsgBox "Error trying to edit Order #" & _
        varOrderID & _
        ".  Someone else may be editing this Order.", _
        vbCritical, gstrAppTitle
      ' Close out
      rstPOProducts.Close
      Set rstPOProducts = Nothing
      rstPORedo.Close
      Set rstPORedo = Nothing
      rstOrder.Close
      Set rstOrder = Nothing
      PostPOProducts = False
      Exit Function
  End If
  ' Reset the error trap
  On Error GoTo POPost_ERR
  ' Open a recordset on tblOrderProducts for this Order and PO
  Set rstOrderProducts = db.OpenRecordset("SELECT * " & _
    "FROM tblOrderProducts " & _
    "WHERE OrderID = " & varOrderID & " AND OrderPONo = " & lngPONumber)
  intOrderYes = True
  ' Calculate "next" order line number in case we have to add some
  '   (received < ordered)
  varRet = DMax("[LineNo]", "tblOrderProducts", _
    "[OrderID] = " & varOrderID)
  If IsNull(varRet) Then
    lngNextOrderLine = 1
  Else
    lngNextOrderLine = varRet + 1
  End If
End If
' Protect everything in a transaction in case we have to bail
BeginTrans
intTrans = True
```

Processing Purchase Order Rows

The code begins a loop to process all the unposted rows in the tblPOProducts table for the specified purchase order. At the beginning of the loop, the code edits the current row to lock it. If the purchase order is for a customer order, the code finds the related row in the tblOrder-Products table. If the code can't find the customer order row, it displays an error message, rolls back all previous updates, and exits. The code is as follows:

```
Do Until rstPOProducts.EOF
' Lock the tblPOProducts row
rstPOProducts.Edit
' If there's a related Order,
'   find the current Product on tblOrderProducts
If (intOrderYes = True) Then
  rstOrderProducts.FindFirst "[ProductID] = " & _
    rstPOProducts![ProductID] & _
    " AND [Quantity] = " & rstPOProducts![SellQuantity] & _
    " AND [OrderPOLineNo] = " & rstPOProducts!LineNo & _
    " AND [Status] = " & OrderStatus.OnOrder
  If rstOrderProducts.NoMatch Then   ' Uh oh!
    If Not intSilent Then MsgBox "Can't find matching " & _
      "Order Product request for Product ID " & _
      rstPOProducts![ProductID] & "!  Post cancelled.", _
      vbCritical, gstrAppTitle
    Rollback
    intTrans = False
    PostPOProducts = False
    ' Close out
    rstPOProducts.Close
    Set rstPOProducts = Nothing
    rstPORedo.Close
    Set rstPORedo = Nothing
    rstOrder.Close
    Set rstOrder = Nothing
    rstOrderProducts.Close
    Set rstOrderProducts = Nothing
    Exit Function
  End If
  ' Found the row - edit it
  rstOrderProducts.Edit
End If
```

Next, the code opens a recordset on the product row from the tblInventory table. If it doesn't find the row, it creates a new row—this might be the first time the product has appeared in inventory. If it finds the row, it locks it by editing it. The code then attempts to find the matching row in the tblStock table. If the purchase order row is adding products to inventory, the code adds a new stock record if the product didn't previously exist or edits the record to lock it. If the quantity in the purchase order is negative—indicating a product being returned—the code displays an error and exits if the row isn't found because the product must have been previously ordered and posted to be able to return it. The code is as follows:

```
' Get the matching master Inventory row
Set rstInventory = db.OpenRecordset("SELECT * FROM tblInventory " & _
  "WHERE [ProductID] = " & rstPOProducts![ProductID] & ";")
If rstInventory.EOF Then ' New Product in inventory -- add it!
  rstInventory.AddNew
  rstInventory![ProductID] = rstPOProducts![ProductID]
Else
  ' Lock the tblInventory row
  rstInventory.Edit
End If
```

```
          ' Attempt to find a matching Stock row for this Product and Cost
          rstStock.FindFirst "[ProductID] = " & rstPOProducts![ProductID] & _
            " AND [Cost] = " & rstPOProducts![Cost]
        If rstPOProducts![QuantityReceived] > 0 Then
          ' Positive quantity received - maybe create a new stock record
          If rstStock.NoMatch Then   ' If not found, then add it
            rstStock.AddNew
            rstStock![ProductID] = rstPOProducts![ProductID]
            rstStock![VendorID] = lngVendorID
            rstStock![Cost] = rstPOProducts![Cost]
            rstStock![Quantity] = 0
          Else
            rstStock.Edit
          End If
        Else
          ' Returning stock (negative quantity)
          ' -- find the matching Stock record
          If rstStock.NoMatch Then   ' Uh oh!
            If Not intSilent Then MsgBox "Can't find matching " & _
              "Stock record for Product ID " & _
              rstPOProducts![ProductID] & "!  Post cancelled.", _
              vbCritical, gstrAppTitle
            Rollback
            intTrans = False
            PostPOProducts = False
            ' Close out
            rstPOProducts.Close
            Set rstPOProducts = Nothing
            rstPORedo.Close
            Set rstPORedo = Nothing
            If (intOrderYes = True) Then
              rstOrder.Close
              Set rstOrder = Nothing
              rstOrderProducts.Close
              Set rstOrderProducts = Nothing
            End If
            rstStock.Close
            Set rstStock = Nothing
            rstInventory.Close
            Set rstInventory = Nothing
            Exit Function
          Else
            rstStock.Edit
          End If
        End If
```

When the code finds the existing stock record or has created a new stock record for a product being added to inventory, it updates the last date received in the stock record. Remember that a vendor ships products in units that might be a multiple of the unit sold to customers. Because inventory is maintained in customer sell units, the code calculates the inventory quantity by multiplying the quantity received times the order multiple.

When the quantity received doesn't match the quantity originally requested (the BuyQuantity value), the code asks the user if the remaining amount should be left pending in the purchase order and, potentially, any related customer order. (A purchase order might have asked for a quantity of 10, but the vendor shipped only 8.) If the user chooses to keep the remaining amount, the code calculates the difference (the lngDiffB variable) and sets the intRedoThis variable to tell code later in the procedure to insert a row to the zttblPOAddProducts working table and ultimately back to the purchase order and the customer order. The code then adjusts the quantity in the current purchase order record. The code is as follows:

```
' Update the stock record date received
rstStock![DateReceived] = rstPOProducts![DateReceived]
' We stock in "sell" units, so calc the real amount received
lngRealQty = rstPOProducts![QuantityReceived] * _
  rstPOProducts![OrderMultiple]
' Reset the "redo" flag (received < ordered)
intRedoThis = False
If rstPOProducts![QuantityReceived] <> rstPOProducts![BuyQuantity] Then
  ' If running in silent mode,
  If intSilent = True Then
    ' Always keep unreceived quantity
    intKeepQty = vbYes
  Else
    ' Ask the user
    intKeepQty = MsgBox("Quantity received for Product " & _
      rstPOProducts!ProductID & _
      " does not equal quantity ordered.  Click YES to keep " & _
      "the outstanding order amount in this purchase order.   " & _
      "Click NO to set quantity ordered equal to quantity received.", _
      vbInformation + vbYesNo, gstrAppTitle)
  End If
  If intKeepQty = vbYes Then
    ' Set flag to insert a new PO Products row
    intRedoThis = True
    ' Save the difference
    lngDiffB = rstPOProducts![BuyQuantity] - _
      rstPOProducts![QuantityReceived]
  End If
  ' Adjust the buy and sell quantities to match what was received
  rstPOProducts![BuyQuantity] = rstPOProducts![QuantityReceived]
  ' If receiving products
  If lngRealQty > 0 Then
    ' then if sellable quantity less than qty needed
    If lngRealQty < rstPOProducts![SellQuantity] Then
      ' Adjust the sell quantity
      rstPOProducts![SellQuantity] = lngRealQty
    End If
  Else
    ' Returning products - if sellable quantity less than qty needed
    '   (returning less)
    If lngRealQty > rstPOProducts![SellQuantity] Then
      ' Adjust the sell quantity
      rstPOProducts![SellQuantity] = lngRealQty
    End If
  End If
End If
```

Next, the code adjusts the stock record to reflect what was actually received. When adding stock to inventory, the code adds the quantity received to the Quantity field. When posting a return credit, the code adds to the QuantityReturned field (subtracts the negative quantity) and subtracts from the QuantityAllocated field. If the resulting QuantityReturned value is larger than the total previously received minus what has been allocated and billed, the code displays an error, rolls back all updates, and exits because the amount attempted to return exceeds what was available to return in inventory. The code is as follows:

```
' Update the Stock record Quantity
' If receiving stock
If lngRealQty > 0 Then
  ' Add to quantity received
  rstStock![Quantity] = rstStock![Quantity] + lngRealQty
Else
  ' Returning add to quantity returned (keep in separate bucket)
  rstStock![QuantityReturned] = rstStock![QuantityReturned] - _
    lngRealQty
  ' .. and subtract from the amount allocated
  rstStock![QuantityAllocated] = rstStock![QuantityAllocated] + _
    lngRealQty
  ' Verify that Returned does not exceed total received (Quantity)
  '  minus allocated product and sold product
  If rstStock!QuantityReturned > _
    (rstStock!Quantity - rstStock!QuantityAllocated - _
    rstStock!QuantitySold) Then
    ' Very bad - issue message and bail
    If Not intSilent Then MsgBox "Attempting to return " & _
      "more of product " rstStock!ProductID & _
      " than is left in inventory.  Total in inventory = " & _
      (rstStock!Quantity - rstStock!QuantityAllocated - _
      rstStock!QuantitySold) & _
      ", but total returned = " & rstStock!QuantityReturned & _
      ".  Post to inventory cancelled!", vbCritical, gstrAppTitle
    Rollback
    intTrans = False
    PostPOProducts = False
    ' Close out
    rstPOProducts.Close
    Set rstPOProducts = Nothing
    rstPORedo.Close
    Set rstPORedo = Nothing
    If (intOrderYes = True) Then
      rstOrder.Close
      Set rstOrder = Nothing
      rstOrderProducts.Close
      Set rstOrderProducts = Nothing
    End If
    rstStock.Close
    Set rstStock = Nothing
    rstInventory.Close
    Set rstInventory = Nothing
    Exit Function
  End If
End If
```

When the purchase order is for a customer order, the code next updates the related customer order row. If the amount to be posted to the customer order is less than what was received from the vendor (remember, a customer might need a quantity of 3, but the vendor shipped or credited a case of 12), the amount to be posted to the customer order is calculated (the intSell variable). When the amount is positive (not a return), the code adds the amount to the QuantityAllocated field in the Stock table. If not enough was received to satisfy the customer request, the code calculates the amount to be added back to the order as a new product request in the lngDiffS variable and changes the Quantity in the tblOrderProducts table to what was actually received. Finally, the code updates the Cost, Price, VendorID, DateAlloc, and Status fields in the tblOrderProducts table and saves the changes. The code is as follows:

```
' Make sure some temp variables are zero
intSell = 0
lngDiffS = 0
' If an Order, then
If (intOrderYes = True) Then
  intSell = rstPOProducts![SellQuantity]
  ' Only do an "enough" check
  If intSell > 0 Then
    ' Positive value - is actual less than required?
    If lngRealQty < intSell Then
      ' Quantity actually received not enough to fill Order request
      intNotEnough = True
      rstPOProducts![SellQuantity] = lngRealQty
      intSell = lngRealQty
    End If
    ' Also allocate in Stock
    rstStock!QuantityAllocated = rstStock!QuantityAllocated + intSell
  Else
    ' Negative value - is actual more (logically less) than required?
    If intSell < lngRealQty Then
      ' Qty actually credited not enough to fill Order request
      intNotEnough = True
      rstPOProducts![SellQuantity] = lngRealQty
      intSell = lngRealQty
    End If
    ' No need to update stock on return -
    '  QuantityReturned already updated
  End If
  ' If not enough received
  If (intRedoThis = True) Then
    ' Calculate the difference for later insert
    lngDiffS = rstOrderProducts![Quantity] - intSell
    ' Reset the quantity in the order
    rstOrderProducts![Quantity] = intSell
  End If
  curCost = rstPOProducts![Cost]
  ' Set the posted Cost in the order
  rstOrderProducts![Cost] = curCost
  curListPrice = rstPOProducts![SellPrice]
  If curListPrice < 0.1 Then curListPrice = 0.1
  ' Update the order with the latest price
```

```
rstOrderProducts![Price] = curListPrice
' Adjust the price if less than cost
If rstOrderProducts![Price] < rstOrderProducts![Cost] Then
  rstOrderProducts!Price = rstOrderProducts!Cost + 0.01
End If
' Set the Vendor ID in the Order
rstOrderProducts![VendorID] = lngVendorID
' Set the allocated date
rstOrderProducts![DateAlloc] = rstPOProducts![DateReceived]
' Set status = allocated
rstOrderProducts!Status = OrderStatus.Allocated
' Save the order row
rstOrderProducts.Update
End If
```

Next, the code sets the HighCost field in the tblInventory record and calculates the new
QuantityInStock and QuantityOnHand values, saves the changes, and closes the inventory
recordset. The code makes a final adjustment to the QuantityRemaining field in the tblStock
table and saves the change. The code is as follows:

```
' If latest cost is greater than previous high cost,
'   then update Inventory
If rstPOProducts![Cost] > rstInventory![HighCost] Then
  rstInventory![HighCost] = rstPOProducts![Cost]
End If
' Update the Inventory record to reflect stock changes
rstInventory!QuantityInStock = rstInventory!QuantityInStock + _
  lngRealQty
rstInventory!QuantityOnHand = rstInventory!QuantityOnHand + _
  lngRealQty - intSell
rstInventory.Update
rstInventory.Close
Set rstInventory = Nothing
' Update the Stock record quantities
rstStock![QuantityRemaining] = rstStock![Quantity] - _
  (rstStock![QuantityAllocated] + rstStock![QuantitySold] + _
  rstStock![QuantityReturned])
rstStock.Update
```

When less was received than requested for the current row, code earlier in the procedure has
set the intRedoThis variable to True. The code sets the intRedo variable to True to let code at
the end of the procedure know that one or more rows have been inserted into the working
table. The code then adds a new row to the working table to save the data required to create
new purchase order and customer order rows to reflect the quantity not received and resets
the intRedoThis variable. Finally, the code sets the current purchase order row posted, saves
the change, moves to the next row to process, and loops back to the Do statement found on
page 271. The code is as follows:

```
If (intRedoThis = True) Then
  ' Didn't receive enough, so set up to add row(s) to this PO
  intRedo = True
  rstPORedo.AddNew
```

```
      ' Save the PO Number
      rstPORedo![PONumber] = lngPONumber
      ' Save the "new" line number to be added to PO
      rstPORedo![LineNo] = lngNextLine
      ' Increment for possible next one
      lngNextLine = lngNextLine + 1
      ' Save the ProductID
      rstPORedo![ProductID] = rstPOProducts![ProductID]
      ' Save the Vendor ID
      rstPORedo![VendorID] = lngVendorID
      ' Calculate the sell amount difference
      If lngDiffS = 0 Then
        lngDiffS = rstPOProducts![OrderMultiple] * lngDiffB
      End If
      ' Set the Sell amount
      rstPORedo![SellQuantity] = lngDiffS
      ' Set the buy amount
      rstPORedo![BuyQuantity] = lngDiffB
      ' Save the stock cost
      rstPORedo![Cost] = rstPOProducts![Cost]
      ' Set the Price
      curPrice = rstPOProducts![SellPrice]
      If curPrice < 0.1 Then curPrice = 0.1
      rstPORedo![Price] = curPrice
      ' Copy OrderBy, Order Multiple, and Sell By
      rstPORedo![OrderBy] = rstPOProducts![OrderBy]
      rstPORedo![OrderMultiple] = rstPOProducts![OrderMultiple]
      rstPORedo![SellBy] = rstPOProducts![SellBy]
      ' If also must set new Order rows ...
      If (intOrderYes = True) Then
        ' Save the OrderID
        rstPORedo![OrderID] = rstOrderProducts![OrderID]
        ' Set the "next" order line number
        rstPORedo![OrderLineNo] = lngNextOrderLine
        ' Increment for next one
        lngNextOrderLine = lngNextOrderLine + 1
        ' Save the Vendor ID to stuff in the new Order record
        rstPORedo![VendorID] = lngVendorID
      End If
      ' Save the row for later insert into PO and possible Order
      rstPORedo.Update
      ' Reset the "redo this one" flag for next row
      intRedoThis = False
    End If
    ' Set the PO record posted and go get the next one
    rstPOProducts![Posted] = True
    rstPOProducts.Update
    rstPOProducts.MoveNext
  Loop
```

Creating Insufficient Quantity Rows and Closing

After processing all the purchase order product request rows, the code checks to see if any rows were added because an insufficient quantity was received for one or more requests. If so, the code executes the zqappAddPOProducts append query to insert the data into the tblPOProducts table. If the purchase order is for a customer order, the code also executes the zqappAddOrderProductPO append query to add the appropriate rows to the tblOrderProducts table. Finally, the code commits all updates, closes all the open recordsets, and exits. At the end of the procedure you can see the error trapping code that writes a record to the error log, displays the error message, rolls back any pending updates, and exits. The code is as follows:

```
' Done processing PO rows - now insert any "left over" amounts
If (intRedo = True) Then
  ' Insert Purchase Order rows
  db.Execute "zqappAddPOProducts", dbFailOnError
  ' If related order
  If (intOrderYes = True) Then
    ' Also insert matching order rows
    db.Execute "zqappAddOrderProductsPO", dbFailOnError
  End If
End If
' Commit the entire ball of wax
CommitTrans
intTrans = False
' Close out
rstPORedo.Close
Set rstPORedo = Nothing
rstPOProducts.Close
Set rstPOProducts = Nothing
rstStock.Close
Set rstStock = Nothing
' If matching order
If (intOrderYes = True) Then
  ' Also close the two order recordsets
  rstOrderProducts.Close
  Set rstOrderProducts = Nothing
  rstOrder.Close
  Set rstOrder = Nothing
  ' If the orders form is open,
  '   requery the subform to display new rows (if any)
  If IsFormLoaded("frmOrders") Then
    Forms!frmOrders!fsubOrderProducts.Requery
  End If
End If
' Give JET a chance to free all locks
DBEngine.Idle dbFreeLocks
' Return successful
PostPOProducts = True
' If had to re-order some, then tell the user
If (intNotEnough = True) Then
  If Not intSilent Then
    MsgBox "Some Products received weren't enough to fill " & _
      "original Order Products request.  " & _
      "You must re-run Products allocation on the Order.", _
      vbExclamation, gstrAppTitle
  End If
```

```
    End If
POPost_Exit:
  Exit Function
POPost_ERR:
Dim strError As String, lngErr As Long
  strError = Error
  lngErr = Err
  If (intTrans = True) Then Rollback
  DoCmd.Hourglass False
  ErrorLog "PostPOProducts", lngErr, strError
  If Not intSilent Then MsgBox "Unexpected error: " & lngErr & _
    ", " & strError & "  Error has been logged.", _
    vbCritical, gstrAppTitle
  Resume POPost_Exit
End Function
```

At this point, you've learned how the application processes customer order requests, creates purchase orders, edits vendor invoices, and posts received products to inventory and to customer orders. The only remaining tasks are to send the customer a bill, which you'll learn about in the next chapter, and creating reports, discussed in Chapter 14.

Chapter 13

Creating Customer Invoices

In the previous three chapters, you learned how an order entry clerk can enter product requests in a customer order and allocate products from inventory. You also learned how the application can automatically generate a vendor purchase order when there is insufficient stock in inventory to satisfy a product request. Finally, you learned how a clerk can enter the vendor invoice when the products are received and post the received products to inventory and any related customer order. In this chapter, you'll see how a clerk can run the billing process to mark the products sold in inventory and create an invoice to send with the shipment to the customer.

Creating a Partial Bill

When the user enters an order for a customer and allocates products to the order, one or more products might be on back order pending receipt of products on a related purchase order. The application allows the user to create a partial bill for the products that were allocated from inventory. After all products have been allocated to the order, the user can create a final bill and close out the order.

To see how this works, open the Inventory Management application (Inventory.mdb), and after the splash form closes, open the frmOrders form. If you have been following along to this point, the first order in the sample database for the customer Around the Horn should have all products allocated and ready to bill. To see how a partial bill works, go to the new row in the Products subform window and add a request for Tourtière in the Meat/Poultry category and ask for a quantity of 10. Click the Allocate button, reply Yes to the offer to generate purchase orders, click Done in the Verify Vendor dialog box, and close the Purchase Order report window. The order should now look something like Figure 13-1 on the next page.

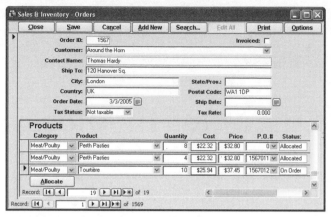

Figure 13-1   A customer order that has most products allocated but has one product request still pending.

Because at least one product is still on order, you won't be able to create a final bill for the customer order, but you can create a partial bill for the products that are allocated. To bill the order, click the Options button and then click the Bill It! button in the Order Options dialog box. The application displays the Bill Order dialog box as shown in Figure 13-2.

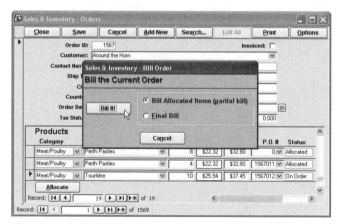

Figure 13-2   Selecting the option to create a partial bill for a customer order.

Choose the option to **Bill Allocated Items (partial bill)**—the default—and click the Bill It! button. The application posts the sold status of the allocated items in inventory, changes the product request status in the customer order to Invoiced, and creates the invoice for the customer order, as shown in Figure 13-3.

Notice that the invoice tells the customer that the Tourtière is on order, so no charge has been included in this invoice. Also, even though the order contains several detail lines for Chartreuse verte and Perth Pasties, the invoice displays one summary line for each product. The record source for the report uses the qryOrderProductSum query to total the items by product, status, invoice number, and price charged to the customer. (If a product was allocated to the order, the price changed, and more was added to the order later, the product could appear with more than one price.) Close the Customer Invoice report and return to the Orders form.

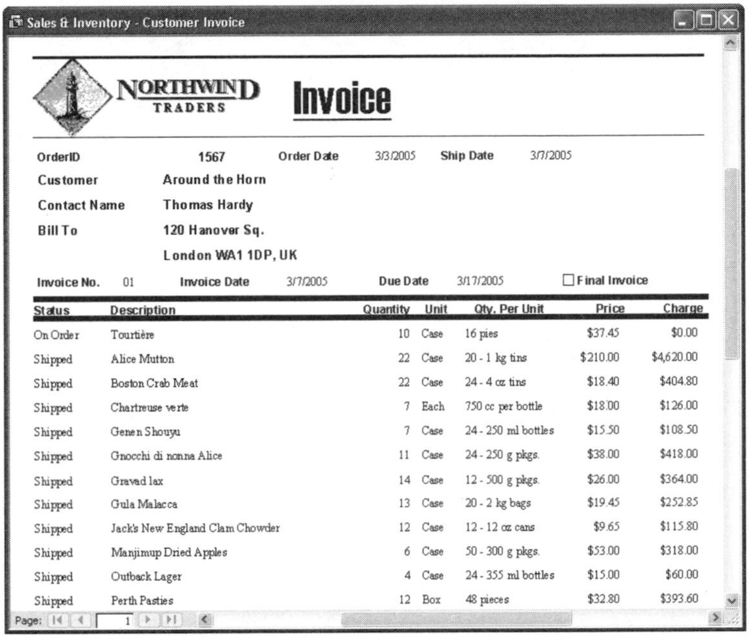

Status	Description	Quantity	Unit	Qty. Per Unit	Price	Charge
On Order	Tourtière	10	Case	16 pies	$37.45	$0.00
Shipped	Alice Mutton	22	Case	20 - 1 kg tins	$210.00	$4,620.00
Shipped	Boston Crab Meat	22	Case	24 - 4 oz tins	$18.40	$404.80
Shipped	Chartreuse verte	7	Each	750 cc per bottle	$18.00	$126.00
Shipped	Genen Shouyu	7	Case	24 - 250 ml bottles	$15.50	$108.50
Shipped	Gnocchi di nonna Alice	11	Case	24 - 250 g pkgs.	$38.00	$418.00
Shipped	Gravad lax	14	Case	12 - 500 g pkgs.	$26.00	$364.00
Shipped	Gula Malacca	13	Case	20 - 2 kg bags	$19.45	$252.85
Shipped	Jack's New England Clam Chowder	12	Case	12 - 12 oz cans	$9.65	$115.80
Shipped	Manjimup Dried Apples	6	Case	50 - 300 g pkgs.	$53.00	$318.00
Shipped	Outback Lager	4	Case	24 - 355 ml bottles	$15.00	$60.00
Shipped	Perth Pasties	12	Box	48 pieces	$32.80	$393.60

Figure 13-3 The partial bill for a customer order.

Validating the Customer Order Before Final Billing It

With the Orders form open on order ID 1567, click the Options button again, click Bill It! in the Order Options dialog box, choose the Final Bill option, and click the Bill It! button. The application displays an error message telling you that you cannot produce a final invoice, as shown in Figure 13-4 on the next page. If you think about it, it doesn't make sense to create a "final" invoice for a customer order when product requests are still outstanding–either not allocated or on order.

Click the OK button in the error dialog box, and the application also tells you about any vendor invoices for this order that have not yet been marked final (not shown). If all the products in the order are allocated but one or more related vendor invoices have not been marked final, the application displays a warning message when the user tries to create a final bill but gives the user the option to create the invoice anyway.

The code that performs the checks for allocated products and related vendor invoices is in the fdlgOrderBillOptions form–the Bill Order dialog box. When you click the Bill It! button, the code in that command button's Click event procedure calls the *BillIt* procedure and passes it the value of the option group containing the Bill Allocated Items (value 2) and Final Bill (value 1) options. The *BillIt* procedure is also in the module for the fdlgOrderBillOptions form.

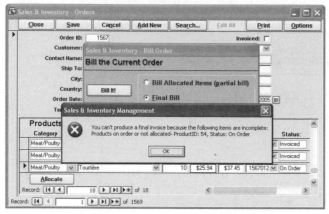

Figure 13-4   You can't final bill a customer order when products are still on order.

The procedure begins by setting an error trap. If the user has asked for a final invoice (intType = 1), the code opens a recordset on the tblOrderProducts table that looks for any products in the customer order that have not yet been allocated (status is None or On Order). When it finds one or more products, it sets the intNoFinal variable to True to let code later in the procedure know to cancel the invoice creation, and then loops through all the records to build (but not yet display) an error message string. Note that the code that builds the error message string uses the *Choose* function to map the Status values of 0 and 1 to "None" and "On Order," respectively. The code is as follows:

```
Private Sub BillIt(intType As Integer)
Dim db As DAO.Database, rst As DAO.Recordset, frm As Form
Dim strMsg As String, varRtn As Variant, _
  strInvoiceNo As String, intNoFinal As Integer
Dim strMsg1 As String, intAskFinal As Integer
  ' Set an error trap
  On Error GoTo BillIt_Err
  ' Get a pointer to the Orders window
  Set frm = Forms!frmOrders
  ' .. and to this database
  Set db = DBEngine(0)(0)
  ' If final, then do some special checks
  If intType = 1 Then
    ' Put a nice message on the status bar
    varRtn = SysCmd(acSysCmdSetStatus, "Checking final status ...")
    ' .. and show the Hourglass to indicate this might take a sec.
    DoCmd.Hourglass True
    ' ** Check products
    ' Products on the Order with status "none" or "On Order"
    Set rst = db.OpenRecordset("SELECT ProductID, Status " & _
      "FROM tblOrderProducts " & _
      "WHERE OrderID = " & frm!OrderID & _
      " AND Status < " & OrderStatus.Allocated)
    ' If we got some, then assemble the error message
    If rst.RecordCount <> 0 Then
      ' Set flag that we can't final bill
```

```
    intNoFinal = True
    ' Set up the error message
    strMsg = "Products on order or not allocated- ProductID: " & _
      rst!ProductID & ", Status: " & _
      Choose(rst!Status + 1, "None", "On Order")
    rst.MoveNext
    Do Until rst.EOF
      ' Loop through all rows to display all products
      strMsg = strMsg & "; ProductID: " & rst!ProductID & _
        ", Status: " & _
        Choose(rst!Status + 1, "None", "On Order")
      rst.MoveNext
    Loop
  End If
  ' Close the recordset
  rst.Close
  Set rst = Nothing
```

> **Note**   You can find OrderStatus declared as an Enum in the modGlobals module. An Enum is a good way to assign meaningful names to code values. In this case, the OrderStatus Enum maps the value 0 to None, 1 to OnOrder, 2 to Allocated, and 3 to Invoiced.

Next, when checking a final invoice, the procedure opens a recordset on any vendor invoices related to the customer order to find any that are not marked final. When it finds one or more records, it sets the intAskFinal variable to True to let code later in the procedure know to display a warning message, and then loops through all the records to build (but not yet display) an error message. The code is as follows:

```
  ' ** Check Vendor Invoices
  Set rst = db.OpenRecordset("SELECT VendorID, InvoiceNumber " & _
    "FROM tblVendInvoices " & _
    "WHERE OrderID = " & frm!OrderID & " And Final = False")
  ' If found some invoices not final
  If rst.RecordCount <> 0 Then
    ' Set flag for warning message
    intAskFinal = True
    ' Set up the message
    strMsg1 = "Vendor Invoices not final- Vendor: " & rst!VendorID & _
        ", Invoice #: " & rst!InvoiceNumber
    rst.MoveNext
    Do Until rst.EOF
      ' Loop through all rows to display all invoices
      strMsg1 = strMsg1 & "; Vendor: " & rst!VendorID & _
        ", Invoice #: " & rst!InvoiceNumber
      rst.MoveNext
    Loop
  End If
  ' Close the recordset
  rst.Close
  Set rst = Nothing
```

After performing the two recordset verifications, the code checks to see if the first one failed (intNoFinal = True). If so, the code displays the two error messages one at a time and exits. If the first test didn't fail, but the second test produced a warning (intAskFinal = True), the code displays the warning and asks the user if he or she wants to proceed. If the user responds No, the code exits. The code is as follows:

```
' Done checking - turn off the hourglass
DoCmd.Hourglass False
' .. and clear the status bar
varRtn = SysCmd(acSysCmdClearStatus)
' *** Did any fail?  If so, tell them and bail
If (intNoFinal = True) Then
  ' Display the error message
  MsgBox "You can't produce a final invoice " & _
    "because the following items " & _
    "are incomplete:" & vbCrLf & strMsg, vbCritical, gstrAppTitle
  ' If warning message, display that, too
  If (intAskFinal = True) Then
    MsgBox "The following non-critical items were also found:" & _
      vbCrLf & strMsg1, vbExclamation, gstrAppTitle
  End If
  ' Can't produce final bill, so exit
  Exit Sub
End If
' No failures, but are there any warnings?
If (intAskFinal = True) Then
  If vbNo = MsgBox("Order is ready to final bill " & _
    "except for the following issues:" & _
    vbCrLf & strMsg1 & vbCrLf & _
    "Are you SURE you want to proceed?", _
    vbQuestion + vbYesNo, gstrAppTitle) Then
    Exit Sub
  End If
End If
End If
```

If the customer order has been pending for a while and the price of one or more products changed during that period, it's possible that a product can appear multiple times in the order with different prices. It's probably not a good idea to send a customer an invoice with the same product listed at different prices, so the code in the *BillIt* procedure next checks for this condition.

The code clears the zttblDupOrderProductPrice working table and executes an append (insert) query that loads product rows from the current customer order that have more than one price for the same product. If the table contains rows after running the query, the code opens the fdlgDupOrderProductPrices form as a dialog box that displays the products, their prices, and the highest price found for each product in the order. Instructions displayed in this dialog box inform the user of the problem and give the user the opportunity to make all the prices the same. If the user clicks the Cancel button in the dialog box, the form sets a cancel indicator in a hidden control and hides itself. When the code in the *BillIt* procedure finds the form still open and the cancel flag set, the code closes the form and exits without producing an invoice. The code is as follows:

```
' Now, check for multiple product prices..
' Clear the working table
db.Execute "DELETE * FROM zttblDupOrderProductPrice;"
' Use append query to insert duplicate product prices, if any
db.Execute "INSERT INTO zttblDupOrderProductPrice " & _
  "(OrderID, ProductID, MaxPrice) " & _
  "SELECT qdp.OrderID, qdp.ProductID, Max(qdp.Price) AS MaxOfPrice " & _
  "FROM (SELECT DISTINCT tblOrderProducts.OrderID, & _
  tblOrderProducts.ProductID, " & _
  "tblOrderProducts.Price FROM tblOrderProducts " & _
  "WHERE tblOrderProducts.OrderID = " & frm!OrderID & ") AS qdp " & _
  "GROUP BY qdp.OrderID, qdp.ProductID HAVING Count(qdp.Price)>1;", _
  dbFailOnError
' Refresh TableDefs to get an accurate count
db.TableDefs.Refresh
' If a product has more than one price, give 'em a chance to edit
If db.TableDefs("zttblDupOrderProductPrice").RecordCount > 0 Then
  ' Open the duplicate price edit form
  DoCmd.OpenForm "fdlgDupOrderProductPrices", , , , , acDialog
  ' Form just closes if they OK the prices
  If IsFormLoaded("fdlgDupOrderProductPrices") Then
    ' Check the form flag to see if they canceled
    If Forms!fdlgDupOrderProductPrices!chkCancel Then
      ' Close out the form
      DoCmd.Close acForm, "fdlgDupOrderProductPrices"
      ' .. and bail
      Exit Sub
    End If
    ' AOK - just close the form
    DoCmd.Close acForm, "fdlgDupOrderProductPrices"
  End If
End If
```

When all checks have completed successfully, the code calls the *MakeInvoice* function that you can find in the modInventory module, and passes it the OrderID field from the customer order form and the final billing indicator (the intType variable). When the *MakeInvoice* function returns the value 0 indicating it has encountered an error, the code displays a message and exits. (As you'll see later, the *MakeInvoice* function displays the exact nature of the error.)

If the *MakeInvoice* function completes successfully, it returns the number of the invoice created, which the code converts into a two-digit string to use later in a filter to open the Customer Invoice report. If the user asked for a final invoice, the code executes an update query to set the FinalInvoice field in the customer order record to True (−1). The code then hides the fdlgOrderBillOptions form (the form where this code is running) to prevent focus problems, opens the rptOrderInvoice report filtered for the current customer order and invoice number, closes the form, and exits. The code is as shown on the next page.

```
' ** all checks complete -- call the invoice create function
varRtn = MakeInvoice(CLng(frm!OrderID), intType)
' If False return, nothing happened
If varRtn = 0 Then
  ' Tell user
  MsgBox "No invoice was created.", vbInformation, gstrAppTitle
  ' .. and bail
  Exit Sub
End If
' Convert returned number to string invoice number
strInvoiceNo = Format(varRtn, "00")
' If Final bill,
If intType = 1 Then
  ' Set the order status to final
  db.Execute "UPDATE tblOrders SET FinalInvoice = -1 " & _
    "WHERE OrderID = " & frm!OrderID, dbFailOnError
End If
' Hide me
Me.Visible = False
' Open the invoice just produced
DoCmd.OpenReport "rptOrderInvoice", acPreview, , _
  "[OrderID] = " & frm!OrderID & _
  " And [InvoiceNo] = """ & strInvoiceNo & """"
BillIt_Exit:
  Exit Sub
BillIt_Err:
Dim lngErr As Long, strError As String
  lngErr = Err
  strError = Error
  ErrorLog Me.Name & ".BillIt", lngErr, strError
  MsgBox "Unexpected Error: " & lngErr & ", " & strError & _
    " Has been logged.", _
    vbCritical, gstrAppTitle
  DoCmd.Hourglass False
  Resume BillIt_Exit
End Sub
```

Creating the Customer Invoice

All the work to post sold items to inventory, mark products invoiced, and create the customer invoice record is performed in the *MakeInvoice* function in the modInventory module.

Initializing and Validating the Data to Be Posted

The code in the *MakeInvoice* function begins by establishing a date to use for the invoice. This procedure can be called by the code in the zfrmLoadData form that you can use to load sample data. When called from that form, the procedure uses the optional date passed by the code, and when called from the fdlgOrderBillOptions form, the procedure uses today's date. Next, the code opens the customer order record and locks it, and then opens the tblCust-Invoices table to add the new customer invoice. The code uses a totals query to determine the previous last invoice number for the customer order and adds one to it to generate the next invoice number. (Remember, an order might have several partial invoices as well as a final one.) Finally, the code opens a recordset on all products in the customer order that have been allocated but not invoiced and obtains a count of the rows to process to display a progress meter on the status bar. The code is as follows:

```
Function MakeInvoice(lngOrder As Long, intType As Integer, _
  Optional varInvoiceDate As Variant) As Integer
Dim db As DAO.Database, qd As DAO.QueryDef, rstInvoice As DAO.Recordset
Dim rstI As DAO.Recordset, rstS As DAO.Recordset, rst As DAO.Recordset
Dim rstOrder As DAO.Recordset, rstProducts As DAO.Recordset
Dim lngQty As Long, dblTaxRate As Double, curProductsTot As Currency
Dim varNextInv As Variant, strInvNo As String
Dim varRtn As Variant, lngRecCount As Long, _
  lngI As Long, intGotSome As Integer
Dim intTrans As Integer, strSQL As String, datInvoiceDate As Date
'
'  Procedure to create either a partial or final invoice for an Order
'
'  Inputs: OrderID, Invoice Type (1 = Final), and optional Invoicing date
'          (Optional date implemented to load sample data.)
'
'  Output: Tags order product rows as invoiced and adds invoice number.
'          Creates a summary row in tblCustInvoices
'          Returns False if any failure or nothing to Invoice
On Error GoTo MakeInv_ERR
  ' Default: use today as Invoicing date
  datInvoiceDate = Date
  ' See if passed a date
  If Not IsMissing(varInvoiceDate) Then
    ' See if it's a valid date
    If IsDate(varInvoiceDate) Then
      ' Use it
      datInvoiceDate = varInvoiceDate
    End If
  End If
  ' Point to this database
  Set db = DBEngine(0)(0)
  ' Protect all in a transaction
  BeginTrans
  intTrans = True
  ' Turn on the hourglass
  DoCmd.Hourglass True
  ' Get the order record
  Set rstOrder = db.OpenRecordset("SELECT * FROM tblOrders " & _
    "WHERE [OrderID] = " & lngOrder)
  ' If cannot find it...
  If rstOrder.RecordCount = 0 Then
    ' Tell the user, close out, and bail
    MsgBox "Fatal error: Unable to find Order # " & lngOrder & _
      ".  Invoice creation cancelled!", vbCritical, gstrAppTitle
    Rollback
    intTrans = False
    rstOrder.Close
    Set rstOrder = Nothing
```

```
    Exit Function
  End If
  ' Lock the Order by editing it
  rstOrder.Edit
  ' Open a tblCustInvoices to add one row
  Set rstInvoice = db.OpenRecordset("tblCustInvoices", _
    dbOpenDynaset, dbAppendOnly)
  ' Calculate the next invoice number for this Order
  ' Figure out highest previous InvoiceNo using a recordset
  Set rst = db.OpenRecordset("SELECT Max(CInt([InvoiceNo])) AS MaxNo " & _
    "FROM tblCustInvoices WHERE [OrderID] = " & lngOrder)
  ' If no previous invoices
  If rst.EOF Then
    ' Set next to 1
    varNextInv = 1
  Else
    ' Also check for Null
    If IsNull(rst!MaxNo) Then
      ' .. and set to 1
      varNextInv = 1
    Else
      ' Otherwise, add 1 to previous max
      varNextInv = rst!MaxNo + 1
    End If
  End If
  rst.Close
  Set rst = Nothing
  ' Create the string equivalent of the invoice number
  strInvNo = Format(varNextInv, "00")
  '*** Process Products
  Set rstProducts = db.OpenRecordset("SELECT tblOrderProducts.* " & _
    "FROM tblOrderProducts " & _
    "WHERE OrderID = " & lngOrder & " AND Status = " & _
    OrderStatus.Allocated)
  ' Make sure we got some
  If rstProducts.RecordCount <> 0 Then
    ' Go to the last row to get an accurate record count
    rstProducts.MoveLast
    ' Save the count
    lngRecCount = rstProducts.RecordCount
    ' Move back to first row
    rstProducts.MoveFirst
    ' Start the status bar meter
    varRtn = SysCmd(acSysCmdInitMeter, "Processing Products ...", _
      lngRecCount)
    lngI = 0
  End If
```

Updating the Customer Order Product Rows and Locating the Inventory Record

The real work in the procedure to produce a customer invoice occurs as the code processes each of the unbilled product request records. The code saves the quantity for use in later calculations. The code calculates the extended price for the product, rounds it to pennies, and adds it to the curProductsTot variable. The code places the invoice number in the product row and sets the status to Invoiced. Next, the code opens a recordset on the related product record in the tblInventory table. If the code can't find the record, it displays an error message, rolls back all previous updates, and exits. When it finds the inventory record, the code locks the record by editing it. The code is as follows:

```
' Loop through all allocated products
Do Until rstProducts.EOF
  rstProducts.Edit
  ' Save the quantity to allocate
  lngQty = rstProducts!Quantity
  ' Add to the total charge
  curProductsTot = curProductsTot + _
    Round((lngQty * rstProducts!Price), 2)
  ' Set the invoice number in this product row
  rstProducts!InvoiceNo = strInvNo
  ' Set the status to Invoiced
  rstProducts!Status = OrderStatus.Invoiced
  ' Get Inventory row for this Product
  Set rstI = db.OpenRecordset("Select * From tblInventory " & _
    "Where [ProductID] = " & rstProducts!ProductID)
  ' Fatal error if not found...
  If rstI.RecordCount = 0 Then
    MsgBox "Fatal error: unable to find master " & _
      Inventory record for Product " & _
      rstProducts!ProductID & ".  Invoice creation cancelled!", _
      vbCritical, gstrAppTitle
    ' Bail out
    Rollback
    rstI.Close
    Set rstI = Nothing
    rstProducts.Close
    Set rstProducts = Nothing
    rstInvoice.Close
    Set rstInvoice = Nothing
    rstOrder.Close
    Set rstOrder = Nothing
    intTrans = False
    DoCmd.Hourglass False
    varRtn = SysCmd(acSysCmdClearStatus)
    Exit Function
  End If
  ' Found it - lock it for editing
  rstI.Edit
```

Updating the Stock and Inventory Totals

Because the customer is being invoiced for products, the application now considers the product sold. The code opens a recordset on the tblStock table to find the stock record that matches the product, vendor, and cost. If it can't find the record, the code displays an error message, rolls back all previous changes, and exits. When the code finds the record, it subtracts the product quantity from the amount previously allocated (this might be an addition if the product request is returning the product) and adds the quantity to the amount previously sold. The code also updates the quantity remaining value that indicates the quantity of the product that is still available to be allocated or sold from this vendor and at this cost. The code saves the stock record and closes the recordset.

Next, the code opens the query definition of the zqrySumStockParm query. This query recalculates the highest cost, total in stock (including allocated but not invoiced), and total on hand (amount available to allocate to other orders) for the specified product. The code sets the product filter using a parameter called ItemToFind in the query. The code opens a recordset on the query and then uses the values returned by the query to update the calculated values in the tblInventory record (the rstI recordset). Finally, the code saves the inventory record, saves the product request record from the customer order, sets the intGotSome variable to True to indicate at least one product has been processed, moves to the next product request row, and loops to the Do statement explained on the previous page. The code is as follows:

```
' Get Stock row for this Product
strSQL = "Select * From tblStock Where ([ProductID] = " & _
   rstProducts!ProductID & ")"
strSQL = strSQL & " AND ([Cost] = " & rstProducts!Cost & ")"
strSQL = strSQL & " AND ([VendorID] = " & rstProducts!VendorID & ")"
Set rstS = db.OpenRecordset(strSQL)
' Fatal error if not found
If rstS.RecordCount = 0 Then
  MsgBox "Fatal error: unable to find Product " & _
    rstProducts!ProductID & _
    " for Vendor ID " & rstProducts!VendorID & " at cost " & _
    Format(rstProducts!Cost, "Currency") & _
    " in Stock.  Invoice creation cancelled!", vbCritical, gstrAppTitle
  Rollback
  intTrans = False
  rstS.Close
  Set rstS = Nothing
  rstI.Close
  Set rstI = Nothing
  rstProducts.Close
  Set rstProducts = Nothing
  rstInvoice.Close
  Set rstInvoice = Nothing
  rstOrder.Close
  Set rstOrder = Nothing
```

```
      DoCmd.Hourglass False
      varRtn = SysCmd(acSysCmdClearStatus)
      Exit Function
    End If
    ' Edit the stock record
    rstS.Edit
    ' "Subtract" the amount allocated
    rstS!QuantityAllocated = rstS!QuantityAllocated - lngQty
    ' "Add" the amount sold
    rstS!QuantitySold = rstS!QuantitySold + lngQty
    ' Update the quantity remaining
    rstS!QuantityRemaining = rstS!Quantity - _
      (rstS!QuantityAllocated + rstS!QuantitySold + rstS!QuantityReturned)
    ' Save the stock update
    rstS.Update
    ' And close the stock record
    rstS.Close
    Set rstS = Nothing
    ' Refresh the master inventory totals...
    Set qd = db.QueryDefs("zqrySumStockParm")
    qd!ItemToFind = rstProducts!ProductID
    Set rst = qd.OpenRecordset()
    ' Update the calc values in the Inventory row
    If Not rst.EOF Then
      rstI!HighCost = rst!MaxCost
      rstI!QuantityInStock = rst!Available
      rstI!QuantityOnHand = rst!Remain
    Else
      rstI!QuantityInStock = 0
      rstI!QuantityOnHand = 0
    End If
    ' Update and close the Inventory stuff
    rstI.Update
    rst.Close
    Set rst = Nothing
    qd.Close
    Set qd = Nothing
    rstI.Close
    Set rstI = Nothing
    ' Save the changes to Order Products
    rstProducts.Update
    ' Indicate we actually Invoiced something
    intGotSome = True
    ' Ready to do the next one - update the status bar
    lngI = lngI + 1
    varRtn = SysCmd(acSysCmdUpdateMeter, lngI)
    ' Get the next Order Product row
    rstProducts.MoveNext
  ' Loop until we're done
  Loop
```

Creating the Invoice Record

After processing all of the product request rows in the customer order, the code clears the status bar and closes the recordset on the tblOrderProducts table. If no product request rows were processed and this is not a final invoice, there's no point in creating a new invoice that has no charges in it. When this is the case, the code rolls back any updates (there should have been none) and exits. Because the code is not returning an invoice number, the code in the fdlgOrderBillOptions form shown earlier on page 288 informs the user that no invoice has been created.

If this is a final invoice or at least one product request row was processed, the code creates a new record in the tblCustInvoices table (the rstInvoice recordset). The code sets the OrderID, InvoiceNo, CustomerID, InvoiceDate, and Final fields. If this is a final invoice, the code sets the due date 30 days in the future; otherwise, payment is due in 10 days. The code next sets the InvoiceSubTotal from the total cost of all products calculated while processing order request rows. If the customer is taxable, the code calculates the tax amount by multiplying the customer's tax rate times the product total, rounding the amount to pennies. The code adds the product total and the tax amount and stores the sum in the InvoiceTotal field. After saving the new invoice, the code updates the ship date in the customer order, sets the FinalInvoice field to True (−1) if this was a final invoice, updates the order, and closes the recordset. The code is as follows:

```
' Clear the status bar
varRtn = SysCmd(acSysCmdClearStatus)
' .. and close Order Products
rstProducts.Close
Set rstProducts = Nothing
'*** Wrap up totals and write invoice row
' If we found nothing to Invoice on a partial Invoice, then bail!
If (intGotSome = False) And (intType <> 1) Then
  Rollback
  intTrans = False
  rstInvoice.Close
  Set rstInvoice = Nothing
  rstOrder.Close
  Set rstOrder = Nothing
  varRtn = SysCmd(acSysCmdClearStatus)
  DoCmd.Hourglass False
  Exit Function
End If
' Start a new Invoice row
rstInvoice.AddNew
' Set the OrderID
rstInvoice!OrderID = lngOrder
' .. Invoice Number
rstInvoice!InvoiceNo = strInvNo
' .. CustomerID
rstInvoice!CustomerID = rstOrder!CustomerID
' .. today's date
rstInvoice!InvoiceDate = datInvoiceDate
```

```
' .. and Final
rstInvoice!Final = (intType = 1)
' If this is a final invoice,
If rstInvoice!Final Then
  ' Give them 30 days to pay
  rstInvoice!DueDate = datInvoiceDate + 30
Else
  ' .. but set 10 days on a partial Invoice
  rstInvoice!DueDate = datInvoiceDate + 10
End If
' Subtotal = total charge for products
rstInvoice!InvoiceSubTotal = curProductsTot
' Get the tax rate from the Order row
dblTaxRate = rstOrder!TaxRate
' See if taxable
Select Case rstOrder!TaxStatus
  Case 0
    ' No, set tax to zero
    rstInvoice!Tax = 0
  Case 1
    ' Yes, calculate tax and round it
    rstInvoice!Tax = CCur(CLng((curProductsTot) * _
      (dblTaxRate) * 100) / 100)
End Select
' Set the grand total
rstInvoice!InvoiceTotal = curProductsTot + rstInvoice!Tax
' Save the row
rstInvoice.Update
' .. and close out
rstInvoice.Close
Set rstInvoice = Nothing
' Finally, set the ship date in the order
rstOrder!ShipDate = datInvoiceDate
' If this is final,
If (intType = 1) Then
  ' .. also set final invoice
  rstOrder!FinalInvoice = -1
End If
rstOrder.Update
' .. and close it
rstOrder.Close
Set rstOrder = Nothing
```

Committing All Changes and Closing

To complete the invoice creation process, the code instructs the Access database engine to save all record changes (CommitTrans) and then gives the database engine a chance to finish saving all the records to the database. The code finally returns the invoice number created and exits. The remainder of the statements are the error handling code. The code is as follows:

```
' Commit all changes
CommitTrans
intTrans = False
' Give JET a chance to catch up
```

```
    DBEngine.Idle dbFreeLocks
    ' Turn off the hourglass
    DoCmd.Hourglass False
    ' Return the number of the invoice we created
    MakeInvoice = varNextInv
MakeInv_Exit:
    ' Done
    Exit Function
MakeInv_ERR:
Dim lngErr As Long, strError As String
    lngErr = Err
    strError = Error
    ErrorLog "MakeInvoice", lngErr, strError
    MsgBox "Unexpected Error: " & lngErr & ", " & strError & _
      " Has been logged.", _
      vbCritical, gstrAppTitle
    DoCmd.Hourglass False
    If (intTrans = True) Then Rollback
    varRtn = SysCmd(acSysCmdClearStatus)
    Resume MakeInv_Exit
End Function
```

After studying all the mechanics of a complete sales and inventory management application, you should now understand why neither the original Northwind sample database nor the Inventory Control template provided with Access come close to solving this complex business problem completely. Admittedly, this particular design maintains more calculated fields than is absolutely necessary. The only calculated fields that are really important are the Quantity and QuantityRemaining fields in the tblStock table. However, the additional calculated fields make it easy to create status and sales reports, as you'll learn in the next chapter.

Chapter 14

Designing Sales and Inventory Reports

In this chapter:

For a sales and inventory application, at a minimum you need a report to print customer invoices. You can probably think of dozens of other reports that would be useful, such as an order packing list for your warehouse personnel, a report to display current inventory levels, and various reports to analyze sales by category, customer type, or vendor. In this chapter, you'll explore how to build some of the more interesting reports you'll find in the Inventory Management sample application (Inventory.mdb).

Printing a Customer Order Packing List

In the previous chapter, you learned how the application builds and displays a customer invoice. You could certainly print an extra copy to send to your warehouse so that the employees packaging the order know what to send to the customer. However, the warehouse employees need to see the products listed in a sequence that will make pulling the products more efficient rather than by category or product description. The warehouse personnel also do not need to see the prices. So it makes sense to create a separate report—a packing list—for each order.

To see a packing list, open the Inventory Management database (Inventory.mdb), and after the splash form closes, open the frmOrders form. The original sample data includes one customer order that has a large number of different products. To find this order and open the Print Order dialog box, perform the following steps:

1. Click in the Order ID text box control.

2. Click the binoculars (Find) on the toolbar, and find order number 1469 for customer Princesa Isabel Vinhos.

3. Click the Options button on that order.

4. Click the Invoices button in the Order Options dialog box. (The Order Options dialog box disappears and displays the related invoice.)

5. Click the Print button in the Customer Invoices form.

6. Choose the **Print the Packing List** option.

Your screen should now look something like Figure 14-1.

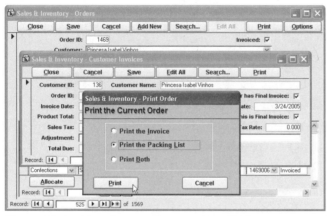

Figure 14-1 Choosing to print a packing list for a customer invoice.

Click the Print button to open the Order Packing List report as shown in Figure 14-2.

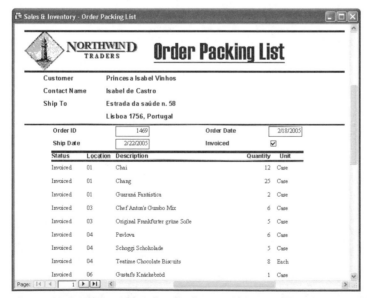

Figure 14-2 The packing list displays products in the sequence of locations in the warehouse.

If you scan down the report, you can see that the products are in order by packaged and dry goods, canned and bottled goods, and products that require refrigeration. When putting together an order, it makes sense to load the least perishable items first.

Designing the Report Record Source

As with any report, constructing the queries to fetch the data is more than half the battle. Remember that the same product can appear in a customer order more than once, but it makes more sense to list the item once in a packing list with a total quantity required. Doing that requires a totals query that fetches the relevant product information and sums the quantity. The qryRptOrderProductSumPack query listed below solves that part of the problem.

```
SELECT tblOrderProducts.OrderID, tblOrderProducts.ProductID, tblProducts.Description,
Sum(tblOrderProducts.Quantity) AS Quantity, tblProducts.SellBy, tblOrderProducts.InvoiceNo,
tblOrderProducts.Status
FROM tblProducts
INNER JOIN tblOrderProducts
ON tblProducts.ProductID = tblOrderProducts.ProductID
WHERE tblOrderProducts.Status > 0
GROUP BY tblOrderProducts.OrderID, tblOrderProducts.ProductID, tblProducts.Description,
tblProducts.SellBy, tblOrderProducts.InvoiceNo, tblOrderProducts.Price,
tblOrderProducts.Status;
```

To retrieve the remainder of the data required for the report, the application uses the tblCustomers and tblOrders tables and the qryRptOrderProductSumPack query to bring together all the fields needed for the report. The qryRptOrderDetails query performs this task, and the SQL for the query is as follows:

```
SELECT tblCustomers.CustomerName, tblCustomers.ContactName, tblOrders.ShipAddress,
tblOrders.ShipCity, tblOrders.ShipRegion, tblOrders.ShipPostalCode, tblOrders.ShipCountry,
tblCustomers.SalesRepID, tblOrders.OrderID, tblOrders.OrderDate, tblOrders.ShipDate,
tblOrders.FinalInvoice, qryRptOrderProductSumPack.Description,
qryRptOrderProductSumPack.Quantity, qryRptOrderProductSumPack.SellBy,
qryRptOrderProductSumPack.Status, qryRptOrderProductSumPack.InvoiceNo
FROM tblCustomers
INNER JOIN (tblOrders
INNER JOIN qryRptOrderProductSumPack
ON tblOrders.OrderID = qryRptOrderProductSumPack.OrderID)
ON tblCustomers.CustomerID = tblOrders.CustomerID;
```

Designing the Packing List

The design of the actual report is very straightforward, as shown in Figure 14-3 on the next page. The report groups by the OrderID field and sorts on the Status, Location, and Description fields. Sorting on the Status field displays all the products that are On Order, followed by those marked as Allocated and Invoiced. All the fields related to the customer order are in the OrderID Header section, and that section has the Force New Page property set to Before Section, the Keep Together property set to Yes, and the Repeat Section property set to Yes.

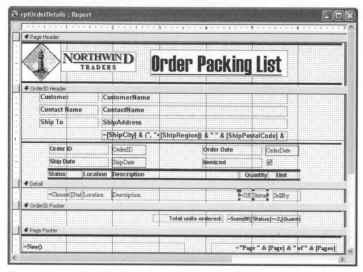

Figure 14-3   The design of the packing list report (rptOrderDetails).

The fields for each product appear in the Detail section. Because the Status field is a code, the text box control that displays that field uses an expression that calls the *Choose* function to convert the number (0, 1, 2, or 3) to text by adding 1 to the Status value to calculate an index into the list of string values. The expression is as follows:

```
=Choose([Status]+1,"None","On Order","Allocated","Invoiced")
```

Note that the qryRptOrderProductSumPack query shown earlier excludes all products that have a Status value of 0, but the expression includes that status so that the *Choose* function displays the correct value. If the status is On Order (1), the packing list should not display the quantity because the product has not yet been allocated from inventory. The txtQuantity text box also uses an expression to display the actual quantity or zero, as follows:

```
=IIf([Status]>=2,[Quantity],0)
```

The total in the OrderID Footer section uses the same expression in the *Sum* function so that the total includes only allocated and invoiced products.

When you print the packing list from an invoice, the application filters the rows by both the OrderID and InvoiceNo fields. All the products that have a value in the InvoiceNo field should be invoiced, so the previous two expressions might seem superfluous. However, you can also print the packing list directly from the order by clicking the Print button. In that case, the report displays all products in the current order, including ones that have not yet been invoiced, so displaying a quantity of 0 for products still on order makes sense.

You might be wondering why I didn't design the report with a subreport to display the products. Frankly, unless the report requires two or more subreports, I avoid using subreports altogether because it's difficult to produce the correct headings on a page when all the rows in the subreport won't fit on one page. To demonstrate this problem, I designed a sample report that uses a record source on customers and customer orders in the outer report. The report includes a subreport that uses the qryRptOrderProductSumPack query as its record source. You can examine this report by opening the rptXmplOrderDetails report in Design view, as shown in Figure 14-4.

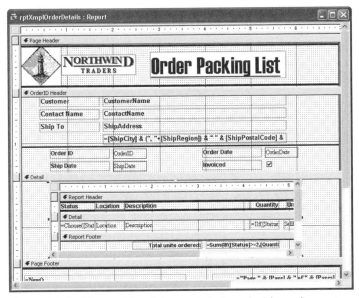

Figure 14-4   The packing list report designed with a subreport.

I expanded the size of the subreport control in Figure 14-4 so that you can see most of the design of the subreport. If you want to display headings in a report embedded within a subreport control, you must put those headings in the Report Header section. However, Access prints this section only once as it formats the contents in the subreport window. To see why this is a problem, open the rptXmplOrderDetails report in Print Preview and move to the second page. (The record source for the report is filtered to print one customer order that has more products than will fit on one page.) The result you see should look like Figure 14-5, on the next page.

As you can see, the Status, Location, Description, Quantity, and Unit headings are missing. One solution would be to forego the Report Header section in the subreport and place the headings at the bottom of the OrderID Header section in the outer report. One drawback is that it is more difficult to align the headings properly. Also, this technique won't work in a report where you are not repeating the OrderID Header on each new page.

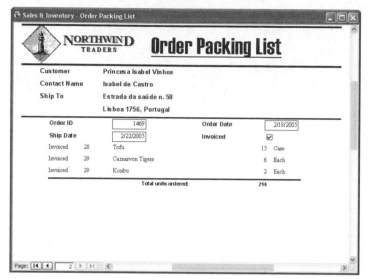

Figure 14-5   When using a subreport, the headers in the report don't repeat when the subreport overflows to a second page.

Designing a Customer Invoice

In Chapter 13, "Creating Customer Invoices," you saw the customer invoice produced by the invoicing process. Figure 14-6 shows you that invoice again.

Sales & Inventory - Customer Invoice

NORTHWIND TRADERS **Invoice**

OrderID	1567	Order Date	3/3/2005	Ship Date	3/7/2005

Customer   Around the Horn
Contact Name   Thomas Hardy
Bill To   120 Hanover Sq.
                London WA1 1DP, UK

Invoice No.	01	Invoice Date	3/7/2005	Due Date	3/17/2005	☐ Final Invoice

Status	Description	Quantity	Unit	Qty. Per Unit	Price	Charge
On Order	Tourtière	10	Case	16 pies	$37.45	$0.00
Shipped	Alice Mutton	22	Case	20 - 1 kg tins	$210.00	$4,620.00
Shipped	Boston Crab Meat	22	Case	24 - 4 oz tins	$18.40	$404.80
Shipped	Chartreuse verte	7	Each	750 cc per bottle	$18.00	$126.00
Shipped	Genen Shouyu	7	Case	24 - 250 ml bottles	$15.50	$108.50
Shipped	Gnocchi di nonna Alice	11	Case	24 - 250 g pkgs.	$38.00	$418.00
Shipped	Gravad lax	14	Case	12 - 500 g pkgs.	$26.00	$364.00
Shipped	Gula Malacca	13	Case	20 - 2 kg bags	$19.45	$252.85
Shipped	Jack's New England Clam Chowder	12	Case	12 - 12 oz cans	$9.65	$115.80
Shipped	Manjimup Dried Apples	6	Case	50 - 300 g pkgs.	$53.00	$318.00
Shipped	Outback Lager	4	Case	24 - 355 ml bottles	$15.00	$60.00
Shipped	Perth Pasties	12	Box	48 pieces	$32.80	$393.60

Figure 14-6   A partial invoice for an order that displays products still on order as well as products shipped with the invoice.

Let's take a look at how the report is designed.

Designing the Report Record Source

As with the packing list report, the customer product request rows need to be summarized so that a product appears only once. The qryRptOrderProductSum query to perform this task is very similar to the one used for the packing list report. The SQL for the query is as follows:

```
SELECT tblOrderProducts.OrderID, tblOrderProducts.ProductID, tblProducts.Description,
Sum(tblOrderProducts.Quantity) AS QtyOrdered, tblProducts.SellBy, tblProducts.QtyPerUnit,
tblOrderProducts.InvoiceNo, tblOrderProducts.Price, tblOrderProducts.Status,
Sum(CCur(CLng([Quantity]*[Price]*100)/100)) AS Charge
FROM tblProducts
INNER JOIN tblOrderProducts
ON tblProducts.ProductID = tblOrderProducts.ProductID
WHERE tblOrderProducts.Status In (1,3)
GROUP BY tblOrderProducts.OrderID, tblOrderProducts.ProductID, tblProducts.Description,
tblProducts.SellBy, tblProducts.QtyPerUnit, tblOrderProducts.InvoiceNo,
tblOrderProducts.Price, tblOrderProducts.Status;
```

Notice that this query includes only products that are on order (Status = 1) or invoiced (Status = 3). When the user has produced a partial invoice for a customer order, this query also returns rows for products that were ordered from a vendor but are not yet received.

The record source for the report is the qryRptOrderInvoice query. This query includes the necessary fields from the tblCustomers, tblOrders, and tblCustInvoices tables and the qryRptOrderProductSum query. The SQL for the query is as follows:

```
SELECT tblCustomers.CustomerName, tblCustomers.ContactName, tblCustomers.Address,
tblCustomers.City, tblCustomers.Region, tblCustomers.PostalCode, tblCustomers.Country,
tblCustomers.SalesRepID, tblOrders.OrderID, tblOrders.OrderDate, tblOrders.ShipDate,
tblCustInvoices.InvoiceNo, tblCustInvoices.CustomerID, tblCustInvoices.InvoiceDate,
tblCustInvoices.DueDate, tblCustInvoices.InvoiceSubTotal, tblCustInvoices.Tax,
tblCustInvoices.Adjustment, tblCustInvoices.AdjustmentReason, tblCustInvoices.InvoiceTotal,
tblCustInvoices.Final, qryRptOrderProductSum.Description, qryRptOrderProductSum.QtyOrdered,
qryRptOrderProductSum.SellBy, qryRptOrderProductSum.QtyPerUnit, qryRptOrderProductSum.Price,
qryRptOrderProductSum.Charge, qryRptOrderProductSum.Status
FROM (tblCustomers
INNER JOIN tblOrders
ON tblCustomers.CustomerID = tblOrders.CustomerID)
INNER JOIN (tblCustInvoices
INNER JOIN qryRptOrderProductSum
ON tblCustInvoices.OrderID = qryRptOrderProductSum.OrderID)
ON tblOrders.OrderID = tblCustInvoices.OrderID
WHERE ((qryRptOrderProductSum.InvoiceNo = [tblCustInvoices].[InvoiceNo])
Or (qryRptOrderProductSum.InvoiceNo Is Null));
```

Notice that the query joins the tblCustInvoices table with the qryRptOrderProductSum query only on the OrderID field. The WHERE clause further restricts the rows in qryRptOrderProductSum to those that match the invoice number or that have no invoice number. This allows the products that are on back order to appear as informational lines on the customer invoice.

Designing the Customer Invoice

As you can see in Figure 14-7, the design of the invoice is very similar to the packing list. The major difference is this report includes a group on the concatenation of the OrderID and the InvoiceNo fields and displays the extended price (Charge) and the invoice totals. Also, the report displays all the quantities but displays the charge for a product only if the product has been invoiced. The control source for the Charge text box control is as follows:

```
=IIf([Status]=3,[Charge],0)
```

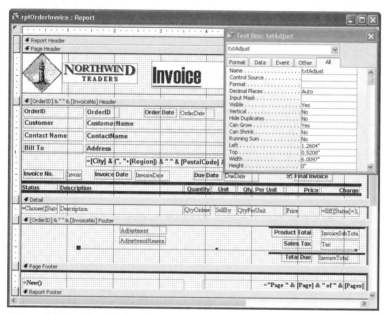

Figure 14-7   The design of the customer invoice report (rptOrderInvoice).

After creating an invoice for a customer order, the user can edit the invoice and enter an adjustment and adjustment reason. You can see two controls in the group footer for these two fields, but the Visible property for both is set to No. The fields must be on the report to ensure that the report engine includes the fields in the dynamic query it builds for the report. Code in the Format event of the group footer references these fields and sets the value of the txtAdjust text box control when appropriate. Note that the height of the text box control is 0″, and the Can Grow property is set to Yes. When the value of the control is Null, the height won't change, and nothing appears on the report. When the code sets the value of the control to something other than Null, the report engine expands the text box height to display the data.

You can find the code for the Format event of the group footer in the report's module. When the Adjustment field is not Null or zero, the code calculates the length of the formatted currency amount and assigns the reason and amount to the txtAdjust text box control, adding spaces so that the text always appears aligned correctly. If the Adjustment field is Null or zero, the code assigns Null to the text box so that it won't expand or display anything. The code is as follows:

```
Private Sub GroupFooter2_Format(Cancel As Integer, FormatCount As Integer)
Dim intLen As Integer
  ' Display adjustment if not zero
  If Not IsNothing(Me.Adjustment) Then
    intLen = Len(Format(Me.Adjustment, "Currency")) - 5
    Me.txtAdjust = "Adjustment Reason: " & Me.AdjustmentReason & _
      Space(10) & "Adjustment:" & Space(18 - intLen) & _
      Format(Me.Adjustment, "Currency")
  Else
    Me.txtAdjust = Null
  End If
End Sub
```

As with the packing list report, the invoice report does not use a subreport to display the product request details. This makes it easier to line up the column headings, and you don't have to worry about an order that won't fit on one page.

Displaying Current Inventory Levels

Although you can certainly look up the quantities in inventory at any time by using the form provided to edit inventory, it will be useful from time to time to produce a printed report that lists the current inventory for all or selected products. For example, all companies that stock inventory must annually take a physical inventory for tax purposes, so a printed inventory report will be needed to be able to compare the physical inventory with the quantities stored in the application.

The Inventory Management sample application contains a basic report that lists both the master inventory record for each product as well as each of the stocking detail records. To see this report, open the Inventory Management database (Inventory.mdb), and after the splash form closes, open the fdlgProductPrintOptions2 form, as shown in Figure 14-8 on the next page.

As you can see, this form that opens as a dialog box provides several options to allow the user to filter the report by product, price, category, vendor, or quantity on hand. Leave the criteria blank, select the Inventory Report option, and click the Print button. Because you did not specify any search criteria, the application prompts you to verify that you want to open the report to display all products. Click Yes, and the Inventory report opens, as shown in Figure 14-9 on the next page.

In the sample data, none of the products were purchased at more than one cost, so you should see only one stock detail row per product. If this were an active application used by a company over several months or years, you could expect to see the pricing history of each product in the stock detail rows.

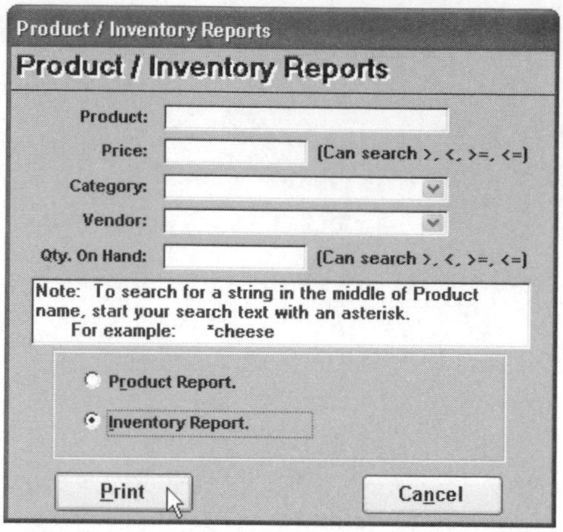

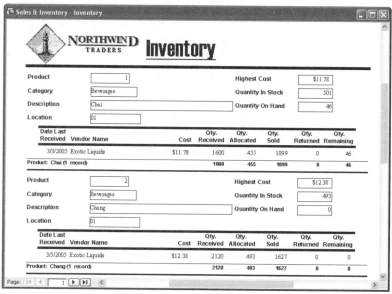

Figure 14-8   Specifying criteria for the Inventory report.

Figure 14-9   The Inventory report displays the current stock levels for all or selected products.

Selecting the Inventory and Stocking Data

You might be tempted to display the stock detail records from the tblStock table in a sub-report, but you can gather all the data needed for the report with a single query. The report needs fields from the tblProducts, tblInventory, tblStock, and tblVendors tables. The SQL for the query that is the record source of the report (qryRptInventory) is as follows:

```
SELECT tblProducts.Category, tblProducts.ProductID, tblProducts.Description,
tblInventory.Location, tblInventory.HighCost, tblInventory.QuantityInStock,
tblInventory.QuantityOnHand, tblVendors.VendorName, tblStock.Cost, tblStock.DateReceived,
tblStock.Quantity, tblStock.QuantityAllocated, tblStock.QuantitySold,
tblStock.QuantityReturned, tblStock.QuantityRemaining
FROM tblProducts
INNER JOIN (tblInventory
INNER JOIN (tblStock
INNER JOIN tblVendors
ON tblStock.VendorID = tblVendors.VendorID)
ON tblInventory.ProductID = tblStock.ProductID)
ON tblProducts.ProductID = tblInventory.ProductID;
```

Notice that you do not need the tblCategories table. The tblProducts table contains the category name instead of a reference ID, so you don't need to include an extra join to the tblCategories table in order to fetch the actual name. See the topic "Avoid Artificial Primary Keys in Tables" on page 26 for more details.

Designing the Inventory Report

You could print the data for the inventory report by vendor, by category, by warehouse location, or simply by product name. For the sample report, I chose to organize the data by category and then sort on the product name (the Description field). You can see design for the rptInventory report in Figure 14-10.

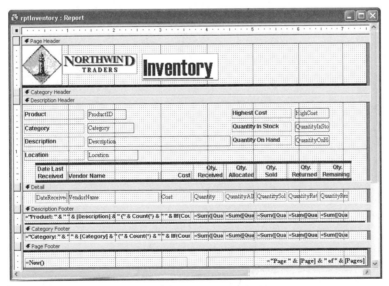

Figure 14-10 The design of the Inventory report.

The Force New Page property of the Category header is set to Before Section so that each category begins on a new page. The detail information from the tblInventory table displays in the Description header, and the Keep Together property of the Description group in the Sorting and Grouping Properties window is set to Whole Group so that all the detail stock rows print with the information from the tblInventory table.

Analyzing Sales by Category and Product

At various times, the management of the company is going to want to know how various products are selling. You can certainly create PivotCharts (Access 2002 and later) and graphs to give high-level managers a pictorial view of sales progress over time. But product line managers are probably more interested in the raw sales numbers to help identify the best and worst selling items in each category.

The Inventory Management database contains a simple example of a report to print total quantity, sales, and profit by category and product for a specific time period. To run this report, open the Inventory Management database (Inventory.mdb), and after the splash form closes, open the fdlgSalesPrintOptions form, as shown in Figure 14-11.

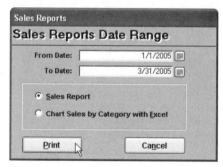

Figure 14-11   The Sales Reports Date Range dialog box lets you specify the dates and the type of report you want to produce.

When the form opens, it sets the From Date to the first date of the current quarter and the To Date to the last date of the current quarter. However, the sample database contains data from September 1, 2004, through March 3, 2005, so you should pick a range of dates that will return some results. Select the Sales Report option (the default) and click the Print button to see the report as shown in Figure 14-12.

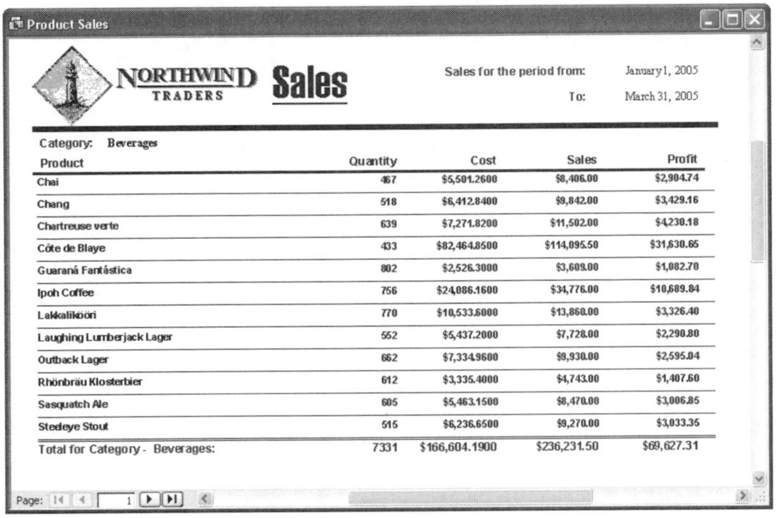

Product Sales

NORTHWIND TRADERS **Sales**

Sales for the period from: January 1, 2005
To: March 31, 2005

Category: Beverages

Product	Quantity	Cost	Sales	Profit
Chai	467	$5,501.2600	$8,406.00	$2,904.74
Chang	518	$6,412.8400	$9,842.00	$3,429.16
Chartreuse verte	639	$7,271.8200	$11,502.00	$4,230.18
Côte de Blaye	433	$82,464.8500	$114,095.50	$31,630.65
Guaraná Fantástica	802	$2,526.3000	$3,609.00	$1,082.70
Ipoh Coffee	756	$24,086.1600	$34,776.00	$10,689.84
Lakkalikööri	770	$10,533.6000	$13,860.00	$3,326.40
Laughing Lumberjack Lager	552	$5,437.2000	$7,728.00	$2,290.80
Outback Lager	662	$7,334.9600	$9,930.00	$2,595.04
Rhönbräu Klosterbier	612	$3,335.4000	$4,743.00	$1,407.60
Sasquatch Ale	605	$5,463.1500	$8,470.00	$3,006.85
Steeleye Stout	515	$6,236.6500	$9,270.00	$3,033.35
Total for Category - Beverages:	7331	$166,604.1900	$236,231.50	$69,627.31

Page: 1

Figure 14-12 The sales data for the Beverages category for the first quarter of 2005.

Fetching the Sales Data by Date Range

The query you need to produce sales data by category and product is relatively straightforward. Again, because the tblProducts table contains the actual category name, you don't need to include the tblCategories table. However, you do need information from the tblProducts, tblOrders, and tblOrderProducts tables. You can have the query calculate the extended cost (Quantity × Cost), extended price (Quantity × Price), and the profit amount (extended price minus extended cost) using expressions.

The only difficult part of the query is the WHERE clause that includes only products that have been allocated (Status = 2) or invoiced (Status = 3) and filters the rows based on the dates you enter in the fdlgSalesPrintOptions form. Because you can clear the From Date or To Date or both, the WHERE clause must contain predicates that cover the case when you enter both dates, only one of the dates, or neither date. The SQL for the query (qryRptSales) is as follows:

```
PARAMETERS [Forms]![fdlgSalesPrintOptions]![txtFromDate] DateTime,
[Forms]![fdlgSalesPrintOptions]![txtToDate] DateTime;
SELECT tblProducts.Category, tblProducts.ProductID, tblProducts.Description,
tblOrders.OrderDate, tblOrderProducts.Quantity,
tblOrderProducts.Cost, [Quantity]*[Cost] AS CostAmount,
tblOrderProducts.Price, [Quantity]*[Price] AS SaleAmount,
([Quantity]*[Price])-([Quantity]*[Cost]) AS Profit,
[Forms]![fdlgSalesPrintOptions]![txtFromDate] AS StartDate,
[Forms]![fdlgSalesPrintOptions]![txtToDate] AS EndDate, tblOrderProducts.Status
FROM tblProducts
INNER JOIN (tblOrders
INNER JOIN tblOrderProducts
ON tblOrders.OrderID = tblOrderProducts.OrderID)
ON tblProducts.ProductID = tblOrderProducts.ProductID
WHERE ((tblOrders.OrderDate>=[Forms]![fdlgSalesPrintOptions]![txtFromDate] AND
```

```
tblOrders.OrderDate<=[Forms]![fdlgSalesPrintOptions]![txtToDate])
AND (tblOrderProducts.Status>=2))
OR (((tblOrders.OrderDate)>=[Forms]![fdlgSalesPrintOptions]![txtFromDate]) AND
((([Forms]![fdlgSalesPrintOptions]![txtToDate]) Is Null) AND ((tblOrderProducts.Status)>=2))
OR (((tblOrders.OrderDate)<=[Forms]![fdlgSalesPrintOptions]![txtToDate]) AND
((([Forms]![fdlgSalesPrintOptions]![txtFromDate]) Is Null) AND ((tblOrderProducts.Status)>=2))
OR ((([Forms]![fdlgSalesPrintOptions]![txtFromDate]) Is Null) AND
((([Forms]![fdlgSalesPrintOptions]![txtToDate]) Is Null) AND ((tblOrderProducts.Status)>=2));
```

I decided to use the date the order was originally placed (the OrderDate field in the tblOrders table) as the date of the product sale. If an order might not be filled for several days or weeks, the ShipDate field in the tblOrders table (the date the invoice was created) or the DateAlloc field in the tblOrderProducts table (the date the product was allocated from inventory) might provide a more accurate portrayal of the actual sales date for each product. Here is another case where the business rules of the company will ultimately dictate the query design.

Designing the Sales Report

The sample sales report is very simple, but with a twist. Although the qryRptSales query returns one row per product sold, the report displays only the totals for each product. If you open the rptSales report in Design view, as shown in Figure 14-13, you can see that the Detail section has no height and no controls in it. All the information for the report is produced by using text box controls that use the *Sum* function to add the totals by product and category. As you might expect, the Force New Page property of the Category Header section is set to Before Section so that each category starts on a new page.

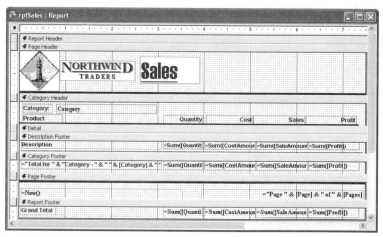

Figure 14-13 The design of the rptSales report.

Once you understand the basic principles, designing additional sales reports to summarize the data in different ways is easy. You can create reports to summarize the data by product, vendor, or customer in just a few minutes.

Creating a Sales Chart Using Microsoft Excel

One of the really powerful features in all the Microsoft Office products is the ability to dynamically start one product from another, exchange data, and execute commands. In Chapter 8, "Sending Out Notices," you learned how to start a session with Microsoft Outlook from Access to construct and send e-mails. The Inventory Management application contains an example that starts a session with Microsoft Excel and commands Excel to chart data loaded from the database. You can imagine how you can extend this example to create a sales report and chart in Excel and then send it via e-mail to the appropriate sales managers.

To see how this works, open the Inventory Management database (Inventory.mdb), and after the splash form closes, open the fdlgSalesPrintOptions form, as shown earlier in Figure 14-11 on page 308. Choose a date range between September 1, 2004, and March 3, 2005, select the **Chart Sales by Category with Excel** option, and click the Print button. The Inventory Management application sends commands to Excel to create a new workbook, load the appropriate data into one worksheet, chart the data, and display the result, as shown in Figure 14-14.

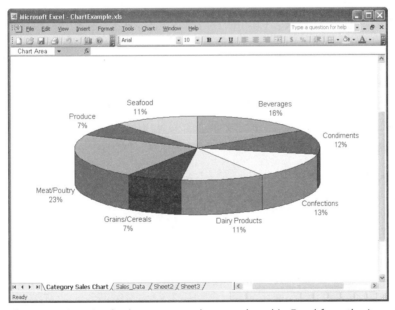

Figure 14-14   A sales by category chart produced in Excel from the Inventory Management application.

Code that responds to the cmdPrint command button Click event on the fdlgSalesPrint-Options form calls the *MakeXLChart* function that you can find in the modExcel module and passes it the two dates that you specified. The code in that function first builds an SQL statement to retrieve the data in the date range you specified. As it builds the SQL, the code validates the two dates passed to it and fails with an error message if either value is not a valid date. After completing the SQL statement, the code opens a recordset and checks to see that some rows were returned. When the recordset is empty, the code exits. The code is as follows:

```
Option Compare Database
Option Explicit
' Excel constant values for late binding
Const Excel3DPie As Integer = -4102
Const ExcelColumns As Integer = 2
Const ExcelLocationAsNewSheet As Integer = 1
Const ExcelThin As Integer = 2
Const ExcelNone As Integer = -4142
Const ExcelSolid As Integer = 1


Public Function MakeXLChart(Optional varStartDate As Variant, _
  Optional varEndDate As Variant) As Integer
' Creates a pie chart by product category in Microsoft Excel
' Inputs: Optional start and end dates
'         Data in filtered query qrySalesByCategory
' Output: File ChartExample.xls loaded with data and a pie chart
'
' Function displays the result in Excel if successful
'   and returns True to caller
' Function returns False on any error or no input records.
Dim objXL As Object, objXLSheet As Object
Dim objXLBook As Object
Dim db As DAO.Database, rst As DAO.Recordset
Dim intRow As Integer, strSQL As String, intExcelRunning As Integer
  ' Set an error trap
  On Error GoTo MakeXLChart_ERR
  ' Set up the query string with start of predicate
  strSQL = "SELECT Category, Sum(Sales) As TotSales " & _
    "FROM qrySalesByCategory " & _
    "WHERE Category > '' "
  ' Add date criteria if dates supplied
  ' Do start date first
  If Not IsMissing(varStartDate) Then
    ' Make sure it's a date value
    If IsDate(varStartDate) Then
      ' Add the predicate
      strSQL = strSQL & " And (OrderDate >= #" & _
        Format(varStartDate, "dd mmm yyyy") & "#) "
    Else
      MsgBox "Invalid start date supplied to MakeXLChart.", _
        vbCritical, gstrAppTitle
      MakeXLChart = False
      Exit Function
    End If
  End If
  ' Do end date
  If Not IsMissing(varEndDate) Then
    ' Make sure it's a date value
    If IsDate(varEndDate) Then
      ' Add the predicate
      strSQL = strSQL & " And (OrderDate <= #" & _
        Format(varEndDate, "dd mmm yyyy") & "#) "
```

```
      Else
        MsgBox "Invalid end date supplied to MakeXLChart.", _
          vbCritical, gstrAppTitle
        MakeXLChart = False
        Exit Function
      End If
    End If
    ' Finish the SQL
    strSQL = strSQL & "Group By Category;"
    ' Point to this database
    Set db = DBEngine(0)(0)
    ' Open a recordset on sales
    Set rst = db.OpenRecordset(strSQL)
    ' Make sure we got some
    If rst.RecordCount = 0 Then
      ' Nope - set false return
      MakeXLChart = False
      ' Close out
      rst.Close
      Set rst = Nothing
      Set db = Nothing
      ' .. and bail
      Exit Function
    End If
```

Next, the code checks to see if the sample Excel file already exists using the *Dir* function. If the file exists, the code deletes it. The code starts an automation session with Excel, setting the objXL object variable to point to the Application object. In Excel, the Application object works similarly to the Application object in Access—it is the root object from which you can execute all the commands specific to Excel.

The code uses the Add method of the Excel Workbooks collection to create a new Workbook object and obtain a pointer to the workbook to the objXLBook object variable. The code next uses the SaveAs method of the Workbook object to tell the Workbook object to save itself using the sample file name. The code acquires a pointer to the active worksheet in the new workbook, names the worksheet, and puts column headings in the first two cells. The code uses the CopyFromRecordset method of a range defined on the worksheet to copy the data from the open recordset and place the data starting in the first cell in the second row (cell A2). Finally, the code gets the count of records sent to Excel and uses the NumberFormat method of the range defining the sales column in the worksheet to set the format of the second column to "$#,##0.00"—similar to the Currency format in Access. The code is as follows:

```
  ' If the file we want to build already exists
  If "" <> Dir(CurrentProject.Path & "\ChartExample.xls") Then
    ' Delete it
    Kill CurrentProject.Path & "\ChartExample.xls"
  End If
  ' Start Excel - using late binding to avoid library problems
  Set objXL = CreateObject("Excel.Application")
  ' Set flag to indicate Excel started OK
  intExcelRunning = True
  ' Create a new workbook
```

```
Set objXLBook = objXL.Workbooks.Add
' Save it
objXLBook.SaveAs CurrentProject.Path & "\ChartExample.xls"
' Point to worksheet
Set objXLSheet = objXLBook.ActiveSheet
' Name it
objXLSheet.Name = "Sales_Data"
' Insert column headings
objXLSheet.Cells(1, 1) = "Category"
objXLSheet.Cells(1, 2) = "Sales"
' Ask Excel to copy the data from the recordset
objXLSheet.Range("A2").CopyFromRecordset rst
' Calculate the end row
intRow = rst.RecordCount + 1
' Set a currency number format for sales
objXLSheet.Range("B2:B" & intRow).NumberFormat = "$#,##0.00"
' Close out the recordset
rst.Close
Set rst = Nothing
```

Now the fun begins. The code uses the Add method of the Charts collection of the Workbook object to start a new chart. The code sets the chart type to 3D Pie, tells the chart that the data is in the Sales_Data worksheet (using the SetSourceData method), and places the chart in a new worksheet named "Category Sales Chart." Next, the code points to the active chart, turns on the title and sets the text, places a thin and transparent border around the chart, and sets the interior and pattern colors. The code adds data labels with category names and percentages. Finally, the code saves the workbook and sets the Visible property of the Excel application object to True to make Excel visible so you can see the result. The code is as follows:

```
' Start a new Chart
objXLBook.Charts.Add
' Set type to 3D Pie chart
objXLBook.ActiveChart.ChartType = Excel3DPie
' Point to the data we just loaded as the source
objXLBook.ActiveChart.SetSourceData _
   Source:=objXLBook.Sheets("Sales_Data").Range( _
   "A1:B" & intRow), PlotBy:=ExcelColumns
' Put the chart in a new worksheet and name it
objXLBook.ActiveChart.Location Where:=ExcelLocationAsNewSheet, _
   Name:= "Category Sales Chart"
' Now fixup the chart
With objXLBook.ActiveChart
   ' Turn on the title
   .HasTitle = True
   ' Set the title and font
   .ChartTitle.Characters.Text = "Sales By Category"
   .ChartTitle.Font.Bold = True
   .ChartTitle.Font.Size = 14
   ' Set a thin border around the entire chart
   .PlotArea.Border.Weight = ExcelThin
   ' .. and the line style to transparent
   .PlotArea.Border.LineStyle = ExcelNone
   ' Set interior color to white
   .PlotArea.Interior.ColorIndex = 2
```

```
       ' .. and pattern to black
       .PlotArea.Interior.PatternColorIndex = 1
       ' Plot solid colors
       .PlotArea.Interior.Pattern = ExcelSolid
       ' Set up labels
       .ApplyDataLabels AutoText:=True, LegendKey:=False, _
         HasLeaderLines:=False, ShowSeriesName:=False, _
         ShowCategoryName:=True, _
         ShowValue:=False, ShowPercentage:=True, ShowBubbleSize:=True
   End With
   ' Save what we've changed
   objXLBook.Save
   ' Clear the worksheet and workbook objects
   Set objXLSheet = Nothing
   Set objXLBook = Nothing
   ' Make Excel visible on the screen
   objXL.Visible = True
   ' Clear the object
   Set objXL = Nothing
   ' Set good return
   MakeXLChart = True
MakeXLChart_EXIT:
   ' Done
   Exit Function
MakeXLChart_ERR:
   ' Display and log any errors
   MsgBox "Unexpected Error: " & Err & ", " & Error, _
     vbCritical, gstrAppTitle
   ErrorLog "MakeXLChart", Err, Error
   MakeXLChart = False
   ' Try to close Excel if it's running
   If intExcelRunning = True Then
     ' Reset flag so we don't come back here
     intExcelRunning = False
     ' Make Excel visible
     objXL.Visible = True
     ' .. and try to make it close
     objXL.Quit
   End If
   Resume MakeXLChart_EXIT
End Function
```

Although some of the reports you need for an application are obvious (such as the customer invoice report), most of the reports you create will be the result of a user request. I hope this chapter has given you a few ideas about the types of reports you might create for a sales and inventory management application.

This concludes the review of features specific to the Inventory Management application. As you explore the forms and reports in the application, you're likely to discover additional interesting features that you can use in any application. You can find some of these features described in Appendix E, "Implementing Generic Features." The next part of this book discusses the Customer Service application that is designed to support 50 or more concurrent users.

Part IV
Implementing a Customer Support Application

Chapter 15

The Customer Support Application

One large category of applications most often implemented using Microsoft Access is contact management. A basic contact management application is relatively simple—information about the people you contact or who contact you, details about each contact, and follow-up reminders. To make the concept of contact management more interesting, I decided to create a sample application that manages contacts for a specific purpose: tracking customer support calls for a fictitious household appliance manufacturer.

When you think of a contact management application, you probably have the idea that such an application is useful only for people who must track frequent contacts with other people. But if you consider the problem thoroughly, a contact management application can cover a broad range of job functions. Here are just a few of the applications:

- A sales representative tracking contacts with customers

- An executive assistant logging contacts for his or her boss

- A political organization tracking voter contacts

- A nonprofit organization handling requests for information

- The secretary of a parent-teacher association tracking contacts with parents

- A recruiting officer logging contacts with prospective recruits

- A marketing organization tracking the results of a promotional campaign

- A seller at an auction Web site logging bids from potential customers

- A stockbroker tracking calls to or meetings with clients

- A customer support organization tracking support calls and results

Basically, any time you need to keep a record of contacts between a person or an organization and many other people or organizations, you need a contact management application.

Understanding the Customer Support Application

The sample Customer Support application (Support.mdb and SupportData.mdb) is designed to track contacts from customers needing to register home appliances they have purchased, request information about products the company sells, or resolve problems they're having with a product. It also tracks follow-up contacts made by a support representative to customers. In any contact management application, you need to keep track of the person or organization with whom you made the contact, the type of contact, the resolution of the contact, and any follow-up contacts required in the future. The Customer Support application includes all these features and more. Although it is specifically designed to manage support contacts, you can use many of the features in any contact management application.

> **Note**   The Customer Support sample application also assumes that many more than 50 users might need to be running the application simultaneously. To provide adequate performance when sharing a data file in the Access desktop database format (.mdb file), the application uses no forms or reports that are bound to data on the server. To understand the architectural design of this application, you should read the section "Pushing the Envelope" on page 85.

Identifying Tasks and Data

Just like creating any other database application, you should start by making lists of the tasks that the application must support and the data needed by those tasks. You should interview the potential users and determine how they're performing the tasks without a database or find out what it is they expect the database to do for them. You'd be surprised how many different ways there are to look at contact management and, specifically, customer support.

Here are the tasks implemented in the Customer Support application:

- Define product categories.
- Enter product information, including product name, category, and description.
- Specify the types of warranties offered.
- Identify the warranties offered for each product.
- Enter customer information, including the preferred home or business contact data.
- Register the products owned by each customer, including the purchase date, serial number, and warranty applicable to the product.
- Enter employee information, including login ID, password, and level of permission in the application.

- Create customer support cases, track the status of each case, and assign a category to each case.

- Log contact events for each support case, including who answered the call and the action taken.

- Create future reminders for a support case, including a deadline date and a range of best times to call.

- Display a list of outstanding and overdue reminders.

- Print case totals or case details for a specified date range, filtering by case status, employee, or customer.

- List customer registration details for a specified date range.

- Export selected data to Microsoft Excel for analysis in PivotTables and PivotCharts.

In addition, a supervisor or manager can perform these tasks:

- Define employee permission levels.

- Define new employee profiles and edit existing ones.

- Create new product categories.

- Add and change products.

- Define warranties and assign warranties to products.

- Create and edit issue categories for cases.

- Define resolution actions for case events.

From the preceding list, you can begin to identify the subjects and actions that should be represented by tables in the application. These include the following:

- Product Categories

- Products

- Warranties

- Product Warranties

- Customers

- Customer Product Registrations

- Employees

- Permissions

- Support Cases

- Case Categories

- Support Case Events

- Case Event Actions
- Reminders

When you see a subject name that lists the simple name of two other subjects, such as Product Warranties or Customer Product Registrations, that subject is probably going to be the many-to-many link between the two other subjects. So, Product Warranties is the many-to-many link between Products and Warranties, and Customer Product Registrations is the many-to-many link between Customers and Product Warranties.

You might wonder why Customer Product Registrations isn't a many-to-many link between Customers and Products. But notice the requirement to "Register the products owned by each customer, including the purchase date, serial number, and warranty applicable to the product." So, a customer doesn't simply own a product—a customer owns a product and an associated warranty. There is no provision in this sample to track charges for service calls out of warranty. However, knowing the applicable warranty will be important if this application is ever extended to bill for parts shipped or service calls scheduled out of warranty. You can see that understanding both the tasks required and the data for those tasks is critical to designing the application correctly. You cannot do one without the other.

Understanding Business Rules

As you identify the tasks required to be supported by your application, you'll also learn something about the business rules that restrict those tasks. From the discussion in "Identifying Tasks and Data," you can already surmise one business rule: A Product Registration record must contain information about the owning customer, the product, and the relevant warranty.

A contact management application isn't particularly complex—certainly not as complex as the Inventory Management application discussed in the previous part of this book. But just like any other application, if you don't understand the business rules the application must support, your application won't work correctly. In addition to the tasks the application must support and the data subjects in the database, you need to find out how these tasks and data interact. One of the best ways to find out the applicable business rules is to ask as many questions as come to mind—and the answers to some questions will inevitably lead you to other questions. Some of the questions that I considered as I designed the Customer Support application (and the answer I chose for each) are as follows:

- Can a customer own more than one product? Yes.
- Can a product have more than one available warranty? Yes, all products have a standard warranty, but extended warranties are also available for some products.
- Can a customer have more than one warranty for a product? No.
- Can a customer register a product during a support call? Yes.

- Must a customer own a product to receive support? No. A support case can be opened to provide product or warranty information.

- When calling for support for a registered product, must the customer be the owner of the product? No. For example, one spouse might be the registered owner of the product, but the other spouse calls in.

- What information must the customer provide to open a support case? The customer must provide first and last name, a phone number, and a home mailing address.

- Must all support calls be logged? Yes. Even when a customer disconnects before providing all information, the customer support representative must log a dropped call.

- Must a case have a reference to a registered product? No, but a case must have a related customer record.

- Must a case have a case category? Yes, all cases must be categorized by type of support problem.

- Can any employee define a new issue category? No, only supervisors and application administrators can add issue categories.

- Can an employee take a call about an existing case started by another employee? Yes.

- Can an employee modify or delete a case event entered by another employee? No.

- Can a case be saved with no events? No.

- Can an employee delete a case event? Yes, if the employee created the event.

- Can an employee delete the last event for a case? No.

- Must a case event have a defined action? Yes.

- Can any employee define a new event action? No, only supervisors and application administrators can add event actions.

- Can a reminder be added for any case? Yes.

- Can a case have multiple reminders? Yes, a case can acquire a reminder history.

- Can an employee enter a reminder in the past? No.

- Can an employee delete a reminder? Yes, if the reminder is still in the future.

- Can an employee change a reminder entered by another employee? Yes.

- Can an employee change the date and time of a saved reminder? Only if the original date and time are in the future.

Keep in mind that no question is too trivial, and sometimes you have to think "outside the box" to conjure up questions that your user or client needs to answer. Think like a good investigative reporter and find out not only what the user needs to do, but also when they need to do the task, where they need to be when they do the task, how they need to perform the task, and, most importantly, *why* they need to do it.

Designing the Tables

If you have identified all the tasks, the data required for all the tasks, and all the business rules, designing the tables you need to store and manage the data should be straightforward. You should never sit down and start creating tables without all the necessary background information. If some of the data exists in other files (such as a spreadsheet), create your properly normalized tables first, and then figure out what you need to do to import the existing data into your correct table structure.

The only tricky issues in designing any contact management application are deciding how to categorize the contact events, whether to treat each event as a single item or to group related events, and how to track reminders or follow-ups. In the Customer Support application, an initial contact opens a support case. Each discrete contact event is part of a case that describes a particular customer problem. A case has an overall issue category, and a support representative opens a new case when the same customer calls with a different issue about a different product. A case has one or more case events (contact events), individual case events must include the action taken, and reminders are tied to cases, not case events.

From the list of subjects determined earlier, you can see that the Customer Support application needs the following tables:

- tlkpProductCategoriesServer
- tlkpProductsServer
- tlkpWarrantiesServer
- tlkpProductsWarrantiesServer
- tblCustomers
- tblRegistrations
- tlkpEmployeesServer
- tlkpPermissionLevelsServer
- tblCases
- tlkpCaseCategoriesServer
- tblCasesEvents
- tlkpActionsServer
- tblReminders

Note   Remember, in Chapter 3 you learned that the architecture of the Customer Support application is designed to support 50 or more users. The application maintains local copies of all tables that are not likely to change frequently—the tables with a "tlkp" prefix. For tables that change often (table names beginning with "tbl"), the application fetches only the data needed for a specific task and stores that data in a local copy (table name beginning with "tvw").

Now, you're ready to begin defining the tables you need and the relationships between them. As you create the tables, you should also define as many of the business rules as possible using the validation rule features of Access. Figure 15-1 shows you the final design for the tables for the customer, product, and warranty tracking part of the Customer Support application.

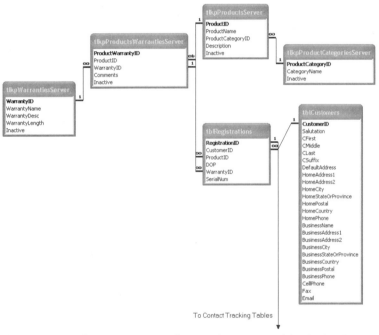

Figure 15-1   The customer, product, and warranty tables in the Customer Support application.

Figure 15-2, on the next page, shows you the tables for the case tracking portion of the Customer Support application. You can see that tblRegistrations is the key link between the two major sets of functions. You can find a detailed listing of the fields and indexes for all the tables in Appendix B, "Sample Database Schemas."

As you can see, the table and relationship design is significantly more complex than the design for the Membership Tracking application that you studied in Part 2 of this book, but far less complex than the Inventory Management application in Part 3. In the remainder of this part of the book, you can explore specific tasks implemented in the Customer Support sample database (Support.mdb). Each chapter describes the tables needed for a particular set of tasks and the code that performs those tasks.

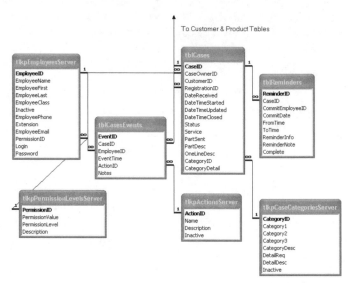

Figure 15-2 The support case tables in the Customer Support application.

Chapter 16

Organizing Customer Information

As noted in the previous chapter, the sample Customer Support application (Support.mdb and SupportData.mdb) is an example of an application in the generic class of contact management applications. In any contact management application, you need to store information about the people or organizations whom you contact.

In the Customer Support application, people call the support center asking for information about or help with household appliances. So naturally, the application needs a "customers" table to identify the people. Because many support calls involve a specific appliance owned by the customer, and a customer might own more than one appliance, the application also needs a "registered appliances" table to identify the specific appliance for each support case. This chapter explains the design of those tables and explores how the application works with the data in those tables.

 Note The Customer Support sample application assumes that more than 50 users might need to be running the application simultaneously. To provide adequate performance when sharing a data file in the Access desktop database format (.mdb file), the application uses no forms or reports that are bound to data on the server. To understand the architectural design of this application, you should read the section "Pushing the Envelope" on page 85.

Understanding the Tables Involved

The table that stores customer information contains the typical information about a person and how to contact the person, including both home and business addresses, phone numbers, and e-mail address, as shown in Table 16-1. Because the theme of this application is support calls for appliances, you might wonder why the table includes business information. But remember that any good table design must handle all the possibilities. Companies do purchase appliances such as microwave ovens and small refrigerators. Individual employees might purchase small appliances that they keep in their offices and also own appliances at home, so the application must be able to handle two sets of addresses for a particular customer.

Table 16-1   The Fields in the tblCustomers Table

Field Name	Data Type	Required	Description
CustomerID	AutoNumber	N/A	Unique customer identifier.
Salutation	Text, Field Size 10	No	Mr., Mrs., Ms., Dr., etc.
CFirst	Text, Field Size 20	Yes	Customer first name.
CMiddle	Text, Field Size 20	Yes	Customer middle name or initial.
CLast	Text, Field Size 30	Yes	Customer last name.
CSuffix	Text, Field Size 10	No	Jr., Sr., III, etc.
DefaultAddress	Integer	Yes	Default address indicator: Home = 1, Business = 2.
HomeAddress1	Text, Field Size 50	No*	Home address line 1.
HomeAddress2	Text, Field Size 50	No	Home address line 2.
HomeCity	Text, Field Size 50	No*	Home city.
HomeStateOrProvince	Text, Field Size 20	No*	Home state or province.
HomePostal	Text, Field Size 15	No*	Home postal (ZIP) code.
HomeCountry	Text, Field Size 50	No	Home country.
HomePhone	Text, Field Size 20	No*	Home phone number.
BusinessName	Text, Field Size 50	No	Business name.
BusinessAddress1	Text, FieldSize 50	No*	Business address line 1.
BusinessAddress2	Text, FieldSize 50	No	Business address line 2.
BusinessCity	Text, FieldSize 50	No*	Business city.
BusinessStateOrProvince	Text, Field Size 20	No*	Business state or province.
BusinessPostal	Text, Field Size 15	No*	Business postal (ZIP) code.
BusinessCountry	Text, Field Size 50	No	Business country.
BusinessPhone	Text, Field Size 20	No*	Business phone number.
CellPhone	Text, Field Size 20	No	Mobile phone number.
Fax	Text, Field Size 20	No	Fax phone number.
Email	Text, Field Size 255	No	E-mail address.

* Validation code in the frmCustomers form checks the setting specified for the DefaultAddress field and requires either the Home or Business fields to be entered accordingly.

Note that in this table the Email field is plain text, not the Hyperlink data type. In a standard application that uses bound forms, the Hyperlink data type can be useful to allow the user to click the bound control to activate the hyperlink (in this case, send an e-mail to the customer). However, this application exclusively uses unbound controls.

Although you can set the Is Hyperlink property of an unbound text box control to Yes, setting that property merely changes the font color to blue and underlines the text. If code in the application were to assign data in hyperlink form to an unbound control, the control would display the hyperlink as though it is plain text (including the # delimiters for up to four parts of the hyperlink), and clicking the control would not activate the hyperlink. In this application it's simpler to use plain text and have the user enter the e-mail address without the hyperlink delimiters. As you'll learn later in this chapter, application code in the control's DoubleClick event procedure does allow the user to "activate" the e-mail address as though it is a hyperlink.

The second table containing information directly related to a customer is the tblRegistrations table, as shown in Table 16-2. Like all the main data tables, the tblRegistrations table uses an AutoNumber data type as the primary key to avoid an extra round trip to the server when inserting new records. (See "Pushing the Envelope" on page 85 for details.) The registration ID is not displayed to the user. The table does have a unique index on the combination of the CustomerID, ProductID, and SerialNumber fields to ensure that the exact same product isn't entered more than once for any customer. Including the SerialNumber field in the unique index is essential because a customer might own two or more of the same product.

Table 16-2   The Fields in the tblRegistrations Table

Field Name	Data Type	Required	Description
RegistrationID	AutoNumber	N/A	Unique registration identifier.
CustomerID	Long Integer	Yes	Customer who owns this product.
ProductID	Long Integer	Yes	Related product.
DOP	Date/Time	Yes	Date of purchase.
WarrantyID	Long Integer	Yes	Related warranty.
SerialNum	Long Integer	Yes	Product serial number.

As you'll learn in Chapter 17, "Capturing Support Cases," a support case always has a related customer ID and will have a related registration ID when the support case is for a specific product owned by the customer.

Working with Customer Data

Before the user can create a support case, the customer must be defined in the database. If the customer record already exists, the user can take advantage of the search facility to find the customer. When the user is entering a new customer record or editing an existing one, the application assists with city and state lookup on ZIP code and helps ensure that the same customer isn't entered in the database twice. Finally, the application makes it easy for the user to start an e-mail to the customer. All these features are discussed in the following section.

Searching for Customers

When a customer calls the support center, the user needs to be able to quickly find out if that customer is already in the database. As you'll learn in the next chapter, the user can start a new support case and execute a search from the support case editing form. More commonly, the user will initiate the search from the main switchboard in the application.

To see how this works, open the Customer Support application—Support.mdb. To get to the main switchboard, open the frmSplash form to start the application and sign on as me—User Name **jviescas** and Password **password**. The application displays the main switchboard form (frmCSMain) as shown in Figure 16-1.

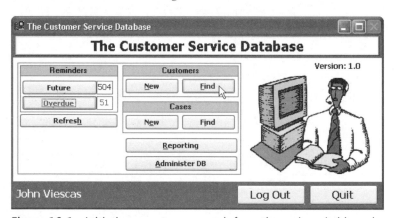

Figure 16-1   Initiating a customer search from the main switchboard.

The sample database contains support cases and reminders from January 1, 2005, through July 5, 2005. The main switchboard displays outstanding reminders based on your current system date and time, so you might see more or fewer overdue reminders depending on the date you run the application. To see how a customer search works, click the Find button under Customers. The application opens the Find Customer form (fpopCustomersFind) that allows you to perform a search on one or more of customer name, home phone number, business phone number, e-mail address, and business name.

When the form first opens, you won't see any customers listed. Enter the letters **de** in the Last Name field to search for customers whose last name begins with those letters and click the Search button. The form performs the search on the criteria you specified, loads the result into a local table, and expands to show you the result, as shown in Figure 16-2.

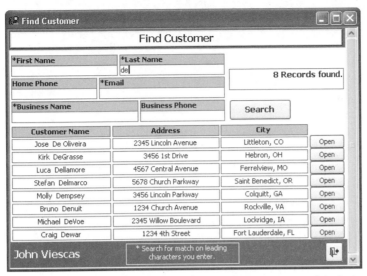

Figure 16-2   Performing a search for customers on part of the last name.

In many ways, this search form works just like any other custom Query By Form—it examines the criteria you entered and builds an appropriate search predicate to find the result. The code examines the unbound text boxes one at a time to build the search string and then exits if you clicked the Search button without entering any criteria. The code in the Click event procedure of the Search command button is as follows:

```
Private Sub cmdSearch_Click()
Dim db As DAO.Database
Dim strSQL As String, varSQLWhere As Variant, intRCount As Integer
  ' User wants to search for customers
  ' Clear the Where clause
  varSQLWhere = Null
  ' If entered a customer first name,
  If Not IsNothing(Me.txtCFirst) Then
    ' Create a wildcard search for leading characters
    '  (C is the alias for tblCustomers)
    varSQLWhere = "(C.CFirst Like '" & Me.txtCFirst & "*')"
  End If
  ' If entered a customer last name,
  If Not IsNothing(Me.txtCLast) Then
    ' Create a wildcard search for leading characters
    varSQLWhere = (varSQLWhere + " AND ") & _
      "(C.CLast Like '" & Me.txtCLast & "*')"
  End If
  ' If entered an email address,
  If Not IsNothing(Me.txtEmail) Then
    ' Create a wildcard search for leading characters
    varSQLWhere = (varSQLWhere + " AND ") & _
      "(C.Email Like '" & Me.txtEmail & "*')"
  End If
  ' If entered a business name,
  If Not IsNothing(Me.txtBusinessName) Then
```

```
  ' Create a wildcard search for leading characters
  varSQLWhere = (varSQLWhere + " AND ") & _
    "(C.BusinessName Like '" & Me.txtBusinessName & "*')"
End If
' If entered a home phone number,
If Not IsNothing(Me.txtHomePhone) Then
  ' Create a search on home phone
  varSQLWhere = (varSQLWhere + " AND ") & _
    "(C.HomePhone = '" & Me.txtHomePhone & "')"
End If
' If entered a business phone number,
If Not IsNothing(Me.txtBusinessPhone) Then
  ' Create a search on business phone
  varSQLWhere = (varSQLWhere + " AND ") & _
    "(C.BusinessPhone = '" & Me.txtBusinessPhone & "')"
End If
' Must enter at least one criterion
If IsNothing(varSQLWhere) Then
  Call CustomError("You must enter at least one search criterion.", _
    OK, "Find Customers")
  Exit Sub
End If
```

> **Caution**   Remember that the Customer Support sample application is specifically designed to handle 50 or more simultaneous users. It manages to do this by strictly minimizing connections to the shared data on the server. If you haven't read the topic "Pushing the Envelope" beginning on page 85, you should do so now before continuing further.

Unlike most custom Query By Form examples, the Find Customers form does not use the predicate it constructs to open a bound form to display the result. The fpopCustomersFind form is actually bound to the local tvwCustomers table but the form's Detail section is hidden (the Visible property is set to No) until the code in the Click event procedure for the Search button performs the search.

After building the predicate, the code includes the condition string in an SQL insert query that fetches the requested data from the linked tblCustomers table on the server into the local tvwCustomers table. After building the SQL statement, the code calls the *fctPlugFind* function (in the same form module) to clear the tvwCustomers table and execute the insert using the filter. If that function executes correctly, the code refreshes the TableDef collection to get an accurate record count, displays the count in a text box control, unhides the Detail section of the form, and expands itself to show up to the first 10 rows. The code is as follows:

```
  ' Build the SQL to insert customers
  strSQL = "INSERT INTO tvwCustomers ( CustomerID, CFirst, CLast, " & _
    "DefaultAddress, HomeAddress1, HomeCity, HomeStateOrProvince, " & _
    "BusinessAddress1, BusinessCity, BusinessStateOrProvince ) " & _
    "SELECT C.CustomerID, C.CFirst, C.CLast, C.DefaultAddress, " & _
    "C.HomeAddress1, C.HomeCity, C.HomeStateOrProvince, " & _
    "C.BusinessAddress1, C.BusinessCity, C.BusinessStateOrProvince " & _
```

```
    "FROM tblCustomers AS C " & _
    "WHERE " & varSQLWhere
' Call the function to clear and load the selected customers
If fctPlugFind(strSQL) = False Then
  ' Got an error - tell the user and exit
  Call CustomError("There was a problem with the search. " & _
    "Please close this window and try again.", , "Search Failure")
  Exit Sub
End If
' Point to this database
Set db = DBEngine(0)(0)
' Refresh TableDefs to get a good count
db.TableDefs.Refresh
' Get the loaded record count
intRCount = db.TableDefs("tvwCustomers").RecordCount
' Set up the form message
If intRCount <> 1 Then
  Me.RecordCount = intRCount & " Records found."
Else
  Me.RecordCount = intRCount & " Record found."
End If
' Reveal the result
Me.RecordCount.Visible = True
' Clear the database object
Set db = Nothing
' If 10 or fewer
If intRCount <= 10 Then
  ' Expand the form to show them all
  Me.InsideHeight = Me.FormHeader.Height + Me.FormFooter.Height + _
    (intRCount * Me.Detail.Height)
Else
  ' Show the first 10
  Me.InsideHeight = Me.FormHeader.Height + Me.FormFooter.Height + _
    (10 * Me.Detail.Height)
End If
' Reload my recordset
Me.Requery
' Unhide the detail section
Me.Detail.Visible = True
End Sub
```

The *fctPlugFind* function is very straightforward. It executes a delete query to clear the existing
rows from the tvwCustomers table and then executes the insert query passed to it as a parameter. As a result, the application connects to the server only for the few milliseconds required
to perform the insert. The code is as follows:

```
Function fctPlugFind(strSQL As String) As Boolean
' Clear the tvwCustomers table and reload using
'   criteria in the SQL string
Dim db As DAO.DataBase
  ' Set an error trap
  On Error GoTo ErrPlugFind
  ' Point to this database
  Set db = DBEngine(0)(0)
```

```
  ' Clear out the table
  db.Execute "DELETE * FROM tvwCustomers", dbFailOnError
  ' Load the search rows
  db.Execute strSQL, dbFailOnError
  ' All OK - return success
  fctPlugFind = True
PlugFindOk:
  Set db = Nothing
  Exit Function
ErrPlugFind:
  ' Got an error - return failure
  fctPlugFind = False
  Resume PlugFindOk
End Function
```

After asking the form to execute the search, the user can scan the returned list to find the customer needed and click the Open button to select the customer. The code in the Click event procedure for the cmdOpen command button first checks to make sure the current row has a valid customer ID.

As you'll learn in Chapter 17, the fpopCustomersFind form can also be opened from the frmCases form to directly search for the customer to be associated with the current case. When called from the frmCases form, the OpenArgs property contains the word "Cases"—and the code returns the selected customer ID to the frmCases form instead of opening the frmCustomers form.

When called from the main switchboard form, the OpenArgs property is empty, so the code checks to see if the frmCustomers form is already open. If it is, the code calls that form's *fctCheckSaved* function to ensure that any pending edits are saved before loading the new customer record to edit. If that function returns "OK" indicating a successful save, the code copies the selected customer ID to the frmCustomers form and calls that form's *fctReLoadRecord* function to load the selected customer data. If the frmCustomers form is not already open, the code opens it and passes it the customer ID to load and display the selected record. The code is as follows:

```
Private Sub cmdOpen_Click()
  ' User wants to open a customer
  ' Hide me
  Me.Visible = False
  ' Make sure we have a customer ID
  If IsNothing(Me.CustomerID) Then Exit Sub
  ' If we were called from the cases form,
  If Me.OpenArgs = "Cases" Then
    ' It should be open,
    If Not IsFormLoaded("frmCases") Then
      ' .. but make sure.
      DoCmd.OpenForm "frmCases"
    End If
    ' Put the selected customer ID on the
    '  cases form
    Form_frmCases.txtCustomerID = Me.CustomerID
```

```
     ' Set the customer name
    Form_frmCases.txtCustomerName = Me.CustomerName
     ' Call that form's "dirty" function
    Form_frmCases.fctDirty
     ' Make sure the focus is on cases
    Form_frmCases.SetFocus
  Else
    ' Regular customer search
    ' If the customer form is open,
    If IsFormLoaded("frmCustomers") Then
      ' Call that form's check & save function
      ' - Reply is "OK" if an error and user
      '     wants to try to fix it.
      If Form_frmCustomers.fctCheckSaved <> "Ok" Then
        ' Set the customer ID
        Form_frmCustomers.txtCustomerID = Me.CustomerID
        ' .. and tell the form to load it
        Form_frmCustomers.fctReLoadRecord
        ' Put the focus there
        Form_frmCustomers.SetFocus
      End If
    Else
      ' Not open yet - just open & pass parameter
      DoCmd.OpenForm "frmCustomers", OpenArgs:=Me.CustomerID
    End If
  End If
  ' Close me
  DoCmd.Close acForm, Me.Name
End Sub
```

Remember from Chapter 3, "Designing a Client/Server Application," that all the data editing forms in the Customer Support application are unbound. You can find a detailed discussion of the *fctReLoadRecord* function in the frmCustomers form in that chapter.

Helping with Postal Codes

If you have followed along to this point, click the Open button next to Stefan Delmarco shown in Figure 16-2 to open that record to edit it in the frmCustomers form. Tab down to the Postal field under Home Address, type a different ZIP code in the Postal field (I used my home ZIP code in Austin, Texas, in the example), and press Enter. The application displays a message offering to change the City and State / Prov fields for you as shown in Figure 16-3 on the next page.

Click No to not change the City and State / Prov fields and then click Undo Edits to restore the record.

As you might imagine, code in the AfterUpdate event procedure of both of the Postal fields on the form performs a lookup to help the user pick the correct city and state for a given postal code. In fact, this same code automatically fills in the city and state values when the user is entering data on a new record.

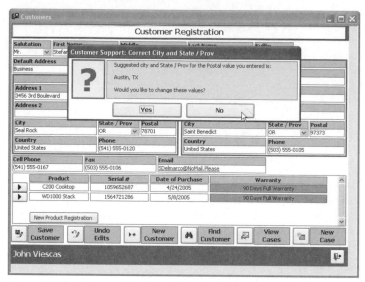

Figure 16-3 The application offers to change city and state when you enter a new postal code.

> **Note** The sample database contains a United States Post Office (USPS) ZIP code table that lists all the ZIP codes and the related city, state, county, and area codes in the United States. It would be a simple matter to modify the sample code to use a similar postal code list for any country.

The code in the AfterUpdate event procedure of the txtHomePostal text box (you can find similar code in the AfterUpdate event procedure of the txtBusinessPostal text box) first calls the *CheckFieldSize* function (described in Chapter 3) to make sure the data entered is not longer than the size of the field. After marking the record changed, the code next verifies that the text box contains data and exits if the control is empty. The code looks for a hyphen within the string (separating the five-digit and four-digit parts of a U.S. ZIP code) and extracts the first five characters preceding the hyphen.

If the remaining characters are numeric, the code passes the data to the *fctGetZipCityState* function that you can find in the form's module. When the data isn't numeric, the procedure does nothing. The *fctGetZipCityState* function returns True when it successfully finds a matching ZIP code in the local tlkpZips table. If there is nothing in the city and state controls on the form, the code updates those controls with the values returned by the function. If the city or state controls contain a value, the code compares the values returned by the function with the values in the controls. If either doesn't match, the code displays the new city and state and asks the user if the values should be changed. The code is as follows:

```
Private Sub txtHomePostal_AfterUpdate()
Dim strCity As String, strState As String
Dim strZip As String, intI As Integer
    ' Call the length validator
```

```
      Call CheckFieldSize(Me.txtHomePostal, "Home Postal", 15)
      ' Mark the record changed
      fctDirty
      ' Do nothing else if postal code is empty
      If IsNothing(Me.txtHomePostal) Then Exit Sub
      ' Extract numbers before the "-", if any
      intI = InStr(Me.txtHomePostal, "-")
      If intI = 0 Then
        strZip = Me.txtHomePostal
      Else
        strZip = Left(Me.txtHomePostal, intI)
      End If
      ' If numeric,
      If IsNumeric(strZip) Then
        ' Attempt to get city and state
        If fctGetZipCityState(strZip, strCity, strState) Then
          ' If existing city and state are empty
          If IsNothing(Me.txtHomeCity) And _
            IsNothing(Me.cmbHomeStateOrProvince) Then
            ' Update with the values returned by the lookup
            Me.txtHomeCity = strCity
            Me.cmbHomeStateOrProvince = strState
          Else
            ' If what user entered doesn't match
            If (strCity <> Me.txtHomeCity) Or _
              (strState <> Me.cmbHomeStateOrProvince) Then
              ' Ask user if want to update
              If "Yes" = CustomError("Suggested city and State / Prov " & _
                "for the Postal value you entered is: " & vbCrLf & vbCrLf & _
                strCity & ", " & strState & vbCrLf & vbCrLf & _
                "Would you like to change these values?", _
                YesNo, "Correct City and State / Prov", Question) Then
                ' Correct the values
                Me.txtHomeCity = strCity
                Me.cmbHomeStateOrProvince = strState
              End If
            End If
          End If
        End If
      End If
    End Sub
```

The *fctGetZipCityState* function is designed to take any string of numbers up to five digits long and attempt to find a matching ZIP code in the tlkpZips local table. The code first strips off the leftmost five digits and then pads the result to the left with zeros to obtain a five-character search string. For example, if you type **2101** in the Postal field, the function uses a search string of "02101" and returns Boston, MA.

The code opens a recordset using the qlkpZips query that eliminates the one copyright record you'll find in the tlkpZips table. Note that many five-digit ZIP codes have more than one entry in the table, but the code returns only the first one it finds. When the table contains a matching record, the code returns the related city and state fields and responds with a True result. The code is as follows:

```
Function fctGetZipCityState(strZipCode As String, _
   strCity As String, strState As String) As Integer
' Called from the two zip code AfterUpdate procedures
' to attempt to find the matching city and state for
' a given ZIP code.
Dim db As DAO.DataBase, rst As DAO.Recordset
Dim strZip5 As String
  ' Point to this database
  Set db = DBEngine(0)(0)
  ' Make sure we're working with only 5 digits
  strZip5 = Left(strZipCode, 5)
  ' Now left pad with zeros if necessary
  strZip5 = Format(strZip5, "00000")
  ' Try to find a matching record
  Set rst = db.OpenRecordset("SELECT * FROM qlkpZips " & _
    "WHERE ZIPCode = '" & strZip5 & "'")
  ' If got one
  If Not rst.EOF Then
    ' Return the first city & state
    strCity = rst!City
    strState = rst!State
    ' Success
    fctGetZipCityState = True
  Else
    ' Failed
    fctGetZipCityState = False
  End If
  ' Close out
  rst.Close
  Set rst = Nothing
  Set db = Nothing
End Function
```

Warning   The United States Postal Service (USPS) holds the copyright to all ZIP code data. If you wish to use this data in your applications, you must first obtain a license either from the USPS or a licensed vendor. My company, Viescas Consulting, Inc., obtained an unlimited license to distribute the data contained in the tlkpZips table you can find in the sample databases from CD Light, LLC: *http://www.zipinfo.com/products/z5/z5.htm*. You can also purchase a monthly subscription from FMS, Inc.: *http://www.fmsinc.com/products/zipcode/index.html*. For information about how to purchase the data directly from the USPS, download the file: *http://ribbs.usps.gov/files/addressing/PUBS/AIS.PDF*.

Checking for Duplicates

In any database that stores information about people, you should take steps to avoid storing more than one record for the same person. The rules of normalization tell you that you should, whenever possible, choose a simple set of natural values as the primary key of your tables and use the primary key to avoid duplicates. When you're dealing with person names and addresses, finding a simple combination of fields that will always be unique is usually difficult if not impossible. So, you end up generating an artificial primary key—usually an integer number—to uniquely identify each row.

In Chapter 5, "Verifying Names," you learned how to use the *Soundex* function to detect similar last names. The Customer Support application goes one step further by checking the last name, the city, and the state entered. You can see how this works by entering information for a new customer that is similar to a customer already in the database. If you have been following along to this point, you can click New Customer on the Customers form to clear the record you were editing and start a new one. You can also click the New button under Customers on the main switchboard form. Or, you can simply open the Customer Support database (Support.mdb) and then open the frmCustomers form from the Database window.

In the blank Customers form, enter **Mr.** in the Salutation field, any name you like in the First Name field, **Wilsen** in the Last Name field, any address of your choosing in the Home Address 1 field, **01541** (the ZIP code for Princeton, MA) in the Postal field, **United States** in the Country field, and any phone number in the Phone field, and then click Save Customer. The application responds with a warning message as shown in Figure 16-4.

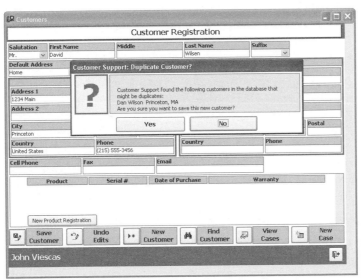

Figure 16-4 The application detects when the user enters a similar last name in the same city.

As it turns out, there's already a Dan Wilson in Princeton, MA. Note that the last name doesn't match exactly, but "sounds like" the name you entered. Code in the *fctCheckSaved* function in the form's module (previously described in Chapter 3) opens a recordset on the tblCustomers table to see if another customer record has a last name with the same Soundex code in the same city name. If the code finds any records, it builds a message containing all the names it found and asks the user if the record should be saved. The code is as shown on the next page.

```
' But if this is a new record,
If blnNewRec Then
  ' See if a potential duplicate
  ' Point to this database
  Set db = DBEngine(0)(0)
  ' Open a recordset using Soundex to find duplicates
  '   and match on city name
  ' Set up the SQL depending on default address
  If Me.cmbDefaultAddress = 1 Then
    ' Home address
    strSQL = "SELECT C.CFirst, C.CLast, " & _
      "C.HomeCity As City, C.HomeStateOrProvince As State " & _
      "FROM tblCustomers As C " & _
      "WHERE Soundex(C.CLast) = '" & Soundex(Me.txtCLast) & _
      "' AND C.HomeCity = '" & Me.txtHomeCity & _
      "' AND C.HomeStateOrProvince = '" & _
      Me.cmbHomeStateOrProvince & "'"
  Else
    ' Business address
    strSQL = "SELECT C.CFirst, C.CLast, " & _
      "C.BusinessCity As City, C.BusinessStateOrProvince As State " & _
      "FROM tblCustomers As C " & _
      "WHERE Soundex(C.CLast) = '" & Soundex(Me.txtCLast) & _
      "' AND C.BusinessCity = '" & Me.txtBusinessCity & _
      "' AND C.BusinessStateOrProvince = '" & _
      Me.cmbBusinessStateOrProvince & "'"
  End If
  Set rst = db.OpenRecordset(strSQL)
  ' If got some,
  If Not rst.EOF Then
    ' Build a warning message
    strErrMsg = "Customer Support found the following " & _
      "customers in the database that might be duplicates:" & vbCrLf
    ' Get all the duplicates
    Do Until rst.EOF
      strErrMsg = strErrMsg & rst!CFirst & " " & rst!CLast & _
        " " & rst!City & ", " & rst!State & vbCrLf
      rst.MoveNext
    Loop
    ' Add the end of the message
    strErrMsg = strErrMsg & "Are you sure you want to save this " & _
      "new customer?"
    ' See if user wants to cancel the save
    If "No" = CustomError(strErrMsg, YesNo, "Duplicate Customer?", _
      Question, SecondButton) Then
      ' Return that edit was canceled
      fctCheckSaved = "Cancel"
      ' Clear all data to a new screen
      Call fctReLoadRecord
      ' Skip the save
      blnSkipSave = True
    End If
  End If
  ' Close the recordset
  rst.Close
```

```
      Set rst = Nothing
      Set db = Nothing
   End If
```

As you can see, when the user chooses to not save the record the code clears the form without saving the record so the user can either search for the already saved customer record or enter another one.

Keep in mind that the technique just described might produce too many false positive results (and annoying message prompts) in a database with many customers in each city. Consider including a match on the first letter of the first name or the street name to reduce the number of incorrect matches.

Activating an Unbound Hyperlink

Although most customer support contacts will be by phone, it's possible that some information can be conveyed by e-mail. For example, the customer support representative might want to send a promotional document or a URL to the company Web site. To make sending an e-mail simple, the application supports creating a new message to the customer.

Remember, in the discussion of the tblCustomers table earlier in this chapter, you learned that the Email field is simple text, not a hyperlink. Because none of the data is bound to a form, hyperlink data won't display or link properly when assigned to an unbound text box. However, the application does allow the user to activate an e-mail address as though it is a hyperlink by double-clicking the unbound text box.

To see how this works, you can open the record for Stefan Delmarco again. You can open frmCustomers from the Database window, click Find Customer, enter **de** in the Last Name field, click Search, and then click Open next to Mr. Delmarco's record (see Figure 16-2). To start an e-mail to Mr. Delmarco, double-click the Email field as shown in Figure 16-5 on the next page.

You should see a new message open in the program that is your default e-mail handler with the To address filled in. The code to make this happen is in the DblClick event of the txtEmail text box control. The code verifies that the text box contains a value and then uses the FollowHyperlink method of the Application object using the MailTo protocol to get the job done. The code is as follows:

```
Private Sub txtEmail_DblClick(Cancel As Integer)
  ' User double-clicked to send email
  ' Make sure not empty
  If Not IsNothing(Me.txtEmail) Then
    ' Fire as a hyperlink
    Application.FollowHyperlink "MailTo:" & Me.txtEmail
  End If
End Sub
```

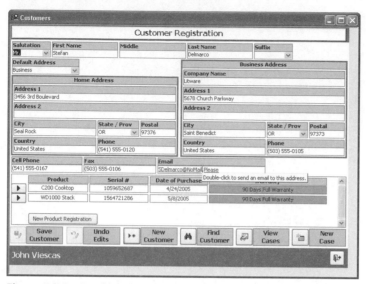

Figure 16-5   Double-click the Email field to start a new message to the current customer.

> **Note**   All the e-mail addresses in the sample database point to an invalid domain name, so you won't be able to successfully send the message.

Editing Product Registrations

Entering customer information fulfills the requirement to identify a customer for each support case, but most cases will also be about a specific product that the customer owns. You can see that the frmCustomers form (Figure 16-5) displays products already registered to the customer in a subform window. In Chapter 3, you learned how the *fctRefreshReg* function in the form's module loads the related product registration records into the local tvwRegistrations table. The fsubCustomersRegistrations form that's used as a subform in the frmCustomers form is bound to this local table.

You can create a new product registration for the current customer by clicking the New Product Registration button you can see in the subform. Code in the subform opens the fdlgRegistration form, and that form grabs the current customer ID and customer name from the frmCustomers form to start a new record. You can click that button, choose Grills in the Product Category combo box, select the GG100 Grill in the Product combo box, enter a date of purchase, select an available warranty for that product, and enter a serial number. Your result should now look like Figure 16-6.

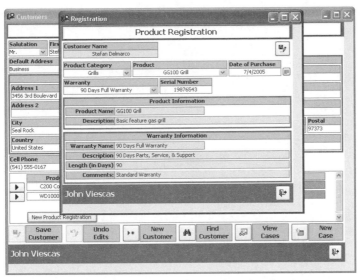

Figure 16-6   Creating a new product registration for a customer.

You might have noticed that the Warranty combo box was dimmed when you first opened the Registration form. You must choose the product before you can choose an available warranty for the product. Note also that when you choose a product, the form displays the product details in the Product Information area. When you choose a warranty, the form displays the details in the Warranty Information area. Click the Save button (upper right corner) to save the new record. The form also saves the record when you close it. When you return to the Customers form, you should see the new product registered, as shown in Figure 16-7.

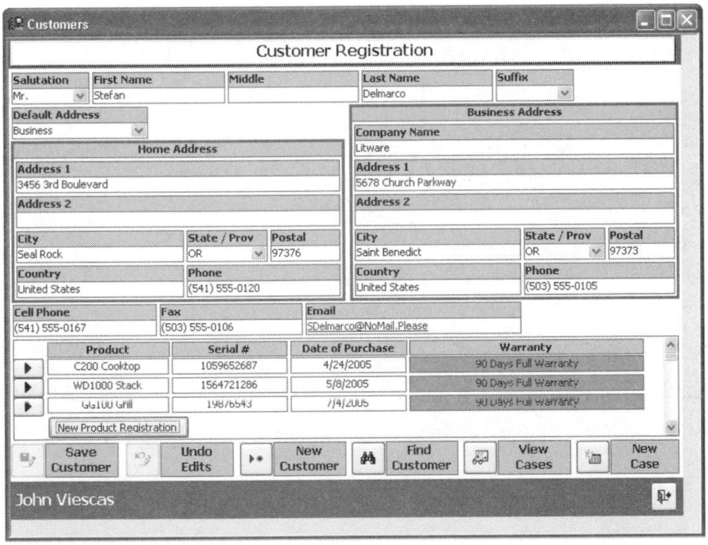

Figure 16-7   The new barbecue grill is now registered.

The code that gets this process started is in the Click event procedure of the cmdNewReg command button control in the fsubCustomersRegistrations form. The code ensures that any changes in the parent customer form were saved by calling that form's *fctCheckSaved* function. If the parent form has a valid customer ID, the form opens the fdlgRegistration form. The code is as follows:

```
Private Sub cmdNewReg_Click()
  ' User wants to create a new product registration for this customer
  ' Make sure any changes here are saved
  If Form_frmCustomers.blnSaved = False Then
    If Form_frmCustomers.fctCheckSaved <> "Saved" Then Exit Sub
  End If
  ' Must have a customer ID to create a product registration
  If IsNothing(Me.Parent.txtCustomerID) Then Exit Sub
  ' Open the form - new registration for current customer
  DoCmd.OpenForm "fdlgRegistration"
End Sub
```

To better understand how the fdlgRegistration form works, it's useful to look at the form in Design view, as shown in Figure 16-8. Notice that all the controls in the top part of the form are unbound. The controls that display the product and warranty details actually extract their information from the columns of the respective combo boxes.

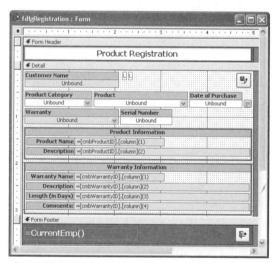

Figure 16-8   The design of the fdlgRegistration form.

The Row Source property of the cmbProductID combo box control (the Product field on the form) contains the following query:

```
SELECT tlkpProducts.ProductID, tlkpProducts.ProductName, tlkpProducts.Description
FROM tlkpProducts
WHERE (((tlkpProducts.Inactive)=False)
AND ((tlkpProducts.ProductCategoryID) = [Forms]![fdlgRegistration]![cmbProductLine]
OR ([Forms]![fdlgRegistration]![cmbProductLine]=0)))
ORDER BY tlkpProducts.ProductName;
```

When the user chooses a new product category in the cmbProductLine control (the Product Category field on the form), code in that control's AfterUpdate event procedure requeries the cmbProductID combo box so that it displays only products in the selected category. If the user leaves the cmbProductLine control set to the default All selection, the value of the combo box is 0, which will select all products.

The Row Source property of the cmbWarrantyID combo box control (the Warranty field on the form) contains the following query:

```
SELECT tlkpWarranties.WarrantyID, tlkpWarranties.WarrantyName, tlkpWarranties.WarrantyDesc,
tlkpWarranties.WarrantyLength, tlkpProductsWarranties.Comments
FROM tlkpWarranties
INNER JOIN tlkpProductsWarranties
ON tlkpWarranties.WarrantyID = tlkpProductsWarranties.WarrantyID
WHERE (((tlkpWarranties.Inactive)=False)
AND ((tlkpProductsWarranties.ProductID) = [forms]![fdlgRegistration].[cmbProductID]))
ORDER BY tlkpWarranties.WarrantyName;
```

As you might expect, code in the AfterUpdate event of the cmbProductID combo box control requeries the cmbWarrantyID control so that it displays only warranties for the selected product. That procedure also unlocks the warranty combo box so that you can select a warranty.

When you click the Save button or close the form, the *fctCheckSaved* procedure in the form runs. As with the same function you studied in Chapter 3 for the frmCustomers form, the code calls the *ValidateRecord* function in the modRecordEditor module to verify that all required fields have been entered. If that function returns an error message, the code formats and displays the message and gives the user a chance to correct the error or undo the changes. If the *ValidateRecord* function returns no error, the code calls the *SaveRecord* function (also in the modRecordEditor module) to save the new product registration. If this is a new registration, the code calls the *fctRefreshReg* function in the frmCustomers form module to reload the list of displayed products. The code is as follows:

```
Public Function fctCheckSaved() As String
' This code checks that the required information is complete and then
' saves the record and flags the linked table for an update
Dim strErrMsg As String      'Stores the total error message
Dim lngID As Long, blnNewRecord As Boolean
  ' Set an error trap
  On Error GoTo errfctCheckSaved
  ' If got a registration ID
  If Not IsNothing(Me.txtRegistrationID) Then
    ' Grab it
    lngID = Me.txtRegistrationID
  Else
    ' Set new record
    blnNewRecord = True
  End If
  'If the current record already saved,
  If blnSaved = True Then
    ' Confirm saved and exit
```

```
        fctCheckSaved = "Saved"
    Else
        ' Validate the registration data - returns ZLS if successful
        strErrMsg = ValidateRecord("fdlgRegistration", "fdlgRegistration")
        ' If the error string not empty,
        If strErrMsg <> "" Then
            ' Set up the message to display
            strErrMsg = "The record could not be saved " & _
                "because the following fields are not complete: " & _
                vbCrLf & strErrMsg & vbCrLf & "What would you like to do?"
            ' Display the message - if user clicked cancel,
            If CustomError(strErrMsg, OkCancel, "Could not save record", _
                Question) = "Cancel Changes" Then
                ' Return that edit was canceled
                fctCheckSaved = "Cancel"
                ' Clear all data to a new screen
                Call fctReLoadRecord
            Else
                ' User clicked - OK, wants to work on it some more
                ' Return that edit failed, but still dirty
                fctCheckSaved = "Ok"      'The user chose to keep working.
                ' Make sure record not marked saved
                fctDirty
            End If
        Else
            'This might take a while...
            DoCmd.Hourglass True
            ' If there was no error message,
            '  and the record hasn't been saved then:
            ' Save the Registration - returns the RegistrationID if successful
            lngID = SaveRecord("fdlgRegistration", "fdlgRegistration", _
                "tblRegistrations", lngID, , "Registration")
            ' If save successful,
            If lngID <> 0 Then
                ' Save the registrationID in the form
                Me.txtRegistrationID = lngID
                ' Set up return success
                fctCheckSaved = "Saved"
                ' Mark the record saved
                blnSaved = True      'The current record is saved
                ' If this was a new record,
                If blnNewRecord Then
                    ' Rebuild the data in the subform on frmCustomers
                    Form_frmCustomers.fctRefreshReg Me.txtCustomerID
                End If
            End If
        End If
    End If
    'Done!
okfctCheckSaved:
    ' Make sure hourglass is off
    DoCmd.Hourglass False
    Exit Function
errfctCheckSaved:
    ' Display and log error
```

```
     ErrTryingTo "save registration data"
     ' Clear so we don't get an unending loop
     Me.txtRegistrationID = 0
     fctReLoadRecord
     Resume okfctCheckSaved
End Function
```

Note that you can also edit an existing product registration by clicking the small arrow button to the left of any record in the subform window on the frmCustomers form. The code in the Click event procedure for the cmdViewRegistration command button control is identical to the code to open a new registration except the code passes the RegistrationID field value to the fdlgRegistration form via the OpenArgs property. When the Open event procedure of that form detects a value in the OpenArgs property, it loads that registration record rather than clearing the form.

Although editing customer and product registration information is somewhat more complicated using the unbound architecture of this application, the basic design would be the same using bound forms in a standard client/server application. Now that you understand how the Customer Support application handles customers and their product registration records, you're ready to move on to working with support cases in the next chapter.

Chapter 17

Capturing Support Cases

The core of any customer support application is capturing and tracking support contacts. Whenever a customer calls with a new problem, the customer support representative must open a new support case and log all the events that occur in the course of solving the problem.

As mentioned in Chapter 15, the sample Customer Support application (Support.mdb and SupportData.mdb) is similar in many ways to any contact management application that you might need. A support case and the related case events, although tailored in this example to customer support, could just as easily be any contact issue and the specific contacts related to that issue. A sales representative might create a case to track a particular prospect's interest in a specific product line. A nonprofit organization might use a case to track contacts about a specific program by month. A seller at an online auction site might create a case for each product put up for sale.

Note   The Customer Support sample application assumes that more than 50 users might need to be running the application simultaneously. To provide adequate performance when sharing a data file in the Access desktop database format (.mdb file), the application uses no forms or reports that are bound to data on the server. To understand the architectural design of this application, you should read the section "Pushing the Envelope" on page 85.

Understanding the Tables Involved

The table that categorizes support contacts by case (shown in Table 17-1 on the next page) contains fields that are useful in any contact management application that needs to categorize contacts in some way. The table contains the ID of the support representative who opened the case; the subjects of the case (CustomerID and RegistrationID in this application); the status of the case; the date case was received; the date and time the case was started, last updated, and closed; and a description of the case. Fields specific to customer support include indicators for whether service was ordered or parts were sent, the description of the part, and the support category.

Table 17-1   The Fields in the tblCases Table

Field Name	Data Type	Required	Description
CaseID	AutoNumber	N/A	Unique case identifier.
CaseOwnerID	Long Integer	Yes	The employee who owns the case.
CustomerID	Long Integer	Yes	Related customer for this case.
RegistrationID	Long Integer	No	Related product registration, if any.
DateReceived	Date/Time	Yes	Date the case was received.
DateTimeStarted	Date/Time	No	Date and time the support representative started working on the case.
DateTimeUpdated	Date/Time	No	Date and time the case was last updated.
DateTimeClosed	Date/Time	No	Date and time the case was closed.
Status	Text, Field Size 15	Yes	Status of the case.
Service	Yes/No	No	Was service ordered?
PartSent	Yes/No	No	Was a part sent?
PartDesc	Text, Field Size 50	No	Description of the part sent.
OneLineDesc	Text, Field Size 150	Yes	Short description of the case problem.
CategoryID	Long Integer	Yes	Related support category for this case.
CategoryDetail	Text, Field Size 255	No	Category details, if any.

Each case should have one or more case event records (shown in Table 17-2) that document the date and time of the event, the resolution or action taken, and notes about what was discussed. As you'll learn later in this chapter, the Customer Support application is designed to disallow a case that does not have at least one case event. The application does allow the user to delete individual case events that the user created, but the user must always leave at least one case event associated with each case.

Table 17-2   The Fields in the tblCasesEvents Table

Field Name	Data Type	Required	Description
EventID	AutoNumber	N/A	Unique case event identifier.
CaseID	Long Integer	No[*]	Related case for this event.
EmployeeID	Long Integer	Yes	Employee who handled the event.
EventTime	Date/Time	Yes	Date and time the event occurred.
ActionID	Long Integer	Yes	Related action taken from tlkpActions.
Notes	Memo	Yes	Notes about the event.

* Field is automatically set by code in the frmCases form.

Working with Support Case Data

A customer support representative can edit an existing support case and create new support cases but cannot delete a case once it has been saved. You might want to take this approach in any application where it is important, for legal or other reasons, to not lose any data entered. Although the sample Customer Support application does not include a capability to allow a user with appropriate authority to mark a record inactive or deleted, the feature would be easy to add.

As noted earlier, each case must have at least one case event record. In addition, a user cannot modify or delete a case event created by another user. The following sections describe how the application implements these features.

Searching for Cases

A customer support representative should always add information to an existing case where appropriate rather than create a new support case for each customer contact. The application makes it easy to quickly find existing support cases when the support representative answers a new call.

You can explore the search capabilities by opening the Customer Support sample application (Support.mdb) and then starting the application by opening the frmSplash form. Sign on as me (User Name is **jviescas**, and the Password is **password**) to see the main switchboard shown in Figure 17-1 on the next page.

The sample database contains support cases and reminders from January 1, 2005, through July 5, 2005. The main switchboard displays outstanding reminders based on your current system date and time, so you might see more or fewer overdue reminders depending on the date you run the application. To see how a case search works, click the Find button under Cases. The application opens the Find Case form (fpopCasesFind) that allows you to perform a search on one or more of the fields for from date, to date, case number, case status, case owner, and all or part of a customer last name.

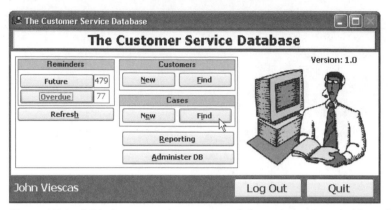

Figure 17-1   Initiating a support case search from the main switchboard.

When the form first opens, you won't see any cases listed. Set the search date to the first quarter of 2005, ask for cases that have a status of Pending, select my name from the Owner list, enter the letter **S** in the Customer Last field to search for customers whose last name begins with that letter, and click the Search button. The form performs the search on the criteria you specified, loads the result into a local table, and expands to show you the result, as shown in Figure 17-2.

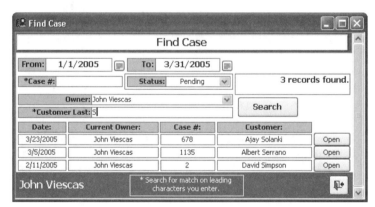

Figure 17-2   Searching for pending cases for a specific case owner and customer last name beginning with the letter *S*.

In many ways, this search form works just like any other custom Query By Form—it examines the criteria you entered and builds an appropriate search predicate to find the result. The code examines the unbound text boxes one at a time to build the search string. The code displays a message and exits if you click the Search button without entering any criteria. The code in the Click event procedure of the Search command button is as follows:

```
Public Sub cmdSearch_Click()
' User wants to perform the search
' Also called from frmCustomers when user wants to
'   find cases for the current customer
```

```vba
Dim strSQL As String, varWhere As Variant, intRCount As Integer
  ' Create the insert command to perform the search
  strSQL = "INSERT INTO tvwCases " & _
    "SELECT C.*, (Cu.CFirst + ' ') & Cu.CLast AS CustomerName " & _
    "FROM tblCases AS C INNER JOIN tblCustomers AS Cu " & _
    "ON C.CustomerID = Cu.CustomerID WHERE "
  ' If have a start date,
  If Not IsNothing(Me.StartDate) Then
    ' Create a predicate
    varWhere = "(C.DateReceived >= #" & Me.StartDate & "#)"
  End If
  ' If have an end date,
  If Not IsNothing(Me.EndDate) Then
    ' Add the predicate
    varWhere = (varWhere + " AND ") & _
      "(C.DateReceived <= #" & Me.EndDate & "#)"
  End If
  ' If something in case ID,
  If Not IsNothing(Me.txtCaseID) Then
    ' Add it to the predicate - match on leading characters
    varWhere = (varWhere + " AND ") & _
      "(C.CaseID Like '" & Me.txtCaseID & "*')"
  End If
  ' If the frmCustomers form gave me a customer ID,
  If Not IsNothing(Me.txtCustomerID) Then
    ' Add it to the predicate - exact match
    varWhere = (varWhere + " AND ") & _
      "(C.CustomerID = " & Me.txtCustomerID & ")"
  End If
  ' If the user specified a case owner (employee),
  If Not IsNothing(Me.cmbOwnerID) Then
    ' Add it to the predicate - exact match
    varWhere = (varWhere + " AND ") & _
      "(C.CaseOwnerID = " & Me.cmbOwnerID & ")"
  End If
  ' If the user specified a case status,
  If Not IsNothing(Me.cmbStatus) Then
    ' Add it to the predicate - exact match
    varWhere = (varWhere + " AND ") & _
      "(C.Status = '" & Me.cmbStatus & "')"
  End If
  ' If the user specified a customer last name,
  If Not IsNothing(Me.txtCLast) Then
    ' Add it to the predicate - match on leading characters
    varWhere = (varWhere + " AND ") & _
      "(Cu.CLast Like '" & Me.txtCLast & "*') "
  End If
  ' Must enter at least one criterion
  If IsNothing(varWhere) Then
    Call CustomError("You must enter at least one search criterion.", _
      OK, "Find Cases")
    Exit Sub
  End If
```

Unlike most custom Query By Form examples, the Find Case form does not use the predicate it constructs to open a bound form to display the result. The fpopCasesFind form is actually bound to the local tvwCases table but the form's Detail section is hidden (the Visible property is set to No) until the code in the Click event procedure for the Search button performs the search.

After building the predicate, the code includes the condition string in an SQL insert query that fetches the requested data from the linked tblCases table on the server into the local tvwCases table. Note that the local table (tvwCases) contains one additional field—CustomerName—which the INSERT command fetches from the related customer record. After building the SQL statement, the code calls the *fctPlugFind* function (in the same form module) to clear the tvwCases table and execute the insert using the filter. If that function executes correctly, the code refreshes the TableDef collection to get an accurate record count, displays the count in a text box control, unhides the Detail section of the form, and expands itself to show up to the first 10 rows. The code is as follows:

```
' Call the function to clear the tvwCases table and
'  insert rows that match the search string
If fctPlugFind(strSQL & varWhere) = False Then
  ' Something failed - notify user and bail
  Call CustomError("There was a problem with the search. " & _
    "Please close this form and try again.", , "Search Failure", Severe)
  Exit Sub
End If
' Refresh the TableDefs collection to get a good count
DBEngine(0)(0).TableDefs.Refresh
' Get the count of rows
intRCount = DBEngine(0)(0).TableDefs("tvwCases").RecordCount
' Set up the label display of records found
If intRCount = 1 Then
  Me.RecordCount = intRCount & " record found."
Else
  Me.RecordCount = intRCount & " records found."
End If
' If 10 or fewer rows
If intRCount <= 10 Then
  ' Size detail to show them all
  Me.InsideHeight = Me.FormHeader.Height + Me.FormFooter.Height + _
    (intRCount * Me.Detail.Height)
Else
  ' Show only the first 10
  Me.InsideHeight = Me.FormHeader.Height + Me.FormFooter.Height + _
    (10 * Me.Detail.Height)
End If
' Make sure form loads the found records
Me.Requery
' Display the count label
Me.RecordCount.Visible = True
' .. and reveal it.
Me.Detail.Visible = True
End Sub
```

The *fctPlugFind* function is very straightforward. It executes a delete query to clear the existing rows from the tvwCases table and then executes the insert query passed to it as a parameter. As a result, the application connects to the server only for the few milliseconds required to perform the insert. The code is as follows:

```
Function fctPlugFind(strSQL As String) As Boolean
Dim db As DAO.DataBase
  ' Set an error trap
  On Error GoTo ErrPlugFind
  ' Point to this database
  Set db = DBEngine(0)(0)
  ' Clear the tvwCases table
  db.Execute "DELETE * FROM tvwCases", dbFailOnError
  ' Run the insert query passed to us
  db.Execute strSQL, dbFailOnError
  ' No errors - return success
  fctPlugFind = True
PlugFindOk:
  Exit Function
ErrPlugFind:
  ' Got an error - set failed
  fctPlugFind = False
  Resume PlugFindOk
End Function
```

Opening a Case Found in a Search

After asking the form to execute the search, the user can scan the returned list to find the case needed and click the Open button to edit the case. In this example, click the Open button next to case 1135 for customer Albert Serrano shown in Figure 17-2 to see the case data in the frmCases form as shown in Figure 17-3 on the next page.

As you can see, the frmCases form is divided into three sections. The top part of the form contains controls to show the customer, the product owned by the customer, the status of the case, the case owner, and the date the case was received. The form provides option buttons to specify if service was ordered or a part was sent and a text box to describe the parts. Next, you can see the short case description, the case category, and a text box to enter required details for certain case categories. In this example, because the case is categorized as having missing parts, the form displays the required information in a label next to the text box. When further detail is not required by the category selected, the caption displays Category Details.

The middle part of the form provides an area to define a new case event for the current case or to edit or view an existing event. Code in the form automatically fills in the name of the current user that will be related to the event and the date and time. The support representative need only select an action description from the Action combo box, enter notes about the case event, and click Save Case to save the new event. The bottom part of the form (the fsubCasesEvents form in a subform window) lists the events that were already recorded for the current case. The support representative can click the arrow button next to an existing event record to move it to the editing area in the middle part of the form so that it can be edited (if the current user created the event record) or viewed (if another user created the event record).

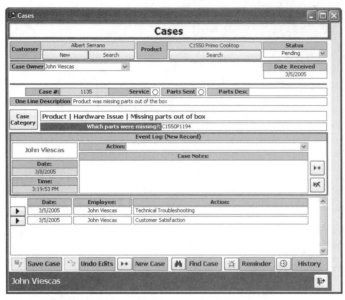

Figure 17-3 Editing an existing case record.

The code that opens the frmCases form in the fpopCasesFind form is very similar to the code you saw in the previous chapter for fpopCustomersFind. The code first checks to see if the frmCases form is already open. If it is, the code calls that form's *fctCheckSaved* function to ensure that any pending edits are saved before loading the new case record to edit. If that function returns "OK" (indicating a save error but the user wants to keep working), the code exits. If that function returns anything else, the code copies the selected case ID to the frmCases form and calls that form's *fctReLoadRecord* function to load the selected customer data. If the frmCases form is not already open, the code opens it and passes it the case ID to load and display the selected record. The code is as follows:

```
Private Sub cmdOpenCase_Click()
  ' User has asked to open this case
  ' Make sure we have a case ID
  If IsNothing(Me.CaseID) Then Exit Sub
  ' Hide me to prevent focus problems
  Me.Visible = False
  ' If the case form already open
  If IsFormLoaded("frmCases") Then
    ' Call the save routine in that form
    ' User replies OK when save error and user
    '  wants to keep working
    If Form_frmCases.fctCheckSaved = "Ok" Then
      ' Close me
      DoCmd.Close acForm, Me.Name
```

```
         ' Bail
        Exit Sub
    End If
    ' Set this case ID
    Form_frmCases.txtCaseID = Me.CaseID
    ' Call the form's reload function
    Form_frmCases.fctReLoadRecord
    ' Put the focus there
    Form_frmCases.SetFocus
  Else
    ' Open the cases form and tell it we
    '  want this case ID
    DoCmd.OpenForm "frmCases", OpenArgs:=Me.CaseID
  End If
  ' Close me
  DoCmd.Close acForm, Me.Name
End Sub
```

Remember from Chapter 3 that all the data editing forms in the Customer Support application are unbound. The *fctReLoadRecord* function that moves the case data into unbound controls on the frmCases form is very similar to the code described in Chapter 3 for the frmCustomers form.

When you click the New button under Cases on the main switchboard (Figure 17-1 on page 352), code in that button's Click event procedure opens the frmCases form without specifying a case ID. When no case ID is specified, the code clears or sets default values for all the unbound controls. When a case ID exists because the form that opened frmCases (fpopCasesFind) specifies a case ID, the code calls the *LoadRecord* function (described in Chapter 3) to fetch the case record from the server and load the values into the unbound controls.

Next the code calls the *fctRefreshEvents* function in the form's module to load the related case events into the subform window at the bottom of the form. After loading the related customer name and product name and formatting the case issue category (*fctCatFormatDetails* function), the code checks for a nonzero event ID and either clears the event edit area or loads the event data. The code is as follows:

```
Function fctReLoadRecord() As Boolean
' Called when the form opens, the user asks to start a new
'  record, or the user cancels an edit after a save failure
' Function either clears all editable controls or reloads
'  the case specified by the current CaseID
Dim db As DAO.DataBase, rst As DAO.Recordset, strSQL As String
  On Error GoTo errfctReLoadRecord
  ' If the CaseID is empty,
  If IsNothing(Me.txtCaseID) Then
    ' Clear the form to create an empty record
    ' Clear case controls
    Me.txtCaseID = Null
    Me.txtCustomerID = Null
    Me.txtCustomerName = Null
    Me.txtRegistrationID = Null
```

```
      Me.txtProductName = Null
      ' Default owner of case is current user
      Me.cmbOwnerID = CurrentID()
      Me.cmbStatus = "Pending"
      ' Use today as the date for a new case
      Me.txtDateReceived = Date
      Me.txtStarted = Now
      Me.txtUpdated = Null
      Me.txtDateClosed = Null
      Me.chkService = False
      Me.chkPartSent = False
      Me.txtPartDesc = Null
      Me.txtOneLineDesc = Null
      Me.CategoryVal = Null
      Me.txtCategoryDetail = Null
      Call fctCatFormatDetails(0)
      ' Clear the event log area
      Me.txtEventID = Null
      Me.cmbActionID = Null
      Me.txtNotes = Null
      ' Default employee for new event is current user
      Me.cmbEmployeeID = CurrentID()
      ' Initialize the event time
      Me.txtEventTime = Now
      ' Indicate on a new record in the event log edit area
      Me.lblEventLog.Caption = "Event Log: (New Record)"
      ' Make sure the New event button is enabled
      Me.cmdNewLog.Enabled = True
      ' Make sure the Delete event button is enabled
      Me.cmdDeleteLog.Enabled = True
   Else
      ' Otherwise, load the record using the CaseID
      ' Call the function that loads the record
      Call LoadRecord("frmCases", "tblCases", Me.txtCaseID, "Case")
      ' Load the related case events into the view table
      If fctRefreshEvents(Me.txtCaseID) = False Then
         'We got an error, bail
         Exit Function
      End If
      ' Get the related customer information
      Me.txtCustomerName = fctGetCustomer
      ' Get the related registration information
      Me.txtProductName = fctGetRegistration
      ' Format the category display
      If IsNothing(Me.CategoryVal) Then
         ' There is no Category, show a clear display
         Call fctCatFormatDetails(0)
      Else
         ' Format the display to show the category
         Call fctCatFormatDetails(Me.CategoryVal)
      End If
      ' If Event ID is empty then show this is a new Event Record
      If IsNothing(Me.txtEventID) Then
         ' Clear the event log area
         Me.txtEventID = Null
```

```
            Me.cmbActionID = Null
            Me.txtNotes = Null
            ' Default employee for new event is current user
            Me.cmbEmployeeID = CurrentID()
            ' Initialize the event time
            Me.txtEventTime = Now
            ' Indicate on a new record in the event log edit area
            Me.lblEventLog.Caption = "Event Log: (New Record)"
            ' Make sure the New event button is enabled
            Me.cmdNewLog.Enabled = True
            ' Make sure the Delete event button is enabled
            Me.cmdDeleteLog.Enabled = True
          Else
            ' Call the function on the sub form to load the call events
            Me.fsubCasesEvents.Form.fctRefreshLog
          End If
      End If
      ' After loading the new case, set the Boolean 'saved' marker
      ' to true (or saved).
      blnSaved = True
      ' .. and hide the save instruction label
      Me.lblSaveCase.Visible = False
      ' .. and mark the event "not dirty"
      blnEventDirty = False
      ' Put the focus in a safe place
      Me.cmbOwnerID.SetFocus
      ' Disable save and undo
      Me.cmdSave.Enabled = False
      Me.cmdUndo.Enabled = False
      'Refresh the sub form display
      Me.fsubCasesEvents.Requery
      ' Return success
      fctReLoadRecord = True
  okfctReLoadRecord:
    Exit Function
  errfctReLoadRecord:
      ' Got an error - set failure
      fctReLoadRecord = False
      ' Display and log the error
      ErrTryingTo "load the case and event data"
      Resume okfctReLoadRecord
  End Function
```

To be able to see all the events for a case, the subform at the bottom of the form is a form in Continuous Forms view that is bound to a local table. When loading a case, the code in the form must also load the related event information into the tvwCasesEvents table. As you saw previously, the *fctReLoadRecord* function calls the *fctRefreshEvents* function to perform this task. The code in that function clears the tvwCases table and executes an insert query to load the rows from the tblCasesEvents table on the server for local viewing. The code is as follows:

```
Function fctRefreshEvents(lngID As Long) As Boolean
' Called from the fctReLoadRecord function
'  to reload the local view of the events for
'  the current case.  Input: CaseID
```

```
Dim db As DAO.DataBase
  ' Set an error trap
  On Error GoTo ErrRefresh     'Enable error trapping
  ' Point to this database
  Set db = DBEngine(0)(0)
  ' Empty the local Call Events table (delete everything).
  db.Execute "DELETE * FROM tvwCasesEvents", dbFailOnError
  ' Update the table with the call events from
  ' the source table on the server
  db.Execute "INSERT INTO tvwCasesEvents " & _
    "SELECT tblCasesEvents.* FROM tblCasesEvents " & _
    "WHERE tblCasesEvents.CaseID = " & lngID
  'Refresh the view of the call events on the form
  Me.fsubCasesEvents.Requery
  ' Clear the database object
  Set db = Nothing
  ' Return successful
  fctRefreshEvents = True
RefreshOk:
  Exit Function
ErrRefresh:
  ' Error - set failure
  fctRefreshEvents = False
  ' Display and log the error
  ErrTryingTo "reload case events"
  ' Bail
  Resume RefreshOk
End Function
```

Of course, if you're using forms bound directly to linked tables in the shared data file on the server, you can avoid most of this extra code. But keep in mind that this extra effort is necessary to support 50 or more simultaneous users.

Editing Cases and Case Events

To understand how a customer support representative might work with the frmCases form, you can create a new case. If you still have the frmCases form open from the previous section, click the New Case button at the bottom of the form. Or, you can return to the main switchboard (shown in Figure 17-1 on page 352) and click the New Case button.

Let's assume an existing customer is calling to register a new product just purchased. First, the support representative needs to find the customer record. Click the Search button under Customer at the top of the form to open the fpopCustomersFind form. The customer says her last name is Dellamore, so type the letters **del** in the Last Name field and click the Search button to obtain the list of customers, as shown in Figure 17-4.

After verifying that the customer is, indeed, Luca Dellamore in Ferrelview, Missouri, click the Select button on the fpopCustomersFind form to select that customer for the case. When you return to the frmCases form, you should find that customer name filled in. Next, click the Search button under Product to open the Select A Product window (the fdlgCasesProducts form) that lists the products registered for the current customer. Because the customer wants to register a new product, click the New Registration button in the Select A Product window to open the fdlgRegistration form, as shown in Figure 17-5.

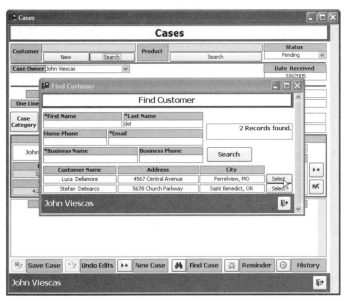

Figure 17-4 Selecting a customer for a new case.

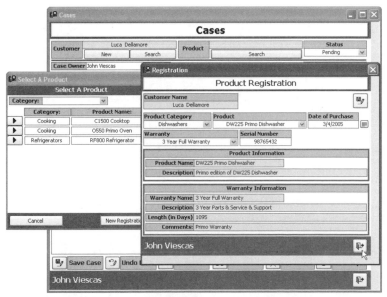

Figure 17-5 Registering a new product while creating a new case record.

Select Dishwashers in Product Category, select the DW225 model in Product, enter the date the customer purchased the product in Date of Purchase, select the warranty, and type the serial number the customer supplies. Click the Close button at the bottom of the form, and you should see the product added to the list of products in the Select A Product window. Click the arrow button next to that product to add it to the case.

When you click the Search button on the frmCases form for products, code in the Click event procedure for the button first makes sure you have specified a customer. When a customer ID exists, the code clears the tvwRegistrations table, loads the registration records for the current customer into that table, and then opens the fdlgCasesProducts form (the Select A Product window) that is bound to the local table. The code is as follows:

```
Private Sub cmdProductSearch_Click()
Dim db As DAO.DataBase
  ' Set an error trap
  On Error GoTo errCmdProductSearch      'Enable error trapping
  ' Make sure a customer has been selected
  If IsNothing(Me.txtCustomerID) Then
    ' Tell user to pick customer first
    CustomError "You must select a customer " & _
      "before searching for a product."
    ' Put the focus on customer search
    Me.cmdCustomerSearch.SetFocus
    ' Exit
    Exit Sub
  End If
  ' Point to this database
  Set db = DBEngine(0)(0)
  ' Empty the local Registrations table (delete everything).
  db.Execute "DELETE * FROM tvwRegistrations", dbFailOnError
  ' Update the table with the registrations
  '  from the source table on the server
  db.Execute "INSERT INTO tvwRegistrations " & _
    "SELECT tblRegistrations.* FROM tblRegistrations " & _
    "WHERE tblRegistrations.CustomerID = " & Me.txtCustomerID
  'Open the form that displays the available registered products
  DoCmd.OpenForm "fdlgCasesProducts"
okCmdProductSearch:
  ' Clear the database object
  Set db = Nothing
  Exit Sub
errCmdProductSearch:
  ' Display and log the error
  ErrTryingTo "load product search records for a case"
  Resume okCmdProductSearch
End Sub
```

On the fdlgCasesProducts form, the code in the Click event procedure for the cmdNewReg button (New Registration) opens the fdlgRegistration form. As it opens the form, the code passes an open argument to let the form know that it is being called from the context of editing a case, not from editing a customer. The code is as follows:

```
Private Sub cmdNewReg_Click()
    ' Open the new product registration form
```

```
'    - pass it a parameter telling it to
'       create a new product for a case
   DoCmd.OpenForm "fdlgRegistration", OpenArgs:="Cases"
End Sub
```

The code in the Open event procedure of the fdlgRegistration form examines the argument passed to it to determine which forms the code needs to verify are open and to obtain customer information from the correct calling form. When called from the fdlgCasesProducts form (OpenArgs set to "Cases"), the code verifies that both the fdlgCasesProducts form and the frmCases form are open. If the correct forms are open, the code sets the default customer ID and name fields on the form. The code is as follows:

```
Private Sub Form_Open(Cancel As Integer)
  ' Emulate form icon - Access 2000
  SetFormIcon Me.hWnd, IconPath
  ' If called from fdlgCasesProducts
  If Me.OpenArgs = "Cases" Then
    ' Always adding a new one - clear Registration ID
    Me.txtRegistrationID = Null
    ' Make sure the correct forms are open
    If (Not IsFormLoaded("fdlgCasesProducts")) _
      Or (Not IsFormLoaded("frmCases")) Then
      ' Tell the user about the problem
      CustomError "The Cases window and the " & _
        "Select a Product window must be open."
      ' Cancel the open
      Cancel = True
      Exit Sub
    End If
    ' Grab the customer ID from frmCases
    Me.txtCustomerID = Form_frmCases.txtCustomerID
    ' Grab the customer name
    Me.txtCustomerName = Form_frmCases.txtCustomerName
```

When called from the frmCustomers form, the OpenArgs parameter is blank or contains the registration ID of a product to edit. The code verifies that the frmCustomers form is open and copies the customer ID and name from that form. Finally, the code calls the *fctReLoadRecord* function in that form's module to either clear the form for a new record or load the record specified from the frmCustomers form. The code is as follows:

```
  Else
    ' Won't work if frmCustomers not open
    If Not IsFormLoaded("frmCustomers") Then
      CustomError "The Customers window must be open."
      ' Cancel the open
      Cancel = True
      Exit Sub
    End If
    ' If not passed a registration ID,
    If IsNothing(Me.OpenArgs) Then
      ' Clear it
      Me.txtRegistrationID = Null
```

```
    Else
      ' Set the registration ID
      Me.txtRegistrationID = Me.OpenArgs
    End If
    ' Get the customer ID
    Me.txtCustomerID = Form_frmCustomers.txtCustomerID
    ' Get the customer name
    Me.txtCustomerName = Form_frmCustomers.txtCustomerName
  End If
  ' Load (or clear) the record
  Call fctReLoadRecord
End Sub
```

Sure enough, when you return to your new case record in the frmCases form, you can see both the customer and the product set for the case. In One Line Description, indicate that the customer is registering a new purchase. Click the Case Category button and select Product, Assistance, and Registration in the list boxes that appear. Choose Product Information / Assistance as the Action, enter details in Case Notes, and click Save Case, as shown in Figure 17-6.

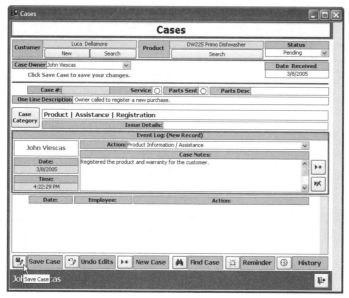

Figure 17-6   Saving the completed case record.

You should see the new case event appear in the list in the subform window at the bottom of the form. Congratulations! You have just successfully created your first case.

Ensuring Cases Have at Least One Case Event

Remember, at the beginning of the chapter you learned that all cases must have at least one case event. Enforcing this rule is actually much simpler using an unbound form because the user has no way to try to save a case without using the Save Case button. In a bound form with a subform, navigating to another record would save the case in the outer form without guaranteeing that the user had entered at least one case event. The alternative to using a bound form would be to use a record source that joined tblCases with tblCasesEvents, but that would make it difficult to edit the case data without affecting (and locking) the case event data.

The code that ensures that the user has entered at least one case event for a case is in the *fctCheckSaved* function in the frmCases form. This code works similarly to the code you have already seen described for products in Chapter 3 and customers in Chapter 16. Near the beginning of the function, the code checks to see if a new case is being added (the txtCaseID text box control does not yet have a value). If it is a new record, the code sets the blnNewRec variable to True.

When the data hasn't been saved (at least one control has changed), the code calls the *ValidateRecord* function that you can find in the modRecordEditor module to verify that the user has supplied all the values required for a case record. Next the code checks the border color of the txtCategoryDetail control to see if it has been set to red. Code that runs when the user clicks the Case Category toggle button sets this color when the user selects a category that requires additional detail explanation. (The DetailReq field for the selected category is True in the tlkpCaseCategories table.) When the border of the txtCategoryDetail control is red, the user must enter something in the txtCategoryDetail text box.

Finally, the code checks to see if any control in the case event area has changed (blnEventDirty = True) or if this is a new record (blnNewRec = True). If so, the code calls the *ValidateRecord* function again to ask it to verify that all required fields for the case event have been entered. So, if the user enters only the case data for a new record but doesn't fill out at least one case event, the edit will fail, and the *ValidateRecord* function returns an error message. Because code validates both the case and the case event before saving anything, the user must enter both the case data and the case event data for a new case. The code is as follows:

```
' If no Case ID yet,
If IsNothing(Me.txtCaseID) Then
  ' Set the new record flag
  blnNewRec = True
Else
  ' Have case ID - save it
  lngID = Me.txtCaseID
  blnNewRec = False
End If
' Save the Event ID, if any
If Not IsNothing(Me.txtEventID) Then
  lngEID = Me.txtEventID
End If
'If the current record already saved,
If blnSaved = True Then
  ' Confirm saved and exit
  fctCheckSaved = "Saved"
```

```
    Else
      ' Validate the case data - returns ZLS if successful
      strErrMsg = ValidateRecord("frmCases", "frmCases")
      ' If the user chose a category that requires
      '  a detailed explanation, the border color is red (255).
      ' If detail required, and nothing supplied,
      If Me.txtCategoryDetail.BorderColor = vbRed _
        And IsNothing(Me.txtCategoryDetail) Then
        ' Add to the error message
        strErrMsg = strErrMsg & " -Category Details" & vbCrLf
      End If
    ' Check event if changed or a new record
    '  (Force at least one event for a new case.)
    If (blnEventDirty = True) Or (blnNewRec = True) Then
      ' Validate the case event data - returns ZLS if successful
      strEventMsg = ValidateRecord("frmCases", "frmCasesEvents")
    End If
    ' If one of the two error strings is not empty,
    If strErrMsg <> "" Or strEventMsg <> "" Then
      ' If had a case event error,
      If strEventMsg <> "" Then
        ' Put a heading on it
        strEventMsg = vbCrLf & "*****Case Event*****" & _
          vbCrLf & strEventMsg
      End If
      ' Set up the error message display
      strErrMsg = "The Record could not be saved because " & _
        "the following fields are incomplete: " & _
        vbCrLf & vbCrLf & "*****Case*****" & vbCrLf & _
        strErrMsg & strEventMsg & vbCrLf & _
        "What would you like to do?"
      ' Display the message - if user clicked cancel,
      If CustomError(strErrMsg, OkCancel, "Could not save record", _
        Question, SecondButton) = "Cancel Changes" Then
        ' Return that edit was canceled
        fctCheckSaved = "Cancel"
        ' Clear all data to a new screen
        Call fctReLoadRecord
      Else
        ' User clicked - OK, wants to work on it some more
        ' Return that edit failed, but still dirty
        fctCheckSaved = "Ok"
        ' Make sure record not marked saved
        fctDirty
      End If
```

You might think that the user can enter a "dummy" case event, save the case, then delete the event, but you'd be wrong. If you still have the new case open that you created in the previous section, try editing the single case event and then clicking the Delete Event Log button to the right of the event editing area. The application tells you that you cannot delete the event because it is the last (only) one, as shown in Figure 17-7.

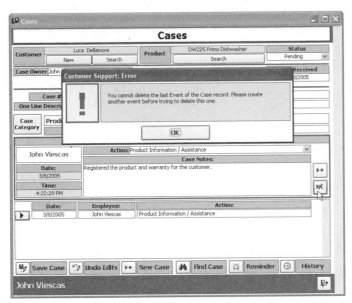

Figure 17-7   The application will not let the user delete the only event for a case.

As you might expect, code in the Click event procedure for the command button is doing the checking. The code obtains the RecordCount property from the RecordSetClone object in the subform that lists all the events for the case. If the count is greater than 1, the code calls the *DeleteRecord* function in the modRecordEditor module to delete the event from both the server and local tables, requeries the subform, clears the edit area, and exits. If only one record is left, the code displays the error message you saw in Figure 17-7. The code is as follows:

```
Private Sub cmdDeleteLog_Click()
'Delete the current call event
Dim intI As Integer
Dim strMsg As String
  On Error GoTo errcmdDeleteLog
  ' If nothing in EventID, nothing to delete
  If IsNothing(Me.txtEventID) Then Exit Sub
  ' Get the count of rows in the subform
  intI = Me.fsubCasesEvents.Form.RecordsetClone.RecordCount
  'If there are more than one call events, OK to delete the current event
  If intI > 1 Then
    ' Call the function that deletes the record
    If DeleteRecord("frmCases", "frmCasesEvents", "tblCasesEvents", _
      Me.txtEventID, True, _
      "tvwCasesEvents", "Event") = True Then
      ' Delete worked - requery the subform
      Me.fsubCasesEvents.Requery
      ' Clear the event log editable data
      cmdNewLog_Click
    End If
```

```
    Else
      ' The last case event of the case cannot be deleted.
      strMsg = "You cannot delete the last Event " & _
        "of the Case record. Please create another event " & _
        "before trying to delete this one."
      Call CustomError(strMsg, OK, , Caution)
    End If
okcmdDeleteLog:
  Exit Sub
errcmdDeleteLog:
  ' Display and log the error
  ErrTryingTo "delete event record"
  Resume okcmdDeleteLog
End Sub
```

Restricting Users to Editing Their Own Case Events

Any customer support representative can answer the next call, so the original support representative might not handle all subsequent calls on a case. When editing a case, a support representative should be able to view the detailed history of previous events but not change or delete events entered by other representatives.

To try this out, you can edit a case opened by another support representative. If you're still signed on as me, go to the main switchboard (shown in Figure 17-1 on page 352) and click the Find button under Cases. In the fpopCasesFind (Find Case) form (shown in Figure 17-2 on page 352), set the date range for the first quarter of 2005, enter **484** in the Case # box, and click the Search button. The search should return one case for customer Ken Myer that was entered by support representative Bonnie Kearney. Click the Open button on the Find Case form to open that case.

As with any case that has already been saved, you can see a list of case events in the subform window in the bottom of the form. Click the arrow button next to any event to move it to the edit/view area in the middle of the form. You should see the details of that event, as shown in Figure 17-8, but you can't change any of the values (they appear with a gray background), and the Delete Event Log button is disabled.

The code that loads the details for the selected event to the edit/view area in the middle of the frmCases form is in the Click event procedure for the cmdViewEvent button on the fsubCasesEvents form. The code first calls the *fctCheckSaved* function in the parent form (frmCases) to ensure that all previous changes have been saved. If an error occurs and the user chooses to keep working, the code exits. If the current row has a valid event ID, the code copies that ID to the edit/view area on the outer form and calls the *fctRefreshLog* function to load the record.

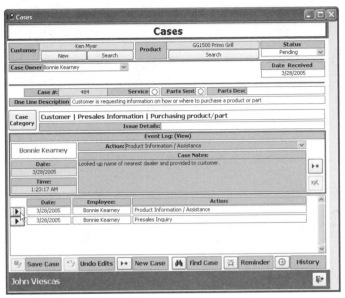

Figure 17-8   You cannot edit or delete a case event created by another user.

The code is as follows:

```
Private Sub cmdViewEvent_Click()
  ' User wants to edit the current event
  ' Call the outer form save routine -
  '  If not saved, bail
  If Me.Parent.fctCheckSaved <> "Saved" Then Exit Sub
  ' Make sure I have an Event ID
  If IsNothing(Me.txtEventID) Then
    ' Bail if none
    Exit Sub
  End If
  ' Copy my event ID to the parent
  Me.Parent.txtEventID = Me.txtEventID
  ' Refresh my rows
  Me.Refresh
  ' Load this record
  fctRefreshLog
End Sub
```

The *fctRefreshLog* function moves the data for the selected event to the frmCases form and controls whether the current user can edit or delete the data. The code first makes sure it has a valid event ID. (This should always be the case, but it doesn't hurt to check.) If an event ID exists, the code obtains a copy of the form's recordset. (Remember, this form is bound to the tvwCasesEvents table containing all the events for the current case.) It tries to find the requested event ID in the form's recordset. If the event ID is not found, the code clears the event controls in the frmCases form and exits.

When the code finds the record, it compares the employee ID of the event record with the ID of the current user. (The *CurrentID* function in the modGlobals module returns the ID of the current user.) If the IDs do not match, the code locks all the controls, sets the back color of the controls to light gray, and disables the Delete command button. If the record was originally created by the current user, the code unlocks all the controls, sets the back color of the controls to white, and enables the Delete command button. Finally, the code copies the data from the selected record to the outer form. The code is as follows:

```
Public Function fctRefreshLog()
' Called from cmdViewEvent click and parent form
'  reload procedure to load event data into
'  editable controls on the outer form.
Dim rst As Recordset
Dim frm As Form
  ' If there is no current event ID, nothing to do
  If IsNothing(Me.Parent.txtEventID) Then Exit Function
  ' Point to the outer form
  Set frm = Me.Parent
  ' Get a copy of this form's recordset
  Set rst = Me.RecordsetClone
  ' Try to find the event requested
  rst.FindFirst "EventID = " & Me.Parent.txtEventID
  ' If not found
  If rst.NoMatch Then
    ' Clear the outer form controls and bail
    frm.txtEventID = Null
    frm.txtEventTime = Null
    frm.cmbActionID = Null
    frm.txtNotes = Null
    ' Set the caption
    frm.lblEventLog.Caption = "Event Log: (New Record)"
    ' Clear the recordset
    Set rst = Nothing
    ' and the form object
    Set frm = Nothing
    ' And bail
    Exit Function
  End If
  ' Move to the found record
  Me.Bookmark = rst.Bookmark
  ' Clear the recordset
  Set rst = Nothing
  ' If record created by another employee
  If CurrentID() <> Me.EmployeeID Then
    ' Lock the controls and
    '  set back color to gray
    frm.txtNotes.Locked = True
    frm.txtNotes.BackColor = RGB(192, 192, 192)
    frm.cmbActionID.Locked = True
    frm.cmbActionID.BackColor = RGB(192, 192, 192)
    frm.cmdDeleteLog.Enabled = False
    ' Set the caption to indicate read-only
    frm.lblEventLog.Caption = "Event Log: (View)"
```

```
    Else
        ' Unlock the controls and
        '  set back color to white
        frm.txtNotes.Locked = False
        frm.txtNotes.BackColor = vbWhite
        frm.cmbActionID.Locked = False
        frm.cmbActionID.BackColor = vbWhite
        frm.cmdDeleteLog.Enabled = True
        ' Indicate this is editable
        frm.lblEventLog.Caption = "Event Log: (Edit)"
    End If
    ' Copy the data to the outer form
    frm.txtEventID = Me.EventID
    frm.cmbEmployeeID = Me.EmployeeID
    frm.txtEventTime = Me.EventTime
    frm.cmbActionID = Me.ActionID
    frm.txtNotes = Me.Notes
    ' Clear the form object
    Set frm = Nothing
End Function
```

Note that the txtEventID, cmbEmployeeID, and txtEventTime controls are not visible on the frmCases form, so the user can't directly edit these values. The setting of these fields is controlled completely by the code in the frmCases and fsubCasesEvents forms.

You should now have a good idea of how cases and case events are handled in the Customer Support sample application. In the next chapter, you'll see how a customer support representative can set a reminder for a callback. You'll also learn how code in the main switchboard tracks pending reminders and allows the user to edit them and go directly to related cases.

Chapter 18

Tracking Reminders

A key component of any contact management or customer support application is the ability to set a future reminder to follow up on an outstanding issue. In the Customer Support sample application, users can define one or more reminders for a support case and establish a date and a range of times for that date to follow up with the customer.

To add a reminder feature to any application, you need a table to store the reminders, a method for creating reminders in the appropriate context, and a way to notify the user when a reminder is about to be due or is overdue. The user must also be able to mark reminders complete so that they no longer show up in any alert list. This chapter explains how these features have been implemented in the Customer Support sample application (Support.mdb).

Note The Customer Support sample application assumes that more than 50 users might need to be running the application simultaneously. To provide adequate performance when sharing a data file in the Access desktop database format (.mdb file), the application uses no forms or reports that are bound to data on the server. To understand the architectural design of this application, you should read the section "Pushing the Envelope" on page 85.

Understanding the Table Structure

In some applications, you might be able to store reminder information directly in the table related to the reminder as long as you need no more than one reminder for any particular event. The Customer Support application uses a separate tblReminders table to store reminders because an individual support case might need more than one reminder.

The fields in the tblReminders table, shown in Table 18-1 on the next page, contain the ID of the related support case, the ID of the employee who is responsible for the reminder, the date on which the reminder should be completed, and a range of times on that date that the customer indicated would be the best times to call. The reminder also includes a short description, a memo field to add extensive notes, and a Yes/No field that the user can set when the reminder has been completed.

Table 18-1   The Fields in the tblReminders Table

Field Name	Data Type	Required	Description
ReminderID	AutoNumber	N/A	Unique reminder identifier.
CaseID	Long Integer	Yes	Related customer case.
CommitEmployeeID	Long Integer	Yes	Employee responsible for the reminder.
CommitDate	Date/Time	Yes	Date to complete the reminder.
FromTime	Date/Time	Yes	Earliest time to handle the reminder.
ToTime	Date/Time	Yes	Time reminder must be completed by.
ReminderInfo	Text, Field Size 100	No	Short description of the reminder.
ReminderNote	Memo	Yes	Detailed notes about the reminder.
Complete	Yes/No	No	Reminder has been completed.

Creating and Editing Reminders

An application that has a reminder feature should provide a simple way for the user to create and edit or view a reminder when working on the task or event for which the reminder should be set. You might have noticed in the previous chapter that the form to edit cases has a convenient command button in the form footer to go directly to reminders.

Creating a New Reminder for a Case

In Chapter 17, "Capturing Support Cases," you learned how a user might typically create a new support case for a customer who called to register a new product purchase. Open the Customer Support database (Support.mdb) and then open the frmSplash form to start the application and sign on as me. (Enter **jviescas** in the User Name field and **password** in the Password field.)

If, in the previous chapter, you created the new support case for Luca Dellamore, click Find under Cases on the main switchboard, search for that case, and open it. You can also click Find under Cases on the main switchboard and open any case that has a Pending status. To create a new reminder for the case, click the Reminder button at the bottom of the window, as shown in Figure 18-1.

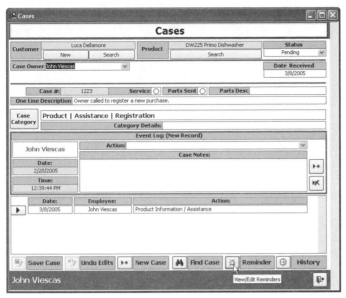

Figure 18-1   Choosing the option to create a reminder for a support case.

Let's assume that management has asked all support representatives to schedule a callback within 30 days to ask the customer if he or she is satisfied with the new purchase. On the Edit Reminders form, enter a date one month in the future, set the Time From field to 9:00 AM and the To field to 5:00 PM, and then enter an appropriate short description in the Info field and a detailed description in the Reminder Notes field. Click the Save button as shown in Figure 18-2 to save the reminder.

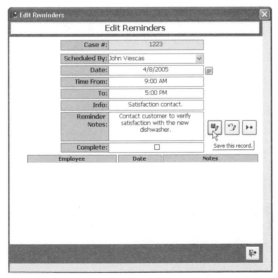

Figure 18-2   Creating and saving a new reminder.

As soon as you click the Save button, you should see your new reminder appear in the list of reminders for the case in the bottom of the form. Click the Close button in the lower right corner to return to the Cases window.

As with all forms in this application, the fdlgReminderSetup form shown in Figure 18-2 is not bound to any data on the server. When you click the Reminder button on the frmCases form, code in that button's Click event procedure clears existing rows in the tvwReminders local table, fetches existing reminders for the current case into that table, and opens the fdlgReminderSetup form. The code is as follows:

```
Private Sub cmdSetReminder_Click()
Dim db As DAO.DataBase
  ' User has asked to set a reminder
  ' Set an error trap
  On Error GoTo errCmdSetReminder
  ' If data not saved,
  If (blnSaved = False) Then
    ' Save the case first, but bail if fails
    If fctCheckSaved() <> "Saved" Then
      Exit Sub
    End If
  End If
  ' Bail if no CaseID
  If IsNothing(Me.txtCaseID) Then Exit Sub
  ' Point to this database
  Set db = DBEngine(0)(0)
  ' Empty the local reminders table (delete everything).
  db.Execute "DELETE * FROM tvwReminders", dbFailOnError
  ' Update the table with the reminders for this case
  '  from the source table on the server
  db.Execute "INSERT INTO tvwReminders " & _
    "SELECT tblReminders.* FROM tblReminders " & _
    "WHERE tblReminders.CaseID = " & Me.txtCaseID
  ' Clear the database object
  Set db = Nothing
  ' Open the reminder setup form
  DoCmd.OpenForm "fdlgReminderSetup"
okCmdSetReminder:
  Exit Sub
errCmdSetReminder:
  'Log and return the error
  ErrTryingTo ("retrieve reminder information")
  Resume okCmdSetReminder
End Sub
```

When you enter data for a new reminder in the fdlgReminderSetup form, you are updating unbound controls. Code in the Click event procedure for the cmdSave command button calls the *fctCheckSaved* function in the form's module to perform the save. (The *fctCheckSaved* function for reminders is very similar to the same function for customers and cases that you studied in previous chapters.) If the save is successful, the code requeries the form to display the new record in the list of reminders in the bottom part of the form. If the *fctCheckSaved* function returns an error indicating that the user wants to cancel all edits, the code calls the *fctReLoadRecord* function to either clear the new record or load a previously selected existing record. The code is as follows:

```
Public Sub cmdSave_Click()
Dim strAnswer As String
  ' User wants to save changes
  ' If not saved,
  If blnSaved = False Then
    ' Call the record saver
    strAnswer = fctCheckSaved
    ' If saved,
    If strAnswer = "Saved" Then
      ' Rebuild my recordset
      Me.Requery
    ' If user wants to cancel
    ElseIf strAnswer = "Cancel" Then
        ' Reload the record
        Call fctReLoadRecord
    End If
  End If
End Sub
```

The *fctCheckSaved* function for saving reminders is very similar to the ones described in previous chapters for customers, cases, and case events. The code first calls the *ValidateRecord* function in the modRecordEditor module to verify that the user has provided all required fields. If that function returns an error message, the code displays the error and asks the user if the changes should be cleared (Cancel Changes) or the user wants to keep working on the current record (OK). The code returns the answer to the code that called it in the Click event of the cmdSave command button. The code is as follows:

```
Private Function fctCheckSaved()
' This code checks that the required information
' is complete and then saves the record and
' flags the linked table for an update
Dim strMsg As String, lngID As Long
  ' Set an error trap
  On Error GoTo errfctCheckSaved
  ' If already saved,
  If blnSaved = True Then
    ' Return success
    fctCheckSaved = "Saved"
    ' and exit
    Exit Function
  End If
  ' Grab the current reminder ID
  lngID = Nz(Me.txtReminderID, 0)
  ' Call record validation to check for required data
  strMsg = ValidateRecord("fdlgReminderSetup", "fdlgReminderSetup")
  ' Return message is zero length string (ZLS) if OK
  If strMsg <> "" Then
    ' Build the error message
```

```
    strMsg = "The record could not be saved because " & _
      "the following fields must be completed: " & _
      vbCrLf & vbCrLf & strMsg & vbCrLf & _
      "What would you like to do?"
  ' Ask the user what to do
  If CustomError(strMsg, OkCancel, "Save Reminder Record", _
      Question) = "Cancel Changes" Then
      ' User gives up - return cancel
      fctCheckSaved = "Cancel"
  Else
      ' User wants to continue edit - return OK
      fctCheckSaved = "Ok"
  End If
  ' Make sure still marked not saved
  blnSaved = False
```

When the validation is successful, the code calls the *SaveRecord* function in the modRecord-Editor module to save the changes to both the tblReminders table on the server and the tvwReminders local table. If the save is successful, the code marks the record saved, requeries the form's recordset to display any changes, makes sure the focus is not on a command button about to be disabled, and disables the Undo and Save command buttons. (These buttons become enabled again if the user makes a subsequent change to one of the editable controls.) If the save fails, the code assumes that the user wants to keep working after the error (the *SaveRecord* function displays the cause of the error), so it returns OK to the calling procedure and leaves the record marked unsaved. The code is as follows:

```
Else
    ' Call the record saver to
    ' update both the remote table
    ' and the local copy.
    If SaveRecord("fdlgReminderSetup", "fdlgReminderSetup", _
      "tblReminders", lngID, _
      "tvwReminders", "Reminder") <> 0 Then
      ' Got a nonzero answer - OK
      ' Return success
      fctCheckSaved = "Saved"
      ' Mark the record saved
      blnSaved = True
      ' Rebuild my recordset to show any added record
      Me.Requery
      ' Put the focus in a safe place
      Me.cmbEmployeeID.SetFocus
      ' Disable the Undo button
      Me.cmdUndo.Enabled = False
      ' .. and the Save button
      Me.cmdSave.Enabled = False
    Else
      ' Something failed -
      fctCheckSaved = "Ok"
      ' Leave record marked not saved
      blnSaved = False
    End If
End If
```

```
   'Done!
okfctCheckSaved:
  Exit Function
errfctCheckSaved:
  ' Display and log error
  ErrTryingTo "save reminder data"
  ' Clear the record so we don't get an unending loop
  Me.txtReminderID = 0
  fctReLoadRecord
  Resume okfctCheckSaved
End Function
```

Editing an Existing Reminder

Let's assume that it's now a month later and the user needs to update the reminder created earlier—perhaps to note that a call was attempted but was unsuccessful and to change the scheduled date. The user can return to the case record, click the Reminder button, and see all reminders previously saved for the current case listed in the bottom portion of the fdlgReminderSetup form. The user can click the arrow button to the left of the reminder that needs to be edited, as shown in Figure 18-3. Code in the form's module moves the record to the editing area in the top part of the form. A conditional formatting specification highlights the record being edited.

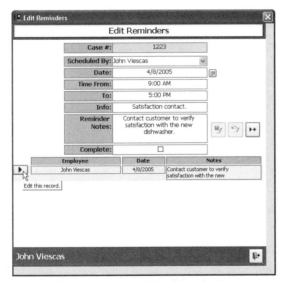

Figure 18-3 Click the **Edit this record** button to edit a saved reminder.

The Click event procedure of the cmdEditRecord command button first makes sure any previous changes are saved by calling the *fctCheckSaved* function. If an error occurred (the function returned an answer other than "Saved"), the code exits. If the save was successful, the code copies the ID of the selected record to the edit area (the txtReminderID text box is hidden) and calls the *fctReLoadRecord* function to move the selected record to the edit area. The code is as follows:

```
Private Sub cmdEditRecord_Click()
  ' User wants to edit this record
  ' If not saved,
  If blnSaved = False Then
    ' Call the record saver
    ' Returns "Saved" if no errors
    If fctCheckSaved <> "Saved" Then Exit Sub
  End If
  ' Set the reminder ID in the edit area
  Me.txtReminderID = Me.ReminderID
  ' Load this record
  Call fctReLoadRecord
End Sub
```

The *fctReLoadRecord* function in the form's module works similarly to the function with the same name that you saw in previous chapters to fetch a record to edit for customers or cases. If the reminder ID is Null or zero, the code assumes that the user wants to edit a new record, so it clears all the editable controls in the top part of the form. The reminder ID is set to zero when the user clicks the New Record button or when the form first opens. The code is as follows:

```
Private Function fctReLoadRecord()
Dim rst As DAO.Recordset
  ' Set an error trap
  On Error GoTo errfctReLoadRecord
  ' If Reminder ID is zero,
  If IsNothing(Me.txtReminderID) Then
    ' User wants to start a new record
    ' Clear all the controls
    Me.txtReminderID = Null
    Me.cmbEmployeeID = CurrentID()
    ' Set default reminder date in 2 weeks
    Me.txtDate = Date + 14
    Me.txtTimeFrom = Null
    Me.txtTimeTo = Null
    Me.txtReminderInfo = Null
    Me.txtRNotes = Null
    Me.chkComplete = False
```

When the reminder ID is not zero, the code uses the form's RecordsetClone property to obtain a copy of the form's recordset and uses that copy to search for the selected reminder. If the record is not found, the code displays an error and exits. If the code finds the record, it makes sure that that record is the current record for the form and then copies the field values to the unbound controls in the edit area. Before exiting, the code makes sure the record is marked saved (not changed) and disables the Save and Undo command buttons. (Code in the AfterUpdate event procedures for all the editable controls marks the record not saved and enables the command buttons whenever the user changes any value.) The code is as follows:

```
    Else
      ' Record should be in the current row source
      Set rst = Me.RecordsetClone
      ' Try to find it
      rst.FindFirst "ReminderID = " & Me.txtReminderID
      ' If not found,
      If rst.NoMatch Then
        ' Clear the recordset
        Set rst = Nothing
        ' Raise an error
        Err.Raise vbObjectError + 8199, , _
          "Reminder record requested not found."
      End If
      ' Move to the correct row
      Me.Bookmark = rst.Bookmark
      ' Clear the recordset
      Set rst = Nothing
      ' Copy the values
      Me.txtReminderID = Me.ReminderID
      Me.cmbEmployeeID = Me.CommitEmployeeID
      Me.txtDate = Me.CommitDate
      Me.txtTimeFrom = Me.FromTime
      Me.txtTimeTo = Me.ToTime
      Me.txtReminderInfo = Me.ReminderInfo
      Me.txtRNotes = Me.ReminderNote
    End If
    ' Mark the record saved
    blnSaved = True
    ' Refresh myself
    Me.Refresh
    ' Put the focus in a safe place
    Me.cmbEmployeeID.SetFocus
    ' Disable the Undo button
    Me.cmdUndo.Enabled = False
    ' .. and the Save button
    Me.cmdSave.Enabled = False
okfctReLoadRecord:
  Exit Function
errfctReLoadRecord:
  ' Display and log the error
  ErrTryingTo "load reminder record"
  ' Bail
  Resume okfctReLoadRecord
End Function
```

Tracking Future and Overdue Reminders

An important aspect of tracking reminders is to provide a way for the user to easily find
reminders that are due soon or that are overdue. You have probably noticed that the main
switchboard in the Customer Support application displays counts for future and overdue
reminders. Because I'm an administrator in the tblEmployees table, the form displays future
and overdue reminders for all employees.

To see a more interesting result, you should log in as one of the regular employees. If you still have the application running, return to the main switchboard and click the Log Out button to log in as a different user. If the application is not running, open the Customer Support database (Support.mdb) and then open the frmSplash form to start the application. Log in as Bonnie Kearney by entering **bkearney** in the User Name field and **password** in the Password field. When I set my system date to February 18, 2005, the main switchboard form displayed 453 future reminders and 14 overdue ones for Bonnie Kearney, as shown in Figure 18-4.

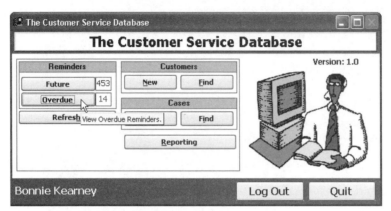

Figure 18-4   Each customer support representative can see current reminder status on the main switchboard.

The code that calculates these values is in the *fctCheckReminders* function in the module of the frmCSMain form. This function runs when the form first opens and again every 4 minutes to refresh the values. The code first constructs an SQL statement to count the number of rows in the tblReminders table where the commit date is earlier than the current date or the commit date is the current date but the deadline time has passed and the reminder has not been marked completed. If the class of the currently logged in user is "Agent" (not a manager or administrator), the code adds a filter for the employee's ID. The code executes the query to find the count, and if the count is zero, the code disables the overdue reminders command button. When the count is not zero (it can't be negative), the code enables the overdue reminders command button and displays the value in red. The code is as follows:

```
Private Function fctCheckReminders() As Boolean
' Function to check for overdue reminders
'  - Called from fctRefreshMain
Dim db As DAO.Database, rst As DAO.Recordset, strSQL As String
  fctCheckReminders = True
  On Error GoTo errfctCheckReminders
  ' Set up the query to count overdue reminders
  strSQL = "SELECT Count(tblReminders.ReminderID) " & _
    "AS CountOfReminderID " & _
    "FROM tblReminders " & _
    "WHERE (tblReminders.CommitDate = Date() " & _
    "AND tblReminders.ToTime < Time()) " & _
    "OR (tblReminders.CommitDate < Date()) " & _
```

```
     "AND tblReminders.Complete=False "
   ' If current user is an Agent
   If CurrentClass() = "Agent" Then
     ' Add a filter on employee ID
     strSQL = strSQL & " AND tblReminders.CommitEmployeeID = " & CurrentID()
   End If
   ' Point to this database
   Set db = DBEngine(0)(0)
   ' Open overdue reminders
   Set rst = db.OpenRecordset(strSQL, dbOpenDynaset, dbSeeChanges)
   'If count of reminders is zero
   If rst!CountOfReminderID = 0 Then
     ' Set the text color to black
     Me.Reminders0.ForeColor = vbBlack
     ' Display none overdue
     Me.Reminders0 = 0
     ' Make sure focus not on cmdReminders0
     Me.cmdRefresh.SetFocus
     ' Disable the command button
     Me.cmdReminders0.Enabled = False
   Else
     ' Set the text color to RED
     Me.Reminders0.ForeColor = vbRed
     ' Display the overdue count
     Me.Reminders0 = rst!CountOfReminderID
     ' Enable the command button
     Me.cmdReminders0.Enabled = True
   End If
   ' Close the recordset
   rst.Close
```

Next, the code constructs the SQL for a query to count the reminders that are in the future and not marked completed. Again, if the logged in user is an agent, the code adds a filter for the employee ID. When the count is zero, the code displays that value and disables the future reminders command button. When the count is not zero, the code displays the count and enables the command button. The code is as follows:

```
   ' Set up the query to count future reminders
   strSQL = "SELECT Count(tblReminders.ReminderID) " & _
     "AS CountOfReminderID " & _
     "FROM tblReminders " & _
     "WHERE (tblReminders.CommitDate = Date() " & _
     "AND tblReminders.ToTime > Time()) " & _
     "OR (tblReminders.CommitDate > Date()) " & _
     "AND tblReminders.Complete = False"
   ' If current user is an Agent
   If CurrentUser = "Agent" Then
     ' Add a filter on employee ID
     strSQL = strSQL & " AND tblReminders.CommitEmployeeID = " & CurrentID()
   End If
   ' Open the recordset
   Set rst = db.OpenRecordset(strSQL, dbOpenDynaset, dbSeeChanges)
   'If no records are found,
   If rst!CountOfReminderID = 0 Then
```

```
  ' Show no future reminders
  Me.RemindersC = 0
  ' Make sure the focus is not on cmdRemindersC button
  Me.cmdRefresh.SetFocus
  ' Disable the button
  Me.cmdRemindersC.Enabled = False
Else
  ' Show how many future reminders
  Me.RemindersC = rst!CountOfReminderID
  ' Enable the command button
  Me.cmdRemindersC.Enabled = True
End If
' Close the recordset
rst.Close
okfctCheckReminders:
  ' Clean up
  Set rst = Nothing
  Set db = Nothing
  Exit Function
errfctCheckReminders:
  ' Got an error - return failure
  fctCheckReminders = False
  Resume okfctCheckReminders
End Function
```

To view the overdue reminders, click the Overdue command button in the main switchboard. The application opens the frmReminders form to display the reminders that should have been completed in the past and that have not been marked complete. The form displays the oldest reminders first, as shown in Figure 18-5.

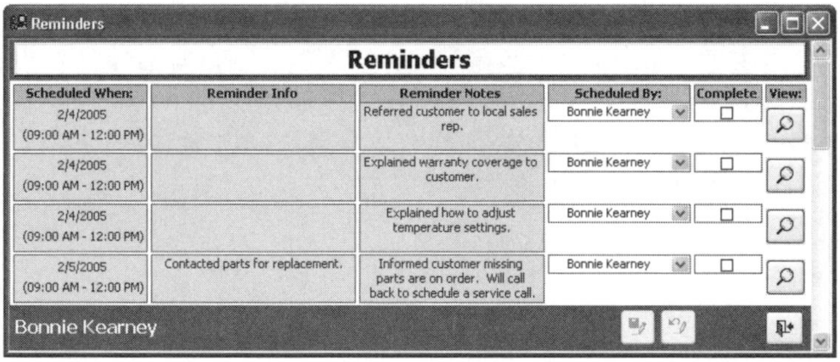

Figure 18-5 Reviewing overdue reminders for Bonnie Kearney on February 18, 2005.

The code in the Click event procedure for the cmdRemindersO command button closes the Reminders form if it is open and then reopens it. The code passes a parameter to the form to ask it to display overdue reminders for a specific class of employee based on the class of the currently logged in employee. The code is as follows:

```
Public Sub cmdRemindersO_Click()
  'If there are no overdue Reminders for the employee, exit
  If Me!RemindersO = 0 Then Exit Sub
  'If the Reminders form is open, close it
```

```
      If IsFormLoaded("frmReminders") = True Then
        DoCmd.Close acForm, "frmReminders"
      End If
      ' Open the frmReminders form and pass it a
      ' parameter based on the logged in employee's class
      Select Case CurrentClass
        Case "Supervisor", "Support", "Manager"
          DoCmd.OpenForm "frmReminders", OpenArgs:="SupO"
        Case Else
          DoCmd.OpenForm "frmReminders", OpenArgs:="EmpO"
      End Select
End Sub
```

As you might expect, the frmReminders form is not bound to data in the tblReminders table
on the server. Code in the Open event procedure of the frmReminders form examines the
parameter value and loads the appropriate records from the tblReminders table on the server
into the tvwReminders local table. It does this by first examining the value of the OpenArgs
property and building an SQL INSERT statement to load overdue agent records, overdue
supervisor records (for all employees), future agent records, or future supervisor records. If
the parameter doesn't match one of the four expected values, the code displays an error message, cancels opening the form, and exits. The code is as follows:

```
Public Sub Form_Open(Cancel As Integer)
Dim db As DAO.Database
Dim strSQL As String, intEmpID As Integer
  ' Set an error trap
  On Error GoTo errLoadReminders
  ' Emulate form icon in Access 2000
  SetFormIcon Me.hWnd, IconPath
  ' Get the current employee ID
  intEmpID = CurrentID()
  ' Set up the basic SQL for Insert
  strSQL = "INSERT INTO tvwReminders " & _
    "SELECT tblReminders.* FROM tblReminders "
  ' Test OpenArgs to see what records to load
  Select Case Me.OpenArgs
    Case "EmpO"
      ' Employee Overdue.  Load overdue
      ' reminders for the current employee (intEmpID)
      strSQL = strSQL & _
        "WHERE (tblReminders.CommitEmployeeID = " & intEmpID & _
        " And tblReminders.CommitDate = Date() And " &_
        "tblReminders.ToTime < Time() " & _
        "And tblReminders.Complete = False) Or " & _
        "(tblReminders.CommitEmployeeID = " & _
        intEmpID & " And tblReminders.CommitDate < Date() " & _
        "And tblReminders.Complete = False)"
    Case "EmpC"
      ' Employee Current.  Load current
      ' Reminders for the current employee (intEmpID)
      strSQL = strSQL & _
        "WHERE (tblReminders.CommitEmployeeID = " & intEmpID & _
        " And tblReminders.CommitDate = Date() And " & _
```

```
        "tblReminders.ToTime > Time() " & _
        "And tblReminders.Complete = False) Or " & _
        "(tblReminders.CommitEmployeeID = " & _
        intEmpID & " And tblReminders.CommitDate > Date() " & _
        "And tblReminders.Complete = False)"
    Case "SupO"
      ' Supervisor / Support / Manager Overdue.
      ' Load ALL overdue Reminders.
      strSQL = strSQL & _
        "WHERE (tblReminders.CommitDate = Date() And " & _
        "tblReminders.ToTime < Time() " & _
        "And tblReminders.Complete = False) Or " & _
        "(tblReminders.CommitDate < Date() " & _
        "And tblReminders.Complete = False)"
    Case "SupC"
      ' Supervisor  / Support / Manager Current.
      ' Load ALL current Reminders.
      strSQL = strSQL & _
        "WHERE (tblReminders.CommitDate = Date() And " & _
        "tblReminders.ToTime > Time() " & _
        "And tblReminders.Complete = False) Or " & _
        "(tblReminders.CommitDate > Date() " & _
        "And tblReminders.Complete = False)"
    Case Else
      CustomError "Invalid parameter passed to the Reminders form.", _
        OK, , Severe
      Cancel = True
      Exit Sub
  End Select
```

After building the appropriate SQL INSERT statement, the code clears the local tvwReminders table using an SQL DELETE statement and then executes the INSERT statement to load the correct records from the server. Finally, the code requeries the form to ensure that the form displays the correct data. The code is as follows:

```
  ' Point to this database
  Set db = DBEngine(0)(0)
  ' Clear out the local table
  db.Execute "DELETE tvwReminders.* FROM tvwReminders", dbFailOnError
  ' Load the data
  db.Execute strSQL, dbFailOnError
  ' Make sure the form sees the new data
  Me.Requery
okLoadReminders:
  Exit Sub
errLoadReminders:
  ' Display and log the error
  ErrTryingTo "load reminder data"
  ' Cancel the open
  Cancel = True
  ' Bail
  Resume okLoadReminders
End Sub
```

Editing Related Cases

When the user sees the list of reminders displayed in the frmReminders form, the user can scan the list and click the magnifying glass button next to the case of interest to view the details. When I clicked the first overdue reminder for Bonnie Kearney, the application opened the related support case, as shown in Figure 18-6.

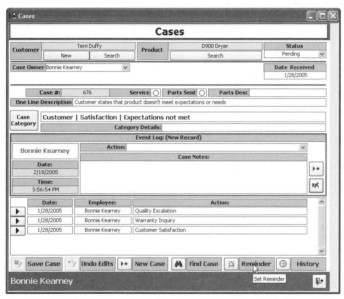

Figure 18-6   Editing a case that has an overdue reminder.

The code in the Click event procedure for the cmdViewOriginal command button on the frmReminders form first makes sure that the row selected has a valid case ID. If the frmCases form is already open, the code calls that form's *fctCheckSaved* function to ensure that any changes have been saved. If an error occurred while attempting to save the record and the user chose to keep working, the function returns "Ok" and the code exits. If the save completed successfully, the code sets the case ID on the frmCases form and calls that form's *fctReLoadRecord* function to open the requested case. If the frmCases form is not open, the code opens the form and passes it the case ID so that the frmCases form will load the requested case. The code is as follows:

```
Private Sub cmdViewOriginal_Click()
  ' Set an error trap
  On Error GoTo errViewReminder
  ' Make sure we have a CaseID
  If IsNothing(Me.CaseID) Then Exit Sub
  ' If cases already open
  If IsFormLoaded("frmCases") Then
    ' Call that form's save function
    '  - Returns OK if there's an error and user
    '     wants to keep working
```

```
    If Form_frmCases.fctCheckSaved = "Ok" Then Exit Sub
    ' Set the CaseID
    Form_frmCases.txtCaseID = Me.CaseID
    ' Ask the form to load that record
    Form_frmCases.fctReLoadRecord
    ' Put the focus there
    Form_frmCases.SetFocus
  Else
    ' Open the form and give it the case to display
    DoCmd.OpenForm "frmCases", _
      OpenArgs:=Me.CaseID
  End If
  ' Close me
  DoCmd.Close acForm, Me.Name
okViewReminder:
  Exit Sub
errViewReminder:
  ' Display and log the error
  ErrTryingTo "open related case for a reminder"
  Resume okViewReminder:
End Sub
```

Marking Reminders Complete

The user has two choices for marking a reminder complete. If the user wants to add comments to the reminder to document what happened, the user can find the reminder on the frmReminders form, open the related case, and then click the Reminder button at the bottom of the frmCases form to edit the reminders. The user can then return to the specific case and add one more case event to further document the call.

After I opened case #676 for Bonnie Kearney, I clicked the Reminder button on the frmCases form to view all three outstanding reminders for the case, as shown in Figure 18-7. I edited the first reminder, added comments to the Reminder Notes field, set the reminder as Complete, and clicked the Save button.

It was a simple matter to close the Reminders window to return to the case, add a case event to document the call, and close the case. After returning to the main switchboard and clicking the Refresh button or waiting 4 minutes, the Overdue count refreshed to show one less overdue reminder.

You might have noticed that the user can also mark the reminder complete on the frmReminders form. When the user marks a reminder complete on that form, code in the BeforeUpdate event procedure of the form asks the user to confirm the change, as shown in Figure 18-8. The application asks for a confirmation on this form because the user is simply marking the reminder complete without editing the reminder or the related case to add comments about how the reminder was completed.

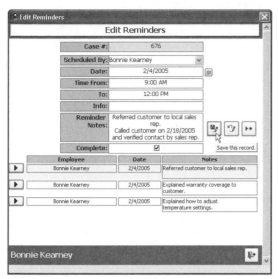

Figure 18-7   Updating a reminder and marking it complete.

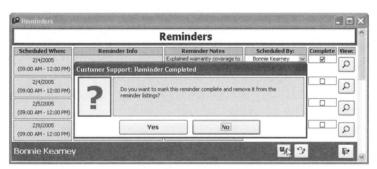

Figure 18-8   Marking a reminder complete on the Reminders form.

The code in the BeforeUpdate event of the frmReminders form checks to see if the user is changing the value of the Complete field to True. If so, the code displays the warning message and cancels saving the record if the user replies No. The code is as follows:

```
Private Sub Form_BeforeUpdate(Cancel As Integer)
  ' If setting reminder complete,
  If Me.Complete = True Then
    ' Verify user really wants to do this
    If "No" = CustomError("Do you want to mark this reminder " & _
      "complete and remove it from the reminder listings?", _
      YesNo, "Reminder Completed", Question, SecondButton) Then
      ' Cancel the update
      Cancel = True
    End If
  End If
End Sub
```

Remember that the frmReminders form displays data from a local table that is a copy of the data on the server. Whenever the user changes a row in this form, code in the form's AfterUpdate event procedure ensures that the same change is made to the copy of the record on the server. The code creates an SQL UPDATE statement to copy the potentially changed values for the Complete and CommitEmployeeID fields (the only two fields the user can change on the form) and then executes the update. The code is as follows:

```
Private Sub Form_AfterUpdate()
Dim db As DAO.Database, strSQL As String
  ' Replicate the change to the server
  ' Set an error trap
  On Error GoTo errAfterUpdate
  ' Point to this database
  Set db = DBEngine(0)(0)
  ' Set up the update SQL
  strSQL = "UPDATE tblReminders " & _
    "SET Complete = " & Me.Complete & _
    ", CommitEmployeeID = " & Me.CommitEmployeeID & _
    " WHERE ReminderID = " & Me.ReminderID & ";"
  ' Execute the update
  db.Execute strSQL, dbFailOnError
  ' Put focus in a safe place
  Me.ReminderInfo.SetFocus
  ' Disable the save and undo buttons
  Me.cmdSave.Enabled = False
  Me.cmdUndo.Enabled = False
okAfterUpdate:
  ' Clear the database object
  Set db = Nothing
  Exit Sub
errAfterUpdate:
  ' Log and display the error
  ErrTryingTo "update reminder on server"
  Resume okAfterUpdate
End Sub
```

At this point, you should have a good understanding of how to implement the major features of a customer support application—or, for that matter, any contact management application. Although the code in the Customer Support sample application is more complicated because it attempts to optimize performance using unbound forms, the basic principles are the same. In the next and final chapter in this part of the book, you'll learn about the design of some of the reporting features in the sample application.

Chapter 19

Reporting and Analyzing Support Cases

Unless an application is designed specifically as a report engine for data loaded from other sources, the majority of the work is done in forms designed to capture and validate data. But even the most data entry–intensive applications will have at least a handful of reports to allow the user to analyze and print the data collected.

Reports tend to be the most resource-intensive elements in any application because, unlike forms that usually focus on the data from one or two tables, many reports must collect data from three, four, five, or more tables to properly display the needed data. When a database contains a lot of data and is shared by many users over a network, a user opening one badly designed report can literally bring the network to its knees. This is particularly true if the tables do not have indexes to help link the tables, the report contains many calculated fields, and the report always opens to display all the available data.

As a database application designer, you can certainly take care to add appropriate indexes to your tables. You should also ensure that any report is filtered to fetch and display only the data needed to solve the user's problem. When you must create a report that fetches hundreds of thousands of rows and the users need to page back and forth through the data displayed in Print Preview, you should consider fetching the data to a local table and then using that table as the record source of the report. You might need to employ this technique even for reports on smaller amounts of data if the report includes percentage calculations in group footers that depend on grand total calculations at the end of the report. When a report includes these features, the report engine must often fetch the data four or more times and might need to re-fetch the entire recordset when the user pages back through the report.

As you learned in Chapter 3 and in the preceding chapters in this part of the book, the Customer Support sample application (Support.mdb) is specifically designed to minimize the connections to the shared data on a network server and to minimize the amount of data fetched to satisfy any particular task. Reports in this sample are no exception. In fact, all reports in the Customer Support application run from data in local tables that has been fetched from the server.

To run the available reports in the Customer Support application, open the database (Support.mdb) and open the frmSplash form to start the application. Sign on as me—enter **jviescas** in the User Name field and **password** in the Password field. Click the Reporting button on the main switchboard to see the Reporting switchboard (the frmReporting form), as shown in Figure 19-1.

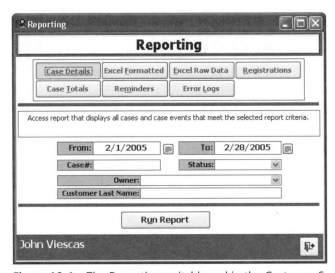

Figure 19-1   The Reporting switchboard in the Customer Support application.

Each toggle button in the top part of the form represents one of the reports available in the database. The available reports are:

- Case Details—Prints information about cases and case events, filtered on a date range, case number, case status, case owner, or customer last name.

- Excel Formatted—Exports case data to an Excel workbook that contains PivotTables to analyze statistics by employee, case category, and product. The data can be filtered on a date range, case number, case status, case owner, or customer last name.

- Excel Raw Data—Exports case and case event data to an Excel workbook but performs no formatting. The data can be filtered on a date range, case number, case status, case owner, or customer last name.

- Registrations—Prints information about product registrations for a specified date range or customer last name.

- Case Totals—Prints case statistics by employee for number of cases handled, services ordered, and parts sent for a specified date range.

- Reminders—Prints statistics for reminders scheduled and completed within the specified date range.

- Error Logs—Prints any error log records saved by the application for a specified date range or employee.

Notice that as you click each button, the lower part of the form displays filter options applicable to each report. At a minimum, you must specify a date range to filter the report. After entering parameters, click the Run Report button to open the selected report in Print Preview.

The following sections explore three of the more interesting reports—Case Details, Product Registrations, and Reminders. The final section explains the Excel Formatted report that is actually a Microsoft Excel spreadsheet that has been designed with several PivotTables to further analyze data extracted from the application.

Printing Case Details

A manager of a customer support organization might need a printed record of certain support cases from time to time. The Customer Support sample application provides a Case Details report that allows the user to print the details for a specific date span, support case number, case status, owning employee, or customer last name.

To run the Case Details report, select the Case Details toggle button on the Reporting switchboard, enter a date range that includes any dates from January 1, 2005, through July 1, 2005, and click the Run Report button. Figure 19-2 shows the result when selecting closed cases in March 2005.

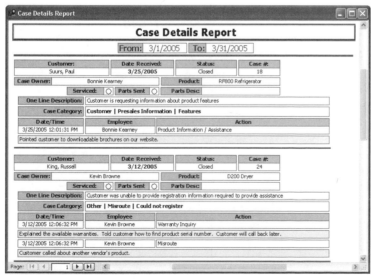

Figure 19-2   The Case Details report.

As you can see, the report prints all the details for each case, including the details for all case events.

Fetching the Required Data

As noted in the beginning of this chapter, all reports use local tables as the record source. When you click the Run Report button, code in the Click event of the command button examines the value of the ogReportButtons option group and calls the appropriate sub procedure to run the report. When you select the Case Details report, the code calls the *CaseDetailsRpt* sub procedure. Code in that procedure calls the *fctBuildQuery* function in the form's module to load the data into a local table, and if the load is successful, the code opens the report in Print Preview. The code is as follows:

```
Private Sub CaseDetailsRpt()
  ' If the query builds successfully, open the report
  If fctBuildQuery = True Then
    DoCmd.OpenReport "rptCaseDetails", acViewPreview
  End If
End Sub
```

The *fctBuildQuery* function first examines the From (the StartDate text box control) and To (the EndDate text box control) values, and if the user cleared (set to Null) either text box, the code sets a default range of dates to include all records. Next, the code examines the blnCasesOnly parameter to determine which query template to load. (As you'll learn later in this chapter, the code to run the Excel Formatted report also calls this function but sets the blnCasesOnly parameter to True to avoid including the case event data.) The code loads the appropriate query as a template and extracts the SQL property of the query definition to use as a base for adding filters specified by the user. Because the *CaseDetailsRpt* procedure calls the *fctBuildQuery* function with no parameter, the blnCasesOnly parameter is False, so the code uses the qryRptCaseDetails query to load both case and case event data. The code is as follows:

```
Private Function fctBuildQuery(Optional blnCasesOnly As Boolean) As Boolean
'This function builds the qryRptCaseDetails query
'   that is used by several reports
Dim db As DAO.Database, qdf As DAO.QueryDef
Dim strSQL As String, varWhere As Variant
  ' Set an error trap
  On Error GoTo errBuildQuery
  ' Clear the Where clause variable
  varWhere = Null
  ' Point to this database
  Set db = DBEngine(0)(0)
  ' Based on the value of blnCasesOnly, fetch the SQL code
  ' from the appropriate template querydef
  If blnCasesOnly Then
    ' Get the query to do case data only
    Set qdf = db.QueryDefs("qryRptCaseDetailsCases")
    ' Fetch the SQL code
    strSQL = qdf.SQL
  Else
    ' Get the query to do cases and events
    Set qdf = db.QueryDefs("qryRptCaseDetails")
```

```
   ' Fetch the SQL code
     strSQL = qdf.SQL
End If
' Close the query object
qdf.Close
Set qdf = Nothing
' Trim off semicolon and start the WHERE clause
strSQL = Left(strSQL, InStrRev(strSQL, ";") - 1) & " WHERE "
```

Next, the code examines each control on the form that can contain a filter value and adds the appropriate predicate using an SQL WHERE clause. The code performs a wildcard search on the case number and customer last name. The code executes a delete query to clear all previous rows from the local tvwRptCaseDetails table, and then executes the insert query that it has modified with additional predicates to load the required data into the table. After refreshing the TableDefs collection to obtain an accurate record count for the tvwRptCaseDetails table, the code checks for zero rows loaded. If the criteria selected no data, the code displays an error message and sets an error return. If the table contains data after executing the insert, the code returns success. The code is as follows:

```
   ' Start building the criteria string for use in the
   ' report by fetching the date range
   strCriteria = "Date Range: " & Me.StartDate & " - " & Me.EndDate & vbLf
   ' Start building the SQL string for the append query
   ' If have a start date
   If Not IsNothing(Me.StartDate) Then
     ' Create the predicate
     varWhere = "(tblCases.DateReceived >= #" & _
       Me.StartDate & "#)"
   End If
   ' If have an end date
   If Not IsNothing(Me.EndDate) Then
     ' Create the predicate
     varWhere = (varWhere + " AND ") & _
       "(tblCases.DateReceived <= #" & Me.EndDate & "#)"
   End If
   ' If the Case Number parameter was specified,
   ' append to the criteria and SQL strings
   If Not IsNothing(Me.txtCaseNum) Then
     strCriteria = strCriteria & "Case Number: Like " & _
       Me.txtCaseNum & "*" & vbLf
     varWhere = (varWhere + " AND ") & _
       "(tblCases.CaseID Like '" & Me.txtCaseNum & "*') "
   End If
   ' If the Customer Last Name parameter was specified,
   ' append to the criteria and SQL strings
   If Not IsNothing(Me.txtCustomerLast) Then
     strCriteria = strCriteria & "Customer Last Name: Like " & _
       Me.txtCustomerLast & "*" & vbLf
     varWhere = (varWhere + " AND ") & _
       "(tblCustomers.CLast Like '" & Me.txtCustomerLast & "*') "
   End If
   ' If the Owner parameter was specified,
   ' append to the criteria and SQL strings
```

```
If Not IsNothing(Me.cmbOwnerID) Then
    strCriteria = strCriteria & "Case Owner: " & _
      Me.cmbOwnerID.Column(1) & vbLf
    varWhere = (varWhere + " AND ") & _
      "(tblCases.CaseOwnerID = " & Me.cmbOwnerID & ") "
End If
' If the Status parameter was specified,
' append to the criteria and SQL strings
If Not IsNothing(Me.cmbStatus) Then
    strCriteria = strCriteria & "Case Status: " & _
      Me.cmbStatus & vbLf
    varWhere = (varWhere + " AND ") & _
      "(tblCases.Status = '" & Me.cmbStatus & "') "
End If
' Make sure have at least one criterion
If IsNothing(varWhere) Then
    CustomError "You must specify at least one criterion."
    Set db = Nothing
    fctBuildQuery = False
    Exit Function
End If
' Delete the records in the view table
db.Execute "DELETE * FROM tvwRptCaseDetails"
' Execute the query
db.Execute strSQL & varWhere
' Refresh the TableDefs collection to get accurate count
db.TableDefs.Refresh
' See if any data was appended.
If db.TableDefs("tvwRptCaseDetails").RecordCount = 0 Then
    ' There was no data. Display an error and set the function to false
    CustomError "There was no data for this report. " & _
      "Change the parameters and try again.", , "No Data"
    fctBuildQuery = False
Else
    ' The function successfully returned data
    fctBuildQuery = True
End If
okBuildQuery:
  Set db = Nothing
  Exit Function
errBuildQuery:
  fctBuildQuery = False
  ErrTryingTo "build the report query"
  Resume okBuildQuery
End Function
```

The template used by the *fctBuildQuery* function to load data for the Case Details report is the qryRptCaseDetails query. The query contains a complex SELECT clause that joins 10 tables (including two copies of the tblEmployees table) to fetch all the data needed by the report. Unlike a typical record source for a report, this query is an append (INSERT INTO) query to fetch the complex set of data once from the server into a local table. The SQL for the query is as follows:

```
INSERT INTO tvwRptCaseDetails ( CaseID, CaseOwner, CategoryName, ProductName, Customer,
Status, DateReceived, Service, PartSent, PartDesc, OneLineDesc, Category1, Category2,
Category3, CategoryDetail, EventID, EmployeeName, EventTime, [Action], Notes )
SELECT tblCases.CaseID, O.EmployeeName AS Owner, tlkpProductCategories.CategoryName,
tlkpProducts.ProductName,
[CLast] & ", " & [CFirst] AS Customer, tblCases.Status, tblCases.DateReceived,
tblCases.Service, tblCases.PartSent, tblCases.PartDesc, tblCases.OneLineDesc,
tlkpCaseCategories.Category1, tlkpCaseCategories.Category2, tlkpCaseCategories.Category3,
tblCases.CategoryDetail, tblCasesEvents.EventID, tlkpEmployees.EmployeeName,
tblCasesEvents.EventTime,
tlkpActions.Name AS [Action], tblCasesEvents.NotesFROM ((tlkpProductCategories
INNER JOIN tlkpProducts
ON tlkpProductCategories.ProductCategoryID = tlkpProducts.ProductCategoryID)
INNER JOIN tblRegistrations
ON tlkpProducts.ProductID = tblRegistrations.ProductID)
INNER JOIN ((((tlkpEmployees AS O
INNER JOIN tblCases
ON O.EmployeeID = tblCases.CaseOwnerID)
INNER JOIN tlkpCaseCategories
ON tblCases.CategoryID = tlkpCaseCategories.CategoryID)
INNER JOIN tblCustomers
ON tblCases.CustomerID = tblCustomers.CustomerID)
INNER JOIN ((tblCasesEvents
INNER JOIN tlkpEmployees
ON tblCasesEvents.EmployeeID = tlkpEmployees.EmployeeID)
INNER JOIN tlkpActions
ON tblCasesEvents.ActionID = tlkpActions.ActionID)
ON tblCases.CaseID = tblCasesEvents.CaseID)
ON tblRegistrations.RegistrationID = tblCases.RegistrationID;
```

Because all the tables have indexes on related keys and indexes on all the fields that might potentially be used in the WHERE clause, the query runs very quickly on the small set of sample data provided. However, if the user needs to run the report for a large date range that would retrieve tens of thousands of rows, the query could take up to a minute to run. The good news is the user need wait only once to load the data. The user will experience no delays paging through the data, and the report won't have to connect to the server again if the user makes several passes back and forth in the report.

Designing the Report

Notice that the process to load the data needed for the Case Details report inserts rows into only one table, and the result is very unnormalized. A report actually runs more efficiently on a single unnormalized data source. When you design a report using a record source with many tables or include a subreport to display related data from another table, the report engine has to do a lot more work.

Using a single unnormalized record source makes the report design simple. To examine the design, open the rptCaseDetails report in Design view, as shown in Figure 19-3.

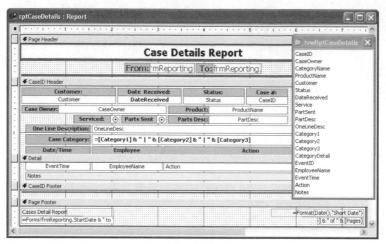

Figure 19-3   The design of the Case Details report.

The report has a group header on the CaseID field value, and the report displays all the fields related to the case in that header. The report displays the data for each of the case events in the Detail section. The only unique aspect of the report is that it displays the date range in the page header and footer by referencing the StartDate and EndDate controls on the frmReporting form that remains open when the report runs.

Listing Product Registrations

One key indicator of potential future support loads is the number of product registrations during the preceding 3 or 6 months. A support manager can obtain a list of the registrations recorded for any period by requesting the Registrations report on the Reporting switchboard. If you open the Reporting switchboard (frmReporting) and select the Registrations toggle button, you'll find that the user can also ask to filter the listing by customer last name. Run the report for the first quarter of 2005, and you should see a listing similar to Figure 19-4.

Notice that the report lists not only the details of each registration but also the number of days that are remaining in the covered warranty period. I ran the sample report with my machine date set to Feb 19, 2005, to obtain the list shown in the figure. On the last page of the report, you can see calculated values for the total number of registrations and the average warranty days remaining for all registrations listed.

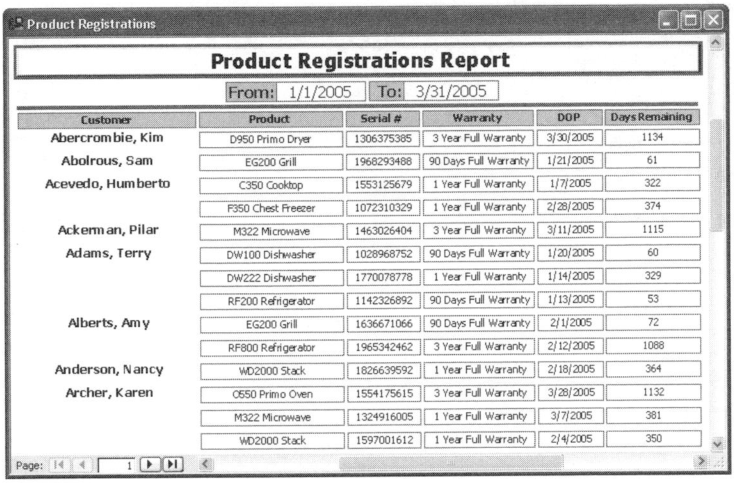

Product Registrations

Product Registrations Report

From: 1/1/2005 To: 3/31/2005

Customer	Product	Serial #	Warranty	DOP	Days Remaining
Abercrombie, Kim	D950 Primo Dryer	1306375385	3 Year Full Warranty	3/30/2005	1134
Abolrous, Sam	EG200 Grill	1968293488	90 Days Full Warranty	1/21/2005	61
Acevedo, Humberto	C350 Cooktop	1553125679	1 Year Full Warranty	1/7/2005	322
	F350 Chest Freezer	1072310329	1 Year Full Warranty	2/28/2005	374
Ackerman, Pilar	M322 Microwave	1463026404	3 Year Full Warranty	3/11/2005	1115
Adams, Terry	DW100 Dishwasher	1028968752	90 Days Full Warranty	1/20/2005	60
	DW222 Dishwasher	1770078778	1 Year Full Warranty	1/14/2005	329
	RF200 Refrigerator	1142326892	90 Days Full Warranty	1/13/2005	53
Alberts, Amy	EG200 Grill	1636671066	90 Days Full Warranty	2/1/2005	72
	RF800 Refrigerator	1965342462	3 Year Full Warranty	2/12/2005	1088
Anderson, Nancy	WD2000 Stack	1826639592	1 Year Full Warranty	2/18/2005	364
Archer, Karen	O550 Primo Oven	1554175615	3 Year Full Warranty	3/28/2005	1132
	M322 Microwave	1324916005	1 Year Full Warranty	3/7/2005	381
	WD2000 Stack	1597001612	1 Year Full Warranty	2/4/2005	350

Page: 1

Figure 19-4 Product registrations in the first quarter of 2005.

Fetching the Required Data

As with all reports in the Customer Support sample database, the Product Registrations report uses data loaded into a local table. When the user clicks the Run Report button on the Reporting switchboard, code in the Click event procedure for that button examines the value of the ogReportButtons option group control and calls the *ProductRegistrationsRpt* sub procedure in the form's module to load the data and open the report.

The procedure first checks that the user has entered start and end date criteria, and displays an error and exits if these are not supplied. The code then establishes a pointer to the current database and executes a delete query to remove all rows previously loaded into the tvwRptProductRegistrations local table. Next, the code opens the query definition for the qryRptProductRegistrations query that contains three parameters to match the three filter values on the Reporting switchboard (StartDate, EndDate, and CustomerLast). The code sets the three parameters and executes the query to load the requested rows into the local table. Finally, the code opens the rptProductRegistrations report in Print Preview. That report has a NoData event procedure (not shown) that displays a message and cancels the open if no rows were loaded into the table. Note that the error trapping code at the end of the *ProductRegistrationsRpt* procedure ignores the 2501 cancel error code that would result when the report has no data. The code is as follows:

```
Private Sub ProductRegistrationsRpt()
' This sub builds the Product Registrations Report query
' and displays the report
Dim db As DAO.Database, qry As DAO.QueryDef, strSQL As String
  ' Set an error trap
  On Error GoTo errProductRegistrations
```

```
' Check for valid parameters
If IsNothing(Me.StartDate) Or IsNothing(Me.EndDate) Then
  CustomError "You must provide From and To dates for this report."
  Exit Sub
End If
' Populate the database object
Set db = DBEngine(0)(0)
' Build query string to delete the current view records
strSQL = "DELETE * FROM tvwRptProductRegistrations"
' Run the query
db.Execute strSQL
' Populate the query object
Set qry = db.QueryDefs("qryRptProductRegistrations")
' Provide values for the query parameters
qry.Parameters("StartDate") = Me.StartDate
qry.Parameters("EndDate") = Me.EndDate
qry.Parameters("CustomerLast") = Me.txtCustomerLast & "*"
' Run the append query
qry.Execute
' Open the report
DoCmd.OpenReport "rptProductRegistrations", acViewPreview
okProductRegistrations:
  Exit Sub
errProductRegistrations:
  ' If the error is not a 'no data' error, return it
  If Err.Number <> 2501 Then ErrTryingTo "fetch Product Registration data"
  Resume okProductRegistrations
End Sub
```

The qryRptProductRegistrations query selects data from four tables to provide the information for the rptProductRegistrations report. The query includes a calculation that adds the WarrantyLength field (in days) to the DOP field (the date of purchase) and subtracts today's date to obtain the number of days remaining in the warranty. When the value is negative, the expression returns a zero. The SQL for the query is as follows:

```
PARAMETERS StartDate DateTime, EndDate DateTime, CustomerLast Text ( 255 );
INSERT INTO tvwRptProductRegistrations
( Customer, ProductName, DOP, SerialNum, WarrantyName, WarrantyDaysRemaining )
SELECT [CLast] & ', ' & [CFirst] AS Customer, tlkpProducts.ProductName, tblRegistrations.DOP,
tblRegistrations.SerialNum, tlkpWarranties.WarrantyName,
IIf((([DOP]+[WarrantyLength])-Date())<1,0,([DOP]+[WarrantyLength])-Date()) AS
WarrantyDaysRemaining
FROM tblCustomers
INNER JOIN (tlkpWarranties
INNER JOIN (tblRegistrations
INNER JOIN tlkpProducts
ON tblRegistrations.ProductID = tlkpProducts.ProductID)
ON tlkpWarranties.WarrantyID = tblRegistrations.WarrantyID)
ON tblCustomers.CustomerID = tblRegistrations.CustomerID
WHERE (((tblRegistrations.DOP) Between [StartDate] And [EndDate])
AND ((tblCustomers.CLast) Like [CustomerLast]));
```

You might wonder why the query parameters (StartDate, EndDate, and CustomerLast) don't point directly to the controls on the open form using an expression like

```
[Forms]![frmReporting]![StartDate]
```

Remember that when you open or directly execute a parameter query in code, the database engine knows very little about the source of the command. You could execute the same query from a Web page or code in a Word document, so the database engine has no visibility to the fact that the frmReporting form might be open. You could use a **DoCmd.OpenQuery**, but you would also need to execute **DoCmd.SetWarnings False** to avoid prompting the user, and your code would not be able to trap any error that occurred. Opening the query and directly assigning the parameters is the best way to accomplish this task.

Designing the Report

The only complicated part of the rptProductRegistrations report is the calculation of warranty days remaining for each registration, but that calculation is performed in the query that fetches the data from the server. To examine the design, open the rptProductRegistrations report in Design view, as shown in Figure 19-5.

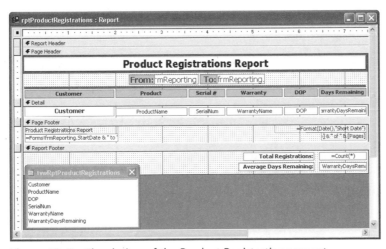

Figure 19-5   The design of the Product Registrations report.

The report as designed sorts the data in ascending sequence by customer name so that you can see multiple products owned by the same customer grouped together. It would be a simple matter to change the sort to the ProductName, DOP (date of purchase), or WarrantyDaysRemaining field to obtain a different result. (The tvwRptProductRegistrations table already has indexes defined on these fields to make changing the sorting order efficient.) As you can see, the calculation of total registrations in the report footer is a simple count of the records. The average calculation uses the Avg aggregate function to calculate the average of the WarrantyDaysRemaining field.

Reporting Reminders

Another important statistic any customer support organization needs is an indicator of how effectively the individual employees are in handling reminders on time. To run the Reminders report, select the Reminders toggle button on the Reporting switchboard, select a range of dates between January 1, 2005, and July 1, 2005, and click the Run Report button. You should see a result similar to Figure 19-6.

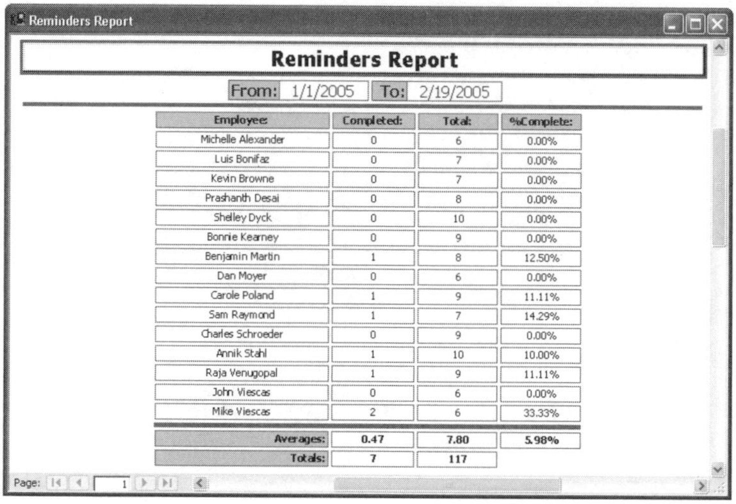

Reminders Report

From: 1/1/2005   **To:** 2/19/2005

Employee:	Completed:	Total:	%Complete:
Michelle Alexander	0	6	0.00%
Luis Bonifaz	0	7	0.00%
Kevin Browne	0	7	0.00%
Prashanth Desai	0	8	0.00%
Shelley Dyck	0	10	0.00%
Bonnie Kearney	0	9	0.00%
Benjamin Martin	1	8	12.50%
Dan Moyer	0	6	0.00%
Carole Poland	1	9	11.11%
Sam Raymond	1	7	14.29%
Charles Schroeder	0	9	0.00%
Annik Stahl	1	10	10.00%
Raja Venugopal	1	9	11.11%
John Viescas	0	6	0.00%
Mike Viescas	2	6	33.33%
Averages:	**0.47**	**7.80**	**5.98%**
Totals:	**7**	**117**	

Figure 19-6   Reminder statistics as of February 19, 2005.

When I ran the report, I had my system date set to February 19, 2005, and I selected that date as the To date. Because the report includes all records up through the To date, it doesn't make sense to pick records from the future if you're interested in past performance. The report counts all records, so including future ones will make the total completed look unusually low. However, a manager might want to run the report using future dates to get an idea of how many reminders might need to be handled in the next week or month. Of course, the sample data is just that—a random sample of values. As you can see in Figure 19-6, any support manager might be worried about the low completion rates shown on the report for all employees!

Fetching the Required Data

When you click the Run Report button, code in the Click event procedure of that button calls the *RemindersRpt* sub procedure in the form's module. As with the Product Registrations report, the code first verifies that the user has entered start and end date values, and it displays an error message and exits if not. The code removes all previously loaded rows from the tvwRptReminders local table by executing a delete query. The code loads the qryRptReminders parameter query (an insert query), sets the date parameters, and executes it. Finally the code opens the report and traps any cancel (error code 2501) due to no data loaded in the procedure's error processing code. The code is as follows:

```
Private Sub RemindersRpt()
' This sub builds the Reminders Report query
' and displays the report
Dim db As DAO.Database, qry As DAO.QueryDef, strSQL As String
  ' Set an error trap
  On Error GoTo errReminders
  ' Check for valid parameters
  If IsNothing(Me.StartDate) Or IsNothing(Me.EndDate) Then
    CustomError "You must provide From and To dates for this report."
    Exit Sub
  End If
  ' Populate the database object
  Set db = DBEngine(0)(0)
  ' Build query string to delete the current view records
  strSQL = "DELETE * FROM tvwRptReminders"
  ' Run the query
  db.Execute strSQL
  ' Populate the query object
  Set qry = db.QueryDefs("qryRptReminders")
  ' Provide values for the query parameters
  qry.Parameters("StartDate") = Me.StartDate
  qry.Parameters("EndDate") = Me.EndDate + 1
  ' Run the append query
  qry.Execute
  ' Open the report
  DoCmd.OpenReport "rptReminders", acViewPreviewokReminders:
okReminders:
  Exit Sub
errReminders:
  ' If the error is not a 'no data' error, return it
  If Err.Number <> 2501 Then ErrTryingTo "fetch Reminders data"
  Resume okReminders
End Sub
```

The qryRptReminders insert query uses a totals query to calculate the number of completed reminders and the count of reminders for each employee. The SQL for the query is as follows:

```
INSERT INTO tvwRptReminders ( EmployeeName, EmployeeFirst,
    EmployeeLast, Completed, Total )
SELECT tlkpEmployees.EmployeeName, tlkpEmployees.EmployeeFirst,
    tlkpEmployees.EmployeeLast, Abs(Sum([Complete])) AS Completed,
    Count(tblReminders.ReminderID) AS Total
FROM tlkpEmployees
INNER JOIN tblReminders
ON tlkpEmployees.EmployeeID = tblReminders.CommitEmployeeID
WHERE (((tblReminders.CommitDate) Between [StartDate] And [EndDate]))
GROUP BY tlkpEmployees.EmployeeName;
```

Remember that a Yes/No field contains the value −1 for True or Yes and 0 for False or No. The query returns the absolute value of the sum of this field using the Abs function to reverse the sign of the total.

Designing the Report

The design of the rptReminders report is very simple. You can view the design by opening the rptReminders report in Design view as shown in Figure 19-7.

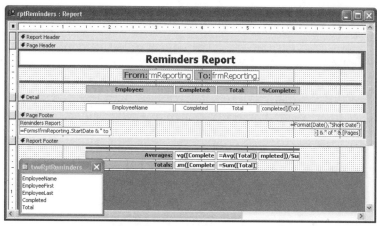

Figure 19-7   The Reminders report design.

The report calculates the percentages by dividing the Completed amount by the Total number of reminders for each employee. The report also displays the average completed, the average of total reminders, and the average percent complete as well as the total completed and the total of all reminders in the requested dates.

Analyzing Case Data with Microsoft Excel

Access 2002 introduced a new feature that lets you design a Microsoft Excel PivotTable or PivotChart directly in a form. This powerful analytical tool lets you "slice and dice" statistical data in various ways very easily. PivotTables and PivotCharts were available in Excel 2000, but not in Access 2000.

As noted in the Introduction to this book, you can run any of the sample databases using Access 2000, 2002 (XP), or 2003. So, to demonstrate analyzing data with PivotTables, I had to export the data to analyze to an Excel workbook that I preformatted with several PivotTable worksheets. You can execute an analysis of the data in the sample database by selecting the Excel Formatted option on the Reporting switchboard, choosing a range of dates between January 1, 2005, and July 1, 2005, entering optional filters for Case #, Status, Owner, or Customer Last Name, and clicking the Run Report button. The code prompts you to verify where you want to save the resulting Excel workbook. You can change the folder or file name and click Save, or just click Save to accept the default location and file. After a few seconds, you should see Excel open and display three different PivotTables on the data you selected, as shown in Figure 19-8.

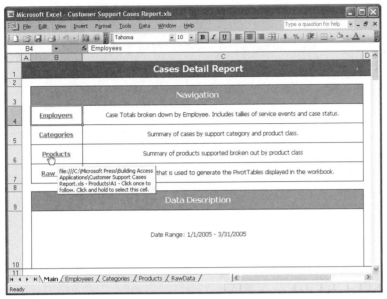

Figure 19-8 The main worksheet in the support cases analysis workbook.

Even if I had restricted the samples to be executed using only Access 2002 (XP) and later, I wouldn't have been able to create such a powerful sample that has three different ways to look at the data in one form. A form in PivotTable view in Access 2002 and later can display only one PivotTable at a time. In this example, the user can analyze statistics by employee and product category, by support case category, or by individual product all in one workbook. The sample workbook includes hyperlinks on the first worksheet to make it easy to navigate to the various results. You can click the Products link (or click the Products tab at the bottom of the workbook) to view the analysis by Product, as shown in Figure 19-9 on the next page.

You can build a workbook like this for any application. Load the data you need into one of the worksheets and then build PivotTables or PivotCharts on that data in other worksheets linked to that data. The following sections show you how to reload the data from Access using Excel automation.

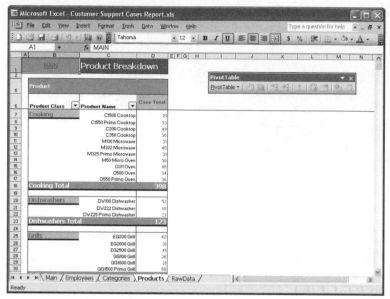

Figure 19-9   The product analysis PivotTable in the support cases analysis workbook.

Fetching the Required Data

The process to set up the Excel PivotTable "reports" starts just like all the other reports in the sample application—code in the frmReporting form loads the selected data into a local table. When the user selects the Excel Formatted option and clicks the Run Report button, code in the Click event procedure of that button calls the *ExcelFormattedRpt* sub procedure in the form's module. That procedure calls the *fctBuildQuery* function described earlier in this chapter and asks it to omit the case event details data by setting the blnCasesOnly parameter to True. If that function completes successfully, the code calls the *fctCasesExcel* function that you can find in the modExcel module and passes it the description of the criteria used. The code is as follows:

```
Private Sub ExcelFormattedRpt()
    ' Build the query for the export code to use
    If fctBuildQuery(True) = True Then
        ' Call the format to Excel export code
        Call fctCasesExcel(strCriteria)
    End If
End Sub
```

As you might recall from the discussion of the *fctBuildQuery* function on page 394, that function uses one of two template queries to load the data requested into the tvwRptCaseDetails table. When called from the *ExcelFormattedRpt* procedure, the code uses the qryRptCase-DetailsCases query that does not include case event data. The SQL for the query is as follows:

```
INSERT INTO tvwRptCaseDetails ( CaseID, CaseOwner, CategoryName,
    ProductName, Customer, Status, DateReceived, Service, PartSent,
```

```
    PartDesc, OneLineDesc, Category1, Category2, Category3,
    CategoryDetail )
SELECT tblCases.CaseID, tlkpEmployees.EmployeeName AS Owner,
    tlkpProductCategories.CategoryName, tlkpProducts.ProductName,
    [CLast] & (", "+[CFirst]) AS Customer, tblCases.Status,
    tblCases.DateReceived, tblCases.Service, tblCases.PartSent,
    tblCases.PartDesc, tblCases.OneLineDesc, tlkpCaseCategories.Category1,
    tlkpCaseCategories.Category2, tlkpCaseCategories.Category3,
    tblCases.CategoryDetail
FROM (tlkpCaseCategories
  INNER JOIN (tlkpEmployees
    INNER JOIN (tblCases
      INNER JOIN tblCustomers
      ON tblCases.CustomerID = tblCustomers.CustomerID)
    ON tlkpEmployees.EmployeeID = tblCases.CaseOwnerID)
  ON tlkpCaseCategories.CategoryID = tblCases.CategoryID)
  INNER JOIN (tlkpProductCategories
    INNER JOIN (tblRegistrations
      INNER JOIN tlkpProducts
      ON tblRegistrations.ProductID = tlkpProducts.ProductID)
    ON tlkpProductCategories.ProductCategoryID =
      tlkpProducts.ProductCategoryID)
  ON tblCustomers.CustomerID = tblRegistrations.CustomerID;
```

Exporting the Data to Excel

After the *fctBuildQuery* function loads the selected data into the tvwRptCaseDetails table, the *fctCasesExcel* function moves the data to a copy of the workbook template, refreshes the Pivot-Tables, and displays the result in Excel. The function begins by opening a recordset on the tvwRptCaseDetails table using a query that excludes the case event columns not used by the PivotTables in the workbook. If the recordset is empty, the code displays a message, closes the recordset, and exits.

Next, the code uses the current path of the application to create the path and name of the file it expects to use as the template for the PivotTables. (If the CaseDetails.xls file isn't in the same folder as the Support.mdb database file, this code will fail.) The code uses the ComDlg class module to open a Windows Save As dialog box initialized to point to the current path and with a default file name of Customer Support Cases Report.xls. Executing the *ShowSave* method opens the dialog box that asks the user to confirm the name and location of the output file. If that method returns True, code in the class module has saved the path and name selected in the FileName property. If *ShowSave* doesn't return True, the code closes the recordset opened previously and exits. If *ShowSave* was successful, the code uses the *Dir* function to check to see if the file already exists. If the file exists, the code uses the *Kill* statement to delete the file so the user isn't prompted again to overwrite the file by Excel. The code is as follows:

```
Public Function fctCasesExcel(strCriteria As String)
' Function to load selected data into an Excel
' workbook that analyzes the data using PivotTables.
' Function makes a copy of a "template" workbook,
' loads the data into the copy, refreshes the PivotTables,
```

```
' and displays the result
Dim objXLApp As Object, objXLws As Object
Dim db As DAO.Database, rst As DAO.Recordset
Dim strField As String, strDocPath, strPath As String
  Const xlPasteValues As Integer = 7
  ' Enable error trapping
  On Error GoTo errfctCasesExcel
  ' Populate database object
  Set db = DBEngine(0)(0)
  ' Open a recordset on the query for the data to export
  ' Data loaded by code in frmReports to the tvwRptCaseDetails table
  Set rst = db.OpenRecordset("qryRptExcelFormatted")
  ' If there are no records, return an error and exit function
  If rst.EOF Then
    Call CustomError("There are no records to export.")
    rst.Close
    Set rst = Nothing
    Set db = Nothing
    Exit Function
  End If
  ' Make sure the path variable is populated
  IconPath
  ' Build the path to the template
  strDocPath = gstrRoot & "CaseDetails.xls"
  ' Use the ComDlg class to locate the path to export the report
  With New ComDlg
    .DialogTitle = "Save Export File"
    ' Specify the default file name
    .FileName = CAppName & " Cases Report.xls"
    ' Specify the default file extension
    .Extension = "xls"
    .Filter = "Excel File (*.xls)|*.xls"
    ' ShowSave method returns true if successful
    If .ShowSave Then
      ' Save the file name selected
      strPath = .FileName
    Else
      rst.Close
      Set rst = Nothing
      Set db = Nothing
      Exit Function
    End If
  End With
  ' If the file we want to build already exists
  If "" <> Dir(strPath) Then
    ' Delete it
    Kill strPath
  End If
```

Now comes the fun part. The code starts Excel by calling the *CreateObject* function. Next, the code instructs Excel to open the template workbook using the *Open* method of the Workbooks collection. The code immediately executes a *SaveAs* method to save the template to the new file name selected by the user. The code then selects the RawData worksheet, activates it, and uses the *CopyFromRecordset* method to instruct Excel to copy the data from the recordset opened earlier into the worksheet beginning at cell A5.

Next, the code activates the Main worksheet, sets a pointer to it, and inserts the criteria description into the second column on the tenth row (cell B10 in Figure 19-8). The code closes the recordset, disables alerts in Excel, and uses the *RefreshTable* method to cause all the PivotTables to recalculate using the new data. Finally, the code sets the Visible property of the Excel application to True to reveal the result and exits. The code is as follows:

```
 ' This might take a while, turn on the hourglass
 DoCmd.Hourglass True
 ' Populate the excel object
 Set objXLApp = CreateObject("Excel.Application")
 ' Open the template workbook
 objXLApp.Workbooks.Open (strDocPath)
 ' Save the template as the file specified by the user
 objXLApp.ActiveWorkbook.SaveAs (strPath)
 ' Select the 'Raw Data' worksheet
 Set objXLws = objXLApp.ActiveWorkbook.Worksheets("RawData")
 ' Activate the selected worksheet
 objXLws.Activate
 ' Ask Excel to copy the data from the recordset
 objXLws.Range("A5").CopyFromRecordset rst
 ' Select the main worksheet
 objXLApp.Worksheets("Main").Activate
 ' Activate the selected worksheet
 Set objXLws = objXLApp.ActiveWorkbook.Worksheets("Main")
 ' Populate the criteria box on the main form
 '   (so the user knows what was exported)
 objXLws.Cells(10, 2).Value = strCriteria
 ' Destroy the recordset and database objects
 rst.Close
 Set rst = Nothing
 Set db = Nothing
 ' Hide warnings on the spreadsheet
 objXLApp.DisplayAlerts = False
 ' Refresh the root PivotTable (which refreshes all)
 objXLApp.Worksheets("Employees").PivotTables(1).RefreshTable
 ' Save the workbook
 objXLApp.ActiveWorkbook.Save
 ' Turn spreadsheet warnings back on
 objXLApp.DisplayAlerts = True
 ' Make it visible
 objXLApp.Visible = True
okfctCasesExcel:
 ' Turn the hourglass off
 DoCmd.Hourglass False
 Set objXLws = Nothing
 Set objXLApp = Nothing
 Exit Function
errfctCasesExcel:
 ErrTryingTo "format to Excel"
 Resume okfctCasesExcel
End Function
```

This concludes the examination of the Customer Support sample application. In the final part of the book, you'll learn the inner workings of an application to manage reservations—in this case, reservations for computer science classes at a local business college.

Part V
Creating a Registration
Management Application

Chapter 20

The Registration Management Application

When deciding what to call this final sample application, I had several choices. I originally thought I would call it Reservations Management, but I could also have used something more generic like Resource Management. Because the sample application demonstrates registering students for courses in a fictitious business school, I settled on Registration Management. The fundamental problem that the application demonstrates is tracking a limited resource that is available only for a specific period of time. Think of resource management as inventory management with a limited amount of product and a time element.

The generic class of resource management applications covers a wide range of business problems. Here are just a few of the applications:

- A school registering students for classes
- An airline selling seats on scheduled flights
- A hotel booking rooms
- A car rental agency renting vehicles
- A passenger line selling cabins on a cruise
- An equipment rental agency renting tools
- A project manager planning staff allocation for a project that has a deadline
- A theater group selling seats for a performance
- A doctor's office scheduling appointments or surgeries
- A library loaning books or tapes

■ A media store renting movies or games

■ A beauty salon booking appointments

Notice that in all of these cases, the amount of product available to sell is limited in some way. A school has just so many classrooms and instructors. A hotel has only so many rooms. A project manager has been given a certain staff with specific talents. A doctor can't be in two places at once. Also, the limited resource is available only for a specific time period. Once the time has passed, an unsold "product" will remain unsold forever. So, a resource management application must not only maximize the use of available product but also try to plan the future availability of product.

Understanding the Registration Management Application

You might think that building a sample for the travel industry would be "just the ticket." (Pun intended.) However, I tried to make all the sample applications complete—each one covers nearly all aspects of the business problem modeled. Building a sample application for the travel industry would be subject to too many variables and would be much more complex than I could adequately describe in four or five chapters.

Consider that travel companies intentionally overbook resources because they know a certain percentage of people fail to show up. They also reserve some of the resource (the best aisle seats on an airplane or the upgraded rooms in a hotel) for "frequent" or "honored" customers until the last minute. They also set aside a portion of the seats or rooms to sell at various discounts to people who book early in the hopes of selling out the resource—but the quantity of set-aside resources varies over time as does the amount of the discounts. The bottom line is it would take a PhD to understand the formulas for maximizing revenue in the travel industry!

So, the sample school registration application for this final part of the book (Registration.mdb and RegistrationData.mdb) tackles a slightly less daunting problem. The prices can change over time but are static for any given semester of study. Every class has a limit to the number of students who can enroll, but an instructor can choose to accommodate additional students up to the size of the room allocated for the class.

> **Note** As with all the other sample applications, the Registration Management application uses fictitious data but with one exception. Many years ago, Microsoft established its Most Valuable Professional (MVP) program to acknowledge individuals who are the "best, most active customers who have demonstrated a technical passion and willingness to share their expertise with others." Several of my fellow Access MVPs graciously agreed to allow me to use their names for the instructors in this sample application.

Identifying Tasks and Data

As with creating any other database application, you should start by making lists of the tasks that the application must support and the data needed by those tasks. You should interview the potential users and determine how they're performing the tasks without a database or find out what it is they expect the database to do for them. You'd be surprised how many different ways there are to look at resource management and, specifically, registration management.

Here are the tasks implemented in the Registration Management application:

- Define course categories.

- Enter course information, including title, description, maximum students, and credit hours.

- Define course plans that lead to a certificate or degree.

- Specify the courses needed to satisfy a course plan.

- Identify any prerequisites for a course and whether a student can obtain instructor approval in lieu of the necessary prerequisites. Allow one of several courses (either/or) to satisfy a prerequisite.

- Define multiple segments for a course—for example, lecture, discussion, or lab segments.

- Enter instructor information, including name, address, and a short biography.

- Specify which instructors are qualified to teach which courses.

- Enter administrator information, including name and address.

- Define course sessions (semesters).

- Specify what courses and how many sections of a course should be taught in a session.

- Define the rooms, room types, and room sizes available for classes.

- Schedule course sections and segments for a session, assign instructors, and adjust the schedule as necessary.

- Enter student information, including name, address, and the student's selected course plan.

- Allow a student to enter requested courses and specific course sections for the coming semester.

- Identify which students do or do not have the prerequisites for requested courses.

- Allow instructors to authorize a student registration without prerequisites satisfied.

- Schedule students into course sections and identify which students must be assigned to an alternate section or placed on a wait list.

- Create invoices for student enrollments.

- Enter student payments for invoices.

- Allow instructors to set a final status for a student enrollment and enter a grade.

- Print teaching schedules for instructors.

- Send instructor schedules via e-mail.

- Print class schedules for students.

- Send student class schedules via e-mail.

- Print a course catalog.

- Analyze instructor class load.

- Analyze student class load.

- Analyze course enrollments to determine offerings for future semesters.

From the preceding list, you can begin to identify the subjects and actions that should be represented by tables in the application. These include the following:

- Course Categories

- Courses

- Course Plans

- Course Plan Courses

- Course Prerequisites

- Course Segments

- Instructors

- Instructor Courses

- Administrators

- Sessions

- Session Courses (to schedule)

- Rooms

- Session Courses (scheduled) and session course segments

- Students

- Student Courses

- Student Invoices

- Student Payments

When you see a subject name that lists the simple name of two other subjects, such as Course Plan Courses or Instructor Courses, that subject is probably going to be the many-to-many link between the two other subjects. So, Course Plan Courses is the many-to-many link between Courses and Course Plans, and Instructor Courses is the many-to-many link between Instructors and Courses.

You might wonder why there appear to be two tables for Session Courses. As you'll learn in Chapter 21, "Scheduling Courses," an administrator can create a generic list of courses to schedule for an upcoming semester and specify the number of sections to be scheduled for each course. The administrator can then ask the application to create the actual schedule, balancing the course sections across rooms and instructors. After letting the application do most of the work, the administrator can subsequently adjust the generated schedule to meet the needs of the school and individual instructors. You can see that understanding both the tasks required and the data for those tasks is critical to designing the application correctly. You cannot do one without the other.

Understanding Business Rules

As you identify the tasks required to be supported by your application, you'll also learn something about the business rules that restrict those tasks. A registration or resource management application has the potential to be more complex than the Inventory Management application that you studied in Part 3 of this book. The resources are limited, so you don't have to worry about purchase orders and vendor invoices to track incoming resources. But the time element and—in the Registration Management sample—tracking prerequisites add to the complexity.

Just like any other application, if you don't understand the business rules the application must support, your application won't work correctly. In addition to the tasks the application must support and the data subjects in the database, you need to find out how these tasks and data interact. One of the best ways to find out the applicable business rules is to ask as many questions as come to mind—and the answers to some questions will inevitably lead you to other questions. Some of the questions that I considered as I designed the Registration Management application (and the answer I chose for each) are as follows:

- Can a student change his or her student record? No, only an administrator can define and change student records.

- Can a student select or change a course plan? No, only an administrator can approve a course plan for a student.

- Can a student choose courses? Yes.

- Can a student choose courses outside his or her course plan? Yes, but the application warns a student if he or she chooses a course not in the course plan.

- Can a student register for a course more than once? Yes, but not in the same semester.

- Is a student allowed to register for a class for which he or she has not completed the prerequisite classes? A student can request a class without taking the prerequisites provided the class allows staff approval. Prerequisites are satisfied only if the student completed the class with a grade of 72 or better.

- Can a student change a course registration? A student can delete an unconfirmed (requested, awaiting approval, or wait list) registration request but cannot make any other changes.

- Is an instructor allowed to change his or her instructor record? Yes, an instructor can make changes to the address, phone, e-mail, Web site, bio, and password fields. An instructor cannot change any name field or the user ID field.

- Can an instructor change or delete assigned courses? No, only an administrator can assign courses or change course assignments.

- Is an instructor allowed to modify assigned course sections? No, only an administrator can assign sections or change section assignments.

- Can an instructor enroll students in course sections taught by the instructor? No.

- Can an instructor change a student enrollment record? Yes, an instructor can approve an enrollment awaiting prerequisite approval, enroll a student on the wait list (provided the enrollment does not exceed room size), and mark a class enrollment completed and enter a grade.

- Can an instructor modify the records for any other instructor? No.

- Is an administrator allowed to define, change, or delete student or instructor records? Yes.

- Can an administrator define and change course categories, courses, prerequisites for courses, instructors for courses, and segments for courses? Yes. However, an administrator must mark inactive any instructor who has taught a course but is no longer teaching that course or mark inactive a course segment that was previously part of a course but has been eliminated.

- Can an administrator define or change a course plan? Yes.

- Can an administrator define semester sessions? Yes.

- Is an administrator allowed to define a course schedule? Yes.

- Must an administrator define a course schedule before scheduling courses? No. An administrator can schedule courses individually.

- Can an administrator change or delete a course schedule? An administrator cannot change a course schedule once students have enrolled in any of the courses.

- Can an administrator enroll students in course sections? Yes.

- Can an administrator delete a student enrollment? Yes, as long as the enrollment was never confirmed.

- Can an administrator change the assigned instructor or room for a scheduled course? Yes. The administrator can change the room assignment as long as the new room has sufficient capacity and is the correct room type to hold the class.

- Must the administrator generate invoices for student enrollments and enter payments? Yes, only an administrator can do this.

Keep in mind that no question is too trivial, and sometimes you have to think "outside the box" to conjure up questions that your user or client needs to answer. Think like a good investigative reporter and find out not only what the user needs to do, but also when they need to do the task, where they need to be when they do the task, how they need to perform the task, and, most importantly, *why* they need to do it.

Designing the Tables

If you have identified all the tasks, the data required for all the tasks, and all the business rules, designing the tables you need to store and manage the data should be straightforward. You should never sit down and start creating tables without all the necessary background information. If some of the data exists in other files (such as a spreadsheet), create your properly normalized tables first, and then figure out what you need to do to import the existing data into your correct table structure.

The only tricky element about designing any registration management application is tracking the status of students enrolled in courses. A student can enter the original course request and ask the application to attempt to confirm enrollment. When a student does not have the prerequisite courses, the status must change to "awaiting approval" and the responsible instructor must be notified about the approval request. If the requested course section is full, the application must offer the student any available alternative or place the student on a wait list. After a student is successfully enrolled, the instructor is responsible for setting a withdrawn, incomplete, or completed status and entering a grade.

From the list of subjects determined earlier, you can see that the Registration Management application needs the following tables:

- tlkpCourseCategories
- tblCourses
- tblCoursePlans
- tblCoursePlanCourses
- tblCoursePrerequisites
- tblCourseSegments
- tblInstructors
- tblInstructorCourses

- tblAdministrators

- tblSessions

- tblSessionCoursesToSchedule

- tlkpRooms

- tblSessionCourses

- tblSessionCourseSegments

- tblStudents

- tblStudentCourses

- tblStudentInvoices

- tblStudentPayments

Now, you're ready to begin defining the tables you need and the relationships between them. As you create the tables, you should also define as many of the business rules as possible using the validation rule features of Access. Figure 20-1 shows you the final design for the tables related to courses and course scheduling in the Registration Management application.

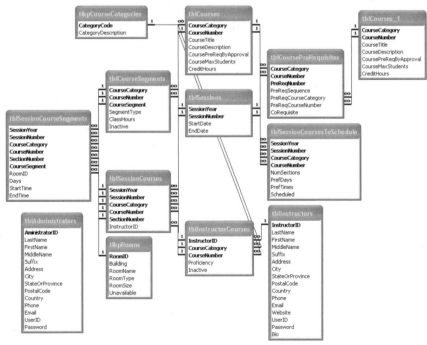

Figure 20-1   The course scheduling tables in the Registration Management application.

Note that a second copy of the tblCourses table (tblCourses_1) appears in the relationship diagram. You must do this when a table has more than one foreign key that is related to a single other table. Adding the second copy allowed me to define a referential integrity rule to ensure that any prerequisite course specified is also a valid course.

Figure 20-2 shows you the tables for the student scheduling portion of the Registration Management application. You can see that seven of the tables are related to both course and student scheduling, and the tblSessionCourseSegments table provides the common link between course scheduling and student scheduling. You can find a detailed listing of the fields and indexes for all the tables in Appendix B, "Sample Database Schemas."

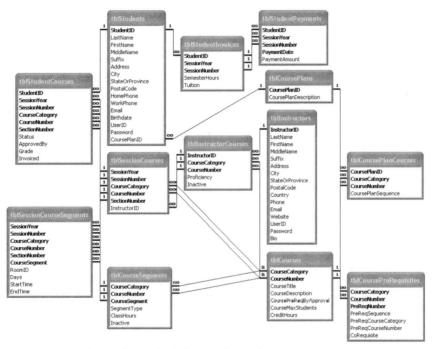

Figure 20-2   The student scheduling tables in the Registration Management application.

As you can see, the table and relationship design is significantly more complex than the design for the Membership Tracking application that you studied in Part 2 of this book, and nearly as complex as the Inventory Management application in Part 3. In the remainder of this part of the book, you can explore specific tasks implemented in the Registration Management sample application (Registration.mdb). Each chapter describes the tables needed for a particular set of tasks and the code that performs those tasks.

Chapter 21
Scheduling Courses

Before any school can enroll students, the school administrators must decide what courses the school offers, sign up instructors, acquire classroom space, and announce a schedule for the courses. On a relative scale, the first three steps are easy. But as anyone who has ever tried to create a complex schedule with limited resources will tell you, allocating the resources and attempting to create a balance can be daunting tasks. This chapter explores the mechanics of creating a schedule and explains the code that can help automate at least part of the process.

Understanding the Tables Involved

The Registration Management sample application (Registration.mdb and Registration-Data.mdb) demonstrates how a typical business or technical school might keep its records. The school offers mostly technical courses and a variety of technical and associate degree programs. The school schedules three sessions or semesters a year—a 16-week session in the spring (weeks 2 through 20), an 8-week session in the summer (weeks 22 through 30), and a 16-week session in the fall (weeks 32 through 50). Table 21-1 describes the fields in the tblSessions table that defines each session. Note that each session includes an extra calendar week or two to allow for holidays and final exams. As you'll learn later in this chapter, code in the application helps set the start and end dates for each session.

Table 21-1 The Fields in the tblSessions Table

Field Name	Data Type	Description
SessionYear	Integer	Year this course session is scheduled.
SessionNumber	Integer	Session semester: 1 = Spring, 2 = Summer, 3 = Fall.
StartDate	Date/Time	First day of class for the session.
EndDate	Date/Time	Last day of class for the session.

For each session, the school schedules a variety of courses and often offers more than one section for each course to provide day of week and time of day choices for students. Each section might have a different instructor. Table 21-2 describes the fields in the tblSessionCourses table that stores the information about each course and section offered.

Table 21-2 The Fields in the tblSessionCourses Table

Field Name	Data Type	Description
SessionYear	Integer	Year this course session is scheduled.
SessionNumber	Integer	Session semester: 1 = Spring, 2 = Summer, 3 = Fall.
CourseCategory	Text, Field Size 3	Course category code.
CourseNumber	Integer	Course number within category.
SectionNumber	Integer	Section number of the course.
InstructorID	Long Integer	ID of the instructor teaching this course section.

Although quite a few courses consist of only one class segment—perhaps a discussion or lecture class—many courses, especially in a school that teaches technical subjects, also have lab segments. In this sample, a class might have up to four segments taught on different days of the week and at different times. Table 21-3 describes the tblSessionCourseSegments table that stores information about scheduled course segments, including the room reserved for the segment, the days of the week the segment is taught, and the start and end time for the class segment. As you'll learn later, one of the scheduling challenges is to ensure that no two segments offered for a class overlap—a student must be able to attend all the segments of a course during each week.

Table 21-3 The Fields in the tblSessionCourseSegments Table

Field Name	Data Type	Description
SessionYear	Integer	Year this course session is scheduled.
SessionNumber	Integer	Session semester: 1 = Spring, 2 = Summer, 3 = Fall.
CourseCategory	Text, Field Size 3	Course category code.
CourseNumber	Integer	Course number within category.
SectionNumber	Integer	Section number of the course.
CourseSegment	Integer	Course segment number (lecture, discussion, or lab).
RoomID	Long Integer	ID of the room where this segment is taught.
Days	Integer	Days of the week this segment is taught. (1 = Mon, 2 = Tue, 3 = Wed, 4 = Thu, 5 = Fri, 6 = Sat, 8 = TuTh, 9 = MWF, 10 = TuThSat)
StartTime	Date/Time	Start time of the class.
EndTime	Date/Time	End time of the class.

The basic tables to define sessions, courses, and course segments seem relatively straight-forward, but you can imagine how tedious it could be for an administrator to lay out a schedule and enter it into the database without producing any conflicts. Not only must a room not be double-booked, but also instructors must not be scheduled to teach two different course segments at the same time. Keep in mind that the different courses might require 2, 3, 4, or more classroom hours per week, so plotting a time schedule to efficiently use the room and instructor resources could be very difficult.

Fortunately, the sample application includes a feature to automate the scheduling process. Rather than schedule each individual course, course segment, instructor, and room, an administrator can specify how many of each course should be taught and on which days and general time of day. The administrator can then ask the application to generate an actual course schedule from the specification.

Table 21-4 describes the fields in the tblSessionCoursesToSchedule table. This table stores the course scheduling preferences for each session, including the specific courses, the number of sections for each course, the preferred days of the week, and the preferred time of day (morning, afternoon, evening). Later in this chapter, you'll learn how code in the application uses this specification to create a course schedule automatically.

Table 21-4   The Fields in the tblSessionCoursesToSchedule Table

Field Name	Data Type	Description
SessionYear	Integer	Year this course session is scheduled.
SessionNumber	Integer	Session semester: 1 = Spring, 2 = Summer, 3 = Fall.
CourseCategory	Text, Field Size 3	Course category code.
CourseNumber	Integer	Course number within category.
NumSections	Integer	Number of sections to schedule.
PrefDays	Integer	Preferred days of the week the course should be taught. (1 = Mon, 2 = Tue, 3 = Wed, 4 = Thu, 5 = Fri, 6 = Sat, 8 = TuTh, 9 = MWF, 10 = TuThSat)
PrefTimes	Integer	Preferred time of day to schedule the sections. (1 = Morning: 8a to Noon, 2 = Afternoon: Noon to 5p, 3 = Evening: 5p to 10p)
Scheduled	Yes/No	The course has been scheduled.

Entering Course Scheduling Requests

Let's assume an administrator needs to define courses for the Fall semester of 2005. To see how this works, you must first sign on to the Registration Management application as an administrator. Open the database (Registration.mdb) and then open the frmSplash form. When the Sign On form opens, enter **tmichaels** as the User Name, enter **password** as the Password, and press Enter or click the Sign On button. To start a new session, click the Sessions button on the main switchboard form and then click the New button on the Select

Sessions form. Select or enter 2005 in the Year combo box and select or enter Fall in the Semester combo box. Notice that as soon as you choose the semester, the form fills in the appropriate start and end dates for you. The form should now look like Figure 21-1. Click the Save Record button on the toolbar to save the new session.

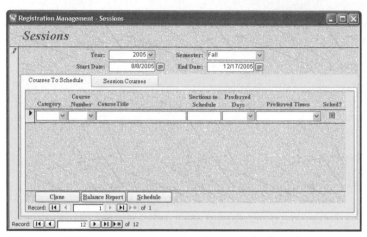

Figure 21-1   Defining a new semester to schedule.

Before going any further, let's explore how the application calculates the start and end dates. The process is triggered by code in the AfterUpdate event procedure for both the cmbYear and cmbSessionNumber (Semester) combo box controls. The code for the cmbSessionNumber control is as follows:

```
Private Sub cmbSessionNumber_AfterUpdate()
Dim datStart As Date, datEnd As Date
  ' Call the default start / end calc
  If CalcStartEnd(Me.SessionYear, Me.SessionNumber, datStart, datEnd) Then
    ' Update the form controls
    Me.StartDate = datStart
    Me.EndDate = datEnd
  End If
End Sub
```

All the hard work is done in the *CalcStartEnd* function that you can find in the modRegistration module. The code first verifies that it has been passed a nonzero year and session number. For the specified year, the code next calculates the first Monday of the year using the *DateSerial* and *Weekday* functions. Finally the code examines the session number (1 = Spring, 2 = Summer, 3 = Fall) and calculates the appropriate start and end dates. The code is as follows:

```
Public Function CalcStartEnd(intYear As Integer, intSession As Integer, _
  datStart As Date, datEnd As Date) As Integer
Dim datFirstMonday As Date
  ' Calculate default start and end days
```

```
' Make sure we have two values
If IsNothing(intYear) Or _
  IsNothing(intSession) Then
    CalcStartEnd = False
    Exit Function
End If
' Set up for a successful return
CalcStartEnd = True
' Calculate the first Monday of the year
datFirstMonday = DateSerial(intYear, 1, 1) + _
    ((8 - Weekday(DateSerial(intYear, 1, 1), vbMonday)) Mod 7)
' Set days based on semester
Select Case intSession
    ' Spring - weeks 2 - 20
    Case 1
        ' Spring semester starts on second Monday
        datStart = datFirstMonday + 7
        ' .. and ends on Saturday of 20th week
        datEnd = datFirstMonday + (7 * 19) + 5
    ' Summer short semester
    Case 2
        ' Summer semester starts on 22nd Monday
        datStart = datFirstMonday + (7 * 21)
        ' .. and ends on Saturday of 30th week
        datEnd = datFirstMonday + (7 * 29) + 5
    ' Fall semester
    Case 3
        ' Fall semester starts on 32nd Monday
        datStart = datFirstMonday + (7 * 31)
        ' .. and ends on Saturday of 50th week
        datEnd = datFirstMonday + (7 * 49) + 5
    Case Else
        ' Not a valid semester number
        CalcStartEnd = False
End Select
End Function
```

Note that the code uses the first Monday of the period as the starting day and the last Saturday of the period as the ending day. As explained earlier, session 1 (Spring) is weeks 2 through 20, session 2 (Summer) is weeks 22 through 29, and session 3 (Fall) is weeks 32 through 50. The administrator is free to adjust the starting and ending dates to reflect the actual needs of the school.

Specifying Sections to Schedule

After creating the session record, the administrator can begin entering the courses that need to be scheduled. You can go to the subform window on the Courses To Schedule tab and select a course category and a course number in that category. Notice that when you select the course number, Access automatically displays the related course title. You can enter the number of sections to schedule, the preferred days, and the preferred times. You cannot change the

Sched? check box—it is there to indicate which requests have already been scheduled by the automated process. As you enter selections, the form should look something like Figure 21-2.

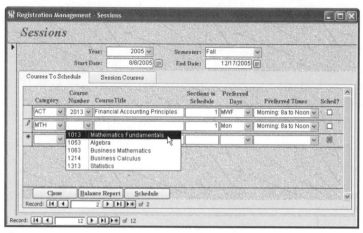

Figure 21-2   Specifying courses to be scheduled.

Notice that when you open the list under Course Number, the list displays only courses in the category you selected. The query that is the row source for the Course Number combo box (qlkpCoursesForSessionCoursesToSchedule) is a parameter query filtered on the Category field. The SQL for the query is as follows:

```
PARAMETERS [Forms]![frmSessions]![fsubSessionCoursesToSchedule].[Form]![cmbCourseCategory]
Text ( 255 );
SELECT tblCourses.CourseNumber, tblCourses.CourseTitle
FROM tblCourses
WHERE tblCourses.CourseCategory =
[Forms]![frmSessions]![fsubSessionCoursesToSchedule].[Form]![cmbCourseCategory]
ORDER BY tblCourses.CourseNumber;
```

As you might expect, code in the AfterUpdate event procedure for the Category combo box requeries the Course Number combo box so that it displays only the courses in the category selected. Code in the Current event procedure for the form also requeries the Course Number combo box to keep that combo box row source updated as you move from row to row in the subform window.

Cloning a Previous Schedule

The first time an administrator enters a schedule request, it must all be done manually. However, once a selection is made for any of the sessions in a year, the schedule request is likely to change only slightly for the same session in another year. To make it easy to copy and modify an existing schedule request, the application includes a "clone" feature. Rather than enter each request for the Fall session in 2005, you can simply clone the request from Fall in 2004.

To do this, first close the Sessions form and click the Sessions button again on the main switchboard. Select 2004 for Year and Fall for Semester and click the Edit button—you should see the 191 requests for that session. Click the Clone button at the bottom of the Courses To Schedule tab, and the application opens the Clone Semester dialog box as shown in Figure 21-3.

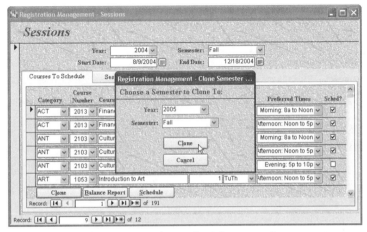

Figure 21-3   Cloning a previous schedule to another semester.

Select 2005 for the Year and Fall for the Semester and click the Clone button. If you previously entered a few requests for the Fall 2005 session, the application displays a warning dialog box, as shown in Figure 21-4. Because the cloning process deletes all previous records before making the copy, it's nice to see that it warns you just in case you chose the wrong semester to clone to. Click Yes to clone the records.

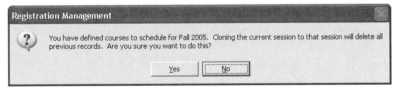

Figure 21-4   The cloning procedure warns you before overwriting records.

You can find the code that performs this task in the Click event procedure of the cmdClone command button on the fsubSessionCoursesToSchedule form—the subform you see on the Courses To Schedule tab of the Sessions window. The code begins by verifying that the current session (the one to be cloned) has courses scheduled. If not, there's nothing to clone, so the code displays a message and exits. Next, the code opens the fdlgCloneSemesterSchedule form—the Clone Semester dialog box shown in Figure 21-3. Because the code opens the fldg-CloneSemesterSchedule form in Dialog mode, the code waits until that form closes or hides itself. As you might expect, the code for the Clone button on the fdlgCloneSemesterSchedule form sets the Visible property of the form to False, and the code for the Cancel button simply closes the form.

When the code resumes, it checks to see if the dialog form is still open. If not, the user must have clicked the Cancel button, so the code exits. If the form is still open, the code fetches the selected values for Year and Semester (session number) and closes the form. If the user selected the year and session for the current session record on the parent form (the frmSessions form), the code displays an error message and exits. The code is as follows:

```
Private Sub cmdClone_Click()
Dim intSession As Integer, intYear As Integer, _
  datStart As Date, datEnd As Date
Dim db As DAO.Database, blnTrans As Boolean
  ' Set an error trap
  On Error GoTo cmdClone_Err
  ' Make sure there is something to clone
  If Me.Recordset.RecordCount = 0 Then
    MsgBox "You must enter courses to schedule " & _
      "in order to clone this semester.", _
      vbInformation, gstrAppTitle
    Exit Sub
  End If
  ' Open the dialog - code will wait as long as form is displayed
  DoCmd.OpenForm "fdlgCloneSemesterSchedule", WindowMode:=acDialog
  ' If form not still open,
  If Not IsFormLoaded("fdlgCloneSemesterSchedule") Then
    ' User canceled
    Exit Sub
  End If
  ' Grab the values from the form
  intYear = Form_fdlgCloneSemesterSchedule.cmbSessionYear
  intSession = Form_fdlgCloneSemesterSchedule.cmbSessionNumber
  ' Close the form
  DoCmd.Close acForm, "fdlgCloneSemesterSchedule"
  ' Make sure they didn't select current session
  If (intYear = Me.Parent.SessionYear) And _
    (intSession = Me.Parent.SessionNumber) Then
    MsgBox "You cannot clone a session course schedule to itself.", _
      vbCritical, gstrAppTitle
    ' Bail
    Exit Sub
  End If
```

If all went well to this point, the code next sets a pointer to the current database and starts a transaction to protect all the changes. Next, the code checks to see if any records exist in the tblSessionCoursesToSchedule table for the target session. If any exist, the code displays the warning message you saw in Figure 21-4, and cancels the transaction and exits if the user clicks the No button in the dialog box. If the user clicks the Yes button, the code deletes the existing records.

If the code found no records in the tblSessionCoursesToSchedule table, it next checks to see if a record exists in the tblSessions table. (If there were records in the tblSessionCoursesTo-Schedule table, then a companion record must already exist in the tblSessions table because of referential integrity rules.) If the record doesn't exist, the code calls the *CalcStartEnd* function to determine the start and end dates and adds the record by executing an SQL INSERT statement. The code is as follows:

```
' Point to this database
Set db = DBEngine(0)(0)
' Start a transaction
BeginTrans
blnTrans = True
' See if any courses to schedule already entered
If Not IsNothing(DLookup("SessionYear", "tblSessionCoursesToSchedule", _
  "SessionYear = " & intYear & _
  " AND SessionNumber = " & intSession)) Then
  ' Tell user we're gonna delete and start over
  If vbNo = MsgBox("You have defined courses to schedule for " & _
    Choose(intSession, "Spring", "Summer", "Fall") & " " & _
    intYear & ".  Cloning the current session to that session " & _
    "will delete all previous records.  Are you sure you want " & _
    "to do this?", vbQuestion + vbYesNo + vbDefaultButton2, _
    gstrAppTitle) Then
    ' Cancel the transaction
    Rollback
    blnTrans = False
    ' Bail
    Exit Sub
  End If
  ' Delete the previous rows
  db.Execute "DELETE * FROM tblSessionCoursesToSchedule " & _
    "WHERE SessionYear = " & intYear & _
    " AND SessionNumber = " & intSession, dbFailOnError
Else
  ' If the session not already set up
  If IsNothing(DLookup("SessionYear", "tblSessions", _
    "SessionYear = " & intYear & _
    " AND SessionNumber = " & intSession)) Then
    ' Need to insert a row
    ' Calculate the default start and end dates
    Call CalcStartEnd(intYear, intSession, datStart, datEnd)
    ' Insert the new row
    db.Execute "INSERT INTO tblSessions " & _
      "(SessionYear, SessionNumber, " & _
      "StartDate, EndDate) VALUES(" & intYear & ", " & intSession & _
      ", #" & datStart & "#, #" & datEnd & "#)", dbFailOnError
  End If
End If
```

Finally, the code executes an SQL INSERT statement to copy the records from the current session to the new one, changing the year and session number as it does so. When that completes successfully, the code commits the transaction, requeries the outer form to ensure that the new session is in the recordset, and moves the form to the newly created session. The code clears the database object and exits. The code at the end of the function handles any errors, including rolling back any updates that occurred up to the point of the error. The code is as follows:

```
' Clone the rows
db.Execute "INSERT INTO tblSessionCoursesToSchedule " & _
  "SELECT " & intYear & " As SessionYear, " & _
  intSession & " As SessionNumber, CourseCategory, " & _
  "CourseNumber, NumSections, PrefDays, PrefTimes, 0 As Scheduled " & _
  "FROM tblSessionCoursesToSchedule " & _
  "WHERE SessionYear = " & Me.Parent.SessionYear & _
  " AND SessionNumber = " & Me.Parent.SessionNumber, dbFailOnError
' Commit all updates
CommitTrans
blnTrans = False
' Requery the outer form
Forms!frmSessions.Requery
' Reposition to newly cloned records
Forms!frmSessions.Recordset.FindFirst "SessionYear = " & intYear & _
  " AND SessionNumber = " & intSession
cmdClone_Exit:
  ' Clear the database object
  Set db = Nothing
  ' Done
  Exit Sub
cmdClone_Err:
  ' Display the error
  MsgBox "Unexpected error attempting to clone courses to schedule:" & _
    vbCrLf & Err.Number & ", " & Err.Description, vbCritical, gstrAppTitle
  ' If a transaction pending
  If blnTrans Then
    ' Reset and roll back
    blnTrans = False
    Rollback
  End If
  ' Log it
  ErrorLog Me.Name & "_cmdClone", Err.Number, Err.Description
  ' Bail
  Resume cmdClone_Exit
End Sub
```

You can use this sort of cloning feature in any application where you need to replicate a large number of dependent records for a new task. As you can imagine, it was a bit tedious entering a sample scheduling request for the first session you see in the sample data, but I used this cloning feature to quickly create the data for the additional sessions.

Verifying Schedule Balance

In the sample application, each course day consists of 4 available hours each morning, afternoon, and evening (a total of 12 hours). This fictitious school also has a total of 12 classrooms available, so it's not possible to schedule more than 48 classroom hours in part of a day or more than a total of 144 classroom hours per day. After entering a course schedule request, it would be nice to see a display of the potential classroom-hour load balance to ensure that no day is overscheduled and that each time slot has roughly the same number of hours requested.

You can open the Sessions form, move to any session you like, and click the Balance Report button at the bottom of the Courses To Schedule tab. The application displays the Schedule Load Analysis report as shown in Figure 21-5. As you can see from the sample cloned for the Fall 2005 semester, Monday mornings might be a little underscheduled, but no day portion or full day exceeds the potential maximum. In truth, trying to schedule more than 100 classroom hours per day might also be limited by the number of instructors available.

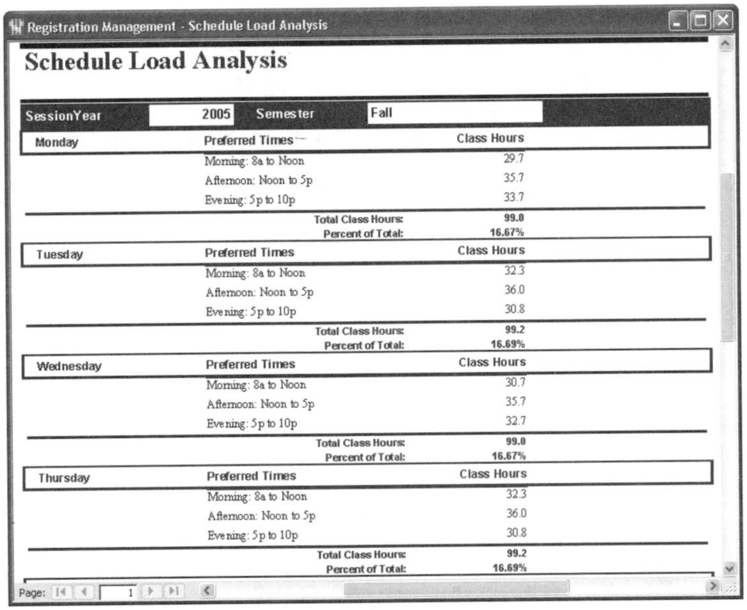

Figure 21-5   The Schedule Load Analysis report.

The report design is actually very simple—it lists the total calculated hours for each time slot and each day of the week. It also calculates the percentage of the total hours for each day. The real work is done in the qryRptScheduleLoadAnalysis query that is the record source for the report. The SQL for the query is as follows:

```
SELECT tblSessionCoursesToSchedule.SessionYear,
  tblSessionCoursesToSchedule.SessionNumber, ztblDays.DayNumber,
  ztblDays.DayName, tblSessionCoursesToSchedule.PrefTimes,
  SUM(IIf([SessionNumber]=2, IIf([PrefDays]<7, [CreditHours]*2,
    IIf([PrefDays]=8, [CreditHours], [CreditHours]*2/3)),
    IIf([PrefDays]<7, [CreditHours],
    IIf([PrefDays]=8, [CreditHours]/2, [CreditHours]/3)))) AS Hours
FROM tblCourses
  INNER JOIN (ztblDays
    INNER JOIN tblSessionCoursesToSchedule
    ON ztblDays.Days = tblSessionCoursesToSchedule.PrefDays)
```

```
ON (tblCourses.CourseNumber = tblSessionCoursesToSchedule.CourseNumber)
  AND (tblCourses.CourseCategory =
       tblSessionCoursesToSchedule.CourseCategory)
GROUP BY tblSessionCoursesToSchedule.SessionYear,
  tblSessionCoursesToSchedule.SessionNumber, ztblDays.DayNumber,
  ztblDays.DayName, tblSessionCoursesToSchedule.PrefTimes;
```

The query uses the credit hours specified for each requested course, but the credit hours aren't straightforward. The credit hours number for a course in most schools reflects the number of classroom hours that the student should attend each week for a full 16-week period. When a class is scheduled on multiple days (such as Monday-Wednesday-Friday or Tuesday-Thursday), the total credit hours must be divided among the days. If the class session is shorter than 16 weeks—as with the 8-week Summer session—the number of classroom hours must be adjusted accordingly.

Remember from the table design explained earlier that the PrefDays field is a code number indicating the days to be scheduled: 1 = Mon, 2 = Tue, 3 = Wed, 4 = Thu, 5 = Fri, 6 = Sat, 8 = TuTh, 9 = MWF, and 10 = TuThSat. Also, the SessionNumber field contains the value 1 for Spring, 2 for the short Summer session, and 3 for Fall. Knowing this, you can analyze the complex IIf expression in the Sum aggregate function as follows.

If this is the Summer session and the class is scheduled on a single day (PrefDays < 7), then multiply the credit hours by 2. If this is the Summer session and the class is on a two-day schedule (PrefDays = 8, or TuTh), use the credit hours value. If this is the Summer session and the class is on a three-day schedule (PrefDays wasn't less than 7 or equal to 8, so PrefDays must be 9 or 10, MWF or TuThSat), multiply credit hours times 2 and divide by 3.

If this isn't the Summer session and the class is scheduled on a single day (PrefDays < 7), then use the credit hours. If this isn't the Summer session and the class is on a two-day schedule (PrefDays = 8, or TuTh), divide the credit hours by 2. Otherwise, divide the credit hours by 3 to obtain the classroom hours per day.

Of course, this calculation is just an estimate. A course might have 4 credit hours, but that could be broken into 3 hours of lecture and 1 hour of lab work each week. The lecture time might spread across three days, but the 1-hour lab is probably scheduled on one day only. Nonetheless, this report helps an administrator determine if the requested schedule is going to be unbalanced or overscheduled.

Creating the Course Schedule

If you have explored the frmSessions form, you know that you can click the Session Courses tab and enter individual course sections and segment schedules. As noted earlier, this could be an arduous task for most schools. In this section, you'll learn how the automated scheduling process works and how an administrator can adjust or enter additional courses after running the process.

Running the Automated Scheduling Process

If you cloned the course schedule request from the Fall session in 2004 to the Fall session in 2005, your form should now look like Figure 21-6.

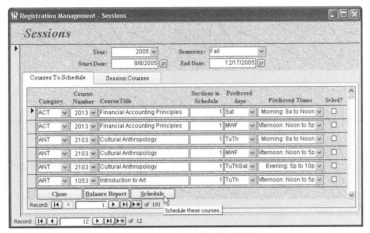

Figure 21-6   Starting the automated scheduling process.

To ask the application to schedule the requested courses, click the Schedule button at the bottom of the Courses To Schedule tab. Depending on the speed of your machine, the scheduler might take several minutes to complete, and you can see a progress meter on the status bar in the bottom of the Access window. When the automated scheduling process is complete, the process will most likely display a count of course requests it was unable to schedule, as shown in Figure 21-7.

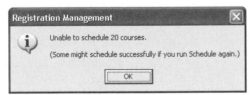

Figure 21-7   The scheduler might not be able to schedule all requested courses.

The message hints that you might be able to schedule additional courses if you run the process again. As you'll learn later when you study the code that performs the automated scheduling, the code first finds an available time and room and then looks for an instructor. If all instructors who can teach the course are already scheduled for other courses at the same time, the code skips scheduling that course without checking additional available times. If subsequent course requests in the first attempt use up all the rooms at the first chosen time, running the scheduling process again might pick a different time for which an instructor can be found.

If the scheduling process was able to honor all the requests, the administrator sees a confirmation message. When the administrator clicks OK in the confirmation message box, the application selects the Session Courses tab to display the full results. If some requests were not scheduled, the application displays the Courses Not Scheduled report, as shown in Figure 21-8, when the administrator clicks the OK button.

Course	Course Title	# Sect.	Days	Preferred Times	No Instr.	No Room / Time
ENG1003	English Composition	1	TuTh	Afternoon: Noon to 5p	☑	☐
CSC2764	Administering Novell Networks	1	TuTh	Afternoon: Noon to 5p	☑	☐
CSC2513	Database Programming: SQL Server	1	TuTh	Evening: 5p to 10p	☑	☐
CSC2473	Advanced JAVA programming	1	TuTh	Afternoon: Noon to 5p	☑	☐
CSC2413	Intermediate Web Programming	1	MWF	Afternoon: Noon to 5p	☐	☑
CSC1023	Personal Computer Skills	1	MWF	Evening: 5p to 10p	☑	☐
CSC1043	Introduction to Spreadsheets	1	MWF	Evening: 5p to 10p	☑	☐
CSC1053	Introduction to Database	1	MWF	Afternoon: Noon to 5p	☐	☑
CSC1053	Introduction to Database	1	MWF	Evening: 5p to 10p	☑	☐
CSC1013	Introduction to Computers	1	MWF	Evening: 5p to 10p	☑	☐
CSC2333	Object-Oriented Programming	1	MWF	Evening: 5p to 10p	☑	☐
SPC1153	Fundamentals of Public Speaking	1	MWF	Evening: 5p to 10p	☑	☐
CSC2543	SQL Server Administration	1	MWF	Evening: 5p to 10p	☑	☐
HUMI203	Arts in Society	1	MWF	Evening: 5p to 10p	☑	☐
CSC1803	UNIX Fundamentals	1	TuThSat	Morning: 8a to Noon	☑	☐

Figure 21-8   The Courses Not Scheduled report helps you analyze how to adjust the schedule requests.

If the administrator wants to schedule all the courses, the report can be invaluable to help determine how to change the unprocessed requests. If no instructor is available, the administrator can run the scheduling report for the instructors assigned to teach the course to find an available time slot. If no room or time is available, the administrator can run the scheduling report for courses by room to find an available room and time slot. You'll learn about both of these additional reports in Chapter 23, "Printing and E-Mailing Schedules."

Understanding the Automated Scheduling Process

You can imagine what you might have to do to lay out an actual course schedule that avoids all time, room, and instructor conflicts. I have a vision of a large conference room with the walls lined with scheduling charts. Not a pretty picture.

Of course, the code to automate the scheduling process isn't simple, either. You can find the *ScheduleCourses* function that performs this task in the modRegistration module. The code performs the scheduling process in the following steps:

1.   Initializes variables and opens the requests recordset and all output recordsets.

2.   Starts a loop to process all course requests.

3. Starts a loop to process all segments for a course request.

4. Finds a time and room for each segment of the course.

5. Finds an instructor available to teach all segments.

6. Schedules the course if a room, time, and instructor are found for all segments.

7. Closes out after processing all requests.

Initializing the Scheduling Process

The code begins by defining all the variables needed for the process. After establishing a pointer to the current database, the code deletes all rows from the ztblNotScheduled table that is the basis for the Courses Not Scheduled report you saw previously. Next, the code starts a transaction to protect all changes made to tables during the process. If an error occurs, the error trapping code at the end of the procedure rolls back all changes.

The code executes the Randomize statement to set a seed[1] based on the system clock for all calls to the *Rnd* function used to pick a random instructor later in the code. The code then opens a recordset on the courses to schedule, the tblSessionCourses table (to insert records only), the tblSessionCourseSegments table (insert only), and the ztblNotScheduled table (insert only).

> **Note**   The query to fetch requests sorts the requests to return single-day courses first, two-day courses (Tuesday-Thursday) next, and finally three-day courses (Monday-Wednesday-Friday and Tuesday-Thursday-Saturday). I designed it this way because the single-day courses are more likely to need larger blocks of time (three hours on one day instead of one hour each for three days). If the code scheduled the one-hour-per-day courses first, there might not be any large time blocks left to schedule a course for three hours on one day.

If there are some courses to schedule, the code moves to the last record to get an accurate count for the progress meter and starts the meter. The code is as follows:

```
Public Function ScheduleCourses(intYear As Integer, _
  intSession As Integer) As Integer
' Schedule the courses listed in tblSessionCoursesToSchedule
'   for the specified year and semester.
' Database object, Courses to Schedule recordset,
' Instructor Courses recordset, Room recordset
Dim db As DAO.Database, rstCtoS As DAO.Recordset, _
  rstIC As DAO.Recordset, rstRooms As DAO.Recordset
' Courses & Segments recordset, Session Courses Recordset,
' Session Course Segments recordset
```

---

1 All random number generators accept a "seed" number to begin creating a random sequence of numbers on each call to the generator. If you don't set the seed before calling the random number function, you'll get the same sequence of random numbers every time.

```
Dim rstCourses As DAO.Recordset, rstSessCourses As DAO.Recordset, _
  rstSessCourseSegs As DAO.Recordset
' Find highest section number recordset, Log of not scheduled recordset
Dim rstHighSec As DAO.Recordset, rstNotSched As DAO.Recordset
' Some working variables
Dim blnTrans As Boolean, intMove As Integer, intI As Integer
Dim intJ As Integer, intK As Integer, intDay As Integer
Dim intRoom As Integer, intMaxSection As Integer, intScheduled As Integer
Dim intProgress As Integer, varReturn As Variant
Dim intFailedThisCourse As Integer, intFailed As Integer
Dim intFailedRoom As Integer, intFailedInstructor As Integer
' Variables to set start and end values for segments
Dim datStartTime As Date, datEndTime As Date, intSegs As Integer
Dim datFullClassTime As Date, datClassTimePerDay As Date
' Found flags for room, time, and instructor overlap searches
Dim intFoundInstructor As Integer, intFoundRoom As Integer, _
  intFoundTime As Integer
' Places to save found segment info until all segments found
Dim intSegments(1 To 4) As Integer, intRooms(1 To 4) As Integer, _
  intDays(1 To 4) As Integer
Dim datStart(1 To 4) As Date, datEnd(1 To 4) As Date
  ' Set an error trap
  On Error GoTo Schedule_Err
  ' Point to this database
  Set db = DBEngine(0)(0)
  ' Clear out the not scheduled table
  db.Execute "DELETE * FROM ztblNotScheduled", dbFailOnError
  ' Start a transaction
  BeginTrans
  blnTrans = True
  ' Set the randomizer seed
  Randomize
  ' Open courses to schedule -
  '   Recordset returns single day courses, then TuTh,
  ' and finally MWF and TuThSat
  Set rstCtoS = db.OpenRecordset("SELECT * FROM zqryCoursesToSchedule " & _
    "WHERE SessionYear = " & intYear & _
    " AND SessionNumber = " & intSession, dbOpenDynaset)
  ' Open session courses, append only
  Set rstSessCourses = db.OpenRecordset("tblSessionCourses", _
    dbOpenDynaset, dbAppendOnly)
  ' Open session course segments, append only
  Set rstSessCourseSegs = db.OpenRecordset("tblSessionCourseSegments", _
    dbOpenDynaset, dbAppendOnly)
  ' Open not scheduled, append only
  Set rstNotSched = db.OpenRecordset("ztblNotScheduled", _
    dbOpenDynaset, dbAppendOnly)
  ' If got some to schedule
  If Not rstCtoS.EOF Then
    ' Move to last to get a count
    rstCtoS.MoveLast
    ' Show hourglass - might take a while
    DoCmd.Hourglass True
    ' Show progress meter
    varReturn = SysCmd(acSysCmdInitMeter, "Scheduling courses...", _
```

```
      rstCtoS.RecordCount)
   ' Start from the beginning
   rstCtoS.MoveFirst
End If
```

Next, the code starts a main loop to process all the request records one at a time. The code opens a recordset using the zqryCourseSegments query that returns the course and course segment information for the currently requested course. The code also opens a recordset using the zqryInstructorCourses query that returns all the available instructors for the current course.

If both the course segment and instructor recordsets contain records, the code moves to the last row in both recordsets to get an accurate count. If either recordset is empty, the code continues at the Else statement on page 449 that sets the course as failed. The code also clears the array used to contain up to four segments per course. (The code must be able to schedule all segments to schedule the course.) Finally, the code uses a totals query to find out the previous high section number for the course and add 1 for the section about to be created. The code is as follows:

```
' Loop through all to schedule
Do Until rstCtoS.EOF
   ' Open Courses and Course segments for this course
   Set rstCourses = db.OpenRecordset("SELECT * FROM zqryCoursesSegments" & _
     " WHERE CourseCategory = '" & rstCtoS!CourseCategory & _
     "' AND CourseNumber = " & rstCtoS!CourseNumber)
   ' Open Instructor Courses for this course
   Set rstIC = db.OpenRecordset("SELECT * FROM zqryInstructorCourses" & _
     " WHERE CourseCategory = '" & rstCtoS!CourseCategory & _
     "' AND CourseNumber = " & rstCtoS!CourseNumber)
   ' Clear the failed count for this course
   intFailedThisCourse = 0
   ' If have records in both,
   If (Not rstCourses.EOF) And (Not rstIC.EOF) Then
     ' Move to last instructor to get a good count
     rstIC.MoveLast
     ' Move to last Course Segment to get a good count
     rstCourses.MoveLast
     ' Save the count
     intSegs = rstCourses.RecordCount
     ' Clear the segment saved data array
     For intI = 1 To 4
       intSegments(intI) = 0
       intRooms(intI) = 0
     Next intI
     ' Find the highest previous section for this course
     ' Must use a recordset to get correct value inside transaction
     Set rstHighSec = db.OpenRecordset("SELECT MAX(SectionNumber) As MaxSec " & _
       "FROM tblSessionCourses " & _
       "WHERE SessionYear = " & intYear & _
       " AND SessionNumber = " & intSession & _
       " AND CourseCategory = '" & rstCtoS!CourseCategory & _
       "' AND CourseNumber = " & rstCtoS!CourseNumber, dbOpenSnapshot)
```

```
' If none yet
If rstHighSec.EOF Then
  intMaxSection = 1
Else
  intMaxSection = Nz(rstHighSec!MaxSec, 0) + 1
End If
' Close the recordset
rstHighSec.Close
```

Processing the Number of Course Sections Requested

Next, the code starts a loop to create the number of sections requested. The code makes sure the course segments recordset is positioned on the first segment for the current course. The code examines the preferred times field to establish beginning and ending search times. If the preferred time is morning, the start time is 8:00 AM and the end time is either 12:00 noon or 12:30 PM depending on the preferred days requested. The later end time on a Tuesday-Thursday schedule allows for up to three 1.5 hours time slots for three 3-credit-hour courses (the most common) spread across the two days.

If the preferred time is afternoon, the start time is set to 1:30 PM and the end time is set to 6:00 PM on a Tuesday-Thursday schedule. For all other days, the afternoon times are 1:00 PM to 5:00 PM. Finally, for evening classes, the start time is set to 7:00 PM and the end time is set to 10:00 PM for a Tuesday-Thursday schedule (to allow for up to two 3-hour courses); the start time is set to 6:00 PM and the end time to 10:00 PM for all other days. The code is as follows:

```
' Loop to create multiple sections
For intI = intMaxSection To (rstCtoS!NumSections + intMaxSection - 1)
  ' Move to the first course segment
  rstCourses.MoveFirst
  ' Figure out the start and end times
  Select Case rstCtoS!PrefTimes
    ' Morning
    Case 1
      datStartTime = #8:00:00 AM#
      ' If PrefDays is TuTh (2 day schedule)
      If rstCtoS!PrefDays = ClassDays.TuTh Then
        ' End time is later
        datEndTime = #12:30:00 PM#
      Else
        datEndTime = #12:00:00 PM#
      End If
    ' Afternoon
    Case 2
      ' If PrefDays is TuTh (2 day schedule)
      If rstCtoS!PrefDays = ClassDays.TuTh Then
        ' Times are different on TuTh schedules
        datStartTime = #1:30:00 PM#
        datEndTime = #6:00:00 PM#
      Else
        datStartTime = #1:00:00 PM#
        datEndTime = #5:00:00 PM#
      End If
```

```
        ' Evening
        Case Else
          ' If PrefDays is TuTh (2 day schedule)
          If rstCtoS!PrefDays = ClassDays.TuTh Then
            ' Times are different on TuTh schedules
            datStartTime = #7:00:00 PM#
            datEndTime = #10:00:00 PM#
          Else
            datStartTime = #6:00:00 PM#
            datEndTime = #10:00:00 PM#
          End If
    End Select
```

Next, the code attempts to find a room and time for each of the segments. The code must first establish both the amount of actual class time per day and the amount of time the class occupies on the schedule. The times are different by 10 minutes to allow students time to move from one class to another. For example, if a class segment for a 3-credit-hour class is to be taught three days a week, the class time per day is 50 minutes, and the time allocated on the schedule is 1 hour.

A class for a lab section should be taught all on one day rather than split across multiple days. If the course segment is a lab or the class is requested on only one day, the code divides the number of hours by 24 to obtain a true date/time value and subtracts 10 minutes to obtain the actual class time. (Note that the literal #12:10:00 AM# represents 10 minutes.) In reality, an instructor teaching a 3-hour class is probably going to take one or two breaks in the middle. And if the class is the last one before lunch, dinner, or the end of the day, the class might run the entire 3 hours. But for purposes of listing the class on the schedule, subtracting 10 minutes ensures that students have time to get to the next class, if any.

If the class is spread across multiple days, the code multiplies by 6, divides by the number of days, divides by 6 to round to the nearest 10 minutes, and divides by 24 to obtain a date/time value for the time on the schedule. The code also subtracts 10 minutes to obtain the actual class time.

If the segment is a lab, the code uses the requested day if the class is requested to be scheduled on one day. If the class is scheduled for multiple days and the segment is a lab, the code sets the search value to the first day (Tuesday for Tuesday-Thursday or Tuesday-Thursday-Saturday and Monday for Monday-Wednesday-Friday). In all other cases, the code uses the requested day code. Finally, the code clears the flags that indicate the time was found or the room was not found. The code is as follows:

```
' Loop through all the segments
For intJ = 1 To intSegs
  ' Calculate the hours per day
  ' If a lab class or all on one day
  If rstCourses!SegmentType = ClassSegType.Lab _
    Or rstCtoS!PrefDays <= ClassDays.Sat Then
    ' Labs all on one day
    ' Calculate time to next class slot
```

```
datFullClassTime = CDate(rstCourses!ClassHours / 24)
    ' Subtract 10 minutes for actual class time
    datClassTimePerDay = datFullClassTime - #12:10:00 AM#
Else
    ' Divide class equally by days available
    Select Case rstCtoS!PrefDays
      Case ClassDays.TuTh
        ' Split into two days
        ' Calculate time to next class slot
        datFullClassTime = CDate(((CInt(rstCourses!ClassHours * 6 / 2)) _
          / 6) / 24)
        ' Subtract 10 minutes for actual class time
        datClassTimePerDay = datFullClassTime - #12:10:00 AM#
      Case ClassDays.MWF, ClassDays.TuThSat
        ' Split into three days
        ' Calculate time to next class slot
        datFullClassTime = CDate(((CInt(rstCourses!ClassHours * 6 / 3)) _
          / 6) / 24)
        ' Subtract 10 minutes for actual class time
        datClassTimePerDay = datFullClassTime - #12:10:00 AM#
    End Select
  End If
' Set the search day value
' If a lab segment
If rstCourses!SegmentType = ClassSegType.Lab Then
  ' Set the search day to the first one
  Select Case rstCtoS!PrefDays
    Case Is <= ClassDays.Sat
      intDay = rstCtoS!PrefDays
    Case ClassDays.MWF
      intDay = ClassDays.Mon
    Case Else
      intDay = ClassDays.Tue
  End Select
Else
  ' Set search days to whatever is in request
  intDay = rstCtoS!PrefDays
End If
' Clear the found time flag
intFoundTime = 0
' Clear the failed room flag
intFailedRoom = 0
```

Searching for an Available Room and Time for Each Segment

Now the code is ready to search for a room and time. The code examines the segment type and opens a recordset on available lab rooms for lab segments or lecture and discussion rooms for non-lab segments. The recordset includes only rooms large enough to hold the maximum class size and is sorted in ascending sequence by room size. After creating the appropriate recordset, the code resets the found room flag. The code is as follows:

```
' Loop until found
Do Until (intFoundTime = -1) Or (datStartTime >= datEndTime)
  ' Open a recordset on rooms - based on segment type
```

```
Select Case rstCourses!SegmentType
  Case ClassSegType.Lab
    ' Lab - choose lab rooms only
    Set rstRooms = db.OpenRecordset("SELECT * FROM tlkpRooms " & _
      "WHERE RoomSize >= " & rstCourses!CourseMaxStudents & _
      " AND RoomType = " & ClassSegType.Lab & _
      " AND Unavailable = 0" & _
      " ORDER BY RoomSize ASC", dbOpenDynaset)
  Case ClassSegType.Discussion
    ' Discussion - choose lecture & discussion, but
    '  put discussion rooms in list first
    Set rstRooms = db.OpenRecordset("SELECT * FROM tlkpRooms " & _
      "WHERE RoomSize >= " & rstCourses!CourseMaxStudents & _
      " AND ((RoomType = " & ClassSegType.Discussion & _
      ") OR (RoomType = " & ClassSegType.Lecture & _
      ")) AND Unavailable = 0" & _
      " ORDER BY RoomType ASC, RoomSize ASC", dbOpenDynaset)
  Case Else
    ' Lecture - choose lecture & discussion rooms, but
    '  put lecture rooms in list first
    Set rstRooms = db.OpenRecordset("SELECT * FROM tlkpRooms " & _
      "WHERE RoomSize >= " & rstCourses!CourseMaxStudents & _
      " AND ((RoomType = " & ClassSegType.Discussion & _
      ") OR (RoomType = " & ClassSegType.Lecture & _
      ")) AND Unavailable = 0" & _
      " ORDER BY RoomType DESC, RoomSize ASC", dbOpenDynaset)
End Select
' Clear the found flag
intFoundRoom = 0
```

The code next starts a loop to look at each of the available rooms. The code calls the *CheckDupRoom* function, also in the modRegistration module, to find out if the current room is available for the current start time and duration. This function is very similar to the *CheckDupInstructor* function you'll see used later in this procedure. You can find a detailed description of how these functions work in "Understanding the Check Duplicates Procedures" on page 451.

The check duplicates functions all return a Variant array containing the information about overlapping segments already scheduled. However, if the first element of the array contains a True (−1) value, the function did not find any duplicates. When a room is found, the code sets the intFoundRoom flag variable to exit the loop. If the room overlaps with a segment already scheduled, the code moves to the next available room to try again. The code is as follows:

```
' Loop until looked at all rooms or found
Do Until (rstRooms.EOF) Or (intFoundRoom = -1)
  ' See if this room is available
  varReturn = CheckDupRoom(intYear, intSession, _
    rstCtoS!CourseCategory, rstCtoS!CourseNumber, _
    intI, rstCourses!CourseSegment, rstRooms!RoomID, _
    intDay, datStartTime, datStartTime + datClassTimePerDay)
  ' If got one
  If varReturn(1) = -1 Then
```

```
        ' Set the found a usable room flag
        intFoundRoom = -1
        ' Save the room
        intRoom = rstRooms!RoomID
    Else
        ' Try the next room
        rstRooms.MoveNext
    End If
Loop  ' .. to room search
' Close the rooms recordset
rstRooms.Close
```

If the previous loop found a room, the code sets the intFoundTime flag variable to exit the Do loop started on page 442. If a room was not found, then the code checks to see if the search day isn't equal to the days requested. When this is the case, the segment is a lab segment that must be scheduled on one day but can be scheduled on any of the preferred days. So, if the preferred days are Tuesday-Thursday and the code just tried to look for a room on Tuesday, the code resets to try Thursday next. Likewise, the code loops through all the days in a Tuesday-Thursday-Saturday and in a Monday-Wednesday-Friday request. If all the days have been tested, the code sets the search day back to the first day and increments the search time to the next time slot. If the segment isn't a lab, the code increments to the next time slot. Finally, the code loops back to the start of the time search loop—the Do statement on page 442. The code is as follows:

```
' If found a room
If intFoundRoom = -1 Then
    ' Good!  Set time found also
    intFoundTime = -1
Else
    ' If trying to schedule a single day segment
    '  on a multi-day class
    If intDay <> rstCtoS!PrefDays Then
        ' Try other days first
        Select Case rstCtoS!PrefDays
            ' TuTh
            Case ClassDays.TuTh
                ' If just tried Tuesday
                If intDay = ClassDays.Tue Then
                    ' Try Thursday next
                    intDay = ClassDays.Thu
                Else
                    ' Go back to Tuesday
                    intDay = ClassDays.Tue
                    ' And bump time slot instead
                    datStartTime = datStartTime + datFullClassTime
                End If
            ' Mon, Wed, Fri
            Case ClassDays.MWF
                ' If just tried Monday
                If intDay = ClassDays.Mon Then
                    ' Try Wednesday next
                    intDay = ClassDays.Wed
```

```
                          ' .. or just tried Wed
                        ElseIf intDay = ClassDays.Wed Then
                          ' Try Friday next
                          intDay = ClassDays.Fri
                        Else
                          ' Go back to Monday
                          intDay = ClassDays.Mon
                          ' And bump time slot instead
                          datStartTime = datStartTime + datFullClassTime
                        End If
                      ' Tue, Thur, Sat
                      Case ClassDays.TuThSat
                        ' If just tried Tuesday
                        If intDay = ClassDays.Tue Then
                          ' Try Thursday next
                          intDay = ClassDays.Thu
                        ' .. or just tried Thursday
                        ElseIf intDay = ClassDays.Thu Then
                          ' Try Saturday next
                          intDay = ClassDays.Sat
                        Else
                          ' Go back to Tuesday
                          intDay = ClassDays.Tue
                          ' And bump time slot instead
                          datStartTime = datStartTime + datFullClassTime
                        End If
                    End Select
                Else
                    ' Bump to next time slot
                    datStartTime = datStartTime + datFullClassTime
                End If
            End If
        Loop  ' .. to time search
```

After falling out of the time search loop, either because a time was found or the start time was incremented beyond the end time of the requested preferred times, the code checks to see if both a room and a time were found. If found, the code saves the found data for the current segment in local array variables. If not found, the code sets the loop variable for the current segment to the total segments to exit the loop searching on segments. There's no point in searching for rooms and times for additional segments for a course if one of them fails completely. The code also sets a flag indicating that the room search failed. Finally, the code increments the start time, moves to the next course segment, and loops to the start of the segment search loop—the For statement on page 440. The code is as follows:

```
            ' If found both a room and a time
            If (intFoundRoom = -1) And (intFoundTime = -1) Then
              ' Save the data for this segment
              intSegments(intJ) = rstCourses!CourseSegment
              intRooms(intJ) = intRoom
              intDays(intJ) = intDay
              datStart(intJ) = datStartTime
              datEnd(intJ) = datStartTime + datClassTimePerDay
            Else
```

```
                    ' Failed on one of the segments - don't process any more
                    intJ = intSegs
                    ' .. and set room failed flag
                    intFailedRoom = True
                End If
                ' Bump to next time slot
                datStartTime = datStartTime + datFullClassTime
                ' Move to the next segment
                rstCourses.MoveNext
            Next intJ  ' .. process all segments
```

Searching for an Instructor for All Segments

After processing all segments for a course, the code sets up to search for an instructor. However, the next block of code executes only if a room and time were found for all segments of the course (the intFailedRoom variable is 0 or False). The code first calculates a random offset to pick an instructor for the class. After moving to the first instructor record, the code moves forward the offset amount if the amount is not zero. (The code would get an error attempting to move 0 rows.)

The code clears the intFoundInstructor flag variable and the intScheduled flag variable and then starts a loop through all instructors. Although the code moved forward to a random instructor record, you'll find code at the end of the loop later that moves back to the start if the search falls off the end. The code then looks at each segment saved in the array variables. Although all segments should contain a valid room number if intFailedRoom was not True, the code double-checks and bumps the loop counter to exit if it finds a zero room number. If the segment has valid schedule information, the code calls the *CheckDupInstructor* function (described later in this chapter) to find out if the current segment causes an overlap with any other segment already scheduled for the instructor. As with the *CheckDupRoom* function, this function returns a True (–1) value in the first element of the returned array if there is no overlap. When no overlap exists, the code adds 1 to the intFoundInstructor flag variable. The code is as follows:

```
            ' Clear the instructor failed flag
            intFailedInstructor = 0
            ' If didn't fail on the room
            If Not intFailedRoom Then
                ' Get a random instructor
                intMove = Int(Rnd * rstIC.RecordCount)
                ' Move to first
                rstIC.MoveFirst
                ' Use the random move number to pick an instructor
                If intMove <> 0 Then rstIC.Move intMove
                ' Clear the found instructor flag
                intFoundInstructor = 0
                ' .. and the scheduled flag
                intScheduled = 0
                ' Potentially loop through all instructors
                For intK = 1 To rstIC.RecordCount
                    ' See if available for all segments
```

```
For intJ = 1 To intSegs
  ' If no room in this segment
  If intRooms(intJ) = 0 Then
    ' Don't process any more - failure
    intJ = intSegs
  Else
    ' See if instructor available for this segment
    varReturn = CheckDupInstructor(intYear, intSession, _
      rstCtoS!CourseCategory, rstCtoS!CourseNumber, _
      intI, intSegments(intJ), rstIC!InstructorID, _
      intDays(intJ), datStart(intJ), datEnd(intJ))
    ' If OK,
    If varReturn(1) = -1 Then
      ' Add 1 to instructor found count
      intFoundInstructor = intFoundInstructor + 1
    End If
  End If
' Process all segments for instructor
Next intJ
```

After processing all segments, the count in the intFoundInstructor flag variable will equal the count of segments if the selected instructor is available for all the segments. When that is the case, the code can then schedule the course. The code first adds a row to the tblSessionCourses table. The code next adds a row for each segment for the course. The code sets the intScheduled flag variable and sets the loop variable to exit at the end of the instructor search loop.

If the instructor was not found for all segments, the code moves to the next instructor row. If that moves off the end of the recordset (remember, the code starts with some random offset), the code moves back to the first record. It makes sure the intFoundInstructor flag variable is reset and loops to the start of the instructor search loop—the For intK statement on the preceding page. The code is as follows:

```
' If found the instructor for ALL segments,
If intFoundInstructor = intSegs Then
  ' Add the course section
  With rstSessCourses
    .AddNew
    ' Set all fields
    !SessionYear = intYear
    !SessionNumber = intSession
    !CourseCategory = rstCtoS!CourseCategory
    !CourseNumber = rstCtoS!CourseNumber
    !SectionNumber = intI
    !InstructorID = rstIC!InstructorID
    .Update
  End With
  ' Add the segments
  For intJ = 1 To intSegs
    ' Add each segment
    With rstSessCourseSegs
      .AddNew
```

```
                       ' Set all fields
                      !SessionYear = intYear
                      !SessionNumber = intSession
                      !CourseCategory = rstCtoS!CourseCategory
                      !CourseNumber = rstCtoS!CourseNumber
                      !SectionNumber = intI
                      !CourseSegment = intSegments(intJ)
                      !RoomID = intRooms(intJ)
                      !Days = intDays(intJ)
                      !StartTime = datStart(intJ)
                      !EndTime = datEnd(intJ)
                      .Update
                    End With
                  Next intJ
                  ' Set scheduled
                  intScheduled = -1
                  ' Set loop counter to exit
                  intK = rstIC.RecordCount
                Else  ' Instructor not found
                  ' Attempt to move to next instructor
                  rstIC.MoveNext
                  ' If fell off the end,
                  If rstIC.EOF Then
                    ' Go back to start
                    rstIC.MoveFirst
                  End If
                  ' Reset the instructor count
                  intFoundInstructor = 0
                End If
              ' Try another instructor
              Next intK
```

After trying all the available instructors (or falling out of the loop because one was found), the code checks the intScheduled flag variable to see if the request was scheduled. If it was not scheduled, the code sets the intFailedInstructor flag variable. It also adds 1 to the number of failed course schedules and then loops to process all sections if multiple sections were requested. The Else statement matches the If statement on page 439 that tests to see if course segments and instructors are available for the requested course. If both were not available, the code sets the intFailedThisCourse flag variable to the number of sections requested. If no class was scheduled for the current request, the code writes a row to the ztblNotScheduled table that is the record source for the rptNotScheduled report and adds 1 to the total failed count. If the course was scheduled, the code edits the request recordset and sets the Scheduled field. The code is as follows:

```
              ' If not scheduled
              If Not intScheduled Then
                ' Set instructor search failed
                intFailedInstructor = -1
              End If
            End If
            ' See if not successful
            If intScheduled = 0 Then
```

```
            ' Failed to schedule - add 1 to failed count
            intFailedThisCourse = intFailedThisCourse + 1
        End If
    Next intI  ' .. process all sections
Else
    ' Set all failed
    intFailedThisCourse = rstCtoS!NumSections
End If  ' .. end of got course & instructor code
' If any failed,
If intFailedThisCourse <> 0 Then
    ' Write a log record
    With rstNotSched
        .AddNew
        !SessionYear = intYear
        !SessionNumber = intSession
        !CourseCategory = rstCtoS!CourseCategory
        !CourseNumber = rstCtoS!CourseNumber
        !NumSections = intFailedThisCourse
        !PrefDays = rstCtoS!PrefDays
        !PrefTimes = rstCtoS!PrefTimes
        !FailedInstructor = intFailedInstructor
        !FailedRoom = intFailedRoom
        .Update
    End With
    ' Add to total failed
    intFailed = intFailed + intFailedThisCourse
Else
    ' Set course scheduled
    rstCtoS.Edit
    rstCtoS!Scheduled = -1
    rstCtoS.Update
End If
```

Processing All Requests and Closing the Procedure

After processing the current request, the code moves to the next schedule request, closes the course segments and instructor courses recordsets, and updates the progress meter. The Loop statement returns to the Do statement on page 439. After processing all requests, the code commits the transaction to save all changes and closes all open recordsets. If all requests were scheduled, the code returns True; otherwise, the code returns the number of requests that were not scheduled. The code at the Schedule_Exit label ignores all subsequent errors as it clears the status bar, turns off the hourglass, clears all object variables, and exits. The code at the end of the function traps any error, displays and logs the error, rolls back any pending changes, and exits the procedure. The code is as follows:

```
' Get next request
rstCtoS.MoveNext
' Close Courses
rstCourses.Close
' Close instructor courses
rstIC.Close
' Add 1 to count processed
```

```
        intProgress = intProgress + 1
        ' Update the meter
        varReturn = SysCmd(acSysCmdUpdateMeter, intProgress)
        ' Give Access some time to update the meter
        DoEvents
    Loop   ' .. process all schedule requests
    ' Commit all changes
    CommitTrans
    blnTrans = False
    ' Close up shop
    rstCtoS.Close
    rstSessCourseSegs.Close
    rstSessCourses.Close
    rstNotSched.Close
    ' If none failed,
    If intFailed = 0 Then
        ' Return success
        ScheduleCourses = True
    Else
        ' Return the failed count
        ScheduleCourses = intFailed
    End If
Schedule_Exit:
    ' Blow past errors after this
    On Error Resume Next
    ' Clean up - clear the meter
    varReturn = SysCmd(acSysCmdClearStatus)
    ' Turn off the hourglass
    DoCmd.Hourglass False
    ' Clear all objects
    Set rstSessCourseSegs = Nothing
    Set rstSessCourses = Nothing
    Set rstCourses = Nothing
    Set rstRooms = Nothing
    Set rstIC = Nothing
    Set rstCtoS = Nothing
    Set rstNotSched = Nothing
    Set db = Nothing
    ' Done
    Exit Function
Schedule_Err:
    ' Got an error - display it
    MsgBox "Unexpected error scheduling courses: " & Err.Number & _
        ", " & Err.Description, _
        vbCritical, gstrAppTitle
    ' Roll back any transaction
    If blnTrans Then
        blnTrans = False
        Rollback
    End If
    ' Log the error
    ErrorLog "ScheduleCourses", Err.Number, Err.Description
    ' Bail
    Resume Schedule_Exit
End Function
```

Understanding the Check Duplicates Procedures

As you learned in the preceding section, the *ScheduleCourses* function calls the *CheckDupRoom* and *CheckDupInstructor* functions to determine if the room or instructor about to be scheduled is already scheduled for another course. You'll also learn later in this chapter that several of the event procedures in the forms to edit course and instructor schedules also use these functions.

The key to both of these functions is the zqryOverlap query that provides the basic query structure to check for overlapping schedules. The query joins the tblCourses, tblSession-Courses, and tblSessionCourseSegments tables, as shown in Figure 21-9, to provide the needed data to analyze.

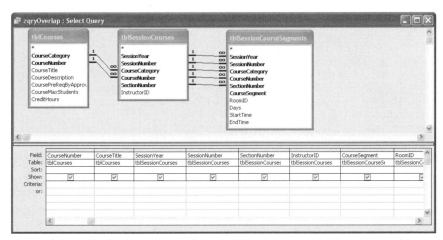

Figure 21-9   The basic query used to check for instructor and room schedule overlaps.

Both the *CheckDupRoom* and *CheckDupInstructor* functions work in similar ways. The only difference is the *CheckDupRoom* function checks for an overlap on RoomID, and the *CheckDupInstructor* function checks for an overlap on InstructorID. The *CheckDupInstructor* function begins by defining local variables and then setting a pointer to the current database. The code opens the QueryDef object for the zqryOverlap query and extracts the SQL minus the ending semicolon to use as a base. The code next adds predicates to test for the session, course, instructor, and times requested. The code also adds predicates to exclude the rows where the course, section, and segment number exactly match the request being scheduled.

Next, the function calls the *BuildDayPredicate* function (discussed on the next page) to add the test for the days requested. If that function returns no predicate string, the code assumes that the code for the days requested was invalid, clears the object variables, returns a failure code, and exits. If the function returned a day predicate string, it adds that predicate to the SQL and opens a recordset to find any overlaps. The code is as follows:

```
Public Function CheckDupInstructor(intSessYear As Integer, _
  intSessNumber As Integer, strCategory As String, intCourseNum As Integer, _
```

```
         intSecNum As Integer, intSegment As Integer, intInstructorID As Integer, _
         intDays As Integer, datStart As Date, datEnd As Date) As Variant
' Check for instructor schedule overlap
' Inputs: Session Year, Session Number, Course Category, Course Number,
'          Section Number, Course Segment, Instructor ID, Days, Start Time, End Time
' Output: Return Variant array for Course Category, Course Number, Course Title,
'          Section Number, and Course Segments that overlap with the request.
'          Array(1) contains the value -1 if no overlaps
'          Array(1) contains the value 0 if an error encountered
Dim db As Dao.Database, rst As Dao.Recordset, qd As Dao.QueryDef
Dim strDayPredicate As String, strWhere As String, strSQL As String
Dim varArray() As Variant, intI As Integer
    ' Set an error trap
    On Error GoTo Err_DupInstructor
    ' Point to this database
    Set db = DBEngine(0)(0)
    ' Get the template query
    Set qd = db.QueryDefs("zqryOverlap")
    ' Extract the SQL
    strSQL = Left(qd.SQL, InStrRev(qd.SQL, ";") - 1)
    ' Start building the predicate
    strWhere = " WHERE tblSessionCourses.SessionYear = " & intSessYear & _
      " AND tblSessionCourses.SessionNumber = " & intSessNumber & _
      " AND InstructorID = " & intInstructorID & _
      " AND StartTime <= #" & datEnd & "#" & _
      " AND EndTime >= #" & datStart & "#" & _
      " AND ((tblCourses.CourseCategory <> '" & strCategory & "') " & _
      " OR (tblCourses.CourseNumber <> " & intCourseNum & ") " & _
      " OR (tblSessionCourses.SectionNumber <> " & intSecNum & ") " & _
      " OR (tblSessionCourseSegments.CourseSegment <> " & intSegment & "))"
    ' Get the days predicate
    strDayPredicate = BuildDayPredicate(intDays)
    ' Make sure we got something
    If IsNothing(strDayPredicate) Then
      ' Oops - must have been passed an invalid day code
      ' Return an error
      CheckDupInstructor = Array(0)
      ' Clear the objects
      Set qd = Nothing
      Set db = Nothing
      ' Bail
      Exit Function
    End If
    ' Add the days predicate
    strWhere = strWhere & " AND " & strDayPredicate
    ' Finish the SQL
    strSQL = strSQL & strWhere
    ' Open the recordset
    Set rst = db.OpenRecordset(strSQL, dbOpenDynaset)
```

Before going further in the *CheckDupInstructor* function, let's take a quick look at the
BuildDayPredicate function. The function examines the days requested input and builds a
predicate to test for all relevant days. If the day requested is Monday, the code builds a

predicate to test both Monday and the Monday-Wednesday-Friday combination. If the day requested is Tuesday, the code builds a predicate to test Tuesday, the Tuesday-Thursday combination, and the Tuesday-Thursday-Saturday combination. The point is to check all potential overlaps—if the request is for a Thursday, you can encounter an overlap with any course scheduled on Thursday, Tuesday-Thursday, or Tuesday-Thursday-Saturday. The code is as follows:

```
Public Function BuildDayPredicate(intDays As Integer) As String
' Build a predicate to check for overlapping days
Dim strWhere As String
  ' Create predicate based on input day
  Select Case intDays
    ' Monday
    Case ClassDays.Mon
      strWhere = "((Days = " & ClassDays.Mon & _
        ") OR (Days = " & ClassDays.MWF & "))"
    ' Tuesday
    Case ClassDays.Tue
      strWhere = "((Days = " & ClassDays.Tue & _
        ") OR (Days = " & ClassDays.TuTh & _
        ") OR (Days = " & ClassDays.TuThSat & "))"
    ' Wednesday
    Case ClassDays.Wed
      strWhere = "((Days = " & ClassDays.Wed & _
        ") OR (Days = " & ClassDays.MWF & "))"
    ' Thursday
    Case ClassDays.Thu
      strWhere = "((Days = " & ClassDays.Thu & _
        ") OR (Days = " & ClassDays.TuTh & _
        ") OR (Days = " & ClassDays.TuThSat & "))"
    ' Friday
    Case ClassDays.Fri
      strWhere = "((Days = " & ClassDays.Fri & _
        ") OR (Days = " & ClassDays.MWF & "))"
    ' Saturday
    Case ClassDays.Sat
      strWhere = "((Days = " & ClassDays.Sat & _
        ") OR (Days = " & ClassDays.TuThSat & "))"
    ' Tue-Thu
    Case ClassDays.TuTh
      strWhere = "((Days = " & ClassDays.Tue & _
        ") OR (Days = " & ClassDays.Thu & _
        ") OR (Days = " & ClassDays.TuTh & _
        ") OR (Days = " & ClassDays.TuThSat & "))"
    ' Mon-Wed-Fri
    Case ClassDays.MWF
      strWhere = "((Days = " & ClassDays.Mon & _
        ") OR (Days = " & ClassDays.Wed & _
        ") OR (Days = " & ClassDays.Fri & _
        ") OR (Days = " & ClassDays.MWF & "))"
    ' Tue-Thu-Sat
    Case ClassDays.TuThSat
```

```
        strwhere = "((Days = " & ClassDays.Tue & _
            ") OR (Days = " & ClassDays.Thu & _
            ") OR (Days = " & ClassDays.Sat & _
            ") OR (Days = " & ClassDays.TuTh & _
            ") OR (Days = " & ClassDays.TuThSat & "))"
  End Select
  ' Return the answer
  BuildDayPredicate = strwhere
End Function
```

Let's say the scheduling process needs to find out if scheduling the third section and the first segment (a lecture segment for a maximum of 25 students) of the Introduction to XML course (CSC1423) overlaps with any other course already scheduled. The instructor is me (John Viescas, instructor number 17), the time is 9:00 AM to 9:50 AM, and the days are Monday-Wednesday-Friday. The code in the *CheckDupInstructor* function will generate the following SQL:

```
SELECT tblCourses.CourseCategory, tblCourses.CourseNumber, tblCourses.CourseTitle,
  tblSessionCourses.SessionYear, tblSessionCourses.SessionNumber,
  tblSessionCourses.SectionNumber, tblSessionCourses.InstructorID,
  tblSessionCourseSegments.CourseSegment, tblSessionCourseSegments.RoomID,
  tblSessionCourseSegments.Days, tblSessionCourseSegments.StartTime,
  tblSessionCourseSegments.EndTime
FROM (tblCourses
  INNER JOIN tblSessionCourses
    ON (tblCourses.CourseNumber = tblSessionCourses.CourseNumber)
    AND (tblCourses.CourseCategory = tblSessionCourses.CourseCategory))
  INNER JOIN tblSessionCourseSegments
    ON (tblSessionCourses.SectionNumber = tblSessionCourseSegments.SectionNumber)
    AND (tblSessionCourses.CourseNumber = tblSessionCourseSegments.CourseNumber)
    AND (tblSessionCourses.CourseCategory = tblSessionCourseSegments.CourseCategory)
    AND (tblSessionCourses.SessionNumber = tblSessionCourseSegments.SessionNumber)
    AND (tblSessionCourses.SessionYear = tblSessionCourseSegments.SessionYear)
WHERE tblSessionCourses.SessionYear = 2005
  AND tblSessionCourses.SessionNumber = 3
  AND InstructorID = 17
  AND StartTime <= #09:50:00 AM#
  AND EndTime >= #09:00:00 AM#
  AND ((tblCourses.CourseCategory <> 'CSC')
    OR (tblCourses.CourseNumber <> 1423)
    OR (tblSessionCourses.SectionNumber <> 3)
    OR (tblSessionCourseSegments.CourseSegment <> 1))
  AND ((Days = 1 ) OR (Days = 3) OR (Days = 5) OR (Days = 9))
```

The above SQL should return to the *CheckDupInstructor* function any other scheduled segment for me on a Monday, Wednesday, or Friday that overlaps with the time span the code is trying to schedule.

After opening a recordset on the constructed query, the *CheckDupInstructor* function checks to see if the query returns any rows. If the query returns nothing, there are no overlaps, so the function sets a True (−1) return and exits. If the recordset contains rows, the rows define the class segments that conflict with the request. The code loops through all the records and builds an array containing the course, course title, section, segment, scheduled days, start time, and end time of the conflicting course. After loading all the conflicts, the function returns the array as an answer. The code at the end of the function traps any errors and returns a failure. The code is as follows:

```
' If we got none
If rst.EOF Then
  ' Return success
  CheckDupInstructor = Array(-1)
  ' Close and clear the objects
  rst.Close
  Set rst = Nothing
  Set qd = Nothing
  Set db = Nothing
  ' Done
  Exit Function
End If
' Process all records
Do Until rst.EOF
  ' Add 8 to the upper bound
  intI = intI + 8
  ' Expand the array to hold another row
  ReDim Preserve varArray(intI)
  ' Set the Course Category
  varArray(intI - 7) = rst!CourseCategory
  ' Set the Course Number
  varArray(intI - 6) = rst!CourseNumber
  ' Set the Course Title
  varArray(intI - 5) = rst!CourseTitle
  ' Set the Section Number
  varArray(intI - 4) = rst!SectionNumber
  ' Set the Segment
  varArray(intI - 3) = rst!CourseSegment
  ' Set the Days
  varArray(intI - 2) = Choose(rst!Days, "Mon", "Tue", "Wed", "Thu", _
    "Fri", "Sat", "", "TuTh", "MWF", "TuThSat")
  ' Set the start time
  varArray(intI - 1) = rst!StartTime
  ' Set the end time
  varArray(intI) = rst!EndTime
  ' Get the next one
  rst.MoveNext
Loop
' Close the recordset
rst.Close
' Assign the variant array as the return value
CheckDupInstructor = varArray
' Done
Exit_DupInstructor:
  ' Clear all objects
  Set rst = Nothing
```

```
  Set qd = Nothing
  Set db = Nothing
  ' Exit
  Exit Function
Err_DupInstructor:
  ' Display the error
  MsgBox "Unexpected error checking duplicate instructor scheduling: " & vbCrLf & _
    Err.Number & ", " & Err.Description, vbCritical, gstrAppTitle
  ' Log it
  ErrorLog "CheckDupInstructor", Err.Number, Err.Description
  ' Return failure
  CheckDupInstructor = Array(0)
  ' Bail
  Resume Exit_DupInstructor
End Function
```

Scheduling Courses "By Hand"

Most of the time, an administrator is going to use the automated process to schedule courses. However, an administrator might also want to schedule a few courses individually or adjust the schedule generated by the automated process. As you might expect, the Sessions form allows the administrator to do that, but it also performs the same overlap checks used by the automated process.

To see how this works, start the application, sign on as **tmichaels** again using **password** as the password, click the Sessions button on the main switchboard, click the New button on the Sessions Select form, and create a new session for the Spring session of 2006. Click the Session Courses tab to begin entering a course schedule.

On the first row, select Category CSC, choose Course Number 1013 (Introduction to Computers), and choose my instructor ID (17). Click the Save Record button on the toolbar to save the record, and click the plus sign next to the course record to begin scheduling the sections. Schedule Segment 1 in the Lecture D room in the Chinook building (Room ID 4), specify that the class should be taught on MWF, and set a Start Time of 9:00 AM. Notice that the form fills in the appropriate End Time for you. Schedule Segment 2 (the lab) in the Lab A room in the Quinault building for Monday starting at 10:00 AM.

Enter a second section of the course to be taught by Lynn Trapp (his instructor ID is 12). Put the lecture portion in the Lecture E room in the Chinook building (Room ID 5) on the same days and time. Schedule the lab portion in Lab C in the Quinault building (Room ID 12) for Monday at 9:40 AM. Your form should now look like Figure 21-10.

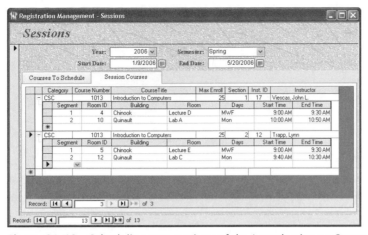

Figure 21-10 Scheduling two sections of the Introduction to Computers course on the same days and times.

Now try to change the instructor for the second section to me (instructor ID 17). As soon as you select me, the application displays an error message, as shown in Figure 21-11.

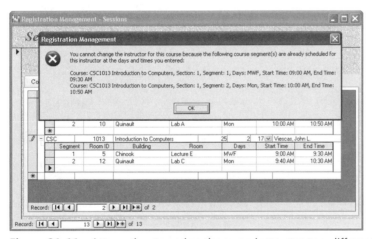

Figure 21-11 Attempting to assign the same instructor to a different section at the same time.

Click OK and then press Esc to clear your edit on the record. Now try to change the Room ID for segment 1 of the second course to the Lecture D room in the Chinook building (Room ID 4). As soon as you pick the new room the application displays an error message, as shown in Figure 21-12 on the next page.

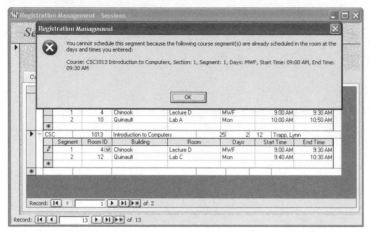

Figure 21-12   Attempting to schedule two segments to the same classroom at the same time.

The check for a duplicate instructor that generates the first error message (shown in Figure 21-11) occurs in the BeforeUpdate event procedure of the cmbInstuctorID combo box on the fsubSessionCoursesDS form. The code in that event procedure first verifies that the user has selected a course category and a course number. Next, if the change is not happening on a new record, the code opens a recordset on the related records that might be in the fsubSubSessionCourseSegmentsDS form.

If related course segments are defined, the code loops through each record and calls the *CheckDupInstructor* function to find out if the new instructor about to be assigned causes any overlaps with other segments already scheduled. Remember from the previous section that the *CheckDupInstructor* function returns a –1 (True) value in the first array element if there are no overlaps or a 0 (False) in the first array element if an error occurred, and it loads the array with data about overlapping course segments if it finds any.

If the function returns something other than a True (–1) value in the first entry in the array, the code assembles an error message for each segment. After processing all segments, if the message string contains text, the code displays the message and cancels the update so the user cannot save the changed instructor. The code is as follows:

```
Private Sub cmbInstructorID_BeforeUpdate(Cancel As Integer)
Dim rst As Dao.Recordset, varArray As Variant, strMsg As String
Dim strMsgInstruct As String, intI As Integer, intJ As Integer
  ' Make sure we have a course category and number
  If IsNothing(Me.CourseCategory) Or _
    IsNothing(Me.CourseNumber) Then
    MsgBox "You must select the course category and " & _
      "number before selecting an instructor.", _
      vbCritical, gstrAppTitle
    ' Cancel the update
    Cancel = True
    Exit Sub
  End If
```

```
' If not a new record,
If (Not Me.NewRecord) Then
  ' Open a recordset on the related segments
  ' (Note: Can't use the subform Recordset because we're in
  '    datasheet/subdatasheet mode.)
  Set rst = DBEngine(0)(0).OpenRecordset( _
    "SELECT * FROM qrySessionCourseSegments " & _
    "WHERE SessionYear = " & Me.SessionYear & _
    " AND SessionNumber = " & Me.SessionNumber & _
    " AND CourseCategory = '" & Me.CourseCategory & _
    "' AND CourseNumber = " & Me.CourseNumber & _
    " AND SectionNumber = " & Me.SectionNumber)
  ' Check for overlapping Instructor schedule
  ' Process all the segments for overlaps with the new instructor
  Do Until rst.EOF
    varArray = CheckDupInstructor(rst!SessionYear, rst!SessionNumber, _
      rst!CourseCategory, rst!CourseNumber, rst!SectionNumber, rst!CourseSegment, _
      Me.cmbInstructorID, rst!Days, rst!StartTime, rst!EndTime)
    ' If an error
    If varArray(1) = 0 Then
      ' Cancel the edit
      Cancel = True
      ' Bail
      Exit Sub
    End If
    ' If some found,
    If varArray(1) <> -1 Then
      ' Loop to build the message - groups of 8
      For intI = 1 To Int(UBound(varArray) / 8)
        ' Calc the upper bound this pass
        intJ = intI * 8
        strMsgInstruct = strMsgInstruct & "Course: " & varArray(intJ - 7) & _
          varArray(intJ - 6) & " " & varArray(intJ - 5) & _
          ", Section: " & varArray(intJ - 4) & _
          ", Segment: " & varArray(intJ - 3) & _
          ", Days: " & varArray(intJ - 2) & _
          ", Start Time: " & Format(varArray(intJ - 1), "hh:mm AM/PM") & _
          ", End Time: " & Format(varArray(intJ), "hh:mm AM/PM") & vbCrLf
      Next intI
    End If
    ' Process the next segment
    rst.MoveNext
  Loop
  ' Close the recordset
  rst.Close
  Set rst = Nothing
  ' If instructor error message is not empty
  If (Not IsNothing(strMsgInstruct)) Then
    ' Build the error message
    strMsg = strMsg & "You cannot change the instructor " & _
      "for this course because the " & _
      "following course segment(s) are already scheduled " & _
      "for this instructor at the days and times you entered:" & vbCrLf & _
      vbCrLf & strMsgInstruct
  End If
```

```
    ' If got a message
    If strMsg <> "" Then
      ' Display it
      MsgBox strMsg, vbCritical, gstrAppTitle
      ' Cancel the update
      Cancel = True
    End If
  End If
End Sub
```

The Advantages and Disadvantages of Subforms in Datasheet View

I designed the forms that display Session Courses as a datasheet (the fsubSession-CoursesDS form) with an embedded subform datasheet (the fsubSessionCourse-SegmentsDS form) to demonstrate how the user can drill down from courses to course segments. Using a datasheet display allows the user to quickly scan a long list of courses without having to navigate one record at a time.

If you would like to see this form using a classic subform in Single Form view with an embedded subform in Continuous Forms view, open the frmSessions form in Design view, select the fsubSessionCourses subform control on the Session Courses tab, and change the Source Object property to **fsubSessionCourses**. When you switch to Form view, you'll notice that the form now displays the courses one at a time. Be sure to not save your changes when you close the form.

There are two distinct disadvantages to using subforms in Datasheet view.

1. The user can change the column widths and even make the columns hidden by shrinking the width to zero.

2. Access doesn't load the subform until the user clicks the plus sign next to the parent row. This means that your code cannot directly reference any property or control in the subform—which explains why the sample code opens a separate recordset that mimics the recordset of the subform rather than just borrowing the subform's RecordSetClone property. You can set the SubDatasheetExpanded property to True to force the subform to load, but that expands the subform for all rows.

As with any design decision, there are tradeoffs. I chose to use Datasheet view to make viewing all of the courses in the potentially long list easier.

The check that produced the second error message shown in Figure 21-12 occurs in the BeforeUpdate event for the fsubSubSessionCourseSegmentsDS form. The code first verifies that the user has selected a course segment, a room number, scheduled days, and start and end times. The code also checks that the start time is earlier than the end time. If any of these values are missing or incorrect, the code displays an appropriate error message and exits. Next, the code uses the *DLookup* function to find out if any other segments already scheduled for the same course and section are scheduled at the same time as the current segment. If the code finds a conflicting segment, it displays an error message and exits. (In the examples in Figures 21-11 and 21-12 you didn't test this case.) The code is as follows:

```
Private Sub Form_BeforeUpdate(Cancel As Integer)
Dim varArray As Variant, strMsgRoom As String, strDaysPredicate As String
Dim intI As Integer, intJ As Integer, strMsgInstruct, strMsg As String
  ' First, check for required fields
  If IsNothing(Me.CourseSegment) Then
    MsgBox "You must select a course segment.", _
      vbCritical, gstrAppTitle
    Me.cmbCourseSegment.SetFocus
    Cancel = True
    Exit Sub
  End If
  If IsNothing(Me.RoomID) Then
    MsgBox "You must select a room.", _
      vbCritical, gstrAppTitle
    Me.cmbRoomID.SetFocus
    Cancel = True
    Exit Sub
  End If
  If IsNothing(Me.Days) Then
    MsgBox "You must select scheduled days.", _
      vbCritical, gstrAppTitle
    Me.cmbDays.SetFocus
    Cancel = True
    Exit Sub
  End If
  If IsNothing(Me.StartTime) Or IsNothing(Me.EndTime) Then
    MsgBox "You must enter a start and end time.", _
      vbCritical, gstrAppTitle
    Me.txtStartTime.SetFocus
    Cancel = True
    Exit Sub
  End If
  ' Make sure end is later than start
  If Me.EndTime <= Me.StartTime Then
    MsgBox "End time must be later than start time.", _
      vbCritical, gstrAppTitle
    Me.txtEndTime.SetFocus
    Cancel = True
    Exit Sub
  End If
  ' Next, make sure no other segment scheduled in this time period
  ' First build the predicate to check for overlapping days
  strDaysPredicate = BuildDayPredicate(Me.Days)
  ' Now see if any other segment for this class scheduled
  '   in the same time and day
  If Not IsNothing(DLookup("CourseSegment", "tblSessionCourseSegments", _
    "SessionYear = " & Me.SessionYear & _
    " AND SessionNumber = " & Me.SessionNumber & _
```

```
            " AND CourseCategory = '" & Me.CourseCategory & _
            "' AND CourseNumber = " & Me.CourseNumber & _
            " AND SectionNumber = " & Me.SectionNumber & _
            " AND CourseSegment <> " & Me.CourseSegment & _
            " AND StartTime <= #" & Me.EndTime & _
            "# AND EndTime >= #" & Me.StartTime & _
            "# AND " & strDaysPredicate)) Then
          MsgBox "You have already scheduled another segment for this " & _
            "section on the same day and within the same time span.", _
            vbCritical, gstrAppTitle
          ' Cancel the update
          Cancel = True
          ' and bail
          Exit Sub
        End If
```

Next, the code calls the *CheckDupRoom* function to find out if the segment about to be saved overlaps with any other course segment already scheduled. If that function returns anything other than a True (–1) value in the first array element, the code constructs a room error message. Finally, the code calls the *CheckDupInstructor* function to find out if the instructor scheduled for the course has an overlap with the new data about to be saved for the segment. If that function returns anything other than a True (–1) value in the first array element, the code constructs an instructor error message. At the end of the procedure, if either the room or instructor message strings are not empty, the code builds the appropriate error message, displays the error, and cancels the update so the changed row cannot be saved. The code is as follows:

```
        ' Check for overlapping room schedule
        varArray = CheckDupRoom(Me.SessionYear, Me.SessionNumber, _
          Me.CourseCategory, Me.CourseNumber, Me.SectionNumber, Me.CourseSegment, _
          Me.RoomID, Me.Days, Me.StartTime, Me.EndTime)
        ' If an error
        If varArray(1) = 0 Then
          ' Cancel the edit
          Cancel = True
          ' Bail
          Exit Sub
        End If
        ' If some found,
        If varArray(1) <> -1 Then
          ' Loop to build the message - groups of 8
          For intI = 1 To Int(UBound(varArray) / 8)
            ' Calc the upper bound this pass
            intJ = intI * 8
            strMsgRoom = strMsgRoom & "Course: " & varArray(intJ - 7) & _
              varArray(intJ - 6) & " " & varArray(intJ - 5) & _
              ", Section: " & varArray(intJ - 4) & _
              ", Segment: " & varArray(intJ - 3) & _
              ", Days: " & varArray(intJ - 2) & _
              ", Start Time: " & Format(varArray(intJ - 1), "hh:mm AM/PM") & _
```

```vba
            ", End Time: " & Format(varArray(intJ)), "hh:mm AM/PM") & vbCrLf
      Next intI
    End If
    ' Check for overlapping Instructor schedule
    varArray = CheckDupInstructor(Me.SessionYear, Me.SessionNumber, _
      Me.CourseCategory, Me.CourseNumber, Me.SectionNumber, Me.CourseSegment, _
      Me.Parent.InstructorID, Me.Days, Me.StartTime, Me.EndTime)
    ' If an error
    If varArray(1) = 0 Then
      ' Cancel the edit
      Cancel = True
      ' Bail
      Exit Sub
    End If
    ' If some found,
    If varArray(1) <> -1 Then
      ' Loop to build the message - groups of 8
      For intI = 1 To Int(UBound(varArray) / 8)
        ' Calc the upper bound this pass
        intJ = intI * 8
        strMsgInstruct = strMsgInstruct & "Course: " & varArray(intJ - 7) & _
          varArray(intJ - 6) & " " & varArray(intJ - 5) & _
          ", Section: " & varArray(intJ - 4) & _
          ", Segment: " & varArray(intJ - 3) & _
          ", Days: " & varArray(intJ - 2) & _
          ", Start Time: " & Format(varArray(intJ - 1), "hh:mm AM/PM") & _
          ", End Time: " & Format(varArray(intJ), "hh:mm AM/PM") & vbCrLf
      Next intI
    End If
    ' If room error message is not empty
    If (Not IsNothing(strMsgRoom)) Then
      ' Build the error message
      strMsg = "You cannot schedule this segment because the " & _
        "following course segment(s) are already scheduled " & _
        "in the room at the days and times you entered:" & vbCrLf & _
        vbCrLf & strMsgRoom & vbCrLf & vbCrLf
    End If
    ' If instructor error message is not emtpy
    If (Not IsNothing(strMsgInstruct)) Then
      ' Build the error message
      strMsg = strMsg & "You cannot schedule this segment because the " & _
        "following course segment(s) are already scheduled " & _
        "for this instructor at the days and times you entered:" & vbCrLf & _
        vbCrLf & strMsgInstruct
    End If
    ' If got a message
    If strMsg <> "" Then
      ' Display it
      MsgBox strMsg, vbCritical, gstrAppTitle
      ' Cancel the update
      Cancel = True
    End If
End Sub
```

You should now have a good understanding of the features and code you need in a scheduling application to make it easy to schedule events and ensure that resources aren't double-booked. In the next chapter, you'll learn about the features in the Registration Management application that handle students requesting courses—including verifying that the sections requested aren't overbooked and the student has the necessary prerequisites to take the course.

Chapter 22

Scheduling Students

Now that you understand how scheduling courses might be automated, you need to know how students schedule themselves for these courses and confirm their enrollments. Before the application can allow a student to request a course, the student must be defined in the system and enrolled for the requested semester. The application also needs to ensure that a student doesn't request two classes on the same day of the week and at the same time. In addition, the application must verify that the student has completed prerequisite courses, ensure that a class isn't overbooked, and provide students with the information about alternate classes they might request when this is the case.

Understanding the Tables Involved

Before a student can begin requesting classes for a semester, the student must be enrolled by an administrator. At most schools and colleges, a new student must apply to attend the school, and the school can accept only the students who are qualified. A continuing student must usually give some notice of intent to enroll in the following semester. Table 22-1 on the next page describes the fields in the tblStudents table that stores the information about each student.

A student can optionally choose a course plan to follow that will lead to a certificate or associate degree in a technical area of expertise. As you'll learn later in this chapter, when a student selects a course plan, the application tracks the student's progress in completing the courses and helps the student request courses that are not completed to schedule for an upcoming semester. Table 22-2 describes the fields in the tblCoursePlans table that defines each available plan, and Table 22-3 describes the fields in the tblCoursePlanCourses table that defines the courses required to complete each plan.

Table 22-1   The Fields in the tblStudents Table

Field Name	Data Type	Description
StudentID	Long Integer	Unique student identifier.
LastName	Text, Field Size 50	Student last name.
FirstName	Text, Field Size 50	Student first name.
MiddleName	Text, Field Size 30	Student middle name or middle initial.
Suffix	Text, Field Size 20	Student name suffix.
Address	Text, Field Size 255	Student street or mailing address.
City	Text, Field Size 50	Student city.
StateOrProvince	Text, Field Size 20	Student state or province.
PostalCode	Text, Field Size 20	Student postal code or ZIP code.
Country	Text, Field Size 50	Student country.
HomePhone	Text, Field Size 30	Student home phone.
WorkPhone	Text, Field Size 30	Student work phone.
Email	Hyperlink	Student e-mail address.
Birthdate	Date/Time	Student birth date.
User ID	Text, Field Size 20	Student sign-on user ID.
Password	Text, Field Size 20	Student sign-on password.
CoursePlanID	Integer	ID of the course plan selected by the student.

Table 22-2   The Fields in the tblCoursePlans Table

Field Name	Data Type	Description
CoursePlanID	Integer	Unique course plan identifier.
CoursePlanDescription	Text, Field Size 100	Description of the certificate or associate degree.

Table 22-3   The Fields in the tblCoursePlanCourses Table

Field Name	Data Type	Description
CoursePlanID	Integer	ID of the related course plan.
CourseCategory	Text, Field Size 3	Course category code.
CourseNumber	Integer	Course number within the category.
CoursePlanSequence	Integer	Sequence in which the courses should be taken. Multiple courses with the same sequence number indicate that the student can complete one of the courses to satisfy the requirement.

In the Registration Management application, the tblStudentInvoices table, as explained in Table 22-4, serves a dual purpose. It is a parent table for the tblStudentCourses table, so a record must exist in this table before a student can begin requesting courses. In that role, it serves as an enrollment record for each student and semester. As you'll learn in Chapter 24, "Producing Student Invoices," this table also contains the calculated total of semester hours and the tuition a student should be charged for a semester. Table 22-4 describes the fields in the tblStudentInvoices table that stores the information about each student registered in each semester.

Table 22-4   The Fields in the tblStudentInvoices Table

Field Name	Data Type	Description
StudentID	Long Integer	ID of the student registered for this session.
SessionYear	Integer	Year this session is scheduled.
SessionNumber	Integer	Session semester: 1 = Spring, 2 = Summer, 3 = Fall.
SemesterHours	Decimal, Precision 7, Scale 1	Total semester hours for which the student is enrolled (calculated by the update invoice process).
Tuition	Currency	Tuition owed for the session (calculated by the update invoice process).

Of course, the Registration Management application needs to store information about each course in which each student enrolls in each semester. The tblStudentCourses table, as described in Table 22-5, contains this information.

Table 22-5   The Fields in the tblStudentCourses Table

Field Name	Data Type	Description
StudentID	Long Integer	ID of the student registered for this course.
SessionYear	Integer	Year this course is scheduled.
SessionNumber	Integer	Session semester: 1 = Spring, 2 = Summer, 3 = Fall.
CourseCategory	Text, Field Size 3	Course category code.
CourseNumber	Integer	Course number within category.
SectionNumber	Integer	Section number of the course.
Status	Integer	Status of the course registration (1 = Requested, 2 = Awaiting Approval, 3 = Approved, 4 = Wait List, 5 = Enrolled, 6 = Withdrawn, 7 = Incomplete, 8 = Completed).
ApprovedBy	Long Integer	ID of the instructor who approved enrollment in a course for which the student did not meet the prerequisites.
Grade	Decimal, Precision 7, Scale 2	Final grade for the course.
Invoiced	Yes/No	Indicator that the course has been invoiced (set by the update invoice process).

This table is similar to the tblOrderProducts table in the Inventory Management application, which tracks the status of an individual product request as it proceeds from Requested to On Order, Allocated, and Invoiced. If you think about it, you're "selling" a course to a student.

In the Registration Management application, a course request might have Awaiting Approval status if the student hasn't completed the prerequisite courses but the course requested allows the instructor or an administrator to approve the enrollment without the prerequisites. If the class is full when the student requests confirmation, the status of the request is set by the confirmation process to Wait List. An instructor or an administrator might choose to override the normal limit of the course enrollment if the scheduled room can accommodate additional students. After a student is enrolled, the student might later withdraw, not complete the course, or complete it.

Last, but certainly not least, the tblCourses table, described in Table 22-6, contains the information about available courses. The fields that are important when scheduling students are the CoursePreReqByApproval field and the CourseMaxStudents field.

Table 22-6   The Fields in the tblCourses Table

Field Name	Data Type	Description
CourseCategory	Text, Field Size 3	Course category code.
CourseNumber	Integer	Course number within the category.
CourseTitle	Text, Field Size 75	Course title.
CourseDescription	Memo	Detailed description of the course.
CoursePreReqByApproval	Yes/No	Can course prerequisites be satisfied by instructor approval?
CourseMaxStudents	Integer	Maximum number of students who can enroll in a section of the course.
CreditHours	Integer	Credit hours for the course.

Enrolling a Student

Before a student can enroll, an administrator must sign on to the application, define the student record and the declared course plan, and create a semester enrollment in the tblStudentInvoices table. Figure 22-1 shows a student record in the frmStudents form as it might have looked when an administrator first defined the student.

As soon as the administrator saves the record with a course plan specified, the form displays the courses the student should take in the window on the Course Plan tab, as shown in Figure 22-2. At the bottom of the window, the Course Plan subform (fsubStudentCoursePlan) displays the total minimum hours needed to complete the plan and the total course hours completed thus far by the student. Note that most course plans have one or more course requirements that can be satisfied by completing one of several courses. As you can see in the figure, a student need complete only one of Web Page Programming, Introduction to Visual

Basic .NET, or Programming Fundamentals to satisfy the second course requirement (Seq# 2) for the Network Administration Certificate.

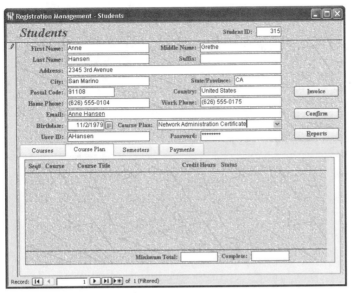

Figure 22-1   Enrolling a student.

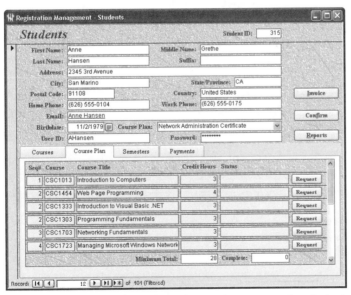

Figure 22-2   The Students form shows what courses the student needs to take to complete the selected course plan.

To display the course plan with the status of completed courses and the total hours, the fsubStudentCoursePlan form uses a complex query, qryStudentCoursePlan, that joins the tblCourses, tblCoursePlanCourses, and tblStudentCourses tables. The subform is filtered on the CoursePlanID specified on the frmStudents form, so the query returns all the courses for that plan. It uses an outer join (LEFT JOIN) with a query on the tblStudentCourses table to fetch the matching courses that the student has in the tblStudentCourses table. The SQL for the query is as follows:

```
PARAMETERS [Forms]![frmStudents]![StudentID] Long;
SELECT tblCoursePlanCourses.CoursePlanID, tblCoursePlanCourses.CoursePlanSequence,
  tblCoursePlanCourses.CourseCategory, tblCoursePlanCourses.CourseNumber,
  tblCourses.CourseCategory & tblCourses.CourseNumber AS Course,
  tblCourses.CourseTitle, tblCourses.CreditHours, SC.StudentID, SC.Status,
  Choose(NZ([Status],0),"Requested","Awaiting Approval","Approved","Wait
    List","Enrolled","Withdrawn","Incomplete","Completed") AS StatusDisp,
  DCount("CoursePlanID","zqryCoursePlanComplete","CoursePlanID = " &
    [CoursePlanID] & " AND CoursePlanSequence = " & [CoursePlanSequence] &
    " AND StudentID = " & [Forms]![frmStudents]![StudentID]) AS SeqComplete
FROM tblCourses
INNER JOIN (tblCoursePlanCourses
  LEFT JOIN (SELECT tblStudentCourses.CourseCategory,
    tblStudentCourses.CourseNumber, tblStudentCourses.StudentID,
    tblStudentCourses.Status
    FROM tblStudentCourses
    WHERE tblStudentCourses.StudentID=[Forms]![frmStudents]![StudentID]) AS SC
  ON (tblCoursePlanCourses.CourseNumber = SC.CourseNumber)
    AND (tblCoursePlanCourses.CourseCategory = SC.CourseCategory))
ON (tblCourses.CourseNumber = tblCoursePlanCourses.CourseNumber)
  AND (tblCourses.CourseCategory = tblCoursePlanCourses.CourseCategory)
ORDER BY tblCoursePlanCourses.CoursePlanSequence;
```

The key to solving this sort of "show all courses and any completed" problem is to first filter the student courses on the StudentID field before joining the data with the tblCoursePlanCourses table. Many novice developers would include the tblStudentCourses table directly in the outer FROM clause and then attempt to apply a filter on StudentID in the WHERE clause. That doesn't return the correct answer because the query engine always performs the joins in the FROM clause first before applying the WHERE clause.

Note that the query also includes a count of courses completed (the SeqComplete field) for each unique sequence number. All the display controls on the form have a conditional formatting specification that highlights the controls when the expression **[SeqComplete]=0** is true. This helps the user see which courses have not been completed in the plan.

Finally, the administrator must click the Semesters tab on the form and create an entry for the upcoming semester, as shown in Figure 22-3. The subform on the Semesters tab edits data in the tblStudentInvoices table, so creating a record in this window "enrolls" the student for the specified semester.

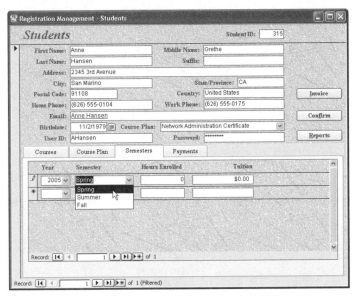

Figure 22-3   Enrolling a student in a semester.

Requesting Enrollment in Courses

After an administrator has enrolled a student, the student can sign on to the Registration Management application and begin to select courses. You can follow along with this part by opening the Registration Management database (Registration.mdb), opening the frmSplash form to start the application, and signing on as student (select Student in the User Type box) Anne Hansen using **ahansen** as the User Name (this is the UserID field in the student record) and **password** as the password. You should see the frmStudents form open displaying the student record for Anne Hansen. Click the Course Plan tab to see the remaining courses that Anne needs to complete her Network Administration Certificate, as shown in Figure 22-4 on the next page.

In the sample data I loaded for the application, Anne has completed all but four courses for her certificate and would like to enroll in them all for the Spring 2005 semester. Scroll down to the first one she needs—course CSC1723, Managing Microsoft Windows Networking. Click in the row and then click the Request button to ask to schedule this course. The application displays the Choose Course Section dialog box, as shown in Figure 22-5 on the next page, where the student can verify the Year and Semester and choose an available course section. If you're following along with the example, set your computer's system to any date in the year 2005, or be sure to select 2005 for Year and Spring for Semester before you open the Section list so you'll see the courses being offered in the Spring 2005 semester.

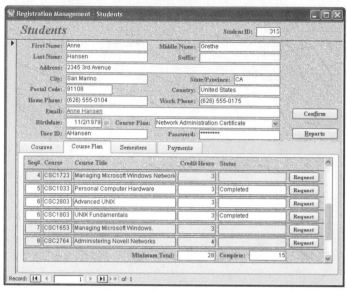

Figure 22-4 The application highlights courses remaining to complete in the student's course plan.

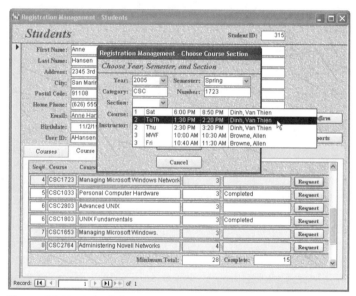

Figure 22-5 Scheduling a course from the course plan.

Choose the Tuesday-Thursday section being taught by Van T. Dinh at 1:30 PM, and click Go to schedule the course. Notice that the list in Figure 22-5 also shows a Section 2 on Thursday from 2:30 PM to 3:20 PM. This is the second segment of the class, and the student will be scheduled for both segments if she chooses either one. Next, scroll down to Seq# 7, click in the row, and then click the Request button to schedule a section of the Managing Microsoft Windows course. Select Spring 2005 again, click the Section box and choose Section 3 taught by Douglas J. Steele on Tuesday mornings, and then click the Go button.

Checking for Overlapping Requests

Scroll down the list on the Course Plan tab once again until you find Seq# 8, a course in Administering Novell Networks. Click in the row and then click the Request button. In the Choose Course Section dialog box, select Spring 2005 again, then click in the Section box and select Section 1 taught by Joe Fallon on Tuesday and Thursday afternoons. Click the Go button, and the application displays an error message, as shown in Figure 22-6.

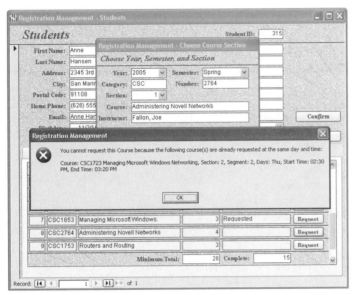

Figure 22-6 The application won't let the student request a course at a conflicting date and time.

In the previous section, you scheduled a class for Tuesday and Thursday afternoons from 1:30 PM until 2:20 PM. This class starts at 3:00 PM, so there shouldn't be a conflict, right? Ah, but remember that the list in Figure 22-5 also showed a lab segment that is scheduled until 3:20 PM on Thursdays. As mentioned earlier, the student is scheduled for all segments of a chosen section, so this new request would, indeed, be an overlap.

Code placed in the Click event procedure of the cmdGo command button on the fdlgSelectCourseSection form performs several checks before attempting to insert a record into the tblStudentCourses table. The code first verifies that the user has specified a session year, session number (semester), and section number. (Code in the form's Open event procedure fetches the course category, course number, and course title from the fsubStudentCoursePlan subform on the frmStudents form.)

Next, the code makes sure the student is registered for the specified year and semester. If the student isn't registered and the student is signed on (the sign-on form sets the gintUserType variable), the code displays an error message and exits. If the student isn't registered and the signed-on user is an administrator or instructor, the code offers to add the registration record to the tblStudentInvoices table. If the user asks the code to perform the insert, the code does so. The code is as follows:

```
Private Sub cmdGo_Click()
Dim varArray As Variant, strMsgStudent As String, strDaysPredicate As String
Dim intI As Integer, intJ As Integer, strMsg As String
Dim lngErr As Long, strError As String
  ' Set an error trap
  On Error GoTo cmdGo_Err
  ' First, check for required fields
  If IsNothing(Me.cmbSessionYear) Then
    MsgBox "You must select a year.", _
      vbCritical, gstrAppTitle
    Me.cmbSessionYear.SetFocus
    Exit Sub
  End If
  If IsNothing(Me.cmbSessionNumber) Then
    MsgBox "You must select a semester.", _
      vbCritical, gstrAppTitle
    Me.cmbSessionNumber.SetFocus
    Exit Sub
  End If
  If IsNothing(Me.cmbSectionNumber) Then
    MsgBox "You must select a course section.", _
      vbCritical, gstrAppTitle
    Me.cmbSectionNumber.SetFocus
    Exit Sub
  End If
  ' Make sure student is "registered" in this semester
  If IsNothing(DLookup("StudentID", "tblStudentInvoices", _
    "StudentID = " & Form_frmStudents.StudentID & _
    " AND SessionYear = " & Me.cmbSessionYear & _
    " AND SessionNumber = " & Me.cmbSessionNumber)) Then
    ' Set up message based on user type
    If gintThisUserType = UserType.Student Then
      ' Student cannot register themselves
      strMsg = "You have not yet been registered for the year and " & _
        "semester you selected.  Contact an Administrator to " & _
        "obtain registration authorization for this semester."
      ' Display the error
      MsgBox strMsg, vbCritical, gstrAppTitle
      ' Bail
      Exit Sub
    Else
      ' Set up instructor, admin message
      strMsg = "This student has not yet been registered for the year and " & _
        "semester selected.  Would you like to register the student now?"
    End If
    ' See if wants to register
    If vbNo = MsgBox(strMsg, _
      vbQuestion + vbYesNo + vbDefaultButton2, gstrAppTitle) Then
      ' Bail - close the form
      DoCmd.Close acForm, Me.Name
      Exit Sub
    End If
```

```
    ' Insert the row
    DBEngine(0)(0).Execute "INSERT INTO tblStudentInvoices " & _
      "(StudentID, SessionYear, SessionNumber) " & _
      "VALUES(" & Form_frmStudents.StudentID & ", " & _
      Me.cmbSessionYear & ", " & Me.cmbSessionNumber & ")", dbFailOnError
    ' Requery the semesters subform
    Form_frmStudents.fsubStudentSemesters.Requery
  End If
```

If the code either finds the registration record or inserts it, the code next calls the *CheckDupStudent* function to find out if the requested course and section would overlap with any course already scheduled. As you'll learn later, the *CheckDupStudent* function returns an array containing information about overlapping sections. The first entry in the array contains a 0 if the function encountered an error, so the code in the cmdGo procedure exits if this is the case. If the first entry contains a True (−1) value, no overlaps were found. When overlaps were found, the array contains information about overlapping segments in groups of 8 items—the course category, course number, course title, section number, segment number, days scheduled, start time, and end time. The code calculates how many items are in the array by dividing the upper bound of the array by 8. If there were no overlapping items, the array contains only one entry, so the For loop that assembles the information never executes.

After exiting the For loop to process all the overlapping entries, the code checks to see if any message was assembled. If the message string is not empty, the code displays the error and exits. The code is as follows:

```
  ' Check for overlapping student schedule
  varArray = CheckDupStudent(Me.cmbSessionYear, Me.cmbSessionNumber, _
    Me.txtCourseCategory, Me.txtCourseNumber, _
    Me.cmbSectionNumber, Form_frmStudents.StudentID)
  ' If an error
  If varArray(1) = 0 Then
    ' Bail
    Exit Sub
  End If
  ' If some found,
  If varArray(1) <> -1 Then
    ' Loop to build the message - groups of 8
    For intI = 1 To Int(UBound(varArray) / 8)
      ' Calc the upper bound this pass
      intJ = intI * 8
      strMsgStudent = strMsgStudent & "Course: " & varArray(intJ - 7) & _
        varArray(intJ - 6) & " " & varArray(intJ - 5) & _
        ", Section: " & varArray(intJ - 4) & _
        ", Segment: " & varArray(intJ - 3) & _
        ", Days: " & varArray(intJ - 2) & _
        ", Start Time: " & Format(varArray(intJ - 1), "hh:mm AM/PM") & _
        ", End Time: " & Format(varArray(intJ), "hh:mm AM/PM") & vbCrLf
    Next intI
  End If
  ' If error message is not empty
  If (Not IsNothing(strMsgStudent)) Then
```

```
    ' Build the error message
    strMsg = "You cannot request this Course because the " & _
        "following course(s) are already requested " & _
        "at the same day and time:" & vbCrLf & _
        vbCrLf & strMsgStudent & vbCrLf & vbCrLf
    ' Display it
    MsgBox strMsg, vbCritical, gstrAppTitle
    ' Let them try again
    Exit Sub
  End If
```

If the student is registered and there are no overlapping courses already requested, the code executes an SQL INSERT statement to create the new record in the tblStudentCourses table. If the INSERT is successful, the code requeries both the student courses and the student course plan subforms and exits. Code at the end of the procedure processes any errors. If the error is a duplicate record, the code informs the user and exits. (The record isn't saved.) If the error was anything else, the code displays and logs the error and exits. The code is as follows:

```
  ' Add the new course request
  DBEngine(0)(0).Execute "INSERT INTO tblStudentCourses " & _
    "(StudentID, SessionYear, SessionNumber, " & _
    "CourseCategory, CourseNumber, SectionNumber) " & _
    "VALUES (" & Form_frmStudents.StudentID & ", " & Me.cmbSessionYear & ", " & _
    Me.cmbSessionNumber & ", '" & Me.txtCourseCategory & "', " & _
    Me.txtCourseNumber & ", " & Me.cmbSectionNumber & ")", dbFailOnError
  ' Requery the student course subform
  Form_frmStudents.fsubStudentCourses.Requery
  ' .. and the course plan
  Form_frmStudents.fsubStudentCoursePlan.Requery
  ' Close me
  DoCmd.Close acForm, Me.Name
cmdGo_Exit:
  Exit Sub
cmdGo_Err:
  lngErr = Err
  strError = Error
  ' If a duplicate record,
  If lngErr = errDuplicate Then
    ' Display a custom error
    MsgBox "You are attempting to request a course and section " & _
      "twice in one semester.", vbInformation, gstrAppTitle
  Else
    ' Log the error
    ErrorLog Me.Name & "_cmdGo", lngErr, strError
    ' Tell user
    MsgBox "Unexpected error: " & lngErr & " " & strError & _
      vbCrLf & "Try again or click Cancel.", _
      vbExclamation, gstrAppTitle
  End If
  ' Bail
  Resume cmdGo_Exit
End Sub
```

In the modRegistration module, you can find the *CheckDupStudent* function that the Click event procedure of the cmdGo command button uses. This function works similarly to the *CheckDupInstructor* function that you studied in Chapter 21, "Scheduling Courses." The function begins by defining variables, setting a pointer to the current database, acquiring the SQL from the zqryOverlapStudent template query, and opening a recordset on the course segments for the course and section number requested. The template query joins the tblCourses, tblStudentCourses, and tblSessionCourseSegments tables and fetches the fields needed to perform the overlap test. The code is as follows:

```
Public Function CheckDupStudent(intSessYear As Integer, intSessNumber As Integer, _
  strCategory As String, intCourseNum As Integer, intSecNum As Integer, _
  lngStudentID As Long) As Variant
' Check for student schedule overlap
' Inputs: Session Year, Session Number, Course Category, Course Number,
'     Section Number, Course Segment, StudentID
' Output: Return Variant array for Course Category, Course Number, Course Title,
'     Section Number, and Course Segments that overlap with the request.
'     Array(1) contains the value -1 if no overlaps
'     Array(1) contains the value 0 if an error encountered
Dim db As DAO.Database, rst As DAO.Recordset, qd As DAO.QueryDef, _
  rstSegs As DAO.Recordset
Dim strDayPredicate As String, strWhere As String, _
  strSQL As String, intSegment As Integer
Dim varArray() As Variant, intI As Integer, intDays As Integer, _
  datStart As Date, datEnd As Date
  ' Set an error trap
  On Error GoTo Err_DupStudent
  ' Point to this database
  Set db = DBEngine(0)(0)
  ' Get the template query
  Set qd = db.QueryDefs("zqryOverlapStudent")
  ' Get the segments for the course the student wants to schedule
  Set rstSegs = db.OpenRecordset("SELECT CourseSegment, Days, StartTime, EndTime " & _
    "FROM tblSessionCourseSegments " & _
    "WHERE SessionYear = " & intSessYear & _
    " AND SessionNumber = " & intSessNumber & _
    " AND CourseCategory = '" & strCategory & _
    "' AND CourseNumber = " & intCourseNum & _
    " AND SectionNumber = " & intSecNum, dbOpenSnapshot)
```

Next, the code begins a loop to process each segment of the requested course and section. After extracting the SQL from the template query, the code begins constructing the complex WHERE clause needed to test for an overlap. The code calls the *BuildDayPredicate* function that was explained in Chapter 21 to create the appropriate test for overlapping days of the week. Finally, the code assembles the two parts of the query and opens a recordset using the generated SQL. The code is as follows:

```
  ' Loop and test all segments
  Do Until rstSegs.EOF
    ' Grab the Segment
    intSegment = rstSegs!CourseSegment
```

```
    ' .. and the days scheduled
    intDays = rstSegs!Days
    ' .. and the start time
    datStart = rstSegs!StartTime
    ' .. and the end time
    datEnd = rstSegs!EndTime
    ' Extract the SQL
    strSQL = Left(qd.SQL, InStrRev(qd.SQL, ";") - 1)
    ' Start building the predicate
    strWhere = " WHERE tblStudentCourses.SessionYear = " & intSessYear & _
        " AND tblStudentCourses.SessionNumber = " & intSessNumber & _
        " AND StudentID = " & lngStudentID & _
        " AND StartTime <= #" & datEnd & "#" & _
        " AND EndTime >= #" & datStart & "#" & _
        " AND ((tblCourses.CourseCategory <> '" & strCategory & "') " & _
        " OR (tblCourses.CourseNumber <> " & intCourseNum & ") " & _
        " OR (tblStudentCourses.SectionNumber <> " & intSecNum & ") " & _
        " OR (tblSessionCourseSegments.CourseSegment <> " & intSegment & "))"
    ' Get the days predicate
    strDayPredicate = BuildDayPredicate(intDays)
    ' Make sure we got something
    If IsNothing(strDayPredicate) Then
        ' Oops - must have been passed an invalid day code
        ' Return an error
        CheckDupStudent = Array(0)
        ' Clear the objects
        rstSegs.Close
        Set rstSegs = Nothing
        Set qd = Nothing
        Set db = Nothing
        ' Bail
        Exit Function
    End If
    ' Add the days predicate
    strWhere = strWhere & " AND " & strDayPredicate
    ' Finish the SQL
    strSQL = strSQL & strWhere
    ' Open the recordset
    Set rst = db.OpenRecordset(strSQL, dbOpenDynaset)
```

The query finds all the classes already scheduled for the student that overlap with the requested section. The query returns one row for each segment and section that overlaps. If the recordset contains rows, the code loops to process them all and builds an array containing the 8 items of information about each row: the course category, course number, course title, section number, segment number, days of the week, start time, and end time. The code dynamically expands the array to accommodate the items for each row. After processing all the rows, the code moves to the next segment of the requested course and section and loops to the Do statement on the preceding page. The code is as follows:

```
    ' Process all records
    Do Until rst.EOF
        ' Add 8 to the upper bound
        intI = intI + 8
```

```
    ' Expand the array to hold another row
    ReDim Preserve varArray(intI)
    ' Set the Course Category
    varArray(intI - 7) = rst!CourseCategory
    ' Set the Course Number
    varArray(intI - 6) = rst!CourseNumber
    ' Set the Course Title
    varArray(intI - 5) = rst!CourseTitle
    ' Set the Section Number
    varArray(intI - 4) = rst!SectionNumber
    ' Set the Segment
    varArray(intI - 3) = rst!CourseSegment
    ' Set the Days
    varArray(intI - 2) = Choose(rst!Days, "Mon", "Tue", "Wed", "Thu", _
      "Fri", "Sat", "", "TuTh", "MWF", "TuThSat")
    ' Set the start time
    varArray(intI - 1) = rst!StartTime
    ' Set the end time
    varArray(intI) = rst!EndTime
    ' Get the next one
    rst.MoveNext
  Loop
  ' Close the recordset
  rst.Close
  ' Move to next segment
  rstSegs.MoveNext
' Process it
Loop
```

After processing all the segments in the requested course and section, the code checks to see if any items were loaded into the dynamic array. If no overlapping segments were found, the code returns an array containing a single element set to True (−1). If the dynamic array contains data, the code returns the array that already has a course category in the first element followed by the data about the overlaps in the remaining elements. The code at the end of the procedure traps and logs any errors and exits. The code is as follows:

```
  ' If got nothing
  If intI = 0 Then
    ' Return success
    CheckDupStudent = Array(-1)
  Else
    ' Assign the variant array as the return value
    CheckDupStudent = varArray
  End If
  ' Close and clear the objects
  rstSegs.Close
  ' Done
Exit_DupStudent:
  ' Clear all objects
  Set rst = Nothing
  Set rstSegs = Nothing
  Set qd = Nothing
  Set db = Nothing
  ' Exit
```

```
    Exit Function
Err_DupStudent:
  ' Display the error
  MsgBox "Unexpected error checking duplicate student scheduling: " & vbCrLf & _
    Err.Number & ", " & Err.Description, vbCritical, gstrAppTitle
  ' Log it
  ErrorLog "CheckDupStudent", Err.Number, Err.Description
  ' Return failure
  CheckDupStudent = Array(0)
  ' Bail
  Resume Exit_DupStudent
End Function
```

To complete the requests for student Anne Hansen, you should request the second section of course CSC2764, Administering Novell Networks (taught on Monday, Wednesday, and Friday mornings), and the second section of course CSC1753, Routers and Routing (taught on Monday, Wednesday, and Friday evenings). You can either use the Course Plan tab to do this, or enter the records yourself in the subform window on the Courses tab. As you might expect, you can find similar overlap checking code in the BeforeUpdate event procedure of the fsubStudentCourses form that displays on the Courses tab.

Requesting Confirmation

After Anne selects all the courses she wants to schedule, she can click the Confirm button on the Students form to attempt to confirm them all. Code in the Click event procedure of the cmdConfirm command button first opens the fdlgConfirmSemester form where the student can specify the year and semester to be confirmed (Spring 2005 in this case). The code then calls the *StudentConfirm* function that you can find in the modRegistration module. If you click the Confirm button on the Students form, verify Spring 2005 in the Confirm Semester dialog box, and click the Confirm button in that dialog box, the application should display the result shown in Figure 22-7.

Figure 22-7   The confirmation process displays the results of a confirmation request.

It doesn't look like Anne is going to have any luck getting the courses she needs. In truth, all the other students have already confirmed their choices in the sample data for Spring 2005, so it's amazing that any courses were confirmed at all. If you click the OK button in the message dialog box, the application opens a detail report, shown in Figure 22-8, that displays details about course requests that were not confirmed.

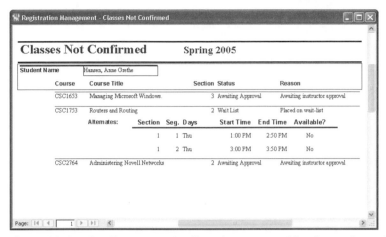

Figure 22-8   The Classes Not Confirmed report provides the student with details about requests that could not be confirmed.

It looks like Anne will have to wait to find out if the instructors for Managing Microsoft Windows and Administering Novell Networks will approve her enrolling in the courses without the required prerequisites. As it turns out, the Managing Microsoft Windows Networking course (CSC1723) that she successfully confirmed is the prerequisite to both these courses, so the instructors might well approve these courses. Note that if course CSC1723 were a co-requisite for either course, the confirmation process would have attempted to schedule the course rather than mark it awaiting approval.

As you can see, there are two alternate sections scheduled for the Routers and Routing course, but both would overlap with the Managing Microsoft Windows Networking course she has already scheduled, and both sections are full. If one of the sections were available, Anne might be able to adjust her course schedule to request the available section. As you'll learn later, an instructor has some leeway to overbook a course as long as the scheduled room is big enough.

The code to confirm a class request must perform the following steps:

1. Verify that each request does not overlap with any other class previously scheduled for the student.

2. If the course has prerequisites and is not approved, check that the student has satisfied the prerequisites or co-requisites. If prerequisites have not been met but the enrollment can be approved by the instructor, the request must be given Awaiting Approval status.

3. Compare the number of students already enrolled in the requested class to the maximum allowed and place the request on the wait list if the class is full.

4. Set the status to Enrolled if there are no overlaps, prerequisites are satisfied, and the class is not full.

Initializing the Confirmation Process

The *StudentConfirm* function begins by declaring all variables and opening a recordset on the year, session, and student passed to the function. The code in the frmStudents form always calls the function with a specific student ID, but code elsewhere in the application can call the function requesting that all students be confirmed. The zqryStudentCourseInfo query returns requests in ascending sequence by prerequisite course count to help ensure that courses that might be prerequisites to others are confirmed first.

If the recordset is empty, the code returns successful execution and zero counts for confirmed, wait-listed, failed prerequisites, awaiting approval, and overlapping schedule items. If the recordset contains requests, the code moves to the last row to obtain an accurate count and then moves back to the first row. The code executes an SQL DELETE query to empty the local ztblNotConfirmed table that will contain details of any requests not confirmed. Finally, the code opens a recordset on that table and starts a transaction to protect all changes. The code is as follows:

```
Public Function StudentConfirm(lngStudentID As Long, _
  intYear As Integer, intSession As Integer, _
  Optional intSilent As Integer = 0) As Variant
' Confirms course requests for a student for the specified year and session
' Inputs: Student ID, Session Year, Session Number (semester)
' Output: Array StudentConfirm(1) = True if completed successfully
'         Array StudentConfirm(1) = False if an error
'         Array StudentConfirm(2) = Count of classes scheduled
'         Array StudentConfirm(3) = The count of wait list items
'         Array StudentConfirm(4) = The count of failed prerequisites
'         Array StudentConfirm(5) = The count of awaiting approval items
'         Array StudentConfirm(6) = The count of overlap items
' Database object, requested courses recordset, count enrolled recordset
Dim db As DAO.Database, rstSC As DAO.Recordset, rstCCount As DAO.Recordset
' Prerequisite lookup recordset, Prerequisite check recordset
Dim rstPreReqs As DAO.Recordset, rstStPreReqs As DAO.Recordset
' Not confirmed log
Dim rstNotConfirmed As DAO.Recordset
' Counts of scheduled, wait list
Dim intSched As Integer, intWait As Integer
' Counts of failed prereq, awaiting approval, overlap schedule
Dim intPreReqFailed As Integer, intApprove As Integer, intOverlap As Integer
' Some working variables
Dim varReturn As Variant, blnTrans As Boolean, intMetThisSeq As Integer
Dim intI As Integer, intMetPreReq As Integer, intLastSeq As Integer
Dim strSQL As String, strWhere As String, intRec As Integer
  ' Set an error trap
  On Error GoTo StudentConfirm_Err
  ' Point to this database
  Set db = DBEngine(0)(0)
  ' Open a recordset on the requested courses
  ' (Query returns courses in ascending sequence by prerequisite count)
  If lngStudentID = 0 Then
    ' Open pending requests for ALL students
```

```
      Set rstSC = db.OpenRecordset("SELECT * FROM zqryStudentCourseInfo " & _
        "WHERE SessionYear = " & intYear & _
        " AND SessionNumber = " & intSession & _
        " AND Status <= " & StudentClassStatus.WaitList, dbOpenDynaset)
    Else
      ' Open pending requests for the requested student
      Set rstSC = db.OpenRecordset("SELECT * FROM zqryStudentCourseInfo " & _
        "WHERE StudentID = " & lngStudentID & _
        " AND SessionYear = " & intYear & _
        " AND SessionNumber = " & intSession & _
        " AND Status <= " & StudentClassStatus.WaitList, dbOpenDynaset)
    End If
    ' If nothing to do,
    If rstSC.EOF Then
      ' Close the recordset
      rstSC.Close
      Set rstSC = Nothing
      Set db = Nothing
      ' Return OK but nothing scheduled
      StudentConfirm = Array(-1, 0, 0, 0, 0, 0)
      ' Done
      Exit Function
    End If
    ' Move to last to get a record count
    rstSC.MoveLast
    ' If not called from zfrmLoadData
    If Not intSilent Then
      ' Show hourglass - might take a while
      DoCmd.Hourglass True
      ' Show progress meter
      varReturn = SysCmd(acSysCmdInitMeter, "Confirming courses...", rstSC.RecordCount)
    End If
    ' Start from the beginning
    rstSC.MoveFirst
    ' Clear out the not confirmed log
    db.Execute "DELETE * FROM ztblNotConfirmed", dbFailOnError
    ' .. and open a recordset on it
    Set rstNotConfirmed = db.OpenRecordset("ztblNotConfirmed", _
      dbOpenDynaset, dbAppendOnly)
    ' Start a transaction to protect all updates
    BeginTrans
    blnTrans = True
```

Checking for an Overlapping Request

Next, the code starts a loop to process all requests. The code first calls the *CheckDupStudent* function to determine if the current request overlaps with any other requested section for the student. This should not occur because code in the various forms to edit or insert requests also performs this check, but it doesn't hurt to check again. If the *CheckDupStudent* function returns anything other than True (−1) in the first element, the function either had an error or found overlaps. When that is the case, the code writes a record to the ztblNotConfirmed table and does no further processing of the request. The code is as shown on the next page.

```
                       ' Loop to process all requests
                       Do Until rstSC.EOF
                         ' First, for overlapping student schedule
                         varReturn = CheckDupStudent(intYear, intSession, rstSC!CourseCategory, _
                           rstSC!CourseNumber, rstSC!SectionNumber, rstSC!StudentID)
                         ' If got an overlap
                         If varReturn(1) <> -1 Then
                           ' No point in processing this one further
                           ' Add 1 to overlap count
                           intOverlap = intOverlap + 1
                           ' Add this request to the not confirmed log
                           With rstNotConfirmed
                             .AddNew
                             !StudentID = rstSC!StudentID
                             !SessionYear = intYear
                             !SessionNumber = intSession
                             !CourseCategory = rstSC!CourseCategory
                             !CourseNumber = rstSC!CourseNumber
                             !SectionNumber = rstSC!SectionNumber
                             !Status = rstSC!Status
                             !Reason = "Schedule Overlap"
                             .Update
                           End With
```

Verifying Prerequisites

Next, the code checks to see if the requested course has any prerequisites, and if so, it checks to see whether those prerequisites have been met. The difficult part about this check is the prerequisite for many courses might be satisfied by completing any one of several courses. When one of several courses would satisfy a prerequisite, the PreReqSequence field contains the same value for each of them. However, the code must check the prerequisite rows one at a time. If a row fails, the code must fetch the next row to see if it is the same sequence. The code looks at all prerequisites within a sequence to determine if any one of them is successful, and it can't make the determination that a sequence has failed until it either finds another row with a different sequence or gets to the end of the recordset.

The request row contains a calculated field, PreReqCount, that indicates if the course has any prerequisites. If that count is zero or the status of the current request indicates enrollment has been approved, the code sets the intMetPreReq variable to True. The Else statement immediately following this assignment matches the End If statement at the end of the code on page 487. Later you'll see that the code immediately following this End If tests this variable to see if prerequisites were met.

If prerequisites exist and the request has not been approved, the code opens a recordset on the prerequisites for the requested course. The code clears the last sequence processed variable (intLastSeq), sets a variable that indicates at least one prerequisite in the sequence was met (intMetThisSeq) to False, and sets the met prerequisites (intMetPreReq) variable to True. This last variable will be set to False if any prerequisite fails in the testing loop. Before starting the loop, the code also sets up a basic SQL statement to fetch courses for the current student. The code is as follows:

```
Else
    ' No schedule overlap - check to see if any prerequisites
    ' Clear the met prerequisites flag
    intMetPreReq = False
    ' If no prerequisites or already approved,
    If (rstSC!PreReqCount = 0) _
      Or (rstSC!Status = StudentClassStatus.Approved) Then
        ' No prerequisites or has been approved - set met
        intMetPreReq = True
    Else
        ' Open a recordset on the prerequisite courses
        Set rstPreReqs = db.OpenRecordset( _
          "SELECT PrereqCourseCategory, PreReqCourseNumber, " & _
          "CoRequisite, PreReqSequence " & _
          "FROM tblCoursePreRequisites " & _
          "WHERE CourseCategory = '" & rstSC!CourseCategory & _
          "' AND CourseNumber = " & rstSC!CourseNumber & _
          " ORDER BY PreReqSequence ASC", dbOpenDynaset)
        ' Clear the last sequence processed
        intLastSeq = 0
        ' .. And met this sequence flag
        intMetThisSeq = False
        ' Assume prereqs met unless one fails
        intMetPreReq = True
        ' Set up the basic test query
        strSQL = "SELECT StudentID FROM tblStudentCourses " & _
          "WHERE (StudentID = " & rstSC!StudentID & ")"
```

Next, the code begins a loop to test each prerequisite row one at a time. Remember that within a given sequence number the prerequisite is met as long as one of the prerequisites in the sequence is met. So, even if the code finds that a prerequisite failed, it must move to the next row to see if the next one is in the same sequence. The process is also complicated because some prerequisites can be met as long as the student is enrolled in the prerequisite course in the same semester (the CoRequisite field is True).

As the code processes each prerequisite row, if the sequence number is different and this is not the first record, the code checks to see if the intMetThisSeq variable is still False. If it is, then one prerequisite sequence has failed, so the code sets the intMetPreReq variable to False and uses the Exit Do statement to end processing any more prerequisites.

If no prerequisite sequences have failed yet, the code constructs a predicate to find out if the student has completed the prerequisite course or is enrolled in a co-requisite course. If the course is a prerequisite, the student must have completed the course in a previous semester with a grade of 72 or better. If the course is a co-requisite, the student must have completed the course in a previous semester with a grade of 72 or better or be already enrolled in the course in the current semester.

After assembling the predicate, the code opens a recordset on the tblStudentCourses table to search that table for the prerequisite course. If the recordset returns a row, the prerequisite is met, so the code sets the intMetThisSeq variable to True. If the recordset is empty, the code leaves that variable set to False. The code will finally test this variable when it encounters a different sequence number or gets to the end of the recordset.

The code moves to the next prerequisite and loops to the Do statement at the beginning of this section of the code. After processing all prerequisites, the code checks to see if the last prerequisite sequence was met and sets the intMetPreReq variable to False if it was not met. Remember, the code can't determine if a prerequisite sequence has failed until it encounters a row with a different sequence or falls off the end—so the code must perform one final test on the last sequence processed when it gets to the end of the recordset. The code is as follows:

```
' Loop to process them all
Do Until rstPreReqs.EOF
  ' If not the first record and sequence different
  If (intLastSeq <> 0) _
    And (intLastSeq <> rstPreReqs!PreReqSequence) Then
    ' If failed all in the sequence,
    If intMetThisSeq = False Then
      ' Set prerequisites failed
      intMetPreReq = False
      ' And bail - no need to check further
      Exit Do
    End If
  End If
  ' Update last sequence
  intLastSeq = rstPreReqs!PreReqSequence
  ' Set basic test for the prerequisite course
  strWhere = " AND (CourseCategory = '" & _
    rstPreReqs!PreReqCourseCategory & _
    "') AND (CourseNumber = " & _
    rstPreReqs!PreReqCourseNumber & ")"
  ' If this is a Co-requisite
  If rstPreReqs!CoRequisite = True Then
    ' Set up to test for both prior completed or
    '  enrolled this semester
    strWhere = strWhere & _
      " AND (((tblStudentCourses.SessionYear = " & intYear & _
      ") AND (tblStudentCourses.SessionNumber < " & intSession & _
      ") AND (tblStudentCourses.Status = " & StudentClassStatus.Completed & _
      ") AND (tblStudentCourses.Grade >= 72)) " & _
      "OR ((tblStudentCourses.SessionYear < " & intYear & _
      ") AND (tblStudentCourses.Status = " & StudentClassStatus.Completed & _
      ") AND (tblStudentCourses.Grade >= 72)) " & _
      "OR ((tblStudentCourses.SessionYear = " & intYear & _
      ") AND (tblStudentCourses.SessionNumber = " & intSession & _
      ") AND (tblStudentCourses.Status IN (" & StudentClassStatus.Enrolled & _
      ", " & StudentClassStatus.Completed & ")))) "
  Else
    ' Test only for prior completed
    strWhere = strWhere & _
```

```
                " AND (((tblStudentCourses.SessionYear = " & intYear & _
                ") AND (tblStudentCourses.SessionNumber < " & intSession & _
                ") AND (tblStudentCourses.Status = " & StudentClassStatus.Completed & _
                ") AND (tblStudentCourses.Grade >= 72)) " & _
                "OR ((tblStudentCourses.SessionYear < " & intYear & _
                ") AND (tblStudentCourses.Status = " & StudentClassStatus.Completed & _
                ") AND (tblStudentCourses.Grade >= 72)))"
          End If
          ' Open a recordset to see if the prerequisite course exists
          Set rstStPreReqs = db.OpenRecordset(strSQL & strWhere, dbOpenSnapshot)
          ' If got a match
          If Not rstStPreReqs.EOF Then
            ' Set matched at least one in this sequence
            intMetThisSeq = True
          End If
          ' Close the recordset
          rstStPreReqs.Close
          ' Move to the next prerequisite record
          rstPreReqs.MoveNext
        ' Loop to process
        Loop
        ' Close the recordset
        rstPreReqs.Close
        ' Check the last sequence
        If intMetThisSeq = False Then
          ' Set failed
          intMetPreReq = False
        End If
      End If
```

After looping through all the prerequisite rows, the code checks to see if the intMetPreReq variable has been set to False, indicating that at least one of the prerequisite sequences was not met. The student must meet at least one of the prerequisites in all the prerequisite sequences to meet the prerequisite requirements. If any one prerequisite sequence failed (intMetPreReq = False), the code checks the CoursePreReqByApproval field for the course to see if the course requested is eligible for approval by the instructor or an administrator. If so, the code updates the status of the request to Awaiting Approval, adds 1 to the awaiting approval counter, and writes a record to the ztblNotConfirmed table. If the course is not eligible for approval, the code adds 1 to the failed prerequisite count and writes an appropriate record to the ztblNotConfirmed table. The code is as follows:

```
      ' If met prereq flag not on
      If intMetPreReq = False Then
        ' If approval can be obtained from instructor,
        If rstSC!CoursePreReqByApproval = True Then
          ' Add 1 to awaiting approval count
          intApprove = intApprove + 1
          ' Update the record to "Awaiting Approval" status
          rstSC.Edit
          rstSC!Status = StudentClassStatus.AwaitingApproval
          rstSC.Update
          ' Add this request to the not confirmed log
```

```
With rstNotConfirmed
  .AddNew
  !StudentID = rstSC!StudentID
  !SessionYear = intYear
  !SessionNumber = intSession
  !CourseCategory = rstSC!CourseCategory
  !CourseNumber = rstSC!CourseNumber
  !SectionNumber = rstSC!SectionNumber
  !Status = rstSC!Status
  !Reason = "Awaiting instructor approval"
  .Update
End With
Else
  ' Add 1 to prereq failed count
  intPreReqFailed = intPreReqFailed + 1
  ' Add this request to the not confirmed log
  With rstNotConfirmed
    .AddNew
    !StudentID = rstSC!StudentID
    !SessionYear = intYear
    !SessionNumber = intSession
    !CourseCategory = rstSC!CourseCategory
    !CourseNumber = rstSC!CourseNumber
    !SectionNumber = rstSC!SectionNumber
    !Status = rstSC!Status
    !Reason = "Failed to meet prerequisites"
    .Update
  End With
End If
```

Checking Whether the Section Is Overbooked

If there were no prerequisites or all prerequisite sequences were met, the code performs a final check to see if the class and section is already overbooked. The code opens a recordset to count the number of students already enrolled in the requested course and section. If the number already enrolled exceeds the value in the CourseMaxStudents field, the code adds 1 to the wait list count and writes a record to the ztblNotConfirmed table. The code is as follows:

```
Else
  ' Prerequisites met - See if overbooked
  Set rstCCount = db.OpenRecordset( _
    "SELECT Count(*) As NumEnrolled FROM tblStudentCourses " & _
    "WHERE SessionYear = " & intYear & _
    " AND SessionNumber = " & intSession & _
    " AND CourseCategory = '" & rstSC!CourseCategory & _
    "' AND CourseNumber = " & rstSC!CourseNumber & _
    " AND (Status = " & StudentClassStatus.Enrolled & _
    " OR Status = " & StudentClassStatus.Completed & _
    ") AND SectionNumber = " & rstSC!SectionNumber & _
    " AND StudentID <> " & rstSC!StudentID, dbOpenSnapshot)
  ' If class is full,
  If rstCCount!NumEnrolled >= rstSC!CourseMaxStudents Then
    ' Add 1 to wait list count
```

```
intWait = intWait + 1
' Update the record to "Wait List" status
rstSC.Edit
rstSC!Status = StudentClassStatus.WaitList
rstSC.Update
' Add this request to the not confirmed log
With rstNotConfirmed
  .AddNew
  !StudentID = rstSC!StudentID
  !SessionYear = intYear
  !SessionNumber = intSession
  !CourseCategory = rstSC!CourseCategory
  !CourseNumber = rstSC!CourseNumber
  !SectionNumber = rstSC!SectionNumber
  !Status = rstSC!Status
  !Reason = "Placed on wait-list"
  .Update
End With
```

> **Note**   The test for Completed status is included when counting enrolled students to accommodate code in the zfrmLoadData form that you can use to load new sample data. Because code in the zfrmLoadData form marks a course completed as soon as it schedules it, this code tests for both Enrolled and Completed status to get a correct count. In actual use, no student should have already completed a class at the time another student is requesting enrollment.

Enrolling the Student Request

Finally, if there is no schedule overlap, all prerequisites have been met, and the course is not full, the code changes the request status to Enrolled and writes it back. After processing all requests, the code commits the transaction to make all changes to the tables permanent. The code at the end of the function traps errors, displays them, and writes a record to the error log table. The code is as follows:

```
        Else
          ' Can enroll the student!
          ' Add one to scheduled count
          intSched = intSched + 1
          ' Update the record to "Enrolled" status
          rstSC.Edit
          rstSC!Status = StudentClassStatus.Enrolled
          rstSC.Update
        End If
    End If
End If
' Move to the next class
rstSC.MoveNext
' Update the processed count
intRec = intRec + 1
' If not called from zfrmLoadData
If Not intSilent Then
  ' Update the meter
```

```
        varReturn = SysCmd(acSysCmdUpdateMeter, intRec)
        ' Let Access update the display
        DoEvents
      End If
    ' Process them all
    Loop
    ' Commit all updates
    CommitTrans
    blnTrans = False
    ' Return success and counts
    StudentConfirm = Array(-1, intSched, intWait, intPreReqFailed, _
      intApprove, intOverlap)
    ' Close the class request recordset
    rstSC.Close
    ' .. and the confirmation log
    rstNotConfirmed.Close
StudentConfirm_Exit:
    ' Blow past errors after this
    On Error Resume Next
    ' If not called from zfrmLoadData
    If Not intSilent Then
      ' Clean up - clear the meter
      varReturn = SysCmd(acSysCmdClearStatus)
      ' Turn off the hourglass
      DoCmd.Hourglass False
    End If
    ' Clear all objects
    Set rstNotConfirmed = Nothing
    Set rstStPreReqs = Nothing
    Set rstPreReqs = Nothing
    Set rstCCount = Nothing
    Set rstSC = Nothing
    Set db = Nothing
    ' Done
    Exit Function
StudentConfirm_Err:
    ' Got an error - display it
    MsgBox "Unexpected error confirming student courses: " & _
      Err.Number & ", " & Err.Description, _
      vbCritical, gstrAppTitle
    ' Roll back any transaction
    If blnTrans Then
      blnTrans = False
      Rollback
    End If
    ' Log the error
    ErrorLog "StudentConfirm", Err.Number, Err.Description
    ' Return error
    StudentConfirm = Array(0)
    ' Bail
    Resume StudentConfirm_Exit
End Function
```

You can now close the Students form (you will be prompted to confirm that you want to exit) to return to the Database window.

Approving Student Requests

As you saw in the previous sections, student Anne Hansen asked for two courses that require approval and one course that is wait-listed because the section she requested is full. To see how instructors deal with requests for approval and the wait list, start the application again by opening the frmSplash form. This time, sign on as an instructor and enter **jfallon** as the User Name and **password** as the Password. You'll see Joe Fallon's instructor record and, if your machine date is set to a date between January 1, 2005, and May 21, 2005, you'll also see a notification that several items require his attention, as shown in Figure 22-9.

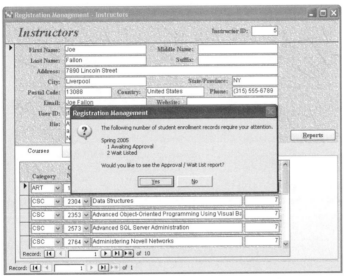

Figure 22-9   The application notifies the instructor of pending approval and wait list requests when the instructor signs on.

If the application displays this message dialog box, click the Yes button, and the application opens the Students Awaiting Approval or On Wait List report, as shown in Figure 22-10 on the next page, to give Joe the details of the courses he needs to review.

You can find the code that checks pending approval and wait list requests in the Load event procedure of the frmInstructors form. If the user is an instructor (an administrator can also open this form), the code sets a pointer to the current database and opens a recordset on the tblSessions table to find out the session year and session number values for the current semester and the one following.

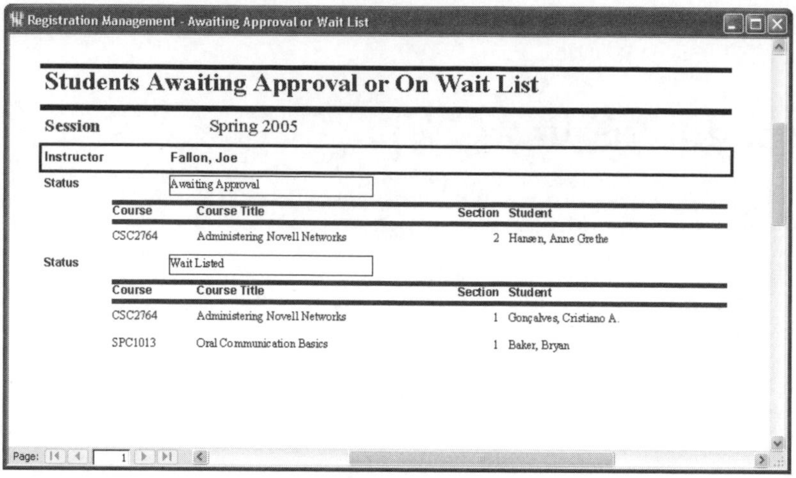

Figure 22-10   The Students Awaiting Approval or On Wait List report.

The code next starts a loop to process the one or two semester records. For each record, the code builds or adds to a predicate string in the strWhere variable that it might use later to open the report. It then uses the *DCount* function to obtain a count of the students awaiting approval and the students on the wait list for the semester. If either count was not zero, the code creates a message string to display the counts for the current semester. The code moves to the next semester record and loops to process it. The code is as follows:

```
Private Sub Form_Load()
Dim db As DAO.Database, rst As DAO.Recordset
Dim strWhere As String, strMsg As String, intApproval As Integer, intWait As Integer
  ' If instructor logged on,
  If gintThisUserType = UserType.Instructor Then
    ' Point to this database
    Set db = DBEngine(0)(0)
    ' Find out the current semester and the one following
    Set rst = db.OpenRecordset("SELECT SessionYear, SessionNumber " & _
      "FROM tblSessions " & _
      "WHERE (#" & Date & "# BETWEEN StartDate AND EndDate) " & _
      "OR StartDate = (SELECT MIN(StartDate) FROM tblSessions " & _
      "WHERE StartDate > #" & Date & "#)")
    ' Process what we got
    Do Until rst.EOF
      ' Add to the potential report filter string
      ' If something already in the string
      If strWhere <> "" Then
        ' Add the Or operator
        strWhere = strWhere & " OR "
      End If
      ' Build the predicate
      strWhere = strWhere & "(SessionYear = " & rst!SessionYear & _
        " AND SessionNumber = " & rst!SessionNumber & ")"
      ' Get awaiting approval for this semester & instructor
      intApproval = DCount("StudentID", "qryRptApprovalWaitList", _
```

```
        "InstructorID = " & Me.OpenArgs & _
        " AND SessionYear = " & rst!SessionYear & _
        " AND SessionNumber = " & rst!SessionNumber & _
        " AND Status = " & StudentClassStatus.AwaitingApproval)
      ' Get wait list count for this semester and instructor
      intWait = DCount("StudentID", "qryRptApprovalWaitList", _
        "InstructorID = " & Me.OpenArgs & _
        " AND SessionYear = " & rst!SessionYear & _
        " AND SessionNumber = " & rst!SessionNumber & _
        " AND Status = " & StudentClassStatus.WaitList)
      ' If one or both not zero
      If (intApproval + intWait) <> 0 Then
        ' Set up message
        strMsg = strMsg & vbCrLf & _
          Choose(rst!SessionNumber, "Spring", "Summer", "Fall") & _
          " " & rst!SessionYear & vbCrLf & _
          "   " & intApproval & " Awaiting Approval" & vbCrLf & _
          "   " & intWait & " Wait Listed" & vbCrLf
      End If
      ' Get the next semester
      rst.MoveNext
    Loop
```

After processing the semester records, the code checks to see if a message string was created. If so, the code makes sure the user can see the form by setting the focus to it. The code then displays the approval and wait counts and asks the user if the report should be opened. If the user clicks the Yes button, the code opens the rptApprovalWaitList report, waits one second to let the report open, and then puts the focus on the report. The code is as follows:

```
    ' Close the recordset
    rst.Close
    Set rst = Nothing
    Set db = Nothing
    ' If built a message,
    If strMsg <> "" Then
      ' Paint me first
      Me.SetFocus
      ' Display and ask if they want to see the report
      If vbYes = MsgBox("The following number of student enrollment " & _
        "records require your attention." & vbCrLf & strMsg & vbCrLf & _
        "Would you like to see the Approval / Wait List report?", _
        vbQuestion + vbYesNo, gstrAppTitle) Then
        ' Open the report
        DoCmd.OpenReport "rptApprovalWaitList", acViewPreview, _
          WhereCondition:="InstructorID = " & Me.OpenArgs & _
            " AND (" & strWhere & ")"
        ' Give Access a chance to open it
        WaitASec 1
        ' Put the focus on the report
        DoCmd.SelectObject acReport, "rptApprovalWaitList"
      End If
    End If
  End If
End Sub
```

The user can now print the report and then examine the student course request records to decide whether the requests can be approved.

> **Note** You can find the *WaitASec* procedure in the modUtility module. It waits the number of seconds specified in a loop that uses the DoEvents statement to release Access to perform other tasks.

Approving an Enrollment

There are several ways that an instructor can approach approving requests. To work with Anne Hansen's pending request for prerequisite approval, Joe can click the Students tab, set the Display filter at the bottom of the form to include the year of data he needs (if he's looking for next semester, he might need to set the filter to Next Year), and then scan down the list to find the requests that need attention. For any student, he can double-click the Student field to open the Students form to review that student's prior record. If he decides to approve an Awaiting Approval request, he simply needs to choose Approved from the list in the Status field, as shown in Figure 22-11.

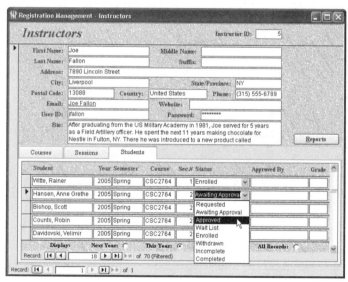

Figure 22-11 Deciding to approve an Awaiting Approval request.

When he changes a status from Awaiting Approval to Approved, the application prompts him to also confirm the enrollment, as shown in Figure 22-12.

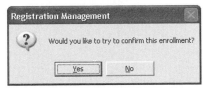

Figure 22-12   The instructor can also confirm an enrollment for a request changed to Approved status.

If the instructor chooses to confirm the enrollment, the application calls the *StudentConfirmed* function and supplies the student ID, year, and session (semester). If any pending requests for that student failed confirmation, the application displays summary counts in a dialog box (shown earlier in Figure 22-7 on page 480) and then opens the rptNotConfirmed report, as shown in Figure 22-13.

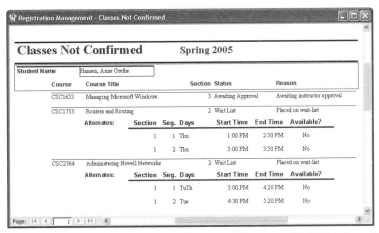

Figure 22-13   Although approved to enroll in course CSC2764, Anne Hansen is now on the wait list for that course and section.

You can find the code that executes the confirmation process in the AfterUpdate event procedure of the cmbStatus combo box control in the fsubInstructorStudents form. If the status was changed to Approved, the code first sets the ApprovedBy field in the record to the ID of the currently signed-on user (in this case, Joe Fallon's instructor ID). The code then displays the message dialog box asking the instructor whether he or she wants to try to confirm the course.

If the instructor clicks the Yes button, the code calls the *StudentConfirm* function that you studied earlier in this chapter. If the function failed, the code exits. If the code completed successfully, the code displays the results of confirmed, wait-listed, failed prerequisites, awaiting approval, and overlapping schedule counts. When the user closes that dialog box, the code opens the rptNotConfirmed report to show the detail results. The code is as follows:

```
Private Sub cmbStatus_AfterUpdate()
Dim varReturn As Variant
  ' If changed to Approved,
  If Me.cmbStatus = StudentClassStatus.Approved Then
    ' Update the approved by
    Me.ApprovedBy = glngUserID
    ' See if the user wants to try to confirm
    If vbYes = MsgBox("Would you like to try to confirm " & _
      "this enrollment?", vbQuestion + vbYesNo, gstrAppTitle) Then
      ' Save the record first
      cmdSave_Click
      ' Call the confirmation routine
      varReturn = StudentConfirm(Me.StudentID, _
        Me.SessionYear, Me.SessionNumber)
      ' If failed,
      If varReturn(1) = 0 Then
        ' Bail
        Exit Sub
      End If
      ' Display the result
      MsgBox "Confirmation Completed." & vbCrLf & vbCrLf & _
        "Confirmed classes: " & varReturn(2) & vbCrLf & _
        "Classes wait-listed: " & varReturn(3) & vbCrLf & _
        "Failed pre-requisites: " & varReturn(4) & vbCrLf & _
        "Awaiting approval: " & varReturn(5) & vbCrLf & _
        "Classes with date/time conflict: " & varReturn(6), _
        vbInformation, gstrAppTitle
      ' Bail past any no data cancel
      On Error Resume Next
      ' Open the results report
      DoCmd.OpenReport "rptNotConfirmed", acViewPreview
    End If
  End If
End Sub
```

Managing a Wait List

Joe still has some work to do. Now that Anne is on the wait list, he needs to check the registration for that particular course and section. He can click the Sessions tab and then click the Details button next to the section he needs to investigate, as shown in Figure 22-14.

When the instructor clicks the Details button next to a specific course section, the application opens the Instructor Sessions form (frmInstructorSessions) displaying the details. Click the Students tab to see the list of students for this instructor, as shown in Figure 22-15. The instructor can look at the total count of students on the navigation bar at the bottom of the subform window and decide whether to add one more student to the class. If Joe decides to approve the extra enrollment, he can change the status from Wait List to Enrolled.

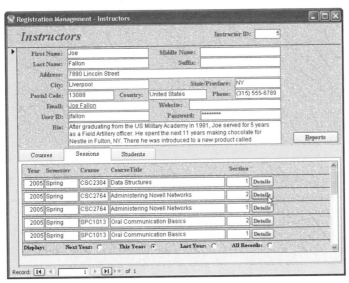

Figure 22-14 An instructor can click the Details button to investigate the detailed enrollment for a particular course and section.

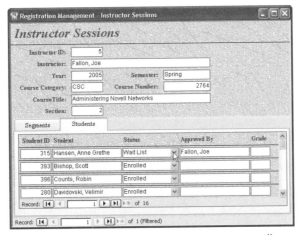

Figure 22-15 An instructor can attempt to enroll a student on the wait list.

Ah, but an instructor cannot book students beyond the capacity of the classrooms scheduled for the course! (Although some classes get scheduled in classrooms that exactly fit the maximum students recommended for the course, most are scheduled in classrooms that are larger.) The application checks the capacity of the smallest room scheduled for any of the segments of the course and displays the dialog box shown in Figure 22-16 on the next page if there is room left.

Figure 22-16   If the additional student can be accommodated, the application asks for confirmation.

You can find the code that performs the check for room size in the BeforeUpdate event procedure for the cmbStatus combo box on the fsubInstructorSessionStudents form. If the current user is an administrator, the code allows all changes. This lets an administrator overbook a course—perhaps stick an extra desk or two in the room! If the user is a student, the code disallows all changes. (A student shouldn't be able to see this form, but the code performs the check anyway.) The code is as follows:

```
Private Sub cmbStatus_BeforeUpdate(Cancel As Integer)
Dim intMinSize As Integer, intNumEnrolled As Integer
  ' If an administrator
  If gintThisUserType = UserType.Administrator Then
    ' Allow all changes
    Exit Sub
  End If
  ' If a student (should not happen - locked)
  If gintThisUserType = UserType.Student Then
    ' Disallow
    MsgBox "You cannot change status.  " & _
      "Press Esc to clear your edit.", vbCritical, gstrAppTitle
    Cancel = True
    Exit Sub
  End If
```

If the user is an instructor, the code first checks to see if the instructor is changing the status from Awaiting Approval to Approved. If so, the code allows the change by exiting. Next, if the previous status was Enrolled and the instructor is changing the value to something higher (Withdrawn, Incomplete, or Completed), the code allows the change by exiting.

The last check the code performs for an instructor is a change from Wait List to Enrolled. When this is the case, the code first uses the *DCount* function to find out the number of students enrolled in the course and section. It then uses the *DMin* function to find out the smallest room size for any segment scheduled for the course and section. If the number enrolled already exceeds the size of the smallest room, the code informs the instructor and disallows the change.

If the smallest room still has capacity, the code displays the counts (the dialog box shown in Figure 22-16), and asks the instructor if the change should be made. The instructor can still change his or her mind at this point, and the code cancels the update. Finally, if the instructor is trying to make any other change, the code displays an error message and cancels the change. The code is as follows:

```vba
' Must be an instructor
' Allowed to change status from Awaiting Approval to Approved
'  .. and from Enrolled to something higher
If (Me.cmbStatus.OldValue = StudentClassStatus.AwaitingApproval) And _
  (Me.cmbStatus = StudentClassStatus.Approved) Then
  ' OK - exit
  Exit Sub
End If
If (Me.cmbStatus.OldValue >= StudentClassStatus.Enrolled) And _
  (Me.cmbStatus > StudentClassStatus.Enrolled) Then
  ' OK - exit
  Exit Sub
End If
' If trying to change from Wait List to Enrolled,
If (Me.cmbStatus.OldValue = StudentClassStatus.WaitList) And _
  (Me.cmbStatus = StudentClassStatus.Enrolled) Then
  ' Get the number currently enrolled
  intNumEnrolled = Nz(DCount("StudentID", "tblStudentCourses", _
    "SessionYear = " & Me.SessionYear & _
    " AND SessionNumber = " & Me.SessionNumber & _
    " AND CourseCategory = '" & Me.CourseCategory & _
    "' AND CourseNumber = " & Me.CourseNumber & _
    " AND SectionNumber = " & Me.SectionNumber & _
    " AND Status = " StudentClassStatus.Enrolled), 0)
  ' Get the smallest room size for any segment of this section
  intMinSize = Nz(DMin("RoomSize", "qrySessionCourseSegments", _
    "SessionYear = " & Me.SessionYear & _
    " AND SessionNumber = " & Me.SessionNumber & _
    " AND CourseCategory = '" & Me.CourseCategory & _
    "' AND CourseNumber = " & Me.CourseNumber & _
    " AND SectionNumber = " & Me.SectionNumber), 0)
  ' See if already over the minimum room size
  If intNumEnrolled >= intMinSize Then
    ' Tell Instructor no can do
    MsgBox "This section has " & intNumEnrolled & _
      " students enrolled, and the smallest room " & _
      " for any segment of this course section is " & _
      intMinSize & ".  You cannot enroll an additional " & _
      "student.  Press Esc to clear your Edit.", vbCritical, gstrAppTitle
    ' Cancel the edit
    Cancel = True
  Else
    ' Inform the instructor and verify
    If vbNo = MsgBox("This section has " & intNumEnrolled & _
      " students enrolled, and the smallest room " & _
      " for any segment of this course section is " & _
      intMinSize & ".  Are you sure you want to enroll " & _
      "this student?", vbQuestion + vbYesNo + vbDefaultButton2, _
      gstrAppTitle) Then
      ' Cancel the edit
      Cancel = True
    End If
  End If
End If
' Do no additional test
Exit Sub
```

```
    End If
    ' Display error and cancel
    MsgBox "You can change Status from 'Awaiting Approval' to " & _
        "'Approved' or from 'Enrolled' to " & _
        "'Withdrawn', 'Incomplete', or 'Completed' only.  " & _
        "Press Esc to clear your edit.", _
        vbCritical, gstrAppTitle    Cancel = True
End Sub
```

You should now understand how the application handles the scheduling of student course requests, including approving courses for which the student does not have prerequisites and enrollment even when the student is on the wait list. In the next chapter, you'll explore how the application prints and sends course schedules, instructor schedules, and student schedules.

Chapter 23

Printing and E-Mailing Schedules

After scheduling courses for the semester, the school needs to be able to publish the course schedule. The school also must inform instructors about the courses they are scheduled to teach. After students enroll in courses, the school should be able to print and send the schedule to each student. You'll learn how the sample Registration Management application accomplishes all these tasks in this chapter.

Printing Course Schedules

An administrator has several options for printing the course schedules for a semester. To see these options, open the Registration Management sample database (Registration.mdb), start the application by opening the frmSplash form, and sign on as an administrator. (Enter **tmichaels** as the User Name and **password** as the Password.) On the main switchboard click the Reports button, and on the Reports switchboard click the Courses button. In the Course Reports dialog box (the fdlgCourseReports form), choose any of the options under Course Schedules to see the semester selection combo boxes enabled, as shown in Figure 23-1 on the next page.

Let's take a look at the complex Course Schedule By Course report that is useful to publish the course schedule for an upcoming semester, perhaps as part of a printed catalog. Select the By Course option, choose 2005 in the Year combo box, choose Spring in the Semester combo box, and click Go to see the course schedule for the Spring 2005 semester, as shown in Figure 23-2 on the next page.

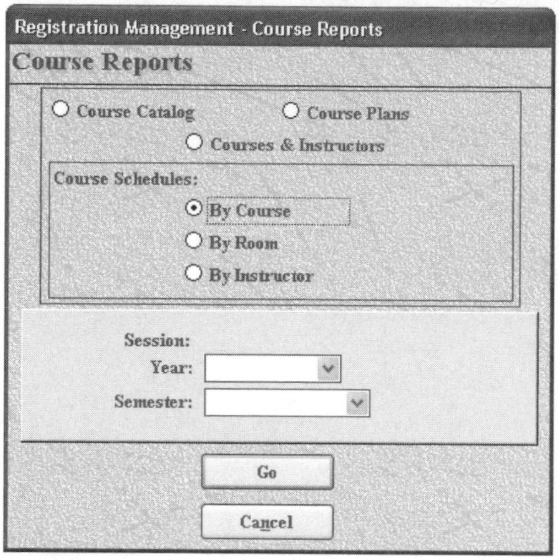

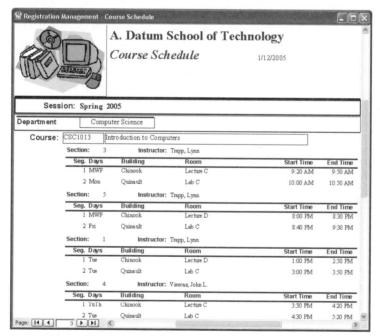

Figure 23-1   Choosing a course report option.

Figure 23-2   The Course Schedule report for the Spring 2005 semester.

Notice that the report keeps the segments for a course section together on the report and sorts the data in an interesting way. The sections are listed in order by the earliest day of the week of any day the section is taught and then by the start time of the earliest section. The report design is relatively simple, but sorting the data in the correct sequence requires some SQL gymnastics in the record source of the report. You'll learn more about the record source design in the section "Understanding the Course Schedule Report Design" on page 505.

Understanding the Course Report Selection Procedure

You probably noticed that the Course Reports dialog box shown in Figure 23-1 offers six different reports related to courses. The Course Catalog is a simple listing of the courses offered by the school, including a detailed description of each course and the course prerequisites. The Course Plans report lists the various certificate and associate degree plans offered by the school and the courses required to complete each plan. The Courses & Instructors report prints all courses and the instructors currently assigned to teach each course.

The application also offers three variations of Course Schedule reports. In the previous example, you took a look at the Course Schedule By Course option that lists all courses, sections, and segments for a particular semester in a complex date and time sequence. The Course Schedule By Room report lists all courses, sections, and segments for a particular semester sorted by the room assigned and then date and time. Finally, the Course Schedule By Instructor report displays all courses, sections, and segments for a semester sorted by instructor and then date and time. This same report is used to produce a schedule for individual instructors, and you'll examine how that report works in the section "Printing and E-Mailing Instructor Schedules" on page 508.

When the user clicks the Go button in the Course Reports dialog box, code in the Click event procedure of that command button (the cmdGo control) examines the options the user selected and the optional year and semester the user specified and opens the appropriate report with a filter. Note that when the user selects any of the first three report options, code in the AfterUpdate event procedure of the ogOptions option group control clears and disables the Year and Semester controls because none of these reports are filtered by year or semester.

The code first tests to see if the user entered a year and semester value. If either value is supplied, the code creates an appropriate predicate to filter the report. Next, the code tests the value of the ogOptions option group control—the control that contains all the option buttons you see in the dialog box. If the user selected one of the first three options, the code opens the appropriate report without a filter.

For the three Course Schedule reports, the code verifies that the user specified either Year or Semester or both. If the predicate string is still null, the code displays an error message and exits. If the predicate string is not empty, the code uses the predicate as a filter to open the appropriate report and then closes the dialog box form. Code at the end of the procedure traps any errors and ignores any cancel error that might have been generated by the NoData event in one of the reports. The code is as follows:

```
Private Sub cmdGo_Click()
Dim lngStudentID As Long, varWhere As String
    ' Build a filter and open the selected report
    ' Set an error trap
    On Error GoTo cmdGo_Err
    ' If have a year
    If Not IsNothing(Me.cmbSessionYear) Then
```

```vba
        ' Create the main predicate
        varWhere = "tblSessionCourses.SessionYear = " & Me.cmbSessionYear
    End If
    ' If have a session number
    If Not IsNothing(Me.cmbSessionNumber) Then
        ' Add to the main predicate
        varWhere = (varWhere + " AND ") & _
            "tblSessionCourses.SessionNumber = " & Me.cmbSessionNumber
    End If
    ' Figure out which report to produce
    Select Case Me.ogOptions
        ' Course Catalog
        Case 1
            ' Hide me
            Me.Visible = False
            ' Open the Course Catalog report
            DoCmd.OpenReport "rptCourseCatalog", acViewPreview
        ' Course Plans
        Case 2
            ' Hide me
            Me.Visible = False
            ' Open the Course Plans report
            DoCmd.OpenReport "rptCoursePlans", acViewPreview
        ' Courses & Instructors
        Case 3
            ' Hide me
            Me.Visible = False
            ' Open the Courses & Instructors report
            DoCmd.OpenReport "rptCoursesInstructors", acViewPreview
        ' Course Schedule by Course
        Case 4
            ' Make sure at least one criterion specified
            If IsNothing(varWhere) Then
                MsgBox "You must specify either year or semester or both.", _
                    vbCritical, gstrAppTitle
                ' Bail
                Exit Sub
            End If
            ' Hide me
            Me.Visible = False
            ' Open the Course Schedule by Course report
            DoCmd.OpenReport "rptCourseSchedule", acViewPreview, _
                WhereCondition:=varWhere
        ' Course Schedule by Room
        Case 5
            ' Make sure at least one criterion specified
            If IsNothing(varWhere) Then
                MsgBox "You must specify either year or semester or both.", _
                    vbCritical, gstrAppTitle
                ' Bail
                Exit Sub
            End If
            ' Hide me
            Me.Visible = False
            ' Open the Course Schedule by Room report
```

```
        DoCmd.OpenReport "rptCourseScheduleRoom", acViewPreview, _
          WhereCondition:=varWhere
    ' Course Schedule by Instructor
    Case 6
      ' Make sure at least one criterion specified
      If IsNothing(varWhere) Then
        MsgBox "You must specify either year or semester or both.", _
          vbCritical, gstrAppTitle
          ' Bail
        Exit Sub
      End If
      ' Hide me
      Me.Visible = False
      ' Open the Course Schedule by Instructor report
      DoCmd.OpenReport "rptCourseScheduleInstructor", acViewPreview, _
        WhereCondition:=varWhere
  End Select
cmdGo_Exit:
  ' Close me
  DoCmd.Close acForm, Me.Name
  Exit Sub
cmdGo_Err:
  ' Bypass any cancel error from no data in a report
  If Err.Number = errCancel Then
    Resume cmdGo_Exit
  End If
  MsgBox "Unexpected error: " & Err & ", " & Error, vbCritical, gstrAppTitle
  ErrorLog Me.Name & "_cmdGo", Err, Error
  Resume cmdGo_Exit
End Sub
```

Understanding the Course Schedule Report Design

The Course Schedule By Course report presents an interesting study in solving a complex sorting problem. The course schedule should list the courses by department and course number—that's simple enough to do. But the report should also list the various sections scheduled for each course in some meaningful way, and it should keep together the segments for any one course section.

One logical way to list the courses is in sequence by day of the week and time. But some course sections have a segment that's taught on Monday-Wednesday-Friday (MWF) with a lab segment on one of those days. Similarly, some course sections have a Tuesday-Thursday (TuTh) segment or Tuesday-Thursday-Saturday (TuThSat) segment with a lab segment taught on just one of those days. It seems logical to sequence the MWF course sections with all other courses that are taught on Monday. Likewise, the TuTh and TuThSat courses should all appear in sequence with any other course taught on Tuesday. Any course that is taught on a single day should appear in sequence by the day of the week. Within a day sequence, the class sections should appear in order of the earliest start time for any section.

The tblSessionCourseSegments table (described in Chapter 21, "Scheduling Courses") contains a code for the day(s) of the week and a start time for each segment. The codes are the numbers 1–6 for Monday-Saturday, 8 for TuTh, 9 for MWF, and 10 for TuThSat. The first trick is to lump any single-day segment of a course with the highest day code for any other segment. This will cause a Friday segment of a course section that also has a MWF segment to sort on the higher code. One way to calculate this value is to create a totals query that returns the MAX value of the Days code, grouped by session year, session number, course category, course number, and section number. The SQL for this query (zqryMaxDayPerSection) is as follows:

```
SELECT MAX(tblSessionCourseSegments.Days) AS MaxDay,
  tblSessionCourseSegments.SessionYear,
  tblSessionCourseSegments.SessionNumber,
  tblSessionCourseSegments.CourseCategory,
  tblSessionCourseSegments.CourseNumber,
  tblSessionCourseSegments.SectionNumber
FROM tblSessionCourseSegments
GROUP BY tblSessionCourseSegments.SessionYear,
  tblSessionCourseSegments.SessionNumber,
  tblSessionCourseSegments.CourseCategory,
  tblSessionCourseSegments.CourseNumber,
  tblSessionCourseSegments.SectionNumber;
```

The next challenge is to calculate the earliest starting time for any segment in a section to be able to sort all segments of a section together. Another totals query that returns the MIN value of the StartTime field, grouped by session year, session number, course category, course number, and section number solves that problem. The SQL for this query (zqryMinTimePerSection) is as follows:

```
SELECT MIN(tblSessionCourseSegments.StartTime) AS MinTime,
  tblSessionCourseSegments.SessionYear,
  tblSessionCourseSegments.SessionNumber,
  tblSessionCourseSegments.CourseCategory,
  tblSessionCourseSegments.CourseNumber,
  tblSessionCourseSegments.SectionNumberFROM tblSessionCourseSegments
GROUP BY tblSessionCourseSegments.SessionYear,
  tblSessionCourseSegments.SessionNumber,
  tblSessionCourseSegments.CourseCategory,
  tblSessionCourseSegments.CourseNumber,
  tblSessionCourseSegments.SectionNumber;
```

Finally, the qryRptCourseSchedule query can be assembled that uses the two totals queries and the tlkpRooms, tlkpCourseCategories, tblCourses, tblSessionCourses, tblInstructors, and tblSessionCourseSegments tables. The SQL for this query is as follows:

```
SELECT tblSessionCourses.SessionYear, tblSessionCourses.SessionNumber,
  tlkpCourseCategories.CategoryDescription,
  tblSessionCourses.CourseCategory,
  Choose([MaxDay],1,2,3,4,5,6,7,2,1,2) AS DaySort,
  CDate([MinTime]) AS TimeSort, tblSessionCourses.CourseNumber,
```

```
  tblCourses.CourseTitle, tblSessionCourseSegments.SectionNumber,
  tblInstructors.InstructorID, tblInstructors.LastName & ", " &
    tblInstructors.FirstName & (" "+tblInstructors.MiddleName) &
    (", "+tblInstructors.Suffix) AS Instructor,
  tblSessionCourseSegments.CourseSegment, tlkpRooms.Building,
  tlkpRooms.RoomName,
  Choose([Days], "Mon", "Tue", "Wed", "Thu", "Fri", "Sat", "", "TuTh",
    "MWF", "TuThSat") AS DaysVal,
  tblSessionCourseSegments.StartTime, tblSessionCourseSegments.EndTime
FROM tlkpRooms
INNER JOIN (tlkpCourseCategories
  INNER JOIN ((tblCourses
    INNER JOIN (((tblSessionCourses
      INNER JOIN tblInstructors
      ON tblSessionCourses.InstructorID = tblInstructors.InstructorID)
      INNER JOIN zqryMaxDayPerSection
      ON (tblSessionCourses.SessionYear = zqryMaxDayPerSection.SessionYear)
        AND (tblSessionCourses.SessionNumber =
          zqryMaxDayPerSection.SessionNumber) AND
        (tblSessionCourses.CourseCategory =
          zqryMaxDayPerSection.CourseCategory) AND
        (tblSessionCourses.CourseNumber =
          zqryMaxDayPerSection.CourseNumber) AND
        (tblSessionCourses.SectionNumber =
          zqryMaxDayPerSection.SectionNumber))
      INNER JOIN zqryMinTimePerSection
      ON (tblSessionCourses.SessionYear =
          zqryMinTimePerSection.SessionYear)
        AND (tblSessionCourses.SessionNumber =
          zqryMinTimePerSection.SessionNumber)
        AND (tblSessionCourses.CourseCategory =
          zqryMinTimePerSection.CourseCategory)
        AND (tblSessionCourses.CourseNumber =
          zqryMinTimePerSection.CourseNumber)
        AND (tblSessionCourses.SectionNumber =
          zqryMinTimePerSection.SectionNumber))
    ON (tblCourses.CourseNumber = tblSessionCourses.CourseNumber)
      AND (tblCourses.CourseCategory = tblSessionCourses.CourseCategory))
    INNER JOIN tblSessionCourseSegments
    ON (tblSessionCourses.SectionNumber =
        tblSessionCourseSegments.SectionNumber)
      AND (tblSessionCourses.CourseNumber =
        tblSessionCourseSegments.CourseNumber)
      AND (tblSessionCourses.CourseCategory =
        tblSessionCourseSegments.CourseCategory)
      AND (tblSessionCourses.SessionNumber =
        tblSessionCourseSegments.SessionNumber)
      AND (tblSessionCourses.SessionYear =
        tblSessionCourseSegments.SessionYear))
  ON tlkpCourseCategories.CategoryCode = tblCourses.CourseCategory)
ON tlkpRooms.RoomID = tblSessionCourseSegments.RoomID;
```

Notice that the query uses the *Choose* function to convert the codes for TuTh, MWF, and TuThSat back to sort with all the other courses on Tuesday, Monday, and Tuesday, respectively. The query has no ORDER BY clause because it is not used for any other purpose, and the sorting criteria are specified in the Sorting and Grouping specification for the report, as shown in Figure 23-3.

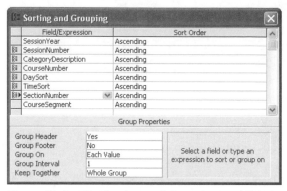

Figure 23-3   The Sorting and Grouping specification for the Course Schedule report.

To get the segments of a course section to appear together and in the correct sequence, the report sorts by the calculated DaySort and TimeSort fields within a course, and then finally sorts by section number and course segment. And no, I didn't get the sort sequence correct on the first try! I originally calculated the DaySort and TimeSort values using the *DMax* and *DMin* functions within the query, but that caused the report to take 10 or more seconds to display on a fast machine. Adding the two totals queries significantly improved performance.

Printing and E-Mailing Instructor Schedules

In addition to publishing the course schedule to help students choose courses at convenient times, the school needs to provide instructors with individual schedules so that the instructors know when they need work at the school. This section shows you how to both print and e-mail instructor schedules.

Printing Instructor Schedules

To print the Instructor Schedule report for a semester, you need to start the application and sign on as an administrator. Open the Registration Management database (Registration.mdb), open the frmSplash form to start the application, select Administrator in the Sign On dialog box, enter **tmichaels** as the User Name and **password** as the Password, and press Enter or click the Sign On button. On the main switchboard form, click the Reports button. On the Reports switchboard, click the Instructors button, and the application opens the Instructor Reports dialog box.

You can ask for an instructor report for specific instructors by entering criteria in the First Name, Last Name, City, State/Province, Course Category, or Course Number fields. In this case, let's look at the schedule for all instructors in the Spring 2005 semester. Select the Instructor Schedule option and choose 2005 for the Year and Spring for the Semester, as shown in Figure 23-4. Notice that when you select the Instructor Schedule option, the form displays the Send via E-Mail check box. You'll explore this option later in this chapter.

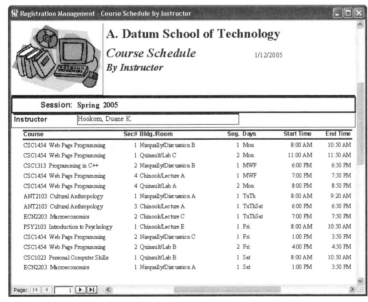

Figure 23-4   Printing the instructor schedules for the Spring 2005 semester.

Click the Go button at the bottom of the dialog box, and the application opens the course schedule for all instructors for the Spring 2005 semester, as shown in Figure 23-5.

Registration Management - Course Schedule by Instructor

A. Datum School of Technology

Course Schedule   1/12/2005

By Instructor

Session: Spring 2005

Instructor	Hookom, Duane K.					
Course		**Sec#**	**Bldg./Room**	**Seg.**	**Days**	**Start Time**	**End Time**

Course	Sec#	Bldg./Room	Seg.	Days	Start Time	End Time
CSC1454 Web Page Programming	1	Nisqually/Discussion B	1	Mon	8:00 AM	10:50 AM
CSC1454 Web Page Programming	1	Quinault/Lab C	2	Mon	11:00 AM	11:50 AM
CSC1313 Programming in C++	2	Nisqually/Discussion B	1	MWF	6:00 PM	6:50 PM
CSC1454 Web Page Programming	4	Chinook/Lecture A	1	MWF	7:00 PM	7:50 PM
CSC1454 Web Page Programming	4	Quinault/Lab A	2	Mon	8:00 PM	8:50 PM
ANT2103 Cultural Anthropology	1	Nisqually/Discussion A	1	TuTh	8:00 AM	9:20 AM
ANT2103 Cultural Anthropology	3	Chinook/Lecture A	1	TuThSat	6:00 PM	6:50 PM
ECN2203 Macroeconomics	2	Chinook/Lecture C	1	TuThSat	7:00 PM	7:50 PM
PSY2103 Introduction to Psychology	1	Chinook/Lecture E	1	Fri	8:00 AM	10:50 AM
CSC1454 Web Page Programming	2	Nisqually/Discussion C	1	Fri	1:00 PM	3:50 PM
CSC1454 Web Page Programming	2	Quinault/Lab B	2	Fri	4:00 PM	4:50 PM
CSC1023 Personal Computer Skills	1	Quinault/Lab B	1	Sat	8:00 AM	10:50 AM
ECN2203 Macroeconomics	1	Nisqually/Discussion A	1	Sat	1:00 PM	3:50 PM

Page: |◄ ◄ 1 ►|►| ◄

Figure 23-5   The Course Schedule By Instructor report for the Spring 2005 semester.

As you might expect, this report uses a sorting sequence that is similar to that used for the Course Schedule By Course report. Notice that the two segments of the Web Page

Programming course appear together in the listing for the first instructor even though some of the segments are taught on different days. You can examine the record source later in this chapter in the section "Understanding the Instructor Schedule Report Design," page 513.

> **Note**   The Course Schedule By Instructor report starts a new page for each instructor, so the administrator can separate and mail or deliver the relevant pages to each instructor. An instructor can also sign on to the application and produce this report for his or her courses only.

Understanding the Instructor Report Selection Procedure

The Instructor Reports dialog box shown in Figure 23-4 offers the administrator various ways to filter any of the instructor reports for a specific instructor. To see the information for one or more specific instructors, the administrator can enter all or the beginning part of the instructor's first name, last name, city, or state/province. The administrator can also select a course category and a course number to see only those instructors who teach in that category or teach a specific course.

As you can see from the dialog box, the application offers four reports related to instructors: a simple name and address list, a display of instructors and the courses they can teach, the instructor schedule for a specific year or semester, and the student log (students enrolled in a course taught by the selected instructor) for a specific year or semester. The administrator also has the option to send the Instructor Schedule report via e-mail, which you'll explore later in this chapter.

When the user clicks the Go button in the dialog box, code in the Click event procedure of the cmdGo command button examines the controls on the form and constructs a predicate to filter the selected report. The code begins by constructing LIKE predicates for the First Name, Last Name, City, and State/Province controls. To filter the reports on course category or course number, the code must use a subquery because not all the reports contain course information to allow directly applying a filter. For the two reports that do contain course information, the filter finds any instructor who teaches the specified course and lists all courses for that instructor. The code is as follows:

```
Private Sub cmdGo_Click()
' Build a filter and open the selected report
Dim varWhere As Variant, varSubquery As Variant
  ' Set an error trap
  On Error GoTo cmdGo_Err
  ' Initialize to Null
  varWhere = Null
  varSubquery = Null
  ' If specified a first name value
  If Not IsNothing(Me.txtFirstName) Then
    ' .. build the predicate
    varWhere = "[tblInstructors].[FirstName] LIKE '" & _
      Me.txtFirstName & "*'"
```

```
End If
' Do last name next
If Not IsNothing(Me.txtLastName) Then
  ' .. build the predicate
  ' Note: taking advantage of Null propogation
  '  so we don't have to test for any previous predicate
  varWhere = (varWhere + " AND ") & _
    "[tblInstructors].[LastName] LIKE '" & Me.txtLastName & "*'"
End If
' Do city next
If Not IsNothing(Me.txtCity) Then
  ' .. build the predicate
  varWhere = (varWhere + " AND ") & _
    "[tblInstructors].[City] LIKE '" & Me.txtCity & "*'"
End If
' Do state / province
If Not IsNothing(Me.txtStateOrProvince) Then
  ' .. build the predicate
  varWhere = (varWhere + " AND ") & _
    "[tblInstructors].[StateOrProvince] LIKE '" & _
    Me.txtStateOrProvince & "*'"
End If
' Do Course Category - must use a subquery
If Not IsNothing(Me.cmbCourseCategory) Then
  ' .. start a predicate for the subquery
  varSubquery = "[CourseCategory] = '" & _
    Me.cmbCourseCategory & "'"
End If
' Finally, do Course Number
If Not IsNothing(Me.cmbCourseNumber) Then
  ' .. build the predicate
  varSubquery = (varSubquery + " AND ") & _
    "[CourseNumber] = " & Me.cmbCourseNumber
End If
' If built a subquery filter,
If Not IsNothing(varSubquery) Then
  ' Add subquery to the main filter
  varWhere = (varWhere + " AND ") & _
    "InstructorID IN (SELECT InstructorID " & _
    "FROM tblInstructorCourses WHERE " & varSubquery & ")"
End If
```

Next, the code examines the Year and Semester controls to determine whether an additional predicate should be constructed. If the user has selected a year, the code must build a subquery for the first two reports (the Name and Address List and Instructor & Courses reports) because these reports do not contain any year or session fields. If the code created a subquery predicate, that predicate is added to the main filter string. The code is as follows:

```
' Clear the subquery
varSubquery = Null
' Do Session Year
If Not IsNothing(Me.cmbSessionYear) Then
  ' If asking for address or instructor course list,
  If (Me.ogOptions < 3) Then
```

```
             ' Set up a subquery predicate
             varSubquery = "SessionYear = " & Me.cmbSessionYear
          Else
             ' Add to the main predicate
             varWhere = (varWhere + " AND ") & _
                "tblSessionCourses.SessionYear = " & Me.cmbSessionYear
          End If
       End If
       ' Finally, do Session Number (semester)
       If Not IsNothing(Me.cmbSessionNumber) Then
          ' If asking for address or instructor course list,
          If (Me.ogOptions < 3) Then
             ' .. add to the subquery predicate
             varSubquery = (varSubquery + " AND ") & _
                "SessionNumber = " & Me.cmbSessionNumber
          Else
             ' Add to the main predicate
             varWhere = (varWhere + " AND ") & _
                "tblSessionCourses.SessionNumber = " & Me.cmbSessionNumber
          End If
       End If
       ' If there's something in the subquery predicate,
       If Not IsNothing(varSubquery) Then
          ' Add the entire subquery
          varWhere = (varWhere + " AND ") & "InstructorID IN " & _
             "(SELECT InstructorID FROM tblSessionCourses WHERE " & _
             varSubquery & ")"
       End If
```

Finally, the code checks to see that at least one criterion was specified. If not, the code displays an error message and exits. If criteria were specified, the code examines the value of the ogOptions option group control and opens the selected report. In the case of the Instructor Schedule report, the code examines the chkEmail check box control to determine whether to print the report or call the *EmailInstructorSchedules* function. (Code in the AfterUpdate event procedure of the option group control hides or shows the chkEmail control as appropriate.) We'll take a look at that function in the section "Sending Instructor Schedules via E-Mail" on page 515. After opening the selected report, the code closes the dialog box and exits. The code at the end of the procedure handles any error, and it bypasses any cancel generated from a report NoData event procedure. The code is as follows:

```
  ' Check to see that we built a filter
  If IsNothing(varWhere) Then
    MsgBox "You must enter at least one search criterion.", _
       vbInformation, gstrAppTitle
    Exit Sub
  End If
  ' Hide me
  Me.Visible = False
  ' Decide which report to open
  Select Case Me.ogOptions
    ' Address
    Case 1
```

```
              ' Open the Name and Address report
              DoCmd.OpenReport "rptInstructors", acViewPreview, _
                WhereCondition:=varWhere
          ' Instructors & Courses
          Case 2
              ' Open the Instructor & Courses report
              DoCmd.OpenReport "rptInstructorCourses", acViewPreview, _
                WhereCondition:=varWhere
          ' Instructor schedule
          Case 3
              ' See if want email or print report
              If Me.chkEmail = True Then
                ' Call the instructor schedule emailer
                Call EmailInstructorSchedules(CStr(varWhere))
              Else
                ' Open the instructor schedule report
                DoCmd.OpenReport "rptCourseScheduleInstructor", acViewPreview, _
                  WhereCondition:=varWhere
              End If
          ' Student log
          Case 4
              ' Open the Instructor Student Log report
              DoCmd.OpenReport "rptInstructorScheduleStudents", acViewPreview, _
                WhereCondition:=varWhere
      End Select
cmdGo_Exit:
    ' Close me
    DoCmd.Close acForm, Me.Name
    Exit Sub
cmdGo_Err:
    ' Bypass any cancel error from no data in a report
    If Err.Number = errCancel Then
      Resume cmdGo_Exit
    End If
    MsgBox "Unexpected error: " & Err & ", " & Error, vbCritical, gstrAppTitle
    ErrorLog Me.Name & "_cmdGo", Err, Error
    Resume cmdGo_Exit
End Sub
```

Understanding the Instructor Schedule Report Design

As noted earlier, the Instructor Schedule report presents the same sorting challenges as did the Course Schedule report. The report should list the courses for each instructor in sequence by day of the week and time while keeping multiple segments of a course section together in the listing. Remember that some course sections have a segment that's taught on Monday-Wednesday-Friday (MWF) with a lab segment on one of those days. Similarly, some course sections have a Tuesday-Thursday (TuTh) segment or Tuesday-Thursday-Saturday (TuThSat) segment with a lab segment taught on just one of those days.

The query that is the record source for the report, the qryRptCourseScheduleInstructor query, uses the zqryMaxDayPerSection query that you examined earlier on page 506 to create a sort value (MaxDay) that keeps any single-day segment of a course with any multiple-day segment. Basically, a Friday segment of a course that also has a Monday-Wednesday-Friday (MWF) segment will sort with the MWF segment. The query also fetches data from the tlkpRooms, tblCourses, tblSessionCourses, tblInstructors, and tblSessionCourseSegments tables. The SQL for the query is as follows:

```
SELECT tblSessionCourses.SessionYear, tblSessionCourses.SessionNumber,
  tlkpRooms.Building, tlkpRooms.RoomName, tblInstructors.InstructorID,
  Choose([MaxDay],1,2,3,4,5,6,7,2,1,2) AS DaySort,
  tblSessionCourses.CourseCategory, tblSessionCourses.CourseNumber,
  tblCourses.CourseTitle, tblSessionCourseSegments.SectionNumber,
  tblInstructors.LastName & ", " & tblInstructors.FirstName &
    (" "+tblInstructors.MiddleName) & (", "+tblInstructors.Suffix)
    AS Instructor,
  Left(Mid(tblInstructors.Email, InStr(tblInstructors.EMail,
    "Mailto:")+7),Len(Mid(tblInstructors.Email, InStr(tblInstructors.EMail,
    "Mailto:")+7))-1) AS EM,
  tblInstructors.FirstName, tblInstructors.LastName, tblInstructors.City,
  tblInstructors.StateOrProvince, tblSessionCourseSegments.CourseSegment,
  Choose([Days], "Mon", "Tue", "Wed", "Thu", "Fri", "Sat", "", "TuTh",
    "MWF", "TuThSat") AS DaysVal,
  tblSessionCourseSegments.StartTime, tblSessionCourseSegments.EndTime
FROM tlkpRooms
INNER JOIN ((tblCourses
  INNER JOIN ((tblSessionCourses
    INNER JOIN tblInstructors
    ON tblSessionCourses.InstructorID = tblInstructors.InstructorID)
    INNER JOIN zqryMaxDayPerSection
    ON (tblSessionCourses.SessionYear = zqryMaxDayPerSection.SessionYear)
      AND (tblSessionCourses.SessionNumber =
        zqryMaxDayPerSection.SessionNumber)
      AND (tblSessionCourses.CourseCategory =
        zqryMaxDayPerSection.CourseCategory)
      AND (tblSessionCourses.CourseNumber =
        zqryMaxDayPerSection.CourseNumber)
      AND (tblSessionCourses.SectionNumber =
        zqryMaxDayPerSection.SectionNumber))
  ON (tblCourses.CourseNumber = tblSessionCourses.CourseNumber)
    AND (tblCourses.CourseCategory = tblSessionCourses.CourseCategory))
  INNER JOIN tblSessionCourseSegments
  ON (tblSessionCourses.SectionNumber =
      tblSessionCourseSegments.SectionNumber)
    AND (tblSessionCourses.CourseNumber =
      tblSessionCourseSegments.CourseNumber)
    AND (tblSessionCourses.CourseCategory =
      tblSessionCourseSegments.CourseCategory)
    AND (tblSessionCourses.SessionNumber =
      tblSessionCourseSegments.SessionNumber)
    AND (tblSessionCourses.SessionYear =
      tblSessionCourseSegments.SessionYear))
ON tlkpRooms.RoomID = tblSessionCourseSegments.RoomID
ORDER BY tblSessionCourses.SessionYear, tblSessionCourses.SessionNumber,
  tblInstructors.InstructorID, Choose([Days],1,2,3,4,5,6,7,2,1,2),
  tblSessionCourseSegments.StartTime;
```

Notice that the query uses the *Choose* function to convert the codes for TuTh, MWF, and TuThSat back to sort with all the other courses on Tuesday, Monday, and Tuesday, respectively. The query has an ORDER BY clause because it is also used by the *EmailInstructorSchedules* function. As with any report that has a Sorting and Grouping specification, the report ignores the ORDER BY clause in the query, but the Sorting and Grouping specification sorts the data in the exact same way for the report.

Sending Instructor Schedules via E-Mail

You probably noticed earlier when you printed the instructor schedules for a semester that the application makes a Send via E-Mail check box available when you select the Instructor Schedule option in the Instructor Reports dialog box. If you're not still signed on as an administrator, start the application by opening the frmSplash form. Use **tmichaels** as the User Name and **password** as the Password in the Sign On dialog box. After signing on, click the Reports button on the main switchboard and then click the Instructors button on the Reports switchboard.

Let's create an e-mail for my course schedule for the Spring 2005 semester. Enter **Viescas** in the Last Name field in the Instructor Reports dialog box, select the Instructor Schedule option, select the Send via E-Mail check box, and choose 2005 for the Year and Spring for the Semester. The Instructor Reports dialog box should now look like Figure 23-6.

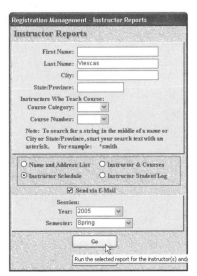

Figure 23-6   Sending an instructor schedule via e-mail.

Click the Go button, and the application generates and displays an e-mail that shows my course schedule, ready to send to me in Microsoft Outlook, as shown in Figure 23-7 on the next page. Looks like I'm going to be busy! Note that a production version of the code would just send the e-mail without displaying it, but because many of the e-mail addresses are fictitious, the sample application simply displays the result.

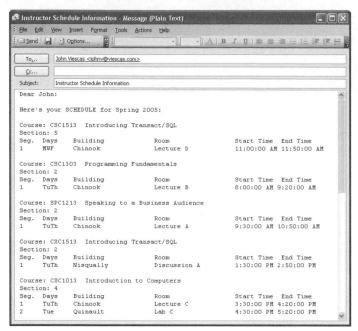

Figure 23-7   An instructor schedule sent via e-mail.

Note   As you'll see when you examine the code in the *EmailInstructorSchedules* function, the application sends an individual e-mail to each instructor. Also, an instructor can sign on to the application and request that an e-mail be sent containing only his or her course schedule.

In the section "Understanding the Instructor Report Selection Procedure" on page 510, you examined the code that deciphers the options the user chooses in the Instructor Reports dialog box. When the user chooses to send the instructor schedule via e-mail, the code in that procedure calls the *EmailInstructorSchedules* function that you can find in the modOutlook module and passes it the predicate it built to filter the result.

The code in that function begins by declaring all variables, setting a pointer to the current database, and opening a recordset on the qryRptCourseScheduleInstructor query using the filter parameter passed from the Instructor Reports dialog box code. If the filter causes the recordset to be empty, the code sets a failed return, closes the recordset, and exits. The code is as follows:

```
Public Function EmailInstructorSchedules(strWhere)
' Function to send instructor schedules via e-mail
' Input:  Predicate string to filter schedules
' Output: True if successful
' Function calls the SendOutlookMsg function for each e-mail
Dim db As DAO.Database, rstSched As DAO.Recordset
Dim lngThisInstructor As Long, intThisYear As Integer, intThisSession As Integer
Dim strMsg As String, strTo As String, strThisCourse As String
```

```
' Set an error trap
On Error GoTo EmailSchedulesI_Err
' Point to this database
Set db = DBEngine(0)(0)
' Open the schedule recordset
'  -- uses the report recordset
Set rstSched = db.OpenRecordset("SELECT * " & _
  "FROM qryRptCourseScheduleInstructor " & _
  "WHERE " & strWhere)
' If got nothing
If rstSched.EOF Then
  ' Set failed return
  EmailInstructorSchedules = False
  ' Close out
  rstSched.Close
  Set rstSched = Nothing
  Set db = Nothing
  ' Bail
  Exit Function
End If
```

If the recordset contains records, the code must process them one at a time in a loop. Because there can be multiple records for each instructor message, the code must wait until it finds either a record for another instructor or semester or the end of the recordset to send the previous message. At the beginning of the loop, if the current record is not the first record and if the instructor or semester is different, the code adds a closing to the previous message and sends it using the *SendOutlookMsg* function that you can find in the same module. If that function returns a failure, the code displays an error message but continues processing. Because the code just sent the last message, it clears out the message string and the saved course information. The code is as follows:

```
' Process all rows
Do Until rstSched.EOF
  ' If not the first one
  '  and if on a different instructor or semester now,
  If (lngThisInstructor <> 0) And _
    ((lngThisInstructor <> rstSched!InstructorID) Or _
    (intThisYear <> rstSched!SessionYear) Or _
    (intThisSession <> rstSched!SessionNumber)) Then
    ' Tack on the closing
    strMsg = strMsg & vbCrLf & "If you have any questions, " & _
      "please contact the A. Datum Technology School " & vbCrLf & _
      "administration at: (512) 555-7238."
    ' Send the message
    If Not SendOutlookMsg("Instructor Schedule Information", _
        strTo, strMsg) Then
      MsgBox "There was a problem sending a schedule e-mail to " & _
        strTo, vbExclamation, gstrAppTitle
    End If
    ' Clear the sent message
    strMsg = ""
    ' Clear the course
    strThisCourse = ""
  End If
```

The code then processes the current record. It first saves the instructor and semester information for comparison with the next record. If the message string is empty, a previous message must have just been sent (or this is the first record), so the code starts a heading for the message. If the course in the current record is not the same as the previous record, the code saves the course information and generates a heading for the course in the message string. Finally, the code formats the detail information for the segment of the course, including the segment number, the days the segment is scheduled, the building and room names, and the start and end times. The code then fetches the next record and loops back to the Do statement in the previous block of code. The code is as follows:

```
' Grab the instructor ID
lngThisInstructor = rstSched!InstructorID
' .. and year
intThisYear = rstSched!SessionYear
' .. and session (semester)
intThisSession = rstSched!SessionNumber
' Set up the To field
strTo = rstSched!FirstName & " " & rstSched!LastName & _
  "<" & rstSched!EM & ">"
' If message is empty,
If strMsg = "" Then
  ' Set up the header
  strMsg = "Dear " & rstSched!FirstName & ":" & vbCrLf & vbCrLf & _
    "Here's your SCHEDULE for " & Choose(intThisSession, "Spring", _
    "Summer", "Fall") & _
    " " & intThisYear & ":" & vbCrLf
End If
' If this is a different course,
If (rstSched!CourseCategory & rstSched!CourseNumber) <> _
  strThisCourse Then
  ' Update the course
  strThisCourse = rstSched!CourseCategory & rstSched!CourseNumber
  ' Add the course header
  strMsg = strMsg & vbCrLf & "Course: " & strThisCourse & _
    "   " & rstSched!CourseTitle & vbCrLf & _
    "Section: " & rstSched!SectionNumber & vbCrLf & _
    "Seg.  Days  Building       Room        " & _
    "Start Time  End Time" & vbCrLf
End If
' Add the detail data
strMsg = strMsg & rstSched!CourseSegment & "    " & _
  Left(rstSched!DaysVal & Space(5), 7) & _
  " " & Left(rstSched!Building & Space(20), 20) & " " & _
  Left(rstSched!RoomName & Space(20), 20) & " " & _
  rstSched!StartTime & " " & rstSched!EndTime & vbCrLf
' Move to the next one
rstSched.MoveNext
Loop
```

After processing the last record, the code must add a closing to the last message and send it. Again, the code uses the *SendOutlookMsg* function and displays an error if the function did not complete successfully. The code then closes the recordset and exits. Code at the end of the procedure handles any errors by displaying the error, logging it, and exiting the procedure. The code is as follows:

```
' Tack on the closing
strMsg = strMsg & vbCrLf & "If you have any questions, " & _
  "please contact the A. Datum Technology School " & vbCrLf & _
  "administration at: (512) 555-7238."
' Send the last message
If Not SendOutlookMsg("Instructor Schedule Information", _
  strTo, strMsg) Then
  MsgBox "There was a problem sending a schedule e-mail to " & _
    strTo, vbExclamation, gstrAppTitle
End If
' Close out
rstSched.Close
EmailSchedulesI_Exit:
  Set rstSched = Nothing
  Set db = Nothing
  Exit Function
EmailSchedulesI_Err:
  MsgBox "Unexpected error: " & Err & ", " & Error, vbCritical, gstrAppTitle
  ErrorLog "EmailSchedulesI", Err, Error
  Resume EmailSchedulesI_Exit
End Function
```

The *SendOutlookMsg* function in this sample application is very similar to the one used in the Membership Tracking application described in Part 2 of this book. The one major difference is the code sends a plain text message rather than use HTML format. You can find the code for the *SendOutlookMsg* function in the modOutlook module. If you look at the references for the Membership project (open the Visual Basic Editor and choose References from the Tools menu), you'll find that I did not include a reference to the Outlook library. I did this so you can run this application on any machine that has Microsoft Outlook 2000, 2002, or 2003 installed. If I referenced a specific library, none of the code would run on a machine that had another version installed because the project would have a library reference error.

To make this code work, I used a coding technique called *late binding*. Rather than declare objects from the Outlook library, I declared the objects the code needs simply As Object. The code uses the *CreateObject* function to start a copy of Outlook and get a reference to its Application object. The code then uses the *CreateItem* method of the Application object to create a new e-mail message, set its Subject property, the To or BCC property, and the Body property using the parameters passed to the function. The code also sets the BodyFormat property of the message to plain text. Finally, the code executes the *Display* method to show you the result. The code is as follows:

```
Public Function SendOutlookMsg(strSubject As String, strTo As String, _
  strMsg As String, Optional intUseBCC As Integer = 0) As Integer
' Function to send an email message using Outlook
' Inputs: Subject of the message
'     List of valid "To" email addresses
'     HTML for the body of the message
```

```
'        Send using BCC flag (optional)
' Output: True if successful
' Note: This demo version only formats and displays a new
'        message.  Use ObjMail.Send instead of .Display
'        to actually send the message
Dim objOL As Object, objMail As Object
  ' Set an error trap
  On Error GoTo SendOutlookMsg_Err
  ' Get a pointer to Outlook - late binding
  Set objOL = CreateObject("Outlook.Application")
  ' Create a new email
  Set objMail = objOL.CreateItem(olMailItem)
  ' Set the subject
  objMail.Subject = strSubject
  ' Set To or BCC
  If intUseBCC = True Then
    objMail.BCC = strTo
  Else
    objMail.To = strTo
  End If
  ' Set the format to plain text
  objMail.BodyFormat = olFormatPlain
  ' Insert the text of the message
  objMail.Body = strMsg
  ' Display it
  objMail.Display
  ' Done - clear objects
  Set objMail = Nothing
  Set objOL = Nothing
  ' Return true
  SendOutlookMsg = True
SendOutlookMsg_Exit:
  Exit Function
SendOutlookMsg_Err:
  ' Log the error
  ErrorLog "SendOutlookMsg", Err, Error
  ' Bail
  Resume SendOutlookMsg_Exit
End Function
```

Printing and E-Mailing Student Schedules

The Registration Management application also includes options to print student schedules or send them via e-mail. As you might expect, these features work similarly to those implemented for instructor schedules.

Printing Student Schedules

To print a student schedule, start the application by opening the frmSplash form. Sign on as an administrator using **tmichaels** as the User Name and **password** as the Password. Click the Reports button on the main switchboard and then click the Students button on the Reports switchboard to open the Student Reports dialog box.

Let's see what the course schedule for Anne Hansen for the Spring semester of 2005 looks like. There's only one student in the database with a last name of Hansen, so enter **Hansen** in the Last Name field. Choose 2005 for the Year and Spring for the Semester, and select the Student Schedule option. The dialog box should now look like Figure 23-8.

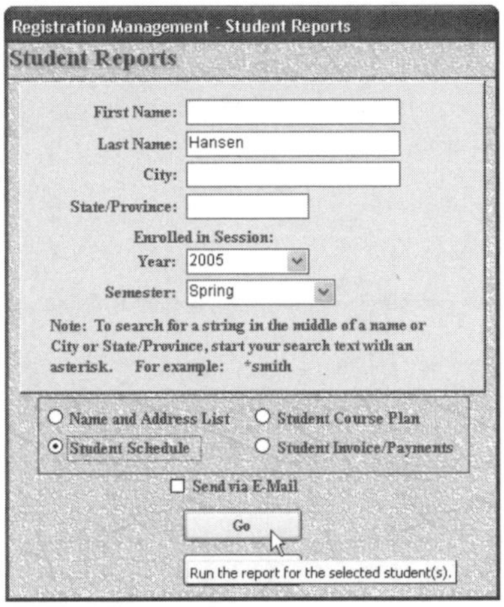

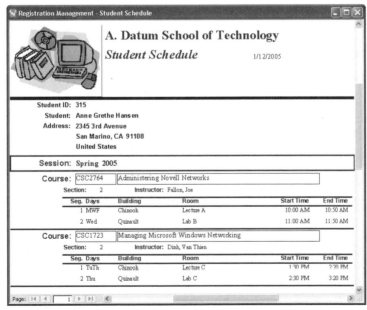

Figure 23-8   Printing a semester schedule for a student.

Click the Go button to see the schedule for Anne Hansen, as shown in Figure 23-9.

Figure 23-9   The Student Schedule report for one student and one semester.

The code in the Click event procedure for the cmdGo button in the Student Reports dialog box is almost identical to the code you examined earlier for the Instructor Reports dialog box.

The primary difference is the code builds a predicate using fields from the tblStudents table and opens student reports rather than instructor reports. You'll examine the design of the student invoice report and the student invoice e-mail in the last chapter of this book, "Producing Student Invoices."

As with the previous scheduling reports, the key to the report design is the query that is the record source for the report. The query uses the zqryMinTimePerSection and zqryMaxDayPerSection queries to obtain calculated values to sort the data correctly. The query also fetches data from the tlkpRooms, tblStudents, tblStudentInvoices, tblCourses, tblSessionCourses, tblInstructors, tblSessionCourseSegments, and tblStudentCourses tables. The SQL for the query (qryRptStudentSchedule) is as follows:

```
SELECT tblStudents.StudentID, tblStudents.FirstName &
    (" "+tblStudents.MiddleName) & " " & tblStudents.LastName &
    (", "+tblStudents.Suffix) AS Student,
  tblStudents.FirstName, tblStudents.MiddleName, tblStudents.LastName,
  tblStudents.Suffix, tblStudents.Address, tblStudents.City,
  tblStudents.StateOrProvince, tblStudents.PostalCode, tblStudents.Country,
  Left(Mid(tblStudents.Email, InStr(tblStudents.EMail, "Mailto:")+7),
    Len(Mid(tblStudents.Email, InStr(tblStudents.EMail, "Mailto:")+7))-1)
    AS EM,
  tblStudentInvoices.SessionYear, tblStudentInvoices.SessionNumber,
  tblSessionCourseSegments.CourseCategory,
  Choose([MaxDay],1,2,3,4,5,6,7,2,1,2) AS DaySort,
  CDate([MinTime]) AS TimeSort, tblSessionCourseSegments.CourseNumber,
  tblCourses.CourseTitle, tblStudentCourses.Status,
  tblSessionCourseSegments.SectionNumber,
  tblSessionCourseSegments.CourseSegment,
  tblInstructors.LastName & ", " & tblInstructors.FirstName &
    (" "+tblInstructors.MiddleName) &
    (", "+tblInstructors.Suffix) AS Instructor,
  tlkpRooms.Building, tlkpRooms.RoomName,
  Choose([Days], "Mon", "Tue", "Wed", "Thu", "Fri", "Sat",
    "", "TuTh", "MWF", "TuThSat") AS DaysVal,
  tblSessionCourseSegments.StartTime, tblSessionCourseSegments.EndTime
FROM tlkpRooms
INNER JOIN (tblStudents
  INNER JOIN (tblStudentInvoices
    INNER JOIN (((tblCourses
      INNER JOIN (((tblSessionCourses
        INNER JOIN tblInstructors
        ON tblSessionCourses.InstructorID = tblInstructors.InstructorID)
        INNER JOIN zqryMinTimePerSection
        ON (tblSessionCourses.SessionYear =
            zqryMinTimePerSection.SessionYear)
          AND (tblSessionCourses.SessionNumber =
            zqryMinTimePerSection.SessionNumber)
          AND (tblSessionCourses.CourseCategory =
            zqryMinTimePerSection.CourseCategory)
          AND (tblSessionCourses.CourseNumber =
            zqryMinTimePerSection.CourseNumber)
          AND (tblSessionCourses.SectionNumber =
            zqryMinTimePerSection.SectionNumber))
```

```
        INNER JOIN zqryMaxDayPerSection
        ON (tblSessionCourses.SessionYear =
             zqryMaxDayPerSection.SessionYear)
          AND (tblSessionCourses.SessionNumber =
             zqryMaxDayPerSection.SessionNumber)
          AND (tblSessionCourses.CourseCategory =
             zqryMaxDayPerSection.CourseCategory)
          AND (tblSessionCourses.CourseNumber =
             zqryMaxDayPerSection.CourseNumber)
          AND (tblSessionCourses.SectionNumber =
             zqryMaxDayPerSection.SectionNumber))
      ON (tblCourses.CourseNumber = tblSessionCourses.CourseNumber)
        AND (tblCourses.CourseCategory = tblSessionCourses.CourseCategory))
      INNER JOIN tblSessionCourseSegments
      ON (tblSessionCourses.SectionNumber =
          tblSessionCourseSegments.SectionNumber)
        AND (tblSessionCourses.CourseNumber =
          tblSessionCourseSegments.CourseNumber)
        AND (tblSessionCourses.CourseCategory =
          tblSessionCourseSegments.CourseCategory)
        AND (tblSessionCourses.SessionNumber =
          tblSessionCourseSegments.SessionNumber)
        AND (tblSessionCourses.SessionYear =
          tblSessionCourseSegments.SessionYear))
      INNER JOIN tblStudentCourses
      ON (tblSessionCourses.SectionNumber =
          tblStudentCourses.SectionNumber)
        AND (tblSessionCourses.CourseNumber =
          tblStudentCourses.CourseNumber)
        AND (tblSessionCourses.CourseCategory =
          tblStudentCourses.CourseCategory)
        AND (tblSessionCourses.SessionNumber =
          tblStudentCourses.SessionNumber)
        AND (tblSessionCourses.SessionYear =
          tblStudentCourses.SessionYear))
    ON (tblStudentInvoices.SessionNumber = tblStudentCourses.SessionNumber)
      AND (tblStudentInvoices.SessionYear = tblStudentCourses.SessionYear)
      AND (tblStudentInvoices.StudentID = tblStudentCourses.StudentID))
  ON tblStudents.StudentID = tblStudentInvoices.StudentID)
ON tlkpRooms.RoomID = tblSessionCourseSegments.RoomID
WHERE (((tblStudentCourses.Status)>=5))
ORDER BY tblStudents.FirstName & (" "+tblStudents.MiddleName) & " " &
  tblStudents.LastName & (", "+tblStudents.Suffix),
  tblStudentInvoices.SessionYear, tblStudentInvoices.SessionNumber,
  Choose([MaxDay],1,2,3,4,5,6,7,2,1,2), CDate([MinTime]),
  tblSessionCourseSegments.CourseNumber, tblCourses.CourseTitle,
  tblSessionCourseSegments.StartTime;
```

Notice that the query uses the *Choose* function to convert the codes for TuTh, MWF, and TuThSat back to sort with all the other courses on Tuesday, Monday, and Tuesday, respectively. The query has an ORDER BY clause because it is also used by the *EmailStudentSchedules* function. As with any report that has a Sorting and Grouping specification, the report ignores the ORDER BY clause in the query, but the Sorting and Grouping specification sorts the data in the exact same way for the report.

Sending Student Schedules via E-Mail

You can return to the Student Reports dialog box and ask that Anne Hansen's schedule for the Spring 2005 semester be sent to her via e-mail. Enter **Hansen** in the Last Name field, choose 2005 for the Year and Spring for the Semester, and select the Student Schedule option. Also select the Send via E-Mail check box and click the Go button. The application generates and displays an e-mail that shows her course schedule, ready to send to Anne in Microsoft Outlook, as shown in Figure 23-10. You can see that the e-mail includes only enrolled classes, not any classes that are still on the wait list or awaiting approval. Note that a production version of the code would just send the e-mail without displaying it, but because all of the student e-mail addresses are fictitious, the sample application simply displays the result.

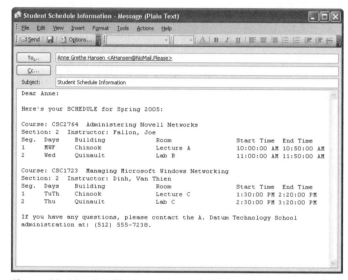

Figure 23-10   Sending a student schedule via e-mail.

The code in the Click event procedure of the cmdGo button in the Student Reports dialog box calls the *EmailStudentSchedules* function that you can find in the modOutlook module. As you might expect, this function is very similar to the function that generates schedule e-mails for instructors.

The code in the function begins by declaring all variables, setting a pointer to the current database, and opening a recordset on the qryRptStudentSchedule query using the filter parameter passed from the Student Reports dialog box code. If the filter causes the recordset to be empty, the code sets a failed return, closes the recordset, and exits. The code is as follows:

```
Public Function EmailStudentSchedules(strWhere As String) As Integer
' Function to send student schedules via e-mail
' Input:  Predicate string to filter schedules
' Output: True if successful
' Function calls the SendOutlookMsg function for each e-mail
Dim db As DAO.Database, rstSched As DAO.Recordset
```

```
Dim lngThisStudent As Long, intThisYear As Integer, intThisSession As Integer
Dim strMsg As String, strTo As String, strThisCourse As String
  ' Set an error trap
  On Error GoTo EmailSchedules_Err
  ' Point to this database
  Set db = DBEngine(0)(0)
  ' Open the schedule recordset
  '   -- uses the report recordset
  Set rstSched = db.OpenRecordset("SELECT * " & _
    "FROM qryRptStudentSchedule " & _
    "WHERE " & strWhere)
  ' If got nothing
  If rstSched.EOF Then
    ' Set failed return
    EmailStudentSchedules = False
    ' Close out
    rstSched.Close
    Set rstSched = Nothing
    Set db = Nothing
    ' Bail
    Exit Function
  End If
```

If the recordset contains records, the code must process them one at a time in a loop. Because there can be multiple records for each student message, the code must wait until it finds either a record for another student or semester or the end of the recordset to send the previous message. At the beginning of the loop, if the current record is not the first record and the student or semester is different, the code adds a closing to the previous message and sends it using the *SendOutlookMsg* function that you studied earlier in this chapter. If that function returns a failure, the code displays an error message but continues processing. Because the code just sent the last message, it clears out the message string and the saved course information. The code is as follows:

```
  ' Process all rows
  Do Until rstSched.EOF
    ' If not the first one and if on a different student or semester now,
    If (lngThisStudent <> 0) And _
      ((lngThisStudent <> rstSched!StudentID) Or _
      (intThisYear <> rstSched!SessionYear) Or _
      (intThisSession <> rstSched!SessionNumber)) Then
      ' Tack on the closing
      strMsg = strMsg & vbCrLf & "If you have any questions, " & _
        "please contact the A. Datum Technology School " & vbCrLf & _
        "administration at: (512) 555-7238."
      ' Send the message
      If Not SendOutlookMsg("Student Schedule Information", _
        strTo, strMsg) Then
        MsgBox "There was a problem sending a schedule e-mail to " & _
          strTo, vbExclamation, gstrAppTitle
      End If
      ' Clear the sent message
      strMsg = ""
      ' Clear the course
```

```
        strThisCourse = ""
    End If
```

The code then processes the current record. It first saves the student and semester information for comparison with the next record. If the message string is empty, a previous message
must have just been sent (or this is the first record), so the code starts a heading for the
message. If the course in the current record is not the same as the previous record, the code
saves the course information and generates a heading for the course in the message string that
includes the course number, course title, and instructor. Finally, the code formats the detail
information for the segment of the course, including the segment number, the days the
segment is scheduled, the building and room names, and the start and end times. The code
then fetches the next record and loops back to the Do statement in the previous block of code.
The code is as follows:

```
    ' Grab the student ID
    lngThisStudent = rstSched!StudentID
    ' .. and year
    intThisYear = rstSched!SessionYear
    ' .. and session (semester)
    intThisSession = rstSched!SessionNumber
    ' Set up the To field
    strTo = rstSched!Student & "<" & rstSched!EM & ">"
    ' If message is empty,
    If strMsg = "" Then
      ' Set up the header
      strMsg = "Dear " & rstSched!FirstName & ":" & vbCrLf & vbCrLf & _
        "Here's your SCHEDULE for " & _
        Choose(intThisSession, "Spring", "Summer", "Fall") & _
        " " & intThisYear & ":" & vbCrLf
    End If
    ' If this is a different course,
    If (rstSched!CourseCategory & rstSched!CourseNumber) <> _
      strThisCourse Then
      ' Update the course
      strThisCourse = rstSched!CourseCategory & rstSched!CourseNumber
      ' Add the course header
      strMsg = strMsg & vbCrLf & "Course: " & strThisCourse & _
        "  " & rstSched!CourseTitle & vbCrLf & _
        "Section: " & rstSched!SectionNumber & _
        "  Instructor: " & rstSched!Instructor & vbCrLf & _
        "Seg. Days  Building       Room          " & _
        "Start Time  End Time" & vbCrLf
    End If
    ' Add the detail data
    strMsg = strMsg & rstSched!CourseSegment & "    " & _
      Left(rstSched!DaysVal & Space(5), 7) & _
      " " & Left(rstSched!Building & Space(20), 20) & " " & _
      Left(rstSched!RoomName & Space(20), 20) & " " & _
      rstSched!StartTime & " " & rstSched!EndTime & vbCrLf
    ' Move to the next one
    rstSched.MoveNext
Loop
```

After processing the last record, the code must add a closing to the last message and send it. Again, the code uses the *SendOutlookMsg* function and displays an error if the function did not complete successfully. The code then closes the recordset and exits. Code at the end of the procedure handles any errors by displaying the error, logging it, and exiting the procedure. The code is as follows:

```
' Tack on the closing
strMsg = strMsg & vbCrLf & "If you have any questions, " & _
  "please contact the A. Datum Technology School " & vbCrLf & _
  "administration at: (512) 555-7238."
' Send the last message
If Not SendOutlookMsg("Student Schedule Information", strTo, strMsg) Then
  MsgBox "There was a problem sending a schedule e-mail to " & _
    strTo, vbExclamation, gstrAppTitle
End If
' Close out
rstSched.Close
EmailSchedules_Exit:
  Set rstSched = Nothing
  Set db = Nothing
  Exit Function
EmailSchedules_Err:
  MsgBox "Unexpected error: " & Err & ", " & Error, vbCritical, gstrAppTitle
  ErrorLog "EmailSchedules", Err, Error
  Resume EmailSchedules_Exit
End Function
```

You should now have a good understanding of some of the challenges you must face when creating or e-mailing complex scheduling reports. In the following chapter, you'll explore how the application handles student invoices and payments.

Chapter 24

Producing Student Invoices

At first glance, it might seem a simple matter to sum the semester hours for any student course that has a status of Enrolled or higher and multiply by the current rate per hour to find out how much a student owes. If this were the case, an administrator could generate an invoice for a student any time after all the courses have been confirmed for a student.

But there's a catch. Many schools set a drop/add date a week or so into each semester—the deadline date for changing courses or withdrawing from a course without owing the fee for the course. After this date, a student might be granted Withdrawn status so that the course is not counted in the student's overall record, but the student still owes the tuition fee. So, an administrator must create all invoices at the end of the day on the drop/add date to get an accurate picture of what each student owes.

After the drop/add date, it's not possible to use the total semester hours for courses that have an Enrolled or higher status to create accurate invoices, so the invoice total must be calculated and stored. This is clearly one of those cases where the business rules of the organization require the developer to design what appears to be an unnormalized table—the tblStudentInvoices table. In this chapter, you'll learn how the invoice totals are updated, payments are entered, and invoices are printed or sent via e-mail.

 Note For the Registration Management application to be complete, it should include code that does not allow an administrator to delete a course enrollment after the drop/add date. The application should ask the administrator whether the student invoice has been updated before allowing a change from Enrolled to Withdrawn after the drop/add date. I did not include this code in the sample application because you would have to reset your computer system date to be able to test all the features.

Understanding the Tables Involved

You took a brief look at the tblStudentInvoices table in Chapter 22, "Scheduling Students," in the context of registering a student for a semester. But the table name implies that the primary purpose of the table is to track the invoice totals for students. Table 24-1 describes the fields in that table.

Table 24-1   The Fields in the tblStudentInvoices Table

Field Name	Data Type	Description
StudentID	Long Integer	ID of the student registered for this session.
SessionYear	Integer	Year this session is scheduled.
SessionNumber	Integer	Session semester: 1 = Spring, 2 = Summer, 3 = Fall.
SemesterHours	Decimal, Precision 7, Scale 1	Total semester hours for which the student is enrolled (calculated by the update invoice process).
Tuition	Currency	Tuition owed for the session (calculated by the update invoice process).

An administrator needs to be able to change the tuition rate charged from time to time, but the application should keep track of all tuition rates charged in the past. As you'll learn later in this chapter, the application uses the tuition rate that was applicable at the start of the semester being invoiced. Table 24-2 describes the fields in the tblTuitionRates table that stores the rate and effective date.

Table 24-2   The Fields in the tblTuitionRates Table

Field Name	Data Type	Description
TuitionEffective	Date/Time	Date the rate is effective.
TuitionAmt	Currency	Amount charged per semester hour.

Any application that includes a billing feature should also track the payments made. Some schools might allow students to make several payments over time, so the table must be able to track multiple payments against an invoice. Table 24-3 describes the fields in the tblStudentPayments table that stores the payment information for the Registration Management sample application.

Table 24-3   The Fields in the tblStudentPayments Table

Field Name	Data Type	Description
StudentID	Long Integer	ID of the student registered for this session.
SessionYear	Integer	Year this session is scheduled.
SessionNumber	Integer	Session semester: 1 = Spring, 2 = Summer, 3 = Fall.
PaymentDate	Date/Time	Date the payment was made.
PaymentAmount	Currency	Amount of the payment.

Creating Invoices

The Registration Management application offers two ways to allow an administrator to update the invoice information. To see how these methods work, open the Registration.mdb file, open the frmSplash form to start the application, and sign on as administrator Tom Michaels. Use **tmichaels** for the User Name and **password** for the Password.

Updating the Invoices for All Students

Click the Students button on the main switchboard, and then click the Update Student Invoices button on the Student Select pop-up form. The application displays the Invoice Semester dialog box as shown in Figure 24-1. As the administrator, you can choose the year and semester for which you want invoices updated and click the Invoice button to run the update invoice process. For now, click the Cancel button in the dialog box to return to the Student Select pop-up window.

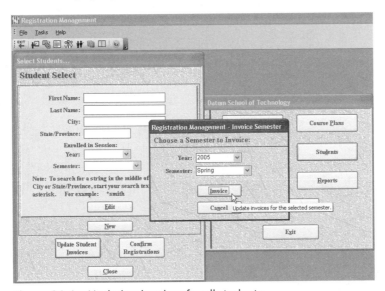

Figure 24-1   Updating invoices for all students.

If you had clicked the Invoice button in the Invoice Semester dialog box, code in the Click event procedure of the cmdInvoice button (Update Student Invoices) on the fpopStudentSelect form would have called the update invoice process for all students for the specified semester. The code in that procedure first opens the fldgInvoiceSemester dialog box form and then waits until that form either hides (when you click Invoice) or closes (when you click Cancel).

When you click the Invoice button in the dialog box, code in that form verifies that you have selected values and then sets the Visible property of the form to False to hide the form so that the code in the Click event procedure of the cmdInvoice command button on the pop-up form can continue. If you click the Cancel button, the form closes itself.

Code in the Click event procedure of the cmdInvoice command button immediately following the OpenForm command checks to see if the fldgInvoiceSemester form is still open. If it isn't, the user must have clicked the Cancel button, so the code exits. If the form is still open (but now hidden), the code obtains the year and session number from that form, closes that form, and calls the *UpdateInvoices* procedure that you can find in the modRegistration module. Notice that the code uses a 0 value as the first argument. When you study the code for the *UpdateInvoices* procedure in the section "Understanding the Update Invoice Process" on page 534, you'll see that this procedure processes invoices for all students when the first parameter has a value of 0. The code for the Click event procedure of the cmdInvoice command button is as follows:

```
Private Sub cmdInvoice_Click()
Dim intYear As Integer, intSession As Integer, varReturn As Variant
    ' Admin wants to invoice courses for all students for a semester
    ' Open the dialog form to pick semester to confirm
    '  - code will wait as long as form is displayed
    DoCmd.OpenForm "fdlgInvoiceSemester", WindowMode:=acDialog
    ' If form not still open,
    If Not IsFormLoaded("fdlgInvoiceSemester") Then
        ' User canceled
        Exit Sub
    End If
    ' Grab the values from the form
    intYear = Form_fdlgInvoiceSemester.cmbSessionYear
    intSession = Form_fdlgInvoiceSemester.cmbSessionNumber
    ' Close the form
    DoCmd.Close acForm, "fdlgInvoiceSemester"
    ' Call the scheduler
    If UpdateInvoices(0, intYear, intSession) = True Then
        ' Tell user all went well
        MsgBox "Invoices updated successfully.", vbInformation, gstrAppTitle
    End If
    ' Close me
    DoCmd.Close acForm, Me.Name
End Sub
```

Updating an Invoice for One Student

The administrator can also update the invoice for a particular student—which might be useful if the administrator has just changed a student's enrollment before the drop/add date. In Chapter 22, you saw how Anne Hansen requested some courses and an instructor approved and enrolled her in one of the courses. If you followed along with the examples, your copy of the database should now have Anne enrolled in two courses and wait-listed in two others.

To find the student record for Anne, enter **Hansen** in the Last Name field of the Student Select pop-up form and click the Edit button. The application opens the Students form displaying her record. You can click the Semesters tab to see that she has not yet been invoiced for the Spring 2005 semester. (She did not enroll in any courses in the Fall 2004 semester.) Click the Invoice button, and the application displays the Invoice Semester dialog box again, as shown in Figure 24-2.

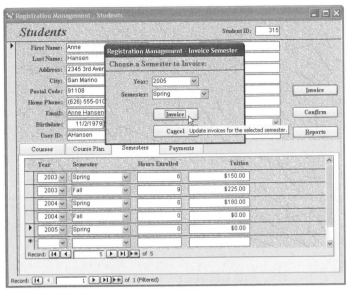

Figure 24-2   Updating an invoice for one student.

Select 2005 in the Year combo box and Spring in the Semester combo box, and click the Invoice button. After updating the invoice, the application displays a dialog box confirming that the invoice has been updated. Click OK in the dialog box, and you should see a value for the Spring 2005 semester in the Tuition column.

You can find the code that updates the student invoice in the Click event procedure of the cmdInvoice command button on the frmStudents form. As you might expect, this code is very similar to the code you studied in the previous section to update all the invoices for all students.

The code first opens the fdlgInvoiceSemester form as a dialog box. After that form hides itself or closes, the code checks to see if the form is still open. If it isn't, the user clicked the Cancel button in the dialog box, so the code exits. If the form is still open, the code obtains the values for year and session from that form, closes it, and calls the *UpdateInvoices* procedure. Notice that in this case, the code passes the current student ID as the first parameter. Finally, the code requeries the recordset of the subform that is displaying the student invoices to show the updated result. The code is as follows:

```
Private Sub cmdInvoice_Click()
Dim intYear As Integer, intSession As Integer
  ' Admin wants to invoice courses for this student for a semester
  ' Open the dialog form to pick semester to confirm
  '  - code will wait as long as form is displayed
  DoCmd.OpenForm "fdlgInvoiceSemester", WindowMode:=acDialog
  ' If form not still open,
  If Not IsFormLoaded("fdlgInvoiceSemester") Then
    ' User canceled
    Exit Sub
```

```
      End If
      ' Grab the values from the form
      intYear = Form_fdlgInvoiceSemester.cmbSessionYear
      intSession = Form_fdlgInvoiceSemester.cmbSessionNumber
      ' Close the form
      DoCmd.Close acForm, "fdlgInvoiceSemester"
      ' Call the scheduler
      If UpdateInvoices(Me.StudentID, intYear, intSession) = True Then
        ' Tell user all went well
        MsgBox "Invoices updated successfully.", vbInformation, gstrAppTitle
      End If
      ' Requery the semesters subform
      Me.fsubStudentSemesters.Requery
    End Sub
```

Understanding the Update Invoice Process

You can find the code that performs the update invoice process in the *UpdateInvoices* procedure in the modRegistration module. The code begins by declaring all variables, setting an error trap, and calling the *CalcStartEnd* procedure to find out the starting date of the specified semester. (You learned about the details of the *CalcStartEnd* procedure in Chapter 21, "Scheduling Courses.") If that procedure returned an error, the code displays a message and exits.

If the *CalcStartEnd* procedure ran successfully, the code points to the current database and opens a recordset to find the latest tuition record that has a TuitionEffective value less than or equal to the start date of the semester. If the code cannot find the relevant tuition rate record, it displays an error message and exits. The code next tests to see if the first parameter is not zero. If the parameter is not zero, the code creates an additional predicate to filter the invoices on student ID. Then the code opens a recordset to fetch the invoices for the specified semester for either all students or the specified student. The code is as follows:

```
Public Function UpdateInvoices(lngStudentID As Long, _
  intYear As Integer, intSession As Integer) As Integer
' Update the invoice records for a specified semester
' and optionally, a specific student
' Inputs: StudentID (0 to update all students)
'       Semester Year
'       Semester Session
Dim db As DAO.Database, rstRate As DAO.Recordset
Dim rstCourses As DAO.Recordset, rstInvoices As DAO.Recordset
Dim datStart As Date, datEnd As Date, strWhere As String
Dim lngHours As Long, curTuition As Currency
  ' Set an error trap
  On Error GoTo UpdateInvoices_Err
  ' Get the start date of the session
  If Not CalcStartEnd(intYear, intSession, datStart, datEnd) Then
    ' Bummer - tell user
    MsgBox "Unable to calculate start date for the session " & _
      "you selected.", vbCritical, gstrAppTitle
    ' Set failed and bail
    UpdateInvoices = False
```

```
      Exit Function
  End If
  ' Point to this database
  Set db = DBEngine(0)(0)
  ' Find the rate applicable as of the start of the semester
  Set rstRate = db.OpenRecordset("SELECT TuitionAmt " & _
    "FROM tblTuitionRates " & _
    "WHERE TuitionEffective = " & _
    "(SELECT MAX(TuitionEffective) " & _
    "FROM tblTuitionRates " & _
    "WHERE TuitionEffective <= #" & datStart & "#)")
  ' If didn't get it,
  If rstRate.EOF Then
    ' Bummer - Tell the user
    MsgBox "No valid rate was found for the semester you " & _
      "selected to invoice.", vbCritical, gstrAppTitle
    ' Close out and exit
    rstRate.Close
    Set rstRate = Nothing
    Set db = Nothing
    UpdateInvoices = False
    Exit Function
  End If
  ' If Student ID not zero
  If lngStudentID <> 0 Then
    ' Build the student filter
    strWhere = " AND StudentID = " & lngStudentID
  End If
  ' Get the invoices to bill
  Set rstInvoices = db.OpenRecordset("SELECT StudentID, " & _
    "SemesterHours, Tuition " & _
    "FROM tblStudentInvoices " & _
    "WHERE SessionYear = " & intYear & _
    " AND SessionNumber = " & intSession & strWhere, dbOpenDynaset)
```

Next, the code starts a loop to process the invoice records one at a time. For each invoice record, the code opens a recordset to fetch the courses for the semester and students that have a status of Enrolled, Incomplete, or Completed. After zeroing the total hours variable, the code loops through all the courses, adds the credit hours for each course, and marks the course invoiced. After processing all courses, the code calculates the tuition owed, updates the invoice record, moves to the next one, and loops to process it. The code is as follows:

```
  ' Loop to process them all
  Do Until rstInvoices.EOF
    ' Get the courses to bill
    Set rstCourses = db.OpenRecordset _
      ("SELECT tblStudentCourses.StudentID, " & _
      "tblStudentCourses.SessionYear, tblStudentCourses.SessionNumber, " & _
      "tblStudentCourses.Status, tblStudentCourses.Invoiced, tblCourses.CreditHours " & _
      "FROM tblCourses INNER JOIN tblStudentCourses " & _
      "ON (tblCourses.CourseNumber = tblStudentCourses.CourseNumber) " & _
      "AND (tblCourses.CourseCategory = tblStudentCourses.CourseCategory) " & _
      "WHERE (tblStudentCourses.Status In (" & StudentClassStatus.Enrolled & _
      ", " & StudentClassStatus.Incomplete & ", " & _
```

```
                    StudentClassStatus.Completed & _
                    ")) AND (tblStudentCourses.SessionYear = " & intYear & _
                    ") AND (tblStudentCourses.SessionNumber = " & intSession & _
                    ") AND (tblStudentCourses.StudentID = " & _
                    rstInvoices!StudentID & ")", dbOpenDynaset)
                ' Zero the total
                lngHours = 0
                ' Process all courses
                Do Until rstCourses.EOF
                    ' Add to the total hours
                    lngHours = lngHours + rstCourses!CreditHours
                    ' Edit the row and mark it invoiced
                    rstCourses.Edit
                    rstCourses!Invoiced = True
                    rstCourses.Update
                    rstCourses.MoveNext
                Loop
                ' Close courses
                rstCourses.Close
                ' Edit the Invoice and update it
                rstInvoices.Edit
                rstInvoices!SemesterHours = lngHours
                rstInvoices!Tuition = Round(CCur(lngHours * rstRate!TuitionAmt), 2)
                rstInvoices.Update
                ' Get the next invoice
                rstInvoices.MoveNext
            Loop
```

After processing all the invoices, the code closes all recordsets, sets the return value to True to indicate success, and exits. The code at the end of the procedure handles any errors that occur by displaying a message, logging the error, and returning False to indicate that the update failed. The code is as follows:

```
            ' Close Invoices
            rstInvoices.Close
            ' Close the rate record
            rstRate.Close
            ' Return success
            UpdateInvoices = True
    UpdateInvoices_Exit:
            ' Blow past errors after this
            On Error Resume Next
            ' Clear all objects
            Set rstRate = Nothing
            Set rstInvoices = Nothing
            Set rstCourses = Nothing
            Set db = Nothing
            ' Done
            Exit Function
    UpdateInvoices_Err:
            ' Got an error - display it
            MsgBox "Unexpected error updating invoices: " & _
                Err.Number & ", " & Err.Description, _
                vbCritical, gstrAppTitle
```

```
    ' Log the error
    ErrorLog "UpdateInvoices", Err.Number, Err.Description
    ' Return error
    UpdateInvoices = False
    ' Bail
    Resume UpdateInvoices_Exit
End Function
```

You might be wondering why the code doesn't use SQL UPDATE commands to calculate the totals and update the invoiced courses. Unfortunately, the JET database engine marks any query that contains a Sum as not updatable. The code could have used an update query that calls the *DSum* function, but that would be less efficient than processing the rows in a loop. By using a loop, the code can both calculate the total and update the individual course records without having to execute a second UPDATE command.

Entering Payments

Creating invoices is certainly an important part of the application, but administrators also need to be able to track payments for a student. If you don't have the application still running, you can open the Registration.mdb database, open the frmSplash form to start the application, and sign on using **tmichaels** as the User Name and **password** as the Password. Click the Students button on the main switchboard, enter **Hansen** in the Last Name field, and click the Edit button. If you still have the Students form open to edit the record for Anne Hansen, click the Payments tab to see the payments entered for the student.

> **Note**   A student or instructor can sign on and view this form, but code in the Load event procedure of the fsubStudentPayments form locks all the controls on the form if the current user is a student or an instructor. Only an administrator can edit the data, delete existing rows, or add new ones. The same is true to varying degrees for the other three subforms displayed on the frmStudents form.

Start by attempting to enter a payment for the 2005 Summer semester in the amount of $50. When you tab away from the Amount field, the application displays an error message, as shown in Figure 24-3 on the next page. Of course, Anne hasn't been registered for this semester, so it doesn't make sense to enter a payment. Click OK in the dialog box and press Esc to clear your edits on the form.

You can find the code that performs this and other validations in the BeforeUpdate event procedure in the fsubStudentPayments form. The code first verifies that the user has supplied year, session number (semester), payment date, and payment amount values. If any of these is missing, the code displays an error, cancels the update, and exits.

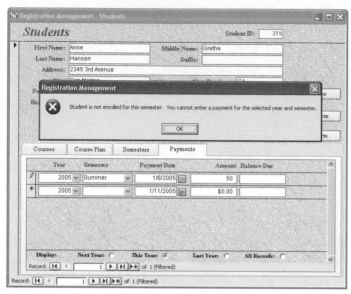

Figure 24-3   Entering a payment for a student.

If the form is about to save a new record, the code uses the *DLookup* function to verify that the current student is registered for the specified year and session number. The *DLookup* function returns a Null if the record doesn't exist, so the *IsNothing* function (that you can find in the modUtility module) returns a True value. If the record does not exist, the code displays the error message that you saw in Figure 24-3, cancels the edit, and exits. The code is as follows:

```
Private Sub Form_BeforeUpdate(Cancel As Integer)
Dim lngErr As Long, strError As String
  ' Set an error trap
  On Error GoTo BeforeUpdate_Err
  ' First, check for required fields
  If IsNothing(Me.cmbSessionYear) Then
    MsgBox "You must select a year.", _
      vbCritical, gstrAppTitle
    Me.cmbSessionYear.SetFocus
    Cancel = True
    Exit Sub
  End If
  If IsNothing(Me.cmbSessionNumber) Then
    MsgBox "You must select a semester.", _
      vbCritical, gstrAppTitle
    Me.cmbSessionNumber.SetFocus
    Cancel = True
    Exit Sub
  End If
  If IsNothing(Me.PaymentDate) Then
    MsgBox "You must enter a payment date.", _
      vbCritical, gstrAppTitle
```

```
      Me.PaymentDate.SetFocus
      Cancel = True
      Exit Sub
    End If
    If IsNothing(Me.PaymentAmount) Then
      MsgBox "You must enter a payment amount.", _
        vbCritical, gstrAppTitle
      Me.PaymentAmount.SetFocus
      Cancel = True
      Exit Sub
    End If
    ' If a new record,
    If Me.NewRecord Then
      ' Make sure student enrolled in this semester
      If IsNothing(DLookup("StudentID", "tblStudentInvoices", _
        "StudentID = " & Me.Parent.StudentID & _
        " AND SessionYear = " & Me.SessionYear & _
        " AND SessionNumber = " & Me.SessionNumber)) Then
        ' Can't enter a payment for a session not enrolled
        MsgBox "Student is not enrolled " & _
          "for this semester.  You cannot enter a payment " & _
          "for the selected year and semester.", vbCritical, gstrAppTitle
        ' Cancel the update
        Cancel = True
        ' Bail
        Exit Sub
      End If
    End If
BeforeUpdate_Exit:
  Exit Sub
BeforeUpdate_Err:
  lngErr = Err
  strError = Error
  ' Log the error
  ErrorLog Me.Name & "_BeforeUpdate", lngErr, strError
  ' Tell user
  MsgBox "Unexpected error: " & lngErr & " " & strError & _
    vbCrLf & "Try again or press Esc to clear your edits.", _
    vbExclamation, gstrAppTitle
  ' Cancel the save
  Cancel = True
  ' Bail
  Resume BeforeUpdate_Exit
End Sub
```

Next, try entering a payment for the 2005 Spring semester in the amount of $50. As soon as you tab out of the Amount field, you should see the Balance Due update, as shown in Figure 24-4 on the next page.

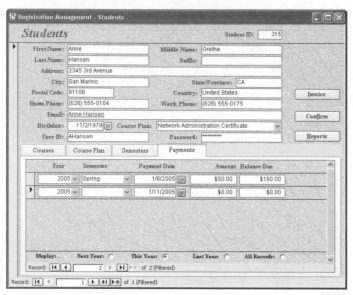

Figure 24-4 The application displays the current balance due after saving a payment.

Code in the AfterUpdate event procedure of the PaymentAmount text box control forces a save of the record to update the balance due, but the real work is done in the query that is the record source for the fsubStudentPayments form. The qryStudentPayments query uses the *DLookup* function to find the tuition amount and the *DSum* function to sum the total payments saved. The BalanceDue field is a result of subtracting the total payments from the tuition. The SQL for the query is as follows:

```
SELECT tblStudentPayments.StudentID, tblStudentPayments.SessionYear,
  tblStudentPayments.SessionNumber, tblStudentPayments.PaymentDate,
  tblStudentPayments.PaymentAmount,
  NZ(DLookUp("[Tuition]","tblStudentInvoices","StudentID = " &
    [tblStudentPayments].[StudentID] & " AND SessionYear = " &
    NZ([tblStudentPayments].[SessionYear],0) & " AND SessionNumber = " &
    NZ([tblStudentPayments].[SessionNumber],0)),0) -
    DSum("[PaymentAmount]","tblStudentPayments","StudentID = " &
    [tblStudentPayments].[StudentID] & " AND SessionYear = " &
    NZ([tblStudentPayments].[SessionYear],0) & " AND SessionNumber = " &
    NZ([tblStudentPayments].[SessionNumber],0) & " AND PaymentDate <= #" &
    [tblStudentPayments].[PaymentDate] & "#") AS BalanceDue
FROM tblStudentPayments
ORDER BY tblStudentPayments.SessionYear, tblStudentPayments.SessionNumber,
  tblStudentPayments.PaymentDate;
```

Notice that the query expression uses the *NZ* (Null to Zero) function to avoid attempting to calculate using Null values when either the SessionYear or SessionNumber haven't been specified in the record yet. If the expression didn't include these calls to the *NZ* function, the Balance Due column would display *#Error* for any row that didn't have a SessionYear or SessionNumber—the new row at the end of the form display.

Printing and E-Mailing Invoices

Now that you understand how invoices are updated and payments entered, the only piece missing is printing the invoice or sending the invoice and payment information via e-mail to the student.

Printing an Invoice

An administrator can print an invoice for one, some, or all students for a specific semester, all semesters in a year, or all semesters. To see how this works, start the application by opening the frmSplash form, sign on using **tmichaels** as the User Name and **password** as the Password, click the Reports button on the main switchboard, and then click the Students button on the Reports switchboard. The application displays the Student Reports dialog box (the fdlgStudentReports form). To print the invoice for the Spring 2005 semester for Anne Hansen, enter **Hansen** in the Last Name field (this selects invoices for all students whose last name begins with "Hansen," but there's only one in the database), select 2005 in the Year combo box, and select Spring in the Semester combo box, as shown in Figure 24-5.

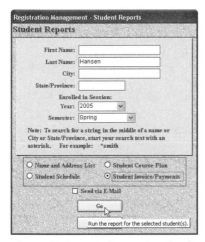

Figure 24-5   Printing an invoice for a specific semester for all students whose last name begins with "Hansen."

Note that because the code in the fdlgStudentReports form filters on the leading part of the first name, last name, city, and state or province, the administrator could easily print invoices in batches by first letter of the last name or by state or province. The administrator can also leave the Year and Semester fields blank to print all invoices for the selected students, enter only a year value to print invoices for that year, or enter a year and semester to print invoices for a specific semester.

Select the Student Invoice/Payments option and click the Go button, as shown in the figure. The application opens the Invoice report (rptStudentInvoice), displaying Anne's invoice, as shown in Figure 24-6 on the next page.

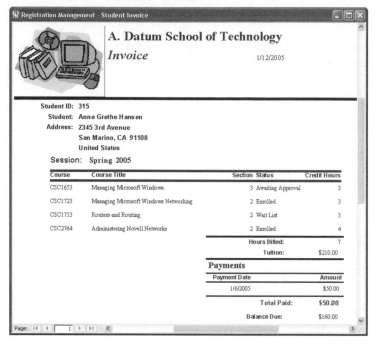

Figure 24-6 The printed invoice for Anne Hansen for the Spring 2005 semester.

The report design is actually quite simple. The payments print from a subreport, the rsubStudentPayments report. If the subreport has no records (there are no payment records), the subreport won't display at all. Because a student isn't likely to sign up for more than six or seven courses in a semester and probably won't make more than one or two payments, the report isn't likely to require more than one page per student. Should the student have more payments than will fit below the course list, the subreport is actually in a group footer for the semester with the Keep Together property set to Yes. If the subreport won't fit at the bottom of the page, it will print all together at the top of the second page.

As with most reports, the complex part of the report design is the report record source—the qryRptStudentInvoice query. The query combines the tblStudents, tblStudentInvoices, tblStudentCourses, and tblCourses tables to fetch all the fields needed for the report. The SQL for the query is as follows:

```
SELECT tblStudents.StudentID, [FirstName] & (" "+[MiddleName]) & " " &
  [LastName] & (", "+[Suffix]) AS Student, tblStudents.FirstName,
  tblStudents.LastName, tblStudents.Address, tblStudents.City,
  tblStudents.StateOrProvince, tblStudents.PostalCode, tblStudents.Country,
  tblStudents.Email, tblStudentInvoices.SessionYear,
  tblStudentInvoices.SessionNumber, tblStudentInvoices.SemesterHours,
  tblStudentInvoices.Tuition, tblCourses.CourseCategory,
  tblCourses.CourseNumber, tblCourses.CourseTitle, tblCourses.CreditHours,
  tblStudentCourses.SectionNumber, tblStudentCourses.Status
FROM tblStudents
INNER JOIN (tblStudentInvoices
```

```
INNER JOIN (tblStudentCourses
  INNER JOIN tblCourses
  ON (tblStudentCourses.CourseNumber = tblCourses.CourseNumber)
  AND (tblStudentCourses.CourseCategory = tblCourses.CourseCategory))
 ON (tblStudentInvoices.SessionNumber = tblStudentCourses.SessionNumber)
 AND (tblStudentInvoices.SessionYear = tblStudentCourses.SessionYear)
 AND (tblStudentInvoices.StudentID = tblStudentCourses.StudentID))
ON (tblStudents.StudentID = tblStudentInvoices.StudentID)
AND (tblStudents.StudentID = tblStudentCourses.StudentID)
ORDER BY tblStudents.StudentID, tblStudentInvoices.SessionYear,
  tblStudentInvoices.SessionNumber, tblCourses.CourseCategory,
  tblCourses.CourseNumber;
```

Sending an Invoice via E-Mail

Although a school might need to print a copy of the invoice to keep in a file, in this modern day of electronic communications, administrators will probably prefer to send out invoices by e-mail. A student can also sign on to the application and request that the invoice be sent by e-mail.

To see how a student might request an e-mail copy of the invoice, start the application by opening the frmSplash form. (If you're still running the application as an administrator, click the Exit button on the main switchboard first.) Sign on using **ahansen** as the User Name and **password** as the Password. The application will open the Students form (frmStudents) displaying only the record for Anne Hansen. Notice that the form does not display the Invoice button when a student is signed on. On the Students form, click the Reports button to see the Student Reports dialog box for the student—the fdlgStudentReportsS form—as shown in Figure 24-7.

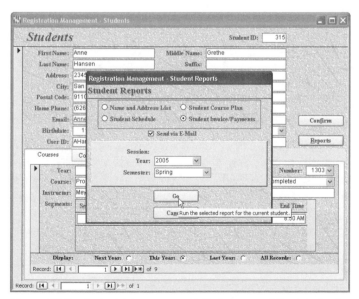

Figure 24-7   A student can request that a copy of the invoice be sent by e-mail.

Select the Student Invoice/Payments option and select the Send via E-Mail check box. Select 2005 in the Year combo box and Spring in the Semester combo box, and click Go to send the report via e-mail. The e-mail should open in your copy of Microsoft Outlook, ready to send, as shown in Figure 24-8. (Of course, the student wouldn't normally see the e-mail displayed on the screen. This sample displays it because all the student e-mail addresses are fictitious, so the e-mail can't be sent.)

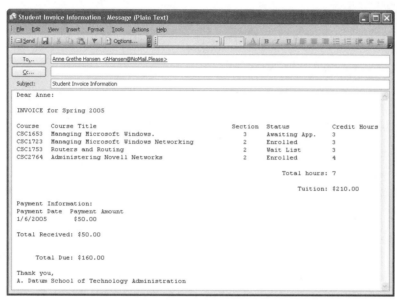

Figure 24-8   The invoice for Anne Hansen for the Spring 2005 semester sent via e-mail.

When code in the fdlgStudentReportsS form determines that you want to send the invoice via e-mail, it calls the *EmailStudentInvoices* procedure that you can find in the modOutlook module and passes it the filter string needed to fetch the correct records. Code in the *EmailStudentInvoices* procedure begins by declaring all variables, setting an error trap, and opening a recordset on the qryRptStudentInvoice query with the filter specified by the calling procedure applied. Note that this is the same query that is the record source for the rptStudentInvoice report. If the recordset is empty, the code sets the return value to False to indicate an error, closes the recordset, and exits. The code is as follows:

```
Public Function EmailStudentInvoices(strWhere As String) As Integer
' Function to send student invoices via e-mail
' Input:  Predicate string to filter invoices
' Output: True if successful
' Function calls the SendOutlookMsg function for each e-mail
Dim db As DAO.Database, rstInv As DAO.Recordset, rstPay As DAO.Recordset
Dim lngThisStudent As Long, intThisYear As Integer, intThisSession As Integer
Dim strMsg As String, strTo As String, curTotPay As Currency
Dim curTuition As Currency, intHours As Integer
  ' Set an error trap
  On Error GoTo EmailInvoices_Err
```

```
' Point to this database
Set db = DBEngine(0)(0)
' Open the invoices recordset
'  -- uses the report recordset
Set rstInv = db.OpenRecordset("SELECT * FROM qryRptStudentInvoice " & _
  "WHERE " & strWhere)
' If got nothing
If rstInv.EOF Then
  ' Set failed return
  EmailStudentInvoices = False
  ' Close out
  rstInv.Close
  Set rstInv = Nothing
  Set db = Nothing
  ' Bail
  Exit Function
End If
```

When the filtered recordset contains data, the code begins a loop to process the records one at a time. Because the e-mail requires a heading, the detailed data from each course record, the detailed data from any related payments, and a closing, the code must check each record to see if it represents the beginning of an invoice for another student or semester. It can't complete an invoice until it encounters either a record for a different invoice or the end of the recordset. If this is not the first record and the student ID or semester is different, the code has processed all the detail course lines for the previous invoice, so the code adds the lines for the total hours and tuition to the outgoing message string.

The code then opens a recordset on the related payments. If at least one payment record exists, the code adds the payment heading to the outgoing message string, clears the total payments variable (curTotPay), and starts a loop to process the payments. For each payment, the code creates a line in the message string and adds the amount to the total paid. After processing all payments, the code adds the total received line to the message.

The code then uses the *SendOutlookMsg* procedure that you studied in the previous chapter to send the invoice message. If the send failed, the code displays an error message. The code clears the message string before going on to process the current record. The code is as follows:

```
' Process all rows
Do Until rstInv.EOF
  ' If not the first one and
  '  if on a different student or semester now,
  If (lngThisStudent <> 0) And _
    ((lngThisStudent <> rstInv!StudentID) Or _
    (intThisYear <> rstInv!SessionYear) Or _
    (intThisSession <> rstInv!SessionNumber)) Then
    ' Add the total lines
    strMsg = strMsg & vbCrLf & Space(69) & "Total hours: " & intHours
    strMsg = strMsg & vbCrLf & vbCrLf & _
      Space(73) & "Tuition: " & Format(curTuition, "Currency") & vbCrLf
    ' Get payments for previous invoice
    Set rstPay = db.OpenRecordset("SELECT * FROM tblStudentPayments " & _
```

```
              "WHERE StudentID = " & lngThisStudent & _
              " AND SessionYear = " & intThisYear & _
              " AND SessionNumber = " & intThisSession)
        ' If got some
        If Not rstPay.EOF Then
          ' Add payment header
          strMsg = strMsg & vbCrLf & "Payment Information:" & vbCrLf & _
            "Payment Date  Payment Amount" & vbCrLf
          ' Zero total payments
          curTotPay = 0
          ' Process all the payments
          Do Until rstPay.EOF
            ' Add a payment line
            strMsg = strMsg & rstPay!PaymentDate & "       " & _
              Format(rstPay!PaymentAmount, "Currency") & vbCrLf
            ' Add to total
            curTotPay = curTotPay + rstPay!PaymentAmount
            ' Get the next one
            rstPay.MoveNext
          Loop
          ' Add the total received
          strMsg = strMsg & vbCrLf & "Total Received: " & _
            Format(curTotPay, "Currency") & vbCrLf & vbCrLf
        End If
        ' Close the payments recordset
        rstPay.Close
        Set rstPay = Nothing
        ' Add signature
        strMsg = strMsg & "Thank you," & vbCrLf & _
          "A. Datum School of Technology Administration"
        ' Send the message
        If Not SendOutlookMsg("Student Invoice Information", strTo, strMsg) _
          Then
          MsgBox "There was a problem sending an invoice e-mail to " & _
            strTo, vbExclamation, gstrAppTitle
        End If
        ' Clear the sent message
        strMsg = ""
      End If
```

For each invoice detail row (data about each course), the code saves the student ID, year, session number, semester hours, and total tuition. (The Tuition field from the tblStudentInvoices table repeats with each related row from the tblStudentCourses table.) The code also sets up the e-mail "To" address string by extracting the actual address from the Email hyperlink field.

If the message string is empty (this is the first row for a new student or semester), the code starts the message by adding the headers to the message string. The code then formats and adds the detail line for the course in the current record, moves to the next record, and loops back to process it. The code is as follows:

```
    ' Grab the student ID
    lngThisStudent = rstInv!StudentID
    ' .. and year
```

```
      intThisYear = rstInv!SessionYear
      ' .. and session (semester)
      intThisSession = rstInv!SessionNumber
      ' .. and semester hours
      intHours = rstInv!SemesterHours
      ' .. and total tuition
      curTuition = rstInv!Tuition
      ' Set up the To field
      strTo = rstInv!Student & _
        "<" & Left(Mid(rstInv!Email, InStr(rstInv!Email, "Mailto:") + 7), _
        Len(Mid(rstInv!Email, InStr(rstInv!Email, "Mailto:") + 7)) - 1) & ">"
      ' If message is empty,
      If strMsg = "" Then
        ' Set up the header
        strMsg = "Dear " & rstInv!FirstName & ":" & vbCrLf & vbCrLf & _
          "INVOICE for " & _
          Choose(intThisSession, "Spring", "Summer", "Fall") & _
          " " & intThisYear & vbCrLf & vbCrLf & _
          "Course    Course Title                     " & _
          "Section  Status        Credit Hours" & vbCrLf
      End If
      ' Add the detail data
      strMsg = strMsg & rstInv!CourseCategory & rstInv!CourseNumber & _
        "  " & Left(rstInv!CourseTitle & Space(40), 50) & _
        rstInv!SectionNumber & _
        "   " & Choose(rstInv!Status, "Requested  ", "Awaiting App.", _
        "Approved   ", "Wait List  ", "Enrolled   ", "Withdrawn  ", _
        "Incomplete ", "Completed  ") & _
        "   " & rstInv!CreditHours & vbCrLf
      ' Move to the next one
      rstInv.MoveNext
  Loop
```

After processing the last record, the last message has not been sent yet. Remember, the code must encounter a different student or semester or fall off the end of the records in order to know the previous message is complete. As with encountering a different row, the code must format the Tuition total line, fetch and format the payment lines (if any), and add the closing signature. When the message has been fully assembled, the code calls the *SendOutlookMsg* procedure to send the assembled message string before closing all recordsets and exiting. The code at the end of the procedure traps any error, displays a message and logs the error, and exits with a failure return. The code is as follows:

```
  ' Format the end of the last invoice
  ' Add the total lines
  strMsg = strMsg & vbCrLf & Space(69) & "Total hours: " & intHours
  strMsg = strMsg & vbCrLf & vbCrLf & _
    Space(73) & "Tuition: " & Format(curTuition, "Currency") & vbCrLf
  ' Get payments for previous invoice
  Set rstPay = db.OpenRecordset("SELECT * FROM tblStudentPayments " & _
    "WHERE StudentID = " & lngThisStudent & _
    " AND SessionYear = " & intThisYear & _
    " AND SessionNumber = " & intThisSession)
  ' If got some
```

```
  If Not rstPay.EOF Then
    ' Add payment header
    strMsg = strMsg & vbCrLf & "Payment Information:" & vbCrLf & _
      "Payment Date  Payment Amount" & vbCrLf
    ' Zero total payments
    curTotPay = 0
    ' Process all the payments
    Do Until rstPay.EOF
      ' Add a payment line
      strMsg = strMsg & rstPay!PaymentDate & "       " & _
        Format(rstPay!PaymentAmount, "Currency") & vbCrLf
      ' Add to total
      curTotPay = curTotPay + rstPay!PaymentAmount
      ' Get the next one
      rstPay.MoveNext
    Loop
    ' Add the total received
    strMsg = strMsg & vbCrLf & "Total Received: " & _
      Format(curTotPay, "Currency") & vbCrLf & vbCrLf
  End If
  ' Close the payments recordset
  rstPay.Close
  Set rstPay = Nothing
  ' Add signature
  strMsg = strMsg & "Thank you," & vbCrLf & _
    "A. Datum School of Technology Administration"
  ' Send the message
  If Not SendOutlookMsg("Student Invoice Information", strTo, strMsg) Then
    MsgBox "There was a problem sending an invoice e-mail to " & _
      strTo, vbExclamation, gstrAppTitle
  End If
  ' Close out
  rstInv.Close
EmailInvoices_Exit:
  Set rstInv = Nothing
  Set rstPay = Nothing
  Set db = Nothing
  Exit Function
EmailInvoices_Err:
  MsgBox "Unexpected error: " & Err & ", " & Error, vbCritical, gstrAppTitle
  ErrorLog "EmailInvoices", Err, Error
  Resume EmailInvoices_Exit
End Function
```

This concludes the examination of the Registration Management application. In the appendixes, you'll find several useful reference topics. Be sure to take a look at Appendix E, which shows you how I implemented some generic features in the sample applications that you are sure to find useful in any Access application you design.

Part VI
Appendixes

Appendix A

Recommended Reading

No one book can provide all you need to know about designing and implementing database applications using Microsoft Access. As noted in Part 1 of this book, "Designing Your Application," you must understand database design before you get started. Access is also a very complex product—I've been working with it for more than a dozen years, and I still can't profess to know all the product can do. Most developers I know own four or five books about Access written at different levels. And finally, you can't begin to build any moderately complex database application without understanding SQL.

In the following sections, you can find books I recommend on various topics related to *Building Microsoft Access Applications*. Within each category, I have arranged the books in ascending order by complexity.

Database Design

Database Design for Mere Mortals, Second Edition. Michael J. Hernandez. Addison-Wesley Professional, 2003.

Designing Effective Database Systems. Rebecca M. Riordan. Addison-Wesley Professional, 2005.

Handbook of Relational Database Design. Candace C. Fleming and Barbara von Halle. Addison-Wesley Publishing Company, 1989.

Microsoft Access

> **Note**   In general, any book written for Microsoft Access 2000, XP (2002), or 2003 can be used with any of the three versions. However, some books written for Access 2002 or 2003 have sample databases in the 2002/2003 file format that you will not be able to open with Access 2000.

Microsoft Access 2000 Step-by-Step. Catapult, Inc. Microsoft Press, 1999.

Microsoft Access Version 2002 Step-by-Step. Online Training Solutions, Inc. Microsoft Press, 2001.

Microsoft Office Access 2003 Step-by-Step. Online Training Solutions, Inc. Microsoft Press, 2003.

Running Microsoft Access 2000. John L. Viescas. Microsoft Press, 1999.

Special Edition Using Microsoft Access 2000. Roger Jennings. Que, 1999.

Microsoft Access 2000 Bible. Cary N. Prague and Michael R. Irwin. Wiley & Sons, 1999.

Special Edition Using Microsoft Access 2002. Roger Jennings. Que, 2001.

Microsoft Access 2002 Bible. Cary N. Prague and Michael R. Irwin. Wiley & Sons, 2001.

Microsoft Office Access 2003 Inside Out. John L. Viescas. Microsoft Press, 2003.

Special Edition Using Microsoft Office Access 2003. Roger Jennings. Que, 2003.

Microsoft Office Access 2003 Bible. Cary N. Prague, Michael R. Irwin, and Jennifer Reardon. Wiley & Sons, 2003.

Access Cookbook. Ken Getz, Andy Baron, and Paul Litwin. O'Reilly, 2002.

Access 2000 Developer's Handbook Set. Paul Litwin, Ken Getz, and Mike Gilbert. Sybex, Inc., 1999.

Access 2002 Developer's Handbook Set. Paul Litwin, Ken Getz, and Mike Gunderloy. Sybex, Inc., 2001.

Microsoft Access Developer's Guide to SQL Server. Andy Baron and Mary Chipman. Sams, 2000.

SQL

SQL Queries for Mere Mortals. Michael J. Hernandez and John L. Viescas. Addison-Wesley Professional, 2000.

SQL: The Complete Reference, Second Edition. James R. Groff and Paul N. Weinberg. McGraw-Hill, 2002.

Joe Celko's SQL for Smarties: Advanced SQL Programming. Joe Celko. Morgan Kaufmann, 1999.

A Guide to the SQL Standard, Fourth Edition. Chris J. Date and Hugh Darwen. Pearson Education, 1996.

Appendix B
Sample Database Schemas

Each section of this appendix begins with a diagram showing the table relationships in the sample application followed by a brief description of the fields in each table. The length shown for Text fields is the defined maximum length. The length shown for all other fields is the amount of storage occupied by that data type in each record. Memo, Hyperlink, and OLE Object data types use 8 bytes in the main record to store a pointer to up to 2 gigabytes of extended data.

Membership Tracking

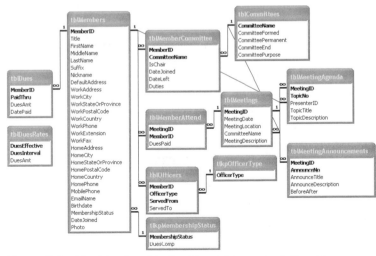

Figure B-1   The Membership Tracking tables and relationships.

tblCommittees

Field Name	Description	Type	Length	Primary Key
CommitteeName	Name of this committee	Text	50	Yes
CommitteeFormed	Date committee was formed	Date/Time	8	
CommitteePermanent	Permanent standing committee?	Yes/No	1	
CommitteeEnd	Date committee disbanded if not permanent	Date/Time	8	
CommitteePurpose	Description of committee purpose	Text	255	

tblDues

Field Name	Description	Type	Length	Primary Key
MemberID	Unique member number	Long Integer	4	Yes
PaidThru	Date membership is paid through	Date/Time	8	Yes
DuesAmt	Amount paid	Currency	8	
DatePaid	Date dues paid	Date/Time	8	

tblDuesRates

Field Name	Description	Type	Length	Primary Key
DuesEffective	Effective date of this dues rate	Date/Time	8	Yes
DuesInterval	Dues payment is for this number of months	Integer	2	Yes
DuesAmt	Dues charged by this organization	Currency	8	

tblMeetingAgenda

Field Name	Description	Type	Length	Primary Key
MeetingID	Unique meeting identifier	Long Integer	4	Yes
TopicNo	Topic sequence number	Integer	2	Yes
PresenterID	(Optional) ID of presenter of this topic	Long Integer	4	
TopicTitle	Title of the agenda item	Text	255	
TopicDescription	Description of the topic	Memo		

tblMeetingAnnouncements

Field Name	Description	Type	Length	Primary Key
MeetingID	Unique meeting identifier	Long Integer	4	Yes
AnnounceNo	Announcement sequence number	Integer	2	Yes
AnnounceTitle	Title of the announcement item	Text	255	
AnnounceDescription	Announcement text	Memo		
BeforeAfter	Print before or after the agenda items	Integer	2	

tblMeetings

Field Name	Description	Type	Length	Primary Key
MeetingID	Unique meeting ID	Long Integer	4	Yes
MeetingDate	Date/time the meeting was held	Date/Time	8	
MeetingLocation	Place where meeting held	Text	255	
CommitteeName	(Optional) Related committee	Text	50	
MeetingDescription	Description of the meeting	Text	50	

tblMemberAttend

Field Name	Description	Type	Length	Primary Key
MeetingID	Unique ID of the meeting	Long Integer	4	Yes
MemberID	Unique ID of member attending	Long Integer	4	Yes
DuesPaid	Were dues paid when user attended meeting?	Yes/No	1	

tblMemberCommittee

Field Name	Description	Type	Length	Primary Key
MemberID	Unique ID of member on this committee	Long Integer	4	Yes
CommitteeName	Name of the committee	Text	50	Yes
IsChair	This person is/was chair of the committee	Yes/No	1	
DateJoined	Date member joined the committee	Date/Time	8	
DateLeft	Date member left the committee	Date/Time	8	
Duties	General description of this member's duties on the committee	Text	255	

tblMembers

Field Name	Description	Type	Length	Primary Key
MemberID	Unique member ID	Long Integer	4	Yes
Title	Member's title (Mr., Mrs., Dr., etc.)	Text	20	
FirstName	Member first name	Text	50	
MiddleName	Member middle name	Text	30	
LastName	Member last name	Text	50	
Suffix	Member name suffix (Jr., Sr., II, etc.)	Text	20	
Nickname	Member's nickname (for badges, etc.)	Text	30	
DefaultAddress	Specify work or home as default address	Integer	2	
WorkAddress	Work address	Text	255	
WorkCity	Work city	Text	50	
WorkStateOrProvince	Work state or province	Text	20	
WorkPostalCode	Work postal/ZIP code	Text	20	
WorkCountry	Work country	Text	50	
WorkPhone	Work phone	Text	30	
WorkExtension	Work phone extension	Text	20	
WorkFax	Work fax number	Text	30	
HomeAddress	Home address	Text	255	
HomeCity	Home city	Text	50	
HomeStateOrProvince	Home state or province	Text	20	
HomePostalCode	Home postal/ZIP code	Text	20	
HomeCountry	Home country	Text	50	
HomePhone	Home phone	Text	30	
MobilePhone	Mobile phone	Text	30	
EmailName	E-mail name	Hyperlink		
Birthdate	Member date of birth	Date/Time	8	
MembershipStatus	Membership status	Text	15	
DateJoined	Date member joined	Date/Time	8	
Photo	Path to member photo	Text	255	

tblOfficers

Field Name	Description	Type	Length	Primary Key
MemberID	Unique member ID	Long Integer	4	Yes
OfficerType	Name of the office held	Text	50	Yes
ServedFrom	Date nominated to this position	Date/Time	8	Yes
ServedTo	Date person left this position	Date/Time	8	

tlkpMembershipStatus

Field Name	Description	Type	Length	Primary Key
MembershipStatus	Membership status	Text	15	Yes
DuesComp	Are dues complimentary?	Yes/No	1	

tlkpOfficerType

Field Name	Description	Type	Length	Primary Key
OfficerType	Description of the office	Text	50	Yes

Inventory Management

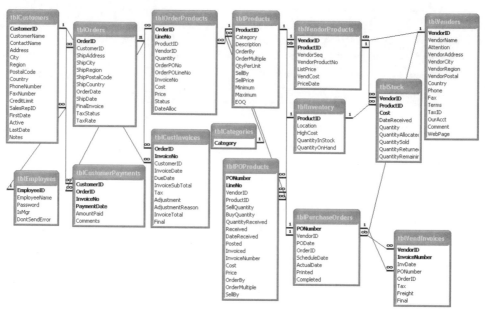

Figure B-2 The Inventory Management tables and relationships.

tblCategories

Field Name	Description	Type	Length	Primary Key
Category	Name of product category	Text	15	Yes

tblCustInvoices

Field Name	Description	Type	Length	Primary Key
OrderID	Unique order number	Long Integer	4	Yes
InvoiceNo	Invoice suffix number	Text	2	Yes
CustomerID	Unique ID for this customer	Long Integer	4	
InvoiceDate	Date invoice issued	Date/Time	8	
DueDate	Payment due date	Date/Time	8	
InvoiceSubTotal	Subtotal for all products billed	Currency	8	
Tax	Sales tax	Currency	8	
Adjustment	Special adjustment	Currency	8	
AdjustmentReason	Reason for adjustment	Text	255	
InvoiceTotal	Total invoice amount	Currency	8	
Final	Final invoice for this order?	Yes/No	1	

tblCustomerPayments

Field Name	Description	Type	Length	Primary Key
CustomerID	Unique ID for this customer	Long Integer	4	Yes
OrderID	Order number; 0 if payment not yet credited to an order invoice	Long Integer	4	Yes
InvoiceNo	Invoice suffix number; 00 if a prepay	Text	2	Yes
PaymentDate	Date of this payment	Date/Time	8	Yes
AmountPaid	Amount of this payment	Currency	8	
Comments	Comments about this payment (check number, etc.)	Text	150	

tblCustomers

Field Name	Description	Type	Length	Primary Key
CustomerID	Unique ID for this customer	Long Integer	4	Yes
CustomerName	Customer name	Text	75	
ContactName	Person to contact at customer	Text	75	
Address	Street or post office box	Text	60	
City	City	Text	15	
Region	State or province	Text	15	
PostalCode	Postal or ZIP code	Text	10	
Country	Country	Text	15	
PhoneNumber	Phone number, including country code or area code	Text	24	
FaxNumber	Fax number, including country code or area code	Text	24	
CreditLimit	Maximum credit allowed	Currency	8	
SalesRepID	Employee ID of this company's sales rep	Long Integer	4	
FirstDate	Date of first business with this customer	Date/Time	8	
Active	Active customer flag	Yes/No	1	
LastDate	Date of most recent business with this customer	Date/Time	8	
Notes	Notes about this customer	Memo		

tblEmployees

Field Name	Description	Type	Length	Primary Key
EmployeeID	Unique employee ID	Long Integer	4	Yes
EmployeeName	Employee name	Text	75	
Password	Sign-on password	Text	20	
IsMgr	Is this employee a manager?	Yes/No	1	
DontSendError	Ignore error report send when this employee exits?	Yes/No	1	

tblInventory

Field Name	Description	Type	Length	Primary Key
ProductID	Unique product ID	Long Integer	4	Yes
Location	Usual storage location for this item	Text	20	
HighCost	Cost of the most expensive item available to sell	Currency	8	
QuantityInStock	Quantity in stock; include products allocated to orders but not sold yet	Long Integer	4	
QuantityOnHand	Quantity available to sell	Long Integer	4	

tblOrderProducts

Field Name	Description	Type	Length	Primary Key
OrderID	Order identifier	Long Integer	4	Yes
LineNo	Unique line number for this entry	Integer	2	Yes
ProductID	Product ordered	Long Integer	4	
VendorID	Vendor for this product	Long Integer	4	
Quantity	Quantity requested by customer	Integer	2	
OrderPONo	Related puchase order number: status On Order	Long Integer	4	
OrderPOLineNo	Related purchase order line number	Integer	2	
InvoiceNo	Related invoice suffix number when billed: status Invoiced	Text	2	
Cost	Cost of each item	Currency	8	
Price	Price charged to customer	Currency	8	
Status	Current status of this order item: None, On Order, Allocated, Invoiced	Integer	2	
DateAlloc	Date this product was allocated to/ from inventory	Date/Time	8	

tblOrders

Field Name	Description	Type	Length	Primary Key
OrderID	Unique order number	Long Integer	4	Yes
CustomerID	Customer for this order	Long Integer	4	
ShipAddress	Shipping street address	Text	60	
ShipCity	Shipping city	Text	15	
ShipRegion	Shipping state or province	Text	15	
ShipPostalCode	Shipping postal or ZIP code	Text	10	
ShipCountry	Shipping country	Text	15	
OrderDate	Date this order was placed	Date/Time	8	
ShipDate	Date of final shipment	Date/Time	8	
FinalInvoice	Final invoice sent?	Yes/No	1	
TaxStatus	Tax status code	Integer	2	
TaxRate	Sales tax rate, if applicable	Decimal	8	

tblPOProducts

Field Name	Description	Type	Length	Primary Key
PONumber	Purchase order number	Long Integer	4	Yes
LineNo	Unique line number for this entry	Integer	2	Yes
VendorID	Vendor for this PO	Long Integer	4	
ProductID	Product ordered	Long Integer	4	
SellQuantity	Quantity required	Integer	2	
BuyQuantity	Quantity ordered	Integer	2	
QuantityReceived	Quantity actually received	Integer	2	
Received	Has item been received?	Yes/No	1	
DateReceived	Date item received	Date/Time	8	
Posted	Received item posted to inventory?	Yes/No	1	
Invoiced	Item invoiced by vendor?	Yes/No	1	
InvoiceNumber	Vendor's Invoice number	Text	20	
Cost	Cost of each item	Currency	8	
Price	Price from vendor invoice, if any	Currency	8	
OrderBy	Order from supplier in this unit ("Each," "Case," etc.)	Text	15	
OrderMultiple	Number of "sell by" units in each "order by" unit	Integer	2	
SellBy	Sell to customers in this unit ("Each," "Case," etc.)	Text	15	

tblProducts

Field Name	Description	Type	Length	Primary Key
ProductID	Unique product ID	Long Integer	4	Yes
Category	Category for this product	Text	15	
Description	Description of this product	Text	75	
OrderBy	Order from supplier in this unit ("Each," "Case," etc.)	Text	15	
OrderMultiple	Number of "sell by" units in each "order by" unit	Integer	2	
QtyPerUnit	Size description of each sales unit	Text	20	
SellBy	Sell to customers in this unit ("Each," "Case," etc.)	Text	15	
SellPrice	Current selling price per unit	Currency	8	
Minimum	When available inventory falls below this number, trigger an order	Long Integer	4	
Maximum	Maximum stocking level	Long Integer	4	
EOQ	Economic order quantity	Long Integer	4	

tblPurchaseOrders

Field Name	Description	Type	Length	Primary Key
PONumber	Unique purchase order number	Long Integer	4	Yes
VendorID	Vendor for this PO	Long Integer	4	
PODate	Date purchase order issued	Date/Time	8	
OrderID	Related order number (if any)	Long Integer	4	
ScheduleDate	Date receipt expected	Date/Time	8	
ActualDate	Date items received	Date/Time	8	
Printed	Has this PO been issued?	Yes/No	1	
Completed	Have all items in this PO been received and posted?	Yes/No	1	

tblStock

Field Name	Description	Type	Length	Primary Key
VendorID	Vendor who supplied this item	Long Integer	4	Yes
ProductID	Product in stock	Long Integer	4	Yes
Cost	Price paid	Currency	8	Yes
DateReceived	Date this item was posted to stock	Date/Time	8	
Quantity	Quantity received	Long Integer	4	

Field Name	Description	Type	Length	Primary Key
QuantityAllocated	Quantity allocated to an order	Long Integer	4	
QuantitySold	Quantity billed to an order	Long Integer	4	
QuantityReturned	Quantity returned to vendor	Long Integer	4	
QuantityRemaining	Quantity remaining in this stock entry (calculated by the system)	Long Integer	4	

tblVendInvoices

Field Name	Description	Type	Length	Primary Key
VendorID	Vendor who sent this invoice	Long Integer	4	Yes
InvoiceNumber	Vendor's invoice number	Text	20	Yes
InvDate	Vendor's invoice date	Date/Time	8	
PONumber	Related PO number	Long Integer	4	
OrderID	Related customer order, if any	Long Integer	4	
Tax	Tax, if any	Currency	8	
Freight	Freight, if any	Currency	8	
Final	Invoice is final?	Yes/No	1	

tblVendorProducts

Field Name	Description	Type	Length	Primary Key
VendorID	Vendor supplying this product	Long Integer	4	Yes
ProductID	Product supplied by vendor	Long Integer	4	Yes
VendorSeq	Vendor priority; −1 = primary vendor	Integer	2	
VendorProductNo	Product number used by this vendor	Text	25	
ListPrice	Vendor's catalog list price	Currency	8	
VendCost	Cost of this part to us	Currency	8	
PriceDate	Date of last pricing update	Date/Time	8	

tblVendors

Field Name	Description	Type	Length	Primary Key
VendorID	Unique ID for this vendor	Long Integer	4	Yes
VendorName	Name of this vendor	Text	40	
Attention	Send mail to attention of	Text	40	
VendorAddress	Mailing address	Text	60	
VendorCity	City	Text	30	
VendorRegion	State or province	Text	2	

Field Name	Description	Type	Length	Primary Key
VendorPostal	Postal or ZIP code	Text	10	
Country	Country	Text	15	
Phone	Phone number	Text	24	
Fax	Fax number	Text	24	
Terms	Usual invoice terms	Text	75	
TaxID	Tax ID	Text	15	
OurAcct	Our account number with this vendor	Text	25	
Comment	Comments about this vendor	Memo		
WebPage	Vendor's home page on World Wide Web	Hyperlink		

Customer Support

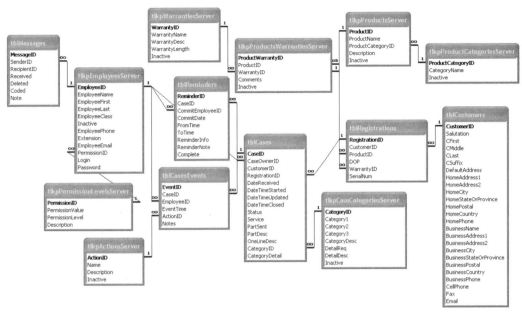

Figure B-3   The Customer Support tables and relationships.

tblCases

Field Name	Description	Type	Length	Primary Key
CaseID	Unique case identifier	AutoNumber	4	Yes
CaseOwnerID	The employee who owns this case	Long Integer	4	
CustomerID	Related customer for this case	Long Integer	4	
RegistrationID	Related product registration, if any	Long Integer	4	
DateReceived	Date the case was received	Date/Time	8	
DateTimeStarted	Date and time employee started working on the case	Date/Time	8	
DateTimeUpdated	Date and time last updated	Date/Time	8	
DateTimeClosed	Date and time the case was closed	Date/Time	8	
Status	Status of this case	Text	15	
Service	Was service ordered?	Yes/No	1	
PartSent	Was a part sent?	Yes/No	1	
PartDesc	Description of the part sent	Text	50	
OneLineDesc	Short description of the case problem	Text	150	

Field Name	Description	Type	Length	Primary Key
CategoryID	Category for this case	Long Integer	4	
CategoryDetail	Category details, if necessary	Text	255	

tblCasesEvents

Field Name	Description	Type	Length	Primary Key
EventID	Unique case event identifier	AutoNumber	4	Yes
CaseID	Related case for this event	Long Integer	4	
EmployeeID	Employee who handled the event	Long Integer	4	
EventTime	Date and time the event was entered	Date/Time	8	
ActionID	Action taken	Long Integer	4	
Notes	Notes about the event	Memo		

tblCustomers

Field Name	Description	Type	Length	Primary Key
CustomerID	Unique customer identifier	AutoNumber	4	Yes
Salutation	Mr., Mrs., Ms., Dr., etc.	Text	10	
CFirst	Customer first name	Text	20	
CMiddle	Customer middle name or initial	Text	20	
CLast	Customer last name	Text	30	
CSuffix	Jr., Sr., III, etc.	Text	10	
DefaultAddress	Default address is home or business	Integer	2	
HomeAddress1	Customer home address line 1	Text	50	
HomeAddress2	Customer home address line 2	Text	50	
HomeCity	Customer home city	Text	50	
HomeStateOrProvince	Customer home state or province	Text	20	
HomePostal	Customer home postal code	Text	15	
HomeCountry	Customer home country	Text	50	
HomePhone	Customer home phone	Text	20	
BusinessName	Customer business name	Text	50	
BusinessAddress1	Customer business address line 1	Text	50	
BusinessAddress2	Customer business address line 2	Text	50	
BusinessCity	Customer business city	Text	50	

Field Name	Description	Type	Length	Primary Key
BusinessStateOrProvince	Customer business state or province	Text	20	
BusinessPostal	Customer business postal code	Text	15	
BusinessCountry	Customer business country	Text	50	
BusinessPhone	Customer business phone number	Text	20	
CellPhone	Customer mobile phone number	Text	20	
Fax	Customer fax number	Text	20	
Email	Customer e-mail	Text	255	

tblMessages

Field Name	Description	Type	Length	Primary Key
MessageID	Unique message identifier	AutoNumber	4	Yes
SenderID	Employee ID of the sender	Long Integer	4	
RecipientID	Employee ID of the recipient	Long Integer	4	
Received	Date and time received	Date/Time	1	
Deleted	Message has been handled	Yes/No	1	
Coded	Set by administrator to indicate a "shutdown" message	Yes/No	1	
Note	Text of the message	Text	255	

tblRegistrations

Field Name	Description	Type	Length	Primary Key
RegistrationID	Unique registration identifier	AutoNumber	4	Yes
CustomerID	Customer who owns this product	Long Integer	4	
ProductID	Product identifier	Long Integer	4	
DOP	Date of purchase	Date/Time	8	
WarrantyID	Warranty included with the product	Long Integer	4	
SerialNum	The product serial number	Long Integer	4	

tblReminders

Field Name	Description	Type	Length	Primary Key
ReminderID	Unique reminder identifier	AutoNumber	4	Yes
CaseID	Related customer case	Long Integer	4	
CommitEmployeeID	Employee responsible for the reminder	Long Integer	4	

Field Name	Description	Type	Length	Primary Key
CommitDate	Date to complete reminder	Date/Time	8	
FromTime	Earliest time to handle the reminder	Date/Time	8	
ToTime	Reminder must be completed by	Date/Time	8	
ReminderInfo	Description of the reminder	Text	100	
ReminderNote	Notes about the reminder	Memo		
Complete	Reminder completed?	Yes/No	1	

tlkpActionsServer

Field Name	Description	Type	Length	Primary Key
ActionID	Unique action identifier	AutoNumber	4	Yes
Name	Name of the action	Text	255	
Description	Description of the action	Memo		
Inactive	This action marked inactive?	Yes/No	1	

tlkpCaseCategoriesServer

Field Name	Description	Type	Length	Primary Key
CategoryID	Unique issue category	AutoNumber	4	Yes
Category1	Primary category for the issue	Text	100	
Category2	Secondary category for the issue	Text	100	
Category3	Final category for the issue	Text	100	
CategoryDesc	Category definition	Text	255	
DetailReq	Employee must enter details for a case in this category?	Yes/No	1	
DetailDesc	Details to be entered	Text	100	
Inactive	Category is inactive?	Yes/No	1	

tlkpEmployeesServer

Field Name	Description	Type	Length	Primary Key
EmployeeID	Unique employee identifier	AutoNumber	4	Yes
EmployeeName	Employee first name and last name for display	Text	50	
EmployeeFirst	Employee first name	Text	50	
EmployeeLast	Employee last name	Text	50	
EmployeeClass	Employee classification	Text	50	
Inactive	Employee is inactive?	Yes/No	1	
EmployeePhone	Employee phone number	Text	20	

Field Name	Description	Type	Length	Primary Key
Extension	Employee extension number	Text	8	
EmployeeEmail	Employee e-mail address	Text	255	
PermissionID	Permission level granted to this employee	Long Integer	4	
Login	Employee login ID	Text	50	
Password	Employee password	Text	15	

tlkpPermissionLevelsServer

Field Name	Description	Type	Length	Primary Key
PermissionID	Unique permission ID	AutoNumber	4	Yes
PermissionValue	Numeric permission value (higher = greater permission)	Long Integer	4	
PermissionLevel	Name of the permission level	Text	50	
Description	Permission level description	Text	255	

tlkpProductCategoriesServer

Field Name	Description	Type	Length	Primary Key
ProductCategoryID	Unique product category identifier	AutoNumber	4	Yes
CategoryName	The name of the product category	Text	50	
Inactive	Indicates whether the product category is currently active in the database	Yes/No	1	

tlkpProductsServer

Field Name	Description	Type	Length	Primary Key
ProductID	Unique product identifier	AutoNumber	4	Yes
ProductName	The name of the product	Text	50	
ProductCategoryID	The category that the product belongs to	Long Integer	4	
Description	A brief description of the product	Text	255	
Inactive	Indicates whether the product is active	Yes/No	1	

tlkpProductsWarrantiesServer

Field Name	Description	Type	Length	Primary Key
ProductWarrantyID	Unique product/warranty identifier	AutoNumber	4	Yes
ProductID	Related product	Long Integer	4	
WarrantyID	Related warranty	Long Integer	4	
Comments	Comments about the product/ warranty combination	Text	50	
Inactive	Is this warranty inactive?	Yes/No	1	

tlkpWarrantiesServer

Field Name	Description	Type	Length	Primary Key
WarrantyID	Unique warranty identifier	AutoNumber	4	Yes
WarrantyName	The name of the warranty	Text	50	
WarrantyDesc	Description of the warranty	Text	255	
WarrantyLength	Length in days	Long Integer	4	
Inactive	The warranty active status	Yes/No	1	

Registration Management

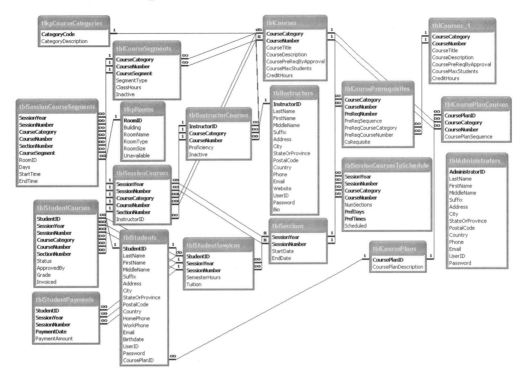

Figure B-4   The Registration Management tables and relationships.

Note   The tblCourses and tblCourses_1 tables shown in Figure B-4 are the same table. Access includes a second copy with a numeric suffix when you define more than one relationship between two tables.

tblAdministrators

Field Name	Description	Type	Length	Primary Key
AdministratorID	Unique administrator identifier	Long Integer	4	Yes
LastName	Administrator last name	Text	50	
FirstName	Administrator first name	Text	50	
MiddleName	Administrator middle name	Text	30	
Suffix	Administrator name suffix	Text	30	
Address	Administrator address	Text	255	
City	Administrator city	Text	50	
StateOrProvince	Administrator state or province	Text	20	

Field Name	Description	Type	Length	Primary Key
PostalCode	Administrator postal code	Text	20	
Country	Administrator country	Text	50	
Phone	Administrator phone	Text	30	
Email	Administrator e-mail address	Hyperlink		
UserID	Administrator logon user ID	Text	20	
Password	Administrator logon password	Text	20	

tblCoursePlanCourses

Field Name	Description	Type	Length	Primary Key
CoursePlanID	Unique course plan identifier	Integer	2	Yes
CourseCategory	Course category	Text	3	Yes
CourseNumber	Course number	Integer	2	Yes
CoursePlanSequence	Sequence number; student may take one of several courses with the same sequence	Integer	2	

tblCoursePlans

Field Name	Description	Type	Length	Primary Key
CoursePlanID	Unique course plan identifier	Integer	2	Yes
CoursePlanDescription	Description of the certificate plan	Text	100	

tblCoursePrerequisites

Field Name	Description	Type	Length	Primary Key
CourseCategory	Course category that has a prerequisite	Text	3	Yes
CourseNumber	Course number that has a prerequisite	Integer	2	Yes
PreReqNumber	Unique ID of the prerequisite within course category and number	Integer	2	Yes
PreReqSequence	Sequence of this prerequisite; "or" prerequisites have the same sequence number	Long Integer	4	
PreReqCourseCategory	Category of the course that is a prerequisite	Text	3	
PreReqCourseNumber	Course number of the course that is a prerequisite	Integer	2	
CoRequisite	Is taking this course concurrently a co-requisite?	Yes/No	1	

tblCourses

Field Name	Description	Type	Length	Primary Key
CourseCategory	Course category	Text	3	Yes
CourseNumber	Course number	Integer	2	Yes
CourseTitle	Course title	Text	75	
CourseDescription	Course description	Memo		
CoursePreReqByApproval	Can course prerequisites be satisfied by instructor approval?	Yes/No	1	
CourseMaxStudents	Maximum number of students in this course	Integer	2	
CreditHours	Credit hours for this course	Integer	2	

tblCourseSegments

Field Name	Description	Type	Length	Primary Key
CourseCategory	Course category	Text	3	Yes
CourseNumber	Course number	Integer	2	Yes
CourseSegment	Course segment number	Integer	2	Yes
SegmentType	Segment type: lecture, discussion, lab	Integer	2	
ClassHours	Class hours for this segment	Decimal	8	
Inactive	Is this segment no longer valid for this course?	Yes/No	1	

tblInstructorCourses

Field Name	Description	Type	Length	Primary Key
InstructorID	Unique instructor identifier	Long Integer	4	Yes
CourseCategory	Course category	Text	3	Yes
CourseNumber	Course number	Integer	2	Yes
Proficiency	Instructor proficiency rating for this course	Integer	2	
Inactive	Is this instructor no longer actively teaching this course?	Yes/No	1	

tblInstructors

Field Name	Description	Type	Length	Primary Key
InstructorID	Unique instructor identifier	Long Integer	4	Yes
LastName	Instructor last name	Text	50	
FirstName	Instructor first name	Text	50	
MiddleName	Instructor middle name	Text	30	

Field Name	Description	Type	Length	Primary Key
Suffix	Instructor name suffix	Text	30	
Address	Instructor address	Text	255	
City	Instructor city	Text	50	
StateOrProvince	Instructor state or province	Text	20	
PostalCode	Instructor postal code	Text	20	
Country	Instructor country	Text	50	
Phone	Instructor phone	Text	30	
Email	Instructor e-mail address	Hyperlink		
Website	Instructor Web site	Hyperlink		
UserID	Instructor logon user ID	Text	20	
Password	Instructor logon password	Text	20	
Bio	Instructor short bio	Memo		

tblSessionCourses

Field Name	Description	Type	Length	Primary Key
SessionYear	Year this course session scheduled	Integer	2	Yes
SessionNumber	Session semester: Spring, Summer, Fall	Integer	2	Yes
CourseCategory	Course category	Text	3	Yes
CourseNumber	Course number	Integer	2	Yes
SectionNumber	Section number	Integer	2	Yes
InstructorID	Instructor for this section	Long Integer	4	

tblSessionCourseSegments

Field Name	Description	Type	Length	Primary Key
SessionYear	Year this course session scheduled	Integer	2	Yes
SessionNumber	Session semester: Spring, Summer, Fall	Integer	2	Yes
CourseCategory	Course category	Text	3	Yes
CourseNumber	Course number	Integer	2	Yes
SectionNumber	Section number	Integer	2	Yes
CourseSegment	Course segment number	Integer	2	Yes
RoomID	ID of the room where this section course segment is taught	Long Integer	4	
Days	Days of the week this section course segment is taught	Integer	2	
StartTime	Start time of the class	Date/Time	8	
EndTime	End time of the class	Date/Time	8	

tblSessionCoursesToSchedule

Field Name	Description	Type	Length	Primary Key
SessionYear	Year this course session scheduled	Integer	2	Yes
SessionNumber	Session semester: Spring, Summer, Fall	Integer	2	Yes
CourseCategory	Course category	Text	3	Yes
CourseNumber	Course number	Integer	2	Yes
NumSections	Number of sections to schedule for this course	Integer	2	
PrefDays	Preferred days of the week course should be taught	Integer	2	Yes
PrefTimes	Preferred time of day to schedule the sections	Integer	2	Yes
Scheduled	This course has been scheduled	Yes/No	1	

tblSessions

Field Name	Description	Type	Length	Primary Key
SessionYear	Year this course session scheduled	Integer	2	Yes
SessionNumber	Session semester: Spring, Summer, Fall	Integer	2	Yes
StartDate	First day of class for the session	Date/Time	8	
EndDate	Last day of class for the session	Date/Time	8	

tblStudentCourses

Field Name	Description	Type	Length	Primary Key
StudentID	Unique student identifier	Long Integer	4	Yes
SessionYear	Year this course scheduled	Integer	2	Yes
SessionNumber	Semester: Spring, Summer, Fall	Integer	2	Yes
CourseCategory	Course category	Text	3	Yes
CourseNumber	Course number	Integer	2	Yes
SectionNumber	Section number	Integer	2	Yes
Status	Enrollment status	Integer	2	
ApprovedBy	ID of instructor who approved this enrollment	Long Integer	4	
Grade	Final grade for this course	Decimal	8	
Invoiced	Course has been invoiced?	Yes/No	1	

tblStudentInvoices

Field Name	Description	Type	Length	Primary Key
StudentID	Unique student identifier	Long Integer	4	Yes
SessionYear	Year this student enrolled	Integer	2	Yes
SessionNumber	Semester: Spring, Summer, Fall	Integer	2	Yes
SemesterHours	Total semester hours	Decimal	8	
Tuition	Tuition owed for the semester	Currency	8	

tblStudentPayments

Field Name	Description	Type	Length	Primary Key
StudentID	Unique student identifier	Long Integer	4	Yes
SessionYear	Year this student enrolled	Integer	2	Yes
SessionNumber	Semester: Spring, Summer, Fall	Integer	2	Yes
PaymentDate	Date payment was made	Date/Time	8	Yes
PaymentAmount	Amount of payment	Currency	8	

tblStudents

Field Name	Description	Type	Length	Primary Key
StudentID	Unique student identifier	Long Integer	4	Yes
LastName	Student last name	Text	50	
FirstName	Student first name	Text	50	
MiddleName	Student middle name	Text	30	
Suffix	Student name suffix	Text	20	
Address	Student address	Text	255	
City	Student city	Text	50	
StateOrProvince	Student state or province	Text	20	
PostalCode	Student postal code	Text	20	
HomePhone	Student home phone	Text	30	
WorkPhone	Student work phone	Text	30	
Email	Student e-mail address	Hyperlink		
Birthdate	Student birth date	Date/Time	8	
UserID	Student logon user ID	Text	20	
Password	Student logon password	Text	20	
CoursePlanID	Primary student course plan	Integer	2	

tlkpCourseCategories

Field Name	Description	Type	Length	Primary Key
CategoryCode	Course category	Text	3	Yes
CategoryDescription	Course category description	Text	50	

tlkpRooms

Field Name	Description	Type	Length	Primary Key
RoomID	Unique room identifier	Long Integer	4	Yes
Building	Name of building	Text	50	
RoomName	Name of room in building	Text	50	
RoomType	Room type: lecture, discussion, lab	Integer	2	
RoomSize	Max students in this room	Integer	2	
Unavailable	Is this room not currently available?	Yes/No	1	

Appendix C
Function Reference

Finding all the most useful functions in Help can be difficult at best. Following is a list of functions, categorized by type, that you might need to use. The tables list the function name and a brief description of what the function does. You can easily find details about the particular function syntax in Help once you know the function name.

Table C-1   Arithmetic Functions

Name	Description
Abs	Returns the absolute value of a number.
Asc	Returns the integer value of a character.
Atn	Returns the arctangent of a number.
Cos	Returns the cosine of a number that is an angle specified in radians.
DDB	Returns a Double value containing the depreciation of a value for a specific time period.
Exp	Returns the value of the base of the natural logarithm (e) raised to the exponent you supply. See also Log.
Fix	Returns the value of the number you supply truncated to an integer. If the number is negative, Fix returns the first integer that is greater than or equal to the number. See also Int.
FV	Calculates the future value of an annuity.
Int	Returns the value of the number you supply truncated to an integer. If the number is negative, Int returns the first integer that is less than or equal to the number. See also Fix.
IPmt	Returns the interest payment for a given period of an annuity.

Table C-1   **Arithmetic Functions**

Name	Description
IRR	Returns the internal rate of return for a series of periodic cash flows.
LBound	Returns the lowest available subscript for the array and dimension you specify. See also UBound.
Log	Returns the natural logarithm of the number you supply. See also Exp.
MIRR	Returns the modified internal rate of return for a series of periodic cash flows.
NPer	Returns the number of payment periods for an annuity.
NPV	Returns the net present value of an investment.
Pmt	Returns the payment required for an annuity.
PPmt	Returns the amount applied to principal for a given payment period of an annuity.
PV	Returns the present value of an annuity.
Rate	Returns the interest rate of an annuity.
Rnd	Returns a random number.
Round	Rounds a number to the specified number of decimal places.
Sin	Returns the sine of a number that is an angle specified in radians.
SLN	Returns the straight-line depreciation of an asset for a single period.
Sqr	Returns the square root of a number.
SYD	Returns the sum-of-the-years' digits depreciation of an asset.
Tan	Returns the tangent of a number that is an angle specified in radians.
UBound	Returns the highest available subscript for the array and dimension you specify. See also LBound.

Table C-2   **Conversion Functions**

Name	Description
CBool	Evaluates an expression and returns True (−1) or False (0).
CByte	Converts a value to Byte data type.
CCur	Converts a value to Currency data type.
CDate	Converts a value to Date/Time data type.
CDbl	Converts a value to Double data type.
CDec	Converts a value to Decimal data type.
CInt	Converts a value to Integer data type. The function rounds fractions.
CLng	Converts a value to Long Integer data type. The function rounds fractions.

Table C-2   **Conversion Functions**

Name	Description
CSng	Converts a value to Single data type.
CStr	Converts a value to a String data type. A Null value generates an error. Boolean values convert to Yes or No. Dates convert to a string in your system's short date format.
CVar	Converts a value to a Variant data type. If the value is a number, the value must be in the ranges valid for CDbl.
Val	Converts the numbers found in a string to a valid numeric data type.

Table C-3   **Date/Time Functions**

Name	Description
Date	Returns the current system date as a Variant data type.
DateAdd	Adds a specified interval to a date value.
DateDiff	Finds the difference between two date/time values in the interval you specify.
DatePart	Returns a requested portion of a date (second, minute, hour, week, weekday, day, day of year, month, quarter, or year).
DateSerial	Returns a date value calculated from supplied integer year, month, and day values. The year value must be between 100 and 9999.
DateValue	Returns the date portion of a date/time value.
Day	Returns the day portion of a date/time value. See also DatePart.
Hour	Returns the hour portion of a date/time value. See also DatePart.
Minute	Returns the minute portion of a date/time value. See also DatePart.
Month	Returns the numeric month portion of a date/time value. See also DatePart.
MonthName	Returns the name of the month of a date/time value.
Now	Returns the current system date and time as a Variant data type.
Second	Returns the seconds portion of a date/time value. See also DatePart.
Time	Returns the current system time as a Variant data type.
Timer	Returns a Double data type containing the number of seconds elapsed since midnight, accurate to .01 second.
TimeSerial	Returns a time value calculated from supplied integer hour, minute, and second values.
TimeValue	Returns the time portion of a date/time value.
WeekDay	Returns the integer day of the week from a date/time value. Sunday is 1, Monday is 2, etc.
WeekDayName	Returns the name of the day from a date/time value.
Year	Returns the year portion of a date/time value. See also DatePart.

Table C-4   **Logic Functions**

Name	Description
Choose	Returns a value from a list based on an integer index in the first argument.
IIf	Evaluates the first argument for True/False. If True, the function evaluates the second argument; otherwise, the function evaluates the third argument.
IsArray	Returns True if the argument you supply is an array.
IsDate	Returns True if the argument you supply can be converted to a date.
IsEmpty	Returns True if the Variant argument you supply has never been initialized.
IsError	Returns True if the number you supply is a valid error value.
IsMissing	Returns True if an optional argument to your Sub or Function procedure has not been supplied.
IsNull	Returns True if the argument you supply is the Null value. Note that you cannot compare a variable to the constant Null (If A = Null Then...).
IsObject	Returns True if the argument you supply is an object variable.
Sgn	Returns an indication whether the number you supply is negative, positive, or zero.
StrComp	Compares two strings. You can optionally specify a comparison that is binary or case-sensitive. (Default string comparison in Access is not case-sensitive.)
Switch	Accepts a series of pairs of expressions (primary and secondary). The primary expression of each pair must be an expression that can be evaluated to True or False. Evaluates the expressions left to right and returns the secondary expression for the first primary expression that evaluates to True.
TypeName	Returns the data type of the variable or expression you supply as a spelled out name of the data type. See also VarType.
VarType	Returns an integer code indicating the data type of the variable or expression you supply. See also TypeName.

Table C-5   **String Functions**

Name	Description
Chr	Returns the character value of an integer character code.
Format	Returns a string containing the value you supply, formatted according to the format string you specify.
FormatCurrency	Formats the number you supply as a currency string.
FormatDateTime	Formats the date/time value you supply as a date and/or time string.
FormatNumber	Formats the number you supply as a string with the specified decimal places and negative indicator characters. See also Str.
FormatPercent	Multiplies the number you supply by 100 and returns a string with a trailing percent (%) sign.

Table C-5   **String Functions**

Name	Description
Hex	Returns a string containing the hexadecimal (base 16) value of the number you supply.
InStr	Returns the integer offset position of a search string within another string, searching the target string from the beginning.
InStrRev	Returns the integer offset position of a search string within another string, searching the target string from the end.
Join	Concatenates the one-dimensional array you supply into a single string separated by the delimiter you specify. See also Split.
LCase	Converts a string to all lowercase characters. See also UCase and StrConv.
Left	Returns the requested number of leftmost characters from a string.
Len	Returns the current length of a string.
LTrim	Returns a string with any leading blanks removed from the string you specify.
Mid	Returns the specified number of characters starting from a specified position in the middle of a string.
Oct	Returns a string containing the octal (base 8) value of the number you supply.
Partition	Returns a string range name for a numeric variable based on the range start, stop, and interval values you supply.
Replace	Examines a string you supply and returns a string with all occurrences of one string replaced by another string.
Right	Returns the requested number of rightmost characters from a string.
RTrim	Returns a string with any trailing blanks removed from the string you specify.
Space	Returns a string containing the specified number of spaces.
Split	Returns a zero-based one-dimensional array. It fills the array with the substrings it finds by parsing a string you supply with a delimiter you specify. See also Join.
Str	Converts a number to a string. See also FormatNumber and Format.
StrConv	Converts a string according to the method you specify. Options include all uppercase, all lowercase, and proper case. See also LCase and UCase.
StrReverse	Returns a string in which the order of characters in the string you supply is reversed.
String	Returns a string of the length you specify filled with the character that you supply.
Trim	Returns a string with any leading and trailing blanks removed from the string you specify.
UCase	Converts a string to all uppercase characters. See also LCase and StrConv.

Table C-6   User Interface/File System Functions

Name	Description
Command	Returns the string of characters following the /cmd switch in the command or shortcut you used to start your application.
CurDir	Returns the current path or the current path on the specified drive.
Dir	Returns a file name based on a supplied path and search criteria. After calling Dir once with a path argument and criteria, you can call Dir without arguments to fetch additional files in the path that also meet the criteria. Dir returns a zero length string when no more files meet the criteria.
FileDateTime	Returns the create date or the last modification date of the file path you specify.
FileLen	Returns the size of the file path you specify.
GetAttr	Returns the attributes of the file or path you specify.
InputBox	Prompts the user with a message you supply and returns the user response.
MsgBox	Displays a message you supply in a dialog box and returns an indication of which button the user clicked in response.
RGB	Returns the RGB value based on red, green, and blue values you supply.
Shell	Executes the program you specify.

Understanding SQL

Underlying every query in Microsoft Access is the SQL database command language. Although you can design most queries using the simple Access design grid (or the view, function, or stored procedure designer in an Access project file), Access stores every query you design as an SQL command. When you use one of the designers, Access creates the SQL for you. However, for advanced types of queries that use the results of a second query as a comparison condition, you need to know SQL in order to define the second query (called a *subquery*). Also, you cannot use the design grid to construct all the types of queries Access is capable of handling; you must use SQL for some of them.

How to Use This Appendix

This appendix contains two major sections: SQL select queries and SQL action queries. Within the first section, you can find keywords used in the SQL language in alphabetical order. You can also find entries for the basic building blocks you need to understand and use in various clauses: Column-Name, Expression, Search-Condition, and Sub-query. If you're new to SQL, you might want to study these building block topics first. You can then study the major clauses of a SELECT statement in the order in which they appear in a SELECT statement: PARAMETERS, SELECT, FROM, WHERE, GROUP BY, HAVING, UNION, and ORDER BY.

In the second section, you can find a discussion of the syntax for the four types of queries that you can use to update your database, also in alphabetical order: DELETE, INSERT, SELECT INTO, and UPDATE. As you study these topics you'll find references to some of the major clauses that you'll also use in a SELECT statement. You can find the details about those clauses in the first section.

Note This appendix does not document all the syntax variants accepted by Access, but it does cover all the features of the SELECT statement and of action queries. Wherever possible, ANSI-standard syntax is shown to provide portability across other databases that also support some form of SQL. You might notice that Access modifies the ANSI-standard syntax to a syntax that it prefers after you define and save a query. You can find some of the examples shown in the following pages in the InventoryData.mdb sample database. When an example is in the sample database, you'll find the name of the sample query in italics immediately preceding the query in the text. For a discussion of the syntax conventions used in this appendix, see the Introduction to this book.

SQL Select Queries

The SELECT statement forms the core of the SQL database language. You use the SELECT statement to select or retrieve rows and columns from database tables. The SELECT statement syntax contains six major clauses: SELECT, FROM, WHERE, GROUP BY, HAVING, and ORDER BY.

In an Access desktop database (.mdb), Microsoft Access implements four significant extensions to the standard language: TRANSFORM, to allow you to build crosstab queries; IN, to allow you to specify a remote database connection or to specify column names in a crosstab query; DISTINCTROW in a SELECT statement, to limit the rows returned from the <*table list*> to rows that have different primary key values in the tables that supply columns in the <*field list*>; and WITH OWNERACCESS OPTION in a SELECT statement, to let you design queries that can be run by users who are authorized to use the query, including those who have insufficient access rights to the tables referenced in the query.

Note When you save a query you have written in SQL in your database, Access often examines your SQL command and adds brackets or extra parentheses to make the command easier to parse and compile. In some cases, Access restates complex predicates or changes the ANSI-standard syntax to one it prefers. For this reason, the examples shown in the book might not exactly match what you see in the sample queries when you open them in SQL view. If you enter the SQL exactly as shown in the book, it will return the same result as the sample query you find in the database.

Aggregate Functions: Avg, Count, Max, Min, StDev, StDevP, Sum, Var, VarP

In a logical table defined by a SELECT statement or a subquery, an aggregate function creates a column value that is the numeric aggregate of the values in the expression or column name specified. You can use the GROUP BY clause to create an aggregate calculation for each group of rows selected from the underlying tables or queries.

The aggregate functions and their purposes are as follows:

Sum	Calculates the sum of all the values for this field in each group. You can specify this function only with number or currency fields.
Avg	Calculates the arithmetic average of all the values for this field in each group. You can specify this function only with number or currency fields. Access does not include any Null values in the calculation.
Min	Returns the lowest value found in this field within each group. For numbers, Min returns the smallest value. For text, Min returns the lowest value in collating sequence ("dictionary"* order), without regard to case. Access ignores Null values.
Max	Returns the highest value found in this field within each group. For numbers, Max returns the largest value. For text, Max returns the highest value in collating sequence ("dictionary"* order), without regard to case. Access ignores Null values.
Count	Returns the count of the rows in which the specified field is not a Null value. You can also enter the special expression COUNT(*) in the Field row to count all rows in each group, regardless of the presence of Null values.
StDev	Calculates the statistical standard deviation of all the values for this field in each group. You can specify this function only with number or currency fields. If the group does not contain at least two rows, Access returns a Null value.
Var	Calculates the statistical variance of all the values for this field in each group. You can specify this function only with number or currency fields. If the group does not contain at least two rows, Access returns a Null value.

* You can change the sort order for new databases you create by choosing Options from the Tools menu and selecting a new order from the **New database sort order** list on the General tab. The default value is General, which sorts your data according to the language specified for your operating system.

Syntax

`<aggregate function>([DISTINCT] {* | <expression>})`

Notes

The JET database engine does not support the DISTINCT keyword. You can use * only with the Count aggregate function.

You cannot use another aggregate function reference within the expression. If you use an SQL aggregate function in the select list of a SELECT statement, any other columns in the select list must be derived using an aggregate function, or the column name must appear in a GROUP BY clause. An expression must contain a reference to at least one column name, and the expression or column name must be a numeric data type for all aggregate functions except Count, Min, and Max.

Null values are not included in the calculation of the result. The data type of the result is generally the same as that of the expression or column name. If the expression or column name is an integer, the resulting average is truncated. For example, AVG(n)—where n is an integer and the values of n in the selected rows are equal to 0, 1, and 1—returns the value 0. The data type of the result of StDev, StDevP, Var, and VarP is a double-precision floating-point number. If there are not at least two members in a group, StdDev and Var return a Null value. StDevP and VarP return an estimate if there is at least one non-Null value in the group.

Examples

To find the average and maximum prices for items in the product catalog by category name, enter the following (qxmplCategoryAvgMaxPrice):

```
SELECT tblProducts.Category,
    Avg(tblProducts.SellPrice) AS AvgOfSellPrice,
    Max(tblProducts.SellPrice) AS MaxOfSellPrice
FROM tblProducts
GROUP BY tblProducts.Category;
```

To find the number of different prices for products in an Access desktop database (.mdb), create the following queries.

1. A query to find each unique price for the books in print (qxmplDistinctPrices):

   ```
   SELECT DISTINCT tblProducts.SellPrice
   FROM tblProducts;
   ```

2. A query to find the number of rows in the first query (qxmplCountDistinctPrice):

   ```
   SELECT COUNT(*) As CountOfDistinctPrices
   FROM qxmplDistinctPrices;
   ```

In Microsoft SQL Server, you can calculate the distinct prices directly.

```
SELECT COUNT(DISTINCT tblProducts.SellPrice)
FROM tblProducts;
```

To find the largest order from any customer within each postal code, create the following queries.

1. A query to calculate the total for each order (qxmplOrderTotals):

   ```
   SELECT tblOrders.OrderID, tblOrders.OrderDate, tblCustomers.CustomerID,
   tblCustomers.City, tblCustomers.Region, tblCustomers.PostalCode,
   Sum([Quantity]*[Price]) AS OrderTot
   FROM (tblCustomers
     INNER JOIN tblOrders
       ON tblCustomers.CustomerID = tblOrders.CustomerID)
     INNER JOIN tblOrderProducts
       ON tblOrders.OrderID = tblOrderProducts.OrderID
   GROUP BY tblOrders.OrderID, tblOrders.OrderDate, tblCustomers.CustomerID,
   tblCustomers.City, tblCustomers.Region, tblCustomers.PostalCode;
   ```

2. A query on the first query to find the largest order (qxmplLargestOrderByPostalCode):

```
SELECT qxmplOrderTotals.PostalCode,
Max(qxmplOrderTotals.OrderTot)
AS MaxOfOrderTot
FROM qxmplOrderTotals
GROUP BY qxmplOrderTotals.PostalCode;
```

To find the product with the lowest price in each category, enter the following (qxmplLowestPricePerCategory):

```
SELECT tblProducts.ProductID, tblProducts.Category, tblProducts.Description,
tblProducts.SellPrice
FROM tblProducts
WHERE tblProducts.SellPrice =
  (Select MIN(SellPrice)
    FROM tblProducts AS P2
    WHERE P2.Category = tblProducts.Category);
```

> **Note** In this example, the subquery makes a reference to the tblProducts table in the SELECT statement by referring to a column in the outer table (tblProducts.ProductID). This forces the subquery to be evaluated for every row in the SELECT statement, which might not be the most efficient way to achieve the desired result. (This type of subquery is also called a *correlated sub-query*.) Whenever possible, the database query plan optimizer solves the query efficiently by reconstructing the query internally as a join between the source specified in the FROM clause and the subquery. In many cases, you can perform this reconstruction yourself, but the purpose of the query might not be as clear as when you state the problem using a subquery.

To find the standard deviation and the population standard deviation of the price of products, grouped by product category, enter the following (qxmplStdDev):

```
SELECT tblProducts.Category, Count(tblProducts.ProductID) AS CountOfProductID,
StDev(tblProducts.SellPrice) AS StDevOfSellPrice, StDevP(tblProducts.SellPrice) AS
StDevPOfSellPrice
FROM tblProducts
GROUP BY tblProducts.Category;
```

To find the total sales for each product, enter the following (qxmplTotalSalesByProduct):

```
SELECT tblProducts.ProductID, tblProducts.Description,
  Sum([Quantity]*[Price]) AS TotSales
FROM tblProducts
  INNER JOIN tblOrderProducts
    ON tblProducts.ProductID = tblOrderProducts.ProductID
GROUP BY tblProducts.ProductID, tblProducts.Description;
```

Also see Expression, GROUP BY Clause, HAVING Clause, IN Predicate, SELECT Statement, Subquery, and WHERE Clause in this appendix.

BETWEEN Predicate

Compares a value with a range of values.

Syntax

`<expression> [NOT] BETWEEN <expression> AND <expression>`

Notes

The data types of all expressions must be compatible. Comparison of alphanumeric literals (strings) in Access or a default installation of Microsoft SQL Server Data Engine (MSDE) is case-insensitive.

Let a, b, and c be expressions. Then, in terms of other predicates, a BETWEEN b AND c is equivalent to the following:

`(a >= b) AND (a <= c)`

a NOT BETWEEN b AND c is equivalent to the following:

`(a < b) OR (a > c)`

The result is undefined if any of the expressions is Null.

Example

To determine whether the SellPrice is greater than or equal to $100 and less than or equal to $500, enter the following:

`SellPrice BETWEEN 100 AND 500`

Also see Expression, SELECT Statement, Subquery, and WHERE Clause in this appendix.

Column-Name

Specifies the name of a column in an expression.

Syntax

```
[[[]{table-name | select-query-name |
  correlation-name}[]].][] field-name[]]
```

Notes

You must supply a qualifier to the field name only if the name is ambiguous within the context of the query or subquery (for example, if the same field name appears in more than one table or query listed in the FROM clause).

The *table-name*, *select-query-name*, or *correlation-name* that qualifies the field name must also appear in the FROM clause of the query or subquery. If a table or query has a correlation name, you must use the alias, not the actual name of the table or query. (A *correlation name* is an alias you assign to the table or query name in the FROM clause.)

You must supply the enclosing brackets in an Access desktop database (.mdb) only if the name contains an embedded blank or the name is also a reserved word (such as *select*, *table*, *name*, or *date*). Embedded blanks and enclosing brackets are not supported in the ANSI standard. You can use names that have embedded blanks in SQL Server by including a SET QUOTED IDENTIFIER ON command and then enclosing each nonstandard name in double quotes ("). When you open a query from an Access project, Access automatically includes this command in the command stream that it sends to SQL Server.

Also see FROM Clause, SELECT Statement, and Subquery in this appendix.

Examples

To specify a field named Customer Last Name in a table named Customer List in an Access desktop database (.mdb), use the following:

```
[Customer List].[Customer Last Name]
```

To reference the same column in a view, stored procedure, or function for SQL Server, use the following:

```
"Customer List"."Customer Last Name"
```

To specify a field named StreetAddress that appears in only one table or query in the FROM clause, enter:

```
StreetAddress
```

Comparison Predicate

Compares the values of two expressions or the value of an expression and a single value returned by a subquery.

Syntax

```
<expression> {= | <> | > | < | >= | <=}
  {<expression> | <subquery>}
```

Notes

Comparison of strings in Access or a default installation of Microsoft SQL Server Data Engine (MSDE) is case-insensitive. The data type of the first expression must be compatible with the data type of the second expression or with the value returned by the subquery. If the subquery returns no rows or more than one row, an error is returned except when the select list of the subquery is COUNT(*), in which case the return of multiple rows yields one value. If either the first expression, the second expression, or the subquery evaluates to Null, the result of the comparison is undefined.

Examples

To determine whether the allocation date was in 2003, enter the following:

```
Year(DateAlloc) = 2003
```

To determine whether the invoice ID is not equal to 50, enter the following:

```
InvoiceID <> 50
```

To determine whether a product was allocated to an order in the first half of the year, enter the following:

```
Month(DateAlloc) < 7
```

To determine whether the date allocated in the current row is less than the earliest order for ProductID 1, enter the following:

```
DateAlloc <
  (SELECT MIN(DateAlloc)
    FROM tblOrderProducts
    WHERE ProductID = 1)
```

Also see Expression, SELECT Statement, Subquery, and WHERE Clause in this appendix.

EXISTS Predicate

Tests the existence of at least one row that satisfies the selection criteria in a subquery.

Syntax

```
EXISTS (<subquery>)
```

Notes

The result cannot be undefined. If the subquery returns at least one row, the result is True; otherwise, the result is False. The subquery need not return values for this predicate; therefore, you can list any columns in the select list that exist in the underlying tables or queries or use an asterisk (*) to denote all columns.

Example

To find all customers who placed an order in the month of October 2004, enter the following (qxmplCustomersOrderedOct2004):

```
SELECT tblCustomers.CustomerID, tblCustomers.CustomerName
FROM tblCustomers
WHERE EXISTS
  (SELECT tblOrders.*
    FROM tblOrders
    WHERE tblOrders.OrderDate BETWEEN #10/1/2004# AND #10/31/2004#
      AND tblOrders.CustomerID = tblCustomers.CustomerID);
```

> **Note**   In this example, the inner subquery makes a reference to the tblCustomers table in the SELECT statement by referring to a column in the outer table (tblCustomers.CustomerID). This forces the subquery to be evaluated for every row in the SELECT statement, which might not be the most efficient way to achieve the desired result. (This type of subquery is also called a *correlated subquery*.) Whenever possible, the database query plan optimizer solves the query efficiently by reconstructing the query internally as a join between the source specified in the FROM clause and the subquery. In many cases, you can perform this reconstruction yourself, but the purpose of the query might not be as clear as when you state the problem using a subquery.

Also see Expression, SELECT Statement, Subquery, and WHERE Clause in this appendix.

Expression

Specifies a value in a predicate or in the select list of a SELECT statement or subquery.

Syntax

```
[+ | -] {function | [(]<expression>[)] | literal |
  column-name} [{+ | - | * | / | \ | ^ | MOD | &}
  {function | [(]<expression>[)] | literal |
  column-name}]...
```

Notes

function

> You can specify one of the SQL aggregate functions: Avg, Count, Max, Min, StDev, StDevP, Sum, Var, or VarP; however, you cannot use an SQL aggregate function more than once in an expression. In a desktop database (.mdb), you can also use any of the functions built into Access or any function you define using Visual Basic. In a project file (.adp), you can use any of the SQL Server built-in functions.

[(]<*expression*>[)]

You can construct an expression from multiple expressions separated by operators. Use parentheses around expressions to clarify the evaluation order. (See the examples later in this section.)

literal

You can specify a numeric or an alphanumeric constant. You must enclose an alpha-numeric constant in single quotation marks in a project file (.adp) or single or double quotation marks in a desktop database (.mdb). To include an apostrophe in an alpha-numeric constant, enter the apostrophe character twice in the literal string; or, in a desktop database, you can also choose to enclose the literal string in double quotation marks. If the expression is numeric, you must use a numeric constant. In a desktop data-base (.mdb), enclose a date/time literal within pound (#) signs, and any date/time literal you enter in SQL view must follow the U.S. mm/dd/yy (or mm/dd/yyyy) format. This might be different than the format you use in the query design grid, which must follow the format defined for Short Date Style in your regional settings in Windows Control Panel. In a project file (.adp), you must enclose date or time literals in single quotes, and you can use any specification inside the quotes that SQL Server can recognize as a date or time. For example, SQL Server recognizes any of the following as a valid date literal:

```
'April 15, 2004'
'15 April, 2004'
'040415'
'04/15/2004'
'2004-04-15'
```

column-name

You can specify the name of a column in a table or a query. You can use a column name only from a table or query that you've specified in the FROM clause of the statement. If the expression is arithmetic, you must use a column that contains numeric data. If the same column name appears in more than one of the tables or queries included in the query, you must fully qualify the name with the query name, table name, or correlation name, as in *TableA.Column1*. When a table or column name contains a blank or is a reserved word (such as *select, table, name,* or *date*) in a desktop database (.mdb), you must enclose each name in brackets, as in *[Table A].[Column 1]*. When a table or column name contains a blank or is a reserved word in a project file (.adp), you must enclose each name in double quotes, as in *"Table A"."Column 1"*. Note that when you open a query in an Access project, Access includes the required SET QUOTED IDENTIFIER ON command in the command string. However, if you execute a SQL Server query from a desktop database with a pass-through query, you must include this command in the pass-through query. Although in ANSI SQL (and SQL Server) you can reference an *output-column-name* anywhere within an expression, Microsoft Access supports this only within the <*field list*> of a SELECT statement. Access does not support references to named expression columns in GROUP BY, HAVING, ORDER BY, or WHERE clauses.

You must repeat the expression rather than use the column name. See SELECT Statement later in this appendix for details about output-column-name.

+ | - | * | / | \ | ^ | MOD

You can combine multiple numeric expressions with arithmetic operators that specify a calculation. If you use arithmetic operators, all expressions within an expression must evaluate as numeric data types.

&

You can concatenate alphanumeric expressions by using the & operator in a desktop database (.mdb). In a project file (.adp), use + as the concatenation operator.

Also see Column-Name, Predicates (BETWEEN, Comparison, EXISTS, IN, LIKE NULL, and Quantified), SELECT Statement, Subquery, and UPDATE Statement in this appendix.

Examples

To specify the average of a column named COST, enter the following:

`AVG(COST)`

To specify one-half the value of a column named PRICE, enter the following:

`(PRICE * .5)`

To specify a literal for 3:00 PM on March 1, 2004, in a desktop database (.mdb), enter the following:

`#3/1/2004 3:00PM#`

To specify a literal for 3:00 PM on March 1, 2004, in a project file (.adp), enter the following:

`'March 1, 2004 3:00PM'`

To specify a character string that contains the name *Acme Mail Order Company,* enter the following:

`'Acme Mail Order Company'`

To specify a character string that contains a possessive noun (requiring an embedded apostrophe), enter the following:

`'Andy''s Hardware Store'`

or in a desktop database you can also enter:

`"Andy's Hardware Store"`

In a desktop database (.mdb), to specify a character string that is the concatenation of fields from a table named Customer List containing a person's first and last name with an intervening blank, enter the following:

```
[Customer List].[First Name] & " " &
   [Customer List].[Last Name]
```

In a project file (.adp), to specify a character string that is the concatenation of fields from a table named Customer List containing a person's first and last name with an intervening blank, enter the following:

```
"Customer List"."First Name" + ' ' +
   "Customer List"."Last Name"
```

FROM Clause

Specifies the tables or queries that provide the source data for your query.

Syntax

```
FROM {table-name [[AS] correlation-name] |
    select-query-name [[AS] correlation-name] |
    (<select-statement>) AS correlation-name |
    <joined table>},...
  [IN <"source database name"> <[source connect string]>]
```

where <joined table> is

```
({table-name [[AS] correlation-name] |
  select-query-name [[AS] correlation-name] |
  <joined table>}
{INNER | {{LEFT | RIGHT | FULL} [OUTER]} JOIN
  {table-name [[AS] correlation-name] |
  select-query-name [[AS] correlation-name] |
  <joined table>}
ON <join-specification>)
```

where <joined table> is the result of another join operation, and where <join-specification> is a search condition made up of predicates that compare fields in the first table, query, or joined table with fields in the second table, query, or joined table.

Notes

You can supply a correlation name for each table name or query name and use this correlation name as an alias for the full table name when qualifying column names in the <field-list>, in the <join-specification>, or in the WHERE clause and subclauses. If you're joining a table or a query to itself, you must use correlation names to clarify which copy of the table or query you're referring to in the select list, join criteria, or selection criteria. If a table name or a query name is also an SQL reserved word (for example, Order), you must enclose the name in brackets. In SQL Server, you must enclose the name of a table or query that is also an SQL reserved word in double quotes. Note that when you open a query in an Access project, Access includes the required SET QUOTED IDENTIFIER ON command in the command string. However, if you execute a query in SQL Server from a desktop database with a pass-through query, you must include this command in the pass-through query.

Use INNER JOIN to return all the rows that match the join specification in both tables. Use LEFT [OUTER] JOIN to return all the rows from the first logical table (where *logical table* is any table, query, or joined table expression) joined on the join specification with any matching rows from the second logical table. When no row matches in the second logical table, the database returns Null values for the columns from that table. Conversely, RIGHT [OUTER] JOIN returns all the rows from the second logical table joined with any matching rows from the first logical table. A FULL [OUTER] JOIN returns all rows from the tables or queries on both sides of the join, but only SQL Server supports this operation.

When you use only *equals* comparison predicates in the join specification, the result is called an *equi-join*. The joins that Access displays in the design grid are equi-joins. Access cannot display in the design grid any join specification that uses any comparison operator other than equals (=)—also called a *nonequi-join*. If you want to define a join on a nonequals comparison (<, >, <>, <=, or >=) in Access, you must define the query using the SQL view. The query designer in an Access project can display nonequi-joins. When you join a table to itself using an equals comparison predicate, the result is called a *self-join*.

SQL Server also supports a CROSS JOIN (with no ON clause). A CROSS JOIN produces the same result as listing table or query names separated by commas with no JOIN specification (a Cartesian product).

If you include multiple tables in the FROM clause with no JOIN specification but do include a predicate that matches fields from the multiple tables in the WHERE clause, the database in most cases optimizes how it solves the query by treating the query as a JOIN. For example:

```
SELECT *
  FROM TableA, TableB
  WHERE TableA.ID = TableB.ID
```

is solved by the database as though you had specified

```
SELECT *
  FROM TableA
    INNER JOIN TableB
    ON TableA.ID = TableB.ID
```

You cannot update fields in a table by using a recordset opened on the query, the query datasheet, or a form bound to a multiple-table query where the join is expressed using a table-list and a WHERE clause. In many cases you can update the fields in the underlying tables when you use the JOIN syntax.

When you list more than one table or query without join criteria, the source is the *Cartesian product* of all the tables. For example, *FROM TableA, TableB* instructs the database to fetch all the rows of TableA matched with all the rows of TableB. Unless you specify other restricting criteria, the number of logical rows that the database processes could equal the number of rows in TableA *times* the number of rows in TableB. When you include WHERE or HAVING clauses, the database returns the rows in which the selection criteria specified in those clauses evaluate to True.

Example

To select information about all vendors and the products they sell and any products allocated on October 15, 2004, enter the following (qxmplAllVendorsAndProductsAllocOct15):

```
SELECT tblVendors.VendorID, tblVendors.VendorName, tblProducts.ProductID,
tblProducts.Category, tblProducts.Description, ProdOct15.Quantity, ProdOct15.DateAlloc
FROM ((tblVendors
  INNER JOIN tblVendorProducts
  ON tblVendors.VendorID = tblVendorProducts.VendorID)
  INNER JOIN tblProducts
  ON tblProducts.ProductID = tblVendorProducts.ProductID)
  LEFT JOIN
    (SELECT tblOrderProducts.ProductID, tblOrderProducts.Quantity,
      tblOrderProducts.DateAlloc
    FROM tblOrderProducts
    WHERE tblOrderProducts.DateAlloc = #10/15/2004#) AS ProdOct15
  ON tblProducts.ProductID = ProdOct15.ProductID;
```

> **Note**   When you open the above query in Design view and switch to SQL view, you'll find that Access saves the inner <select-statement> with brackets as:
>
> ```
> [SELECT tblOrderProducts.ProductID, tblOrderProducts.Quantity,
> tblOrderProducts.DateAlloc
> FROM tblOrderProducts
> WHERE tblOrderProducts.DateAlloc = #10/15/2004#]. AS ProdOct15
> ```
>
> This is the internal syntax supported by the JET database engine, but the query designer accepts the ANSI-standard syntax shown above.

Also see HAVING Clause, IN Clause, SELECT Statement, Subquery, and WHERE Clause in this appendix.

GROUP BY Clause

In a SELECT statement, specifies the columns used to form groups from the rows selected. Each group contains identical values in the specified column(s). In Access, you use the GROUP BY clause to define a totals query. You must also include a GROUP BY clause in a crosstab query in Access. (See TRANSFORM Statement for details.)

Syntax

`GROUP BY` *column-name,...*

Notes

A column name in the GROUP BY clause can refer to any column from any table in the FROM clause, even if the column is not named in the select list. If the GROUP BY clause is preceded by a WHERE clause, the database creates the groups from the rows selected after it applies the WHERE clause. When you include a GROUP BY clause in a SELECT statement, the select list must be made up of either SQL aggregate functions or column names specified in the GROUP BY clause.

Example

To find the average and maximum prices for products by category name, enter the following (qxmplCategoryAvgMaxPrice):

```
SELECT tblProducts.Category,
    Avg(tblProducts.SellPrice) AS AvgOfSellPrice,
    Max(tblProducts.SellPrice) AS MaxOfSellPrice
FROM tblProducts
GROUP BY tblProducts.Category;
```

Also see Aggregate Functions, HAVING Clause, Search-Condition, SELECT Statement, and WHERE Clause in this appendix.

HAVING Clause

Specifies groups of rows that appear in the logical table (a recordset) defined by a SELECT statement. The search condition applies to columns specified in a GROUP BY clause, to columns created by aggregate functions, or to expressions containing aggregate functions. If a group doesn't pass the search condition, the database does not include it in the logical table.

Syntax

`HAVING` *<search-condition>*

Notes

If you do not include a GROUP BY clause, the select list must be formed by using one or more of the SQL aggregate functions.

The difference between the HAVING clause and the WHERE clause is that WHERE *<search-condition>* applies to single rows before they are grouped, while HAVING *<search-condition>* applies to groups of rows.

If you include a GROUP BY clause preceding the HAVING clause, the *<search-condition>* applies to each of the groups formed by equal values in the specified columns. If you do not include a GROUP BY clause, the *<search-condition>* applies to the entire logical table defined by the SELECT statement.

Example

To find the order amount for all orders that total more than $1,500, enter the following (qxmplTotalOrders>1500):

```
SELECT tblCustomers.CustomerName, tblOrders.OrderID,
  tblOrders.OrderDate, Sum([Quantity]*[Price]) AS OrderTotal
FROM (tblCustomers
  INNER JOIN tblOrders
    ON tblCustomers.CustomerID = tblOrders.CustomerID)
  INNER JOIN tblOrderProducts
    ON tblOrders.OrderID = tblOrderProducts.OrderID
GROUP BY tblCustomers.CustomerName, tblOrders.OrderID, tblOrders.OrderDate
HAVING (((Sum([Quantity]*[Price]))>1500));
```

Also see Aggregate Functions, GROUP BY Clause, Search-Condition, SELECT Statement, and WHERE Clause in this appendix.

IN Clause

In a desktop database (.mdb), specifies the source for the tables in a query. The source can be another Access database; a dBASE, Microsoft FoxPro, or Paradox file; or any database for which you have an ODBC driver. This is an Access extension to standard SQL.

Syntax

```
IN <"source database name"> <[source connect string]>
```

Enter *"source database name"* and *[source connect string]*. (Be sure to include the quotation marks and the brackets.) If your database source is Access, enter only *"source database name"*. Enter these parameters according to the type of database to which you are connecting, as shown in Table D-1.

Table D-1   IN Parameters for Various Database Types

Database Name	Source Database Name	Source Connect String
Access	*"drive:\path\filename"*	(none)
dBASE III	*"drive:\path"*	[dBASE III;]
dBASE IV	*"drive:\path"*	[dBASE IV;]
dBASE 5	*"drive:\path"*	[dBASE 5.0;]
Paradox 3.*x*	*"drive:\path"*	[Paradox 3.x;]

Table D-1   IN Parameters for Various Database Types

Database Name	Source Database Name	Source Connect String
Paradox 4.*x*	*"drive:\path"*	[Paradox 4.x;]
Paradox 5.*x*	*"drive:\path"*	[Paradox 5.x;]
FoxPro 2.0	*"drive:\path"*	[FoxPro 2.0;]
FoxPro 2.5	*"drive:\path"*	[FoxPro 2.5;]
FoxPro 2.6	*"drive:\path"*	[FoxPro 2.6;]
FoxPro 3.0	*"drive:\path"*	[FoxPro 3.0;]
ODBC	(none)	[ODBC; DATABASE= *defaultdatabase*; UID=*user*; PWD= *password*; DSN= *datasourcename*]

Notes

The IN clause applies to all tables referenced in the FROM clause and any subqueries in your query. You can refer to only one external database within a query, but if the IN clause points to a database that contains more than one table, you can use any of those tables in your query. If you need to refer to more than one external file or database, attach those files as tables in Access and use the logical attached table names instead.

For ODBC, if you omit the DSN= or DATABASE= parameters, Access prompts you with a dialog box showing available data sources so that you can select the one you want. If you omit the UID= or PWD= parameters and the server requires a user ID and password, Access prompts you with a login dialog box for each table accessed.

For dBASE, Paradox, and FoxPro databases, you can provide an empty string ("") for *source database name* and provide the path or dictionary file name using the DATABASE= parameter in *source connect string* instead, as in

```
"[dBase IV; DATABASE=C:\MyDB\dbase.dbf]"
```

Example

In a desktop database (.mdb), to retrieve the Company Name field in the Northwind Traders sample database without having to attach the Customers table, you could enter the following:

```
SELECT Customers.CompanyName
FROM Customers
IN "C:\My Documents\Shortcut to NORTHWIND.MDB";
```

Also see SELECT Statement in this appendix.

IN Predicate

Determines whether a value is equal to any of the values or is unequal to all values in a set returned from a subquery or provided in a list of values.

Syntax

```
<expression> [NOT] IN {(<subquery>) |
  ({literal},...) |<expression>}
```

Notes

Comparison of strings in Access or a default installation of Microsoft SQL Server Data Engine (MSDE) is case-insensitive. The data types of all expressions, literals, and the column returned by the subquery must be compatible. If the expression is Null or any value returned by the subquery is Null, the result is undefined. In terms of other predicates, *<expression>* IN *<expression>* is equivalent to the following:

```
<expression> = <expression>
```

<expression> IN (*<subquery>*) is equivalent to the following:

```
<expression> = ANY (<subquery>)
```

<expression> IN (*a*, *b*, *c*,...), where *a*, *b*, and *c* are literals, is equivalent to the following:

```
(<expression> = a) OR (<expression> = b) OR
  (<expression> = c) ...
```

<expression> NOT IN ... is equivalent to the following:

```
NOT (<expression> IN ...)
```

Examples

To test whether Region is on the West Coast of the United States, enter the following:

```
[Region] IN ('CA', 'OR', 'WA')
```

To list all customers who have not purchased Sasquatch Ale, enter the following (qxmplCustomersNotAle):

```
SELECT tblCustomers.CustomerID, tblCustomers.CustomerName
FROM tblCustomers
WHERE tblCustomers.CustomerID Not In
  (SELECT CustomerID
  FROM (tblOrders
    INNER JOIN tblOrderProducts
      ON tblOrders.OrderID = tblOrderProducts.OrderID)
    INNER JOIN
```

```
            ON tblProducts tblProducts.ProductID = tblOrderProducts.ProductID
        WHERE tblProducts.Description = "Sasquatch Ale");
```

Also see Expression, Quantified Predicate, SELECT Statement, Subquery, and WHERE Clause in this appendix.

LIKE Predicate

Searches for strings that match a pattern.

Syntax

column-name [NOT] LIKE *match-string* [ESCAPE *escape-character*]

Notes

String comparisons in Access or a default installation of Microsoft SQL Server Data Engine (MSDE) are case-insensitive. If the column specified by *column-name* contains a Null, the result is undefined. Comparison of two empty strings or an empty string with the special asterisk (*) character (% character in SQL Server) evaluates to True.

You provide a text string as a *match-string* value that defines what characters can exist in which positions for the comparison to be true. Access and SQL Server understand a number of wild-card characters (shown in Table D-2) that you can use to define positions that can contain any single character, zero or more characters, or any single digit.

Table D-2   Wildcard Characters for String Comparisons

Desktop Database	Project File	Meaning
?	_	Any single character
*	%	Zero or more characters (used to define leading, trailing, or embedded strings that don't have to match any of the pattern characters)
#	[0-9]	Any single digit

You can also specify in the match string that any particular position in the text or memo field can contain only characters from a list that you provide. To define a list of comparison characters for a particular position, enclose the list in brackets ([ ]). You can specify a range of characters within a list by entering the low-value character, a hyphen, and the high-value character, as in [A-Z] or [3-7]. If you want to test a position for any characters *except* those in a list, start the list with an exclamation point (!) in a desktop database or a caret symbol (^) in a project file.

If you want to test for one of the special characters *, ?, #, and [, (and _ or % in a project file) you must enclose the character in brackets. Alternatively, in a project file, you can specify an ESCAPE clause. When you place the escape character in the match string, the database ignores the character and uses the following character as a literal comparison value. So, you can include the escape character immediately preceding one of the special characters to use the special character as a literal comparison instead of a pattern character. Desktop databases do not support the ESCAPE clause.

Examples

In a desktop database, to determine whether a customer's name is at least four characters long and begins with *Smi*, enter the following:

```
tblCustomers.CustomerName LIKE "Smi?*"
```

In a project file, write the above test as follows:

```
tblCustomers.CustomerName LIKE 'Smi_%'
```

In a desktop database, to test whether PostalCode is a valid Canadian postal code, enter the following:

```
PostalCode LIKE "[A-Z]#[A-Z] #[A-Z]#"
```

In a project file, to test whether a character column named Discount ends in 5%, enter the following:

```
Discount LIKE '%5$%' ESCAPE '$'
```

Also see Expression, SELECT Statement, Subquery, and WHERE Clause in this appendix.

NULL Predicate

Determines whether the expression evaluates to Null. This predicate evaluates only to True or False and will not evaluate to undefined.

Syntax

```
<expression> IS [NOT] NULL
```

Example

To determine whether the customer fax number column contains the Null value, enter the following:

```
tblCustomers.FaxNumber IS NULL
```

Also see Expression, SELECT Statement, Subquery, and WHERE Clause in this appendix.

ORDER BY Clause

Specifies the sequence of rows to be returned by a SELECT statement or a subquery.

Syntax

ORDER BY {*column-name* | *column-number* [ASC | DESC]},...

Notes

You use column names or relative output column numbers to specify the columns on whose values the rows returned are ordered. (If you use relative output column numbers, the first output column is 1.) You can specify multiple columns in the ORDER BY clause. When you specify multiple columns, the list is ordered primarily by the first column. If rows exist for which the values of that column are equal, they are ordered by the next column in the ORDER BY list, and so on. When multiple rows contain the matching values in all the columns in the ORDER BY clause, the database can return the matching rows in any order. You can specify ascending (ASC) or descending (DESC) order for each column. If you do not specify ASC or DESC, ASC is assumed. Using an ORDER BY clause in a SELECT statement is the only means of defining the sequence of the returned rows.

When you include the DISTINCT keyword or use the UNION query operator in the SELECT statement, the ORDER BY clause can include only columns specified in the SELECT clause. Otherwise, you can include any column in the logical table returned by the FROM clause.

To use ORDER BY in a view, function, or stored procedure in SQL Server, you must also include the TOP keyword in the SELECT clause. To fetch and sort all rows, specify TOP 100 PERCENT.

Examples

To calculate the total product sales for all orders and list the result for each customer and order in descending sequence by order total, enter the following (qxmplOrderTotalSorted):

```
SELECT TOP 100 PERCENT tblCustomers.CustomerID, tblCustomers.CustomerName,
  tblOrders.OrderID, tblOrders.OrderDate,
  SUM([Quantity]*[Price]) AS OrderTotal
FROM (tblCustomers
  INNER JOIN tblOrders
    ON tblCustomers.CustomerID = tblOrders.CustomerID)
  INNER JOIN tblOrderProducts
    ON tblOrders.OrderID = tblOrderProducts.OrderID
GROUP BY tblCustomers.CustomerID, tblCustomers.CustomerName,
  tblOrders.OrderID, tblOrders.OrderDate
ORDER BY SUM([Quantity]*[Price]) DESC;
```

> **Note**   The TOP keyword is optional in a desktop database (.mdb). In SQL Server, you can also specify the calculated column alias name in the ORDER BY clause, such as ORDER BY Invoice-Total DESC. In a desktop database, you must repeat the calculation expression as shown in the example.

In a desktop database (.mdb), to create a mailing list for all customers and all vendors, sorted in ascending order by postal code, enter the following (qxmplSortedMailingList):

```
SELECT tblCustomers.CustomerName, tblCustomers.Address, tblCustomers.City,
    tblCustomers.Region, tblCustomers.PostalCode, tblCustomers.Country
  FROM tblCustomers
UNION ALL
SELECT tblVendors.VendorName, tblVendors.VendorAddress, tblVendors.VendorCity,
    tblVendors.VendorRegion, tblVendors.VendorPostal, tblVendors.Country
  FROM tblVendors
ORDER BY 5;
```

> **Note**   If you decide to use column names in the ORDER BY clause of a UNION query, the database derives the column names from the names returned by the first query. In this example, you could change the ORDER BY clause to read ORDER BY PostalCode.

To create the same mailing list in a view or in-line function in a SQL Server database, enter the following:

```
SELECT TOP 100 PERCENT U.CustomerName, U.Address, U.City,
    U.Region, U.PostalCode, U.Country
FROM
(SELECT tblCustomers.CustomerName, tblCustomers.Address, tblCustomers.City,
    tblCustomers.Region, tblCustomers.PostalCode, tblCustomers.Country
  FROM tblCustomers
UNION ALL
SELECT tblVendors.VendorName, tblVendors.VendorAddress, tblVendors.VendorCity,
    tblVendors.VendorRegion, tblVendors.VendorPostal, tblVendors.Country
  FROM tblVendors) AS U
ORDER BY 5;
```

Notice that you must UNION the rows first and then select and sort them all.

Also see INSERT Statement, SELECT Statement, and UNION Query Operator in this appendix.

PARAMETERS Declaration

In a desktop database (.mdb), precedes an SQL statement to define the data types of any parameters you include in the query. You can use parameters to prompt the user for data values or to match data values in controls on an open form. In a SQL Server database, you declare the parameters for a function or procedure as part of the CREATE statement.

Syntax

PARAMETERS {[*parameter-name*] *data-type*},... ;

Notes

If your query prompts the user for values, each parameter name should describe the value that the user needs to enter. For example, [Print invoices from orders on date:] is much more descriptive than [Enter date:]. If you want to refer to a control on an open form, use the format:

[Forms]![Myform]![Mycontrol]

To refer to a control on a subform, use the format:

[Forms]![Myform]![Mysubformcontrol].[Form]![ControlOnSubform]

Valid data type entries are shown in Table D-3.

Example

To create a parameter query that summarizes the sales and the cost of goods for all items allocated in a given month, enter the following (qxmplMonthSalesParameter):

```
PARAMETERS [Year to summarize:] Short, [Month to summarize:] Short;
SELECT tblProducts.Description,
    Format([DateAlloc],"mmmm""", """yyyy") AS AllocateMonth,
    Sum([Quantity]*[Price]) AS TotalSales
FROM tblProducts
  INNER JOIN tblOrderProducts
  ON tblProducts.ProductID = tblOrderProducts.ProductID
WHERE (Year([DateAlloc]) = [Year to summarize:])
  AND (Month([DateAlloc]) = [Month to summarize:])
GROUP BY tblProducts.Description, Format([DateAlloc],"mmmm""", """yyyy");
```

Table D-3   SQL Parameter Data Types and Access Equivalents

SQL Parameter Data Type	Equivalent Access Data Type
Char, Text(n)*, VarChar	Text
Text*, LongText, LongChar, Memo	Memo
TinyInt, Byte, Integer1	Number, Byte
SmallInt, Short, Integer2	Number, Integer
Integer, Long, Integer4	Number, Long Integer

Table D-3   SQL Parameter Data Types and Access Equivalents

SQL Parameter Data Type	Equivalent Access Data Type
Real, Single, Float4, IEEESingle	Number, Single
Float, Double, Float8, IEEEDouble	Number, Double
Decimal, Numeric	Number, Decimal
UniqueIdentifier, GUID	Number, Replication ID
DateTime, Date, Time	Date/Time
Money, Currency	Currency
Bit, Boolean, Logical, YesNo	Yes/No
Image, LongBinary, OLEObject	OLE Object
Text, LongText, LongChar, Memo	Hyperlink[†]
Binary, VarBinary	Binary[‡]

*   Text with a length descriptor of 255 or less maps to the Access Text data type. Text with no length descriptor is a Memo field.

†   Internally, Access stores a hyperlink in a Memo field, but sets a custom property to indicate a Hyperlink format.

‡   The JET database engine supports a Binary data type (raw hexadecimal), but the Access user interface does not. If you encounter a non-Access table that has a data type that maps to Binary, you will be able to see the data type in the table definition, but you won't be able to successfully edit this data in a datasheet or form. You can manipulate binary data in Visual Basic.

Also see SELECT Statement in this appendix.

Quantified Predicate

Compares the value of an expression to some, any, or all values of a single column returned by a subquery.

Syntax

```
<expression> {= | <> | > | < | >= | <=}
    [SOME | ANY | ALL] (<subquery>)
```

Notes

String comparisons in Access or a default installation of Microsoft SQL Server Data Engine (MSDE) are case-insensitive. The data type of the expression must be compatible with the data type of the value returned by the subquery.

When you use ALL, the predicate is True if the comparison is True for all the values returned by the subquery. If the expression or any of the values returned by the subquery is Null, the result is undefined. When you use SOME or ANY, the predicate is True if the comparison is True for any of the values returned by the subquery. If the expression is a Null value, the result is undefined. If the subquery returns no values, the predicate is False.

Examples

To find the products whose price is greater than all the products in the Confections category, enter the following (qxmplProductPrice>AllConfections):

```
SELECT tblProducts.ProductID, tblProducts.Description, tblProducts.SellPrice
  FROM tblProducts
  WHERE tblProducts.SellPrice > All
    (SELECT tblProducts.SellPrice
     FROM tblProducts
     WHERE tblProducts.Category = 'Confections');
```

To find the products whose price is greater than any of the products in the Confections category, enter the following (qxmplProductPrice>AnyConfections):

```
SELECT tblProducts.ProductID, tblProducts.Description, tblProducts.SellPrice
  FROM tblProducts
  WHERE tblProducts.SellPrice > Any
    (SELECT tblProducts.SellPrice
     FROM tblProducts
     WHERE tblProducts.Category = 'Confections');
```

Also see Expression, SELECT Statement, Subquery, and WHERE Clause in this appendix.

Search-Condition

Describes a simple or compound predicate that is True, False, or undefined for a given row or group. Use a search condition in the WHERE clause of a SELECT statement, a subquery, a DELETE statement, or an UPDATE statement. You can also use a search condition within the HAVING clause in a SELECT statement. The search condition defines the rows that should appear in the resulting logical table or the rows that should be acted upon by the change operation. If the search condition is True when applied to a row, that row is included in the result.

Syntax

```
[NOT] {predicate | (<search-condition>)}
  [{AND | OR | XOR | EQV | IMP}
  [NOT] {predicate | (<search-condition>)}]...
```

Notes

If you include a comparison predicate in the form of *<expression> comparison-operator <subquery>*, the database returns an error if the subquery returns no rows. The database effectively applies any subquery in a predicate within a search condition to each row of the table that is the result of the previous clauses. The database then evaluates the result of the subquery with regard to each candidate row.

The order of evaluation of the Boolean operators is NOT, AND, OR, XOR (exclusive OR), EQV (equivalence), and IMP (implication). You can include additional parentheses to influence the order in which the Boolean expressions are processed. SQL Server does not support the XOR, EQV, or IMP logical operators.

> **Tip** You can express AND and OR Boolean operations directly by using the design grid in Microsoft Access. If you need to use XOR, EQV, or IMP, you must create an expression in the Field row, clear the Show check box, and set the Criteria row to <> False.

When you use the Boolean operator NOT, the following holds: NOT (True) is False, NOT (False) is True, and NOT (undefined) is undefined. The result is undefined whenever a predicate references a Null value. If a search condition evaluates to False or undefined when applied to a row, the row is not selected. The database returns True, False, or undefined values as a result of applying Boolean operators (AND, OR, XOR, EQV, IMP) against two predicates or search conditions according to the tables shown in Figure D-1.

Example

In a desktop database, to find all products for which the unit price is greater than $25 and for which the category description is equal to Condiments or the product has an order multiple of 1, but not both, enter the following (qxmplXOR):

```
SELECT tblProducts.ProductID, tblProducts.Description,
  tblProducts.Category, tblProducts.SellPrice, tblProducts.OrderMultiple
FROM tblProducts
WHERE (tblProducts.SellPrice > 25)
  AND ((tblProducts.Category = 'Condiments')
        XOR (tblProducts.OrderMultiple = 1));
```

In a project file, to find all products for which the unit price is greater than $25 and for which the category description is equal to Condiments or the product has an order multiple of 1, but not both, enter the following:

```
SELECT tblProducts.ProductID, tblProducts.Description,
  tblProducts.Category, tblProducts.SellPrice, tblProducts.OrderMultiple
FROM tblProducts
WHERE (tblProducts.SellPrice > 25)
    AND ((tblProducts.Category = 'Condiments')
    OR (tblProducts.OrderMultiple = 1))
    AND NOT ((tblProducts. Category = 'Condiments')
    AND (tblProducts. OrderMultiple = 1));
```

Also see DELETE Statement, Expression, HAVING Clause, Predicates (BETWEEN, Comparison, EXISTS, IN, LIKE NULL, and Quantified), SELECT Statement, Subquery, UPDATE Statement, and WHERE Clause in this appendix.

AND	True	False	Undefined (Null)
True	True	False	True
False	False	False	False
Undefined (Null)	Null	False	Null

OR	True	False	Undefined (Null)
True	True	True	True
False	True	False	Null
Undefined (Null)	True	Null	Null

XOR	True	False	Undefined (Null)
True	False	True	Null
False	True	False	Null
Undefined (Null)	Null	Null	Null

EQV	True	False	Undefined (Null)
True	True	False	Null
False	False	True	Null
Undefined (Null)	Null	Null	Null

IMP [(Not A) OR B]	True	False	Undefined (Null)
True	True	False	Null
False	True	True	True
Undefined (Null)	True	Null	Null

Figure D-1   Truth tables for SQL Boolean operators.

SELECT Statement

Fetches data from one or more tables or queries to create a logical table (recordset). The items in the select list identify the columns or calculated values to return from the source tables to the new recordset. You identify the tables to be joined in the FROM clause, and you identify the rows to be selected in the WHERE clause. Use GROUP BY to specify how to form groups for an aggregate query, and use HAVING to specify which resulting groups should be included in the result.

Syntax

```
SELECT [ALL | DISTINCT | DISTINCTROW | TOP number
     [PERCENT]] <select-list> FROM {table-name [[AS] correlation-name] |
   select-query-name [[AS] correlation-name] |
   (<select-statement>) AS correlation-name |
   <joined table>},...
 [IN <"source database name"> <[source connect
     string]>]
 [WHERE <search-condition>]
 [GROUP BY column-name,...]
 [HAVING <search-condition>]
 [UNION [ALL] <select-statement>]
 [ORDER BY {column-name [ASC | DESC]},...]
 [WITH OWNERACCESS OPTION];
```

where <select-list> is

```
{* | {<expression> [AS output-column-name] |
  table-name.* | query-name.* |
  correlation-name.*},...}
```

and where <joined table> is

```
({table-name [[AS] correlation-name] |
  select-query-name [[AS] correlation-name] |
  (<select-statement>) AS correlation-name |
  <joined table>}
{INNER | {{LEFT | RIGHT | FULL} [OUTER]} JOIN
  {table-name [[AS] correlation-name] |
  select-query-name [[AS] correlation-name] |
  (<select-statement>) AS correlation-name |
  <joined table>}
ON <join-specification>)
```

Notes

You can supply a correlation name for each table name or query name and use this correlation name as an alias for the full table name when qualifying column names in the <select-list>, in the <join-specification>, or in the WHERE clause and subclauses. If you're joining a table or a query to itself, you must use correlation names to clarify which copy of the table or query you're referring to in the select list, join criteria, or selection criteria. If a table name or a query name is also an SQL reserved word (for example, *Order*), you must enclose the name in brackets. In SQL Server, you must enclose the name of a table or query that is also an SQL reserved word in double quotes. Note that when you open a query in an Access project, Access includes the required SET QUOTED IDENTIFIER ON command in the command string. However, if you execute a query in SQL Server from a desktop database with a pass-through query, you must include this command in the pass-through query.

When you list more than one table or query without join criteria, the source is the *Cartesian product* of all the tables. For example, *FROM TableA, TableB* instructs the database to fetch all the rows of TableA matched with all the rows of TableB. Unless you specify other restricting criteria, the number of logical rows that the database processes could equal the number of rows in TableA *times* the number of rows in TableB. When you include WHERE or HAVING clauses, the database returns the rows in which the selection criteria specified in those clauses are True. See the FROM Clause topic for further details about specifying joins.

You can further define which rows the database includes in the output recordset by specifying ALL, DISTINCT, DISTINCTROW (in a desktop database only), TOP *n*, or TOP *n* PERCENT. ALL includes all rows that match the search criteria from the source tables, including potential duplicate rows. DISTINCT requests that the database return only rows that are different from any other row. You cannot update any columns in a query that uses DISTINCT because the database can't identify which of several potentially duplicate rows you intend to update.

DISTINCTROW (the default in Access version 7.0 and earlier) requests that Access return only rows in which the concatenation of the primary keys from all tables supplying output columns is unique. Depending on the columns you select, you might see rows in the result that contain duplicate values, but each row in the result is derived from a distinct combination of rows in the underlying tables. DISTINCTROW is significant only when you include a join in a query and do not include output columns from all tables. For example, the statement

```
SELECT tblCustomers.City
FROM tblCustomers
  INNER JOIN tblOrders
  ON tblCustomers.CustomerID = tblOrders.CustomerID
WHERE tblOrders.OrderDate BETWEEN #9/1/2004# AND #9/30/2004#;
```

returns 283 rows in the InventoryData.mdb sample database—one row for each order in September 2004. On the other hand, the following statement:

```
SELECT DISTINCTROW tblCustomers.City
FROM tblCustomers
  INNER JOIN tblOrders
  ON tblCustomers.CustomerID = tblOrders.CustomerID
WHERE tblOrders.OrderDate BETWEEN #9/1/2004# AND #9/30/2004#;
```

returns only 89 rows—one for each *distinct row* in the tblCustomers table, the only table with output columns. The equivalent of the second example in ANSI-standard SQL is as follows:

```
SELECT tblCustomers.City
FROM tblCustomers
WHERE tblCustomers.CustomerID
  IN (SELECT tblOrders.CustomerID
      FROM tblOrders
      WHERE tblOrders.OrderDate BETWEEN #9/1/2004# AND #9/30/2004#);
```

I suspect Microsoft implemented DISTINCTROW in version 1 because the first release of Access did not support subqueries.

Specify TOP *n* or TOP *n* PERCENT to request that the recordset contain only the first *n* or first *n* percent of rows. In general, you should specify an ORDER BY clause when you use TOP to indicate the sequence that defines which rows are first, or top. The parameter *n* must be an integer and must be less than or equal to 100 if you include the PERCENT keyword. If you do not include an ORDER BY clause, the sequence of rows returned is undefined. In a TOP query, if the *n*th and any rows immediately following the *n*th row are duplicates, the database returns the duplicates; thus, the recordset might have more than *n* rows. Note that if you specify an order, using TOP does not cause the query to execute any faster; the database must still solve the entire query, order the rows, and return the top rows.

When you include a GROUP BY clause, the select list must be made up of one or more of the SQL aggregate functions or one or more of the column names specified in the GROUP BY clause. A column name in a GROUP BY clause can refer to any column from any table in the FROM clause, even if the column is not named in the select list. If you want to refer to a calculated expression in the GROUP BY clause, you must assign an output column name to the expression in the select list and then refer to that name in the GROUP BY clause. If the GROUP BY clause is preceded by a WHERE clause, the database forms the groups from the rows selected after it applies the WHERE clause.

If you use a HAVING clause but do not include a GROUP BY clause, the select list must be formed using SQL aggregate functions. If you include a GROUP BY clause preceding the HAVING clause, the HAVING search condition applies to each of the groups formed by equal values in the specified columns. If you do not include a GROUP BY clause, the HAVING search condition applies to the entire logical table defined by the SELECT statement.

You use column names or relative output column numbers to specify the columns on whose values the rows returned are ordered. (If you use relative output column numbers, the first output column is 1.) You can specify multiple columns in the ORDER BY clause. When you specify multiple columns, the list is ordered primarily by the first column. If rows exist for which the values of that column are equal, they are ordered by the next column in the ORDER BY list, and so on. When multiple rows contain the matching values in all the columns in the ORDER BY clause, the database can return the matching rows in any order. You can specify ascending (ASC) or descending (DESC) order for each column. If you do not specify ASC or DESC, ASC is assumed. Using an ORDER BY clause in a SELECT statement is the only means of defining the sequence of the returned rows.

In a desktop database, the person running the query not only must have rights to the query but also must have the appropriate rights to the tables used in the query. (These rights include reading data to select rows and updating, inserting, and deleting data using the query.) If your application has multiple users, you might want to secure the tables so that no user has direct access to any of the tables and all users can still run queries defined by you. Assuming you're the owner of both the queries and the tables, you can deny access to the tables but allow access to the queries. To make sure that the queries run properly, you must add the WITH OWNERACCESS OPTION clause to allow users the same access rights as the table owner when accessing the data via the query.

Examples

To select information about all vendors and the products they sell and any products allocated on October 15, 2004, enter the following (qxmplAllVendorsAndProductsAllocOct15):

```
SELECT tblVendors.VendorID, tblVendors.VendorName, tblProducts.ProductID,
tblProducts.Category, tblProducts.Description, ProdOct15.Quantity, ProdOct15.DateAlloc
FROM ((tblVendors
  INNER JOIN tblVendorProducts
  ON tblVendors.VendorID = tblVendorProducts.VendorID)
  INNER JOIN tblProducts
  ON tblProducts.ProductID = tblVendorProducts.ProductID)
  LEFT JOIN
    (SELECT tblOrderProducts.ProductID, tblOrderProducts.Quantity,
      tblOrderProducts.DateAlloc
    FROM tblOrderProducts
    WHERE tblOrderProducts.DateAlloc = #10/15/2004#) AS ProdOct15
  ON tblProducts.ProductID = ProdOct15.ProductID;
```

> **Note** When you open the above query in Design view and switch to SQL view, you'll find that Access saves the inner <select-statement> with brackets as:
>
> ```
> [SELECT tblOrderProducts.ProductID, tblOrderProducts.Quantity,
> tblOrderProducts.DateAlloc
> FROM tblOrderProducts
> WHERE tblOrderProducts.DateAlloc = #10/15/2004#]. AS ProdOct15
> ```
>
> This is the internal syntax supported by the JET database engine, but the query designer accepts the ANSI-standard syntax shown above.

To find the average and maximum prices for items in the product catalog by category name, enter the following (qxmplCategoryAvgMaxPrice).

```
SELECT tblProducts.Category,
    Avg(tblProducts.SellPrice) AS AvgOfSellPrice,
    Max(tblProducts.SellPrice) AS MaxOfSellPrice
FROM tblProducts
GROUP BY tblProducts.Category;
```

To find the order amount for all orders that total more than $1,500, enter the following (qxmplTotalOrders>1500):

```
SELECT tblCustomers.CustomerName, tblOrders.OrderID,
  tblOrders.OrderDate, Sum([Quantity]*[Price]) AS OrderTotal
FROM (tblCustomers
  INNER JOIN tblOrders
    ON tblCustomers.CustomerID = tblOrders.CustomerID)
  INNER JOIN tblOrderProducts
    ON tblOrders.OrderID = tblOrderProducts.OrderID
GROUP BY tblCustomers.CustomerName, tblOrders.OrderID, tblOrders.OrderDate
HAVING (((Sum([Quantity]*[Price]))>1500));
```

To calculate the total product sales for all orders and list the result for each customer and order in descending sequence by order total, enter the following (qxmplOrderTotalSorted):

```
SELECT TOP 100 PERCENT tblCustomers.CustomerID, tblCustomers.CustomerName,
  tblOrders.OrderID, tblOrders.OrderDate,
  SUM([Quantity]*[Price]) AS OrderTotal
FROM (tblCustomers
  INNER JOIN tblOrders
    ON tblCustomers.CustomerID = tblOrders.CustomerID)
  INNER JOIN tblOrderProducts
    ON tblOrders.OrderID = tblOrderProducts.OrderID
GROUP BY tblCustomers.CustomerID, tblCustomers.CustomerName,
  tblOrders.OrderID, tblOrders.OrderDate
ORDER BY SUM([Quantity]*[Price]) DESC;
```

> **Note**   The TOP keyword is optional in a desktop database (.mdb). In SQL Server, you can also specify the calculated column alias name in the ORDER BY clause, such as ORDER BY Invoice-Total DESC. In a desktop database, you must repeat the calculation expression as shown in the example.

In a desktop database (.mdb), to create a mailing list for all customers and all vendors, sorted in ascending order by postal code, enter the following (qxmplSortedMailingList):

```
SELECT tblCustomers.CustomerName, tblCustomers.Address, tblCustomers.City,
    tblCustomers.Region, tblCustomers.PostalCode, tblCustomers.Country
  FROM tblCustomers
UNION ALL
SELECT tblVendors.VendorName, tblVendors.VendorAddress, tblVendors.VendorCity,
    tblVendors.VendorRegion, tblVendors.VendorPostal, tblVendors.Country
  FROM tblVendors
ORDER BY 5;
```

> **Note**   If you decide to use column names in the ORDER BY clause of a UNION query, the database derives the column names from the names returned by the first query. In this example, you could change the ORDER BY clause to read ORDER BY PostalCode.

To create the same mailing list in a view or in-line function in a Microsoft SQL Server database, enter the following:

```
SELECT TOP 100 PERCENT U.CustomerName, U.Address, U.City,
    U.Region, U.PostalCode, U.Country
FROM
(SELECT tblCustomers.CustomerName, tblCustomers.Address, tblCustomers.City,
    tblCustomers.Region, tblCustomers.PostalCode, tblCustomers.Country
  FROM tblCustomers
UNION ALL
SELECT tblVendors.VendorName, tblVendors.VendorAddress, tblVendors.VendorCity,
    tblVendors.VendorRegion, tblVendors.VendorPostal, tblVendors.Country
```

```
  FROM tblVendors) AS U
ORDER BY 5;
```

Notice that you must UNION the rows first and then select and sort them all.

Also see FROM Clause, GROUP BY Clause, HAVING Clause, INSERT Statement, Search-Condition, and UNION Query Operator in this appendix.

Subquery

Selects from a single column any number of values or no values at all for comparison in a predicate. You can also use a subquery that returns a single value in the select list of a SELECT clause.

Syntax

```
(SELECT [ALL | DISTINCT | DISTINCTROW | TOP number
      [PERCENT]] <select-list>
  FROM {table-name [[AS] correlation-name] |
    select-query-name [[AS] correlation-name] |
    <joined table>},...
  [WHERE <search-condition>]
  [GROUP BY column-name,...]
  [HAVING <search-condition>]
  [ORDER BY {column-name [ASC | DESC]},...])
```

where *select-list* is

```
{* | {<expression> | table-name.* | query-name.* | correlation-name.*}}
```

and where *<joined table>* is

```
({table-name [[AS] correlation-name] |
   select-query-name [[AS] correlation-name] |
   (<select-statement>) AS correlation-name |
   <joined table>}
{INNER | {{LEFT | RIGHT | FULL} [OUTER]} JOIN
   {table-name [[AS] correlation-name] |
   select-query-name [[AS] correlation-name] |
   (<select-statement>) AS correlation-name |
   <joined table>} ON <join-specification>)
```

Notes

You can use the special asterisk (*) character in the *<select-list>* of a subquery only when the subquery is used in an EXISTS predicate or when the FROM clause within the subquery refers to a single table or query that contains only one column.

You can supply a correlation name for each table name or query name and use this correlation name as an alias for the full table name when qualifying column names in the *<select-list>*, in the *<join-specification>*, or in the WHERE clause and subclauses. If you're joining a table or a query to itself, you must use correlation names to clarify which copy of the table or query you're referring to in the select list, join criteria, or selection criteria. You must also use a correlation name if one of the tables in the FROM clause is the same as a table in the outer query. If a table name or a query name is also an SQL reserved word (for example, *Order*), you must enclose the name in brackets. In SQL Server, you must enclose the name of a table or query that is also an SQL reserved word in double quotes. Note that when you open a query in an Access project, Access includes the required SET QUOTED IDENTIFIER ON command in the command string. However, if you execute a query in SQL Server from a desktop database with a pass-through query, you must include this command in the pass-through query.

When you list more than one table or query without join criteria, the source is the *Cartesian product* of all the tables. For example, *FROM TableA, TableB* instructs the database to fetch all the rows of TableA matched with all the rows of TableB. Unless you specify other restricting criteria, the number of logical rows that the database processes could equal the number of rows in TableA *times* the number of rows in TableB. When you include WHERE or HAVING clauses, the database returns the rows in which the selection criteria specified in those clauses are True. See the FROM Clause topic for further details about specifying joins.

You can further define which rows the database includes in the output recordset by specifying ALL, DISTINCT, DISTINCTROW (in a desktop database only), TOP *n*, or TOP *n* PERCENT. ALL includes all rows that match the search criteria from the source tables, including potential duplicate rows. DISTINCT requests that the database return only rows that are different from any other row.

DISTINCTROW (the default in Access version 7.0 and earlier) requests that Access return only rows in which the concatenation of the primary keys from all tables supplying output columns is unique. Depending on the columns you select, you might see rows in the result that contain duplicate values, but each row in the result is derived from a distinct combination of rows in the underlying tables. DISTINCTROW is significant only when you include a join in a query and do not include output columns from all tables. See the SELECT Statement topic for more information about DISTINCTROW.

Specify TOP *n* or TOP *n* PERCENT to request that the recordset contain only the first *n* or first *n* percent of rows. In general, you should specify an ORDER BY clause when you use TOP to indicate the sequence that defines which rows are first, or top. The parameter *n* must be an integer and must be less than or equal to 100 if you include the PERCENT keyword. If you do not include an ORDER BY clause, the sequence of rows returned is undefined. In a TOP query, if the *n*th and any rows immediately following the *n*th row are duplicates, the database returns the duplicates; thus, the recordset might have more than *n* rows. Note that if you specify an order, using TOP does not cause the query to execute any faster; the database must still solve the entire query, order the rows, and return the top rows.

In the search condition of the WHERE clause of a subquery, you can use an outer reference to refer to the columns of any table or query that is defined in the outer queries. You must qualify the column name if the table or query reference is ambiguous.

A column name in the GROUP BY clause can refer to any column from any table in the FROM clause, even if the column is not named in the *<select-list>*. If the GROUP BY clause is preceded by a WHERE clause, the database creates the groups from the rows selected after the application of the WHERE clause.

When you include a GROUP BY or HAVING clause in a SELECT statement, the select list must be made up of either SQL aggregate functions or column names specified in the GROUP BY clause. If a GROUP BY clause precedes a HAVING clause, the HAVING clause's search condition applies to each of the groups formed by equal values in the specified columns. If you do not include a GROUP BY clause, the HAVING clause's search condition applies to the entire logical table defined by the SELECT statement.

Examples

To find all customers who placed an order in the month of October, 2004, enter the following (qxmplCustomersOrderedOct2004):

```
SELECT tblCustomers.CustomerID, tblCustomers.CustomerName
FROM tblCustomers
WHERE EXISTS
  (SELECT tblOrders.*
    FROM tblOrders
    WHERE tblOrders.OrderDate BETWEEN #10/1/2004# AND #10/31/2004#
      AND tblOrders.CustomerID = tblCustomers.CustomerID);
```

> **Note**   In this example, the inner subquery makes a reference to the tblCustomers table in the SELECT statement by referring to a column in the outer table (tblCustomers.CustomerID). This forces the subquery to be evaluated for every row in the SELECT statement, which might not be the most efficient way to achieve the desired result. (This type of subquery is also called a *correlated subquery*.) Whenever possible, the database query plan optimizer solves the query efficiently by reconstructing the query internally as a join between the source specified in the FROM clause and the subquery. In many cases, you can perform this reconstruction yourself, but the purpose of the query might not be as clear as when you state the problem using a subquery.

To select customers who first placed an order before September 15, 2004, and list them in ascending order by postal code, enter the following (qxmplCustomersPurchaseBefore-15Sep2004):

```
SELECT TOP 100 PERCENT tblCustomers.CustomerName, tblCustomers.Address,
  tblCustomers.City, tblCustomers.Region, tblCustomers.PostalCode,
  tblCustomers.Country
FROM tblCustomers
```

```
WHERE #9/15/2004# >
  (SELECT Min(tblOrders.OrderDate)
   FROM tblOrders
   WHERE tblOrders.CustomerID = tblCustomers.CustomerID)
ORDER BY tblCustomers.PostalCode;
```

> **Note**   The preceding query also uses a correlated subquery.

To list all customers who have not purchased Sasquatch Ale, enter the following (qxmplCustomersNotAle):

```
SELECT tblCustomers.CustomerID, tblCustomers.CustomerName
FROM tblCustomers
WHERE tblCustomers.CustomerID Not In
  (SELECT CustomerID
  FROM (tblOrders
    INNER JOIN tblOrderProducts
      ON tblOrders.OrderID = tblOrderProducts.OrderID)
    INNER JOIN
      ON tblProducts tblProducts.ProductID = tblOrderProducts.ProductID
  WHERE tblProducts.Description = "Sasquatch Ale");
```

To find the products whose price is greater than any of the products in the Confections category, enter the following (qxmplProductPrice>AnyConfections):

```
SELECT tblProducts.ProductID, tblProducts.Description, tblProducts.SellPrice
  FROM tblProducts
  WHERE tblProducts.SellPrice > Any
    (SELECT tblProducts.SellPrice
     FROM tblProducts
     WHERE tblProducts.Category = 'Confections');
```

Also see Expression, Predicates (BETWEEN, Comparison, EXISTS, IN, LIKE NULL, and Quantified), and SELECT Statement in this appendix.

TRANSFORM Statement

In a desktop database, produces a crosstab query that lets you summarize a single value by using the values found in a specified column or in an expression as the column headers and using other columns or expressions to define the grouping criteria to form rows. The result looks similar to a spreadsheet and is most useful as input to a graph object. This is an Access extension to standard SQL.

Syntax

```
TRANSFORM <aggregate-function-expression>
  <select-statement> PIVOT <expression>
[IN (<column-value-list>)]
```

where *<aggregate-function-expression>* is an expression created with one of the aggregate functions, *<select-statement>* contains a GROUP BY clause, and *<column-value-list>* is a list of required values expected to be returned by the PIVOT expression, enclosed in quotes and separated by commas. (You can use the IN clause to force the output sequence of the columns.)

Notes

The *<aggregate-function-expression>* parameter is the value that you want to appear in the "body" of the crosstab datasheet. PIVOT *<expression>* defines the column or expression that provides the column headings in the crosstab result. You might, for example, use this value to provide a list of months with aggregate rows defined by product categories in the *<select-statement>* GROUP BY clause. You can use more than one column or expression in the SELECT statement to define the grouping criteria for rows.

Example

To produce a total sales amount for each month in the year 2005, categorized by product, enter the following (qxmpl2005SalesByProductXtab):

```
TRANSFORM Sum([Quantity]*[Price]) AS SumOfSales
SELECT tblProducts.ProductID, tblProducts.Description,
  Sum([Quantity]*[Price]) AS TotSales
FROM tblProducts
  INNER JOIN tblOrderProducts
  ON tblProducts.ProductID = tblOrderProducts.ProductID
GROUP BY tblProducts.ProductID, tblProducts.Description
PIVOT Format([DateAlloc],"mmm yyyy")
  IN ("Jan 2005","Feb 2005","Mar 2005","Apr 2005","May 2005",
      "Jun 2005","Jul 2005","Aug 2005","Sep 2005","Oct 2005",
      "Nov 2005","Dec 2005");
```

> **Note**   This example shows a special use of the IN keyword to define not only which months should be selected but also the sequence in which Access displays the months in the resulting recordset.

Also see GROUP BY Clause, HAVING Clause, SELECT Statement, and Total Functions in this appendix.

UNION Query Operator

Produces a result table that contains the rows returned by both the first SELECT statement and the second SELECT statement.

Syntax

```
<select-statement> UNION [ALL]
  <select-statement>
[ORDER BY {column-name | column-number
[ASC | DESC]},...]
```

Notes

When you specify ALL, the database returns all rows in both logical tables. When you do not specify ALL, the database eliminates duplicate rows. The tables returned by each *<select-statement>* must contain an equal number of columns, and each column must have identical attributes.

You must not use the ORDER BY clause in the *<select-statements>* that are joined by query operators; however, you can include a single ORDER BY clause at the end of a statement that uses one or more query operators. This action will apply the specified order to the result of the entire statement. The database derives the column names of the output from the column names returned by the first *<select-statement>*. If you want to use column names in the ORDER BY clause, be sure to use names from the first query. You can also use the output column numbers to define ORDER BY criteria.

In a project file, you can include the ORDER BY clause at the end of the statement in a stored procedure, but you cannot include this clause in a view or in-line function. To sort a UNION in a view or in-line function, you must create a view on the query containing the UNION and then sort the view. You can also embed the UNION query in a FROM clause of a query and then sort the result.

You can combine multiple SELECT statements using UNION to obtain complex results. You can also use parentheses to influence the sequence in which the database applies the operators, as shown here:

```
SELECT...UNION (SELECT...UNION SELECT...)
```

Example

In a desktop database (.mdb), to create a mailing list for all customers and all vendors, sorted in ascending order by postal code, enter the following (qxmplSortedMailingList):

```
SELECT tblCustomers.CustomerName, tblCustomers.Address, tblCustomers.City,
    tblCustomers.Region, tblCustomers.PostalCode, tblCustomers.Country
  FROM tblCustomers
UNION ALL
SELECT tblVendors.VendorName, tblVendors.VendorAddress, tblVendors.VendorCity,
    tblVendors.VendorRegion, tblVendors.VendorPostal, tblVendors.Country
  FROM tblVendors
ORDER BY 5;
```

> **Note**   If you decide to use column names in the ORDER BY clause of a UNION query, the database derives the column names from the names returned by the first query. In this example, you could change the ORDER BY clause to read ORDER BY PostalCode.

To create the same mailing list in a view or in-line function in a Microsoft SQL Server database, enter the following:

```
SELECT TOP 100 PERCENT U.CustomerName, U.Address, U.City,
    U.Region, U.PostalCode, U.Country
FROM
(SELECT tblCustomers.CustomerName, tblCustomers.Address, tblCustomers.City,
    tblCustomers.Region, tblCustomers.PostalCode, tblCustomers.Country
  FROM tblCustomers
UNION ALL
SELECT tblVendors.VendorName, tblVendors.VendorAddress, tblVendors.VendorCity,
    tblVendors.VendorRegion, tblVendors.VendorPostal, tblVendors.Country
  FROM tblVendors) AS U
ORDER BY 5;
```

Notice that you must UNION the rows first and then select and sort them all.

Also see ORDER BY Clause and SELECT Statement in this appendix.

WHERE Clause

Specifies a search condition in an SQL statement or an SQL clause. The DELETE, SELECT, and UPDATE statements and the subquery containing the WHERE clause operate only on those rows that satisfy the condition.

Syntax

WHERE *<search-condition>*

Notes

The database applies the *<search-condition>* to each row of the logical table assembled as a result of executing the previous clauses, and it rejects those rows for which the *<search-condition>* does not evaluate to True. If you use a subquery within a predicate in the *<search-condition>* (often called an *inner query*), the database must first execute the subquery before it evaluates the predicate.

In a subquery, if you refer to a table or a query that you also use in an outer FROM clause (often called a *correlated subquery*), the database must execute the subquery for each row being evaluated in the outer table. If you do not use a reference to an outer table in a subquery, the database must execute the subquery only once. A correlated subquery can also be expressed as a join, which generally executes more efficiently. If you include a predicate in the *<search-condition>* in the form

```
<expression> <comparison-operator> <subquery>
```

the database returns an error if the subquery returns no rows.

The order of evaluation of the logical operators used in the *<search-condition>* is NOT, AND, OR, XOR (exclusive OR), EQV (equivalence), and then IMP (implication). (SQL Server does not support the XOR, EQV, or IMP logical operators.) You can include additional parentheses to influence the order in which the database processes expressions.

Example

In a desktop database, to find all products for which the unit price is greater than $25 and for which the category description is equal to Condiments or the product has an order multiple of 1, but not both, enter the following (qxmplXOR):

```
SELECT tblProducts.ProductID, tblProducts.Description,
  tblProducts.Category, tblProducts.SellPrice, tblProducts.OrderMultiple
FROM tblProducts
WHERE (tblProducts.SellPrice > 25)
  AND ((tblProducts.Category = 'Condiments')
       XOR (tblProducts.OrderMultiple = 1));
```

In a project file, to find all products for which the unit price is greater than $25 and for which the category description is equal to Condiments or the product has an order multiple of 1, but not both, enter the following:

```
SELECT tblProducts.ProductID, tblProducts.Description,
  tblProducts.Category, tblProducts.SellPrice, tblProducts.OrderMultiple
FROM tblProducts
WHERE (tblProducts.SellPrice > 25)
    AND ((tblProducts.Category = 'Condiments')
    OR (tblProducts.OrderMultiple = 1))
    AND NOT ((tblProducts. Category = 'Condiments')
    AND (tblProducts. OrderMultiple = 1));
```

Also see DELETE Statement, Expression, Predicates (BETWEEN, Comparison, EXISTS, IN, LIKE NULL, and Quantified), Search-Condition, SELECT Statement, Subquery, and UPDATE Statement in this appendix.

SQL Action Queries

Use SQL action queries to delete, insert, or update data or to create a new table from existing data. Action queries are particularly powerful because they allow you to operate on sets of data, not single rows. For example, an UPDATE statement or a DELETE statement affects all rows in the underlying tables that meet the selection criteria you specify.

DELETE Statement

Deletes one or more rows from a table or a query. The WHERE clause is optional. If you do not specify a WHERE clause, all rows are deleted from the table or the query that you specify in the FROM clause. If you specify a WHERE clause, the database applies the search condition to each row in the table or the query, and only those rows that evaluate to True are deleted.

Syntax

```
DELETE [DISTINCTROW] [<select-list>]
  FROM {table-name [[AS] correlation-name] |
    select-query-name [[AS] correlation-name] |
    <joined table>},...
  [IN <source specification>]
  [WHERE <search-condition>];
```

where *<select-list>* is

```
[* | table-name.*]
```

and where *<joined table>* is

```
({table-name [[AS] correlation-name] |
  select-query-name [[AS] correlation-name] |
  (<select-statement>) AS correlation-name |
  <joined table>}
{INNER | {{LEFT | RIGHT | FULL} [OUTER]} JOIN
  {table-name [[AS] correlation-name] |
  select-query-name [[AS] correlation-name] |
  (<select-statement>) AS correlation-name |
  <joined table>}
ON <join-specification>)
```

Notes

When you specify a query name in a DELETE statement, the query must not be constructed using the UNION query operator. The query also must not contain an SQL aggregate function, the DISTINCT keyword, a GROUP BY or HAVING clause, or a subquery that references the same base table as the DELETE statement.

When you join two or more tables in the FROM clause, you can delete rows only from the many side of the relationship if the tables are related one to many; if the tables are related one to one, you can delete rows from either side. When you include more than one table in the FROM clause, you must also specify from which table the rows are to be deleted by using *tablename.** in the *<select-list>*. Microsoft Access also requires that you include the DISTINCTROW keyword and specify only one table as the target of the delete operation. When you specify only one table in the FROM clause, you do not need to provide a *<select-list>*.

You can supply a correlation name for each table or query name. You can use this correlation name as an alias for the full table name when qualifying column names in the WHERE clause and in subclauses. You must use a correlation name when referring to a column name that occurs in more than one table in the FROM clause.

If you use a subquery in the *<search-condition>*, you must not reference the target table or the query or any underlying table of the query in the subquery.

Examples

To delete all rows in the tblOrderProducts table, enter the following:

```
DELETE tblOrderProducts.* FROM tblOrderProducts;
```

To delete all rows in the tblOrderProducts table for orders placed before January 1, 2004, enter the following (qxmplDeleteOldOrderProducts):

```
DELETE DISTINCTROW tblOrderProducts.*
FROM tblOrders
INNER JOIN tblOrderProducts
ON tblOrders.OrderID = tblOrderProducts.OrderID
WHERE tblOrders.OrderDate < #1/1/2004#;
```

To delete all rows in the tblOrders table for orders placed before January 1, 2004, enter the following (qxmplDeleteOldOrders):

```
DELETE tblOrders.*
FROM tblOrders
WHERE tblOrders.OrderDate < #1/1/2004#;
```

Also see IN Clause, INSERT Statement, Predicates (BETWEEN, Comparison, EXISTS, IN, LIKE NULL, and Quantified), Search-Condition, and Subquery in this appendix.

INSERT Statement (Append Query)

Inserts one or more new rows into the specified table or query. When you use the VALUES clause, the database inserts only a single row. If you use a SELECT statement, the number of rows inserted equals the number of rows returned by the SELECT statement.

Syntax

```
INSERT INTO table-name [({column-name},...)]
[IN <source specification>]
{VALUES({literal},...) | select-statement}
```

Notes

If you do not include a column name list, you must supply values for all columns defined in the table in the order in which they were declared in the table definition. If you include a column name list, you must supply values for all columns in the list, and the values must be compatible with the receiving column attributes. You must include in the list all columns in the underlying table whose Required attribute is Yes and that do not have a default value.

If you include an IN clause in both the INSERT and the FROM clause of the SELECT statement, both must refer to the same source database.

If you supply values by using a SELECT statement, the statement's FROM clause cannot have the target table of the insert as its table name or as an underlying table. The target table also cannot be used in any subquery.

Because Access allows you to define column-value constraints (validation rules in a desktop database), table constraints (validation rules in a desktop database), and referential integrity checks, any values that you insert must pass these validations before Access will allow you to run the query.

Examples

To insert a new row in the tblEmployees table, enter the following:

```
INSERT INTO tblEmployees (EmployeeID,
      EmployeeName, Password, IsMgr)
VALUES (99, 'Allen, Michael', 'allen', -1);
```

To insert old order records into a history table and avoid duplicates, enter the following (qxmplArchiveOrdersByDate):

```
PARAMETERS LastDateToKeep DateTime;
INSERT INTO tblOrdersArchive
  ( OrderID, CustomerID, ShipAddress, ShipCity, ShipRegion,
  ShipPostalCode, ShipCountry, OrderDate, ShipDate, FinalInvoice,
  TaxStatus, TaxRate )
SELECT tblOrders.OrderID, tblOrders.CustomerID, tblOrders.ShipAddress,
  tblOrders.ShipCity, tblOrders.ShipRegion, tblOrders.ShipPostalCode,
  tblOrders.ShipCountry, tblOrders.OrderDate, tblOrders.ShipDate,
  tblOrders.FinalInvoice, tblOrders.TaxStatus, tblOrders.TaxRate
FROM tblOrders
LEFT JOIN tblOrderProductsArchive
ON tblOrders.OrderID = tblOrderProductsArchive.OrderID
WHERE ((tblOrders.OrderDate < [LastDateToKeep])
  AND (tblOrderProductsArchive.OrderID Is Null));
```

Although Access accepts the ANSI-standard VALUES clause, you will discover that in a desktop database, Access converts a statement such as

```
INSERT INTO MyTable (ColumnA, ColumnB)
VALUES (123, "Jane Doe");
```

to

```
INSERT INTO MyTable (ColumnA, ColumnB)
SELECT 123 As Expr1, "Jane Doe" as Expr2;
```

Also see DELETE Statement, IN Clause, SELECT Statement, and Subquery in this appendix.

SELECT . . . INTO Statement (Make-Table Query)

Creates a new table from values selected from one or more other tables. Make-table queries are most useful for providing backup snapshots or for creating tables with rolled-up totals at the end of an accounting period.

Syntax

```
SELECT [ALL | DISTINCT | DISTINCTROW |
        TOP number PERCENT]] <select-list> INTO new-table-name
  [IN <source specification>]
  FROM {table-name [[AS] correlation-name] |
    select-query-name [[AS] correlation-name] |
    <joined table>},...
  [IN <source specification>]
  [WHERE <search-condition>]
  [GROUP BY column-name,...]
  [HAVING <search-condition>]
[UNION [ALL] <select-statement>]
  [[ORDER BY {column-name [ASC | DESC]},...] |
  IN <"source database name">
    <[source connect string]>
  [WITH OWNERACCESS OPTION];
```

where *<select-list>* is

```
{* | {<expression> [AS output-column-name] |
  table-name.* | query-name.* | correlation-name.*},...}
```

and where *<joined table>* is

```
({table-name [[AS] correlation-name] |
  select-query-name [[AS] correlation-name] |
  (<select-statement>) AS correlation-name |
  <joined table>}
{INNER | {{LEFT | RIGHT | FULL} [OUTER]} JOIN
  {table-name [[AS] correlation-name] |
  select-query-name [[AS] correlation-name] |
  (<select-statement>) AS correlation-name |
  <joined table>}
ON <join-specification>)
```

Notes

A SELECT...INTO query creates a new table with the name specified in *new-table-name*. If a table with that name already exists, the database displays a dialog box that asks you to confirm the deletion of the table before it creates a new one in its place. The columns in the new table inherit the data type attributes of the columns produced by the *<select-list>*.

If you include an IN clause for both the INTO and the FROM clauses, both must refer to the same source database.

Example

To create a new table that summarizes all sales by product and by month, enter the following (qxmplProductSalesMakeTable):

```
SELECT tblProducts.ProductID, tblProducts.Category,
  tblProducts.Description, Format([DateAlloc],"yyyy mm") AS DateSold,
  Sum([Quantity]*[Price]) AS TotalSales
INTO tblMonthSalesSummary
FROM tblProducts
INNER JOIN tblOrderProducts
ON tblProducts.ProductID = tblOrderProducts.ProductID
GROUP BY tblProducts.ProductID, tblProducts.Category,
  tblProducts.Description, Format([DateAlloc],"yyyy mm");
```

Also see IN Clause, Search-Condition, and SELECT Statement in this appendix.

UPDATE Statement

In the specified table or query, updates the selected columns (either to the value of the given expression or to Null) in all rows that satisfy the search condition. If you do not enter a WHERE clause, all rows in the specified table or query are affected.

Syntax

```
UPDATE {table-name [[AS] correlation-name] |
  select-query-name [[AS] correlation-name] |
  <joined table>},...
[IN <source specification>]
SET {column-name = {<expression> | NULL}},...
[WHERE <search-condition>]
```

where *<joined table>* is

```
({table-name [[AS] correlation-name] |
  select-query-name [[AS] correlation-name] |
  (<select-statement>) AS correlation-name |
  <joined table>}
{INNER | {{LEFT | RIGHT | FULL} [OUTER]} JOIN
  {table-name [[AS] correlation-name] |
  select-query-name [[AS] correlation-name] |
  (<select-statement>) AS correlation-name |
  <joined table>}
ON <join-specification>)
```

Notes

If you provide more than one table name, you can update columns only in the table on the many side of a one-to-many relationship. If the tables are related one to one, you can update columns in either table. You can also update columns in the table on the one side of a relationship as long as the query returns unique rows for that table. The database must be able to determine the relationship between tables or queries in order to update columns in a query. In general, if a table is joined by its primary key to a query, you can update columns in the query (because the primary key indicates that the table is on the *one* side of the join). If you want to update a table with the results of a query, you must insert the query results into a temporary table that can be defined with a one-to-many or one-to-one relationship with the target table and then use the temporary table to update the target.

If you specify a *<search-condition>*, you can reference only columns found in the target table or query. If you use a subquery in the *<search-condition>*, you must not reference the target table or the query or any underlying table of the query in the subquery.

In the SET clause, you cannot specify a column name more than once. Values assigned to columns must be compatible with the column attributes. If you assign the Null value, the column cannot have the Required property set to Yes.

Both Access and SQL Server let you define column-value constraints (validation rules in a desktop database), table constraints (validation rules in a desktop database), and referential integrity checks, so any values that you update must pass these validations or the database will not let you run the query.

Example

To mark customers inactive who haven't placed an order since April 1, 2004, enter the following (qxmplSetInactive):

```
UPDATE tblCustomers
SET tblCustomers.Active = False
WHERE tblCustomers.CustomerID Not In
  (SELECT CustomerID
   FROM tblOrders
   WHERE OrderDate >=#4/1/2004#);
```

Also see Expression, IN Clause, Predicates (BETWEEN, Comparison, EXISTS, IN, LIKE NULL, and Quantified), Search-Condition, and WHERE Clause in this appendix.

Appendix E

Implementing Generic Features

Any developer who has been working with Microsoft Access for a while has created generic features and bits of code that can help make any application more robust. Sprinkled throughout the sample databases, you can find a host of neat features that you might find useful in any application you build using Access. This appendix shows you where to find and how to use some of the generic features that I've collected for use in any application I build. These include:

■ A custom calendar form that does not depend on the Calendar ActiveX control

■ A procedure for automatically creating a backup of the linked data tables when the user exits the application

■ A technique to call a form event procedure from a custom toolbar or menu bar

■ Keeping two open forms synchronized using form events

■ Managing tabbing across pages in a tab control on a form

■ Providing a way for the user to edit image files that are linked to the database via a text path link instead of embedded in the application tables

The following sections show you where to find these features and explain how they work. Although I used many of the features in all the sample databases, this appendix explores them as implemented in the Membership Tracking sample application (Membership.mdb).

Creating a Custom Calendar

When I first started creating applications in Access to be installed at a client site or used as an example in one of my books, I made use of the Calendar custom control that comes with Access. However, I found that when I created a Runtime installation of my application and installed my application on a client's machine, the forms that used the Calendar control would sometimes not work because of a version conflict with the control already installed on the client's machines. I could have included the version that my application used in the installation procedure, but that could have caused existing applications on the client's machine to break.

I eventually came up with a way to create a calendar on a form that did not depend on the ActiveX control, so my applications could be completely version independent. You can find a couple of versions of this form in the sample applications included with this book. To see one in action, open the Membership Tracking application (Membership.mdb) and open the frmMembers form. Notice the tiny command button with a calendar image next to the Birth Date field. Click the button to see my custom calendar form, as shown in Figure E-1.

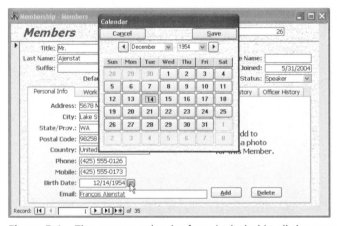

Figure E-1   The custom calendar form included in all the sample applications.

The user can navigate forward and backward one month at a time or choose a different month or year from the combo box controls. The main body of the calendar is an option group with six rows of seven option buttons each. As you'll learn later, code in the form dynamically assigns values and captions to the buttons and enables only the buttons for the current month when the user moves to a new month. To select a date, the user need only click the button representing the date wanted and then click the Save button to return the value to the calling form.

Understanding the *GetDate* Function

The code in the Click event of the tiny command button with the calendar icon calls the *GetDate* function that you can find in the modCalendar module. The code begins by moving the focus to the control about to be updated with a date/time value. The code then calls the *GetDate* function and passes it the control to be updated and an indicator to tell the function that the control needs a date value only. Because the BirthDate control on the frmMembers form also has a BeforeUpdate validation procedure, the code calls that procedure if the *GetDate* function indicates that the date was updated successfully. (The BeforeUpdate procedure disallows a birth date later than the current date.) The code is as follows:

```
Private Sub cmdMemberBirthCal_Click()
Dim varReturn As Variant
  ' Clicked the calendar icon asking for graphical help
  ' Put the focus on the control to be updated
  Me.BirthDate.SetFocus
  ' Call the get a date function - date only
  ' If returned a value,
  If GetDate(Me.BirthDate, True) = True Then
    ' Fire the control's Before Update event
    BirthDate_BeforeUpdate (varReturn)
  End If
End Sub
```

It's the *GetDate* function that opens the calendar (the fdlgCalendar form) that the user sees. The code begins by validating the type of control to be updated. If the control is not a text box, combo box, or list box, the code sets a failed return and exits. If the control currently has no value and the caller asked for a date value only, the code sets today as the default date. If the control has no value and the caller asked for a date and a time (the optional intDateOnly parameter is False or 0), the code sets the current date and time as the default value. If the control has a value, the code fetches it and verifies that it yields a true Date/Time data type. If the value is some other data type, the code sets a failed return and exits. The code is as follows:

```
Public Function GetDate(ctl As Control, _
  Optional intDateOnly As Integer = 0) As Integer
'----------------------------------------------------------
' Inputs: A Control object containing a date/time value
'     Optional "date only" (no time value) flag
' Outputs: Sets the Control to the value returned by fdlgCalendar
' Created By: JLV 09/05/01
' Last Revised: JLV 09/05/01
'----------------------------------------------------------
Dim varDateTime As Variant, strDateTime As String, frm As Form
  ' Error trap just in case
  On Error GoTo Error_Date
  ' First, validate the kind of control passed
  Select Case ctl.ControlType
    ' Text box, combo box, and list box are OK
    Case acTextBox, acListBox, acComboBox
    Case Else
      GetDate = False
      Exit Function
  End Select
  ' If the control has no value
  If IsNothing(ctl.Value) Then
```

```
      If intDateOnly Then
        ' Set default date
        varDateTime = Date
      Else
        ' .. or default date and time
        varDateTime = Now
      End If
    Else
      ' Otherwise, pick up the current value
      varDateTime = ctl.Value
      ' Make sure it's a date/time
      If vbDate <> VarType(varDateTime) Then
        GetDate = False
        Exit Function
      End If
    End If
  End If
```

Next, the code converts either the default value or the value in the form control into a string that can be passed to the calendar form. If the calendar form is still open (perhaps because a previous call failed without closing the form), the code closes it. The code then opens the fdlgCalendar form as a dialog box and passes it the starting date/time value in the OpenArgs property. (The OpenArgs property is a string, which explains why the code converted the value before passing it to the form.)

Because the code opens the form as a dialog box, the code waits until the form disappears from the screen—the form either closes or becomes hidden (the Visible property is set to False). When the code resumes running after the OpenForm command, it checks to see if the calendar form is still open. If it is not open, the user must have clicked the Cancel button that closes the form, so the code exits. If the form is still open, the code sets a pointer to the form and fetches the selected value from a hidden text box called ctlCalendar. If the caller asked for a time value, the code appends the hour and minute selected from the txtHour and txtMinute text boxes on the form. The code converts the date and time components back to a true date/time value, assigns the value to the control on the calling form, sets a successful return, and exits. The code at the end of the function traps and logs any errors. The code is as follows:

```
  ' Turn the date and time into a string to pass to the form
  strDateTime = Format(varDateTime, "mm/dd/yyyy hh:nn")
  ' Make sure we don't have an old copy of fdlgCalendar hanging around
  If IsFormLoaded("fdlgCalendar") Then DoCmd.Close acForm, "fdlgCalendar"
  ' Open the calendar as a dialog box so this code waits,
  '   and pass the date/time value
  DoCmd.OpenForm "fdlgCalendar", WindowMode:=acDialog, _
    OpenArgs:=strDateTime & "," & intDateOnly
  ' If the form is gone, user canceled the update
  If Not IsFormLoaded("fdlgCalendar") Then Exit Function
  ' Get a pointer to the now-hidden form
  Set frm = Forms!fdlgCalendar
  ' Grab the date part off the hidden text box
  strDateTime = Format(frm.ctlCalendar.Value, "mm/dd/yyyy")
  If Not intDateOnly Then
    ' If looking for date and time, also grab the hour and minute
```

```
      strDateTime = strDateTime & " " & frm.txtHour & ":" & frm.txtMinute
    End If
    ' Stuff the returned value back in the caller's control
    ctl.Value = DateValue(strDateTime) + TimeValue(strDateTime)
    ' Close the calendar form to clean up
    DoCmd.Close acForm, "fdlgCalendar"
    GetDate = True
Exit_Date:
    Exit Function
Error_Date:
    ' This code is pretty simple and does check for a usable control type,
    '  .. so this should never happen.
    ' But if it does, log it...
    ErrorLog "GetDate", Err, Error
    GetDate = False
    Resume Exit_Date
End Function
```

Exploring the Design of the fdlgCalendar Form

To understand how the fdlgCalendar form works, select the form in the Database window of
the Membership Tracking database (Membership.mdb) and open it in Design view, as shown
in Figure E-2. Notice that the form design includes controls to set the hour and time at the
bottom of the form that you do not see in Figure E-1. As you'll learn later, code in the form's
Load event procedure shrinks the form window to hide these controls when the calling form
has asked for a date value only.

Figure E-2   The design of the fdlgCalendar form.

Even though you might think that a month typically has four weeks and a few days, to properly display all months the form needs six rows of seven columns. The longest months of the
year have 31 days, and if the first day of the month is on a Friday or Saturday, the 31st day
needs to appear in the first or second column of the sixth week.

To provide a visual clue of the day selected, the form design uses an option group control to contain the six rows of seven columns of toggle buttons. Each toggle button that can be clicked for a given month is assigned a unique day value by code in the form that "draws" the calendar when the form opens and each time the user changes the month or year values or navigates to a different month. The result is that only one of the toggle buttons appears selected to show the current date value selected.

First, let's take a look at the code in the Load event procedure that runs when the form opens. The code first checks to see if the OpenArgs property contains a value. If the OpenArgs property is empty, the code sets the default value to the current date. (The varDate variable is declared in the form module's Declarations section.) If the OpenArgs property contains data, the code extracts the date, hour, and minute portions of the date/time string that was formatted by the *GetDate* function. If the end of the string contains a −1 value indicating that the caller wants a date value only, the code hides the hour and minute text boxes, the label control that separates the two text boxes, and the label control that contains instructions at the bottom of the form. The code then resizes the form window so that the user sees only the calendar. Finally, the code sets the value of the month and year combo box controls, calls the *SetDays* procedure in the form module to format the days for the current month, saves the date value in a hidden text box on the form, and sets the value of the option group control so that the correct toggle button appears selected. The code is as follows:

```
Private Sub Form_Load()
  ' Establish an initial value for the date
  If IsNothing(Me.OpenArgs) Then
    varDate = Date
  Else
    ' Should have date, time, and "DateOnly" indicator in OpenArgs:
    '   mm/dd/yyyy hh:mm,-1
    varDate = Left(Me.OpenArgs, 10)
    Me.txtHour = Mid(Me.OpenArgs, 12, 2)
    Me.txtMinute = Mid(Me.OpenArgs, 15, 2)
    ' If "date only"
    If Right(Me.OpenArgs, 2) = "-1" Then
      ' Hide some stuff
      Me.txtHour.Visible = False
      Me.txtMinute.Visible = False
      Me.lblColon.Visible = False
      Me.lblTimeInstruct.Visible = False
      Me.SetFocus
      '  .. and resize my window
      DoCmd.MoveSize , , , 4295
    End If
  End If
  ' Initialize the month selector
  Me.cmbMonth = Month(varDate)
  ' Initialize the year selector
  Me.cmbYear = Year(varDate)
  ' Call the common calendar draw routine
```

```
      SetDays
      ' Place the date/time value in a hidden control -
      '  The calling routine fetches it from here
      Me.ctlCalendar = varDate
      ' Highlight the correct day box in the calendar
      Me.optCalendar = Day(varDate)
End Sub
```

The last big piece of the puzzle is the *SetDays* procedure that "draws" the calendar. As you have just seen, this procedure is called when the form opens. Code in the AfterUpdate event of the year and month combo box controls and in the Click event of the two arrow controls also calls this procedure to update the toggle buttons in the option group.

First, the code moves the focus temporarily to the month combo box control. The code is about to enable and disable the toggle buttons, and an error would occur if the code tried to disable a button that had the focus. Next, the code loops through all 42 toggle buttons and clears and disables them all by setting the Caption property to an empty string, the OptionValue property to 0, the ForeColor property to Black, and the Enabled property to False. Note that the name of each toggle button is tglnn, where nn is the numbers 01 to 42. This makes it simple for the code to generate the names to create a reference to each control easily in a loop. The code is as follows:

```
Private Sub SetDays()
Dim intI As Integer, intJ As Integer, strNum As String, ctl As Control
   ' Move the focus so we can dink with the calendar
   Me.cmbMonth.SetFocus
   ' First, clear all the boxes
   For intI = 1 To 42
     ' Controls are named "tglnn"
     ' Where nn = 01 to 42
     ' Using Format to get 2 digits
     strNum = Format(intI, "00")
     ' Establish a pointer to the control
     Set ctl = Me("tgl" & strNum)
     ' Clear the day number
     ctl.Caption = ""
     ' Reset the Option Value
     ctl.OptionValue = 0
     ' Reset the ForeColor to black
     ctl.ForeColor = vbBlack
     ' And disable it
     ctl.Enabled = False
   Next intI
```

Next, the code gets the value of the current month and year from the combo box controls and calculates the day of the week of the first day of the month, the day number of the last day of the month, and the offset of the toggle button that represents the last day of the month. The code then starts a loop to set up all the toggle buttons that represent the days of the current month. The code sets the Caption property and the OptionValue property of the toggle button to the day number, the ForeColor property to Blue, and the Enabled property to True. The code is as follows:

```
intMonth = Me!cmbMonth
intYear = Me!cmbYear
' The first box to set is the weekday of the first day of the month
intFirst = WeekDay(DateSerial(intYear, intMonth, 1), vbSunday)
' Calculate the last day number
'    by adding 1 month to Day 1 and subtracting one
intLastDay = Day(DateAdd("m", 1, DateSerial(intYear, intMonth, 1)) - 1)
' .. and the last box to set
intLast = intFirst + intLastDay - 1
' Now set up all the boxes for the current month
intJ = 1
For intI = intFirst To intLast
  strNum = Format(intI, "00")
  ' Establish a pointer to the control
  Set ctl = Me("tgl" & strNum)
  ' Put the day number in the associated label caption
  ctl.Caption = intJ
  ' Set the value of the Toggle
  ctl.OptionValue = intJ
  ' Set the Fore Color to Blue
  ctl.ForeColor = vbBlue
  ' and Enable it
  ctl.Enabled = True
  intJ = intJ + 1
Next intI
```

Finally, the code sets the captions of the disabled buttons following the last day of the month to the day numbers that represent the start of the following month. The code also calculates the last day of the previous month and fills in the captions of the buttons that represent the last days of the preceding month. Keep in mind that these buttons have their OptionValue property set to 0 but remain disabled, so the user can't click them and set an invalid date. The code is as follows:

```
Set ctl = Nothing
' Fill in the remaining buttons with days for the next month
If intLast <> 42 Then
  intJ = 1
  For intI = intLast + 1 To 42
    strNum = Format(intI, "00")
    ' Put the day number in the associated label caption
    Me("tgl" & strNum).Caption = intJ
    intJ = intJ + 1
  Next intI
End If
' .. and the days from the previous month
If intFirst <> 1 Then
  intJ = Day(DateSerial(intYear, intMonth, 1) - 1)
```

```
   For intI = intFirst - 1 To 1 Step -1
     strNum = Format(intI, "00")
     ' Put the day number in the associated label caption
     Me("tgl" & strNum).Caption = intJ
     intJ = intJ - 1
   Next intI
 End If
 ' Put the focus back
 Me.optCalendar.SetFocus
End Sub
```

If you examine the rest of the code in the module for the fdlgCalendar form, you'll find that the AfterUpdate event procedures for the cmbYear and cmbMonth combo box controls and the Click event procedures for the cmdNext and cmdPrevious command button controls all calculate the current month, update the varDate value, and call the *SetDays* procedure to redraw the calendar. The AfterUpdate event procedure also updates the varDate value but does not redraw the calendar.

> **Tip**   The graphic calendar form is one generic feature that you can implement in your application by simply copying the fdlgCalendar form and the modCalendar module into any database. Add a call to the *GetDate* function in your application anywhere you want to use the calendar form.

Automating a Backup on Exit

In the Membership Tracking, Inventory Management, and Registration Management applications, you can find an automated procedure that offers to create a backup of the data file every 10th time you exit the application or every 14 days, whichever occurs first. I set the last backup date for these applications to July 1, 2005, so you won't see the application offer to create a backup unless you have opened the application 10 times or more or the date on your machine is after July 14, 2005.

To be sure you see the message, open the Membership Tracking application and then open the ztblVersion table. Set the LastBackup field to a date more than two weeks in the past or set the OpenCount field to **9** and save the one record in the table. Start the application by opening the frmSplash form. Click the Exit button on the main switchboard and confirm that you want to exit in the first dialog box. The application then asks you if you want to create a backup, as shown in Figure E-3 on the next page.

Click the Yes button in the dialog box, and the application creates a new BackupData subfolder and makes a backup of the data file in that folder. You can find the code that performs this task in the Click event procedure of the cmdExit command button on the frmMain form. After verifying that the user wants to exit, code at the beginning of the procedure loops through all open forms and closes them. (This code is not shown.)

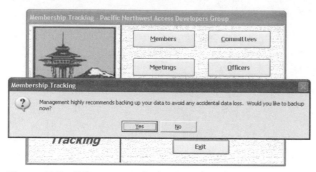

Figure E-3 When you exit the Membership Tracking application, it asks if you want to create a backup if you have opened the application more than 10 times or the last backup was more than two weeks ago.

After closing all forms (except the frmMain form) successfully, the code then points to the current database and opens a recordset on the ztblVersion table. The code fetches the values for the OpenCount and LastBackup fields and closes the recordset. (Code called by the frmSplash form updates the open count each time you start the application.) If the open count is an even multiple of 10 or the last backup was more than 14 days ago, the code asks the user if a new backup file should be created. The code is as follows:

```
Set db = DBEngine(0)(0)
' Open ztblVersion to see if we need to do a backup
Set rst = db.OpenRecordset("ztblVersion", dbOpenDynaset)
rst.MoveFirst
lngOpen = rst!OpenCount
datBackup = rst!LastBackup
rst.Close
Set rst = Nothing
' If the user has opened 10 times
'   or last backup was more than 2 weeks ago...
If (lngOpen Mod 10 = 0) Or ((Date - datBackup) > 14) Then
   ' Ask if they want to backup...
   If vbYes = MsgBox("Management highly recommends backing up " & _
      "your data to avoid " & _
      "any accidental data loss.  Would you like to backup now?", _
      vbYesNo + vbQuestion, gstrAppTitle) Then
```

If the user clicks the Yes button in the dialog box, the code uses the Connect property of the ztblVersion table (a linked table) to find out the location of the data file. The code then uses the *Dir* function to find out if a BackupData subfolder exists in that location. If the folder doesn't exist, the code uses the MkDir command to create the new subfolder.

Next, the code uses the *Dir* function again to find any database files in the subfolder with names that begin with the characters MembershipBkp. The code examines each name in a loop and keeps the name of the oldest file. After searching for all the backup files, if the number of backup files is greater than two, the code uses the Kill statement to delete the oldest file. The objective is to keep no more than three backup files in the subfolder. Finally, the code uses today's date to generate a new backup file name, deletes the file if a file with today's date already exists, and uses the *CompactDatabase* method of the DBEngine object to create the new backup. If the backup doesn't cause an error, the code updates the last backup date in the ztblVersion table. The code is as follows:

```
' Get the name of the data file
strData = Mid(db.TableDefs("ztblVersion").Connect, 11)
' Get the name of its folder
strDir = Left(strData, InStrRev(strData, "\"))
' See if the "BackupData" folder exists
If Len(Dir(strDir & "BackupData", vbDirectory)) = 0 Then
  ' Nope, build it!
  MkDir strDir & "BackupData"
End If
' Now find any existing backups - keep only three
strBkp = Dir(strDir & "BackupData\MembershipBkp*.mdb")
Do While Len(strBkp) > 0
  intBkp = intBkp + 1
  If (strBkp < strLowBkp) Or (Len(strLowBkp) = 0) Then _
    strLowBkp = strBkp
  strBkp = Dir
Loop
If intBkp > 2 Then
  Kill strDir & "BackupData\" & strLowBkp
End If
' Now, setup new backup name based on today's date
strBkp = strDir & "BackupData\MembershipBkp" & _
  Format(Date, "yymmdd") & ".mdb"
' Make sure the target file doesn't exist
If Len(Dir(strBkp)) > 0 Then Kill strBkp
' Create the backup file using Compact
DBEngine.CompactDatabase strData, strBkp
' Now update the backup date
db.Execute "UPDATE ztblVersion SET LastBackup = #" & _
  Date & "#", dbFailOnError
MsgBox "Backup created successfully!", vbInformation, gstrAppTitle
    End If
  End If
Set db = Nothing
```

You can't use the *CompactDatabase* method to copy a file that is open, so you can't create a backup of the current application file that's open and running this code. This process works because all the sample applications use a separate database containing the shared data tables. At the point this code runs, it has closed all recordsets and forms that might have any of the shared data tables open. If another user has the application that is using the shared data file open on another machine when the code attempts to create the backup, the *CompactDatabase* method generates an error. However, that error is trapped by the error handling code at the end of the procedure, and the application exits successfully (but without creating a backup).

Executing Form Procedures from a Custom Toolbar or Menu Bar

You might have noticed as you ran any of the sample applications that all the forms and reports use custom toolbars and menu bars. You should always define custom toolbars and menu bars for any application that is designed to be used by others. You don't want a user to be able to get into the Design view of your forms and reports, and you might want to disable some other features as well. If you plan to distribute your application to execute in Runtime mode, you must define custom toolbars and menu bars because the built-in toolbars and menu bars are not available in Runtime mode.

One useful feature to add to your custom toolbars or menu bars for switchboard forms is the ability for the user to click an option on the toolbar or menu bar and have it execute code in the switchboard. You can see how this works by opening the Membership Tracking sample application (Membership.mdb) and starting the application by opening the frmSplash form. Notice that the custom toolbar contains one icon that matches each of the navigation options on the switchboard, as shown in Figure E-4. You can click any of the toolbar buttons or choose an option from the Tasks menu to execute the related option on the switchboard.

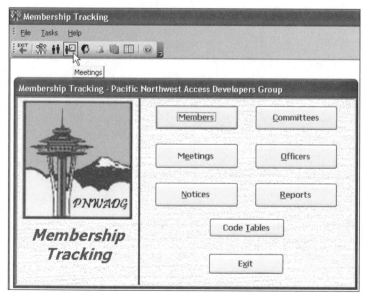

Figure E-4   The switchboard forms in all the sample applications have companion custom toolbars and menu bars.

You can explore how this works by right-clicking the toolbar and choosing Customize from the shortcut menu. (I didn't disable this feature for any of the toolbars in the sample applications.) When you have the Customize dialog box open, you can edit any existing toolbar or menu bar or create new ones. Right-click the Meetings toolbar button and choose Properties from the shortcut menu to see the properties for this button, as shown in Figure E-5.

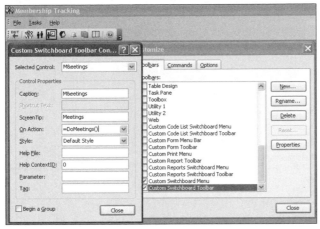

Figure E-5   Setting up a custom toolbar button to call a public function.

Notice that the On Action property of the button names the *DoMeetings* function. You can find this function and all the functions that handle toolbar and menu bar actions in the modSwitchboard module. The code is very simple—it makes sure that the relevant form is open and then attempts to execute the Click event procedure of the related command button inside an error trap. The code is as follows:

```
Public Function DoMeetings() As Integer
  ' Function called by main switchboard menu and toolbar
  ' to call cmdMeetings_Click on frmMain
  ' Ignore errors not trapped at lower level
  On Error Resume Next
  ' Do nothing if form not loaded - SNO
  If Not IsFormLoaded("frmMain") Then Exit Function
  ' Execute the requested command
  Form_frmMain.cmdMeetings_Click
End Function
```

The other piece of the puzzle is you must declare any procedure within a form that you want to execute in this manner as a Public procedure. When you do that, the procedure effectively becomes a method of the form's class module. So, you'll find that the Click event procedures for all the command buttons on the frmMain form are declared Public, not Private. As you can see in the preceding code, the name of any form's class module is the characters *Form_* followed by the form name. (If you include spaces or special characters in your form name, those spaces and characters are replaced with underscores.)

Synchronizing Two Forms with Form Events

You might find it necessary in some applications to have two forms showing related information at the same time. One form might be showing an overview of information from a table on the one side of a one-to-many relationship, and the second form might be displaying the details from the table on the many side of the relationship. As the user moves to a new record on the first form, it would be nice to have the detail form stay synchronized.

You can find an example of this sort of problem in the Membership Tracking sample database (Membership.mdb). Open the database and then start the application by opening the frmSplash form. Click the Meetings button on the main switchboard, ask for all meetings between October 1, 2004, and January 31, 2005, in the Select Meetings window, and click the Edit button. Click the Attendees button on the Meetings form, choose the **Open the pop-up attendee list** option in the Attendee Options dialog box, and click the Go button. (You can also choose the **Open the meeting sign-in form** option—that form is also synchronized with the Meetings form.) Your screen should now look something like Figure E-6.

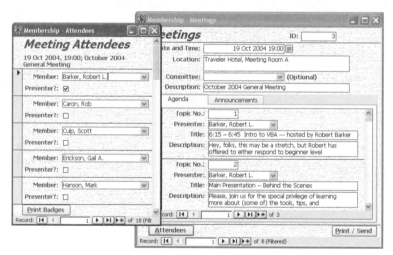

Figure E-6   The Meetings form displays basic information about a meeting, and the Meeting Attendees form displays related information about the members who attended the meeting.

Now click forward one record on the Meetings form using the bottom set of navigation buttons. Notice that the Meeting Attendees form stays synchronized with the Meetings form—it now displays the members who attended the second meeting, as shown in Figure E-7.

This synchronization happens because the frmMeetings form defines a custom event, the fpopMeetingAttendees form notifies Access that it wants to "listen" for that event when it opens, and code in the frmMeetings event signals the event and passes the current meeting ID as a parameter every time the user moves to a new record. You don't need to worry about writing code in the frmMeetings form to check whether the related form is open—the code simply signals the custom event, and any form that is open and listening for the event can respond to it.

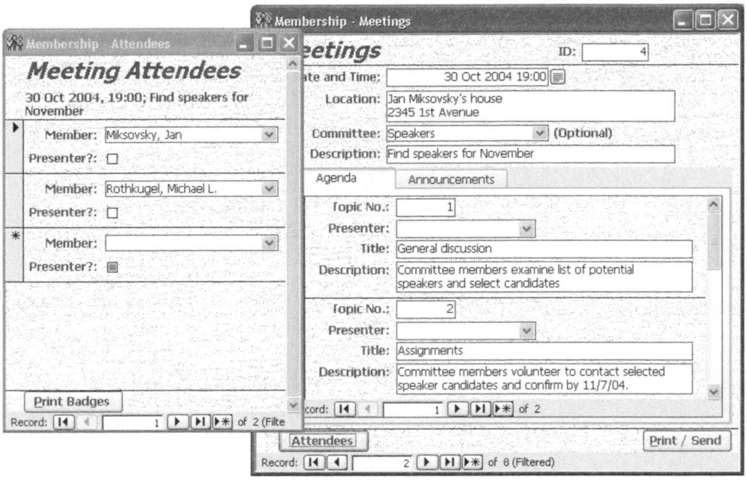

Figure E-7   The Meeting Attendees form synchronizes with the Meetings form when the user moves to a new record on the Meetings form.

First, the code in the module for the frmMeetings form must declare the custom event and any parameters that are passed when the event is signaled. In the Declarations section of that module, you can find the following code:

```
' Declare event that is "hooked" by both Agenda and Attendee popup forms
Public Event NewMeeting(varMeetingID As Variant)
```

Next, the code in the module of the frmMeetings form must make sure the event is signaled whenever any form that needs to synchronize with it is opened. When the user clicks the cmdAttendees command button, code in the Click event procedure first checks to see if either of the synchronized forms is already open. (Remember, earlier you could have also opened the meeting sign-in form—frmMemberAttendance—that is also synchronized.) If either is open, the form puts the focus on that form and exits. The code then checks to see if the current meeting record is for a meeting that is scheduled in the future. If this is the case, the code asks whether the user wants to enter attendance for a meeting in the future. If the user clicks the No button in the message dialog box, the code exits. The code is as follows:

```
Private Sub cmdAttendees_Click()
  ' See if form already open
  ' If short meeting popup open,
  If IsFormLoaded("fpopMeetingAttendees") Then
    ' Put the focus there
    Form_fpopMeetingAttendees.SetFocus
    ' Done
    Exit Sub
  End If
  ' If Meeting attendance sign-in open,
```

```
If IsFormLoaded("frmMemberAttendance") Then
  ' Put the focus there
  Form_frmMemberAttendance.SetFocus
  ' Done
  Exit Sub
End If
' See if meeting is in the future
If Me.MeetingDate > Date Then
  ' Verify they want to enter attendance
  If vbNo = MsgBox("Are you sure you want to enter attendance for a " & _
    "meeting in the future?", vbYesNo + vbQuestion + vbDefaultButton2, _
    gstrAppTitle) Then
    ' Bail
    Exit Sub
  End If
End If
```

Next, the code opens the fdlgAttendanceChoice form to find out which of the two attendance forms the user wants to see. Because the code opens the form in Dialog mode, the code waits until the user either selects an option or closes the form. When the user selects an option and clicks the Go button, the fdlgAttendanceChoice form hides itself so that the code in the frmMeetings form can continue.

If the fdlgAttendanceChoice form is still open, the user must have selected an option. The code looks at the option group on that form and opens the appropriate companion form with a filter that returns no records. The code then executes the DoEvents statement to let Access process events on the form just opened. Code in the companion form must let Access know that it wants to respond to events in this form. Finally, the code raises the custom NewMeeting event and passes the ID of the current meeting as a parameter. The code closes the dialog box before it exits. The code is as follows:

```
' Ask which window they want open
DoCmd.OpenForm "fdlgAttendanceChoice", WindowMode:=acDialog
' Form either hides or closes
If IsFormLoaded("fdlgAttendanceChoice") Then
  ' Open form based on what they chose
  Select Case Form_fdlgAttendanceChoice.optOptions
    Case 1  ' Popup form
      ' Open it with a "null" filter
      DoCmd.OpenForm "fPopMeetingAttendees", _
        WhereCondition:="MeetingID = 0"
      ' Release to Access to give the form
      '  a chance to "hook" the NewMeeting event
      DoEvents
    Case 2  ' Meeting sign-in form
      ' Open it with a "null" filter
      DoCmd.OpenForm "frmMemberAttendance", _
        WhereCondition:="MeetingID = 0"
      ' Release to Access to give the form
      '  a chance to "hook" the NewMeeting event
      DoEvents
  End Select
```

```
    ' .. and then signal the event to sync the form
    RaiseEvent NewMeeting(Me.MeetingID)
    ' Close the form
    DoCmd.Close acForm, "fdlgAttendanceChoice"
  End If
End Sub
```

As you might expect, the Current event procedure of the frmMeetings form also uses the RaiseEvent statement to signal any form that is responding to the event that the form is now positioned on a different meeting. Keep in mind that the code in the Current event procedure doesn't need to check whether any responding form is open or not. It merely raises the event and lets Access deal with it.

In the code in any form that you want to respond to events in another form, you must declare and set a pointer to the second form's class module. You can find the following code in the Declarations section of the fpopMeetingAttendees form's module:

```
' Declare the meetings form to hook the NewMeeting event
Dim WithEvents frmMtg As Form_frmMeetings
```

The Load event procedure of the form sets a pointer to the frmMeetings form, which enables code in the fpopMeetingAttendees form's module to respond to any declared public events. The code is as follows:

```
Private Sub Form_Load()
  ' Set the frmMtg object
  Set frmMtg = Form_frmMeetings
End Sub
```

Finally, the module for the fpopMeetingAttendees form has a procedure to respond specifically to the NewMeeting event signaled by the frmMeetings form. The code checks the ID passed by the event, and if it is Null, the frmMeetings form must be on a new record, so the code hides the synchronized form. If the ID is not Null, the form modifies its Filter property to fetch attendance records for the current meeting and sets the FilterOn property to True to apply the filter. The code also copies some descriptive information from controls on the frmMeetings form. Note that the name of the procedure is the name of the object that points to the form followed by an underscore and the name of the event. The code is as follows:

```
Private Sub frmMtg_NewMeeting(varID As Variant)
  ' Respond to the NewMeeting event on frmMeetings
  ' Save the ID passed
  varMeetingID = varID
  ' If the meeting ID is empty - on a new row
  If isNothing(varID) Then
    ' Just hide me for now
    Me.Visible = False
  Else
    ' Change my filter
    Me.Filter = "MeetingID = " & varID
    Me.FilterOn = True
```

```
    ' Copy meeting info
    Me.txtDescription = Format(frmMtg.MeetingDate, "dd mmm yyyy, hh:nn") & _
        "; " & frmMtg.MeetingDescription
    ' Make sure I'm not hidden
    Me.Visible = True
  End If
End Sub
```

Last but not least, when the frmMeetings form closes, code in the Close event procedure checks to see if either companion form is open. If it finds a companion form open, it closes the form. The code is as follows:

```
Private Sub Form_Close()
  ' Close the companion forms
  If IsFormLoaded("fpopMeetingAttendees") Then
    ' Use the Cancel procedure in case edit in progress
    Form_fpopMeetingAttendees.cmdCancel_Click
  End If
  If IsFormLoaded("frmMemberAttendance") Then
    Form_frmMemberAttendance.cmdCancel_Click
  End If
End Sub
```

Controlling Tabbing on a Tab Control

The tab control can be useful to segregate data to edit in a table with many fields into manageable chunks. One such example is the frmMembers form in the Membership Tracking sample application. Open the Membership Tracking database (Membership.mdb) and open the frmMembers form from the Database window. (If you still have the application running from the previous section, click the Exit button on the main switchboard to return to the Database window.) You should see the first member record displayed in the form, as shown in Figure E-8.

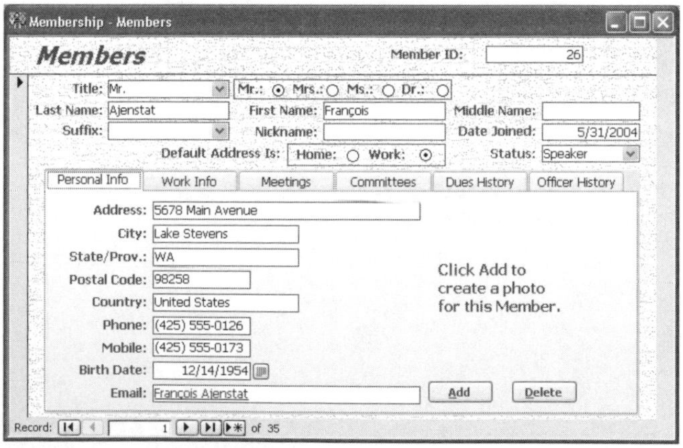

Figure E-8   Editing member records in the Membership Tracking database.

Notice that the first two tabs contain fields from the tblMembers table—the personal information fields on the first tab and the work information fields on the second tab. The other four tabs contain related information displayed in subforms.

One problem with a tab control is when the user tabs into a field on a tab page using the Tab key, the user cannot use the Tab key to move into a field on the second tab page. Pressing Tab merely cycles through the controls on that tab page. However, I fixed this form so that when the user presses the Tab key in the Email field at the end of the first tab, the display moves to the second tab and puts the focus on the Address field (the work address), as shown in Figure E-9.

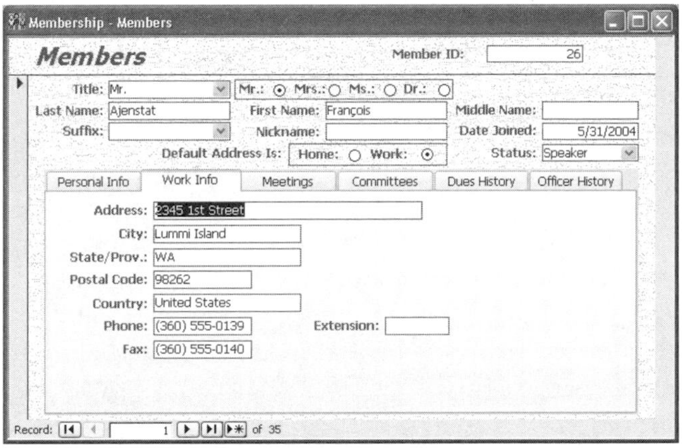

Figure E-9   Pressing the Tab key in the Email field on the first tab takes the user to the Address field on the second tab.

Likewise, when the user presses the Tab key in the Fax field on the second tab, the focus moves to the third tab. And when the user presses Shift+Tab in the Address field, the focus moves back to the Email field on the first tab. To make the Tab key work this way in controls on a tab control, you need some code in the KeyDown event of the relevant controls. For example, the code in the KeyDown event of the EmailName text box control on the first tab looks for the user pressing the Tab key but not the Shift key. If the user pressed the Tab key, the code cancels the keystroke by setting the KeyCode to 0 and moves the focus to the WorkAddress control on the second tab. The code is as follows:

```
Private Sub EmailName_KeyDown(KeyCode As Integer, Shift As Integer)
    ' This is the last control on this "page"
    ' If user just pressed Tab (not Shift-Tab),
    If KeyCode = vbKeyTab And (Shift And acShiftMask) = 0 Then
        ' Cancel the key
        KeyCode = 0
        ' .. And put the focus on the first control
        ' on the next page
        Me.WorkAddress.SetFocus
    End If
End Sub
```

Similarly, code in the KeyDown event of the WorkAddress text box control on the second tab looks for the user pressing the Shift+Tab key combination. If this is what the user pressed, the code cancels the keystroke and puts the focus back on the EmailName text box control on the previous page. The code is as follows:

```
Private Sub WorkAddress_KeyDown(KeyCode As Integer, Shift As Integer)
  ' This is the first control on this "page"
  ' If user just pressed Shift-Tab,
  If KeyCode = vbKeyTab And (Shift And acShiftMask) > 0 Then
    ' Cancel the key
    KeyCode = 0
    ' .. And put the focus on the last control
    ' on the previous page
    Me.EmailName.SetFocus
  End If
End Sub
```

Working with Image Links

Although you can certainly store and display photos in an Access application using the OLE Object data type, if your application might need to interact with a Web application, you cannot use this feature. Web applications, including data access pages, cannot handle the internal format of a stored OLE Object data type. Also, if your application needs to handle hundreds or thousands of photos, you could easily exceed the 2 gigabyte file size limit for an .mdb file. The alternative method is to store the pictures as files and save the picture path as a text field in your tables. However, you'll need to write code in your application to display the pictures.

The frmMembers form in the Membership Tracking sample application (Membership.mdb) is designed to display linked images of the members, not store them in the database. Open the database, open the frmMembers form from the Database window, and scroll down to my record. You should see my picture displayed on the form, as shown in Figure E-10.

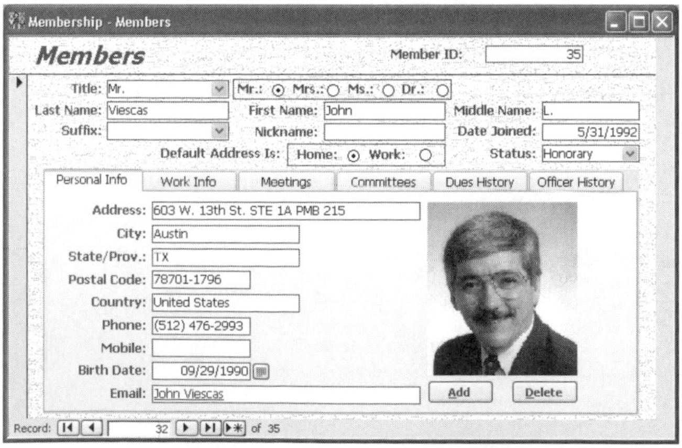

Figure E-10   The picture on the Members form is loaded from a picture path.

Displaying a Linked Photo

The frmMembers form uses an image control that does not have its Picture property set in advance. The Picture property defines the path to the image that the control should display. You might have noticed that as you moved from record to record to find my record, some of the other members also have pictures. Code in the Current event procedure loads the pictures you see from information stored in the Photo field in the tblMembers table being edited by the form.

The code first checks the form's NewRecord property to see if the user has moved to a new row that won't have a picture path stored yet. If so, the code hides the image control, sets the caption of an informative label (the lblMsg control) behind the image and makes the label visible, and then exits the procedure. When not on a new row, the code checks to see if the Photo field that contains the picture path is empty. If so, it hides the image control and displays the message as though the form is on a new record. If there's something in the path, the code checks to see if a full path and file name are stored (a value containing a colon to indicate a drive letter, or a path containing the characters \\ that indicate a Universal Naming Convention path). If the Photo field does not contain what appears to be a full path, the code inserts the path of the current database in front of the file name.

Finally, the code sets an error trap and then attempts to set the Picture property of the image control to the full path to load the picture into the control. If that fails, the code displays a warning message in the label behind the image and hides the image. If the picture load is successful, the code helps ensure that the colors in the picture are true by setting the form's PaintPalette property equal to the color palette used in the image. The code is as follows:

```
Private Sub Form_Current()
' Load the current image, if any, when moving to new row
Dim strPath As String
  ' If on new record,
  If Me.NewRecord Then
    ' Then set the message
    Me.lblMsg.Caption = "Click Add to create a photo for this member."
    ' Make it visible
    Me.lblMsg.Visible = True
    ' .. and hide the image frame
    Me.imgMember.Visible = False
    Exit Sub
  End If
  ' Try to load image - set error trap
  On Error Resume Next
  ' If nothing in the photo text,
  If IsNothing(Me.Photo) Then
    ' Then set the message
    Me.lblMsg.Caption = "Click Add to create a photo for this Member."
    ' Make it visible
    Me.lblMsg.Visible = True
    ' .. and hide the image frame
    Me.imgMember.Visible = False
```

```
  Else
    strPath = Me.Photo
    ' Check for characters that indicate a full path
    If (InStr(strPath, ":") = 0) And (InStr(strPath, "\\") = 0) Then
      ' Just a file name, so add the current path
      strPath = CurrentProject.Path & "\" & strPath
    End If
    ' Attempt to assign the file name
    Me.imgMember.Picture = strPath
    ' If got an error,
    If Err <> 0 Then
      ' Then set the message
      Me.lblMsg.Caption = "Photo not found.  Click Add to correct."
      ' Make it visible
      Me.lblMsg.Visible = True
      ' .. and hide the image frame
      Me.imgMember.Visible = False
    Else
      ' Reveal the picture
      Me.imgMember.Visible = True
      ' And set the form palette so the picture displays correctly
      Me.PaintPalette = Me.imgMember.ObjectPalette
    End If
  End If
End Sub
```

> **Note**   To display an image from a path, you can use the image control. When you first add
> the control to your form, a wizard asks you for the image you want to display. You can choose
> any image file on your hard drive just to keep the wizard happy. After the wizard finishes, clear
> the Picture property of the image control, and reply Yes to the "Do you want to remove this
> picture from the form?" warning message.

Deleting and Updating an Image Path

Clearing the file name saved in the record is the easy part, so let's take a look at that first.
Behind the Delete button that you can see on the frmMembers form, you can find the following code:

```
Private Sub cmdDelete_Click()
' User asked to remove the picture
  ' Clear photo
  Me.txtPhoto = Null
  ' Hide the frame
  Me.imgMember.Visible = False
  ' Clear the image
  Me.imgMember.Picture = ""
  ' Set the message
  Me.lblMsg.Caption = "Click Add to create a photo for this member."
  ' Make it visible
  Me.lblMsg.Visible = True
  ' Put focus in a safe place
```

```
     Me.FirstName.SetFocus
End Sub
```

When the user clicks the command button asking to delete the photo, the code sets the photo path to Null, hides the image, and displays the informative label. But what if the user deletes the picture and then decides to clear pending edits by pressing the Esc key or by choosing Undo from the Edit menu? You need some code in the form's Undo event to put the picture back.

Every editable bound control on a form has an OldValue property that has the value of the control before the user changed it. When the user hasn't changed the value, the OldValue of the control equals the current value. The code checks to see if there's a picture path in the OldValue property of the Photo field that's different from the current value. If so, the code uses the OldValue to reload the picture. The code for the Undo event procedure for the frmMembers form is as follows:

```
Private Sub Form_Undo(Cancel As Integer)
Dim strPath As String
' User trying to undo changes.  See if we need to reload the picture
  ' See if Photo has changed
  If Me.txtPhoto = Me.txtPhoto.OldValue Then
    ' Nope - nothing to do
    Exit Sub
  End If
  ' Try to load image - set error trap
  On Error Resume Next
  ' If nothing in the photo text,
  If IsNothing(Me.txtPhoto.OldValue) Then
    ' Then set the message
    Me.lblMsg.Caption = "Click Add to create a photo for this member."
    ' Make it visible
    Me.lblMsg.Visible = True
    ' .. and hide the image frame
    Me.imgMember.Visible = False
  Else
    strPath = Me.txtPhoto.OldValue
    ' Check for characters that indicate a full path
    If (InStr(strPath, ":") = 0) And (InStr(strPath, "\\") = 0) Then
      ' Just a file name, so add the current path
      strPath = CurrentProject.Path & "\" & strPath
    End If
    ' Attempt to assign the file name
    Me.imgMember.Picture = strPath
    ' If got an error,
    If Err <> 0 Then
      ' Then set the message
      Me.lblMsg.Caption = "Photo not found.  Click Add to correct."
      ' Make it visible
      Me.lblMsg.Visible = True
      ' .. and hide the image frame
      Me.imgMember.Visible = False
    Else
```

```
          ' Reveal the picture
          Me.imgMember.Visible = True
          ' And set the form palette so the picture displays correctly
          Me.PaintPalette = Me.imgMember.ObjectPalette
      End If
  End If
End Sub
```

Finally, you need to provide the user with a way to enter the picture path to add or update a picture in a record. Although you could certainly use the *InputBox* function to ask the user for the path, it's much more professional to call the Windows Open File dialog box so that the user can navigate to the desired picture using familiar tools. You can find the code to accomplish this task in the Click event procedure of the cmdAdd button on the frmMembers form.

The code begins by establishing a copy of the ComDlg class module. This class module provides a simple way to interface with the Microsoft Windows Open File dialog box. The code can set properties of the class rather than deal with the complex Windows structure needed to call the dialog box. The code disallows selecting multiple files; sets the title of the dialog box, the default path (directory) to begin the search (the Pictures subfolder where the database is located), the default file extension, and the filter for file extensions displayed; and requires that the file and path must exist. The code then calls the ShowOpen method to display the dialog box. If the ShowOpen method returns a True value indicating that a file name was successfully located, the code saves the FileName property of the class module. If the ShowOpen failed, the code exits. The code is as follows:

```
Private Sub cmdAdd_Click()
' User asked to add a new photo
Dim strPath As String
    ' If you want to use the Office FileDialog object,
    ' comment out the following code and remove the
    ' comments from the block below
' ***** Begin ComDlg code
    ' Establish a new ComDlg object
    With New ComDlg
      ' Don't allow multiple files
      .AllowMultiSelect = False
      ' Set the title of the dialog box
      .DialogTitle = "Locate Member picture File"
      ' Set the default directory
      .Directory = CurrentProject.Path & "\Pictures\"
      ' .. and file extension
      .Extension = "bmp"
      ' .. but show all graphics files just in case
      .Filter = "Picture Files (.bmp, .jpg, .gif)|*.bmp;*.jpg;*.gif"
      ' Tell the common dialog box that the file and path must exist
      .ExistFlags = FileMustExist + PathMustExist
      If .ShowOpen Then
        strPath = .FileName
      Else
        Exit Sub
```

```
        End If
    End With
```

The next block of code demonstrates an alternative method for displaying the Windows Open File dialog box if you're using Microsoft Access 2002 or later. If you want to use this code, comment out the previous usage of the ComDlg class, set a reference to the Microsoft Office library (choose References from the Tools menu in the Visual Basic Editor), and remove the comments from this code. The code is as follows:

```
' ***** End ComDlg code
    ' If you're using Access 2002 or later, you can set a
    ' reference to the Office library and use the following
    ' code instead:
' ***** Begin Office FileDialog code
    ' Grab a copy of the Office file dialog
'   With Application.FileDialog(msoFileDialogFilePicker)
        ' Select only one file
'       .AllowMultiSelect = False
        ' Set the dialog box title
'       .Title = "Locate the Member picture file"
        ' Set the button caption
'       .ButtonName = "Choose"
        ' Make sure the filter list is clear
'       .Filters.Clear
        ' Add two filters
'       .Filters.Add "JPEGs", "*.jpg"
'       .Filters.Add "Bitmaps", "*.bmp"
        ' Set the filter index to 2
'       .FilterIndex = 2
        ' Set the initial path name
'       .InitialFileName = CurrentProject.Path & "\Pictures"
        ' Show files as thumbnails
'       .InitialView = msoFileDialogViewThumbnail
        ' Show the dialog box and test the return
'       If .Show = 0 Then
            ' Didn't pick a file - bail
'           Exit Sub
'       End If
        ' Should be only one filename - grab it
'       strPath = Trim(.SelectedItems(1))
'   End With
' ***** End Office FileDialog code
```

> **Note** I used the ComDlg class module method in these samples because they're all intended to run successfully using Microsoft Access 2000. Microsoft Office 2000 does not include the FileDialog feature, so the code that is commented out won't compile in Access 2000.

After fetching the name of the file, the code sets a local error trap. The code then attempts to set the Picture property of the image control. If the picture stored successfully in the image control, the Err code will be zero, so the code checks to see if the path returned is a subfolder of the path where the database is located. If this is the case, the code strips off the database path and stores only the subfolder name and the file name. The code then stores the result in the txtPhoto control that is bound to the Photo field in the table, hides the label containing the information message, and makes the image control visible. The code is as follows:

```
' Set an error trap
On Error Resume Next
' Set the image
Me.imgMember.Picture = strPath
' Make sure that "took" OK
If Err = 0 Then
  ' Got a good file selection ...
  ' See if the photo is in a subpath of this project
  If Left(strPath, Len(CurrentProject.Path)) = CurrentProject.Path Then
    ' Strip it off and store a relative path
    strPath = Mid(strPath, Len(CurrentProject.Path) + 2)
  End If
  ' Set the path in the record
  Me.txtPhoto = strPath
  ' Hide the message
  Me.lblMsg.Visible = False
  ' and reveal the new photo
  Me.imgMember.Visible = True
```

If setting the Picture property caused an error, the code clears the txtPhoto control, hides the image control, and sets the Picture property of the image control to an empty string. The code also changes the text of the label that displays a message to inform the user that assigning the picture file failed and makes that label visible. Finally, the code moves the focus to the first control on the form and ends. The code is as follows:

```
Else
    ' OOOps.
    ' Clear photo
    Me.txtPhoto = Null
    ' Hide the frame
    Me.imgMember.Visible = False
    ' Clear the image
    Me.imgMember.Picture = ""
    ' Set the message
    Me.lblMsg.Caption = "Failed to load the picture you selected.  " & _
      "Click Add to try again."
    ' Make it visible
    Me.lblMsg.Visible = True
  End If
  ' Put focus in a safe place
  Me.FirstName.SetFocus
End Sub
```

That concludes the discussion of generic features you might find useful in any application. Feel free to copy any of these code examples into your own applications to add new functionality.

Index

John Viescas

John got started in computing long before many of the current employees at Microsoft were starting grade school. It amazes him to think that the laptop he carries with him when he travels has more than 30,000 times the memory, has 1,000 times the disk space, and is many times faster than the first so-called mainframe computer he used to teach himself an obscure language called Autocoder.

John has been working with database systems for most of his career. He began by designing and building a database application using ISAM (indexed sequential access method) files for a magazine and paperback book distributing company in Illinois in 1968. He went on to build large database application systems for El Paso Natural Gas Company in his hometown in the early 1970s using IBM's IMS software. From there, he went to Applied Data Research in Dallas, where he managed the development of database and data dictionary systems for mainframe computers and became involved in the evolution of the SQL database language standard.

Before forming his own company in 1993, he helped market and support NonStop SQL for Tandem Computers in California. In 1991, he became involved in the early testing of a new Microsoft product that was code-named "Cirrus." The first edition of *Running Microsoft Access* was published in 1992. Since then, he has written four more editions of *Running*, co-authored the best-selling *SQL Queries for Mere Mortals*, and wrote *Microsoft Office Access 2003 Inside Out*. John is active in the newsgroups and several of the support groups on Yahoo and has been named a Microsoft MVP every year since 1993 for his continuing help to the Access users' community. You can reach John via his Web site at *http://www.viescas.com*.

Work smarter—conquer your software from the inside out!

Microsoft® Windows®
XP Inside Out, Second
Edition
ISBN: 0-7356-2044-X
U.S.A. $44.99
Canada $64.99

Microsoft Office
System Inside Out—
2003 Edition
ISBN: 0-7356-1512-8
U.S.A. $49.99
Canada $72.99

Microsoft Office
Access
2003 Inside Out
ISBN: 0-7356-1513-6
U.S.A. $49.99
Canada $72.99

Microsoft Office
FrontPage® 2003
Inside Out
ISBN: 0-7356-1510-1
U.S.A. $49.99
Canada $72.99

Hey, you know your way around a desktop. Now dig into the new Microsoft Office products and the Windows XP operating system and *really* put your PC to work! These supremely organized software reference titles pack hundreds of timesaving solutions, troubleshooting tips and tricks, and handy workarounds into a concise, fast-answer format. They're all muscle and no fluff. All this comprehensive information goes deep into the nooks and crannies of each Office application and Windows XP feature. And every INSIDE OUT title includes a CD-ROM packed with bonus content such as tools and utilities, demo programs, sample scripts, batch programs, an eBook containing the book's complete text, and more! Discover the best and fastest ways to perform everyday tasks, and challenge yourself to new levels of software mastery!

Microsoft Press has other INSIDE OUT titles to help you get the job done every day:

Microsoft Office Excel 2003 Programming Inside Out
ISBN: 0-7356-1985-9

Microsoft Office Word 2003 Inside Out
ISBN: 0-7356-1515-2

Microsoft Office Excel 2003 Inside Out
ISBN: 0-7356-1511-X

Microsoft Office Outlook 2003® Inside Out
ISBN: 0-7356-1514-4

Microsoft Office Project 2003 Inside Out
ISBN: 0-7356-1958-1

Microsoft Office Visio® 2003 Inside Out
ISBN: 0-7356-1516-0

Microsoft Windows XP Networking Inside Out
ISBN: 0-7356-1652-3

Microsoft Windows Security Inside Out
for Windows XP and Windows 2000
ISBN: 0-7356-1632-9

To learn more about the full line of Microsoft Press® products, please visit us at:

microsoft.com/mspress

Microsoft Press products are available worldwide wherever quality computer books are sold. For more information, contact your book or computer retailer, software reseller, or local Microsoft Sales Office, or visit our Web site at **microsoft.com/mspress**. To locate your nearest source for Microsoft Press products, or to order directly, call 1-800-MSPRESS in the United States. (In Canada, call 1-800-268-2222.)

Learn the latest *Web database technologies* for the *.NET Framework—* complete with line-by-line explanations and code samples.

U.S.A. **$39.99**
Canada $57.99
ISBN: 0-7356-1637-X

The Microsoft® .NET Framework is all about simplifying the exchange of data among applications across the Internet, regardless of operating system or back-end software. The step-by-step lessons in this easy-to-grasp tutorial detail the major .NET database technologies to demonstrate how to create powerful, flexible Web databases that can serve your needs today and scale for the future. You'll discover the background behind the latest Web database technologies—and see them in action with complete code samples. If you know how to use HTML, know something about databases, and want to integrate the two in the .NET era with Microsoft Visual Basic® .NET, this book is for you.

Microsoft Press® products are available worldwide wherever quality computer books are sold. For more information, contact your book or computer retailer, software reseller, or local Microsoft® Sales Office, or visit our Web site at microsoft.com/mspress. To locate your nearest source for Microsoft Press products, or to order directly, call 1-800-MSPRESS in the United States (in Canada, call 1-800-268-2222).

Prices and availability dates are subject to change.

Microsoft®
microsoft.com/mspress

Take creative control *of the*
built-in programming language
in Microsoft Excel 2002
and Access 2002

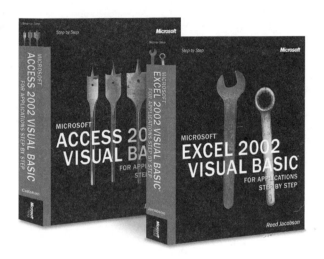

Teach yourself how to use Microsoft Visual Basic for Applications (VBA) to take command of Microsoft Excel 2002 and Access 2002. Choose your own best starting point in these self-paced guides to learn how to automate spreadsheets and databases, write your own functions and procedures, customize menus and toolbars, connect applications to the Web, and more. Easy-to-follow lessons with real-world scenarios and examples show you exactly how to maximize the built-in programming power of the popular desktop applications. Numerous screenshots and a CD-ROM full of practice files in each guide help you master step-by-step programming procedures. Find out how to create custom solutions—and then keep the guides nearby as ongoing desktop references to VBA functions and features.

Microsoft® Excel Version 2002
Visual Basic® for Applications
Step by Step
ISBN: 0-7356-1359-1

Microsoft Access 2002
Visual Basic for Applications
Step by Step
ISBN: 0-7356-1358-3

Microsoft Press® products are available worldwide wherever quality computer books are sold. For more information, contact your book or computer retailer, software reseller, or local Microsoft® Sales Office, or visit our Web site at microsoft.com/mspress. To locate your nearest source for Microsoft Press products, or to order directly, call 1-800-MSPRESS in the United States (in Canada, call 1-800-268-2222).

Prices and availability dates are subject to change.

Microsoft®
microsoft.com/mspress

'n-depth learning solutions *for every software user*

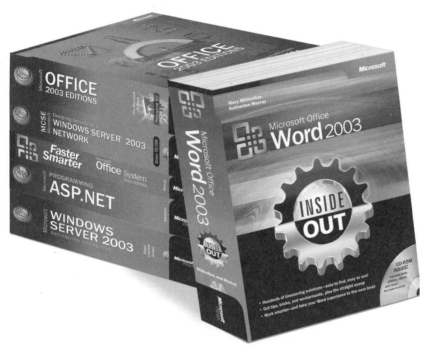

The tools you need to put technology to work.

Microsoft Press produces in-depth learning solutions that empower home and corporate users, IT professionals, and software developers to do more exciting things with Microsoft technology. From beginning PC how-to's to developer reference titles to IT training and technical resources, we offer hundreds of computer books, interactive training software, and online resources, all designed to help build your skills and knowledge—how, when, and where you learn best.

To learn more about the full line of Microsoft Press® products, please visit us at:

microsoft.com/mspress

Microsoft Press products are available worldwide wherever quality computer books are sold. For more information, contact your book or computer retailer, software reseller, or local Microsoft Sales Office, or visit our Web site at **microsoft.com/mspress**. To locate your nearest source for Microsoft Press products, or to order directly, call 1-800-MSPRESS in the United States. (In Canada, call 1-800-268-2222).

What do you think of this book? We want to hear from you!

Do you have a few minutes to participate in a brief online survey? Microsoft is interested in hearing your feedback about this publication so that we can continually improve our books and learning resources for you.

To participate in our survey, please visit:

www.microsoft.com/learning/booksurvey

And enter this book's ISBN, 0-7356-2039-3. As a thank-you to survey participants in the United States and Canada, each month we'll randomly select five respondents to win one of five $100 gift certificates from a leading online merchant.* At the conclusion of the survey, you can enter the drawing by providing your e-mail address, which will be used for prize notification *only*.

Thanks in advance for your input. Your opinion counts!

Sincerely,

Microsoft Learning

Learn More. Go Further.

To see special offers on Microsoft Learning products for developers, IT professionals, and home and office users, visit: *www.microsoft.com/learning/booksurvey*

* No purchase necessary. Void where prohibited. Open only to residents of the 50 United States (includes District of Columbia) and Canada (void in Quebec). Sweepstakes ends 6/30/2005. For official rules, see: *www.microsoft.com/learning/booksurvey*